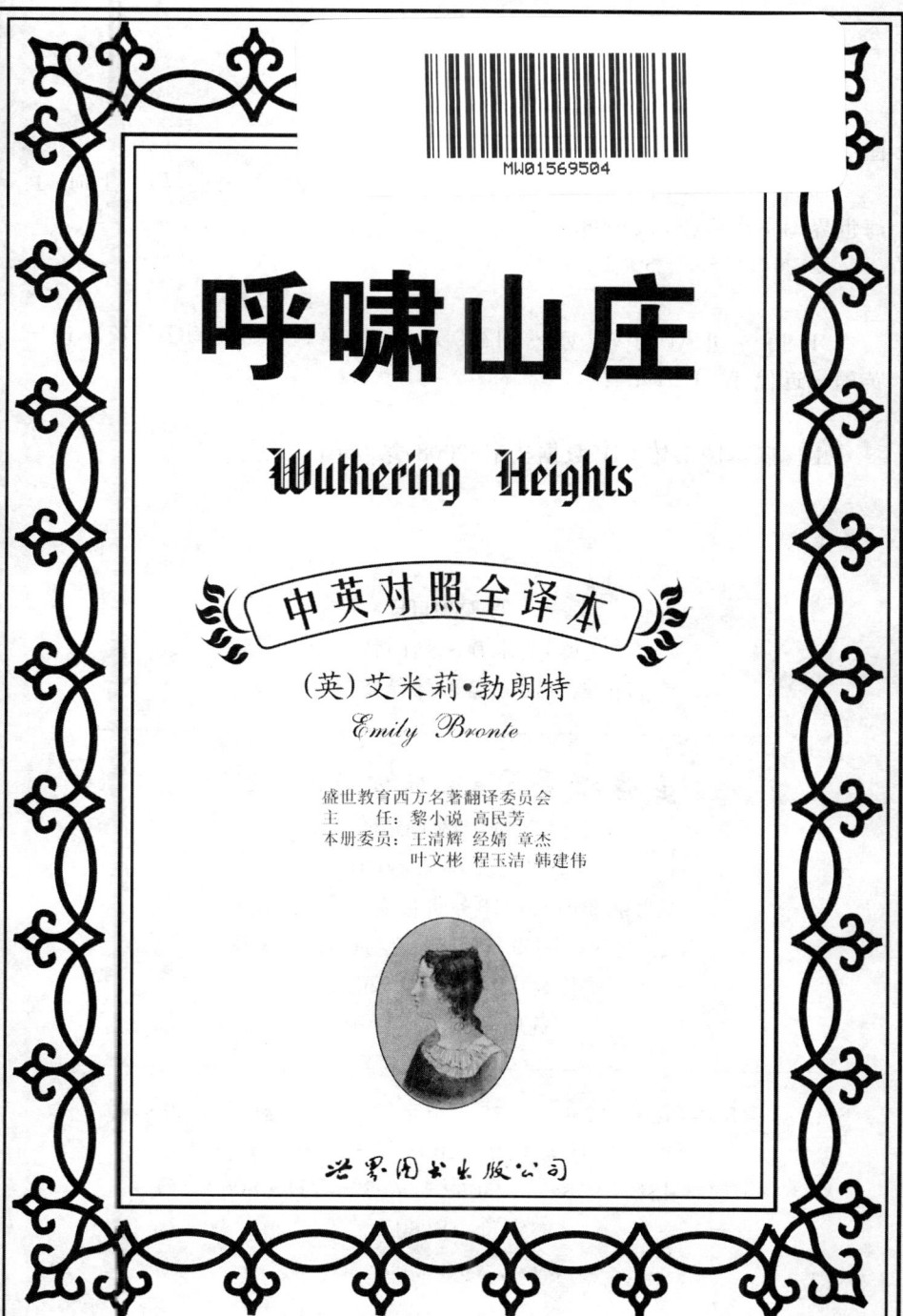

图书在版编目(CIP)数据

呼啸山庄/(英)勃朗特著;盛世教育西方名著翻译委员会译.—上海:上海世界图书出版公司,2008.5
ISBN 978-7-5062-9698-4

.I.呼… Ⅱ.①勃…②盛… Ⅲ.①英语-汉语-对照读物②长篇小说-英国-近代 Ⅳ.H319.4:I

中国版本图书馆 CIP 数据核字(2008)第 056126 号

呼啸山庄

〔英〕艾米莉·勃朗特 著
盛世教育西方名著翻译委员会 译

上海世界图书出版公司 出版发行
上海市尚文路 185 号 B 楼
邮政编码 200010
北京泰山兴业印务责任有限公司印刷
如发现印刷质量问题,请与印刷厂联系
(质检科电话:010-52052501)
各地新华书店经销

开本:880×1230 1/32 印张:13.5 字数:281 000
2008 年 5 月第 1 版 2008 年 5 月第 1 次印刷
ISBN 978-7-5062-9698-4/H·806
定价:18.80 元
www.wpcsh.com.cn

  通过阅读文学名著学语言，是掌握英语的绝佳方法。既可接触原汁原味的英语，又能享受文学之美，一举两得，何乐不为？

  对于喜欢阅读名著的读者，这是一个最好的时代，因为有成千上万的书可以选择；这又是一个不好的时代，因为在浩繁的卷帙中，很难找到适合自己的好书。

  然而，你手中的这套丛书，值得你来信赖。

  这套精选的中英对照名著全译丛书，未改编改写、未删节削减，且配有权威注释、部分书中还添加了精美插图。

  要学语言、读好书，当读名著原文。如习武者切磋交流，同高手过招方能渐明其间奥妙，若一味在低端徘徊，终难登堂入室。积年流传的名著，就是书中"高手"。然而这个"高手"，却有真假之分。初读书时，常遇到一些挂了名著名家之名改写改编的版本，虽有助于了解基本情节，然而所得只是皮毛，你何曾真的就读过了那名著呢？一边是窖藏了五十年的女儿红，一边是贴了女儿红标签的薄酒，那滋味，怎能一样？"朝闻道，夕死可矣。"人生短如朝露，当努力追求真正的美。

  本套丛书的英文版本，是根据外文原版书精心挑选而来；对应的中文译文以直译为主，以方便中英文对照学习，译文经反复推敲，对忠实理解原著极有助益；在涉及到重要文化习俗之处，添加了精当的注释，以解疑惑。

  读过本套丛书的原文全译，相信你会得书之真意、语言之精髓。

  送君"开卷有益"之书，愿成文采斐然之人。

目录

第一章 …… 1	第十八章 …… 238
第二章 …… 8	第十九章 …… 251
第三章 …… 22	第二十章 …… 257
第四章 …… 39	第二十一章 …… 266
第五章 …… 49	第二十二章 …… 289
第六章 …… 54	第二十三章 …… 297
第七章 …… 63	第二十四章 …… 308
第八章 …… 78	第二十五章 …… 321
第九章 …… 90	第二十六章 …… 326
第十章 …… 113	第二十七章 …… 333
第十一章 …… 136	第二十八章 …… 349
第十二章 …… 151	第二十九章 …… 358
第十三章 …… 169	第三十章 …… 366
第十四章 …… 184	第三十一章 …… 375
第十五章 …… 196	第三十二章 …… 383
第十六章 …… 208	第三十三章 …… 398
第十七章 …… 214	第三十四章 …… 409

Chapter 1
第一章

1801—I have just returned from a visit to my landlord—the solitary neighbour that I shall be troubled with. This is certainly a beautiful country! In all England, I do not believe that I could have fixed on a situation so completely removed from the stir of society. A perfect misanthropist's Heaven：and Mr. Heathcliff and I are such a suitable pair to divide the desolation between us. A capital fellow! He little imagined how my heart warmed towards him when I beheld his black eyes withdraw so suspiciously under their brows, as I rode up, and when his fingers sheltered themselves, with jealous resolution, still further in his waistcoat, as I announced my name.

"Mr. Heathcliff?" I said.

A nod was the answer.

"Mr. Lockwood your new tenant, sir. I do myself the honour of calling as soon as possible after my arrival, to express the hope that I have not inconvenienced you by my perseverance in soliciting the occupation of Thrushcross Grange：I heard yesterday you had had some thoughts—"

"Thrushcross Grange is my own, sir," he interrupted, wincing. "I should not allow any

一八零一年——我刚拜访我的房东回来——就是那个我将要费心相处的孤独的邻居。这儿可真是个美丽的乡村！在整个英格兰境内，我不相信还能找到一个像这儿一样与熙熙攘攘的尘世彻底隔绝的地方。一个完美的厌世者的天堂：而希斯克利夫先生和我则是共同分享这荒凉景色的再相配不过的一对。一个绝妙的家伙！我骑着马走到他近前，看到他眉毛下那双乌黑的眼睛满腹狐疑地往里缩，在我通报自己姓名时，他非常警惕地把手指更深地藏到背心袋里。这时，我对他充满了亲切感，他却一点也没有察觉到。

"希斯克利夫先生？"我说。

他点一下头，算是回答。

"先生，我是洛克伍德，您的新房客。为了表达我的敬意，我一到此地就赶来拜访您，希望我坚持要把画眉田庄租下来不会给您带来什么不便。昨天我听说您想——"

"先生，画眉田庄是我的产业。"他打断我的话，闪烁其词："只要我能

1

one to inconvenience me, if I could hinder it—walk in!"

The "walk in" was uttered with dosed teeth, and expressed the sentiment, "Go to the Deuce": even the gate over which he leant manifested no sympathizing movement to the words; and I think that circumstance determined me to accept the invitation: I felt interested in a man who seemed more exaggeratedly reserved than myself.

When he saw my horse's breast fairly pushing the barrier, he did pull out his hand to unchain it, and then sullenly preceded me up the causeway, calling, as we entered the court, —"Joseph, take Mr. Lockwood's horse; and bring up some wine."

"Here we have the whole establishment of domestics, I suppose," was the reflection, suggested by this compound order."No wonder the grass grows up between the flags, and cattle are the only hedge-cutters."

Joseph was an elderly, nay, an old man: very old, perhaps, though hale and sinewy. "The Lord help us!" he soliloquised in an undertone of peevish displeasure, while relieving me of my horse, looking, meantime, in my face so sourly that I charitably conjectured he must have need of divine aid to digest his dinner, and his pious ejaculation had no reference to my unexpected advent.

Wuthering Heights is the name of Mr. Heathcliff's dwelling."Wuthering" being a significant provincial adjective, descriptive of the atmospheric tumult to which its station is exposed in stormy weather. Pure, bracing ventilation they must have up there at all times, indeed: one may guess the power of the north

阻止，我不会让任何人给我造成不便。进来！"

这一声"进来"是从牙缝中挤出来的，表达了这样一种情绪："见鬼！"甚至他靠的那扇大门也没有因他的话作出相应的移动，而我认为这样的情况决定了我必须接受他的邀请：我对这个仿佛比我还要冷淡的人很感兴趣。

当看见我的马胸部快要压上栅栏时，他倒也伸手解开了门链，然后郁郁不乐地领我走上石路。我们一进到院子里，他就喊道："约瑟夫，把洛克伍德先生的马牵走，再拿些酒。"

"我想这是他所有的家仆了，"这个双重任务的吩咐暗示我。"这也就怪不得石板缝里长满了草，树篱只有靠牛在修剪呢。"

约瑟夫是个上了年纪的人，不，是个老头儿——尽管健壮结实，但是非常老。当牵过我的马时，他恨声怨气地小声嘟哝着："主保佑我们！"同时还那么愤怒地盯着我的脸，以至于我好心地推测，他一定是需要神的帮助来消化他的晚餐，而他突然说出来的虔诚祈祷与我这个不速之客是毫不相干的。

呼啸山庄是希斯克利夫先生住所的名称。"呼啸"是一个意味深长的当地的形容词，形容这地方在暴风雨天气里空气的喧嚷。的确，他们这儿一定随时都流通着清新凉爽的空气。从房屋那头那几棵过度倾斜的矮小的冷杉，还有那一排瘦削的荆棘——它们

wind blowing over the edge, by the excessive slant of a few stunted firs at the end of the house; and by a range of gaunt thorns all stretching their limbs one way, as if craving alms of the sun. Happily, the architect had foresight to build it strong: the narrow windows are deeply set in the wall, and the corners defended with large jutting stones.

Before passing the threshold, I paused to admire a quantity of grotesque carving lavished over the front, and especially about the principal door; above which, among a wilderness of crumbling griffins and shameless little boys, I detected the date "1500", and the name "Hareton Earnshaw". I would have made a few comments, and requested a short history of the place from the surly owner; but his attitude at the door appeared to demand my speedy entrance, or complete departure, and I had no desire to aggravate his impatience previous to inspecting the penetralium.

One step brought us into the family sitting-room, without any introductory lobby or passage: they call it here "the house" preeminently. It includes kitchen and parlour, generally; but I believe at Wuthering Heights the kitchen is forced to retreat altogether into another quarter: at least I distinguished a chatter of tongues, and a clatter of culinary utensils, deep within; and I observed no signs of roasting, boiling, or baking, about the huge fire-place; nor any glitter of copper saucepans and tin cullenders on the walls. One end, indeed, reflected splendidly both light and heat from ranks of immense pewter dishes, interspersed with silver jugs and tankards, towering row after row, on a vast oak dresser, to the very roof. The lat-

的分支伸向一侧，仿佛在渴求太阳的布施，我们就可以猜想北风刮过房檐的威力了。所幸的是，建筑师很有远见地把房子建得很坚固：狭窄的窗子深深地嵌在墙里，两边都用凸出的大石块保护着。

在跨进门槛之前，我驻足观赏布满了整个房屋正面，尤其是正门周围的许多形状怪异的雕刻；在正门上，除了许多碎裂的狮身鹰首兽和不知害羞的小男孩外，我还发现了"1500"这个年份和"哈旦顿·恩肖"这个名字。我本该评论一番，向这位乖戾的主人请教一下这个地方的简要历史，可从他站在门口的架式看来，是要我要么赶快进屋，要么就赶紧走人，而我可不愿意在参观内部之前就把主人惹恼，让他越发不耐烦。

根本不用经过任何会客室或是走道，我一步就跨进了起居室，这就是典型的他们所谓的"屋子"，通常的屋子连厨房带客厅都包括在内，但是我认为，在呼啸山庄里，厨房必定是被挤到另一个角落去了：至少我听出来在里屋有喋喋的说话声和厨房用具的碰撞声；而在大壁炉四周我看不出什么烤、煮或烘焙的痕迹；在墙上也没有发现有铜制炖锅和锡制滤勺之类的东西在闪闪发光。倒是在屋子的另一头，在一个巨大的橡木橱柜里陈列着白镴盘子，中间夹杂着银壶、银杯，一排一排的垒到樑顶，反射出非常壮观的光线和热气。橱柜从没上过漆，它的整个结构一览无遗。只有一处，

ter had never been underdrawn: its entire anatomy lay bare to an inquiring eye, except where a frame of wood laden with oatcakes and clusters of legs of beef, mutton, and ham, concealed it. Above the chimney were sundry villanous old guns, and a couple of horse-pistols: and, by way of ornament, three gaudily painted canisters disposed along its ledge. The floor was of smooth, white stone; the chairs, high-backed, primitive structures, painted green and one or two heavy black ones lurking in the shade. In an arch under the dresser, reposed a huge, liver-coloured bitch pointer, surrounded by a swarm of squealing puppies; and other dogs haunted other recesses.

The apartment and furniture would have been nothing extraordinary as belonging to a homely, northern farmer, with a stubborn countenance, and stalwart limbs set out to advantage in knee-breeches and gaiters. Such an individual seated in his armchair, his mug of ale frothing on the round table before him, is to be seen in any circuit of five or six miles among these hills, if you go at the right time after dinner. But Mr. Heathcliff forms a singular contrast to his abode and style of living. He is a dark-skinned gypsy in aspect, in dress and manners a gentleman: that is, as much a gentleman as many a country squire: rather slovenly, perhaps, yet not looking amiss with his negligence, because he has an erect and handsome figure; and rather morose. Possibly, some people might suspect him of a degree of underbred pride; I have a sympathetic chord within that tells me it is nothing of the sort. I know, by instinct, his reserve springs from an aversion to showy displays of feeling to mani-

被搁着麦饼、牛腿、羊肉还有火腿的木架遮住了一部分。壁炉台上挂着各式各样的蹩脚的老式枪，以及一对马枪。还有三个涂色很俗气的茶叶罐排列在壁架上，当作装饰。地板是平滑的白石铺砌的，椅子是高背的，结构粗糙，涂着绿漆，还有一两只笨重的黑椅子躲在阴暗处。橱柜下面的圆拱里，睡着一条巨大的、深褐色的母猎狗，身边围着一群尖叫着的小狗，还有些别的狗在其他地方安身。

要是主人是一个普通的北方庄稼汉，长着一张倔强的脸，拥有一双被绑腿马裤衬托得尤为粗壮的腿，那么像这样的屋子和陈设倒也没什么特别。只要你去的时间恰巧是午饭之后，那么在这山中周围五六英里内，随处都可以看到这样的人，他坐在扶手椅上，一大杯冒着泡沫的啤酒放在他面前的圆桌上。然而希斯克利夫先生和他的住宅，以及生活方式，却形成了一种奇怪的对比。从容貌来说，他是个深色皮肤的吉普赛人，从衣着和言谈举止来说，他是个绅士——也就是说，像乡绅那样的绅士：也许有点不修边幅，可这点疏忽并不见得就叫人看不顺眼，因为他的身材挺拔、外表英俊，只是有点郁郁不乐。可能有人会猜想，他多少带点缺乏教养的傲慢，然而我和他有一种感情上的共鸣，告诉我并不是那么一回事。我凭着本能，知道他的沉默源于他对浮华的反感——互相表示亲热的厌恶。他

festations of mutual kindliness. He'll love and hate equally under cover, and esteem it a species of impertinence to be loved or hated again. No, I'm running on too fast. I bestow my own attributes over liberally on him. Mr. Heathcliff may have entirely dissimilar reasons for keeping his hand out of the way when he meets a would-be acquaintance, to those which actuate me. Let me hope my constitution is almost peculiar: my dear mother used to say I should never have a comfortable home; and only last summer I proved myself perfectly unworthy of one.

While enjoying a month of fine weather at the sea coast, I was thrown into the company of a most fascinating creature: a real goddess in my eyes, as long as she took no notice of me. I "never told my love" vocally; still, if looks have language, the merest idiot might have guessed I was over head and ears. She understood me at last, and looked a return—the sweetest of all imaginable looks. And what did I do? I confess it with shame—shrunk icily into myself, like a snail; at every glance retired colder and farther; till finally the poor innocent was led to doubt her own senses, and, overwhelmed with confusion at her supposed mistake, persuaded her mamma to decamp. By this curious turn of disposition I have gained the reputation of deliberate heartlessness; how undeserved, I alone can appreciate.

I took a seat at the end of the hearthstone opposite that towards which my landlord advanced, and filled up an interval of silence by attempting to caress the canine mother, who had left her nursery, and was sneaking wolfishly to the back of my legs, her lip curled up,

把爱和恨全都埋在心里,却又把被人爱或恨看作是不合时宜的事情。不,我扯得太远了,我把自己的喜好强加于他了。希斯克利夫先生可能就有他完全不同于我的理由,才在遇见一个准熟人的时候,便把手收起来。但愿我的天性算是非常特别的:我那亲爱的母亲总是说我永远也不会有一个舒适的家。就在去年夏天,我证实了我的确不配有那样一个家。

那时候我正在海滨享受着一个月的好天气,遇见了一个迷人的同伴:在我看来她简直就是女神,即便她根本就没有注意到我。我从来没有把自己的爱情说出口,可是,如果眉目也可以传情的话,就连傻子也能猜得出我坠入了爱河。最后她明白了我的意思,送我一个秋波——这是可以想像到的最甜蜜的秋波。而我做了什么呢?说出来丢人——我冷冰冰地退缩了,像个蜗牛似的;她的每一瞥都让我退缩得更冷更远。直到最后这可怜的天真的人儿开始怀疑她自己的感觉,疑惑自己推测错了,于是说服她母亲离开了。因为这样奇怪的性情,我得了个冷酷无情的名声,只有我自己才明白,这是多么的不应该啊。

我坐到壁炉的一头,我的房东上前坐到我对面。为了打破这一刻的沉默,我想去抚摸那只才离开待喂养的狗崽的母狗。它像狼一般偷偷地溜到我的腿后,龇牙咧嘴地,白牙上淌着口水,只准备咬我一口。我的抚摸激

and her white teeth watering for a snatch. My caress provoked a long, guttural gnarl.

"You'd better let the dog alone," growled Mr. Heathcliff in unison, checking fiercer demonstrations with a punch of his foot. "She's not accustomed to be spoiled—not kept for a pet." Then, striding to a side door, he shouted again, "Joseph!"

Joseph mumbled indistinctly in the depths of the cellar, but gave no intimation of ascending; so his master dived down to him, leaving me vis-à-vis the ruffianly bitch and a pair of grim shaggy sheep-dogs, who shared with her a jealous guardianship over all my movements. Not anxious to come in contact with their fangs, I sat still; but, imagining they would scarcely understand tacit insults, I unfortunately indulged in winking and making faces at the trio, and some turn of my physiognomy so irritated madam, that she suddenly broke into a fury, and leapt on my knees. I flung her back, and hastened to interpose the table between us. This proceeding roused the whole hive. Half-a-dozen four-footed fiends, of various sizes and ages, issued from hidden dens to the common centre. I felt my heels and coat-laps peculiar subjects of assault; and, parrying off the larger combatants as effectually as I could with the poker, I was constrained to demand, aloud, assistance from some of the household in establishing peace.

Mr. Heathcliff and his man climbed the cellar steps with vexatious phlegm. I don't think they moved one second faster than usual, though the hearth was an absolute tempest of worrying and yelping. Happily, an inhabitant of the kitchen made more dispatch: a lusty

起它一声长长的嗥叫。

"你最好别理那只狗，"希斯克利夫先生同时喊道，顿了一下脚来制止凶恶的示威。"它不习惯被宠——它可不是宠物。"而后他跨进一个侧门，再次大声喊道："约瑟夫！"

约瑟夫在地窖的深处喃喃而语，并没有要上来的意思。因此他的主人就亲自下去找他，丢下我和那条凶猛的母狗四目相对，还有一对令人害怕的蓬毛守羊狗，它们同那母狗一起警惕地监视着我的一举一动。我并不想和它们的犬牙打交道，只能一动不动地坐着。可是，我以为它们不会理解非言语的冒犯，非常不幸地对这三个畜生挤眉弄眼，做鬼脸，我脸上某个面部表情的变化是如此惹恼了狗太太，以至于它忽然暴跳起来，直扑我的膝盖。我把它猛推回去，慌忙拉来一张桌子挡在中间。这一举动可激起了全体狗的公愤了：六只不同体形、不同年龄的四脚恶魔，一窝蜂地从隐蔽的洞穴窜到了中间。我觉得我的脚后跟和衣摆都是容易受到攻击的地方，就一面极力的用拨火棒来挡开较大的斗士，一面被迫大声呼救，希望这家的主人快来维持秩序。

希斯克利夫和他的仆人迈着令人伤脑筋的懒散的步子，爬上了地窖的梯阶。我觉得他们没有比平常快一秒钟，尽管壁炉这边已经是又嗥又咬，闹得天翻地覆。幸亏厨房里有个人出来的比较快：一个健壮的女人，长袍

dame, with tucked-up gown, bare arms, and fire-flushed cheeks, rushed into the midst of us flourishing a frying-pan: and used that weapon, and her tongue, to such purpose, that the storm subsided magically, and she only remained, heaving like a sea after a high wind, when her master entered on the scene.

"What the devil is the matter?" he asked, eyeing me in a manner I could ill endure after this inhospitable treatment.

"What the devil, indeed!" I muttered. "The herd of possessed swine① could have had no worse spirits in them than those animals of yours, sir. You might as well leave a stranger with a brood of tigers!"

"They won't meddle with persons who touch nothing," he remarked, putting the bottle before me, and restoring the displaced table. "The dogs do right to be vigilant. Take a glass of wine?"

"No thank you."

"Not bitten, are you?"

"If I had been, I would have set my signet on the biter."

Heathcliff's countenance relaxed into a grin.

"Come, come," he said, "you are flurried, Mr. Lockwood. Here, take a little wine. Guests are so exceedingly rare in this house that I and my dogs, I am willing to own, hardly know how to receive them. Your health, sir!"

I bowed and returned the pledge; beginning to perceive that it would be foolish to sit

的袖子卷着,露出胳臂,两颊火红,她冲到我们中间,挥舞着一个煎锅。她运用的武器和她的舌头颇为见效,暴乱奇迹般地平息了。等她的主人上场的时候,她像大风过后的海洋一般平静。

"见什么鬼了?"他问道,向我瞪了一眼。我受了这样不友好的接待,他还这样对我,可真难以忍受。

"是,真是见鬼!"我懊恼地抱怨。"先生,就算有一群着了魔的猪,也不可能比您的那些畜生更恶毒。您倒不如把一个生客丢给一群老虎的好!"

"他们不会对不碰它们的人乱来的。"他说,把酒瓶放在我面前,又把移位的桌子复原。"狗保持警觉是对的。喝杯酒吧?"

"不,谢谢。"

"没有被咬着,是吧?"

"要是我给咬着了,我会在咬我的狗的身上打下我的印记。"

希斯克利夫先生的脸上露出了笑容。

"行啦,行啦,"他说,"你受惊了,洛克伍德先生。来,喝点酒。这儿真难得有客人光临,所以我愿意承认,我和我的狗简直都不知道该怎么接待客人。祝你健康,先生。"

我鞠了一躬并回敬了他,我开始意识到如果因为一群狗的失礼而坐在

---

① 着了魔的猪:见《圣经·新约·路加福音》第八章第三十一节到第三十三节:"鬼就央求耶稣,不要吩咐他们到无底坑里去。那里有一大群猪,在山上吃食。鬼央求耶稣,准他们进入猪里去。耶稣准了他们。鬼就从那人身上出来,进入猪里去。于是那群猪闯下山崖,投在湖里淹死了。"

sulking for the misbehaviour of a pack of curs. Besides, I felt loath to yield the fellow further amusement at my expense; since his humour took that turn. He—probably swayed by prudential considerations of the folly of offending a good tenant—relaxed a little in the laconic style of chipping off his pronouns and auxiliary verbs, and introduced what he supposed would be a subject of interest to me, —a discourse on the advantages and disadvantages of my present place of retirement. I found him very intelligent on the topics we touched; and before I went home, I was encouraged so far as to volunteer another visit tomorrow. He evidently wished no repetition of my intrusion. I shall go, notwithstanding. It is astonishing how sociable I feel myself compared with him.

那儿生闷气，可有点傻。再说，我也觉得让这个家伙继续在我付出的代价上寻开心实在是讨厌，因为他的兴致已经转移到取乐上来了。他呢，也许是出于谨慎的考虑，觉得把一个好房客给得罪了是件愚蠢的事，就开始略微改变他谈话的简洁风格，比如省掉代词和辅助动词，提起了他以为我会有兴趣的话题——谈到我现在要住的地方的优点与缺点。我发现在我们所谈到的话题上，他是非常睿智的，于是在我回家之前，受到鼓励以至于有勇气提出明天再来拜访。他显然并不希望我再来打搅。无所谓，我还是要去。我觉得，与他相比我是多么喜欢交际啊，这可真是令人吃惊。

Chapter 2
第二章

Yesterday afternoon set in misty and cold. I had half a mind to spend it by my study fire, instead of wading through heath and mud to Wuthering Heights. On coming up from dinner① however, (N. B.—I dine between twelve and one o'clock; the housekeeper, a matronly lady,

昨天下午又有雾又冷。我本想就在火炉旁看看书什么的消磨一下午，而不是踩着泥路，穿过石楠树丛走到呼啸山庄。但是，吃过午饭（注——我的吃饭时间是在十二点与一点钟之间；这里的女管家，一位庄重的太

---

① 正餐。英国人一般在午间用正餐。然而在十八、十九世纪，人们以推迟正餐时间为时尚以标榜自己的社会地位。洛克伍德来自城里，喜欢把正餐安排在晚上；而管家太太却根据当地习惯在中午安排正餐。

taken as a fixture along with the house, could not, or would not, comprehend my request that I might be served at five), on mounting the stairs with this lazy intention, and stepping into the room, I saw a servant-girl on her knees, surrounded by brushes, and coal-scuttles; and raising an infernal dust as she extinguished the flames with heaps of cinders. This spectacle drove me back immediately; I took my hat, and, after a four miles' walk, arrived at Heathcliff's garden gate just in time to escape the first feathery flakes of a snow-shower.

On that bleak hill-top the earth was hard with a black frost, and the air made me shiver through every limb. Being unable to remove the chain, I jumped over, and, running up the flagged causeway bordered with straggling gooseberry bushes, knocked vainly for admittance, till my knuckles tingled, and the dogs howled.

"Wretched inmates!" I ejaculated, mentally, "you deserve perpetual isolation from your species for your churlish inhospitality. At least, I would not keep my doors barred in the daytime. I don't care—I will get in!" So resolved, I grasped the latch and shook it vehemently. Vinegarfaced Joseph projected his head from a round window of the barn.

"Whet are ye for?" he shouted. "T' maister's dahn i' t' fowld. Goa rahnd by th' end ut' laith, if yah went tuh spake tull him."

"Is there nobody inside to open the door?" I hallooed, responsively.

"They's nobbut t' missis; and shoo'll nut oppen 't an ye mak yer flaysome dins till neeght."

"Why," I began, "Cannot you tell her who I am,

太,却不能,或者并不愿理会我在五点钟开饭的请求),我怀着这个懒惰的想法登上楼梯,走进房间,恰巧看见一个女仆跪在地上,周围堆着刷子和煤斗。她正在用一堆堆煤渣来封火,搞起一片如恶魔般的灰尘。这情形立刻促使我回去。我拿了帽子,走了四里路,到达希斯克利夫的花园门口时,天上飘起了第一片鹅毛般的雪花,我刚好逃过了这场大雪。

在这个荒凉的山头上,盖着黑霜的泥土已冻得坚硬,冷空气使我手脚都在哆嗦。由于弄不开门链,我就跳了进去,跑过两边乱长着醋栗树丛的石板道,敲起了门。敲到我的手节骨都痛了,狗也嚎叫起来,却没有人来开门。

"倒霉的人家!"我在心里叫道,"就冲你的无礼怠慢,就该永远跟人类隔绝。至少,我是不会在白天把门锁起来的。我才不管呢——我要进去!"打定了主意,我就抓住门上的插销猛烈地摇。约瑟夫从谷仓上一个圆形窗户里探出头来,一脸的不高兴。

"你要干什么?"他喊道。"主人在羊圈里,如果你要找他的话,打谷仓那边绕过去。"

"屋里没有人开门吗?"我大声回喊道。

"没有人,只有太太在家。就算你闹到半夜,她也不会来开门的。"

"为什么?你就不能告诉她我是

eh, Joseph?"

"Nor-ne me! Aw'll hae noa hend wi't," muttered the head vanishing.

The snow began to drive thickly. I seized the handle to essay another trial; when a young man without coat, and shouldering a pitchfork, appeared in the yard behind. He hailed me to follow him, and, after marching through a wash-house, and a paved area containing a coalshed, pump, and pigeon-cote, we at length arrived in the huge, warm, cheerful apartment, where I was formerly received. It glowed delightfully in the radiance of an immense fire, compounded of coal, peat, and wood; and near the table, laid for a plentiful evening meal, I was pleased to observe the "missis," an individual whose existence I had never previously suspected. I bowed and waited, thinking she would bid me take a seat. She looked at me, leaning back in her chair, and remained motionless and mute.

"Rough weather!" I remarked. "I'm afraid, Mrs. Heathcliff, the door must bear the consequence of your servants' leisure attendance. I had hard work to make them hear me!"

She never opened her mouth. I stared—she stared also. At any rate, she kept her eyes on me in a cool, regardless manner, exceedingly embarrassing and disagreeable.

"Sit down," said the young man, gruffly. "He'll be in soon."

I obeyed; and hemmed, and called the villain Juno[①], who deigned, at this second interview, to move the extreme tip of her tail, in

谁吗，啊，约瑟夫？"

"别找我！这事儿和我没关系，"咕噜了这么两句后，那个脑袋又不见了。

雪开始下大了。我抓住把手，企图再试一回。这时，后面院子里出现了一个年轻人，没穿外套，肩上扛着一个草耙。他招呼我跟他走，我们穿过一个洗衣房和一片有煤棚、抽水机和鸽笼的铺平的区域，最后进到了那间宽敞、温暖、舒适的房间，我曾在这儿被接待过。在煤、炭和木头混合燃烧产生的熊熊火焰的烘烤下，屋子放着光彩。桌子旁边摆放着丰盛的晚餐，我非常高兴地看到了那位"太太"，我以前从未料到会有这么一个人存在呢。我鞠了一躬，等着，以为她会叫我坐下。她看着我，往后靠着椅子，保持那个姿态，一言不发。

"天气真是糟糕！"我说，"希斯克利夫太太，恐怕大门要承担您的仆人偷懒的后果了，我好容易才让他们听见我敲门！"

她根本不开口说话。我瞪眼——她也瞪眼。反正无论怎样，她总是以一种冷冷的、漠不关心的眼神盯着我，让我觉得非常尴尬和不舒服。

"坐下吧，"那年轻人粗声粗气地说，"他一会儿就来了。"

我依了他的话，轻咳了一下，召唤那只恶狗"朱诺"。临到第二次见面，它屈尊动了动它的尾巴尖，表示

---

① Juno：朱诺，罗马神话中主神朱庇特的妻子，司婚姻、生育和妇女之神，相当于希腊神话中的赫拉。

token of owning my acquaintance.

"A beautiful animal!" I commenced again. "Do you intend parting with the little ones, madam?"

"They are not mine," said the amiable hostess, more repellingly than Heathcliff himself could have replied.

"Ah, your favourites are among these!" I continued, turning to an obscure cushion full of something like cats.

"A strange choice of favourites!" she observed scornfully.

Unluckily, it was a heap of dead rabbits. I hemmed once more, and drew closer to the hearth, repeating my comment on the wildness of the evening.

"You should not have come out," she said, rising and reaching from the chimney-piece two of the painted canisters.

Her position before was sheltered from the light; now, I had a distinct view of her whole figure and countenance. She was slender, and apparently scarcely past girlhood, an admirable form, and the most exquisite little face that I have ever had the pleasure of beholding, small features, very fair; flaxen ringlets, or rather golden, hanging loose on her delicate neck; and eyes, had they been agreeable in expression, they would have been irresistible. Fortunately for my susceptible heart, the only sentiment they evinced hovered between scorn and a kind of desperation, singularly unnatural to be detected there.

The canisters were almost out of her reach; I made a motion to aid her; she turned upon me as a miser might turn if any one attempted to assist him in counting his gold.

接受我是熟人了。

"好漂亮的狗!"我再次开口。"您打算不要这些小东西吗,太太?"

"那不是我的,"这位和善的女主人说,比希斯克利夫本人所能做出的回答还要更令人反感一些。

"啊,那您最喜欢的在这些里面吗?"我接着说,转身望着放在暗处靠垫上一堆像猫似的东西。

"谁会喜欢这些东西才怪呢!"她轻蔑地说。

真倒霉,原来那是一堆死兔子。我又轻咳一声,走到更靠近壁炉的地方,把今晚天气不好的话又评论了一通。

"你本来就不该出来。"她说着,站起来从烟囱上拿下壁炉架上两个漆成彩色的茶叶罐。

之前,她坐在光线被挡住的地方,这会儿我看清了她的全身和面貌。她很苗条,分明还没有过青春期,体态很好,还有一张我生平从未有幸见过的精致的小脸,五官非常漂亮;淡黄色的卷发,或者说是金色的,松松地垂在她那优雅的脖子旁边;至于眼睛,要是眼神和气些,就会让人无法抗拒了。幸运的是,对我这容易动情的心而言,它们所表现出的惟一情绪徘徊在轻蔑与近似绝望之间,叫人觉得异乎寻常的不自然。

她不大够得着茶叶罐。我动了动,想帮她一下。她转过身来对着我,就像一个守财奴看见别人想要帮他数他的金子一样。

"I don't want your help," she snapped; "I can get them for myself."

"I beg your pardon," I hastened to reply.

"Were you asked to tea?" she demanded, tying an apron over her neat black frock, and standing with a spoonful of the leaf poised over the pot.

"I shall be glad to have a cup," I answered.

"Were you asked?" she repeated.

"No," I said, half smiling. "You are the proper person to ask me."

She flung the tea back, spoon and all; and resumed her chair in a pet, her forehead corrugated, and her red under-lip pushed out, like a child's, ready to cry.

Meanwhile, the young man had slung onto his person a decidedly shabby upper garment, and, erecting himself before the blaze, looked down on me, from the corner of his eyes, for all the world as if there were some mortal feud unavenged between us. I began to doubt whether he were a servant or not. His dress and speech were both rude, entirely devoid of the superiority observable in Mr. and Mrs. Heathdiff; his thick, brown curls were rough and uncultivated, his whiskers encroached bearishly over his cheeks, and his hands were embrowned like those of the common labourer. still his bearing was free, almost haughty, and he showed none of a domestic's assiduity in attending on the lady of the house. In the absence of clear proofs of his condition, I deemed it best to abstain from noticing his curious conduct; and, five minutes afterwards, the entrance of Heathcliff relieved me, in some measure, from my uncomfortable state.

"You see, sir, I am come, according to

"我不要你帮忙，"她呵斥道，"我自己可以拿到。"

"请原谅！"我连忙回答。

"你是被请来喝茶的吗？"她问，把一条围裙系在她那干净的黑衣服上，站在那儿，拿一满匙茶叶正要往茶壶里倒。

"我很想喝杯茶。"我回答。

"你是被请来的吗？"她又问。

"没有，"我说，勉强笑笑。"您是邀请我的合适人选。"

她把茶叶丢了回去，连匙带茶叶一起，使性地又坐在椅子上。她的前额皱起，红红的下嘴唇撅起来，像一个要哭的孩子。

同时，那年轻人披上一件相当破旧的上衣，站起来走到炉火前，用眼角瞅着我，简直仿佛我们之间有什么未了的血海深仇似的。我开始怀疑他到底是不是一个仆人了。他的衣着和言谈都很粗俗，完全没有希斯克利夫先生和他太太身上的那种优越感。他那稠密的棕色卷发乱糟糟的，没有修剪过，他的胡子肆无忌惮的布满脸颊，双手都变成了褐色，就像普通工人的手那样。可是另一方面，他的举止很放肆，几乎有点傲慢，还有他在房子的女主人面前并没有表现出任何家仆该有的那种勤勉。既然对他的地位缺乏足够的证据来判断，我觉得最好还是忽略他那古怪的行径。五分钟以后，希斯克利夫的到来在某种程度上把我从不舒服的状态中解救了出来。

"您瞧，先生，我来了，说话算

promise!" I exclaimed, assuming the cheerful; "and I fear I shall be weather-bound for half an hour, if you can afford me shelter during that space."

"Half an hour?" he said, shaking the white flakes from his clothes; "I wonder you should select the thick of a snow-storm to ramble about in. Do you know that you run a risk of being lost in the marshes? People familiar with these moors often miss their road on such evenings; and, I can tell you, there is no chance of a change at present."

"Perhaps I can get a guide among your lads, and he might stay at the Grange till morning-could you spare me one?"

"No, I could not."

"Oh, indeed! Well, then, I must trust to my own sagacity."

"Umph!"

"Are you going to mak' th' tea?" demanded he of the shabby coat, shifting his ferocious gaze from me to the young lady.

"Is *he* to have any?" she asked, appealing to Heathcliff.

"Get it ready, will you?" was the answer uttered so savagely that I started. The tone in which the words were said, revealed a genuine bad nature. I no longer felt inclined to call Heathcliff a capital fellow. When the preparations were finished, he invited me with—"Now, sir, bring forward your chair." And we all, including the rustic youth, drew round the table, an austere silence prevailing while we discussed our meal.

I thought, if I had caused the cloud, it was my duty to make an effort to dispel it. They could not every day sit so grim and taciturn; and

数!"我装着高兴的样子说道:"恐怕因为这天气的缘故,我要困在这儿半个小时呢,如果您容许的话。"

"半个小时?"他说,抖落他衣服上的雪花,"我不知道你为什么要挑这么个大雪天出来闲逛。你知道你是冒着在沼泽地里迷路的危险吗?熟悉这荒野的人,往往都还会在这样的夜晚迷路。而且我可以告诉你,眼下你别指望天气会转好。"

"或许我可以在您的仆人中找一位向导,他可以在田庄住到明天早上——您能派个人给我吗?"

"不,我不能。"

"哦!真是的!那我只能靠自己的智慧啦。"

"哼!"

"你要沏茶了吗?"那个衣着褴褛的人问,把他那凶狠的目光从我身上转到那位年轻的太太身上。

"要给他喝吗?"她向希斯克利夫请示。

"快把茶准备好,好不好?"这就是回答,他说得这么恶狠狠的,把我吓了一跳。这句话的腔调显示出他真实的恶的本性。我再也不想称希斯克利夫为一个好人了。当茶准备好之后,他邀请我:"现在,先生,把你的椅子往前挪挪。"于是我们所有的人,包括那个野小子在内,都围着桌子坐下来。在我们品尝食物时,四下里一片阴郁可怕的沉默。

我想,如果是我造成了这块乌云,那我就有义务努力驱散它。他们不可能每天都这么阴沉缄默地坐着

it was impossible, however ill-tempered they might be, that the universal scowl they wore was their everyday countenance.

"It is strange," I began, in the interval of swallowing one cup of tea and receiving another—"it is strange how custom can mould our tastes and ideas: many could not imagine the existence of happiness in a life of such complete exile from the world as you spend, Mr. Heathcliff; yet, I'll venture to say, that, surrounded by your family, and with your amiable lady as the presiding genius over your home and heart—"

"My amiable lady!" he interrupted, with an almost diabolical sneer on his face."Where is she—my amiable lady?"

"Mrs. Heathcliff, your wife, I mean."

"Well, yes—Oh! you would intimate that her spirit has taken the post of ministering angel, and guards the fortunes of Wuthering Heights, even when her body is gone. Is that it?"

Perceiving myself in a blunder, I attempted to correct it. I might have seen that there was too great a disparity between the ages of the parties to make it likely that they were man and wife. One was about forty; a period of mental vigour at which men seldom cherish the delusion of being married for love, by girls. That dream is reserved for the solace of our declining years. The other did not look seventeen.

Then it flashed upon me—"The clown at my elbow, who is drinking his tea out of a basin and eating his bread with unwashed hands, may be her husband, Heathcliff, junior, of course. Here is the consequence of being buried alive: she has thrown herself away

吧。不管他们的脾气有多坏，也不可能每天都皱着眉。"

"真是奇怪，"在喝完一杯茶，倒第二杯的时候，我说："习惯是如何铸就我们的品味和想法的，这是很奇怪的，许多人无法想像，希斯克利夫先生，像您这样过着一种如此与世隔绝的生活也会有幸福存在。可是我敢说，被家人围绕，还有您那位可爱的太太作为您家庭与您心灵的守护神——"

"我可爱的太太！"他脸上带着近乎恶魔般的讥笑，打断了我："她在哪儿——我可爱的太太？"

"希斯克利夫夫人，我的意思是说，您的太太。"

"哦，是啦——啊！你是说尽管她的肉体不在了，她的灵魂却充当着保护的天使，而且守护着呼啸山庄的财产。是这样吗？"

我自知失言了，就试着去纠正错误。我早该看出双方的年龄相差太大，不像是夫妻。一个大约四十了，正是精力旺盛的时期，这时期的男人很少会抱着幻想，以为女孩子们是由于爱情而嫁给他的。这种梦是留到我们年老时聊以自慰的。而另外那个人呢，看来还不满十七岁。

于是我灵机一动，"那个坐在我胳臂肘旁边正用盆喝茶，用没洗过的手抓面包吃的那个乡巴佬，可能是她的丈夫，当然也是希斯克利夫少爷。这就是活埋的后果：她把自己胡乱嫁给了一个乡巴佬，全然不知天下还有更

upon that boor, from sheer ignorance that better individuals existed! A sad pity—I must beware how I cause her to regret her choice." The last reflection may seem conceited; it was not. My neighbour struck me as bordering on repulsive; I knew, through experience, that I was tolerably attractive.

"Mrs. Heathcliff is my daughter-in-law," said Heathcliff, corroborating my surmise, He turned, as he spoke, a peculiar look in her direction, a look of hatred unless he has a most perverse set of facial muscles that will not, like those of other people, interpret the language of his soul.

"Ah, certainly—I see now: you are the favoured possessor of the beneficent fairy," I remarked, turning to my neighbour.

This was worse than before: the youth grew crimson, and clenched his fist, with every appearance of a meditated assault. But he seemed to recollect himself, presently; and smothered the storm in a brutal curse, muttered on my behalf: which, however, I took care not to notice.

"Unhappy in your conjectures, sir!" observed my host, "we neither of us have the privilege of owning your good fairy; her mate is dead. I said she was my daughter-in-law, therefore, she must have married my son."

"And this young man is—"

"Not my son, assuredly!"

Heathcliff smiled again, as if it were rather too bold a jest to attribute the paternity of that bear to him.

"My name is Hareton Earnshaw," growled the other; "and I'd counsel you to respect it!"

"I've shown no disrespect," was my re-

好的人存在！真是令人伤心的憾事啊——我必须留神点儿，可别让她对她的选择感到后悔。"最后这个念头看上去可能有点自负，其实也不是。我旁边的人在我看来近乎面目可憎。凭经验，我知道我还是有点吸引力的。

"希斯克利夫太太是我的儿媳妇，"希斯克利夫说，这证实了我的猜想。他说着，掉过头来用一种特别的目光望着她：一种憎恨的目光，除非是他脸上的肌肉生得极反常，不能像其他人一样表现出他心灵的语言。

"啊，当然——我明白了：您是这善良的仙女的幸运拥有者。"我转过头来对我旁边那个人说。

比之前更糟：那年轻人涨红了脸，握紧了拳头，简直摆明了要出手了。可他似乎马上空制住自己，只对我咕噜了一句粗野的骂人的话，平息了这场风波，而我只能假装没听见。

"抱歉你猜得不对，先生！"我的主人说，"我们两个都没福气拥有你这位好仙女，她的丈夫已经死啦。我说过她是我的儿媳妇，因此，她当然是嫁给我的儿子了。"

"那么这位年轻人——"

"当然不是我儿子！"

希斯克利夫又笑了，似乎要他来做这头笨熊的父亲，这玩笑简直开得太大了。

"我的姓名是哈里顿·恩肖，"另一个人怒吼道："而且我劝你表示尊重！"

"我并没有不尊重呀。"我回答

ply, laughing internally at the dignity with which he announced himself.

He fixed his eye on me longer than I cared to return the stare, for fear I might be tempted either to box his ears, or render my hilarity audible. I began to feel unmistakably out of place in that pleasant family circle. The dismal spiritual atmosphere overcame, and more than neutralised the glowing physical comforts round me; and I resolved to be cautious how I ventured under those rafters a third time.

The business of eating being concluded, and no one uttering a word of sociable conversation, I approached a window to examine the weather. A sorrowful sight I saw: dark night coming down prematurely, and sky and hills mingled in one bitter whirl of wind and suffocating snow.

"I don't think it possible for me to get home now, without a guide," I could not help exclaiming. "The roads will be buried already; and, if they were bare, I could scarcely distinguish a foot in advance."

"Hareton, drive those dozen sheep into the barn porch. They'll be covered if left in the fold all night and put a plank before them," said Heathcliff.

"How must I do?" I continued, with rising irritation.

There was no reply to my question; and on looking round I saw only Joseph bringing in a pail of porridge for the dogs, and Mrs. Heathcliff leaning over the fire, diverting herself with burning a bundle of matches which had fallen from the chimney-piece as she restored the tea-canister to its place. The former, when he had deposited his burden, took a critical survey of

道，心里却在嘲笑他报出自己姓名时的高傲模样。

他死盯着我看了很长时间，我都不愿意去回瞪他，因为担心这样下去，我也许会给他个耳光或是笑出声来。我这才开始一点不含糊地感到自己不适应这个愉快的家庭。那种精神上的压力不止是抵消，而且压倒了包围着我的温暖的物质享受。我决定第三次再来这屋檐下的时候可要小心谨慎。

用餐完毕，谁也没说句应酬话，我就到一扇窗子前去看看天气。我看到一片悲凉的景象：黑夜早已笼罩着大地，寒冷的旋风和令人窒息的雪把天空和群山混在一起。

"现在没有人带路，我是不可能回家了，"我不禁喊道。"道路应该已经给埋起来了，就算还露出来的话，一步之外我也看不清往哪儿迈步啦。"

"哈里顿，把那些羊都赶到谷仓的门廊上去，要是放它们在羊圈里过夜，就得给它们盖点东西，前面也得挡块木板。"希斯克利夫说。

"我该怎么办呢？"我又说，越发焦急了。

谁也不来搭理我。我四处看看，只见约瑟夫提了一桶粥给那些狗，希斯克利夫太太靠在火炉旁，烧着从壁炉架上掉下来的一把火柴玩，这些火柴是她刚才放茶叶罐回去的时候碰下来的。约瑟夫把他的粥桶放下之后，以审视的目光扫过房间，然后扯着他那沙哑的喉咙嚷起来：

the room; and, in cracked tones, grated out—

"Aw woonder hagh yah can faishion tuh stand thear i' idleness un war, when all on 'em's goan aght! Bud yah're a nowt, and it's noa use talking—yah'll niver mend uh yer ill ways; bud, goa raight tuh t' divil, like yer mother afore ye!"

I imagined, for a moment, that this piece of eloquence was addressed to me; and, sufficiently enraged, stepped towards the aged rascal with an intention of kicking him out of the door. Mrs. Heathcliff, however, checked me by her answer.

"You scandalous old hypocrite!" she replied. "Are you not afraid of being carried away bodily, whenever you mention the devil's name? I warn you to refrain from provoking me, or I'll ask your abduction as a special favour. Stop, look here, Joseph," she continued, taking a long, dark book from a shelf."I'll show you how far I've progressed in the Black Art: I shall soon be competent to make a clear house of it. The red cow didn't die by chance; and your rheumatism can hardly be reckoned among providential visitations!"

"Oh, wicked, wicked!" gasped the elder; "may the Lord deliver us from evil!"

"No, reprobate! you are a castaway—be off, or I'll hurt you seriously! I'll have you all modelled in wax and clay①; and the first who passes the limits I fix, shall—I'll not say what he shall be done to—but, you'll see! Go, I'm looking at you②!"

The little witch put a mock malignity into

"我真不明白别人都出去了,你怎么能让自己无所事事地在那儿站着!不过我看你就是没出息,跟你说也是白说——你的毛病是永远也改不好的,你就等着见魔鬼吧,像你妈那样!"

我一时还以为这番话是对我而发的,我感到非常恼火,往前走去,想把这老流氓踢出门外。可是,希斯克利夫太太的回答止住了我。

"你这胡说八道、假正经的老东西!"她回答,"你提到魔鬼名字的时候,就不怕被魔鬼活活捉去吗?我警告你不要惹我,要不然我就要特地请他把你抓了去。别动!看这儿,约瑟夫,"她从书架上拿出一本大黑书,接着说:"我要给你看看我在这种魔术上的进展:很快我就可以精通。那头红牛的死不是无缘无故的,你的风湿病也还不能算作神意的造访!"

"哦,恶毒,恶毒!"老头喘息着,"愿主让我们远离邪恶!"

"不,堕落的人!你是个被上帝抛弃的人——滚开,不然我要狠狠地伤害你啦!我把你们一个个用蜡和泥捏成模型,谁先越过我定的界限,我就要——我不说他会怎样——可是,你会看见的!出去,我可在看着你呢!"

这个小女巫那双美丽的眼睛闪烁

---

① 女巫信奉一种巫术,用蜡像塑造出所要加害的人,将其放在火中熔化,即诅咒其死亡。
② 施行巫术时,用眼神摄其魂魄,而使对方无法摆脱巫术控制。

her beautiful eyes, and Joseph, trembling with sincere horror, hurried out praying and ejaculating "wicked" as he went. I thought her conduct must be prompted by a species of dreary fun; and, now that we were alone, I endeavoured to interest her in my distress.

"Mrs. Heathcliff," I said, earnestly, "you must excuse me for troubling you—I presume, because, with that face, I'm sure you cannot help being good-hearted. Do point out some landmarks by which I may know my way home: I have no more idea how to get there than you would have how to get to London!"

"Take the road you came," she answered, ensconcing herself in a chair, with a candle, and the long book open before her. "It is brief advice, but as sound as I can give."

"Then, if you hear of me being discovered dead in a bog or a pit full of snow, your conscience won't whisper that it is partly your fault?"

"How so? I cannot escort you. They wouldn't let me go to the end of the garden-wall."

"*You*! I should be very sorry to ask you to cross the threshold, for my convenience, on such a night," I cried. "I want you to *tell* me my way, not to *show* it; or else to persuade Mr. Heathchff to give me a guide."

"Who? There is himself, Earnshaw, Zillah, Joseph, and I. Which would you have?"

"Are there no boys at the farm?"

"No, those are all."

"Then, it follows that I am compelled to stay."

"That you may settle with your host. I have nothing to do with it."

着一种嘲弄的恶毒神气。而约瑟夫真的吓得直发抖,一边跑一边祷告,还喊着"女巫!"我想她的行为无非是由于闷得发慌闹着玩玩罢的。现在只剩下我们两个人了,我试图吸引她来注意到我的不幸。

"希斯克利夫太太,"我诚恳地说,"您一定得原谅我对您的打扰。我相信,凭你这样容貌,我确定你肯定是一个好心人。请指一些回家的路标给我吧。回去该怎么走,我心里一点谱也没有,正如您不知道怎么去伦敦一样!"

"顺着你来的路走回去好啦,"她回答道,仍然稳稳地坐在椅子上,面前点了一支蜡烛,那本大书摊开着。"这是个简单的建议,但也是我能给你的最妥当的建议。"

"那么,如果您以后听说,有人发现我死在沼泽中或是雪坑里,您的良心就不会低声谴责您也有部分的过错吗?"

"为什么会呢?我不能去送你。他们不许我走到花园的墙角。"

"您!在这样一个夜晚,如果为了我自己的方便要求您迈出这个门槛,那我心里真是太难受了!"我叫道,"我要您告诉我怎么走,而不是要您领路。或者您可以说服希斯克利夫先生派一位向导给我。"

"派谁呢?只有他自己、恩肖、希拉、约瑟夫和我。你想要哪个?"

"难道农场上没有男孩子吗?"

"没有,就这些。"

"那么,就是说我不得不留下来了!"

"这个你可以跟你的主人商量。与我无关。"

"I hope it will be a lesson to you, to make no more rash journeys on these hills," cried Heathcliff's stern voice from the kitchen entrance. "As to staying here, I don't keep accommodations for visitors: you must share a bed with Hareton, or Joseph, if you do."

"I can sleep on a chair in this room," I replied.

"No, no! A stranger is a stranger, be he rich or poor: it will not suit me to permit any one the range of the place while I am off guard!" said the unmannerly wretch.

With this insult, my patience was at an end. I uttered an expre-ssion of disgust, and pushed past him into the yard, running against Earnshaw in my haste. It was so dark that I could not see the means of exit; and, as I wandered round, I heard another specimen of their civil behaviour amongst each other. At first, the young man appeared about to befriend me.

"I'll go with him as far as the park," he said.

"You'll go with him to hell!" exclaimed his master, or whatever relation he bore. "And who is to look after the horses, eh?"

"A man's life is of more consequence than one evening's neglect of the horses: somebody must go," murmured Mrs. Heathcliff, more kindly than I expected.

"Not at your command!" retorted Hareton. "If you set store on him, you'd better be quiet."

"Then I hope his ghost will haunt you; and I hope Mr. Heathcliff will never get another tenant, till the Grange is a ruin!" she answered sharply.

"Hearken, hearken, shoo's cursing on em!" muttered Joseph, towards whom I had

"我希望这会给你一个教训，以后少在山区轻率出行。"希斯克利夫严厉的喊声从厨房门口传来："至于住在这儿，我可没有招待客人的设备。你要留在这儿，就得跟哈里顿或者约瑟夫睡一张床！"

"我可以睡在这间屋子里的椅子上。"我回答道。

"不行，不行！生人总归是生人，不论他是富是穷。我是不会允许任何人在我的监视之外活动的！"那个没有礼貌的无赖说。

受到这样的侮辱，我的忍耐到头了。我恨恨地骂了一声，从他的旁边冲过，直奔院子，由于匆忙，一下子撞到了恩肖身上。天太黑了，我根本找不到出口。正在乱转的时候，我听见他们的说话声，而这是他们之间有教养的举止的另一例证：起初那个年轻人好像对我还比较友好。

"我陪他走到山庄那儿去。"他说。

"你会和他一起下地狱的！"他的主人或是他的什么亲属叫道。"那么，谁去看管那些马呢，呃？"

"一条命比一匹马一晚上没人照应要重要些。得有个人去。"希斯克利夫太太咕哝道，比我所想的要友善很多。

"不要你命令我！"哈里顿反攻了："你要是重视他，最好别吭声。"

"那么我希望他的鬼魂会来缠住你，我还希望希斯克利夫先生直到田庄全毁掉，也找不到另一个房客！"她尖刻地回答。

"听吧，听吧，她在咒他们啦！"约瑟夫咕哝着，这会儿，我正向他的

been steering.

He sat within earshot, milking the cows by the light of a lantern, which I seized unceremoniously, and, calling out that I would send it back on the morrow, rushed to the nearest postern.

"Maister, maister, he's staling t' lantern!" shouted the ancient, pursuing my retreat. "Hey, Gnasher! Hey, dog! Hey, Wolf, holld him, holld him!"

On opening the little door, two hairy monsters flew at my throat, bearing me down and extinguishing the light; while a mingled guffaw, from Heathcliff and Hareton, put the copestone on my rage and humiliation. Fortunately, the beasts seemed more bent on stretching their paws, and yawning, and flourishing their tails, than devouring me alive; but they would suffer no resurrection, and I was forced to lie till their malignant masters pleased to deliver me, then hatless, and trembling with wrath, I ordered the miscreants to let me out—on their peril to keep me one minute longer—with several incoherent threats of retaliation that, in their indefinite depth of virulency, smacked of King Lear①.

The vehemence of my agitation brought on a copious bleeding at the nose, and still Heathcliff laughed, and still I scolded. I don't know what would have concluded the scene, had there not been one person at hand rather more rational than myself, and more benevolent than my entertainer. This was Zillah, the stout housewife; who at length issued forth to inquire

方向走去。

他坐在说话听得见的地方，借着一盏灯的光，正在挤牛奶，我就随便抓起灯，大喊着我明天会把它送回来，便急匆匆地向最近的一个边门冲去。

"主人，主人，他把灯偷跑啦！"这老头一面喊叫，一面追我。"嘿，犬牙！嘿，狗！嘿，狼！抓住他，抓住他！"

一开小门，两个长毛的怪物便扑向我的喉咙，把我压倒在地，灯也给弄灭了。同时希斯克利夫与哈里顿两个放声大笑，使我愤怒和羞辱到了极点。所幸的是，这些畜生仿佛只想伸伸他们的爪子，打打哈欠，还有就是摇摇他们的尾巴，并不想把我活活吞下去。但它们也不容我再起来，我被迫躺在地上，直到等它们可恶的主人什么时候高兴时来解救我。我的帽子也掉了，气得直发抖。我命令这些恶棍放我出去——否则他们留我一分钟，就多一分危险——带着对他们的仇恨，我语无伦次的威胁了一番，那股黑森森的怨气，颇有李尔王的味道。

这剧烈的激动引起了我鼻子的大量出血，可希斯克利夫还是在大笑，我也还是在骂。我真不知道这该怎样收场，难道这里就没有一个人比我更理性了吗？就没有一个人比我的主人更慈善些了吗？这人就是希拉，这位健壮的管家婆，她终于挺身而出询问这场骚乱的原因。她以为他们当中有

---

① King Lear：李尔王。威廉·莎士比亚最著名的悲剧人物之一。李尔王曾在黑夜的暴风雨中强烈诅咒他的两个忤逆的女儿。

into the nature of the uproar. She thought that some of them had been laying violent hands on me; and, not daring to attack her master, she turned her vocal artillery against the younger scoundrel.

"Well, Mr. Earnshaw," she cried, "I wonder what you'll have agait next! Are we going to murder folk on our very door-stones? I see this house will never do for me—look at t' poor lad, he's fair choking! Wisht, wisht! you mun n't go on so. Come in, and I'll cure that. There now, hold ye still."

With these words she suddenly splashed a pint of icy water down my neck, and pulled me into the kitchen. Mr. Heathcliff followed, his accidental merriment expiring quickly in his habitual moroseness.

I was sick exceedingly, and dizzy and faint; and thus compelled, perforce, to accept lodgings under his roof. He told Zillah to give me a glass of brandy, and then passed on to the inner room; while she condoled with me on my sorry predicament, and having obeyed his orders, whereby I was somewhat revived, ushered me to bed.

个人对我动了手。由于不敢得罪她的主人，就转向那个年轻的无赖。

"好啊，恩肖先生，"她叫道，"我不知道你下次还要干出什么好事！我们是要在自家门口杀人吗？我看在这个家里我可再也呆不下去啦——瞧瞧这个可怜的小伙子，他都要窒息了！得了，得了！你可不能再这样了。进来，我给你治治。就这样，别动。"

说着这些话，她突然把一桶冰冷的水泼在我的脖子上，又把我拖进了厨房。希斯克利夫先生跟在后面，他难得流露的欢乐很快又消散在他习惯性的忧郁中了。

我难受得厉害，而且头昏目眩，因此不得不勉强在他家借宿一夜。他让希拉给我一杯白兰地，然后就进里屋去了。她对我可怜的困境慰问了一番，并按照主人的吩咐，给了我一杯白兰地，见我略略恢复了一些，就领我上床去睡了。

Chapter 3
第三章

While leading the way upstairs, she recommended that I should hide the candle, and not make a noise; for her master had an odd notion about the chamber she would put me in, and never let anybody lodge there willingly. I asked the reason. She did not know, she answered. She had only lived there a year or two; and they had so many queer goings on, she could not begin to be curious.

Too stupified to be curious myself, I fastened my door and glanced round for the bed. The whole furniture consisted of a chair, a clothespress, and a large oak case, with squares cut out near the top, resembling coach windows. Having approached this structure, I looked inside, and perceived it to be a singular sort of old-fashioned couch, very conveniently designed to obviate the necessity for every member of the family having a room to himself. In fact, it formed a little closet, and the ledge of a window, which it enclosed, served as a table. I slid back the panelled sides, got in with my light, pulled them together again, and felt secure against the vigilance of Heathcliff, and every one else.

The ledge, where I placed my candle, had

领我上楼时,她建议我把蜡烛藏起来,而且不要出声。因为对于她将带我去的那个卧房,她的主人有一种古怪的看法,而且从来不愿让任何人在那儿睡。我问起原因,她回答说不知道。她说她在那儿才住了一两年,他们又有这么多古怪事,她也就不以为意了。

我自己昏昏沉沉的,也不好奇了,我拴上门,向四下里张望,想找张床。全部的家具只有一把椅子,一个大衣橱,还有一个顶部刻着类似马车窗户的方洞的大橡木箱子。我走近这个东西往里瞧,才看出这是一张非常独特的老式卧榻,设计得非常方便,有了它家里就没有每人独占一间屋子的必要了。实际上,它形成一个小小的隔间,里面还有一个窗台,正好可以当作桌子用。我把嵌板的门往两边推开,拿着蜡烛进去了,然后又把嵌板门关上,觉得自己安全了,躲开了希斯克利夫或是其他人的戒备。

在我放蜡烛的窗台的一角堆着几

a few mildewed books piled up in one corner; and it was covered with writing scratched on the paint. This writing, however, was nothing but a name repeated in all kinds of characters, large and small—*Catherine Earnshaw*, here and there varied to *Catherine Heathcliff*, and then again to *Catherine Linton*.

In vapid listlessness I leant my head against the window, and continued spelling over Catherine Earnshaw—Heathcliff—Linton, till my eyes closed; but they had not rested five minutes when a glare of white letters① started from the dark, as vivid as spectres—the air swarmed with Catherines; and rousing myself to dispel the obtrusive name, I discovered my candle wick reclining on one of the antique volumes, and perfuming the place with an odour of roasted calf-skin. I snuffed it off, and, very ill at ease under the influence of cold and lingering nausea, sat up and spread open the injured tome on my knee. It was a Testament, in lean type, and smelling dreadfully musty: a fly-leaf bore the inscription—"Catherine Earnshaw, her book," and a date some quarter of a century back. I shut it, and took up another, and another, till I had examined all. Catherine's library was select②, and its state of dilapidation proved it to have been well used; though not altogether for a legitimate purpose: scarcely one chapter had escaped a pen-and-ink commentary—at least, the appearance of one—covering every morsel of blank that the printer had left. Some were detached sentences; other parts took the form of a regular diary, scrawled in an

---

① 西方的迷信,认为幽灵是白色的。
② 指凯瑟琳的藏书都是被精选出的宣扬基督教教义的"善书"。

unformed, childish hand. At the top of an extra page (quite a treasure, probably, when first lighted on) I was greatly amused to behold an excellent caricature of my friend Joseph, — rudely yet powerfully sketched. An immediate interest kindled within me for the unknown Catherine, and I began, forthwith, to decypher her faded hieroglyphics.

"An awful Sunday!" commenced the paragraph beneath."I wish my father were back again. Hindley is a detestable substitute—his conduct to Heathcliff is atrocious—H. and I are going to rebel—we took our initiatory step this evening.

"All day had been flooding with rain; we could not go to church, so Joseph must needs get up a congregation in the garret; and, while Hindley and his wife basked down stairs before a comfortable fire—doing anything but reading their Bibles, I'll answer for it—Heathcliff, myself, and the unhappy plough-boy were commanded to take our Prayer-books, and mount. We were ranged in a row, on a sack of corn, groaning and shivering, and hoping that Joseph would shiver too, so that he might give us a short homily for his own sake. A vain idea! The service lasted precisely three hours; and yet my brother had the face to exclaim, when he saw us descending, 'What, done already?' On Sunday evenings we used to be permitted to play, if we did not make much noise; now a mere titter is sufficient to send us into corners!

"'You forget you have a master here,' says the tyrant. 'I'll demolish the first who puts me out of temper! I insist on perfect sobriety and silence. Oh, boy! was that you?

出于小孩子之手的笔迹潦草地写下的。在一张空余的书页上面(刚发现它也许还把它当作宝贝呢),我很高兴地看见了一幅我那位相识约瑟夫的绝妙的漫画像——画得虽说粗糙,可是很有力。这使我立刻对这位素昧平生的凯瑟琳产生了兴趣,于是开始辨认她那很难认的已褪色的字迹。

"讨厌的星期天!"底下一段这样写道。"但愿我的父亲还能再回来。辛德雷是个可恶的继父——他对希斯克利夫的态度非常粗暴——希和我准备要反抗了——今天晚上我们要进行第一步。

"一整天都淫雨绵绵。我们不能去教堂,所以约瑟夫非要在阁楼上召集会众不可。而辛德雷和他的妻子则在楼下舒舒服服地烤火——我敢保证,他们随便做什么,也决不会去读《圣经》——而希斯克利夫、我和那可怜的干农活的孩子都被要求带着各自的祈祷书,爬到上面去。我们坐在一口袋粮食上,排成一排,又哼哼唧唧又哆嗦。但愿约瑟夫也哆嗦,这样为了他自己,他也会少给我们传点道了。妄想!礼拜做了整整三个小时。而我的哥哥看见我们下楼的时候,竟然还有脸嚷道,'什么,已经结束啦?'以前星期天的晚上一向是准许我们玩的,只要我们不弄出太多的声音,但是现在,哪怕一点点笑声,我们就得被赶到墙角去罚站。

"'你们忘记了这里是有主人的了,'这暴君说道,'我会把第一个惹我发脾气的家伙毁掉!我坚决要求绝对的肃静。哦,小子!是你吗?亲爱

Frances, darling, pull his hair as you go by: I heard him snap his fingers.' Frances pulled his hair heartily, and then went and seated herself on her husband's knee; and there they were, like two babies, kissing and talking nonsense by the hour—foolish palaver that we should be ashamed of. We made ourselves as snug as our means allowed in the arch of the dresser. I had just fastened our pinafores together, and hung them up for a curtain, when in comes Joseph, on an errand from the stables. He tears down my handywork, boxes my ears, and croaks—

"'T' maister nobbut just buried, and Sabbath nut oe'red, und t' sahnd uh't gospel still i' yer lugs, and yah darr be laiking! shame on ye! sit ye dahn, ill childer! they's good books eneugh if ye'll read 'em. Sit ye dahn, and think uh yer sowls!'

"Saying this, he compelled us so to square our positions that we might receive from the far-off fire a dull ray to show us the text of the lumber he thrust upon us. I could not bear the employment. I took my dingy volume by the scroop, and hurled it into the dog-kennel, vowing I hated a good book. Heathcliff kicked his to the same place. Then there was a hubbub!

"'Maister Hindley!' shouted our chaplain. 'Maister, coom hither! Miss Cathy's riven th' back off 'Th' Helmet uh Salvation,' un' Heathcliff's pawsed his fit intuh t' first part uh "T' Brooad Way to Destruction!" It's fair flaysome ut yah let 'em goa on this gait. Ech! th'owd man ud uh laced 'em properly—bud he's goan!'

"Hindley hurried up from his paradise on the hearth, and seizing one of us by the collar, and the other by the arm, hurled both into the backkitchen; where, Joseph asseverated, 'owd Nick' would fetch us as sure as we were living. And, so comforted, we each sought a separate nook to await his advent. I reached this book, and a pot of ink from the shelf, and pushed the house-door ajar to give me light, and I have got the time on with writing for twenty minutes; but my companion is impatient, and proposes that we should appropriate the dairy woman's cloak, and have a scamper on the moors, under its shelter. A pleasant suggestion—and then, if the surly old man come in, he may believe his prophecy verified-we cannot be damper, or colder, in the rain than we are here."

I suppose Catherine fulfilled her project, for the next sentence took up another subject: she waxed lachrymose.

"How little did I dream that Hindley would ever make me cry so!" she wrote. "My head aches, till I cannot keep it on the pillow; and still I can't give over. Poor Heathcliff! Hindley calls him a vagabond, and won't let him sit with us, nor eat with us any more; and, he says, he and I must not play together, and threatens to turn him out of the house if we break his orders. He has been blaming our father (how dared he?) for treating H. too liberally; and swears he will reduce him to his right place—"

I began to nod drowsily over the dim page, my eye wandered from manuscript to print. I saw a red ornamented title—"Seventy Times Seven, and the First of the Seventy-First. A Pious Discourse delivered by the Reverend Jabes Branderham, in the Chapel of Gimmerden Sough." And while I was, half consciously, worrying my brain to guess what Jabes

约瑟夫断言，'老尼克'准会在那儿把我们给活捉的。得到这样的安慰，我们便各自找了个角落，等待魔鬼降临。我从书架上伸手摸到了这本书和一瓶墨水，又把门推开了一些，漏进几丝亮光，于是我就写了大概二十分钟字。可是我的同伴不耐烦了，他建议我们把挤牛奶女人的外套借来一用，到旷野上去跑一阵。多好的一个主意——这样，要是那个乖戾的老头进来的话，他可能会相信他的预言实现了呢——即使在雨里，我们也不会比在这儿更湿更冷的。"

我猜想凯瑟琳实现了她的计划，因为下一句开始了另一话题，她伤心起来。

"我从来没有想到辛德雷会让我这样哭泣！"她写道，"我头疼，疼得我无法睡在枕头上。即使这样，我还是不能停止哭泣。可怜的希斯克利夫！辛德雷骂他是流氓，并且不许他再跟我们一起坐，一起吃饭。而且他说，他和我不能再在一起玩，并威胁说要是我们违背了他的命令，就把希斯克利夫撵出去。他指责我们的父亲（他怎么敢呀？）待希太宽厚了，还发誓说要把他降到属于他的地位去——"

对着这字迹模糊的书页，我开始打盹，眼睛从手写体转到印刷字体上。我看到一个有花饰的红字标题——"七十乘七，与第七十一的第一条。杰贝兹•伯兰德罕牧师在吉默顿•苏的小教堂宣读的一篇传道经文。"还在我迷迷糊糊、绞尽脑汁地推敲杰贝兹•伯兰德罕牧师将怎样发

第三章

Branderham would make of his subject, I sank back in bed, and fell asleep. Alas, for the effects of bad tea and bad temper! what else could it be that made me pass such a terrible night? I don't remember another that I can at all compare with it since I was capable of suffering.

I began to dream, almost before I ceased to be sensible of my locality. I thought it was morning; and I had set out on my way home, with Joseph for a guide. The snow lay yards deep in our road; and, as we floundered on, my companion wearied me with constant reproaches that I had not brought a pilgrim's staff, telling me that I could never get into the house without one, and boastfully flourishing a heavy-headed cudgel, which I understood to be so denominated. For a moment I considered it absurd that I should need such a weapon to gain admittance into my own residence. Then a new idea flashed across me. I was not going there: we were journeying to hear the famous Jabes Branderham preach from the text—"Seventy Times Seven"; and either Joseph, the preacher, or I had committed the "First of the Seventy-First," and were to be publicly exposed and excommunicated.

We came to the chapel. I have passed it really in my walks, twice or thrice; it lies in a hollow, between two hills: an elevated hollow, near a swamp, whose peaty moisture is said to answer all the purposes of embalming on the few corpses deposited there. The roof has been kept whole hitherto; but as the clergyman's stipend is only twenty pounds per annum, and a house with two rooms, threatening speedily to determine into one, no clergyman will undertake the duties of pastor, especially

挥他这个题目的时候，我已经倒在床上睡着了。咳，这倒霉的茶和坏脾气的影响啊！还能有什么足以使我度过如此糟糕的一夜呢？自从我学会吃苦受难以来，我记不起有哪一次能够和这一夜相比的。

在我几乎快要忘记自己置身何地之前，我开始做梦。我认为是到了早晨，我正一路赶回家去，约瑟夫作我的向导。路上堆着几尺厚的雪，我们挣扎着往前走，我的同伴不停地指责我没有带朝圣的手杖，惹得我心烦。他告诉我不带拐杖就永远也进不了家，还得意洋洋地挥舞着他手中那一根大头棍棒，我只知道那是棍棒而已。一开始，我觉得需要这么一个武器才能进我自己的家也未免太荒谬了。突然一个新的念头闪过我的脑海，我并不是回家，我们是在去听那大名鼎鼎的杰贝兹·伯兰德罕牧师宣讲"七十乘七"的经文的路上，而无论是约瑟夫，还是牧师，我要是犯了这"第七十一的第一条"的罪，就会被人当众揭发，并被逐出教会。

我们来到了小教堂。说真的，我平日散步从那经过过两三回。它位于两山之间的一个山谷里：一个高高的山谷，靠近一片沼泽，据说那儿泥炭的湿气足以保护埋在那儿的几具死尸一点儿也不腐烂。房顶完好地保存至今，可是这儿教士每年的收入仅仅只有二十镑，外带一所有两个房间的屋子，而且眼看恐怕快要决定只给一间了，所以没有一个教士愿意担任牧师的职位，尤其是根据最近的传说；他

as it is currently reported that his flock would rather let him starve than increase the living by one penny from their own pockets. However, in my dream, Jabes had a full and attentive congregation; and he preached—good God! what a sermon: divided into *four hundred and ninety* parts, each fully equal to an ordinary address from the pulpit, and each discussing a separate sin! Where he searched for them, I cannot tell. He had his private manner of interpreting the phrase, and it seemed necessary the brother should sin different sins on every occasion. They were of the most curious character, odd transgressions that I never imagined previously.

Oh, how weary I grew. How I writhed, and yawned, and nodded, and revived! How I pinched and pricked myself, and rubbed my eyes, and stood up, and sat down again, and nudged Joseph to inform me if he would *ever* have done. I was condemned to hear all out, finally, he reached the *"First of the Seventy-First."* At that crisis, a sudden inspiration descended on me; I was moved to rise and denounce Jabes Branderham as the sinner of the sin that no Christian need pardon.

"Sir," I exclaimed, "sitting here within these four walls, at one stretch, I have endured and forgiven the four hundred and ninety heads of your discourse. Seventy times seven times have I plucked up my hat and been about to depart—Seventy times seven times have you preposterously forced me to resume my seat. The four hundred and ninety first is too much. Fellow-martyrs, have at him! Drag him down, and crush him to atoms, that the place which knows him may know him no more!"

的教徒们宁愿让他饿死，也不愿从他们自己腰包里多掏出一分钱来供其生计。但是，在我的梦里，杰贝兹有着聚精会神的满堂会众，而他正在讲道——老天！这是什么布道呀，一共分成四百九十节，每一节都足足相当于通常布道坛上的一篇讲道，每一节单独讨论一种罪过！我不知道他是从哪儿搜集出来这么些罪过的。他用自己的方式讲解那些词语，看上去仿佛必然教友每一次犯的都是不同的罪。这些罪过性质极其奇怪，都是我以前从来不曾想像过的一些古怪的罪过。

哦，我是多么疲倦啊！我是怎样地转来转去、打呵欠、打瞌睡，又清醒过来的啊！我是怎样地掐自己、戳自己、揉眼睛、站起来，又坐下，而且用胳膊肘碰约瑟夫，如果牧师终于把经文讲完的话让他告诉我。我注定是要听完所有的了。最后，他讲到"第七十一的第一条"。就在这个时候，一个念头突然闪现我的脑海，我不由自主地站起来，当众谴责杰贝兹•伯兰德罕是个罪人，他犯了一种没有哪个基督徒能够宽恕的罪过。

"先生，"我大声叫道，"坐在这四堵墙壁之内，我已经一口气儿忍受而且原谅了您这篇经文的四百九十个题目。有七十乘七次我曾拿起我的帽子，准备离开。有七十乘七次，您荒谬地迫使我回到座位上。这第四百九十一我是忍无可忍的了。受难的同伴们，打他！把他拖下来，把他捣烂，这样，这个认识他的地方，也许再也没有他这个人了！"

第三章

"*Thou art the Man*!" cried Jabes, after a solemn pause, leaning over his cushion. "Seventy times seven times didst thou gapingly contort thy visage—seventy times seven did I take counsel with my soul—Lo, this is human weakness: this also may be absolved! The First of the Seventy-First is come. Brethren, execute upon him the judgment written. Such honour have all His saints!"

With that concluding word the whole assembly, exalting their pilgrim's staves, rushed round me in a body; and I, having no weapon to raise in selfdefence, commenced grappling with Joseph, my nearest and most ferocious assailant, for his. In the confluence of the multitude, several clubs crossed; blows, aimed at me, fell on other sconces. Presently the whole chapel resounded with rappings and counter-rappings, every man's hand was against his neighbour; and Branderham, unwilling to remain idle, poured forth his zeal in a shower of loud taps on the boards of the pulpit, which responded so smartly that, at last, to my unspeakable relief, they woke me. And what was it that had suggested the tremendous tumult? What had played Jabes's part in the row? Merely the branch of a fir-tree that touched my lattice, as the blast wailed by, and rattled its dry cones against the panes! I listened doubtingly an instant; detected the disturber, then turned and dosed, and dreamt again: if possible, still more disagreeably than before.

This time, I remembered I was lying in the oak closet, and I heard distinctly the gusty wind, and the driving of the snow; I heard, also, the fir-bough repeat its teasing sound, and ascribed it to the right cause. But it annoyed me

"罪人就是你!"在一阵严静之后,杰贝兹惊呼,靠在他的坐垫上。"七十乘七次你张大嘴作怪相——七十乘七次我和我的灵魂商议着——瞧吧,这是人类的弱点,这也还是可以赦免的!第七十一的第一条来啦。兄弟们,按照写定的判决处死他吧。所有的圣徒都有他这种光荣!"

他的话音刚落,全体与会者举起他们的朝圣手杖,一窝蜂地向我冲来。我没有自卫的武器,于是便开始抓住约瑟夫——这个离我最近、也是最凶猛的攻击者——抢他的手杖。在人潮汇集之中,一些棍子交叉着,向我砸来,却落在别人的脑袋上。霎那间,整个教堂充满了打斗的声音,每个人都在跟旁边的人动手,而伯兰德罕也不愿意闲着,倾注满腔热情猛敲讲坛,非常有力,以至于最后让我醒过来,缓解了我无以言语的痛苦。这样巨大的骚乱意味着什么呢?在这场骚乱中是谁扮演了杰贝兹的角色呢?原来只不过是在狂风呜呜地刮过时,一棵枞树的树枝碰到了我的窗格,它的干果打在玻璃窗上嘎嘎作响而已!我将信将疑地倾听了一阵,弄清了使我不安的根源就是它,然后翻了个身,昏昏睡去,又做了梦:如果可能的话,这个梦比先前的那个更令人不快。

这次,我记得我是躺在那个橡木的壁橱里。我很清晰地听见怒吼的狂风,还有风吹起雪的声音,我也听见那枞树树枝总是发出烦人的声音,而且也知道这是什么原因。可它实在使

so much, that I resolved to silence it, if possible; and, I thought, I rose and endeavoured to unhasp the casement. The hook was soldered into the staple, a circumstance observed by me when awake, but forgotten. "I must stop it, nevertheless!" I muttered, knocking my knuckles through the glass, and stretching an arm out to seize the importunate branch; instead of which, my fingers closed on the fingers of a little, ice-cold hand! The intense horror of nightmare came over me. I tried to draw back my arm, but the hand clung to it, and a most melancholy voice sobbed, "Let me in—let me in!" "Who are you?" I asked, struggling, meanwhile, to disengage myself. "Catherine Linton," it replied shiveringly (why did I think of *Linton*? I had read *Earnshaw* twenty times for Linton). "I'm come home, I'd lost my way on the moor!" As it spoke, I discerned, obscurely, a child's face looking through the window. Terror made me cruel; and, finding it useless to attempt shaking the creature off, I pulled its wrist on to the broken pane, and rubbed it to and fro till the blood ran down and soaked the bedclothes, still it wailed, "Let me in!" and maintained its tenacious gripe, almost maddening me with fear. "How can I!" I said at length. "Let *me* go, if you want me to let you in!" The fingers relaxed, I snatched mine through the hole, hurriedly piled the books up in a pyramid against it, and stopped my ears to exclude the lamentable prayer. I seemed to keep them closed above a quarter of an hour; yet, the instant I listened again, there was the doleful cry moaning on! "Begone!" I shouted, "I'll never let you in, not if you beg for twenty years." "It is twentyyears," mourned the

我太烦了,于是我决定,如果可能的话,要让它安静下来。我觉得我起了床,并且企图去打开那窗子。窗钩是焊在钩环里的,这情况我在清醒时就注意到了,但是又给忘了。"不管怎么样,我都要止住它!"我咕噜着,用拳头打破了玻璃,伸出一个胳臂去抓那捣乱的树枝。可我的手指没抓到它,却碰着了一只冰凉小手的手指!梦魇的强烈恐怖压倒了我,我试图缩回手臂,但是那只手却抓住我不放,一个异常忧郁的声音呜咽着:"让我进去——让我进去!""你是谁?"我问,同时挣扎着想把手挣脱出来。"凯瑟琳·林顿,"那声音颤抖着回答道(为什么我会想到林顿?有二十来次我把林顿都念成了恩肖)。"我回家来了,我在旷野上迷路啦!"在她说话的时候,我模模糊糊地辨认出一张孩子的脸在向窗里探望。恐怖使我变得残忍,发现挣扎摆脱不了这个东西,就把她的手腕拉到那个破了的玻璃面上,来回摩擦,直到鲜血流下来,浸湿了床褥。可她还是哀哭着,"让我进去!"而且还是紧紧抓住我不放,恐惧使我发狂。"我怎么能够呢?"我终于说。"如果你想让我放你进来的话,先放开我!"手指松开了。我从窗洞外把自己的手抽回来,急忙把书堆成金字塔形状抵住窗子,还把耳朵捂住,不想再听那哀痛的祈求声。我捂了耳朵仿佛有一刻多钟。然而当我再听的时候,那悲惨的呼声还继续哀叫着!"走开!"我叫道,"我永远都不会让你进来,哪怕你苦求我二十年也没用。""已经二十年啦,"这声音呜咽着说,"二十年。我已经作了二

voice: "twenty years. I've been a waif for twenty years!" Thereat began a feeble scratching outside, and the pile of books moved as if thrust forward. I tried to jump up; but could not stir a limb; and so yelled aloud, in a frenzy of fright. To my confusion, I discovered the yell was not ideal; hasty footsteps approached my chamber door; somebody pushed it open, with a vigorous hand, and a light glimmered through the squares at the top of the bed. I sat shuddering yet, and wiping the perspiration from my forehead the intruder appeared to hesitate, and muttered to himself. At last, he said in a half-whisper, plainly not expecting an answer, "Is any one here?" I considered it best to confess my presence; for I knew Heathcliff's accents, and feared he might search further, if I kept quiet. With this intention, I turned and opened the panels. I shall not soon forget the effect my action produced.

Heathcliff stood near the entrance, in his shirt and trousers; with a candle dripping over his fingers, and his face as white as the wall behind him. The first creak of the oak startled him like an electric shock; the light leaped from his hold to a distance of some feet, and his agitation was so extreme, that he could hardly pick it up.

"It is only your guest, sir," I called out, desirous to spare him the humiliation of exposing his cowardice further. "I had the misfortune to scream in my sleep, owing to a frightful nightmare. I'm sorry I disturbed you."

"Oh, God confound you, Mr. Lockwood! I wish you were at the —①" com-

十年无家可归的人！"接着，外面就响起细微的刮擦声，那堆书也动起来，像是有人在把它往里推似的。我想要跳起来，可是四肢却动弹不了，于是在狂乱的恐惧中我放声叫声。使我狼狈的是，我发现那大叫并非虚幻，一阵急促的脚步声逼近我的卧房门口。有人用力推开了门，接着，有一道光透过床顶的方洞外微微照了进来。我还坐在那儿哆嗦，揩着我额上的汗。那闯进来的人好像踌躇了一下，自言自语。最后他用近乎耳语的声音问道："有人在这儿吗？"显然，他并不指望有人回答。我觉得最好还是承认我在这儿，因为我听出来，那是希斯克利夫的口音，我怕如果我一声不吭，他还要进一步搜查。打定了主意，我就转身推开嵌板。我的这一举动所带来的后果将令我久久难忘。

希斯克利夫站在门口，身穿衬衣和长裤，手里拿着一支蜡烛，烛油直滴到他的手指上，他的脸色就像他身后的墙壁一样苍白。那橡木门第一声吱吱一响，吓得他犹如触电一样，蜡烛从他手里跳出来，掉在了几尺远的地方，而他极度不安，以至于几乎捡不起蜡烛。

"只不过是你的客人在这儿罢了，先生。"我叫出声来，免得他因过多暴露出胆怯的样子而感到难堪。"因为做梦，我不幸在睡着时尖叫起来。很抱歉，打搅你了。"

"哦，上帝诅咒你，洛克伍德先生！我但愿你是在——"我的主人开

---

① 应为"I wish you were at the hell."当时的书籍把一些诅咒的词汇用"—"代替。

menced my host, setting the candle on a chair, because he found it impossible to hold it steady. "And who showed you up to this room?" he continued, crushing his nails into his palms, and grinding his teeth to subdue the maxillary convulsions."Who was it? I've a good mind to turn them out of the house this moment!"

"It was your servant, Zillah," I replied, flinging myself on to the floor, and rapidly resuming my garments."I should not care if you did, Mr. Heathcliff; she richly deserves it. I suppose that she wanted to get another proof that the place was haunted, at my expense. Well, it is—swarming with ghosts and goblins! You have reason in shutting it up, I assure you. No one will thank you for a dose in such a den!"

"What do you mean?" asked Heathcliff, "and what are you doing? Lie down and finish out the night, since you *are* here; but, for Heaven's sake! Don't repeat that horrid noise; nothing could excuse it, unless you were having your throat cut!"

"If the little fiend had got in at the window, she probably would have strangled me!" I returned."I'm not going to endure the persecutions of your hospitable ancestors again. Was not the Reverend Jabes Branderham akin to you on the mother's side? And that minx, Catherine Linton, or Earnshaw, or however she was called—she must have been a changeling[①]—wicked little soul! She told me she had been walking the earth these twenty years; a just punishment for her mortal transgressions, I've no doubt!"

始说,因为他发现他再也没法稳稳拿住蜡烛了,就把它固定在椅子上。"是谁把你领到这间房里来的?"他接着说,把指甲掐进他的手心,同时磨着牙齿,好抑制上颌骨的抽搐。"是谁带你来的?我真想现在就把他们撵出门去!"

"是你的仆人,希拉,"我回答,同时从床上跳到地板上,很快穿好衣服。"要是你这么做,我也不在乎,希斯克利夫先生。她活该,我猜想她是想利用我来再一次证明这地方闹鬼罢了。嘿,是闹鬼——满屋子妖魔鬼怪!我向你保证,你有理由把它关起来。没有人会为了在这么个洞里睡上一觉而感谢你!"

"你是什么意思?"希斯克利夫问道,"你干什么?既然你已经在这儿了,躺下睡完这一夜。但是,看在上帝的分上!千万别再发出那种可怕的叫声了。那叫人没法原谅,除非你的喉咙正被人割断!"

"如果那个小妖精从窗子钻进来,说不定她会把我掐死的!"我回敬道:"我可不愿再忍受你那些殷勤好客的祖先们的迫害了。那位杰贝兹·伯兰德罕牧师是不是你母亲的亲戚?还有那个疯丫头,凯瑟琳·林顿,或是恩肖,或者管她叫什么名字吧——她一定是个被调包的小妖精——邪恶的小东西!她告诉我,这二十年来她就在地面上流浪,这正是她致命罪行的报应——我一点都不怀疑!"

---

① 在欧洲各国有一个流传甚广的民间故事:每当美丽的婴儿出生,侏儒小鬼戈布林便常常会用自己丑陋的孩子偷偷换走那美丽的婴儿。这个被留下来的丑孩子,就是 changeling(调包婴儿)。

Scarcely were these words uttered, when I recollected the association of Heathcliff's with Catherine's name in the book, which had completely slipped from my memory, till thus awakened. I blushed at my inconsideration; but, without showing further consciousness of the offence, I hastened to add—"The truth is, sir, I passed the first part of the night in"— here I stopped afresh—I was about to say "perusing those old volumes," then it would have revealed my knowledge of their written, as well as their printed, contents; so, correcting myself, I went on—"in spelling over the name scratched on that window-ledge. A monotonous occupation, calculated to set me asleep, like counting, or—"

"What *can* you mean by talking in this way to *me*?" thundered Heathcliff with savage vehemence. "How—how *dare* you, under my roof? —God! he's mad to speak so!" And he struck his forehead with rage.

I did not know whether to resent this language or pursue my explanation; but he seemed so powerfully affected that I took pity and proceeded with my dreams; affirming I had never heard the appellation of "Catherine Linton" before, but reading it often over produced an impression which personified itself when I had no longer my imagination under control. Heathcliff gradually fell back into the shelter of the bed, as I spoke; finally sitting down almost concealed behind it. I guessed, however, by his irregular and intercepted breathing, that he struggled to vanquish an excess of violent emotion. Not liking to show him that I heard the conflict, I continued my toilette rather noisily, looked at my watch, and soliloquised on the length of the

这几句话刚一出口，我就想起在那本书上希斯克利夫与凯瑟琳这两个名字的联系来，我竟忘得一干二净，直到这时才醒过来。我为我的鲁莽而感到脸红，但是，我并没表现出已经察觉到自己的冒失的表情，赶紧补充道："事实上，先生，我前半夜是在这——"说到这儿我又打住了——我本想说"读那些旧书"，但那样就会暴露我不但知道书中印刷的，也知道那些用笔写出的内容了。因此，我改口往下说道——"在拼读刻在窗台上的那些名字，一种非常单调的工作，数着数着使我睡着，就像数数字似的，或者——"

"你这样跟我讲话，到底是什么意思？"希斯克利夫非常激动而粗暴地咆哮道："怎么——你怎么敢在我的家里？——上帝呀！他说这话肯定是发疯啦！"说着他愤怒地敲着自己的额头。

我不知是该生气好，还是继续我的解释。但是他反应如此强烈以至我都同情他了，便继续说我的梦，并断言"凯瑟琳·林顿"这个名字我以前从来没有听过，只是念得次数过多才产生了一个印象，这印象在我的想像力失控的情况下而就把它视为人了。在我说话的时候，希斯克利夫慢慢地往床后退，最后坐下来，几乎是躲在床后面了。然而，从他那不规则的、时断时续的呼吸，我猜想他是拼命平息过于强烈的情绪。我不想让他知道我已听出了他内心的挣扎，就继续穿衣服，还发出很大的声响，又看看我的表，自言自语地抱怨长夜漫漫。"还不到三点钟哪！我简直可以发誓

night; "Not three o'clock yet! I could have taken oath it had been six. Time stagnates here: we must surely have retired to rest at eight!"

"Always at nine in winter, and always rise at four," said my host, suppressing a groan: And, as I fancied, by the motion of his shadow's arm, dashing a tear from his eyes. "Mr. Lockwood," he added, "you may go into my room; you'll only be in the way, coming down stairs so early; and your childish outcry has sent sleep to the devil for me."

"And for me, too," I replied. "I'll walk in the yard till daylight, and then I'll be off; and you need not dread a repetition of my intrusion. I am now quite cured of seeking pleasure in society, be it country or town. A sensible man ought to find sufficient company in himself."

"Delightful company!" muttered Heathcliff. "Take the candle, and go where you please. I shall join you directly. Keep out of the yard, though, the dogs are unchained; and the house—Juno mounts sentinel there, and—nay, you can only ramble about the steps and passages. But, away with you! I'll come in two minutes!"

I obeyed, so far as to quit the chamber; when, ignorant where the narrow lobbies led, I stood still, and was witness, involuntarily, to a piece of superstition on the part of my landlord, which belied, oddly, his apparent sense. He got on to the bed, and wrenched open the lattice, bursting, as he pulled at it, into an uncontrollable passion of tears. "Come in! come in!" he sobbed. "Cathy, do come. Oh do—*once more*! Oh! My heart's darling! hear me *this* time, Catherine, at last!" The spectre showed a spectre's ordinary caprice; it gave no

说已经六点了,时间在这儿静止不动:我们一定是在八点钟就睡觉了!"

"在冬天总是九点钟睡觉,四点起床,"压住一声呻吟,我的主人说。看他胳臂的影子的动作,我想他正在抹去眼里的一滴眼泪。"洛克伍德先生,"他接着说,"你可以到我房间去。这么早下楼,会给别人添麻烦的。你那孩子般的喊叫已经把我的睡意都赶得见鬼去了。"

"我也是。"我回答。"我到院子里去散散步,等到天亮我就离开,你也不用担心我再来打扰你了。我这不管是在城里还是在乡下都喜欢交朋友的毛病现在已经差不多给治好了。一个明智的人应该发现有他自己做伴就够了。"

"愉快的伙伴!"希斯克利夫咕噜着,"拿着蜡烛,你爱去哪儿就去吧。我就去找你。但是,别到院子里去,那几只狗都没拴住。还有大厅里——朱诺在那儿放哨,还有——不,你只能在楼梯和走廊里走走。可是,你去吧!我过两分钟就来。"

我听从他,离开了这间卧室。当时我不知道那条狭窄的走道通向哪里,就站住了,不料却在无意之中看见我那房东做一件迷信的事情,非常奇怪,看来他不过是表面上理智罢了。他爬上了床,猛力扭开窗子,当他用力推时,涌出了抑制不住的热泪。"进来吧!进来吧!"他啜泣着。"凯茜,快来吧!哦,来吧——再来一次!啊!我的心肝儿!这次就听我的吧,凯茜,最后一次!"鬼魂显示出鬼魂素有的反复无常,它没有一点

sign of being; but the snow and wind whirled wildly through, even reaching my station, and blowing out the light.

There was such anguish in the gush of grief that accompanied this raving, that my compassion made me overlook its folly, and I drew off, half angry to have listened at all, and vexed at having related my ridiculous nightmare, since it produced that agony; though *why*, was beyond my comprehension. I descended cautiously to the lower regions, and landed in the back-kitchen, where a gleam of fire, raked compactly together, enabled me to rekindle my candle. Nothing was stirring except a brindled, grey cat, which crept from the ashes, and saluted me with a querulous mew.

Two benches, shaped in sections of a circle, nearly enclosed the hearth; on one of these I stretched myself, and Grimalkin mounted the other. We were both of us nodding, ere any one invaded our retreat, and then it was Joseph, shuffling down a wooden ladder that vanished in the roof, through a trap; the ascent to his garret, I suppose. He cast a sinister look at the little flame which I had enticed to play between the ribs, swept the cat from its elevation, and bestowing himself in the vacancy, commenced the operation of stuffing a three-inch pipe with tobacco. My presence in his sanctum was evidently esteemed a piece of impudence too shameful for remark; he silently applied the tube to his lips, folded his arms, and puffed away. I let him enjoy the luxury unannoyed; and after sucking out the last wreath, and heaving a profound sigh, he got up, and departed as solemnly as he came.

A more elastic footstep entered next; and

第三章

要来的迹象！只有风雪呼呼地灌进来，甚至吹到我站的地方，把蜡烛都吹灭了。

那一堆语无伦次的话中，夹杂着那么一股剧痛，以致我对他的同情使我忽视了他举止的愚蠢。我退了出来，一半是气恼自己听了他这番话，另一半是因自己讲了那荒谬的恶梦而烦恼，因为它招来这许多痛苦。尽管我说不上来为什么会这样。我小心地下了楼，来到后厨房，那儿还留着一星火苗，拨拢在一起，使我重新点着了蜡烛。除了一只斑纹灰猫从灰堆里爬出来，怒气冲冲地喵喵叫了一声向我打个招呼之外，屋里一点动静也没有。

两条圆弧形的长凳，差不多把炉边围了起来。我在一条长凳上躺下来，而那只老母猫跳上了另一条。在没有任何人闯入我们的静居地之前，我们两个都在打瞌睡。那个闯入的人就是约瑟夫，他拖曳着一个木梯下来，木梯在屋顶处消失，穿过一个活门：我猜想那儿是上到阁楼的。他向着被我拨弄起来的火苗狠狠地瞥了一眼，把猫从它的高座上撵了下来，自己占用了那个空出的位子，往他那三英寸长的烟斗里填烟丝。很显然，我在他的圣地出现，被他看作是羞于提及的粗鲁行为。他默默地把烟斗递到嘴里，双臂合抱，喷云吐雾。我让他享受这奢侈，不去打搅他。他抽完最后一口烟，长长地出了一口气，站起来，像他走进来时那样严肃地走出去了。

接着来了一阵更有弹性的脚步。

now I opened my mouth for a "goodmorning," but closed it again, the salutation unachieved; for Hareton Earnshaw was performing his orisons *sotto voce*, in a series of curses directed against every object he touched, while he rummaged a corner for a spade or shovel to dig through the drifts. He glanced over the back of the bench, dilating his nostrils, and thought as little of exchanging civilities with me as with my companion the cat. I guessed, by his preparations, that egress was allowed, and, leaving my hard couch, made a movement to follow him He noticed this, and thrust at an inner door with the end of his spade, intimating by an inarticulate sound that there was the place where I must go, if I changed my locality.

It opened into the house, where the females were already astir. Zillah urging flakes of flame up the chimney with a colossal bellows; and Mrs. Heathcliff, kneeling on the hearth, reading a book by the aid of the blaze. She held her hand interposed between the furnace-heat and her eyes, and seemed absorbed in her occupation; desisting from it only to chide the servant for covering her with sparks, or to push away a dog, now and then, that snoozled its nose over-forwardly into her face. I was surprised to see Heathcliff there also. He stood by the fire, his back towards me, just finishing a stormy scene to poor Zillah; who ever and anon interrupted her labour to pluck up the corner of her apron, and heave an indignant groan.

"And you, you worthless—" he broke out as I entered, turning to his daughter-in-law, and employing an epithet as harmless as duck, or sheep, but generally represented by a dash—."There you are, at your idle tricks again? The

这次，我张开口正要说"早安"，可又闭上了，没能致意，因为哈里顿·恩肖正在偷偷地低声做早祷，其实是一连串的诅咒，他碰到每样东西都要对它发出一串的诅咒，原来他正在屋角找一把铲子或是铁锹去铲除积雪。他向长凳后面扫了一眼，张大鼻孔，根本没有要跟我或我那猫伙伴打招呼的意思。看他所作的准备，我猜他允许我走了，便离开了我的硬座准备跟他走。他发现了，就用他的铲子头戳了戳一扇里门，含糊不清的暗示，如果我要换个地方，就非走那儿不可。

那扇门通向大厅，女人们已经开始四处活动了：希拉正在鼓动着一只巨大的风箱，把火苗吹上烟囱；希斯克利夫太太，则跪在炉边，借着火光读着一本书。她用手遮挡在炉子和她的眼睛之间，似乎完全沉醉其中，只有在斥责仆人把火星溅到她身上，或者不时推开一只总用鼻子向她脸上凑近的狗时才分一下神。我很惊讶地看见希斯克利夫也在那儿。他站在火旁，背对着我。因为刚刚对可怜的希拉暴风雨般地发过一场脾气，她时不时地打断手上的活，扯着围裙角，发出愤愤不平的呻吟声。

"还有你，你这没有用的——"我进去时，他正转过去骂他的儿媳妇，还用了一个如鸭呀、羊呀一类无伤大雅的绰号，可是一般情况下只用的手一挥来表示。"你又在那儿游手好

rest of them do earn their bread—you live on my charity! Put your trash away, and find something to do. You shall pay me for the plague of having you eternally in my sight do you hear, damnable jade?"

"I'll put my trash away, because you can make me, if I refuse," answered the young lady, closing her book, and throwing it on a chair. "But I'll not do anything, though you should swear your tongue out, except what I please."

Heathcliff lifted his hand, and the speaker sprang to a safer distance, obviously acquainted with its weight. Having no desire to be entertained by a cat-and-dog combat, I stepped forward briskly, as if eager to partake the warmth of the hearth, and innocent of any knowledge of the interrupted dispute. Each had enough decorum to suspend further hostilities. Heathcliff placed his fists, out of temptation, in his pockets; Mrs. Heathcliff curled her lip, and walked to a seat far off, where she kept her word by playing the part of a statue during the remainder of my stay. That was not long. I declined joining their breakfast, and, at the first gleam of dawn, took an opportunity of escaping into the free air, now clear and still, and cold as impalpable ice.

My landlord hallooed for me to stop, ere I reached the bottom of the garden, and offered to accompany me across the moor. It was well he did, for the whole hill-back was one billowy, white ocean; the swells and falls not indicating corresponding rises and depressions in the ground: many pits, at least, were filled to a level; and entire ranges of mounds, the refuse of the quarries, blotted out from the chart

闲啦！其他人都能自己挣饭吃——就只你靠我的施舍！把你那没用的东西丢掉，找点事做！你得为因为你总出现在我眼前而给我带来的困扰付出代价，听见没有，该死的荡妇！"

"我会把我的废物扔掉的，因为如果我拒绝的话，你也会强迫我那么做。"少妇回答道，合上她的书，把它扔在一张椅子上。"但就算你咒掉了舌头，我不会做任何事的，除非我自己乐意！"

希斯克利夫举起了手，说话的人立即跳到了一个远处更安全的地方，显然熟悉那只手的分量。我可没有兴趣观赏一场阿猫阿狗的打斗，便轻快地向前走去，仿佛是想急于分享炉边的温暖，对被打断的争吵一无所知似的。双方都还有礼貌地中止了进一步的敌对行为。希斯克利夫把他的拳头放到口袋里，免得再发痒。希斯克利夫太太撅着嘴，走向远处的一张椅子，而且在我待在那儿的一段时间里，她果然依照她的话，像雕像一样地坐在那里。不过时间不长，我谢绝了与他们共进早餐。黎明的第一道微光一出现，我就抓住机会，逃到户外去了，那空气现在已是晴朗、安宁而寒冷得像块无形的冰一样了。

我还没有走到花园的尽头，我的房东就叫住了我，表示愿意陪我穿过旷野。他这样做，因为整个山脊就像一片汹涌的白色海洋。它的起伏并不指示出底下地面的高低：至少，很多坑是被填平了；而且整个山丘的绵亘——石矿的残迹——都从我昨天走过时在我脑海中留下的地图中抹掉了。我曾注意到在路的一边，每隔六

which my yesterday's walk left pictured in my mind. I had remarked on one side of the road, at intervals of six or seven yards, a line of upright stones, continued through the whole length of the barren; these were erected, and daubed with lime on purpose to serve as guides in the dark; and also when a fall, like the present, confounded the deep swamps on either hand with the firmer path. But, excepting a dirty dot pointing up here and there, all traces of their existence had vanished, and my companion found it necessary to warn me frequently to steer to the right or left, when I imagined I was following, correctly, the windings of the road.

We exchanged little conversation, and he halted at the entrance of Thrushcross park, saying I could make no error there. Our adieus were limited to a hasty bow, and then I pushed forward, trusting to my own resources; for the porter's lodge is untenanted as yet. The distance from the gate to the Grange is two miles; I believe I managed to make it four; what with losing myself among the trees, and sinking up to the neck in snow: a predicament which only those who have experienced it can appreciate. At any rate, whatever were my wanderings, the clock chimed twelve as I entered the house; and that gave exactly an hour for every mile of the usual way from Wuthering Heights.

My human fixture and her satellites rushed to welcome me; exclaiming, tumultuously, they had completely given me up: everybody conjectured that I perished last night; and they were wondering how they must set about the search for my remains. I bid them be quiet, now that they saw me returned, and, be-

七码，就有一排直立的石头，连续不断的一直贯穿荒地。它们都竖立着，上面涂着石灰，以便在黑暗中作为路标；也是为了碰上像现在这样的一场大雪，把两边深深的沼泽地和较坚实的小路弄得混淆不清时作路标而设的。但是，除了一个个的黑点不时出现以外，这些石头存在的痕迹全都消失了。当我以为我所走的弯弯曲曲的路是正确的时候，我的同伴却时时发现有必要频繁提醒我向右或是向左转。

我们没有怎么交谈，他在画眉田庄的门口停了下来，说是到了这我就不会再走错了。我们的道别仅限于匆匆的一鞠躬，然后我就继续向前走。我相信自己的能耐，因为山门守卫的小屋还没租出去。从山门到田庄是两英里，我相信我走着像四英里。我在树林里迷了路，雪没到了脖子：那种困境只有经历过的人才能体会。无论如何，不管我怎样的迂回，在钟正敲十二下的时候我踏进了屋子。这意味着通着平常从呼啸山庄到这儿的道路算来，我每一英里路都花了整整一个小时。

我的管家和她的随从都冲出来欢迎我，七嘴八舌地嚷着说，他们已经完全放弃我了：人人都猜想我昨晚已经死掉了，她们正不知该怎么出发去搜寻我的尸体。既然他们看到我回来，我叫她们安静下来，我连心脏都快要冻僵了。我拖着步子上楼去，换

numbed to my very heart, I dragged upstairs; whence, after putting on dry clothes, and pacing to and fro thirty or forty minutes, to restore the animal heat, I am adjourned to my study, feeble as a kitten; almost too much so to enjoy the cheerful fire and smoking coffee which the servant has prepared for my refreshment.

上干衣服以后，来来回回走了三四十分钟，好恢复体温。我又到我的书房里，软弱得像一只小猫，连融融的炉火和仆人为我准备的用于恢复精神的热气腾腾的咖啡，几乎都无法享受了。

Chapter 4
第四章

What vain weather-cocks we are! I, who had determined to hold myself independent of all social intercourse, and thanked my stars that, at length, I had lighted on a spot where it was next to impracticable—I, weak wretch, after maintaining till dusk a struggle with low spirits and solitude, was finally compelled to strike my colours; and, under pretence of gaining information concerning the necessities of my establishment, I desired Mrs. Dean, when she brought in supper, to sit down while I ate it; hoping sincerely she would prove a regular gossip, and either rouse me to animation or lull me to sleep by her talk.

"You have lived here a considerable time," I commenced; "did you not say sixteen years?"

"Eighteen, sir. I came, when the mistress was married, to wait on her; after she died, the

我们是些多么没用的反复无常的人啊！我，本来决定断绝一切社交活动。这得归功于命运，最后我来到一个几乎都不能通行的地方——我，一个软弱不幸的人，坚持与自己的低落情绪和孤独苦苦斗争直到黄昏，最终还是不得不放弃这个计划。当迪安太太来给我送晚饭的时候，我假装想了解一些关于我住所的必要情况，请她能在我吃饭的时候坐下来，我真诚地希望她是一个真正喜欢闲聊的人，希望她讲的话要么能令我精神焕发，要么能催我昏昏入睡。

"你在这里住了相当长的时间吧，"我开始问道，"你说过是十六年？"

"十八年，先生，在女主人嫁过来时我就来了，过来伺候她。她死

master retained me for his housekeeper."

"Indeed."

There ensued a pause. She was not a gossip, I feared; unless about her own affairs, and those could hardly interest me. However, having studied for an interval, with a fist on either knee, and a cloud of meditation over her ruddy countenance, she ejaculated—

"Ah, times are greatly changed since then!"

"Yes," I remarked, "you've seen a good many alterations, I suppose?"

"I have, and troubles too," she said.

"Oh, I'll turn the talk on my landlord's family!" I thought to myself. "A good subject to start—and that pretty girl-widow, I should like to know her history, whether she be a native of the country, or, as is more probable, an exotic that the surly indigenae will not recognise for kin." With this intention I asked Mrs. Dean why Heathcliff let Thrushcross Grange, and preferred living in a situation and residence so much inferior. "Is he not rich enough to keep the estate in good order?" I inquired.

"Rich, sir!" she returned. "He has, nobody knows what money, and every year it increases. Yes, yes, he's rich enough to live in a finer house than this; but he's very near—close-handed; and, if he had meant to flit to Thrushcross Grange, as soon as he heard of a good tenant he could not have borne to miss the chance of getting a few hundreds more. It is strange people should be so greedy, when they are alone in the world!"

"He had a son, it seems?"

"Yes, he had one—he is dead."

"And that young lady, Mrs. Heathcliff, is

his widow?"

"Yes."

"Where did she come from originally?"

"Why, sir, she is my late master's daughter: Catherine Linton was her maiden name. I nursed her, poor thing! I did wish Mr. Heathcliff would remove here, and then we might have been together again."

"What! Catherine Linton?" I exclaimed, astonished. But a minute's reflection convinced me it was not my ghostly Catherine. "Then," I continued, "my predecessor's name was Linton?"

"It was."

"And who is that Earnshaw, Hareton Earnshaw, who lives with Mr. Heathcliff? Are they relations?"

"No; he is the late Mrs. Linton's nephew."

"The young lady's cousin, then?"

"Yes; and her husband was her cousin also: one on the mother's, the other on the father's side. Heathcliff married Mr. Linton's sister."

"I see the house at Wuthering Heights has 'Earnshaw' carved over the front door. Are they an old family?"

"Very old, sir; and Hareton is the last of them, as our Miss Cathy is of us—I mean, of the Lintons. Have you been to Wuthering Heights? I beg pardon for asking; but I should like to hear how she is."

"Mrs. Heathcliff? she looked very well, and very handsome; yet, I think, not very happy."

"Oh dear, I don't wonder! And how did you like the master?"

"A rough fellow, rather, Mrs. Dean. Is

克利夫太太,是他的遗孀?"

"是的。"

"她本来是哪里人呢?"

"唉,先生,她就是我那位过世的主人的女儿,凯瑟琳·林顿是她的闺名。我把她从小带大的,可怜的孩子!我曾经希望希斯克利夫先生搬到这里来住,这样一来我们又可以在一起了。"

"什么!凯瑟琳·林顿?"我惊呼,错愕。不过转念一想,我断定这不是我那个幽灵凯瑟琳。然后,我继续说道,"我的前任房客姓林顿吗?"

"是的。"

"那么恩肖又是谁呢?就是那个跟希斯克利夫先生住在一起的哈里顿·恩肖,他们是亲戚吗?"

"不,他是过世的林顿太太的侄子。"

"那么也就是这位年轻太太的表兄了?"

"是的,她的丈夫也是她的表兄:一个是她母亲那边的亲戚,另一个是她父亲那边的亲戚。希斯克利夫娶了林顿先生的妹妹。"

"我看到呼啸山庄的房子前门上刻有'恩肖'的字样。他们是个古老的家族吗?"

"非常古老,先生;哈里顿是这一家族的最后一个了,而我们的凯茜小姐是我们这边的最后一个——我是指林顿家族。你去过呼啸山庄吧?请原谅我问起这个,我很想知道她现在怎样。"

"希斯克利夫太太吗?她看上去很好,也很漂亮。但是,我想,她不是很快乐。"

"哦,那我不觉得奇怪!你觉得主人怎样?"

"我觉得他是一个粗暴的家伙,

not that his character?"

"Rough as a saw-edge, and hard as whinstone! The less you meddle with him the better."

"He must have had some ups and downs in life to make him such a churl. Do you know anything of his history?"

"It's a cuckoo's①, sir—I know all about it: except where he was born, and who were his parents, and how he got his money, at first. And Hareton has been cast out like an unfledged dunnock! The unfortunate lad is the only one in all this parish that does not guess how he has been cheated."

"Well, Mrs. Dean, it will be a charitable deed to tell me something of my neighbours: I feel I shall not rest, if I go to bed; so be good enough to sit and chat an hour."

"Oh, certainly, sir! I'll just fetch a little sewing, and then I'll sit as long as you please. But you've caught cold. I saw you shivering, and you must have some gruel to drive it out."

The worthy woman bustled off, and I crouched nearer the fire; my head felt hot, and the rest of me chill, moreover I was excited, almost to a pitch of foolishness, through my nerves and brain. This caused me to feel, not uncomfortable, but rather fearful (as I am still) of serious effects from the incidents of today and yesterday. She returned presently, bringing a smoking basin and a basket of work; and, having placed the former on the hob, drew in her seat, evidently pleased to find me so companionable.

迪安太太。那就是他的性格吗？"

"跟锯齿一样粗糙，跟燧石一样硬！你最好少跟他来往。"

"他肯定在人生中经历了很多起起落落，才变成了如此粗暴的一个人吧。你知道一点他的过去吗？"

"这是一只杜鹃鸟的过去，先生——除了他在哪儿出生，他的父母是谁，还有他最初是怎么发财的之外，其余的我全都知道。哈里顿就像个羽毛未丰的鸟雀一样给驱逐了出去！这个可怜的小伙子是这整个教区里惟一料想不到自己被欺骗了的人。"

"啊，迪安太太，如果你能告诉我一些关于我邻居的事情就真是太好了。我觉得我爬上床去也睡不着觉，所以还不如坐在这儿跟你聊上一个小时。"

"哦，当然可以了，先生！我就去拿点针线活过来，这样你想让我坐多久我就坐多久。但是你着凉了。我看见你在打寒颤，你必须喝点粥去去寒气。"

这个可敬的女人匆忙地跑开了，我蜷缩着身子又朝炉火边凑了凑。我感觉脑门发热，其他地方发冷，更重要的是，我的神经和大脑都很兴奋，兴奋到近乎愚蠢的地步。这并没有使我觉得不舒服，而是使我相当害怕（此刻依然如此），害怕今天和昨天的遭遇会导致严重的后果。她很快就回来了，带回一个热气腾腾的粥盆和一个针线篮子。她把粥盆放到铁架上，拉过椅子，显然对发现我如此友好而感到高兴呢。

---

① cuckoo：杜鹃，暗喻希斯克里夫为弃婴。杜鹃不会筑巢，生产之后像抛弃私生子一样，把卵产在别的鸟类的巢中而让别的鸟抚育自己的孩子。

Before I came to live here, she commenced—waiting no further invitation to her story—I was almost always at Wuthering Heights; because my mother had nursed Mr. Hindley Earnshaw, that was Hareton's father, and I got used to playing with the children. I ran errands too, and helped to make hay, and hung about the farm ready for anything that anybody would set me to. One fine summer morning—it was the beginning of harvest, I remember—Mr. Earnshaw, the old master, came down stairs, dressed for a journey; and after he had told Joseph what was to be done during the day, he turned to Hindley, and Cathy, and me—for I sat eating my porridge with them—and he said, speaking to his son, "Now, my bonny man, I'm going to Liverpool today, what shall I bring you? You may choose what you like, only let it be little, for I shall walk there and back: sixty miles each way, that is a long spell!" Hindley named a fiddle, and then he asked Miss Cathy; she was hardly six years old, but she could ride any horse in the stable, and she chose a whip. He did not forget me; for he had a kind heart, though he was rather severe sometimes. He promised to bring me a pocketful of apples and pears, and then he kissed his children, good-bye, and set off.

It seemed a long while to us all—the three days of his absence—and often did little Cathy ask when he would be home. Mrs. Earnshaw expected him by suppertime, on the third evening, and she put the meal off hour after hour; there were no signs of his coming, however, and at last the children got tired of running down to the gate to look. Then it grew dark; she would have had them to bed, but they

在我来这里住之前——她开始讲起了她的故事——不再等我邀请——我几乎没有离开过呼啸山庄。因为我母亲从辛德雷·恩肖先生幼年就开始带他,他就是哈里顿的爸爸,而我也和孩子们一起玩惯了。有时也帮忙干杂活,帮忙弄弄干草,或是在农场上转悠,看看有没有人叫我做点什么。一个晴朗的夏天的早晨——我记得那时正是开始收获的季节——恩肖先生,那位老主人穿着要出远门的衣服下楼来。在他吩咐了约瑟夫这一天要做些什么之后,他转过身来对着辛德雷、凯茜和我——因为我正在和他们一块儿吃粥——他对他的儿子说:"喂,我的漂亮小人儿,我今天要去利物浦了。想要我给你们带点什么回来吗?挑些你们喜欢的东西吧,只是要挑个小点儿的东西,因为我是要走路去,走路回来的:一趟六十英里,是很长的一段路哩!"辛德雷说要一把小提琴,接着他又问凯茜小姐想要什么。她还不到六岁,但她已经能骑上马房里所有的马了,所以她选择了一根马鞭。他也没有忘记我,因为他有一颗善良的心,尽管有时他非常严厉。他答应要给我带回一口袋的苹果和梨,然后他亲了亲孩子们,说了声再见,就出发了。

他离家的三天,对我们所有人来说都觉得仿佛非常漫长,小凯茜总是问起他什么时候回家。第三天晚上,恩肖太太希望他会在晚饭时候回来,于是把晚饭往后推迟一小时又一小时。但却没有任何他回来的迹象。最后,孩子们也对跑到大门口去张望感到厌倦。天黑了下来,她本该让他们

begged sadly to be allowed to stay up; and, just about eleven o'clock, the doorlatch was raised quietly, and in stept the master. He threw himself into a chair, laughing and groaning, and bid them all stand off, for he was nearly killed—he would not have such another walk for the three kingdoms.

"And at the end of it, to be flighted to death!" he said, opening his great-coat, which he held bundled up in his arms. "See here, wife！ I was never so beaten with anything in my life：but you must e'en take it as a gift of God; though it's as dark almost as if it came from the devil."

We crowded round, and over Miss Cathy's head I had a peep at a dirty, ragged, black-haired child; big enough both to walk and talk：indeed, its face looked older than Catherine's; yet, when it was set onits feet, it only stared round, and repeated over and over again some gibberish, that nobody could understand. I was frightened, and Mrs. Earnshaw was ready to fling it out of doors；she did fly up, asking how he could fashion to bring that gipsy brat into the house, when they had their own bairns to feed and fend for? What he meant to do with it, and whether he were mad? The master tried to explain the matter; but he was really half dead with fatigue, and all that I could make out, amongst her scolding, was a tale of his seeing it starving, and houseless, and as good as dumb, in the streets of Liverpool; where he picked it up and inquired for its owner. Not a soul knew to whom it belonged, he said; and his money and time being both limited, he thought it better to take it home with him at once, than run into vain expenses there because he was deter-

上床睡觉，但他们苦苦哀求准许他们再待一会儿。十一点钟左右的时候，门闩被轻轻地抬了起来，主人走了进来。他倒在一把椅子上，又是大笑又是呻吟，叫他们都不要过来，因为他几乎快没命了——就算把英伦三岛送给他，他也不肯再这样走一趟了。

"走到最后，就像是在奔命！"他说着，敞开大衣，这是被他裹成一团抱在怀里的。"看看这儿，太太！我这辈子都没有像这样被任何东西弄得这么狼狈过，但你必须把它当成是上帝赐予的礼物，尽管他黑得简直像从恶魔那儿来的一样。"

我们都围拢过去。从凯茜小姐的头顶上方望去，我窥见一个脏兮兮的、穿得破破烂烂的、黑头发的孩子。他挺大了，已经该能走路和说话了：实际上，他的脸看上去比凯瑟琳还显得大一些。然而，当把他放到地上时，他只会瞪着眼四处张望，不断重复说着一些没人能听懂的莫名其妙的话。我非常害怕，而恩肖太太则打算把他扔出门去。她可真跳起来了，质问他怎么想得出把那样的一个吉普赛小孩带回家来，自己的小孩都已够他们抚养的了。他到底准备怎么处理这个野孩子？他是不是疯了？主人试图把事情解释一下，但他实在累得半死了。从她的斥责声中，我只能听出是这么一回事：他在利物浦的大街上看见这孩子快饿死了，又无家可归，而且又像哑巴一样。于是就带着他询问是谁家的孩子。可没有一个人知道。他说。他的钱有限，时间又紧，想想还不如立刻把他带回家，总比在那儿白白浪费时间和钱要好些，因为

mined he would not leave it as he found it. Well the conclusion was that my mistress grumbled herself calm, and Mr. Earnshaw told me to wash it, and give it clean things, and let it sleep with the children.

  Hindley and Cathy contented themselves with looking and listening till peace was restored; then, both began searching their father's pockets for the presents he had promised them. The former was a boy of fourteen, but when he drew out what had been a fiddle, crushed to morsels in the greatcoat, he blubbered aloud; and Cathy, when she learnt the master had lost her whip in attending on the stranger, showed her humour by grinning and spitting at the stupid little thing; earning for her pains a sound blow from her father to teach her cleaner manners. They entirely refused to have it in bed with them, or even in their room; and I had no more sense, so I put it on the landing of the stairs, hoping it might be gone on the morrow. By chance, or else attracted by hearing his voice, it crept to Mr. Earnshaw's door, and there he found it on quitting his chamber. Inquiries were made as to how it got there; I was obliged to confess, and in recompense for my cowardice and inhumanity was sent out of the house.

  This was Heathcliff's first introduction to the family. On coming back a few days afterwards (for I did not consider my banishment perpetual) I found they had christened him "Heathcliff". It was the name of a son who died in childhood, and it has served him ever since, both for Christian and surname. Miss Cathy and he were now very thick; but Hindley hated him, and to say the truth I did the same; and we

他已经决定，既然发现就不能坐视不管。那么，结果就是，我的女主人抱怨够了，平静下来。恩肖先生吩咐我给他洗个澡，穿上干净衣服，让他和孩子们一起睡觉。

  辛德雷和凯茜先甘心情愿地看着听着，直到一切恢复平静，两人就开始搜他们父亲的口袋，寻找他许诺过的礼物。辛德雷是一个十四岁的男孩，但当他从大衣里拉出那只原本是小提琴、却已经绺成碎片的东西时，他号啕大哭起来。至于凯茜，当她知道主人为照顾这个陌生人而弄丢她的马鞭时，就向那愚蠢的小东西龇牙咧嘴、吐口水以发泄她的脾气，但她得到的是父亲一记狠狠的耳刮子，以此来教训她要礼貌些。他们完全拒绝让他睡到他们的床上，就是在他们屋里睡也不行。我也不知该怎么办，所以就把他放在楼梯口，希望明天他会走掉。不知是巧合还是主人的声音吸引了他，他爬到恩肖先生的门口，而他一出房门就看见了他。于是恩肖先生追问他怎么会到那儿去的，我不得不承认是我干的，作为我懦弱和没有同情心的报应，我被主人赶出了家门。

  这就是希斯克利夫第一次进入这个家庭的情形。几天后我再回来的时候（因为我并不认为对我的放逐是永远的），发现他们已经给他取了名，叫"希斯克利夫"。这原本是他们一个夭折了的儿子的名字，以后这个名字既是他的教名，也是他的姓氏。凯茜小姐和他很亲密，但辛德雷讨厌他。说实话，我也讨厌他，于是我们

plagued and went on with him shamefully, for I wasn't reasonable enough to feel my injustice, and the mistress never put in a word on his behalf when she saw him wronged.

He seemed a sullen, patient child; hardened, perhaps, to ill-treatment; he would stand Hindley's blows without winking or shedding a tear, and my pinches moved him only to draw in a breath and open his eyes, as if he had hurt himself by accident and nobody was to blame. This endurance made old Earnshaw furious, when he discovered his son persecuting the poor, fatherless child, as he called him. He took to Heathcliff strangely, believing all he said (for that matter, he said precious little, and generally the truth), and petting him up far above Cathy, who was too mischievous and wayward for a favourite.

So; from the very beginning, he bred bad feeling in the house; and at Mrs. Earnshaw's death, which happened in less than two years after, the young master had learnt to regard his father as an oppressor rather than a friend, and Heathcliff as a usurper of his father's affections and his privileges, and he grew bitter with brooding over these injuries. I sympathised awhile; but when the children fell ill of the measles, and I had to tend them, and take on me the cares of a woman at once, I changed my ideas. Heathcliff was dangerously sick; and while he lay at the worst he would have me constantly by his pillow. I suppose he felt I did a good deal for him, and he hadn't the wit to guess that I was compelled to do it. However, I will say this, he was the quietest child that ever nurse watched over. The difference between him and the others forced me to be less partial.

两个就折磨他，用粗鄙的方式对待他，因为我还没有理智地认识到自己做的不对，而女主人看到他受欺负时也从来没有帮他说过一句话。

他似乎是个阴郁能忍耐的孩子，或许是受尽虐待已经变得不在乎了，他眼睛都不眨一下就能忍受辛德雷的拳头，也不会掉一滴眼泪。我掐他，也只能让他倒吸一口气，睁大双眼，就像他不小心弄伤自己，没有人应受谴责一样。这种逆来顺受让老恩肖非常生气，当他发现他的儿子这样虐待这个他所谓的可怜的没有父亲的孩子时，他不同寻常地喜欢希斯克利夫，相信他所说的每句话（说到这点，他说的总是很少，并且一般情况下都是实话），而且宠爱他远远胜过凯茜——凯茜太淘气、太任性，难以成为一个宠儿。

所以从一开始，他就给这个家庭带来了不愉快。不到两年，恩肖太太去世了，而小主人已学会把他父亲当作是一个压迫者而不是朋友，把希斯克利夫当作是一个篡夺他父母感情和他特权的人。他把这些伤害牢牢记住，越发怀恨在心。有一段时间我还挺同情他，可当这些孩子们都出麻疹的时候，我得照顾他们，担负起一个女人的责任时，就改变了想法。希斯克利夫病得很严重。当他躺在那儿最难受的时候，他总是要我一直陪在枕边。我猜想他是觉得我帮了他不少忙，还猜不到我是被迫那样做的。不管怎么说，我得说：他可是我曾经照顾过的孩子中最安静的一个。他跟别的孩子不一样，使我不得不少了一些偏见。凯茜和她哥哥把我折磨得筋疲

Cathy and her brother harassed me terribly; *he* was as uncomplaining as a lamb; though hardness, not gentleness, made him give little trouble.

  He got through, and the doctor affirmed it was in a great measure owing to me, and praised me for my care. I was vain of his commendations, and softened towards the being by whose means I earned them, and thus Hindley lost his last ally still I couldn't dote on Heathcliff, and I wondered often what my master saw to admire so much in the sullen boy, who never, to my recollection, repaid his indulgence by any sign of gratitude. He was not insolent to his benefactor, he was simply insensible; though knowing perfectly the hold he had on his heart, and conscious he had only to speak and all the house would be obliged to bend to his wishes. As an instance, I remember Mr. Earnshaw once bought a couple of colts at the parish fair, and gave the lads each one. Heathcliff took the handsomest, but it soon fell lame, and when he discovered it, he said to Hindley—

  "You must exchange horses with me: I don't like mine; and if you won't I shall tell your father of the three thrashings you've given me this week, and show him my arm, which is black to the shoulder." Hindley put out his tongue, and cuffed him over the ears. "You'd better do it at once," he persisted, escaping to the porch (they were in the stable): "you will have to; and if I speak of these blows, you'll get them again with interest." "Off, dog!" cried Hindley, threatening him with an iron weight used for weighing potatoes and hay. "Throw it," he replied, standing still, "and

力尽，而他却像一只羊羔，一点也不抱怨——尽管他不怎么给人添麻烦是因为坚强，而不是因为柔顺。

  他的病好了，医生肯定地说这很大一部分都是我的功劳，并且表扬我照顾得好。我因为他的称赞而得意。对于这个因为他而让我得到称赞的孩子，也就心软了些。就这样，辛德雷失去了他的最后一个同盟者。但我还是无法喜欢希斯克利夫，而且我常常非常不解，我的主人在这个阴郁的孩子身上发现了哪一点让他如此喜欢。在我的印象中，这个孩子从来没有对他的溺爱表示过任何的感激作为回报。他也并不是对他的恩人无礼，只是无动于衷。尽管他完全知道自己在主人心中的分量，而且很清楚，只要他一开口，这个屋子里所有人就不得不服从他的意愿。举个例子吧，我记得有一次恩肖先生在教会的市场上买了两只小马驹，给了两个小伙子一人一匹。希斯克利夫得到了最漂亮的那匹，但没过多久它就跛了，当他发现之后，就对辛德雷说：

  "你必须跟我换马：我不喜欢我那匹了。要是你不换给我，我就告诉你父亲这礼拜你痛打我三次，还要给他看我的胳臂，一直青到肩膀上呢。"辛德雷吐吐舌头，并且又打了他耳光。"你最好立刻就换，"他逃到门廊上（他们原来是在马厩里的），坚持说："你一定得跟我换不可，如果我说出你打我的事儿，你可要连本带利地挨一顿。""滚开，狗！"辛德雷吼道，用一个称土豆和干草的铁秤砣来吓唬他。"扔啊，"他答道，站着一动不动，"那样的话，我就要告诉

then I'll tell how you boasted that you would turn me out of doors as soon as he died, and see whether he will not turn you out directly." Hindley threw it, hitting him on the breast, and down he fell, but staggered up immediately, breathless and white; and, had not I prevented it, he would have gone just so to the master, and got full revenge by letting his condition plead for him, intimating who had caused it. "Take my colt, gipsy, then!" said young Earnshaw. "And I pray that he may break your neck. Take him, And be damned, you beggarly interloper! and wheedle my father out of all he has: only afterwards show him what you are, imp of Satan. —And take that, I hope he'll kick out your brains!"

Heathcliff had gone to loose the beast, and shift it to his own stall; he was passing behind it, when Hindley finished his speech by knocking him under its feet, and without stopping to examine whether his hopes were fulfilled, ran away as fast as he could. I was surprised to witness how coolly the child gathered himself up, and went on with his intention; exchanging saddles and all, and then sitting down on a bundle of hay to overcome the qualm which the violent blow occasioned, before he entered the house. I persuaded him easily to let me lay the blame of his bruises on the horse: he minded little what tale was told since he had what he wanted. He complained so seldom, indeed, of such stirs as these, that I really thought him not vindictive. I was deceived completely, as you will hear.

他你是怎么自吹自擂地说，等他一死你就要把我赶到门外去，看看他会不会立刻把你赶出去。"辛德雷真的扔出了那个秤砣，打在他胸上，他倒了下去，但马上又晃晃悠悠地站了起来，气喘吁吁，脸色苍白。如果不是我去阻止，他肯定会马上去找主人，他只需要把当时的情况说清楚，说出是谁干的，那就会彻底地报了这个仇。"把我的马拿去吧，吉卜赛人！"小恩肖说："我希望这匹马会弄断你的脖子。把它拿去吧，该死的，你这讨饭的闯入者！把我父亲所有的东西全都骗去吧。最后你会让他看出你的真实面目的，你这个小魔鬼——尝尝这个：我希望它把你的脑袋踢开花！"

希斯克利夫走过去解开马，把它带到自己的马厩里。他正从马的身后走过，辛德雷以把希斯克利夫打倒在马蹄下结束了他的咒骂，也没有停下来看看自己的愿望是否实现，就尽快撒腿跑开了。令我惊奇的是，我目睹着这个孩子是如何冷静地挣扎起来，执意于他的意志：换马鞍子，还有其他的一切，然后在他进入房间之前，先坐在一堆干草上平息住那重重的一拳所引起的晕眩。我很轻松就劝服他把那些青肿的责任归于马：他并不在乎一个精心编造的谎言应怎样讲，因为他已经得到他想要的东西。说真的，他很少拿像这样的事情去告状。我真的以为他不是一个有寻仇倾向的人。我完全被欺骗了，接下来你就会听到。

Chapter 5
第五章

In the course of time, Mr. Earnshaw began to fail. He had been active and healthy, yet his strength left him suddenly; and when he was confined to the chimney-corner he grew grievously irritable. A nothing vexed him; and suspected slights of his authority nearly threw him into fits. This was especially to be remarked if any one attempted to impose upon, or domineer over, his favourite: he was painfully jealous lest a word should be spoken amiss to him; seeming to have got into his head the notion that, because he liked Heathcliff, all hated, and longed to do him an ill-turn. It was a disadvantage to the lad; for the kinder among us did not wish to fret the master, so we humoured his partiality; and that humouring was rich nourishment to the child's pride and black tempers. Still it became in a manner necessary; twice, or thrice, Findley's manifestations of scorn, while his father was near, roused the old man to a fury; he seized his stick to strike him, and shook with rage that he could not do it.

At last, our curate, (we had a curate then who made the living answer by teaching the little Lintons and Earnshaws, and farming his bit of land himself,) he advised that the young man should be sent to college; and Mr. Earn-

随着时间逝去,恩肖先生开始垮下来。他曾经活跃和健康,然而他的体力突然就弃他而去了。当他只能待在烟囱旁的角落里时,他的脾气暴躁得让人难以忍受。无关紧要的事就会让他生气,而一旦怀疑有人轻视他的权威,他简直要火冒三丈。特别是有人试图为难或者欺负他的宠儿的话,这点就显得特别明显:他很痛苦地提防着,惟恐有人说他的宠儿有缺点。好像他脑子里已经形成这个观念:那就是因为自己喜欢希斯克利夫,所有人都讨厌他,并且都想加害于他。这对那个小伙子是一个障碍,因为我们中间比较善解人意的人并不愿惹主人生气,所以我们就迁就他的偏袒。那种迁就大大助长了那孩子的骄傲和坏脾气。但不这样做也不行。有两三次,辛德雷在他父亲就在旁边的时候,表现出轻视的神气,这把老人家气坏了,他抓住拐棍就要打辛德雷,但由于打不着,只能气得浑身颤抖。

最后,我们的助理牧师(那时我们有两个助理牧师,靠教小林顿和小恩肖们读书还有自己耕种一点土地维持生计)建议说,该把这个年轻人送到大学去。恩肖先生心里虽然并不情

shaw agreed, though with a heavy spirit, for he said—"Hindley was naught, and would never thrive as where he wandered."

I hoped heartily we should have peace now. It hurt me to think the master should be made uncomfortable by his own good deed. I fancied the discontent of age and disease arose from his family disagreements; as he would have it that it did: really, you know, sir, it was in his sinking frame. We might have got on tolerably, notwithstanding, but for two people, Miss Cathy and Joseph, the servant: you saw him, I dare say, up yonder. He was, and is yet, most likely, the wearisomest, selfrighteous pharisee[①] that ever ransacked a Bible to rake the promises to himself and fling the curses on his neighbours. By his knack of sermonizing and pious discoursing, he contrived to make a great impression on Mr. Earnshaw; and the more feeble the master became, the more influence he gained. He was relentless in worrying him about his soul's concerns, and about ruling his children rigidly. He encouraged him to regard Hindley as a reprobate; and, night after night, he regularly grumbled out a long string of tales against Heathcliff and Catherine: always minding to flatter Earnshaw's weakness by heaping the heaviest blame on the last.

Certainly, she had ways with her such as I never saw a child take up before; and she put all of us past our patience fifty times and oftener in a day: from the hour she came down stairs till the hour she went to bed, we had not a minute's security that she wouldn't be in mischief.

愿，但还是同意了，因为他说："辛德雷是没有什么用的，不管他荡到哪儿也永远不会变好。"

我非常希望我们可以过平静的日子。一想到主人因为做了善事反而弄得心神不宁，我就感到难过。我猜测都是由于家庭不和才让他晚年心怀不满以及病魔缠身。事实上他也得承认就是这样：真的，先生，你知道这日益衰老的身体里就藏着这块心病。其实如果不是因为那两个人——凯茜小姐和约瑟夫，那个佣人：我们本来还可以过得不错。我敢说，你在那边见过他了。他从前是，现在八成依然是，最令人厌烦、自以为是的法利赛人，他翻来倒去看他的《圣经》，搜寻好的希望归于自己，却把诅咒都丢给旁边的人。约瑟夫凭着他精通说教，还有虔诚的讲演，有预谋地给恩肖先生留下一个好印象。而主人越虚弱，他的势力就越大。他无情地让主人担心自己的灵魂所在，大谈该如何苛刻地管束他的孩子们。他鼓励主人将辛德雷当作被上帝摒弃的人，而且，一晚一晚的，他还经常嘟哝抱怨希斯克利夫和凯瑟琳一番：总忘不了把最重的责备加在后者头上，以迎合恩肖的偏爱。

当然，凯瑟琳总是那副样子，那是我从来没有在一个孩子身上见到过的。常常在一天之内，她就能让我们所有人忍无可忍不下五十次：从她下楼直到她上床睡觉为止，我们没有办法保证让她有一分钟不淘气。她总是

---

① Pharisee：法利赛人。古代犹太法利赛教派的教徒，该派标榜墨守传统礼仪，《圣经》中称他们为言行不一的伪善者。

Her spirits were always at high-water mark, her tongue always going— singing, laughing, and plaguing everybody who would not do the same. A wild, wicked slip she was—but she had the bonniest eye, and sweetest smile, and lightest foot in the parish. And, after all, I believe she meant no harm; for when once she made you cry in good earnest, it seldom happened that she would not keep you company, and oblige you to be quiet that you might comfort her. She was much too fond of Heathcliff. The greatest punishment we could invent for her was to keep her separate from him; yet she got chided more than any of us on his account. In play, she liked exceedingly to act the little mistress; using her hands freely, and commanding her companions: she did so to me, but I would not bear slapping and ordering: and so I let her know.

Now, Mr. Earnshaw did not understand jokes from his children; he had always been strict and grave with them; and Catherine, on her part, had no idea why her father should be crosser and less patient in his ailing condition, than he was in his prime. His peevish reproofs wakened in her a naughty delight to provoke him: she was never so happy as when we were all scolding her at once, and she defying us with her bold, saucy look, and her ready words; turning Joseph's religious curses into ridicule, baiting me, and doing just what her father hated most, showing how her pretended insolence, which he thought real, had more power over Heathcliff than his kindness: how the boy would do *her* bidding in anything, and *his* only when it suited his own inclination. After behaving as badly as possible all day, she

精力充沛,舌头动个不停——唱歌、笑,还有就是不断打扰那些不跟着她一起这样做的人。她真是个又野又捣蛋的小姑娘——但她有教区内最好看的眼睛、最甜的微笑和最轻盈的步伐。而且,毕竟,我相信她是没有坏心眼的,因为如果她真的把你给惹哭了,很少不陪着你一起哭的,而且使你不得不安静下来,反过来去安慰她。她特别喜欢希斯克利夫。我们能施于她最大的惩罚莫过于把他俩分开,但是因为他,她受到的训斥比我们谁都多。在玩的时候,她特别喜欢扮演小女主人,总是出手打人,而且指挥她的玩伴们。对我她也这样做过,但我可受不了被掌掴和命令,所以就让她放明白点。

不过,恩肖先生无法理解孩子们的玩笑。他对子女一向都是严厉而严肃的。而凯瑟琳,在她这方,也不理解父亲为什么在生病时比在盛年时脾气要暴躁些,耐性也更少了。他那不满的斥责反而唤起她想激怒他的顽皮乐趣。她最高兴的时候就是我们在一块儿责骂她,而她则用一副无畏无礼的神情和早有准备的话语反抗我们。她把约瑟夫宗教上的诅咒当成是滑稽的废话;激怒我;做她父亲最讨厌的事——展示她那假装出来的傲慢无礼(而他却以为是真的),炫耀她比他的慈爱对希斯克利夫更有影响力:这个男孩子是如何对她惟命是从;而对于他的命令,希斯克利夫只在合自己心意时才肯做。在一整天干尽坏事之后,有时到晚上她又来撒娇主动亲

sometimes came fondling to make it up at night. "Nay, Cathy," the old man would say, "I cannot love thee; thou'rt worse than thy brother. Go, say thy prayers, child, and ask God's pardon. I doubt thy mother and I must rue that we ever reared thee!" That made her cry, at first; and then, being repulsed continually hardened her, and she laughed if I told her to say she was sorry for her faults, and beg to be forgiven.

But the hour came, at last, that ended Mr. Earnshaw's troubles on earth. He died quietly in his chair one October evening, seated by the fire-side. A high wind blustered round the house, and roared in the chimney: it sounded wild and stormy, yet it was not cold, and we were all together—I, a little removed from the hearth, busy at my knitting, and Joseph reading his Bible near the table (for the servants generally sat in the house then, after their work was done). Miss Cathy had been sick, and that made her still; she leant against her father's knee, and Heathcliff was lying on the floor with his head in her lap. I remember the master, before he fell into a doze, stroking her bonny hair—it pleased him rarely to see her gentle—and saying—"Why canst thou not always be a good lass, Cathy?" And she turned her face up to his, and laughed, and answered, "Why cannot you always be a good man, father?" But as soon as she saw him vexed again, she kissed his hand, and said she would sing him to sleep. She began singing very low, till his fingers dropped from hers, and his head sank on his breast. Then I told her to hush, and not stir, for fear she should wake him. We all kept as mute as mice a full half-hour, and should have done longer, only Joseph, having

和。"不，凯茜，"老人家说道："我不能爱你。你比你的哥哥还要更坏些。去，去做祷告吧，孩子，求上帝宽恕你。我想你母亲和我肯定会因为生养了你而感到后悔哩！"起初，她还会为这些话哭一场，到了后来，不断地被数落让她的心肠变硬了。如果我让她为自己的错误道歉，请求父亲的原谅，她反而会大笑起来。

最后，恩肖先生结束尘世烦恼的时刻终于来了。在一个十月的晚上，他坐在炉边椅上，静静地死去。大风绕着屋子咆哮，并在烟囱里怒吼，听起来既狂暴又激烈，天气却并不怎么冷。我们都聚在一起——我，离火炉有点远，忙着我的编织活儿，约瑟夫则在桌子旁边读着他的《圣经》（因为那时佣人们干完活儿之后通常都要在正屋里坐着）。凯茜小姐病了，这让她安静下来。她靠在父亲的膝盖上，而希斯克利夫则躺在地板上，头枕着她的衣襟。我记得主人在打盹之前，还在抚摸着她那美丽的头发——看到她温顺的样子，他少有的高兴——而且说道："为什么你不能永远都做一个好女孩呢，凯茜？"她仰起脸来迎着他的脸大笑着答道："为什么你不能永远都是一个好男人呢，父亲？"可是一看见他又要发火了，凯茜就去吻了吻他的手，还说愿意唱首歌伴他入睡。她开始轻轻地吟唱，直到他的手指从她手中滑落，头耷拉到胸前。这时我还告诉她别再出声，也别动弹，因为怕她把他吵醒。差不多有整整半个小时，我们都像老鼠一样不声不响。本来还应该呆得再久一些的，只是约瑟夫已经读完了那一章，

finished his chapter, got up and said that he must rouse the master for prayers and bed. He stepped forward, and called him by name, and touched his shoulder; but he would not move, so he took the candle and looked at him. I thought there was something wrong as he set down the light; and seizing the children each by an arm, whispered them to "frame upstairs, and make little din—they might pray alone that evening—he had summut to do."

"I shall bid father goodnight first", said Catherine, putting her arms round his neck before we could hinder her. The poor thing discovered her loss directly—she screamed out—"Oh, he's dead, Heathcliff! he's dead!" And they both set up a heart-breaking cry.

I joined my wail to theirs, loud and bitter; but Joseph asked what we could be thinking of to roar in that way over a saint in heaven. He told me to put on my cloak and run to Gimmerton for the doctor and the parson. I could not guess the use that either would be of, then. However, I went, through wind and rain, and brought one, the doctor, back with me; the other said he would come in the morning. Leaving Joseph to explain matters, I ran to the children's room; their door was ajar, I saw they had never laid down, though it was past midnight; but they were calmer, and did not need me to console them. The little souls were comforting each other with better thoughts than I could have hit on; no parson in the world ever pictured heaven so beautifully as they did, in their innocent talk; and, while I sobbed, and listened, I could not help wishing we were all there safe together.

站起身来说他得叫醒主人，让他作了祷告然后上床睡觉。他走上前去，叫了叫主人的名字，碰了碰主人的肩膀，但他一动不动，于是，他就取过蜡烛来看。他一放下蜡烛，我就感到肯定是出事儿了。于是我一手抓着一个孩子的胳膊，轻声跟他们说，快到楼上去，不要弄出什么声音——那天晚上他们可以自己做祷告——他还有事情要做。

"我应该先跟父亲道声晚安，"凯瑟琳说道。我们没来得及阻止她，她已经用胳膊搂住了他的脖子。这可怜的孩子马上发现她失去了父亲，她尖叫道："哦，他死了，希斯克利夫！他死了！"然后他们两个人就开始放声痛哭，哭得令人心碎。

我也跟他们一起痛哭，哭声又大又痛苦。但是约瑟夫问我们，在一位已经进入天堂的圣徒面前，我们怎么能这样大声喊叫。他叫我穿上外套，赶紧跑到吉默顿去请医生和牧师。那时，我猜不透去请这两个人来有什么用。但我还是顶着风雪去了，带回一位医生，另一位说他会在明天早上过来。我把交代情况的事情留给约瑟夫，自己跑到孩子们的房间里去：门半开着，尽管已经过了午夜，他们根本就没躺下来。不过已经平静些了，也不需要我去安慰。这两个小灵魂正在用比我所能想到更好的想法互相安慰：世上没有哪个牧师能把天堂描绘得跟他们天真单纯话语中描绘的那样美丽。当我一边呜咽、一边听着的时候，我情不自禁地希望我们大家都平平安安地一起到那里去。

Chapter 6
第六章

Mr. Hindley came home to the funeral; and—a thing that amazed us, and set the neighbours gossiping right and left—he brought a wife with him. What she was, and where she was born, he never informed us; probably, she had neither money nor name to recommend her, or he would scarcely have kept the union from his father.

She was not one that would have disturbed the house much on her own account. Every object she saw, the moment she crossed the threshold, appeared to delight her; and every circumstance that took place about her; except the preparing for the burial, and the presence of the mourners. I thought she was half silly, from her behaviour while that went on: she ran into her chamber, and made me come with her, though I should have been dressing the children; and there she sat shi-vering and clasping her hands, and asking repeatedly—"Are they gone yet?" Then she began describing with hysterical emotion the effect it produced on her to see black①; and started, and trembled, and, at last, fell weeping—and when I asked what was the matter, answered, she didn't know; but she felt so afraid of dying! I imagined her as little likely to die as myself. She was rather

辛德雷先生回来奔丧了，而且——有一件事让我们非常惊讶，也引来左邻右舍的闲言碎语——他带回来一个妻子。他从来没告诉过我们她是谁，在哪里出生。也许她的财产和门第并不足以让人夸耀，不然他也不会把这门婚事瞒着他的父亲。

她并不是一个为了自己而让家里混乱不堪的人。从跨进门槛的那刻起，她见到的所有东西和发生在她周围的每件事情，除了准备葬礼和吊唁者到访外，似乎都让她高兴。从她的行为举止中，我发现她有点傻里傻气：她跑进她的卧室，叫我也跟着进去，虽然那时我应该给孩子们穿孝服。她坐在那儿发抖，紧握着双手，再三地问我："他们走了没有？"然后，她开始歇斯底里地描述看见黑色会对自己产生什么样的影响，会惊跳，会颤抖，最后就会哭起来。当我问她这是怎么回事时，她又回答说不知道，只是觉得自己非常怕死！我想她和我一样不至于这么快就死吧。她相当瘦，但是很年轻，容光焕发，一双眼睛像钻石一样明亮。不过我也确实注意到，爬楼梯时她的呼吸会变得

thin, but young, and fresh complexioned, and her eyes sparkled as bright as diamonds. I did remark, to be sure, that mounting the stairs made her breathe very quick; that the least sudden noise set her all in a quiver, and that she coughed troublesomely sometimes; but I knew nothing of what these symptoms portended, and had no impulse to sympathise with her. We don't in general take to foreigners, here, Mr. Lockwood, unless they take to us first.

Young Earnshaw was altered considerably in the three years of his absence. He had grown sparer, and lost his colour, and spoke and dressed quite differently; and, on the very day of his return, he told Joseph and me we must thenceforth quarter ourselves in the back-kitchen, and leave the house for him. Indeed, he would have carpeted and papered a small spare room for a parlour; but his wife expressed such pleasure at the white floor and huge glowing fire-place, at the pewter dishes and delf-case, and dog-kennel, and the wide space there was to move about in where they usually sat, that he thought it unnecessary to her comfort, and so dropped the intention.

She expressed pleasure, too, at finding a sister among her new acquaintance; and she prattled to Catherine, and kissed her, and ran about with her, and gave her quantities of presents, at the beginning. Her affection tired very soon, however, and when she grew peevish, Hindley became tyrannical. A few words from her, evincing a dislike to Heathcliff, were enough to rouse in him all his old hatred of the boy. He drove him from their company to the

---

① 在西方，丧服的颜色为黑色。

急促，一点点最轻微的响动就会让她全身发抖，而且有时她的咳嗽声很让人讨厌。不过我不知这些症状预示着什么，也没有想要同情她的冲动。洛克伍德先生，在这里我们通常都不跟外地人亲近，除非他们先跟我们亲近。

年轻的恩肖在这离家的三年里变了很多。他变高变瘦了，脸上失去了血色，谈吐与衣着也跟从前大不相同。他回来的那天，就吩咐约瑟夫和我往后搬去后厨房住，把这间房子留给他。当然，他本可以收拾出一间小空房铺上地毯，糊上墙纸，当作客厅。不过他的妻子对这里的白色地板和熊熊燃烧的大壁炉，对那些锡制盘子和陶瓷容器，还有这狗窝，以及他们通常起坐时可以活动的宽大空间，表现出异常的喜爱，他觉得为了妻子的舒适而收拾客厅有点多此一举，于是放弃了这个念头。

她同时还为能在新认识的人中找到一个妹妹而感到高兴。刚开始时，她跟凯瑟琳唠叨个没完，亲她，跟她跑来跑去，给她很多礼物。不过她这种喜爱之情很快就退却了。当她变得急躁时，辛德雷也变得蛮横起来。她只要说几个暗示自己不喜欢希斯克利夫的词，就足以把他对这孩子的陈年旧恨都勾起来。他把希斯克利夫从家庭成员中赶到佣人堆里去，剥夺他从

servants, deprived him of the instructions of the curate, and insisted that he should labour out of doors instead; compelling him to do so as hard as any other lad on the farm.

He bore his degradation pretty well at first, because Cathy taught him what she learnt, and worked or played with him in the fields. They both promised fair to grow up as rude as savages; the young master being entirely negligent how they behaved, and what they did, so they kept clear of him. He would not even have seen after their going to church on Sundays, only Joseph and the curate reprimanded his carelessness when they absented themselves; and that reminded him to order Heathcliff a flogging, and Catherine a fast from dinner or supper. But it was one of their chief amusements to run away to the moors in the morning and remain there all day, and the after punishment grew a mere thing to laugh at. The curate might set as many chapters as he pleased for Catherine to get by heart, and Joseph might thrash Heathcliff till his arm ached; they forgot everything the minute they were together again; at least the minute they had contrived some naughty plan of revenge; and many a time I've cried to myself to watch them growing more reckless daily, and I not daring to speak a syllable, for fear of losing the small power I still retained over the unfriended creatures. One Sunday evening, it chanced that they were banished from the sittingroom, for making a noise, or a light offence of the kind; and when I went to call them to supper, I could discover them nowhere. We searched the house, above and below, and the yard and stables; they were invisible. And, at last, Hindley in a passion told

副牧师那儿接受教诲的权利，执意让他去外面干活，强迫他跟庄园其他的小伙子一样辛苦劳作。

刚开始，希斯克利夫还很能忍受他的降级，因为凯茜会教他自己学到的知识，还会陪他在地里干活或玩耍。他们都直白地发誓要长得像野人那样鲁莽。少爷完全不理会他们的行为举止和所作所为，因此他们也不跟他往来。他甚至不会留意他们俩礼拜天是否去教堂，只有约瑟夫和副牧师发现他们不在而责备他的疏忽时，才提醒他下令给希斯克利夫一顿鞭打，不准凯瑟琳吃午饭或晚饭。但一大清早跑去荒野，在那儿待上一整天，这已成为他们的主要娱乐之一，随后的惩罚就成了可笑的小插曲。尽管副牧师随心所欲地布置很多章节让凯瑟琳背诵，尽管约瑟夫鞭打希斯克利夫直到他的胳膊受伤，但只要他们再次相聚，至少在他们策划出一些不恰当的报复计划时，就会把什么都忘了。我眼看着他们一天天地越来越莽撞，多少次我只是暗自哭泣，不敢说一个字，惟恐失去我对这两个无依无靠的小家伙保留的一点点权力。一个星期天傍晚，他们碰巧又因为太吵闹这类的小错误被赶出了起居室。当我去叫他们吃晚饭时，到处都找不到他俩。我们找遍了整幢房子，楼上楼下，院子里，马厩里，连个影子都没找到。最后，辛德雷大发雷霆，吩咐我们闩上所有的门，发誓这天夜里谁也不准让他们进来。全家都去睡了，我急得无法入睡，打开我的小窗子，虽然外面在下雨，我还是探出头去听声音，

us to bolt the doors, and swore nobody should let them in that night. The household went to bed; and I, too anxious to lie down, opened my lattice and put my head out to hearken, though it rained, determined to admit them in spite of the prohibition, should they return. In a while, I distinguished steps coming up the road, and the light of a lantern glimmered through the gate. I threw a shawl over my head and ran to prevent them from waking Mr. Earnshaw by knocking. There was Heathcliff, by himself; it gave me a start to see him alone.

"Where is Miss Catherine?" I cried hurriedly."No accident, I hope?" "At Thrushcross Grange," he answered;"and I would have been there too, but they had not the manners to ask me to stay." "Well, you will catch it!" I said: "you'll never be content till you're sent about your business. What in the world led you wandering to Thrushcross Grange?" "Let me get off my wet clothes, and I'll tell you all about it, Nelly," he replied. I bid him beware of rousing the master, and while he undressed and I waited to put out the candle, he continued— "Cathy and I escaped from the wash-house to have a ramble at liberty, and getting a glimpse of the Grange lights, we thought we would just go and see whether the Lintons passed their Sunday evenings standing shivering in corners, while their father and mother sat eating and drinking, and singing and laughing, and burning their eyes out before the fire. Do you think they do? Or reading sermons, and being catechised by their man-servant, and set to learn a column of Scripture names, if they don't answer properly?" "Probably not," I responded. "They are good children, no doubt, and don't

我决定只要他们回来,就会不顾禁令,让他们进来。过了一会儿,我听到路上有脚步声传来,一盏火光闪闪的提灯进了大门。我在头上披了条围巾便跑出去,防止他们的敲门声吵醒恩肖。是希斯克利夫,只有他一个人。见他独自一人回来着实吓了我一跳。

"凯瑟琳小姐在哪儿?"我慌忙叫道,"我希望没出什么意外吧。""在画眉田庄,"他回答,"我本来也在那儿,可他们并没有想要留我过夜。""好了,这下你可要遭殃了!"我说,"一定要到人家赶你出来,你才会满意。到底有什么东西可以吸引你们去画眉田庄闲逛?""先让我把湿衣服脱了,然后再告诉你发生了什么,内莉。"他回答道。我吩咐他小心别吵醒主人。当他脱着衣服,我等着熄蜡烛的时候,他接着说:"凯茜和我从洗衣房跑出去后自由自在地闲逛着,忽然瞥见画眉田庄的灯光,于是我们想过去看看林顿他们是不是站在墙角,颤抖着度过星期日的晚上,而他们的父母却坐在那里吃吃喝喝,又唱又笑,在火炉前面烤火。你猜林顿他们在干什么?是在读讲道吗,而且还被他们的男仆盘问,如果回答得不正确,还要背一段圣经上的名字?""大概不是,"我回答说,"他们都是毋庸置疑的好孩子,不应受到你们这些行为恶劣的孩子该受的惩罚。""别说那么无聊的话,内莉,"他说,"毫无意

deserve the treatment you receive, for your bad conduct." "Don't you cant, Nelly," he said: "nonsense! We ran from the top of the Heights to the park, without stopping—Catherine completely beaten in the race, because she was barefoot. You'll have to seek for her shoes in the bog tomorrow. We crept through a broken hedge, groped our way up the path, and planted ourselves on a flower-plot under the drawing-room window. The light came from thence; they had not put up the shutters, and the curtains were only half closed. Both of us were able to look in by standing on the basement, and clinging to the ledge, and we saw—ah! it was beautiful—a splendid place carpeted with crimson, and crimsoncovered chairs and tables, and a pure white ceiling bordered by gold, a shower of glass-drops hanging in silver chains from the centre, and shimmering with little soft tapers. Old Mr. and Mrs. Linton were not there; Edgar and his sister had it entirely to themselves. Shouldn't they have been happy? We should have thought ourselves in heaven! And now, guess what your good children were doing? Isabella—I believe she is eleven, a year younger than Cathy—lay screaming at the farther end of the room, shrieking as if witches were running red-hot needles into her. Edgar stood on the hearth weeping silently, and in the middle of the table sat a little dog, shaking its paw and yelping; which, from their mutual accusations, we understood they had nearly pulled in two between them. The idiots! That was their pleasure! to quarrel who should hold a heap of warm hair, and each begin to cry because both, after struggling to get it, refused to take it. We laughed outright at the petted things;

义！我们一步未停地从山庄顶上跑去庄园里，凯瑟琳完全被我抛在后面，因为她光着脚。明天你得去泥沼里找找她的鞋了。我们爬过一个破败的篱笆，一路摸索着，最后爬到客厅窗户的下面，站在那里的花坛上。灯光从那儿透出来，他们没有把百叶窗关上，窗帘也是半掩着。我俩站在地基上，手扒在窗台边，就可以看到里面。我们看到了一个富丽堂皇的地方，哇！真漂亮啊！地上铺着深红色的地毯，桌椅上套着深红色的套子，纯白的天花板上镶着金边，一大堆用银链子挂着的玻璃坠子从天花板中央吊下来，在小蜡烛的照耀下变得闪闪发光。老林顿先生和太太都不在那儿，只有埃德加和他妹妹完全霸占着这间房子。这样他们还不高兴吗？换了我们，早就觉得自己到了天堂呢！现在你猜猜这些你嘴里的好孩子在干什么？伊莎贝拉——我相信她有十一岁，比凯茜小一岁——躺在屋子的一边大声尖叫，好像有个巫婆用烧得炽热的针刺进她的身体里一样。埃德加站在壁炉旁边默默地啜泣着，一只小狗坐在桌子中间，抖着它的爪子，汪汪地吠着。从他们相互的控诉看来，我们得知他们差点儿把它扯成了两半。真是两个白痴！这就是他们的乐趣！争吵着谁可以抱那堆暖和的软毛，而且两个都哭起来，就因为两个人拼命抢它之后又都不肯要了。我们痛快地嘲笑了这两个被宠坏的家伙，非常鄙视他们！你什么时候见过我想要凯瑟琳要的东西，或是发现我们分坐在房间的两边又哭又叫，在地上打滚这样的事吗？就是让我再活一千

we did despise them! When would you catch me wishing to have what Catherine wanted? Or find us by ourselves, seeking entertainment in yelling, and sobbing, and rolling on the ground, divided by the whole room? I'd not exchange, for a thousand lives, my condition here, for Edgar Linton's at Thrushcross Grange—not if I might have the privilege of flinging Joseph off the highest gable, and painting the house-front with Hindley's blood!"

"Hush, hush!" I interrupted. "Still you have not told me, Heathcliff, how Catherine is left behind?"

"I told you we laughed," he answered "The Lintons heard us, and with one accord, they shot like arrows to the door; there was silence, and then a cry, 'Oh, mamma, mamma! Oh, papa! Oh, mamma, come here. Oh, papa, oh!' They really did howl out something in that way. We made frightful noises to terrify them still more, and then we dropped off the ledge, because somebody was drawing the bars, and we felt we had better flee. I had Cathy by the hand, and was urging her on, when all at once she fell down. 'Run, Heathcliff, run!' she whispered. 'They have let the bull-dog loose, and he holds me!' The devil had seized her ankle, Nelly, I heard his abominable snorting. She did not yell out—no! She would have scorned to do it, if she had been spitted on the horns of a mad cow. I did, though I vociferated curses enough to annihilate any fiend in Christendom; and I got a stone and thrust it between his jaws, and tried with all my might to cram it down his throat. A beast of a servant came up with a lantern, at last, shouting-'Keep fast, Skulker①, keep fast!' He

次，我也不会拿我在这儿的地位和埃德加在画眉田庄的地位交换；即便是让我有权把约瑟夫从最高的屋顶上扔下来，在房子前面涂上辛德雷的血，我也不干！"

"嘘！嘘！"我打断了他，"希斯克利夫，你还没告诉我为什么凯瑟琳没一起回来？"

"我跟你说过我们笑出了声，"他回答道，"林顿兄妹听到我们，就像箭一样冲到门口，先是一阵沉默，然后大叫起来，'啊，妈妈，妈妈！啊，爸爸！啊，妈妈！快来啊！啊，爸爸，啊！'他们真的就这样大声嚎叫着这些话。我们发出可怕的声音把他们吓得更厉害了，接着就从窗台边上下来，因为有人来开门了，我们觉得最好还是开溜。我拉着凯茜的手，催她快跑，忽然她跌倒了。'快跑，希斯克利夫，快跑，'她小声说，'他们放出牛头犬，它咬住我啦！'那个恶魔咬住了她的脚踝，内莉，我听见那家伙令人讨厌的呼哧声。她没有叫出声来——是的！就算被戳在疯牛的角上，她也不屑于叫喊出来。可是我喊了，大声喊出一些足以消灭基督王国里任何恶魔的咒骂，我捡起一块石头塞到它嘴里，尽力把石头塞进它的喉咙。最后一个野蛮的佣人提着提灯走了过来，叫喊着：'咬紧了，狐儿，咬紧它！'但当他看到狐儿的猎物时，就改变了语气。那狗快不行了，紫色

changed his note, however, when he saw Skulker's game. The dog was throttled off; his huge, purple tongue hanging half a foot out of his mouth, and his pendant lips streaming with bloody slaver. The man took Cathy up; she was sick, not from fear, I'm certain, but from pain. He carried her in; I followed, grumbling execrations and vengeance. 'What prey, Robert?' hallooed Linton from the entrance. 'Skulker has caught a little girl, sir,' he replied; 'and there's a lad here,' he added, making a clutch at me, 'who looks an out-and-outer! Very like, the robbers were for putting them through the window to open the doors to the gang after all were asleep, that they might murder us at their ease. Hold your tongue, you foul-mouthed thief, you! you shall go to the gallows for this. Mr. Linton, sir, don't lay by your gun.' 'No, no, Robert,' said the old fool. 'The rascals knew that yesterday was my rent-day: they thought to have me cleverly. Come in; I'll furnish them a reception. There, John, fasten the chain. Give Skulker some water, Jenny. To beard a magistrate in his stronghold, and on the Sabbath, too! Where will their insolence stop? Oh, my dear Mary, look here! Don't be afraid, it is but a boy—yet the villain scowls so plainly in his face; would it not be a kindness to the country to hang him at once, before he shows his nature in acts as well as features?' He pulled me under the chandelier, and Mrs. Linton placed her spectacles on her nose and raised her hands in horror. The cowardly children crept nearer, also, Isabella lisping—'Frightful thing! Put him in the cellar, papa. He's exactly

---

① Skulker：狐儿——狗名

like the son of the fortune①-teller, that stole my tame pheasant. Isn't he, Edgar?'

"While they examined me, Cathy came round; she heard the last speech, and laughed. Edgar Linton, after an inquisitive stare, collected sufficient wit to recognise her. They see us at church, you know, though we seldom meet them elsewhere. 'That is Miss Earnshaw!' he whispered to his mother, 'and look how Skulker has bitten her—how her foot bleeds!'

"'Miss Earnshaw? Nonsense!' cried the dame; 'Miss Earnshaw scouring the country with a gipsy! And yet, my dear, the child is in mourning—surely it is—and she may be lamed for life!'

"'What culpable carelessness in her brother!' exclaimed Mr. Linton, turning from me to Catheri"e. 'I've understood from Shielders'" (that was the curate, sir) "'that he lets her grow up in absolute heathenism. But who is this? Where did she pick up this companion? Oho! I declare he is that strange acquisition my late neighbour made, in his journey to Liverpool—a little Lascar, or an American or Spanish castaway.'

"'A wicked boy, at all events,' remarked the old lady, 'and quite unfit for a decent house! Did you notice his language, Linton? I'm shocked that my children should have heard it.'

"I recommenced cursing—don't be angry, Nelly—and so Robert was ordered to take me off. I refused to go without Cathy; he dragged me into the garden, pushed the lantern into my hand, assured me that Mr. Earnshaw should be

德加?'"

"正在他们审问我的时候,凯茜走过来。她听到最后这句话,大笑起来。埃德加·林顿好奇地盯着她,总算不傻,认出了她。你知道,他们在教堂见过我们,虽然我们很少在其他地方遇到他们。'那是恩肖小姐!'他轻声对他母亲说:'看看狐儿把她交成什么样了,她的脚上流了很多血呢!'"

"'恩肖小姐? 胡说八道!'那位太太嚷道,'恩肖小姐跟个流浪汉在郡里四处闲逛!不过,亲爱的,这孩子戴着孝呢——当然是了——或许她一辈子就这么跛脚了!'"

"'她哥哥还真是粗心大意!'林顿先生惊叹道,从我这儿转身看着凯瑟琳,'我从希尔德斯那儿听说(就是那个教区副牧师,先生),他放任她在纯粹的异教中长大。这人是谁啊?她从哪儿捡到这么个同伴?哦!我肯定他是我那已故的邻居去利物浦旅行时带回来的奇怪收获——一个印度小水手,或是一个美洲人或西班牙人的弃儿。'"

"'不管是什么人,反正是坏孩子,'那个老女人说道,'而且对一个正派人家来说非常不合适!你有没有注意他说的话,林顿?我们的孩子如果听到这些话,我真不能忍受。'"

"我又开始诅咒起来——别生气,内莉——于是罗伯特就奉命把我带走。没有凯茜我绝不会离开。他把我拖到花园,把提灯塞在我手里,跟我说,一定会把我的行为告知恩肖先

---

① the son of the fortune:算命人的孩子。指希斯克利夫像个小吉普赛人,吉普赛人常以为人算命谋生。

informed of my behaviour, and, bidding me march directly, secured the door again. The curtains were still looped up at one corner, and I resumed my station as spy; because, if Catherine had wished to return, I intended shattering their great glass panes to a million of fragments, unless they let her out. She sat on the sofa quietly. Mrs. Linton took off the grey cloak of the dairy maid which we had borrowed for our excursion, shaking her head and expostulating with her, I suppose she was a young lady, and they made a distinction between her treatment and mine. Then the woman-servant brought a basin of warm water, and washed her feet; and Mr. Linton mixed a tumbler of negus, and Isabella emptied a plateful of cakes into her lap, and Edgar stood gaping at a distance. Afterwards, they dried and combed her beautiful hair, and gave her a pair of enormous slippers, and wheeled her to the fire; and I left her, as merry as she could be, dividing her food between the little dog and Skulker, whose nose she pinched as she ate; and kindling a spark of spirit in the vacant blue eyes of the Lintons—a dim reflection from her own enchanting face. I saw they were full of stupid admiration; she is so immeasurably superior to them—to everybody on earth, is she not, Nelly?"

"There will more come of this business than you reckon on," I answered, covering him up and extinguishing the light. "You are incurable, Heathcliff; and Mr. Hindley will have to proceed to extremities, see if he won't." My words came truer than I desired. The luckless adventure made Earnshaw furious. And then Mr. Linton, to mend matters, paid us a visit himself on the morrow; and read the

生，而且命令我立刻走人，又关上门。窗帘还是半拉在一边，我就继续侦查一番，因为如果凯瑟琳愿意回来，我就打算把他们家的大玻璃窗打得粉碎，除非他们肯让她出来。她安静地坐在沙发上。林顿太太把我们为了出游而借来的乳牛场女工的灰色外套脱下来，摇摇头，我猜是在劝诫她。她是个小姐，他们对待她和她对待我的态度截然不同。然后女仆端来一盆热水给她洗脚，林顿先生还调了一大杯尼格斯酒，伊莎贝拉把满满一盘糕点放在她腿上，而埃德加远远站着，张着嘴看她。后来他们又把她美丽的头发擦干，梳整齐，给她一双大拖鞋，用轮椅把她移到壁炉旁边。于是我便离开了她，因为她正高高兴兴地把她的食物分给小狗和狐儿吃，吃东西时，她还捏了捏小狗的鼻子，这让林顿一家人空虚的蓝眼睛里激发出一丝生机勃勃的火花——是她迷人的脸引起的柔和的反映。我看他们一家人表现出愚笨的钦佩之情，她远远地超过了他们——超过了世上所有人，不是吗，内莉？"

"这件事比你估计的要严重得多，"我一边给他盖好被，熄了灯，一边答道："你真是没得救了，希斯克利夫，辛德雷先生一定会不择手段的，你看他会不会吧。"我的话比我所预想的更为灵验。这次不幸的冒险让恩肖极为愤怒。后来，林顿先生为了补救，第二天早上亲自来拜访我们，还给小主人一大堆说教，教导他

young master such a lecture on the road he guided his family, that he was stirred to look about him, in earnest. Heathcliff received no flogging, but he was told that the first word he spoke to Miss Catherine should ensure a dismissal; and Mrs. Earnshaw undertook to keep her sister-in-law in due restraint when she returned home; employing art, not force; with force she would have found it impossible.

如何领导家庭，说得他真的动了心。希斯克利夫没有受到鞭打，可是被告知：只要他开口跟凯瑟琳小姐说话，就会被撵出家门。恩肖太太承担起等小姑娘回家后约束管制她的任务；用的是计谋，而不是武力；用武力的话她会发现行不通。

Chapter 7
第七章

Cathy stayed at Thrushcross Grange five weeks till Christmas. By that time her ankle was thoroughly cured, and her manners much improved. The mistress visited her often in the interval, and commenced her plan of reform by trying to raise her selfrespect with fine clothes and flattery, which she took readily; so that, instead of a wild, hatless little savage jumping into the house, and rushing to squeeze us all breathless, there lighted from a handsome black pony a very dignified person, with brown ringlets falling from the cover of a feathered beaver, and a long cloth habit, which she was obliged to hold up with both hands that she might sail in. Hindley lifted her from her horse, exclaiming delightedly, "Why, Cathy, you are

凯茜在画眉田庄住了五个星期，直到圣诞节才回家。那时她的脚踝已经痊愈，仪态方面也大有进步。在这期间，这儿的女主人常去看望她，开始执行她的改造计划，试着用漂亮衣服和奉承话来提高她的自尊心，凯茜也欣然接受了。于是，她不再是个疯狂的不戴帽子的小野人，跳进屋冲过来抱得我们都喘不过气，而是从英俊的黑马驹上下来的一位非常高贵的小姐，一头棕色的卷发从一顶插着羽毛的海狸皮帽里垂下来，身上穿着一套长长的布质骑马装，她不得不用双手提着下摆，才能稳稳当当地走进来。辛德雷扶着她下马，欣喜地大叫着："天哪，凯茜，你可真是个美人啊！

quite a beauty! I should scarcely have known you; you look like a lady now. Isabella Linton is not to be compared with her, is she, Frances?" "Isabella has not her natural advantages," replied his wife: "but she must mind and not grow wild again here. Ellen, help Miss Catherine off with her things—Stay, dear, you will disarrange your curls—let me untie your hat."

I removed the habit, and there shone forth, beneath a grand plaid silk frock, white trousers, and burnished shoes; and, while her eyes sparkled joyfully when the dogs came bounding up to welcome her, she dare hardly touch them lest they should fawn upon her splendid garments. She kissed me gently; I was all flour making the Christmas cake, and it would not have done to give me a hug; and, then, she looked round for Heathcliff; Mr. and Mrs. Earnshaw watched anxiously their meeting; thinking it would enable them to judge, in some measure, what grounds they had for hoping to succeed in separating the two friends.

Heathcliff was hard to discover, at first. If he were careless, and uncared for, before Catherine's absence, he had been ten times more so since. Nobody but I even did him the kindness to call him a dirty boy, and bid him wash himself, once a week; and children of his age seldom have a natural pleasure in soap and water. Therefore, not to mention his clothes, which had seen three months' service in mire and dust, and his thick uncombed hair, the surface of his face and hands was dismally beclouded. He might well skulk behind the settle, on beholding such a bright, graceful damsel enter the house, instead of a rough-headed coun-

我简直都快认不出你了,现在你就像个淑女一样。伊莎贝拉·林顿可没法跟她比了,是吧,弗兰西丝?""伊莎贝拉没有她这么天生丽质,"他妻子回答说,"不过她可得记住,千万不要再在这里变野了。艾伦,帮凯瑟琳小姐把外套脱下来,别动,宝贝,你会把自己的卷发弄乱的。让我来把你的帽子解开。"

我脱下她的骑马装,里面露出了一件奢华的格子呢丝衬衣、一条白裤子和一双锃亮的皮鞋。当家里的小狗跳出来欢迎她时,她的眼里充满了喜悦,但她又不敢摸它们,生怕这些狗扑到她漂亮的衣服上去。她轻轻地吻了我一下——那时我正在做圣诞节蛋糕,身上全是面粉,要抱我可不行。然后她就四下张望,寻找着希斯克利夫。恩肖先生和太太急切地注视着他俩的碰面,认为这或多或少可以让他们判断,到底有没有可以成功地拆散这对伙伴的希望。

起初还很难找到希斯克利夫。如果说在凯瑟琳不在家之前他就粗心大意、没人管教的话,那么这之后的他要坏上十倍。除了我之外没人会好心好意地叫他脏孩子,命令他每星期洗一次澡;而像他这个年纪的孩子很少会对水和肥皂有兴趣。因此,暂且不说他那身已经穿了三个月、满是泥巴和尘土的衣服,还有他那浓密而蓬乱的头发,就连他的脸和手上都是一层黑色。他看到这么一位漂亮端庄的小姐,而不是他所期望的、跟他一样蓬头垢面披头散发的人走进屋来,只好躲在高背长椅的后面。"希斯克利夫

terpart of himself, as he expected. "Is Heathcliff not here?" she demanded, pulling off her gloves, and displaying fingers wonderfully whitened with doing nothing and staying in doors.

"Heathcliff, you may come forward," cried Mr. Hindley, enjoying his discomfiture, and gratified to see what a forbidding young blackguard he would be compelled to present himself. "You may come and wish Miss Catherine welcome, like the other servants."

Cathy, catching a glimpse of her friend in his concealment, flew to embrace him; she bestowed seven or eight kisses on his cheek within the second, and then stopped, and drawing back, burst into a laugh, exclaiming, "Why, how very black and cross you look! and how—how funny and grim! But that's because I'm used to Edgar and Isabella Linton. Well, Heathcliff, have you forgotten me?"

She had some reason to put the question, for shame and pride threw double gloom over his countenance, and kept him immoveable.

"Shake hands, Heathcliff," said Mr. Earnshaw, condescendingly; "once in a way, that is permitted."

"I shall not," replied the boy, finding his tongue at last; "I shall not stand to be laughed at. I shall not bear it!"

And he would have broken from the circle, but Miss Cathy seized him again.

"I did not mean to laugh at you," she said; "I could not hinder myself. Heathcliff, shake hands, at least! What are you sulky for? It was only that you looked odd. If you wash your face, and brush your hair, it will be all right, but you are so dirty!"

不在这儿吗?"她一边询问,一边脱下她的手套,露出她那白皙的手指,由于每天待在屋里无所事事,手指变得更白了。

"希斯克利夫,你可以过来了,"辛德雷先生喊道,看着他一脸的尴尬很是高兴,看着他不得不以一个令人讨厌的小流氓形象出场,辛德雷真是心满意足。"你可以过来,和其他佣人一样,欢迎一下凯瑟琳小姐。"

凯茜一瞥见她的朋友躲在那个地方,便飞奔过去抱住他。片刻之内她就在希斯克利夫的脸上亲了七八下,然后停住,向后退了几步,大声笑着,叫道:"怎么了,一脸生气的样子!而且多滑稽多冷酷啊!大概是因为我看惯了埃德加和伊莎贝拉·林顿吧。好呀,希斯克利夫,难道你把我忘了吗?"

她提出这个问题当然有理由的,因为羞耻和自尊在他脸上投下了双重阴影,让他无法动弹。

"握一下手,希斯克利夫。"恩肖先生惺惺作态地说道,"偶尔握一次是允许的。"

"我不,"这男孩终于开口说话了,"我无法忍受别人对我的嘲笑,我受不了!"

他想要冲破人群离开这里,但又被凯茜小姐拉住了。

"我并没有想要嘲笑你,"她说,"刚才是我情不自禁笑出来的。希斯克利夫,至少也该握个手吧!你在生什么气呢?只不过是你的样子有点奇怪罢了,如果你把脸洗干净,把头发梳整齐,就没事啦,不过你现在可真脏啊!"

She gazed concernedly at the dusky fingers she held in her own, and also at her dress; which she feared had gained no embellishment from its contact with his.

"You needn't have touched me!" he answered, following her eye and snatching away his hand. "I shall be as dirty as I please and I like to be dirty, and I will be dirty."

With that he dashed head foremost out of the room, amid the merriment of the master and mistress, and to the serious disturbance of Catherine; who could not comprehend how her remarks should have produced such an exhibition of bad temper.

After playing lady's maid to the new comer, and putting my cakes in the oven, and making the house and kitchen cheerful with great fires, befitting Christmas eve, I prepared to sit down and amuse myself by singing carols, all alone; regardless of Joseph's affirmations that he considered the merry tunes I chose as next door to songs①. He had retired to private prayer in his chamber, and Mr. and Mrs. Earnshaw were engaging Missy's attention by sundry gay trifles bought for her to present to the little Lintons, as an acknowledgment of their kindness. They had invited them to spend the morrow at Wuthering Heights, and the invitation had been accepted, on one condition: Mrs. Linton begged that her darlings might be kept carefully apart from that "naughty swearing boy."

Under these circumstances I remained solitary. I smelt the rich scent of the heating spices and admired the shining kitchen utensils, the polished clock, decked in holly, the silver

她关切地盯着握在自己手里的黑手指，又看看自己的衣服，生怕自己的衣服和他的衣服碰上就会变得不漂亮。

"你用不着碰我！"他回答道，看到她的眼神，便把手抽了回来，"我自己想怎么脏，就怎么脏。我喜欢脏，偏要脏。"

一说完，他就冲到了屋外，这一来正中了主人家的下怀，却让凯瑟琳感到心慌意乱，她无法理解自己的这番话怎么会惹出这么一场坏脾气的爆发。

在给这位新来到者当完女仆之后，我便把蛋糕放进烤箱，在客厅和厨房里升起旺火，搞得很适合圣诞前夜的氛围。所有事情都做完之后，我就准备坐下来，唱几首圣诞颂歌来轻松一下；完全不顾约瑟夫断言说他觉得我选的这些欢快的调子根本算不上是歌。他已经回到自己房里独自祷告去了，而恩肖夫妇正用那些为她买来送给小林顿兄妹的各种漂亮小礼物吸引她的注意力，这些玩意儿是用来答谢他们的款待的。他们已经邀请小林顿兄妹第二天来呼啸山庄，他们接受了这个邀请，不过有一个条件：林顿太太请求把她心爱的宝贝们和那个"淘气、爱骂人的男孩"小心地隔开。

就这样，只剩我一人留在这里。我闻到香料在烹调中发出的香浓味道，欣赏着那些闪闪发光的厨具，冬青叶装饰着的擦得锃亮的钟，排列在

---

① 约瑟夫自命为虔诚的清教徒，认为欢快的歌是"魔鬼的赞美诗(devil's psalmody)"，而对之大加反对。

mugs ranged on a tray ready to be filled with mulled ale for supper; and above all, the speckless purity of my particular care—the scoured and well-swept floor. I gave due inward applause to every object, and then I remembered how old Earnshaw used to come in when all was tidied, and call me a cant lass, and slip a shilling into my hand as a Christmas box; and from that I went on to think of his fondness for Heathcliff, and his dread lest he should suffer neglect after death had removed him; and that naturally led me to consider the poor lad's situation now, and from singing I changed my mind to crying. It struck me soon, however, there would be more sense in endeavouring to repair some of his wrongs than shedding tears over them. I got up and walked into the court to seek him. He was not far; I found him smoothing the glossy coat of the new pony in the stable, and feeding the other beasts, according to custom.

"Make haste, Heathcliff!" I said, "the kitchen is so comfortable; and Joseph is upstairs; make haste, and let me dress you smart before Miss Cathy comes out, and then you can sit together, with the whole hearth to yourselves, and have a long chatter till bedtime."

He proceeded with his task and never turned his head towards me.

"Come—are you coming?" I continued. "There's a little cake for each of you, nearly enough; and you'll need half-an-hour's donning."

I waited five minutes, but getting no answer left him... Catherine supped with her brother and sister-in-law. Joseph and I joined at an unsociable meal, seasoned with reproofs on

盘子里的银杯,它们是准备吃晚饭时盛加料麦芽酒用的,不过我最欣赏的就是经我特别小心打扫清洗后变得干净无瑕的地板。我心里暗暗为所有东西都鼓掌一番,然后便想起老恩肖常常会在一切收拾完毕后走进来,说我是个假正经的姑娘,还会塞一先令给我作为圣诞节的礼物。想到这里我又回忆起老爷对希斯克利夫的喜爱,生怕他死后希斯克利夫会因为没人照管而感到害怕,于是我很自然地想到这可怜的家伙如今的地位。我唱着唱着便哭了起来,不过很快我就想到,与其在这里为他掉眼泪,还不如尽力改正他的缺点来得有意义些。于是我站起身来,走到院子里去找他。他就在不远的地方。我发现他和往常一样,在马厩里给新来的小马驹梳理光滑的毛皮,然后喂其他的牲口。

"快来,希斯克利夫!"我说道,"厨房里面很舒服的,约瑟夫在楼上呢。快过来,在凯茜小姐出来之前让我把你打扮得漂漂亮亮的,那样你们就可以坐在一起了,整个火炉归你们,可以一直谈到睡觉呢。"

他依旧头也不回地继续干活。

"来啊,你来不来?"我接着说,"给你们俩一人一小块蛋糕,差不多够了,你还得花半个小时打扮停当呢。"

我等了五分钟,但他还是没回答,我便走开了。凯瑟琳和她的哥哥嫂嫂一块儿吃晚饭。约瑟夫和我一起吃了顿不和气的饭,一个责难对方,

one side and sauciness on the other. His cake and cheese remained on the table all night for the fairies. He managed to continue work till nine o'clock, and then marched dumb and dour to his chamber. Cathy sat up late, having a world of things to order for the reception of her new friends, she came into the kitchen once to speak to her old one; but he was gone, and she only stayed to ask what was the matter with him, and then went back In the morning he rose early; and as it was a holiday, carried his ill-humour onto the moors; not appearing till the family were departed for church. Fasting and reflection seemed to have brought him to a better spirit. He hung about me for a while, and having screwed up his courage, exclaimed abruptly—

"Nelly, make me decent, I'm going to be good."

"High time, Heathcliff," I said; "you *have* grieved Catherine: she's sorry she ever came home, I dare say! It looks as if you envied her, because she is more thought of than you."

The notion of *envying* Catherine was incomprehensible to him, but the notion of grieving her he understood clearly enough.

"Did she say she was grieved?" he inquired, looking very serious.

"She cried when I told her you were off again this morning."

"Well, I cried last night," he returned, "and I had more reason to cry than she."

"Yes; you had the reason of going to bed with a proud heart and an empty stomach," said I. "Proud people breed sad sorrows for themselves. But, if you be ashamed of your touchiness, you must ask pardon, mind, when

另一个也相当不客气。他的蛋糕和干酪一整夜都放在桌上留给神仙吃了。他一直干活到九点钟，然后一声不响地走到自己的卧室。凯茜为了接待她的新朋友吩咐了一大堆事情，因此留到很晚。她来过厨房一次，想跟她的老朋友说说话，不过他不在，于是凯茜只问了一下他发生了什么事，便回去了。第二天希斯克利夫很早就起来了。那天刚好是节假日，他闷闷不乐地去了荒野，直到全家都出发去教堂时，他才回来。挨饿和反省仿佛让他的精神好了很多。他在我身旁呆了一阵，然后鼓足勇气，突然对我大声说道：

"内莉，帮我打扮得体面些，我要学乖了！"

"正是时候，希斯克利夫，"我说，"你让凯瑟琳好伤心，我想她一定后悔回家来！看样子好像是因为她比你多被人关心，你就嫉妒她了。"

这嫉妒凯瑟琳的想法，他是无法理解的，不过让她伤心的念头，他非常明白。

"她说自己很伤心吗？"他样子很严肃地问道。

"在我今天早上告诉她你又出去了的时候，她哭了。"

"唉，我昨天晚上也哭了，"他回答说，"我比她更有理由哭啊。"

"是啊，你有理由带着一颗自大的心和一个空空的胃上床睡觉。"我说，"自大的人给自己招来悲哀。不过，如果你为自己的牛脾气感到惭愧的话，记住，一定要在她进来的时

she comes in. You must go up and offer to kiss her, and say—you know best what to say; only do it heartily, and not as if you thought her converted into a stranger by her grand dress. And now, though I have dinner to get ready, I'll steal time to arrange you so that Edgar Linton shall look quite a doll beside you and that he does. You are younger, and yet, I'll be bound, you are taller and twice as broad across the shoulders; you could knock him down in a twinkling; don't you feel that you could?"

Heathcliff's face brightened a moment; then it was overcast afresh, and he sighed.

"But, Nelly, if I knocked him down twenty times, that wouldn't make him less handsome or me more so. I wish I had light hair and a fair skin, and was dressed and behaved as well, and had a chance of being as rich as he will be!"

"And cried for mama, at every turn," I added, "and trembled if a country lad heaved his fist against you, and sat at home all day for a shower of rain. Oh, Heathcliff, you are showing a poor spirit! Come to the glass, and I'll let you see what you should wish. Do you mark those two lines between your eyes; and those thick brows, that instead of rising arched, sink in the middle; and that couple of black fiends, so deeply buried, who never open their windows boldly, but lurk glinting under them, like devil's spies? Wish and learn to smooth away the surly wrinkles, to raise your lids frankly, and change the fiends to confident, innocent angels, suspecting and doubting nothing, and always seeing friends where they are not sure of foes. Don't get the expression of a vicious cur that appears to know the

候，请求她的原谅。你一定要走上前去亲亲她，然后说——你知道自己最该说什么话吧。只要你真心诚意地去做就行，不要以为她穿了漂亮衣服就变成了陌生人。尽管我现在还要去准备午饭，不过还可以抽时间把你打扮一番，让埃德加·林顿在你旁边显得像个洋娃娃一样，他确实像个洋娃娃。虽然你比他小，但我可以断定，你比他高，肩膀也比他宽一倍，一眨眼工夫你就可以把他打趴下。你不觉得自己可以吗？"

希斯克利夫脸上的神色变得高兴起来，但很快又阴沉下来，叹了口气。

"但是，内莉，就算我把他打倒二十次，也不会让他变得难看些，或者让我变得英俊些。我希望自己也有浅色的头发、白色的皮肤，衣着举止也和他一样，而且有机会变得和他将来一样富有！"

"而且还动不动就哭着要妈妈，"我附和了一句，"如果有个乡下孩子向你挥挥拳头你就吓得发抖，下大雨就一整天坐在家里。哦，希斯克利夫，你可真没志气啊！到镜子这儿来，让我来给你看看你该许些什么愿。有没有看到你两只眼睛中间那两条纹路，还有这两条粗眉毛，没有在中间弓起来，而是向下凹。还有那对黑色的魔鬼，埋得那么深，从来不敢大胆地打开它们的窗户，在下面一闪一闪地埋伏着，像是魔鬼的探子，但愿你能抚平这些阴沉的皱纹，真诚地抬起你的眼皮，把恶魔变成自信、天真的天使，不怀疑任何东西，把不确定是敌人的人一直当成朋友。不要表现出恶狗的样子，认为挨踢是自己应得的，

kicks it gets are its desert, and yet hates all the world, as well as the kicker, for what it suffers."

"In other words, I must wish for Edgar Linton's great blue eyes and even forehead," he replied. "I do—and that won't help me to them."

"A good heart will help you to a bonny face, my lad," I continued, "if you were a regular black; and a bad one will turn the bonniest into something worse than ugly. And now that we've done washing, and combing, and sulking—tell me whether you don't think yourself rather handsome? I'll tell you, I do. You're fit for a prince in disguise. Who knows but your father was Emperor of China, and your mother an Indian queen, each of them able to buy up, with one week's income, Wuthering Heights and Thrushcross Grange together? And you were kidnapped by wicked sailors and brought to England. Were I in your place, I would frame high notions of my birth; and the thoughts of what I was should give me courage and dignity to support the oppressions of a little farmer!"

So I chattered on; and Heathcliff gradually lost his frown and began to look quite pleasant, when all at once our conversation was interrupted by a rumbling sound moving up the road and entering the court. He ran to the window and I to the door, just in time to behold the two Lintons descend from the family carriage, smothered in cloaks and furs, and the Earnshaws dismount from their horses; they often rode to church in winter. Catherine took a hand of each of the children, and brought them into the house and set them before the fire, which

但又因为自己的遭遇而怨恨全世界的人，以及那个踢它的人。"

"换句话说，我一定要希望自己会有埃德加·林顿蓝色的大眼睛和平坦的额头喽，"他回答，"我确实想要——不过那也不会帮我实现愿望。"

"只要你心地善良，你就会拥有帅气的面孔，我的孩子，"我接着说，"哪怕你是一个真正的黑人。但如果你内心邪恶，就会把最漂亮的脸变得奇丑无比。现在我们已经梳洗完毕，闹完别扭，你告诉我有没有觉得自己挺帅气的啊？我要告诉你，我就这么觉得，觉得你很适合装扮成一位王子呢。谁知道呢？也许你父亲就是中国的皇帝，你母亲是印度女王，他们两个中的任何一个只要用一个星期的收入，就能把呼啸山庄和画眉田庄一起买下来。而你却被邪恶的水手绑架，带到了英国。如果我是你，我就会幻想着自己是高贵的出身，而且一想到我自己曾经是什么人，就能给我勇气和尊严来支撑自己抵抗这个小农场主的压迫！"

我就这样喋喋不休地说着，希斯克利夫也渐渐消除了不快，开始变得高兴起来。这时我们的谈话被一阵从路上传来的隆隆的马车声打断，最后这声音传到院子里。他跑到窗边，我跑到门口，刚好看到林顿兄妹俩从家用马车上走下来，裹着厚厚的裘皮大衣，恩肖一家人也从自己的马上下来，冬天的时候他们常常会骑马去教堂。凯瑟琳一手牵着一个小伙伴，带他们走到家里，来到火炉面前，他们苍白的脸上马上恢复了血色。

quickly put colour into their white faces.

I urged my companion to hasten now and show his amiable humour, and he willingly obeyed; but ill-luck would have it that, as he opened the door leading from the kitchen on one side, Hindley opened it on the other. They met, and the master, irritated at seeing him clean and cheerful; or, perhaps, eager to keep his promise to Mrs. Linton, shoved him back with a sudden thrust, and angrily bade Joseph "keep the fellow out of the room—send him into the garret till dinner is over. He'll be cramming his fingers in the tarts and stealing the fruit, if left alone with them a minute."

"Nay, sir," I could not avoid answering, "he'll touch nothing, not he and I suppose he must have his share of the dainties as well as we."

"He shall have his share of my hand, if I catch him down stairs again till dark," cried Hindley. "Begone, you vagabond! What! you are attempting the coxcomb, are you? Wait till I get hold of those elegant locks—see if I won't pull them a bit longer!"

"They are long enough already," observed Master Linton, peeping from the doorway;"I wonder they don't make his head ache. It's like a colt's mane over his eyes!"

He ventured this remark without any intention to insult; but Heathcliff's violent nature was not prepared to endure the appearance of impertinence from one whom he seemed to hate, even then, as a rival. He seized a tureen of hot apple sauce, the first thing that came under his gripe, and dashed it full against the speaker's face and neck; who instantly commenced a lament that brought Isabella and

我催促着我的同伴眼下动作快点,还要表现得和和气气的;他也欣然服从了。不过倒霉的是,当他从一边打开厨房的门时,辛德雷也从另一边开门,他们不期而遇。主人一见他这么干净而且笑容满面的样子就非常生气,又或者是因为想要保守对林顿太太的诺言吧,突然把希斯克利夫推了回来,还愤怒地吩咐约瑟夫:"不准让这个家伙进客厅,把他送到阁楼去,等吃完晚餐再放他。要是让他跟他们共处一分钟,他准会把手指头伸进果酱蛋糕里,还会偷吃水果呢。"

"不会的,先生,"我忍不住插了句嘴,"他不会碰任何东西,他不会的。而且我想他也一定和我们一样有一份点心吧。"

"如果在天黑以前还让我在楼下抓到他的话,就让他尝尝我的巴掌吧,"辛德雷大吼着,"快滚,你这个小流氓!什么,你想当个贵公子,是不是?等我抓住你这头漂亮的长发,看看我会不会再把它拉长一点!"

"那已经够长啦,"林顿少爷在门口偷看,说道,"我真惊讶这头发怎么没让他头疼呢。他那眼睛上面的刘海真像马鬃毛!'

他大胆地说出这些话并没有侮辱人的意思,但希斯克利夫的暴烈性子并不准备容忍这个让自己憎恨的人的傲慢表现,那时他甚至已经把这人当成了情敌。他顺手拿起一碗滚烫的苹果酱,整碗泼向说话的那个人的脸和脖子。那个人立刻嗷嗷痛哭起来,伊莎贝拉和凯瑟琳闻声急忙跑过来。恩肖先生立刻抓起这个犯人,押送他回

Catherine hurrying to the place. Mr. Earnshaw snatched up the culprit directly and conveyed him to his chamber; where, doubtless, he administered a rough remedy to cool the fit of passion, for he appeared red and breathless. I got the dish-cloth, and, rather spitefully, scrubbed Edgar's nose and mouth, affirming it served him right for meddling. His sister began weeping to go home, and Cathy stood by, confounded, blushing for all.

"You should not have spoken to him!" she expostulated with Master Linton. "He was in a bad temper, and now you've spoilt your visit; and he'll be flogged. I hate him to be flogged! I can't eat my dinner. Why did you speak to him, Edgar?"

"I didn't," sobbed the youth, escaping from my hands, and finishing the remainder of the purification with his cambric pocket-handkerchief. "I promised mamma that I wouldn't say one word to him, and I didn't."

"Well, don't cry," replied Catherine, contemptuously; "you're not killed. Don't make more mischief; my brother is coming; be quiet! Give over, Isabella! Has anybody hurt *you*?"

"There, there, children—to your seats!" cried Hindley, bustling in. "That brute of a lad has warmed me nicely. Next time, Master Edgar, take the law into your own fists-it will give you an appetite!"

The little party recovered its equanimity at sight of the fragrant feast. They were hungry after their ride, and easily consoled, since no real harm had befallen them. Mr. Earnshaw carved bountiful platefuls, and the mistress made them merry with lively talk. I waited behind her chair, and was pained to behold Catherine,

自己的房间里。毫无疑问，在那儿他采取了一种粗暴的方法来让希斯克利夫冷静下来，因为回来的时候，他满脸通红、气喘吁吁。我拿起抹布，不怀好意地擦洗着埃德加的鼻子和嘴，说这就是他多管闲事的报应。他妹妹也开始哭着要回家，凯茜不知所措地站在那里，为这一切感到羞愧。

"你本来就不该跟他说话！"她告诫林顿少爷道，"他脾气很坏。现在可好，你把这一趟拜访搞砸了，他还要挨鞭子，我可不愿他挨鞭子！现在我连饭都吃不下了。你为什么要跟他说话呢，埃德加？"

"我没有，"那小子呜咽着，从我手里挣脱出来，用自己口袋里的白纱手绢擦净身上残余的污渍，"我答应过妈妈不会跟他说一句话的，我真的没有说。"

"好啦，别哭了，"凯瑟琳轻蔑地回答他，"你又没有被杀死，别再淘气了。我哥哥来了，安静点！好啦，伊莎贝拉！有人伤到你了吗？"

"喂，孩子们，回到自己的位子上去吧！"辛德雷匆匆忙忙地走进来，喊着，"那个小畜生可把我搞得热死了。埃德加少爷，下次你见到他就随意惩罚他吧，那会让你有个好胃口的！"

一看到这香味扑鼻的盛宴，这几个人马上就恢复了平静。骑过马之后他们都已经饿了，而且他们也并没有受到什么真正的伤害，因此很容易就被安抚下来。恩肖先生切了满满一盘肉，女主人风趣的谈话也让他们很高兴。我在她椅子背后侍候着，很难过

with dry eyes and an indifferent air, commence cutting up the wing of a goose before her. "An unfeeling child," I thought to myself; "how lightly she dismisses her old playmate's troubles. I could not have imagined her to be so selfish.' She lifted a mouthful to her lips; then she set it down again; her cheeks flushed, and the tears gushed over them. She slipped her fork to the floor, and hastily dived under the cloth to conceal her emotion. I did not call her unfeeling long; for I perceived she was in purgatory throughout the day, and wearying to find an opportunity of getting by herself, or paying a visit to Heathcliff, who had been locked up by the master; as I discovered, on endeavouring to introduce to him a private mess of victuals.

In the evening we had a dance. Cathy begged that he might be liberated then, as Isabella Linton had no partner; her entreaties were vain, and I was appointed to supply the deficiency. We got rid of all gloom in the excitement of the exercise, and our pleasure was increased by the arrival of the Gimmerton band, mustering fifteen strong, a trumpet, a trombone, clarionets, bassoons, French horns, and a bass viol, besides singers. They go the rounds of all the respectable houses, and receive contributions every Christmas, and we esteemed it a first-rate treat to hear them. After the usual carols had been sung, we set them to songs and glees. Mrs. Earnshaw loved the music, and so they gave us plenty.

Catherine loved it too; but she said it sounded sweetest at the top of the steps, and she went up in the dark, I followed. They shut the house door below, never noting our absence, it was so full of people. She made no stay at the stairs' head, but mounted farther, to the garret where Heathcliff was confined, and called him. He stubbornly declined answering for a while; she persevered, and finally persuaded him to hold communion with her through the boards. I let the poor things converse unmolested, till I supposed the songs were going to cease, and the singers to get some refreshment; then, I clambered up the ladder to warn her. Instead of finding her outside, I heard her voice within. The little monkey had crept by the skylight of one garret along the roof, into the skylight of the other, and it was with the utmost difficulty I could coax her out again. When she did come, Heathcliff came with her, and she insisted that I should take him into the kitchen, as my fellow-servant had gone to a neighbour's to be removed from the sound of our "devil's psalmody," as it pleased him to call it. I told them I intended by no means to encourage their tricks; but as the prisoner had never broken his fast since yesterday's dinner, I would wink at his cheating Mr. Hindley that once. He went down; I set him a stool by the fire, and offered him a quantity of good things; but he was sick and could eat little, and my attempts to entertain him were thrown away. He leant his two elbows on his knees, and his chin on his hands, and remained wrapt in dumb meditation. On my inquiring the subject of his thoughts, he answered gravely—

"I'm trying to settle how I shall pay Hindley back. I don't care how long I wait, if I can only do it at last. I hope he will not die before I do!"

"For shame, Heathcliff!" said I. "It is for

God to punish wicked people; we should learn to forgive."

"No, God won't have the satisfaction that I shall," he returned. "I only wish I knew the best way! Let me alone, and I'll plan it out while I'm thinking of that I don't feel pain."

But, Mr. Lockwood, I forget these tales cannot divert you. I'm annoyed how I should dream of chattering on at such a rate and your gruel cold, and you nodding for bed! I could have told Heathcliff's history, all that you need hear, in half a dozen words.

Thus interrupting herself, the housekeeper rose, and proceeded to lay aside her sewing; but I felt incapable of moving from the hearth, and I was very far from nodding. "Sit still, Mrs. Dean," I cried, "do sit still, another half hour! You've done just right to tell the story leisurely. That is the method I like; and you must finish in the same style. I am interested in every character you have mentioned, more or less."

"The clock is on the stroke of eleven, sir."

"No matter—I'm not accustomed to go to bed in the long hours. One or two is early enough for a person who lies till ten."

"You shouldn't lie till ten. There's the very prime of the morning gone long before that time. A person who has not done one half his day's work by ten o'clock, runs a chance of leaving the other half undone."

"Nevertheless, Mrs. Dean, resume your chair because tomorrow I intend lengthening the night till afternoon. I prognosticate for myself an obstinate cold, at least."

"I hope not, sir. Well, you must allow me to leap over some three years; during that space

"惩罚恶人是上帝的事,我们应该学着宽恕。"

"不,上帝得不到我那种满足感,"他回答说,"我只希望能找到最好的办法!让我一个人呆着,我会策划出来,我在想那件事时,就不感到痛苦了。"

不过,洛克伍德先生,我忘记了这些故事不会让你得到消遣。我真是气自己怎么会唠唠叨叨到这种地步。你的粥都冷了,而且你也要睡觉啦!我本来可以把你想听的那些关于希斯克利夫的过去用几个字说完的。

就这样,女管家打断了自己的话,站起身来,放下手里的针线活;但我觉得自己离不开壁炉,而且我也根本不想睡觉。"再坐会儿吧,迪安太太,"我喊道,"再坐半个小时!你这样从从容容讲故事的方式很好。我就喜欢这样;你就用这种方式把故事讲完吧。我对你提及的每个人物或多或少都有点兴趣呢。"

"已经十一点了,先生。"

"没关系——我不习惯在十二点前上床睡觉。对于一个睡到十点才起床的人来说,一两点睡已经够早了。"

"你不该睡到十点才起床。早晨最好的时光在十点前就过去了。如果有人在十点之前还没完成这一天工作的一半,剩下那一半就很有可能也做不完。"

"话虽如此,不过,迪安太太,还是再坐下来吧,因为明天我打算把夜晚延长到下午。我已经预感到自己至少要得一场重感冒了。"

"我希望你不要生病,先生。那好吧,你必须允许我跳过三年时间,

Mrs. Earnshaw—"

"No, no, I'll allow nothing of the sort! Are you acquainted with the mood of mind in which, if you were seated alone, and the cat licking its kitten on the rug before you, you would watch the operation so intently that puss's neglect of one ear would put you seriously out of temper?"

"A terribly lazy mood, I should say."

"On the contrary, a tiresomely active one. It is mine, at present and, therefore, continue minutely. I perceive that people in these regions acquire over people in towns the value that a spider in a dungeon does over a spider in a cottage, to their various occupants; and yet the deepened attraction is not entirely owing to the situation of the lookeron. They *do* live more in earnest, more in themselves, and less in surface change, and frivolous external things. I could fancy a love for life here almost possible; and I was a fixed unbeliever in any love of a year's standing. One state resembles setting a hungry man down to a single dish, on which he may concentrate his entire appetite and do it justice; the other, introducing him to a table laid out by French cooks; he can perhaps extract as much enjoyment from the whole; but each part is a mere atom in his regard and remembrance."

"Oh! here we are the same as anywhere else when you get to know us," observed Mrs. Dean, somewhat puzzled at my speech.

"Excuse me," I responded; "you, my good friend, are a striking evidence against that assertion. Excepting a few provincialisms of slight consequence, you have no marks of the manners which I am habituated to consider pe-

在那期间，恩肖太太……"

"不，不，我不允许你这么做！你知不知道这样一种心情：如果你单独一个人坐着，有只猫在你面前的地毯上舐着它的小猫，你是如此专心致志地看着这个过程，以至于这猫忘记舔一只耳朵时，会让你发脾气？"

"我觉得这是一种很可怕的懒性子。"

"恰恰相反，是一种令人讨厌的急性子。现在我就是这样的心情。因此，请你继续详细讲下去。我发现这一带的人，对城里那些形形色色的居民来说，就好比地牢里的蜘蛛见到茅舍里的蜘蛛一样，从中受益良多。这并不完全因为我是个旁观者，才得出这种日益深刻的印象。他们确实更热忱、更自顾自的生活着，很少顾及那些表面的变化和琐碎的外界事物。我可以想像得到，在这儿几乎有可能存在着一种终生的爱情；而过去我都不相信有什么爱情可以维持到一年。一种情况类似于给一个饥饿的人一盘菜，他可以把全部胃口都集中在这一道菜上，对它作出公正的评价。而另一种情况则是把他领到法国厨子摆下的一桌盛宴面前，或许他依旧可以享用一番这整桌菜肴，但是每种菜肴在他心中、在他记忆里只是极小的一部分而已。"

"哦！只要跟我们熟络了之后，你就知道我们这儿的人跟其他地方是一样的，"迪安太太说，对我这番话感到有些困惑。

"打断一下，"我插了一句，"我的好朋友，你就是一个与这句断言相反的显著证据。除了有点乡土气息外，你完全没有那些我一向认为你们这一

culiar to your class. I am sure you have thought a great deal more than the generality of servants think. You have been compelled to cultivate your reflective faculties for want of occasions for frittering your life away in silly trifles."

Mrs. Dean laughed.

"I certainly esteem myself a steady, reasonable kind of body," she said; "not exactly from living among the hills and seeing one set of faces, and one series of actions, from year's end to year's end; but I have undergone sharp discipline, which has taught me wisdom and then, I have read more than you would fancy, Mr. Lockwood. You could not open a book in this library that I have not looked into, and got something out of also unless it be that range of Greek and Latin, and that of French; and those I know one from another; it is as much as you can expect of a poor man's daughter. However, if I am to follow my story in true gossip's fashion, I had better go on; and instead of leaping three years, I will be content to pass to the next summer—the summer of 1778, that is nearly twenty-three years ago."

阶级的人所特有的习气。我确定你比一般仆人要考虑得周到。你迫使自己培养出了思考的能力，因为你没有必要把光阴虚度在愚蠢的琐事上。"

迪安太太笑了。

"我的确认为自己是个沉着镇定、通情达理的人，"她说，"这并不完全因为自己一年到头住在山里，见到的都是那几张熟面孔和一样的动作，而是因为我受过严格的训练，这训练给了我智慧，而且我读过的书比你能想像到的要多，洛克伍德先生。在这藏书室里，你可找不到我没看过的书，我从每本书中都学到很多。除了那排希腊文和拉丁文的，还有那排法文书，当然那些书我都能分辨出来。对于一个穷人的女儿，你也只能期望这么多了。不过，如果要我像闲聊那样继续说这个故事，那我就这样说下去吧。时间上也不跳过那三年，直接从第二年夏天讲起也可以——就是一七七八年的夏天，差不多二十三年前。"

Chapter 8
第八章

On the morning of a fine June day, my first bonny little nursling, and the last of the ancient Earnshaw stock, was born. We were busy with the hay in a far away field, when the girl that usually brought our breakfasts came running an hour too soon, across the meadow and up the lane, calling me as she ran.

"Oh, such a grand bairn!" she panted out. "The finest lad that ever breathed! But the doctor says missis must go; he says she's been in a consumption these many months. I heard him tell Mr. Hindley and now she has nothing to keep her, and she'll be dead before winter. You must come home directly. You're to nurse it, Nelly, to feed it with sugar and milk, and take care of it day and night. I wish I were you, because it will be all yours when there is no missis!"

"But is she very ill?" I asked, flinging down my rake, and tying my bonnet.

"I guess she is; yet she looks bravely," replied the girl, "and she talks as if she thought of living to see it grow a man. She's out of her head for joy, it's such a beauty! If I were her, I'm certain I should not die; I should get better at the bare sight of it, in spite of Kenneth. I was

在一个晴朗的六月的早晨,第一个需要我照料的漂亮婴儿,也是古老的恩肖家族中最后一个孩子出生了。当时我们正在远处的一块农田里忙着耙干草,那个经常给我们送早饭的姑娘提前一小时就跑来了。她穿过牧场,跑上小路,一边跑一边叫我。

"哦,真是个高贵的小孩!"她气喘吁吁地说,"从没见过这么健康活泼的男孩!但是大夫说太太快不行了,他说这几个月以来太太一直肺痨缠身。我听他跟辛德雷先生说,她现在已经没法保住自己了,冬天之前她就要不行了。你必须马上回家,要你去照顾那孩子呢,内莉,喂他牛奶加糖,白天夜里都得照顾着。真希望我是你啊,因为等到太太不在的时候,这一切都要归你了呢!"

"不过她真的病得很重吗?"我一边问,一边放下耙子,系上帽子。

"我猜是吧,不过她看起来很勇敢,"那姑娘回答说,"而且听她的口气好像还想活下去看着孩子长大成人呢。她肯定高兴得晕过头了,多么漂亮的孩子啊,如果我是她,肯定死不了,光是看他一眼,就会好得差不多,

fairly mad at him. Dame Archer brought the cherub down to master, in the house, and his face just began to light up, then the old croaker steps forward, and says he—'Earnshaw, it's a blessing your wife has been spared to leave you this son. When she came, I felt convinced we shouldn't keep her long; and now, I must tell you, the winter will probably finish her. Don't take on, and fret about it too much; it can't be helped. And besides, you should have known better than to choose such a rush of a lass!'"

"And what did the master answer?" I inquired.

"I think he swore but I didn't mind him, I was straining to see the bairn," and she began again to describe it rapturously. I, as zealous as herself, hurried eagerly home to admire, on my part; though I was very sad for Hindley's sake. He had room in his heart only for two idols—his wife and himself: he doted on both, and adored one, and I couldn't conceive how he would bear the loss.

When we got to Wuthering Heights, there he stood at the front door; and, as I passed in, I asked, "how was the baby?"

"Nearly ready to run about, Nell①!" he replied, putting on a cheerful smile.

"And the mistress?" I ventured to inquire; "the doctor says she's—"

"Damn the doctor!" he interrupted, reddening. "Frances is quite right; she'll be perfectly well by this time next week. Are you going upstairs? will you tell her that I'll come, if she'll promise not to talk. I left her because she would not hold her tongue; and she must—tell

---

① Nell: 内儿, 内莉(Nelly)的爱称。

her Mr. Kenneth says she must be quiet."

I delivered this message to Mrs. Earnshaw: she seemed in flighty spirits, and replied merrily—

"I hardly spoke a word, Ellen, and there he has gone out twice, crying. Well, say I promise I won't speak, but that does not bind me not to laugh at him!"

Poor soul! Till within a week of her death that gay heart never failed her; and her husband persisted doggedly, nay, furiously, in affirming her health improved every day. When Kenneth warned him that his medicines were useless at that stage of the malady, and he needn't put him to further expense by attending her, he retorted—

"I know you need not—she's well—she does not want any more attendance from you! She never was in a consumption. It was a fever; and it is gone; her pulse is as slow as mine now, and her cheek as cool."

He told his wife the same story, and she seemed to believe him; but one night, while leaning on his shoulder in the act of saying she thought she should be able to get up tomorrow, a fit of coughing took her—a very slight one—he raised her in his arms; she put her two hands about his neck, her face changed, and she was dead.

As the girl had anticipated, the child Hareton fell wholly into my hands. Mr. Earnshaw, provided he saw him healthy and never heard him cry, was contented, as far as regarded him. For himself, he grew desperate; his sorrow was of that kind that will not lament. He neither wept nor prayed; he cursed and defied; execrated God and man, and gave himself up to reckless dissipation. The servants could not

静养——告诉她，这是肯尼斯大夫说的。"

我把口信传达给恩肖太太，她看起来有点情绪激动，高兴地对我说：

"艾伦，我几乎没说过一个字，他倒哭着出去两次了。好吧，跟他说我答应不说话，但那并不能保证不笑他！"

可怜的人！直到她临死前的一个星期，那颗快乐的心还是没有放弃她。她的丈夫固执地——不，是偏执地——肯定她的身体会一天天好转。当肯尼斯大夫警告他说，病情到这个阶段，药已经不起作用，而且也没有必要浪费钱来治疗她时，他却反驳说：

"我知道你什么都不用做，她很好，不需要你再来医治她了。她从来没有得过肺痨。只是发烧而已，现在已经退了。现在她的脉搏跟我的一样平稳，脸也和我的一样凉。"

他跟妻子也说了同样的话，她好像相信了他。可是一天夜里，她靠着丈夫的肩膀，正说着她想明天可以下床的时候，忽然咳嗽起来——一阵非常轻微的咳嗽。他把她抱在怀里。她用双手搂着恩肖的脖子，脸色一变，就死了。

正如那姑娘预料的那样，哈里顿这个孩子完全托付给了我。恩肖先生只要见到他健健康康，没听到他哭哭啼啼，就满足了，这就是他所关心的。至于他自己，则变得绝望了，他的悲痛属于哭不出来的那种。他不恸哭，也不祷告，只是诅咒蔑视，痛骂上帝和人类，让自己过着放荡的生活。仆人们忍受不了他的暴虐邪恶的

bear his tyrannical and evil conduct long: Joseph and I were the only two that would stay. I had not the heart to leave my charge; and besides, you know, I had been his foster-sister, and excused his behaviour more readily than a stranger would. Joseph remained to hector over tenants and labourers; and because it was his vocation to be where he had plenty of wickedness to reprove.

The master's bad ways and bad companions formed a pretty example for Catherine and Heathcliff. His treatment of the latter was enough to make a fiend of a saint. And, truly, it appeared as if the lad *were* possessed of something diabolical at that period. He delighted to witness Hindley degrading himself past redemption; and became daily more notable for savage sullenness and ferocity. I could not half tell what an infernal house we had. The curate dropped calling, and nobody decent came near us, at last; unless Edgar Linton's visits to Miss Cathy might be an exception. At fifteen she was the queen of the country-side; she had no peer; and she did turn out a haughty, headstrong creature! I own I did not like her, after her infancy was past; and I vexed her frequently by trying to bring down her arrogance: she never took an aversion to me, though. She had a wondrous constancy to old attachments: even Heathcliff kept his hold on her affections unalterably; and young Linton, with all his superiority, found it difficult to make an equally deep impression. He was my late master: that is his portrait over the fireplace. It used to hang on one side, and his wife's on the other; but her's has been removed, or else you might see something of what she was. Can you make that

第八章

行为，都走了，只有约瑟夫和我两个人愿意留下来。我不忍心丢下自己抚养的孩子，而且，你知道我以前是他的共乳姐妹，比一个陌生人更容易原谅他的行为。约瑟夫一直恐吓那些佃户和劳工，因为留在一个有很多供他责备的事情的地方，就是他的职业。

主人的坏习惯和坏朋友给凯瑟琳与希斯克利夫树立了一个糟糕的榜样。他对希斯克利夫的态度足以让一个圣徒变成恶魔。而且说实话，在那段时期，那孩子好像真的被魔鬼附身一样。他幸灾乐祸地看着辛德雷自甘堕落到不可救药的地步，他那野蛮的阴郁和凶残也一天天地越来越显著。我无法形容我们居住的房子是多么像地狱。副牧师不来拜访了，最后，没有一个体面人物接近我们；埃德加·林顿算是个例外，他常常来看望凯茜小姐。到了十五岁，凯茜已经成为乡间皇后，没人能和她媲美，她也真的变成一个傲慢任性的丫头！我承认，自从她过了幼年时代，我就已经不喜欢她了。为了试着要改掉她傲慢自大的脾气，我常常惹她生气，尽管她从没对我表示出厌恶。她对那些以前的喜爱之物保持着一种怪异的始终如一的感情；甚至从未改变对希斯克利夫的爱慕。尽管年轻的林顿有他的优越之处，但他却发觉很难给她留下一个同等深刻的印象。他是我后来的主人，挂在壁炉上的就是他的画像。本来一直挂在一边的，他妻子的挂在另一边，不过她的已经搬走了，要不然你也许可以看看她以前长什么样。你

out?

Mrs. Dean raised the candle, and I discerned a soft-featured face, exceedingly resembling the young lady at the Heights, but more pensive and amiable in expression. It formed a sweet picture. The long light hair curled slightly on the temples; the eyes were large and serious; the figure almost too graceful. I did not marvel how Catherine Earnshaw could forget her first friend for such an individual. I marvelled much how he, with a mind to correspond with his person, could fancy my idea of Catherine Earnshaw.

"A very agreeable portrait," I observed to the housekeeper. "Is it like?"

"Yes," she answered; "but he looked better when he was animated; that is his everyday countenance: he wanted spirit in general."

Catherine had kept up her acquaintance with the Lintons since her five weeks' residence among them; and as she had no temptation to show her rough side in their company, and had the sense to be ashamed of being rude where she experienced such invariable courtesy, she imposed unwittingly on the old lady and gentleman, by her ingenious cordiality; gained the admiration of Isabella, and the heart and soul of her brother: acquisitions that flattered her from the first, for she was full of ambition, and led her to adopt a double character without exactly intending to deceive any one. In the place where she had heard Heathcliff termed a "vulgar young ruffian," and "worse than a brute," she took care not to act like him; but at home she had small inclination to practise politeness that would only be laughed at, and restrain an unruly nature when it would bring her neither

能看得出来吗？

迪安太太举起蜡烛，我看到了一张温柔的脸，和山庄的那位年轻太太及其相像，但是表情更为忧郁，更加和蔼。那是一幅可爱的画像。鬓角处长长的浅色头发微微地卷曲着，一双眼睛大而严肃，整个轮廓显得非常优雅。凯瑟琳·恩肖为了这个人而忘记她第一个朋友，我一点也不觉得奇怪。但如果他有着和他外形相称的头脑，能猜到此刻我对凯瑟琳·恩肖的想法，那才让我惊讶呢。

"这画像非常讨人喜欢，"我对女管家说，"像不像他本人？"

"像，"她回答道，"不过他在心情好的时候看起来还要帅气；画里是他平日的脸色，总是缺少生气。"

自从凯瑟琳和林顿兄妹住了五个星期之后，就和他们成了朋友。因为在他们相处的过程中，她没有表现出她粗枝大叶的那一面，而且在她身边的人一直都是恭恭敬敬、有礼貌的，她也知道粗鲁无礼是羞耻的，所以她那乖巧而又诚恳的性格在不知不觉中骗过了老太太和老先生，赢得了伊莎贝拉的钦佩，征服了她哥哥的心。刚开始时这些收获还挺让她得意的，因为她野心勃勃，这让她养成一种双重性格，也不是故意想要去欺骗什么人。在她听到希斯克利夫被称为是"没教养的小流氓"和"比畜生还坏"的那些地方，她就很注意自己的举止不要像他。但是一回到家，她就不想去做那些只会被人嘲笑的有礼行为，也不想去克制自己那种蛮横的天性，因为克制也不会给她带来荣誉和赞

credit nor praise.

　　Mr. Edgar seldom mustered courage to visit Wuthering Heights openly. He had a terror of Earnshaw's reputation, and shrunk from encountering him; and yet he was always received with our best attempts at civility: the master himself avoided offending him, knowing why he came; and if he could not be gracious, kept out of the way. I rather think his appearance there was distasteful to Catherine: she was not artful, never played the coquette, and had evidently an objection to her two friends meeting at all; for when Heathcliff expressed contempt of Linton in his presence, she could not half coincide, as she did in his absence; and when Linton evinced disgust and antipathy to Heathcliff, she dare not treat his sentiments with indifference, as if depreciation of her playmate were of scarcely any consequence to her. I've had many a laugh at her perplexities and untold troubles, which she vainly strove to hide from my mockery. That sounds ill-natured: but she was so proud, it became really impossible to pity her distresses, till she should be chastened into more humility. She did bring herself, finally, to confess, and confide in me: there was not a soul else that she might fashion into an adviser.

　　Mr. Hindley had gone from home, one afternoon, and Heathcliff presumed to give himself a holiday on the strength of it. He had reached the age of sixteen then, I think, and without having bad features, or being deficient in intellect, he contrived to convey an impression of inward and outward repulsiveness that his present aspect retains no traces of. In the first place, he had by that time lost the benefit

扬。

　　埃德加先生很少鼓起勇气公开来拜访呼啸山庄。恩肖的名声让他很有戒心，不愿遇到他。不过我们还是尽量有礼貌地招呼他。主人知道他为什么而来，因此也会主动避免去冒犯他，如果不能让自己表现得温文儒雅，他就索性避开。我甚至觉得他的出现让凯瑟琳觉得很讨厌，她本来就不圆滑，从来不会卖弄风骚，显然非常反对她这两位朋友碰面。因为当希斯克利夫当着林顿的面对他表示出轻蔑之情时，她并没有像林顿不在场时那样附和他。而当林顿对希斯克利夫表示出厌恶反感之情时，她又不敢对他态度冷漠，就好象别人轻视她的伙伴跟她完全没有关系似的。我总是一直嘲笑她的那些困惑茫然和无法形容的烦恼，她再怎么努力也没法躲过我的嘲笑。听起来我好像很恶毒，但她真的太自命不凡，让大家无法去怜悯她的悲痛，除非她能克制些，变得更谦逊些。最后她自己也忏悔了，向我倾诉衷肠。除了我，还有谁愿意当她的顾问呢。

　　一天下午，辛德雷先生出门去了，希斯克利夫乘机想给自己放个假。我想他应该有十六岁了吧，相貌不差，智力也不缺乏，可他却要刻意地从内到外都给人留下让人厌恶的印象，当然他现在的外貌并没有留下任何痕迹。首先，在那个时候，他早年所受的教育并没让他从中受益，接连不断的苦差事，每天早起晚睡，已经

of his early education: continual hard work, begun soon and concluded late, had extinguished any curiosity he once possessed in pursuit of knowledge, and any love for books or learning. His childhood's sense of superiority, instilled into him by the favours of old Mr. Earnshaw, was faded away. He struggled long to keep up an equality with Catherine in her studies, and yielded with poignant though silent regret: but he yielded completely; and there was no prevailing on him to take a step in the way of moving upward, when he found he must, necessarily, sink beneath his former level. Then personal appearance sympathised with mental deterioration: he acquired a slouching gait, and ignoble look; his naturally reserved disposition was exaggerated into an almost idiotic excess of unsociable moroseness; and he took a grim pleasure, apparently, in exciting the aversion rather than the esteem of his few acquaintance.

  Catherine and he were constant companions still at his seasons of respite from labour; but he had ceased to express his fondness for her in words, and recoiled with angry suspicion from her girlish caresses, as if conscious there could be no gratification in lavishing such marks of affection on him. On the before-named occasion he came into the house to announce his intention of doing nothing, while I was assisting Miss Cathy to arrange her dress: she had not reckoned on his taking it into his head to be idle; and imagining she would have the whole place to herself, she managed, by some means, to inform Mr. Edgar of her brother's absence, and was then preparing to receive him.

扑灭了他曾经想要追求知识的好奇心，以及他对书本或知识的喜爱。在他童年时因为老恩肖先生的宠爱而慢慢灌输进他心底的优越感，在那时已经荡然无存了。一直以来他努力想要在学习上跟凯瑟琳保持平等的地位，却带着无声而惨痛的遗憾放弃了，而且是完全放弃。当他发觉自己必须，而且不得不沉沦到他以前的水平之下后，谁也没能成功地规劝他向上爬一步。之后他的外表和堕落的心灵变得一致了：他养成了无精打采的走路姿态和一副出身卑贱的外表；他天生就沉默寡言的性格扩大为一种几乎是愚笨般的、极度不爱交际的忧郁性格。而当他极少数的几个熟人对他表现出反感而非尊重时，很显然他会得到一种苦中作乐的乐趣。

  不过在他干活休息的空当，凯瑟琳还是会常常跟他做伴，但他已经不再用言语来表达对她的爱慕了，而是愤怒地、猜疑地躲避她女孩子气的抚爱，好像觉得别人在他身上浪费感情，是不值得的。在我前面提到的那一天，他走进客厅宣布这一天自己不打算做任何事情，那时我正在帮凯茜小姐整理衣服，她没有料到他脑子里会想着要偷懒一下，想像着她可以把整个客厅占为己有，而且已经想办法通知埃德加先生说她哥哥今天出门了，还准备过会儿去接待他。

"Cathy, are you busy this afternoon?" asked Heathcliff. "Are you going anywhere?"

"No, it is raining," she answered.

"Why have you that silk frock on, then?" he said. "Nobody coming here, I hope?"

"Not that I know of," stammered Miss: "but you should be in the field now, Heathcliff. It is an hour past dinner time: I thought you were gone."

"Hindley does not often free us from his accursed presence," observed the boy. "I'll not work any more today: I'll stay with you."

"Oh, but Joseph will tell," she suggested: "you'd better go!"

"Joseph is loading lime on the farther side of Pennistow Crag; it will take him till dark, and he'll never know."

So saying, he lounged to the fire, and sat down. Catherine reflected an instant, with knitted brows—she found it needful to smooth the way for an intrusion. "Isabella and Edgar Linton talked of calling this afternoon," she said, at the conclusion of a minute's silence. "As it rains, I hardly expect them; but they may come, and if they do, you run the risk of being scolded for no good."

"Order Ellen to say you are engaged, Cathy," he persisted; "don't turn me out for those pitiful, silly friends of yours! I'm on the point, sometimes, of complaining that they—but I'll not—"

"That they what?" cried Catherine, gazing at him with a troubled countenance. "Oh, Nelly!" she added petulantly, jerking her head away from my hands, "you've combed my hair quite out of curl! That's enough; let me alone. What are you on the point of complaining

"凯茜,今天下午忙不忙?"希斯克利夫问道,"要去什么地方吗?"

"没有,外面在下雨呢。"她回答。

"那你为什么穿那件丝绸上衣?"他说,"我想,没人来这里吧?"

"我不知道,"小姐结结巴巴地说,"但你现在应该在田里干活才对啊,希斯克利夫。吃完饭已经一个小时啦,我还以为你已经走了呢。"

"可恶的辛德雷在家就很少让我们休息一下,"这男孩子说,"我今天就是不干活,要跟你待在一起。"

"哦,可约瑟夫会告密,"她暗示道,"你最好还是去干活!"

"约瑟夫在遥远的盘尼斯吞岩那边装石灰,他要忙到天黑,肯定不会知道。"

他一边说着,一边懒洋洋地来到火炉边,坐下来。凯瑟琳眉头紧锁,想了片刻,她觉得有必要为即将到访的客人赶走这个人。"伊莎贝拉和埃德加·林顿说过今天下午会来这里,"沉默片刻之后,她说道,"既然下雨了,我也用不着等他们来了。但他们有可能会来的,如果真的来了,你可又要无辜被骂了。"

"让艾伦跟他们说你很忙不就可以了,凯茜,"他坚持着,"你可别为了你那些可怜愚蠢的朋友把我给撵出去!有时候,我真想要抱怨一下他们,不过我不会说的——"

"抱怨他们什么?"凯瑟琳不安地盯着他,叫道,"啊,内莉!"她任性地嚷道,猛地把头从我手里挣脱出来,"我的卷发都被你梳直啦!够了,别来打扰我。你想要抱怨什么,希斯克利夫?"

about, Heathcliff?"

"Nothing—only look at the almanack on that wall," he pointed to a framed sheet hanging near the window, and continued—"The crosses are for the evenings you have spent with the Lintons, the dots for those spent with me. Do you see? I've marked every day."

"Yes—very foolish: as if I took notice!" replied Catherine in a peevish tone."And where is the sense of that?"

"To show that I *do* take notice," said Heathcliff.

"And should I always be sitting with you?" she demanded, growing more irritated. "What good do I get? What do you talk about? You might be dumb, or a baby, for anything you say to amuse me, or for anything you do, either!"

"You never told me before that I talked too little, or that you disliked my company, Cathy!" exclaimed Heathcliff in much agitation.

"It's no company at all, when people know nothing and say nothing," she muttered.

Her companion rose up, but he hadn't time to express his feelings further, for a horse's feet were heard on the flags, and having knocked gently, young Linton entered, his face brilliant with delight at the unexpected summons he had received. Doubtless Catherine marked the difference between her friends, as one came in and the other went out. The contrast resembled what you see in exchanging a bleak, hilly, coal country for a beautiful fertile valley; and his voice and greeting were as opposite as his aspect. He had a sweet, low manner of speaking, and pronounced his words as

"没什么——你看看那墙上的日历。"他指着挂在窗边的一张裱在框里的纸，继续说道，"那些打叉的都是你跟林顿他们一起消磨的傍晚，画点的是你跟我一起度过的傍晚。你看见没有？我每天都在做记号。"

"是的——很傻，好像我会注意到一样！"凯瑟琳回答，显得有些不满，"那又有什么意义呢？"

"说明我注意到了。"希斯克利夫说。

"那我就该一直跟你一起坐吗？"她质问着，变得更加生气了，"我又得到什么好处了？你说什么呢？你跟我说过什么话又做过什么事情逗我开心，你简直是个哑巴，一个小孩子！"

"你之前从没跟我说我说话太少，或者说你不喜欢跟我做伴，凯茜。"希斯克利夫非常激动地说道。

"什么都不知道，什么都不说的人根本算不上同伴，"她咕哝着。

希斯克利夫站了起来，但他没有时间进一步表达自己的感受，因为石板路上传来了一阵马蹄声，年轻的林顿轻轻敲了敲门后便走进房门，因为收到凯瑟琳意外的召唤，他的脸色显得容光焕发。毫无疑问，在这一个进门、另一个出门的时候，凯瑟琳发现这两个朋友的不同之处。这种对比犹如你的目光从一个荒凉陡峭的产煤区，转移到一个美丽肥沃的山谷；而他的声音与问候也和他的相貌一样与之恰恰相反。他说话的声音悦耳低沉，发音吐字跟你一样。跟我们这里的人相比，显得没有那么生硬，要更加柔和。

you do: that's less gruff than we talk here, and softer.

"I'm not come too soon, am I?" he said, casting a look at me: I had begun to wipe the plate, and tidy some drawers at the far end in the dresser.

"No," answered Catherine. "What are you doing there, Nelly?"

"My work, Miss," I replied. (Mr. Hindley had given me directions to make a third party in any private visits Linton chose to pay.)

She stepped behind me and whispered crossly, "Take yourself and your dusters off; when company are in the house, servants don't commence scouring and cleaning in the room where they are!"

"It's a good opportunity, now that master is away," I answered aloud: "he hates me to be fidgeting over these things in his presence. I'm sure Mr. Edgar will excuse me."

"I hate you to be fidgeting in *my* presence," exclaimed the young lady imperiously, not allowing her guest time to speak: she had failed to recover her equanimity since the little dispute with Heathcliff.

"I'm sorry for it, Miss Catherine," was my response; and I proceeded assiduously with my occupation.

She, supposing Edgar could not see her, snatched the cloth from my hand, and pinched me, with a prolonged wrench, very spitefully on the arm. I've said I did not love her, and rather relished mortifying her vanity now and then: besides, she hurt me extremely; so I started up from my knees, and screamed out, "Oh, Miss, that's a nasty trick! You have no right to nip me, and I'm not going to bear it."

"我没有来得太早吧?"他看了我一眼,说道。我正好开始擦盘子,清理柜子上面的几个抽屉。

"没有,"凯瑟琳回答,"你在那儿干什么,内莉?"

"干活啊,小姐,"我回答。(辛德雷先生曾指示过我,只要在林顿私自拜访的时候,我就要充当第三者。)

她走到我身后,生气地低声说道:"马上带着你的抹布消失,有朋友来家做客的时候,仆人不该在客人待的房间里洗洗刷刷!"

"既然主人不在家,这正是个好机会啊,"我大声地回答她,"他不喜欢我在他面前收拾这些东西。我相信埃德加先生会谅解我的。"

"可我讨厌你在我面前收拾,"还没等她的客人回答,小姐就蛮横地大声嚷着。自从跟希斯克利夫发生小小的争执之后,她还没能恢复镇定。

"真是抱歉,凯瑟琳小姐。"我就这样回答她,继续坚持干我的活。

她自以为埃德加看不见她,就从我手里夺走抹布,狠狠地在我胳膊上掐了一把,还停了很长时间。前面已经说过我并不喜欢她,时刻想要克制她的虚荣心,况且她真的把我弄得非常痛,因此本来蹲在地上的我,立马跳起来,对她大叫:"啊,小姐,你这样可真是下流!你没权力掐我,我受不了了。"

"I didn't touch you, you lying creature!" cried she, her fingers tingling to repeat the act, and her ears red with rage. She never had power to conceal her passion, it always set her whole complexion in a blaze.

"What's that, then?" I retorted, showing a decided purple witness to refute her.

She stamped her foot, wavered a moment, and then, irresistibly impelled by the naughty spirit within her, slapped me on the cheek a stinging blow that filled both eyes with water.

"Catherine, love! Catherine!" interposed Linton, greatly shocked at the double fault of falsehood and violence which his idol had committed.

"Leave the room, Ellen!" she repeated, trembling all over.

Little Hareton, who followed me everywhere, and was sitting near me on the floor, at seeing my tears commenced crying himself, and sobbed out complaints against "wicked aunt Cathy," which drew her fury on to his unlucky head: she seized his shoulders, and shook him till the poor child waxed livid, and Edgar thoughtlessly laid hold of her hands to deliver him. In an instant one was wrung free, and the astonished young man felt it applied over his own ear in a way that could not be mistaken for jest. He drew back in consternation. I lifted Hareton in my arms, and walked off to the kitchen with him, leaving the door of communication open, for I was curious to watch how they would settle their disagreement. The insulted visitor moved to the spot where he had laid his hat, pale and with a quivering lip.

"That's right!" I said to myself. "Take warning and begone! It's a kindness to let you

"我又没碰你，你这个爱撒谎的家伙！"她大喊着，手指头咯咯作响，准备再掐一次，她的耳朵因为激动而变得通红。她从来不会掩饰自己的激动，总是自己的脸变得像火烧一样。

"那么，这是什么？"我指着一个明显的紫色印记作为证据，反驳她。

她跺了跺脚，犹豫了一会儿，然后，无法克制自己恶劣情绪的驱使，打了我一耳光，这一刺痛的耳光打得我眼泪都流出来了。

"凯瑟琳，亲爱的！凯瑟琳！"林顿说话了，看到自己的偶像犯了欺骗和暴力的双重错误而大感震惊。

"离开这间房子，艾伦！"她重复说，浑身发抖。

小哈里顿一直都是跟着我到处走，这会正坐在我附近的地板上，一见我流眼泪，他也马上哭了起来，还哽咽着骂道"坏蛋凯茜姑姑"，于是她的怒火又烧到了这不幸的孩子身上。她抓住他的肩膀，一直摇他，直到这可怜的孩子脸色惨白。埃德加想都没想就去抓住她的手，想让她放手。忽然间一只手从中抽了出来，这个惊讶的小伙子才发现这手已经打在自己的耳朵上了，这一打绝不能被误认为是开玩笑。她惊慌失措地缩回了手。我把哈里顿抱在怀里，带着他走去厨房，不过把进出的门开着，因为我很好奇，想看他们怎么解决这场争执。这个被侮辱的客人走到他放帽子的地方，面色苍白，嘴唇颤抖。

"那才像话！"我自言自语着，"引以为戒，快走吧！能让你看清楚

have a glimpse of her genuine disposition."

"Where are you going?" demanded Catherine, advancing to the door.

He swerved aside, and attempted to pass.

"You must not go!" she exclaimed energetically.

"I must and shall!" he replied in a subdued voice.

"No," she persisted, grasping the handle; "not yet, Edgar Linton: sit down; you shall not leave me in that temper. I should be miserable all night, and I won't be miserable for you!"

"Can I stay after you have struck me?" asked Linton.

Catherine was mute.

"You've made me afraid and ashamed of you," he continued;"I'll not come here again!"

Her eyes began to glisten, and her lids to twinkle.

"And you told a deliberate untruth!" he said.

"I didn't!" she cried, recovering her speech;"I did nothing deliberately. Well, go, if you please—get away! And now I'll cry—I'll cry myself sick!"

She dropped down on her knees by a chair, and set to weeping in serious earnest. Edgar persevered in his resolution as far as the court; there he lingered. I resolved to encourage him.

"Miss is dreadfully wayward, sir," I called out. "As bad as any marred child: you'd better be riding home, or else she will be sick, only to grieve us."

The soft thing looked askance through the window: he possessed the power to depart, as much as a cat possesses the power to leave a

她真正的性格，也是件好事。"

"你要去哪里？"凯瑟琳跑到门口追问道。

他侧过身子，想要走过去。

"你可不能走！"她大声嚷着。

"我一定要走，马上就走！"他压低声音回答道。

"不，"她坚持着，抓着门把，"现在不行，埃德加·林顿。坐下，你不能带着这种心情离开我。我会痛苦一整晚，我不想因为你而难过！"

"你打了我，我还能留在这里吗？"林顿问。

凯瑟琳哑巴了。

"你让我害怕，为你而惭愧，"他接着说，"我不会再来这儿了！"

她的眼睛闪现出泪光，眼皮直眨。

"而且你还故意撒谎！"他说。

"我没有！"她哭着，大声说，"我不是故意的。行啊，走吧，只要你喜欢，走啊！现在我要哭了，我要一直哭到半死不活的！"

她跪倒在一把椅子旁边，非常认真地痛哭起来。埃德加坚定着自己的决心走到院子里，可是在那里，他又犹豫了。我决定去怂恿他快点离开。

"小姐确实非常任性，先生，"我对他喊道，"跟其他惯坏了的孩子一样坏。你最好还是骑马回家吧，不然她只会闹得死去活来，让我们伤心难过。"

这软弱的孩子斜着眼看着窗里面：他没法让自己离开这里，正如一只猫没法离开一只半死的老鼠或是一

mouse half killed, or a bird half eaten. Ah, I thought, there will be no saving him—He's doomed, and flies to his fate! And so it was: he turned abruptly, hastened into the house again, shut the door behind him; and when I went in a while after to inform them that Earnshaw had come home rabid drunk, ready to pull the old place about our ears (his ordinary frame of mind in that condition), I saw the quarrel had merely effected a closer intimacy—had broken the out-works of youthful timidity, and enabled them to forsake the disguise of friendship, and confess themselves lovers.

Intelligence of Mr. Hindley's arrival drove Linton speedily to his horse, and Catherine to her chamber. I went to hide little Hareton, and to take the shot out of the master's fowling-piece, which he was fond of playing with in his insane excitement, to the hazard of the lives of any who provoked, or even attracted his notice too much; and I had hit upon the plan of removing it, that he might do less mischief if he did go the length of firing the gun.

只吃了一半的鸟一样。唉！我想他是无药可救了，他命中注定就该如此，而且已经朝着他的命运而去。事实真是如此，他猛地转过身来，再次匆忙地回到家里，关上身后的门。过了一会儿后，我进去通知他们恩肖已经酩酊大醉地回家，准备把这所房子都毁掉（在那种情况下他脑子里想的通常都是这些东西），才发现这场争吵反而促成了他们更为亲密的行为——已经打破了年轻人胆怯的堡垒，使他们抛弃了友谊的伪装，承认他们是情人了。

辛德雷先生回家的消息驱使着林顿迅速策马而去，也把凯瑟琳赶回到她自己的卧室。我赶紧把小哈里顿藏起来，把主人猎枪里的子弹取出来，这是他在疯狂激动的时刻喜欢玩的东西，任何人激怒了他，甚至是太吸引他的注意，就要冒生命危险。因此我想到了把子弹取出来的办法，这样就算他真的闹到要开枪的地步，也不会造成多大的危害。

Chapter 9
第九章

He entered, vociferating oaths dreadful to hear; and caught me in the act of stowing his son away in the kitchen cupboard. Hareton was

他走进屋来，大声地叫着不堪入耳的污言秽语，正好看见我把他儿子藏在厨房的碗橱里。哈里顿遇到他那

impressed with a wholesome terror of encountering either his wild-beast's fondness or his madman's rage; for in one he ran a chance of being squeezed and kissed to death, and in the other of being flung into the fire, or dashed against the wall; and the poor thing remained perfectly quiet wherever I chose to put him.

"There, I've found it out at last!" cried Hindley, pulling me back by the skin of my neck, like a dog."By heaven and hell, you've sworn between you to murder that child! I know how it is, now, that he is always out of my way. But, with the help of Satan, I shall make you swallow the carving-knife, Nelly! You needn't laugh; for I've just crammed Kenneth, head-downmost, in the Blackhorse marsh; and two is the same as one—and I want to kill some of you: I shall have no rest till I do!"

"But I don't like the carving-knife, Mr. Hindley," I answered;"it has been cutting red herrings. I'd rather be shot, if you please."

"You'd rather be damned!" he said;"and so you shall. No law in England can hinder a man from keeping his house decent, and mine's abominable! open your mouth."

He held the knife in his hand, and pushed its point between my teeth: but, for my part, I was never much afraid of his vagaries. I spat out, and affirmed it tasted detestably—I would not take it on any account.

"Oh!" said he, releasing me, "I see that hideous little villain is not Hareton: I beg your pardon, Nell. If it be, he deserves flaying alive for not running to welcome me, and for screaming as if I were a goblin. Unnatural cub, come hither! I'll teach thee to impose on a

野兽般的溺爱或是疯子样的狂暴,都会产生强烈的恐惧感,因为如果是第一种情况,他有可能会被挤死或吻死;而如果是另一种情况,他有可能会被丢进火堆或是猛撞墙壁。因此无论我把他藏在什么地方,这可怜的小家伙总是会保持安静。

"喂,到底还是被我发现了!"辛德雷大叫道,揪着我脖子上的皮,像只狗一样把我往后拖。"天地良心,你们肯定发誓想要谋害这孩子!现在总算知道为什么我老是见不到他了。但是撒旦帮我,我要让你把切肉刀吞下去,内莉!你别笑,因为我刚把肯尼斯头朝下埋在黑马沼泽里了,一个两个都一样,我要杀了你们,不杀了你们我就不得安宁!"

"可我不喜欢切肉刀,辛德雷先生,"我回答他,"这刀刚刚用来切过红鲱鱼。如果你愿意,我宁愿被枪打死。"

"你最好还是下地狱,"他说,"你肯定会下地狱的。在英格兰没有哪一条法律可以阻止一个人把他的家弄得大方得体,但我的家却糟糕透顶!张开你的嘴!"

他拿着刀子,把刀尖往我的牙齿缝里戳。但我从来不畏惧他的怪异行为。我吐了口唾沫,说这味道很恶心,我无论如何都不会吞下去的。

"哦!"他放开我,说道,"我发现那个可恶的小流氓不是哈里顿,请你原谅我,内尔。如果真是他的话,他就应该被活生生地剥皮,居然没有跑来迎接我,而且还大声尖叫,好像

goodhearted, deluded father. Now, don't you think the lad would be handsomer cropped? It makes a dog fiercer, and I love something fierce—get me a scissors—something fierce and trim! Besides, it's infernal affection—devilish conceit it is, to cherish our ears—we're asses enough without them. Hush, child, hush! Well then, it is my darling! Wisht, dry thy eyes—there's a joy; kiss me. What! it won't? Kiss me, Hareton! Damn thee, kiss me! By God, as if I would rear such a monster! As sure as I'm living, I'll break the brat's neck".

Poor Hareton was squalling and kicking in his father's arms with all his might, and redoubled his yells when he carried him up-stairs and lifted him over the banister. I cried out that he would frighten the child into fits, and ran to rescue him. As I reached them, Hindley leant forward on the rails to listen to a noise below; almost forgetting what he had in his hands. "Who is that?" he asked, hearing some one approaching the stair's foot. I leant forward also, for the purpose of signing to Heathcliff, whose step I recognised, not to come further; and, at the instant when my eye quitted Hareton, he gave a sudden spring , delivered himself from the careless grasp that held him, and fell.

There was scarcely time to experience a thrill of horror before we saw that the little wretch was safe. Heathcliff arrived underneath just at the critical moment; by a natural impulse, he arrested his descent, and setting him on his feet, looked up to discover the author of the accident. A miser who has parted with a lucky lottery ticket for five shillings, and finds next day he has lost in the bargain five thousand

我是妖怪一样。不懂规矩的小兔崽子，到这儿来！我要教训教训你，居然欺骗一个好心的、被蒙蔽的父亲。现在你不觉得这小家伙的头发剪短点会变得更漂亮吗？狗毛剪短点可以让狗显得更凶猛，我喜欢凶猛的东西，给我把剪刀，我喜欢凶猛整齐的东西，而且这是恶魔般的伪装，是恶魔的幻想，珍惜我们的耳朵吧，没有了耳朵，我们也真够像驴子的。嘘，孩子，嘘！好啦，我的乖宝宝！不哭，擦干你的眼睛，刚才跟你开玩笑呢。亲亲我。什么！不想亲？亲亲我，哈里顿！该死的，亲我！神啊，好像我愿意养这么个怪物似的！只要我还活着，就要把这毛小子的脖子摔断。"

可怜的哈里顿在他父亲怀里嚎啕大哭，拼命地踢蹬，当辛德雷把他抱上楼梯，然后把他举到栏杆边上的时候，他更加倍地大叫起来。我一边大声叫着他这样会把孩子吓坏的，一边跑过去救孩子。当我来到他们那边时，辛德雷探身向前靠在栏杆上听着楼下的动静，几乎忘记了他手里还拿着什么东西。"谁在下面？"他听到有人走向楼梯跟前，便问道。我也向前探望，想要示意希斯克利夫，叫他不要走过来，我听得出这是他的脚步声。就在我的视线离开哈里顿的那一刹那，孩子猛地一跃，从那抱着他的疏忽的怀抱中挣脱出来，掉了下去。

在看到这个可怜的小家伙安然无恙之前，我们简直没有时间来感受那令人颤抖的恐怖。在这危急关头希斯克利夫赶到楼下，下意识地接住了哈里顿，然后扶他站好，抬头看看是谁酿成了这起意外事故。即使是一个守

pounds, could not show a blanker countenance than he did on beholding the figure of Mr. Earnshaw above. It expressed, plainer than words could do, the intensest anguish at having made himself the instrument of thwarting his own revenge. Had it been dark, I dare say, he would have tried to remedy the mistake by smashing Hareton's skull on the steps; but, we witnessed his salvation; and I was presently below with my precious charge pressed to my heart. Hindley descended more leisurely, sobered and abashed.

"It is your fault, Ellen," he said; "you should have kept him out of sight: you should have taken him from me! Is he injured anywhere?"

"Injured!" I cried angrily. "If he's not killed, he'll be an idiot! Oh! I wonder his mother does not rise from her grave to see how you use him. You're worse than a heathen—treating your own flesh and blood in that manner!"

He attempted to touch the child, who, on finding himself with me, sobbed off his terror directly. At the first finger his father laid on him, however, he shrieked again louder than before, and struggled as if he would go into convulsions.

"You shall not meddle with him!" I continued. "He hates you—they all hate you—that's the truth! A happy family you have; and a pretty state you're come to!"

"I shall come to a prettier, yet, Nelly," laughed the misguided man, recovering his hardness. 'At present, convey yourself and him away. And, hark you, Heathcliff! clear you too, quite from my reach and hearing. . . I

财奴为了五先令而舍弃一张幸运彩票，第二天却发现他在这笔交易上损失了五千英镑，也不会有希斯克利夫看到楼上的人是恩肖先生时表现出的那副茫然若失的表情。这表情比言语更明确地显示出他内心的极端痛苦，因为他竟然成了阻挠自己报仇的工具。如果是在天黑的时候，我敢说他肯定会在楼梯上打爆哈里顿的头，试图来弥补这个错误，但我们亲眼看到他救了哈里顿。我急忙跑下楼抱过我的宝贝，紧紧贴在自己的心头。辛德雷从容不迫地走下来，头脑清醒，觉得很羞愧。

"都是你的错，艾伦，"他说，"你应该把他藏起来，让我找不到才对。你应该把他从我手里抢过去！他有没有摔伤？"

"摔伤！"我愤怒地对他喊道，"就算他没被你摔死，也会摔成一个傻子！啊！我真感到奇怪，他母亲怎么没从坟墓里坐起来看看你是怎样对待他的。你比野蛮人还要恶毒，居然会这样对待自己的亲身骨肉！"

他想要摸摸孩子。这孩子一发现他跟着我，就立刻放声大哭的发泄他的恐惧。但当他父亲的手指头碰到他时，他又大声尖叫起来，叫得比刚才还响亮，还像发羊癫疯一样挣扎着。

"你还是别来碰他了！"我接着说，"他恨你，他们都恨你，这是事实！你有个幸福的家庭，却被你弄到这样一个糟糕的境地！"

"我还要把这家搞得更糟，内莉，"这陷入歧途的男人大笑着，恢复了他的顽强，"现在，你抱着他走吧。还有希斯克利夫，你听着！你也

wouldn't murder you tonight, unless, perhaps, I set the house on fire: but that's as my fancy goes."

While saying this he took a pint bottle of brandy from the dresser, and poured some into a tumbler.

"Nay, don't!" I entreated. "Mr. Hindley, do take warning. Have mercy on this unfortunate boy, if you care nothing for yourself!"

"Any one will do better for him than I shall," he answered.

"Have mercy on your own soul!" I said, endeavouring to snatch the glass from his hand.

"Not I! On the contrary, I shall have great pleasure in sending it to perdition to punish its Maker," exclaimed the blasphemer. "Here's to its hearty damnation!"

He drank the spirits and impatiently bade us go; terminating his command with a sequel of horrid imprecations, too bad to repeat or remember.

"It's a pity he cannot kill himself with drink," observed Heathcliff, muttering an echo of curses back when the door was shut. "He's doing his very utmost; but his constitution defies him. Mr. Kenneth says he would wager his mare, that he'll outlive any man on this side Gimmerton, and go to the grave a hoary sinner; unless some happy chance out of the common course befall him."

I went into the kitchen, and sat down to lull my little lamb to sleep. Heathcliff, as I thought, walked through to the barn. It turned out afterwards that he only got as far as the other side the settle, when he flung himself on a bench by the wall, removed from the fire, and remained silent.

滚得远远的，别让我看到你听到你。今晚我不会杀了你，除非我放火烧了这座房子：不过我只是这么想想罢了。"

他一边说着，一边从柜子里拿出一小瓶白兰地，倒在杯子里。

"不，不要喝了！"我哀求着，"辛德雷先生，请你听听我的劝告吧。如果你不在意你自己，也求你可怜可怜这不幸的孩子吧！"

"任何人都会比我待他更好的。"他回答道。

"可怜可怜你自己的灵魂吧！"我说着，竭力想抢过他手里的杯子。

"我不会这么做的。恰恰相反，我宁愿毁灭自己的灵魂来惩罚它的造物主，"这亵渎上帝的人叫喊着，"为灵魂的衷心毁灭干杯！"

他喝下酒，极不耐烦地吩咐我们快走开，用一连串恐怖而又很难记住或复述的咒骂，来结束他的命令。

"真可惜他不能让自己醉死，"希斯克利夫说。等关上门之后，他也嘀咕了一阵谴责，"他这完全是在作践自己，可他的体格还能支撑得住，肯尼斯先生说过，他愿意拿自己的马打赌，在吉默顿这一带，没人会比他长命百岁，最终他会像个白发罪人一样走向坟墓，除非他能那么好运碰巧遇到了什么意外的事。"

我来到厨房，坐下来哄我的小宝贝睡觉。我以为希斯克利夫去马厩了，后来才知道他只是走到另一边的长靠椅边，躺在一条靠墙的椅子上，远离着火堆，一直没有吭声。

I was rocking Hareton on my knee, and humming a song that began—

It was far in the night, and the bairnies grat, The mither beneath the mools heard that[①]

When Miss Cathy, who had listened to the hubbub from her room, put her head in and whispered—

"Are you alone, Nelly?"

"Yes, Miss," I replied.

She entered and approached the hearth. I, supposing she was going to say something, looked up. The expression of her face seemed disturbed and anxious. Her lips were half asunder, as if she meant to speak, and she drew a breath; but it escaped in a sigh instead of a sentence. I resumed my song; not having forgotten her recent behaviour.

"Where's Heathcliff?" she said, interrupting me.

"About his work in the stable," was my answer.

He did not contradict me; perhaps he had fallen into a dose. There followed another long pause, during which I perceived a drop or two trickle from Catherine's cheek to the flags. Is she sorry for her shameful conduct? I asked myself. That will be a novelty: but she may come to the point as she will—I shan't help her! No, she felt small trouble regarding any subject, save her own concerns.

"Oh, dear!" she cried at last. "I'm very unhappy!"

"A pity," observed I. "You're hard to

我一边把哈里顿放在腿上摇晃着，一边哼着这首曲子：

"夜已经很深，孩子呼喊着，坟土下的母亲听到了……"

这时凯茜小姐探头进来，她已经在房里听见了这吵闹声，轻声地说：

"你一个人吗，内莉？"

"是的，小姐，"我回答。

她走进厨房，来到壁炉边上。我抬头看着她，猜想着她会说什么。她脸上的表情看起来有点烦躁不安。她的嘴半开着，好像要说什么话。她深吸了一口气，但这口气化为一声叹息而不是一句话。我继续哼着我的歌，并没有忘记她刚才的行为。

"希斯克利夫在哪呢？"她打断了我的歌声，问道。

"在马厩里干他的活呢。"我回答她。

希斯克利夫并没有反驳我，也许他已经睡着了。接着又是一阵安静。这期间我发现凯瑟琳的脸颊上有一两滴眼泪落在地板上。她是为自己羞耻的行为而到抱歉吗？我自忖着。那可就新鲜了。但她可能真的知道错了，反正我不去帮她！不，她不会为任何事情感到烦恼，除非这事跟她自己有关。

"哦，哎呀！"她终于叫了起来，"我难过死了！"

"真可怜啊，"我说，"要你高兴

[①] 出自一首古老的丹麦民谣《鬼魂的警告》，英国诗人司各特(W. Walter Scott, 一七七一年至一八三二年)在长诗《湖上夫人(The Lady of the Lake)》的附录里把这个民谣翻译成了苏格兰语。内莉的吟唱和司各特的翻译略有出入。

please: so many friends and so few cares, and can't make yourself content!"

"Nelly, will you keep a secret for me?" she pursued, kneeling down by me, and lifting her winsome eyes to my face with that sort of look which turns off bad temper, even when one has all the right in the world to indulge it.

"Is it worth keeping?" I inquired, less sulkily.

"Yes, and it worries me, and I must let it out! I want to know what I should do. Today, Edgar Linton has asked me to marry him, and I've given him an answer. Now, before I tell you whether it was a consent or denial, you tell me which it ought to have been."

"Really, Miss Catherine, how can I know?" I replied. "To be sure, considering the exhibition you performed in his presence this afternoon, I might say it would be wise to refuse him: since he asked you after that, he must be either hopelessly stupid or a venturesome fool."

"If you talk so, I won't tell you any more," she returned, peevishly, rising to her feet. "I accepted him, Nelly. Be quick, and say whether I was wrong!"

"You accepted him! then what good is it discussing the matter? You have pledged your word, and cannot retract."

"But, say whether I should have done so—do!" she exclaimed in an irritated tone; chafing her hands together, and frowning.

"There are many things to be considered before that question can be answered properly," I said sententiously. "First and foremost, do you love Mr. Edgar?"

"Who can help it? Of course I do," she

还真是困难啊，你有这么多的朋友，这么少的烦恼，还不能让你满足吗！"

"内莉，你能替我保密吗？"她跪在我旁边继续说道，抬起她那迷人的双眼，用那种足以驱走坏脾气的眼神看着我，那眼神甚至可以让一个极有理由发怒的人消气。

"这事值得保密吗？"我问道，心里已经没有了刚才的不高兴。

"有，而且这事情让我很烦恼，我非说出来不可！我想知道自己该怎么办。今天，埃德加·林顿向我求婚，我也已经给了他答复。现在，在我告诉你我的回答是接受还是拒绝之前，你告诉我应该选什么。"

"真是的，凯瑟琳小姐，我怎么会知道？"我回答道，"当然，考虑到今天下午你在他面前表现出来的行为，我想说拒绝他是明智的。既然他是在这之后问你的，那他一定是个无药可救的笨蛋，或是一个敢于冒险的傻瓜。"

"如果你要这么说，我就不再跟你说了，"她生气地站起来，回答道，"我答应他了，内莉。你快告诉我这样做是不是错了！"

"你答应他了？那讨论这件事还有什么意义呢？既然你话已经说出来了，那就不能再收回啦。"

"不过可以说说我是不是应该这么做啊，快说吧！"她擦了擦双手，皱着眉头，用生气的语气叫着。

"在正确地回答那个问题之前，还有许多事情需要考虑，"我很简洁地回答她，"第一个也是最重要的一个问题就是，你爱不爱埃德加先生？"

"谁会不爱他呢？我当然爱啦。"

answered.

Then I put her through the following catechism: for a girl of twentytwo, it was not injudicious.

"Why do you love him, Miss Cathy?"

"Nonsense, I do—that's sufficient."

"By no means; you must say why?"

"Well, because he is handsome, and pleasant to be with."

"Bad!" was my commentary.

"And because he is young and cheerful."

"Bad, still."

"And because he loves me."

"Indifferent, coming there."

"And he will be rich, and I shall like to be the greatest woman of the neighbourhood, and I shall be proud of having such a husband."

"Worst of all. And now say how you love him?"

"As everybody loves—You're silly, Nelly."

"Not at all—Answer."

"I love the ground under his feet, and the air over his head, and everything he touches, and every word he says. I love all his looks, and all his actions, and him entirely and altogether. There now!"

"And why?"

"Nay, you are making a jest of it: it is exceedingly ill-natured! It's no jest to me!" said the young lady, scowling, and turning her face to the fire.

"I'm very far from jesting, Miss Catherine," I replied. "You love Mr. Edgar, because he is handsome, and young, and cheerful, and rich, and loves you. The last, however, goes for nothing: you would love him without that,

接着我就问了下面的这些问题：对于一个二十二岁的姑娘来说，这些问题并不算浅薄。

"那你为什么爱他，凯茜小姐？"

"废话，我爱他，那就够了。"

"不行，一定要说为什么。"

"好吧，因为他很帅气，跟他在一起很快乐。"

"不够！"我评价道。

"还因为他年轻，有活力。"

"还是不够。"

"还因为他也爱我。"

"这些都无关紧要，继续说。"

"他会很有钱，我将会成为这附近最了不起的女人，我会为有这一个丈夫而感到骄傲。"

"糟糕至极。那现在说说你是怎么爱他的吧？"

"跟其他每个恋人一样啊——你真是无聊，内莉。"

"一点也不无聊——回答吧。"

"我爱他脚下的土地，爱他头上的天空，爱他碰过的每样东西，爱他说过的每句话。我爱他所有的表情，爱他所有的动作。我爱他的全部，爱他的一切。这样行了吧！"

"为什么爱呢？"

"不会吧，你是在开玩笑吗，你可真是太恶毒了！我可不是开玩笑的！"小姐皱着眉说道，接着把脸转向火炉。

"我绝没有开玩笑，凯瑟琳小姐！"我回答说，"因为埃德加先生帅气、年轻、活泼、富有、爱你，所以你就爱他。不过这最后一条没什么意义，即使没有这条，你也许还是会

probably; and with it you wouldn't, unless he possessed the four former attractions."

"No, to be sure not: I should only pity him—hate him, perhaps, if he were ugly, and a down."

"But there are several other handsome, rich young men in the world: handsomer, possibly, and richer than he is. What should hinder you from loving them?"

"If there be any, they are out of my way: I've seen none like Edgar."

"You may see some; and he won't always be handsome, and young, and may not always be rich."

"He is now; and I have only to do with the present. I wish you would speak rationally."

"Well, that settles it: if you have only to do with the present, marry Mr. Linton."

"I don't want your permission for that—I *shall* marry him: and yet you have not told me whether I'm right."

"Perfectly right; if people be right to marry only for the present. And now, let us hear what you are unhappy about. Your brother will be pleased... The old lady and gentleman will not object, I think; you will escape from a disorderly comfortless home into a wealthy, respectable one; and you love Edgar, and Edgar loves you. All seems smooth and easy: where is the obstacle?"

"*Here*! And *here*!" replied Catherine, striking one hand on her forehead, and the other on her breast, "in whichever place the soul lives. In my soul and in my heart, I'm convinced I'm wrong!"

"That's very strange! I cannot make it out."

爱他；而有了这条，你倒不一定会爱他，除非他具备前面四个优点。"

"不，当然不会，如果他长相丑陋、性格粗鲁，那我只会可怜他，或许讨厌他。"

"可这世上还有其他很多帅气富有的年轻男人啊，会比他更帅气更富有。你为什么不去爱他们呢？"

"如果有的话，我也见不到他们——我还没有看见过像埃德加这样的人呢。"

"你会看到的，而他不会总是那么帅气、那么年轻，也不会总是那么有钱。"

"他已经是了啊，而我只要想着眼前的人就可以。我希望你能说点合情合理的话。"

"行了，那就好，如果你只想着眼前的人，那就嫁林顿先生。"

"我并不想得到你的允许，我会嫁他，但你还没告诉我这样决定到底对不对。"

"如果人们只顾着眼前的人而结婚是对的话，那就完全是对的。那现在让我们听听为什么你闷闷不乐吧。我想你哥哥会高兴的，那位老太太和老先生也不会反对。你可以逃离这个混乱不堪、毫不舒适的家，到一个富裕、有名望的人家里。而且你爱埃德加，埃德加也爱你。所有的一切看来都那么顺心如意，哪来的阻碍呢？"

"这里，还有这里！"凯瑟琳一边回答，一边用手拍打自己的额头，另一只手则捶着胸，"凡是有灵魂存在的地方都有阻碍。在我的灵魂与内心深处，我感到自己选择错了！"

"那真是奇怪了！我不明白。"

"It's my secret. But if you will not mock at me, I'll explain it: I can't do it distinctly; but I'll give you a feeling of how I feel."

She seated herself by me again: her countenance grew sadder and graver, and her clasped hands trembled.

"Nelly, do you never dream queer dreams?" she said, suddenly, after some minutes' reflection.

"Yes, now and then," I answered.

"And so do I. I've dreamt in my life dreams that have stayed with me ever after, and changed my ideas: they've gone through and through me, like wine through water, and altered the colour of my mind. And this is one: I'm going to tell it—but take care not to smile at any part of it."

"Oh! don't, Miss Catherine!" I cried. "We're dismal enough without conjuring up ghosts and visions to perplex us. Come, come, be merry and like yourself! Look at little Hareton! *he's* dreaming nothing dreary. How sweetly he smiles in his sleep!"

"Yes; and how sweetly his father curses in his solitude! You remember him, I dare say, when he was just such another as that chubby thing: nearly as young and innocent. However, Nelly, I shall oblige you to listen: it's not long; and I've no power to be merry tonight."

"I won't hear it, I won't hear it!" I repeated, hastily.

I was superstitious about dreams then, and am still; and Catherine had an unusual gloom in her aspect, that made me dread something from which I might shape a prophecy, and foresee a fearful catastrophe. She was vexed, but she did not proceed. Apparently taking up another sub-

"这是我的秘密。但如果你不嘲笑，我就解释给你。我也解释不清，但我会让你感同身受。"

她又坐到我的身旁，脸色变得更加哀伤、更加严肃，她那紧攥着的双手颤抖着。

"内莉，你从没做过稀奇古怪的梦吗？"她想了几分钟后，忽然说道。

"不，有时候会做。"我回答。

"我也是。我这辈子做过的梦有些会在梦过之后永远跟着我，还会改变我的想法。这些梦在我心里游来穿去，好像酒在水里流动一样，改变我心思的颜色。这是一个，我要讲了，但你千万不要嘲笑我说的话。"

"唉，别说了，凯瑟琳小姐！"我叫道，"我们已经够凄凉的了，用不着招神引鬼来迷惑自己。来，开心点，像你原来那样！看看小哈里顿，他都不会梦到什么伤心事。看他在梦里笑得多甜啊！"

"是啊，他的父亲在孤独寂寞的时候诅咒得多痛快啊！我猜你应该还记得他和那个胖小子一样大的时候，差不多一样年幼一样天真。但是，内莉，我希望你能听我一句话，并不是很长，而且我今晚也没什么精神可以高兴起来。"

"我不要听，我不要听！"我急忙重复地说。

那时我对梦境非常迷信，现在依旧如此。凯瑟琳的脸色又显得异常忧郁，我担心她的梦会使我有某种预感，让我预见一个可怕的大灾难。她有点生气，不过并没继续说下去。过

ject, she recommenced in a short time.

"If I were in heaven, Nelly, I should be extremely miserable."

"Because you are not fit to go there," I answered. "All sinners would be miserable in heaven."

"But it is not for that. I dreamt once that I was there."

"I tell you I won't harken to your dreams, Miss Catherine! I'll go to bed," I interrupted again.

She laughed, and held me down; for I made a motion to leave my chair.

"This is nothing," cried she: "I was only going to say that heaven did not seem to be my home; and I broke my heart with weeping to come back to earth; and the angels were so angry that they flung me out into the middle of the heath on the top of Wuthering Heights; where I woke sobbing for joy. That will do to explain my secret, as well as the other. I've no more business to marry Edgar Linton than I have to be in heaven; and if the wicked man in there had not brought Heathcliff so low, I shouldn't have thought of it. It would degrade me to marry Heathcliff now; so he shall never know how I love him: and that, not because he's handsome, Nelly, but because he's more myself than I am. Whatever our souls are made of, his and mine are the same; and Linton's is as different as a moonbeam from lightning, or frost from fire."

Ere this speech ended, I became sensible of Heathcliff's presence. Having noticed a slight movement, I turned my head, and saw him rise from the bench, and steal out noiselessly. He had listened till he heard Catherine

了一会儿她又说话了,很显然这次换了个话题。

"内莉,如果我在天堂,一定会非常悲惨的。"

"因为你不配去那儿,"我回答她,"所有有罪的人都会在天堂里过得很悲惨。"

"但并不是因为这个。我曾经梦到过自己在那儿。"

"我跟你说了我不想听你的梦,凯瑟琳小姐!我要上床睡觉了。"我再次打断了她。

她笑了笑,把我按着坐下来,因为我想要起身离开椅子。

"这没有什么呀,"她叫道,"我只是想说天堂好像不是我的家。我伤透了心,哭泣着,因为自己要回到人间。天使们非常生气,就把我扔到呼啸山庄的石楠树丛中间。我就在那里醒过来,高兴地哭着。这就解释了我的秘密,以及其他的事。我无权嫁给埃德加·林顿,就像我无权留在天堂一样。如果那边那个恶毒的人没有把希斯克利夫贬得一文不值,我就不会想到这个。如今要是我嫁给了希斯克利夫就会降低身份,所以他永远不会知道我有多么爱他;那并不是因为他的帅气,内莉,而是因为他比我更像自己。不管我们的灵魂是由什么做成的,他和我的灵魂都是一模一样的;而林顿的灵魂就如闪电中的月光,或者是烈焰中的冰霜,完全不一样。"

这段话还没说完,我就发现希斯克利夫还在这里。当我回头的时候,注意到一个轻微的动静,我看见他从长椅上站起来,悄无声息地溜出去。他一直听到凯瑟琳说嫁给他就会降低

say it would degrade her to marry him, and then he staid to hear no farther. My companion, sitting on the ground, was prevented by the back of the settle from remarking his presence or departure; but I started, and bade her hush!

"Why?" she asked, gazing nervously round.

"Joseph is here," I answered, catching opportunely the roll of his cartwheels up the road;"and Heathcliff will come in with him. I'm not sure whether he were not at the door this moment."

"Oh, he couldn't overhear me at the door!" said she."Give me Hareton, while you get the supper, and when it is ready ask me to sup with you. I want to cheat my uncomfortable conscience, and be convinced that Heathcliff has no notion of these things. He has not, has he? He does not know what being in love is?"

"I see no reason that he should not know, as well as you," I returned;"and if you are his choice, he'll be the most unfortunate creature that ever was born! As soon as you become Mrs. Linton, he loses friends, and love, and all! Have you considered how you'll bear the separation, and how he'll bear to be quite deserted in the world? Because, Miss Catherine—"

"He quite deserted! we separated!" she exclaimed, with an accent of indignation."Who is to separate us, pray? They'll meet the fate of Milo[①]! Not as long as I live, Ellen: for no mortal creature. Every Linton on the face of the earth might melt into nothing, before I could

身份后就没有继续听下去。我的同伴正坐在地上,刚好被高背长椅的椅背挡住了视线,没有注意到他在这儿,也没有看见他走出去。但是我吃了一惊,叫她安静。

她神情紧张地四处张望,问我:"怎么了?"。

"约瑟夫回来了,"我回答道,碰巧听到他的车轮在路上发出的声音,"希斯克利夫会跟他一起进来的。我不确定他这会儿有没有站在门口。"

"唉,他不会站在门口偷听我说话的!"她说,"把哈里顿给我,你去准备晚饭吧,好了以后叫我跟你一起吃饭。我想要欺骗自己不安的良心,而且深信希斯克利夫没有想到这些事情。他没有吧,是不是?他不知道什么叫爱情吧?"

"我找不到理由说明他不了解爱情,你也一样。"我回答,"如果他选择了你,他就会成为天下最不幸的人。一旦你成为林顿太太,他就失去了友谊,失去了爱情,失去了一切!你有没有考虑过你将如何承受这种分离,他又将如何承受完全被人遗弃在这世上?因为,凯瑟琳小姐……"

"他完全被人遗弃!我们分开了!"她带着愤怒的语气惊呼道,"请问谁会把我们分开?他们会遭到米罗的命运的!艾伦,只要我还活着,没有人能把我们分开。世上所有的林顿都可以化为乌有,但我绝不会答应抛

---

① Milo:米罗。原为庞贝的手下人,公元前五十二年谋杀了克劳狄斯,后被控告并放逐。公元前四十八年又组织叛乱,在科萨被捕并被处死。

consent to forsake Heathcliff. Oh, that's not what I intend—that's not what I mean! I shouldn't be Mrs. Linton were such a price demanded! He'll be as much to me as he has been all his lifetime. Edgar must shake off his antipathy, and tolerate him, at least. He will, when he learns my true feelings towards him. Nelly, I see now, you think me a selfish wretch; but did it never strike you that if Heathcliff and I married, we should be beggars? Whereas, if I marry Linton, I can aid Heathcliff to rise, and place him out of my brother's power."

"With your husband's money, Miss Catherine?" I asked. "You'll find him not so pliable as you calculate upon: and though I'm hardly a judge, I think that's the worst motive you've given yet for being the wife of young Linton."

"It is not," retorted she; "it is the best! The others were the satisfaction of my whims: and for Edgar's sake, too, to satisfy him. This is for the sake of one who comprehends in his person my feelings to Edgar and myself. I cannot express it; but surely you and everybody have a notion that there is or should be an existence of yours beyond you. What were the use of my creation, if I were entirely contained here? My great miseries in this world have been Heathcliff's miseries, and I watched and felt each from the beginning: my great thought in living is himself. If all else perished, and *he* remained, I should still continue to be; and if all else remained, and he were annihilated, the universe would turn to a mighty stranger: I should not seem a part of it. My love for Linton is like the foliage in the woods: time will change it, I'm well aware, as winter changes the trees. My love for Heathcliff resembles the eternal rocks beneath: a source of little visible delight, but necessary. Nelly, I *am* Heathcliff! He's always, always in my mind: not as a pleasure, any more than I am always a pleasure to myself, but as my own being. So don't talk of our separation again: it is impracticable; and—"

She paused, and hid her face in the folds of my gown; but I jerked it forcibly away. I was out of patience with her folly!

"If I can make any sense of your nonsense, Miss," I said, "it only goes to convince me that you are ignorant of the duties you undertake in marrying; or else that you are a wicked, unprincipled girl. But trouble me with no more secrets: I'll not promise to keep them."

"You'll keep that?" she asked, eagerly.

"No, I'll not promise," I repeated.

She was about to insist, when the entrance of Joseph finished our conversation; and Catherine removed her seat to a corner, and nursed Hareton, while I made the supper. After it was cooked, my fellowservant and I began to quarrel who should carry some to Mr. Hindley; and we didn't settle it till all was nearly cold. Then we came to the agreement that we would let him ask, if he wanted any; for we feared particularly to go into his presence when he had been some time alone.

"Und hah isn't that nowt comed in frough th' field, be this time? What is he abaht? Girt eedle seeght!" demanded the old man, looking round for Heathcliff.

"I'll call him," I replied. "He's in the

我不会成为这其中的一部分。我对林顿的爱就像是树上的叶子，我完全明白，冬天改变树木的时候，时间也会改变叶子。而我对希斯克利夫的爱就像地上永恒不变的磐石：虽然没有太多明显的快乐，但这点快乐却是必需的。内莉，我就是希斯克利夫！他永远永远地存在于我的心里。他并不是一种乐趣，并没有比我对我自己要有趣些，但他却是作为我自己而存在着。所以不要再说我们会分离了，那是不可能的；而且……"

她停顿一下，把脸藏到我长袍的褶子里。不过我用力地把她推开，我已经无法容忍她的愚蠢了！

"小姐，如果我能够从你这些废话中找出一点意义来，"我说，"也只能是让我确信你忽视了你自己在婚姻中承担的责任；要不然，你就是个恶毒的、没有道德的女孩。不要再拿什么秘密来烦我，我不会答应你保守这些秘密的。"

"之前的秘密你会保守吧？"她急切地问道。

"不，我不答应，"我重复道。

她正想坚持，约瑟夫已进来了，我们的谈话也就此结束。凯瑟琳把她的座位移到角落里，照看着哈里顿，我就去做饭。饭菜都做好之后，我的下房的伙伴就开始跟我争执着谁给辛德雷先生送饭菜，直到饭菜都快冷了，我们还没能决定。之后我们达成了协议，如果他想吃饭，就等他自己来要吧。因为他单独一个人的那段时间里，我们都特别害怕走到他面前。

"都这个时候了，那个坏小子怎么还不从田里回来？他干什么去了？"

barn, I've no doubt."

I went and called, but got no answer. On returning, I whispered to Catherine that he had heard a good part of what she said, I was sure; and told how I saw him quit the kitchen iust as she complained of her brother's conduct regarding him. She jumped up in a fine fright, flung Hareton onto the settle, and ran to seek for her friend herself; not taking leisure to consider why she was so flurried, or how her talk would have affected him. She was absent such a while that Joseph proposed we should wait no longer. He cunningly conjectured they were staying away in order to avoid hearing his protracted blessing. They were "ill eneugh for ony fahl manners," he affirmed. And on their behalf he added that night a special prayer to the usual quarter of an hour's supplication before meat, and would have tacked another to the end of the grace, had not his young mistress broken in upon him with a hurried command that he must run down the road, and, wherever Heathcliff had rambled, find and make him reenter directly!

"I want to speak to him, and I *must*, before I go up-stairs," she said. "And the gate is open: he is somewhere out of hearing; for he would not reply, though I shouted at the top of the fold as loud as I could."

Joseph objected at first; she was too much in earnest, however, to suffer contradiction; and at last he placed his hat on his head, and walked grumbling forth. Meantime, Catherine paced up and down the floor, exclaiming—

"I wonder where he is—I wonder where he *can* be! What did I say, Nelly? I've forgotten. Was he vexed at my bad humour this

又去闲荡了？"这老头子问道，四处张望着寻找希斯克利夫。

"我去叫他，"我回答，"我肯定他在马厩。"

我过去叫他，但没人应答。回来的时候，我轻声对凯瑟琳说，我确信希斯克利夫已经听到她说的大部分话了，还告诉她在她抱怨哥哥对待他的行为时，我是怎么看着他离开厨房的。她非常吃惊地跳起来，把哈里顿扔在靠背椅上，跑出去找她的朋友，也没有抽时间好好想想她为什么这么不安，或是她的那番话会对他产生什么影响。她出去了很长一段时间，因此约瑟夫建议我们不用再等了。他推测他们待在外面是想要避免听他那冗长的祷告，断定他们是"坏得只会做坏事了"。而且，为了他们，那天晚上除了平日在饭前做的一刻钟祈祷外，约瑟夫又加了一个特别祈祷，要不是他年轻的女主人这时冲进来，他还想在祈祷之后再做一段。凯瑟琳匆忙地命令他必须到路上去，不管希斯克利夫游荡到哪里，都必须找到他，并且立刻带他回来！

"我要跟他说话，在我上楼之前，我必须要跟他说话，"她说，"大门是开着的，他肯定在一个听不见叫声的地方，因为尽管我在山谷的最高处放声大喊，他还是不回答。"

刚开始约瑟夫不肯去，但她已经下定决心，不容他反对。最后他还是戴上帽子，满腹牢骚地走了出去。

与此同时，凯瑟琳在房间里踱来走去，叫道，"真奇怪，他会在哪里呢？他能跑到哪里去呢！我说什么了，内莉？我都已经忘记了，他是为

afternoon? Dear! tell me what I've said to grieve him? I do wish he'd come. I do wish he would!"

"What a noise for nothing!" I cried, though rather uneasy myself. "What a trifle scares you! It's surely no great cause of alarm that Heathcliff should take a moonlight saunter on the moors, or even lie too sulky to speak to us in the hay-loft. I'll engage he's lurking there. See if I don't ferret him out!"

I departed to renew my search; its result was disappointment, and Joseph's quest ended in the same.

"Yon lad gets war un war!" observed he on re-entering. "He's left th' yate ut t' full swing, and miss's pony has trodden dahn two rigs uh corn, un plottered through, raight o'er intuh t' meadow! Hahsomdiver, t'maister 'ull play t'devil to morn, and he'll do weel. He's patience itsseln wi' sich careless, offald craters—patience itsseln he is! Bud he'll nut be soa allus—yah's see, all on ye! Yah mum'n't drive him aht uf his heead fur nowt!"

"Have you found Heathcliff, you ass?" interrupted Catherine. "Have you been looking for him, as I ordered?"

"Aw sud more likker look for th' horse," he replied. "It 'ud be tuh more sense. Bud, aw can look for norther horse, nur man uf a neeght loike this—as black as t'chimbley! und Hathecliff's noan t' chap tuh coom ut *maw* whistle—happen he'll be less hard uh hearing wi' *ye*!"

It *was* a very dark evening for summer: the clouds appeared inclined to thunder, and I said we had better all sit down: the approaching rain would be certain to bring him home with-

我今天下午的坏脾气而生气吗？亲爱的，快告诉我，我到底说了什么话让他这么伤心？我真希望他回来，希望他会回来啊！"

"无缘无故吵什么呢！"我对她喊道，尽管自己也非常不安，"这么点儿小事就把你吓成这样了！当然没什么可以大惊小怪的事，也许希斯克利夫在荒野的月下散步，或是躺在干草棚里，生气得不想跟我们说话。我保证他就伏在那里。看看我会不会把他搜出来！"

我又过去重新找了一遍，结果让人失望，约瑟夫那边的结果也是一样。

他一进来就说，"这家伙越来越不像话了！他就这样把大门敞开着，小姐的马驹踩烂了两排小麦，还冲进了牧场！明天早上主人肯定又要闹了，肯定会闹个天翻地覆。他对这样粗心大意的行为，这种废物可没有什么耐心，他可是一点耐心都没有！但他也不能一直这样啊。你们瞧瞧！你们不该让他无缘无故地发疯！"

"找到希斯克利夫没有？你这笨蛋，"凯瑟琳打断了他的话，"你有没有照我的吩咐去找他？"

"我宁愿去找马，"他回答道，"那比找人有意义多了。可在这样一个比烟囱还黑的夜晚，人马我都没有找到！而且希斯克利夫也不是一个听到我的哨声就会回来的人，或许你叫他还更能让他听得到呢！"

在夏天，这样的夜晚已经算是非常黑暗了。乌云密布，好像要打雷了，我建议大家还是先坐下来，这场即将到来的大雨肯定会毫不费力地把他带回家的。不过，我还是没法规劝

out further trouble. However, Catherine would not be persuaded into tranquillity. She kept wandering to and fro, from the gate to the door, in a state of agitation which permitted no repose; and at length took up a permanent position on one side of the wall, near the road: where, heedless of my expostulations and the growling thunder, and the great drops that began to plash around her, she remained, calling at intervals, and then listening, and then crying outright. She beat Hareton, or any child, at a good passionate fit of crying.

About midnight, while we still sat up, the storm came rattling over the Heights in full fury. There was a violent wind, as well as thunder, and either one or the other split a tree off at the corner of the building: a huge bough fell across the roof, and knocked down a portion of the east chimney-stack, sending a clatter of stones and soot into the kitchen fire. We thought a bolt had fallen in the middle of us; and Joseph swung onto his knees, beseeching the Lord to remember the patriarchs Noah① and Lot②, and, as in former times, spare the righteous, though he smote the ungodly. I felt some sentiment that it must be a judgment on us also. The Jonah③, in my mind, was Mr. Earnshaw; and I shook the handle of his den that I might ascertain if he were yet living. He replied audibly enough, in a fashion which made my companion vociferate,

凯瑟琳平静下来。她一直在大门和房门之间来回徘徊，心情焦虑得一刻也不肯休息，最后终于在靠近路边的一面墙旁站住了。她不顾我的劝告，不顾轰隆隆的雷鸣和落在她周围的大雨滴，就这样站在那儿，时不时地叫喊几声，然后听听声音，接着就嚎啕大哭起来。这哭声要比哈里顿或其他小孩子来得大声起劲多了。

临近午夜时分，我们仍旧坐在那儿，暴风雨异常凶猛地袭击着山庄。忽然刮起了一阵狂风，打了一个霹雳，不知是风还是雷或是其他东西把屋角的一棵树劈成了两半。一根粗大的树干掉到了屋顶上，把东面的高烟囱敲掉了一部分，一大堆石头和煤灰掉进厨房。我们还以为是闪电打在这里了呢，约瑟夫跪倒在地上，祈求上帝想一想诺亚和罗得，祈求上帝像以前那样，虽然要惩罚不虔诚的人，但请赦免正直的人。我也觉得这一定是上帝对我们的判决。在我的心里，约拿就是恩肖先生。我过去摇摇他房间的门把，确定一下他是不是还活着。他回答得非常小声，这使得我的同伴比刚才叫得更吵闹了，想要把像他这样的圣人和像他主人这样的罪人彻底

---

① Noah：诺亚，见《圣经·旧约·创世记》第六、七、八、九章。上帝愤怒降洪水于世，诺亚受神示，造方舟将其家和各种家禽置于舟中，得免灾祸。
② Lot：罗得，为亚伯拉罕之侄，见《圣经·旧约·创世记》第十九章。在今死海边曾有一城名所多玛（Sodom），该城居民罪恶深重，故天降大火焚之，义人罗得因敬神幸免于难。
③ Jonah：约拿，见《圣经·旧约·约拿书》第一章。约拿因违抗上帝，乘船逃遁，上帝施以飓风，遂致吹入海中，为巨鱼所吞，而困于鱼腹中三昼夜。

第九章

more clamorously than before, that a wide distinction might be drawn between saints like himself and sinners like his master. But the uproar passed away in twenty minutes, leaving us all unharmed; excepting Cathy, who got thoroughly drenched for her obstinacy in refusing to take shelter, and standing bonnetless and shawlless to catch as much water as she could with her hair and clothes. She came in and lay down on the settle, all soaked as she was, turning her face to the back, and putting her hands before it.

"Well, Miss!" I exclaimed, touching her shoulder; "you are not bent on getting your death, are you? Do you know what o'clock it is? Halfpast twelve. Come, come to bed! there's no use waiting longer on that foolish boy: he'll be gone to Gimmerton, and he'll stay there now. He guesses we shouldn't wake for him till this late hour: at least, he guesses that only Mr. Hindley would be up; and he'd rather avoid having the door opened by the master."

"Nay, nay, he's noan at Gimmerton!" said Joseph. "Aw's niver wonder, bud he's at t' bothom uf a bug-hoile. This visitation worn't for nowt, und aw wod hev ye tuh look aht, Miss—yah muh be t' next. Thank Hivin for all! All warks togither for gooid tuh them as is chozzen, and piked aht froo' th' rubbidge! Yah knaw whet t' Scripture ses—" And he began quoting several texts, referring us to the chapters and verses, where we might find them.

I, having vainly begged the wilful girl to rise and remove her wet things, left him preaching and her shivering, and betook myself to bed with little Hareton, who slept as fast as if

划清界限。但是二十分钟后这场骚动便平息了。大家都相安无事，除了凯茜全身湿透，因为她自己固执地不去避雨，不戴帽子，不穿披肩地站在那儿，结果头发和衣服都湿得不能再湿了。她走进屋里，躺在高背椅上，全身湿淋淋的，把脸朝着椅背，手放在椅背前面。

"好了，小姐！"我拍拍她的肩膀，对她说，"你并没有想寻死吧，是不是？你知道现在几点钟了吗？已经十二点半啦。来！睡觉去吧。不用再等那个傻孩子了，他可能去了吉默顿，可能现在就在那儿。他想这么晚我们应该没有在等他了，至少他会猜到只有辛德雷先生会起来，他宁可避免让主人来给他开门也不会回来。"

"不，不会的，他没有在吉默顿，"约瑟夫说。"我猜他一定是掉进沼泽地了。这场天罚不是没有原因的。我希望你能小心点，小姐，下次就该轮到你了。感谢上帝所做的一切！这一切都是为了他们好，能让他们重新做人！你们知道《圣经》上都是怎么说的吗？"接着他就开始引用好几段经文，告诉我们具体章节，可以在哪里找到这些话。

我祈求这任性的小姑娘起来换掉她这身湿衣服，但都是徒劳，只好留下约瑟夫在那里祈祷，任凭凯瑟琳在那里颤抖，我自己则带着哈里顿上床

every one had been sleeping round him. I heard Joseph read on a while afterwards; then I distinguished his slow step on the ladder, and then I dropt asleep.

Coming down somewhat later than usual, I saw, by the sunbeams piercing the chinks of the shutters, Miss Catherine still seated near the fireplace. The house door was ajar, too; light entered from its unclosed windows; Hindley had come out, and stood on the kitchen hearth, haggard and drowsy.

"What ails you, Cathy?" he was saying when I entered: "you look as dismal as a drowned whelp. Why are you so damp and pale, child?"

"I've been wet," she answered reluctantly, "and I'm cold, that's all."

"Oh, she is naughty!" I cried, perceiving the master to be tolerably sober. "She got steeped in the shower of yesterday evening, and there she has sat the night through, and I couldn't prevail on her to stir."

Mr. Earnshaw stared at us in surprise. "The night through," he repeated. "What kept her up? Not fear of the thunder, surely? That was over hours since."

Neither of us wished to mention Heathcliff's absence, as long as we could conceal it; so I replied, I didn't know how she took it into her head to sit up; and she said nothing. The morning was fresh and cool; I threw back the lattice, and presently the room filled with sweet scents from the garden; but Catherine called peevishly to me, "Ellen, shut the window. I'm starving!" And her teeth chattered as she shrunk closer to the almost extinguished embers.

睡觉去了。小哈里顿睡得很香，仿佛他周围的每个人都睡着了似的。之后我听到约瑟夫读了一阵经书，接着我听见他上楼梯时慢腾腾的脚步声，后来我就睡着了。

我下楼比平时晚了些，透过百叶窗缝中穿进来的一缕缕阳光，我看见凯瑟琳小姐还坐在壁炉旁边，客厅的门也仍旧半开着，光线从那开着的窗户里透进来。辛德雷已经出来了，站在厨房的火炉边上，显得很憔悴很疲倦。

"什么事让你这么烦恼啊，凯茜？"当我进去时他正说着，"看起来像个落水狗一样沮丧。孩子，你身上怎么这么湿，脸色怎么这么苍白？"

"我淋湿的，"她很不情愿地回答道，"而且我感到很冷，就这么回事。"

"唉，她太淘气了！"我大声说，发现主人还比较清醒，"昨天晚上她就在外面淋着雨，还在这里坐了一个通宵，我劝都劝不动她。"

恩肖先生很惊讶地看着我们。"通宵，"他重复着，"有什么事能让她睡不着？应该不是害怕雷声吧？几个小时之前就已经停了啊。"

我们都不愿提起希斯克利夫出走的事情，能瞒多久就瞒多久，于是我回答他，我不知道她脑子怎么会想起来坐在那里不睡觉，她也没说什么。早晨的空气非常新鲜凉爽，我打开窗户，很快房间里就充满了从花园里飘来的芳香。但是凯瑟琳气急败坏地喊道，"艾伦，把窗户关上，我都快冻死了！"她的牙齿直打哆嗦，往那几乎熄灭了的灰烬挪近一些。

"She's ill," said Hindley, taking her wrist;"I suppose that's the reason she would not go to bed. Damn it! I don't want to be troubled with more sickness here. What took you into the rain?"

"Running after t' lads, as usuald!" croaked Joseph, catching an opportunity, from our hesitation, to thrust in his evil tongue."If Aw wur yah, maister, Aw'd just slamt' boards i' their faces all on 'em, gentle and simple! Never a day ut yah're off, but yon cat uh Linton comes sneaking hither; and Miss Nelly Shoo's a fine lass! Shoo sits watching for ye i' t' kitchen; and as yah're in at one door, he's aht at t'other; und, then, wer grand lady goes a coorting uf hor side! It's bonny behaviour, lurking amang t' fields, after twelve ut' night, wi' that fahl, flaysome divil uf a gipsy, Heathcliff! They think *Aw*'m blind; but Aw'm noan, nowt ut t'soart! Aw seed young Linton, boath coming and going, and Aw seed *yah*" (directing his discourse to me)."Yah gooid fur nowt, slattenly witch! Nip up und bolt intuh th'hahs, t'minute yah heard t'maister's horse fit clatter up t'road."

"Silence, eavesdropper!" cried Catherine; "None of your insolence, before me! Edgar Linton came yesterday, by chance, Hindley; and it was *I* who told him to be off: because, I knew you would not like to have met him as you were."

"You lie, Cathy, no doubt," answered her brother, "and you are a confounded simpleton! But never mind Linton at present: tell me, were you not with Heathcliff last night? Speak the truth, now. You need not be afraid of harming him: though I hate him as much as ev-

"她生病了，"辛德雷说，拿起她的手腕，"我想这才是她不肯上床睡觉的原因。该死的！我可不愿这里再有人生病添麻烦，你到底为什么跑去淋雨啊？"

"和往常一样，追男孩子啊！"约瑟夫发着牢骚，趁我们犹豫不决时，抓住机会讲了几句坏话。"主人，如果我是你，不论他们贫富贵贱，我都会扇他们几耳光！如果哪一天你不在家了，那年轻的林顿就会偷偷跑到这里来。还有内莉小姐，好歹也是个不错的小姐！她就坐在厨房等着你，只要你一进这扇门，林顿就从另一扇门出去。还有，我们这个高贵的小姐还给她献殷勤！半夜过了十二点，还跟那个野小子希斯克利夫躲在田里，还真是浪漫啊！他们以为我是瞎子，但我不是，我一点都不瞎！我看着小林顿进来，也看着他离开，我还看见你（他指着我说），你这没出息的老巫婆！一听见主人在路上的马蹄声，你就跳起来跑到客厅去。"

"给我住嘴，你这个偷听话的！"凯瑟琳嚷着，"在我面前还轮不到你放肆！辛德雷，昨天埃德加·林顿是碰巧来这里的，而且是我叫他离开的，因为我知道你一直都不喜欢遇到他。"

"毫无疑问你在撒谎，凯茜，"她哥哥回答，"你这个糊涂的傻瓜！但是现在先别管林顿了。告诉我，昨天夜里你没跟希斯克利夫在一起，对吗？现在给我说实话。你不用担心我会伤害他，虽然我一直都非常讨厌他，但

er, he did me a good turn a short time since, that will make my conscience tender of breaking his neck. To prevent it, I shall send him about his business, this very morning; and after he's gone, I'd advise you all to look sharp: I shall only have the more humour for you."

"I never saw Heathcliff last night," answered Catherine, beginning to sob bitterly: "and if you do turn him out of doors, I'll go with him. But, perhaps, you'll never have an opportunity: perhaps he's gone." Here she burst into uncontrollable grief, and the remainder of her words were inarticulate.

Hindley lavished on her a torrent of scornful abuse, and bade her get to her room immediately, or she shouldn't cry for nothing! I obliged her to obey; and I shall never forget what a scene she acted when we reached her chamber: it terrified me. I thought she was going mad, and I begged Joseph to run for the doctor. It proved the commencement of delirium: Mr. Kenneth, as soon as he saw her, pronounced her dangerously ill; she had a fever. He bled her, and he told me to let her live on whey, and water gruel; and take care she did not throw herself down stairs or out of the window; and then he left: for he had enough to do in the parish, where two or three miles was the ordinary distance between cottage and cottage.

Though I cannot say I made a gentle nurse, and Joseph and the master were no better; and though our patient was as wearisome and headstrong as a patient could be, she weathered it through. Old Mrs. Linton paid us several visits, to be sure, and set things to rights, and scolded and ordered us all; and when Catherine was convalescent, she insisted

"昨天夜里我根本没见过希斯克利夫，"凯瑟琳开始哽咽起来，回答道，"如果你要把他赶出家门，我就跟他一起走。不过，也许你永远都不会有机会啦！也许他已经走啦。"说到这儿，她忍不住悲伤，放声痛哭起来，下面的话也说得不清楚了。

辛德雷对她辱骂一番，叫她立刻回自己房间去，不然就不要无缘无故地哭泣！我劝她服从哥哥的命令。当我们到了她卧室后，我永远都不会忘记她演了怎样的一出戏，真的把我吓坏了。我以为她要疯了，还求约瑟夫快去请大夫来。随后证实这是精神错乱的开始，肯尼斯先生一看见她，就说她病情危急，正在发烧。他给她抽了血，又告诉我只给她吃乳浆和稀饭，小心别让她跳楼，或是跳窗，然后就走了。因为他在这片教区里有很多事情要忙，而这里郡与郡之间通常都相隔两三英里远。

虽然我不能说自己是个温柔的保姆，但约瑟夫和主人也好不到哪去。而且虽然我们的病人比其他病人还要麻烦、任性，但她总算挺了过来。当然喽，林顿老太太来拜访过好几次，而且还对我们指手画脚，臭骂我们，命令我们做这做那。等凯瑟琳身体痊愈的时候，她又坚持把她送去画眉田

on conveying her to Thrushcross Grange: for which deliverance we were very grateful. But the poor dame had reason to repent of her kindness: she and her husband both took the fever, and died within a few days of each other.

Our young lady returned to us, saucier and more passionate, and haughtier than ever. Heathcliff had never been heard of since the evening of the thunder-storm; and, one day, I had the misfortune, when she provoked me exceedingly, to lay the blame of his disappearance on her: where indeed it belonged, as she well knew. From that period, for several months, she ceased to hold any communication with me, save in the relation of a mere servant. Joseph fell under a ban also: he *would* speak his mind, and lecture her all the same as if she were a little girl; and she esteemed herself a woman, and our mistress, and thought that her recent illness gave her a claim to be treated with consideration. Then the doctor had said that she would not bear crossing much; she ought to have her own way; and it was nothing less than murder in her eyes for any one to presume to stand up and contradict her. From Mr. Earnshaw and his companions she kept aloof; and tutored by Kenneth, and serious threats of a fit that often attended her rages, her brother allowed her whatever she pleased to demand, and generally avoided aggravating her fiery temper. He was rather *too* indulgent in humouring her caprices; not from affection, but from pride: he wished earnestly to see her bring honour to the family by an alliance with the Lintons, and as long as she let him alone she might trample us like slaves, for aught he cared! Edgar Linton, as multitudes have been before

庄，我们真是非常感谢她这个意见。可这位可怜的太太有理由对自己的善心感到后悔，她和她丈夫两个人都感染了风寒，几天之后便双双去世了。

我们的小姐回家之后变得比以前更无礼，更暴躁，更傲慢了。自从雷雨之夜后希斯克利夫也一直杳无音讯。有一天她把我激怒了，我自认倒霉居然把他的失踪归咎于她。其实她自己也明白这事确实该由她担当责任。从那时开始，有好几个月她都没有跟我说话，仅仅保持着主仆关系。约瑟夫也受到了责备，虽然他还是会说自己的想法，还把她当小姑娘一样教训，不过她却把自己看作成年人，当成我们的女主人。而且还认为她最近的这场病可以让她有权要求别人体谅她。后来大夫说以后不能过多阻挠她，得由着她的性子才行。在她眼里，任何人想要站起来反对她，就跟谋杀一样。她一直刻意避开恩肖先生和他的同伴们，她的哥哥经过肯尼斯的一番教导，又因为她的暴怒常常会引起一阵癫痫的严重威胁，所以就对她百依百顺，尽量避免去激起她的火爆脾气。他真的太纵容她的任性了，这并不是因为对她的关爱，而是因为他的自大，他真诚地希望能够看到她和林顿家共结连理，从而光宗耀祖，而只要她不去打扰他，她就可以把我们当奴隶一样践踏，他根本不管这些事情！埃德加·林顿像在他以前和以后的大多数人一样，被她迷得神魂颠倒。在他父亲逝世三年后，他把凯瑟琳领到吉默顿教堂的那天，他相信自己是世上最幸福的人。

and will be after him, was infatuated; and believed himself the happiest man alive on the day he led her to Gimmerton chapel, three years subsequent to his father's death.

Much against my inclination, I was persuaded to leave Wuthering Heights and accompany her here. Little Hareton was nearly five years old, and I had just begun to teach him his letters. We made a sad parting; but Catherine's tears were more powerful than ours. When I refused to go, and when she found her entreaties did not move me, she went lamenting to her husband and brother. The former offered me munificent wages; the latter ordered me to pack up: he wanted no women in the house, he said, now that there was no mistress; and as to Hareton, the curate should take him in hand, by and bye. And so I had but one choice left: to do as I was ordered. I told the master he got rid of all decent people only to run to ruin a little faster; I kissed Hareton goodbye; and since then he has been a stranger: and it's very queer to think it, but I've no doubt he has completely forgotten all about Ellen Dean, and that he was ever more than all the world to her, and she to him!

At this point of the housekeeper's story, she chanced to glance towards the time-piece over the chimney; and was in amazement on seeing the minute-hand measure half-past one. She would not hear of staying a second longer: in truth, I felt rather disposed to defer the sequel of her narrative myself. And now that she is vanished to her rest, and I have meditated for another hour or two, I shall summon courage to go, also, in spite of aching laziness of head and limbs.

我很不情愿地被说服离开了呼啸山庄，陪着她来到这里。那时小哈里顿差不多五岁了，我才开始教他认字，我们的分别非常悲伤，但凯瑟琳的眼泪比我们的更有力量。当我拒绝离开山庄，而她发现自己的请求无法打动我的时候，她就跑去她丈夫和她哥哥面前痛哭。她丈夫给了我丰厚的报酬，她哥哥则命令我行李打包，他说，既然现在家里没有女主人，这房子也不需要什么女佣人了。至于哈里顿，不久之后就交给副牧师照管。因此我只有一个选择，按照主人的吩咐照办。我对主人说，他把所有的体面人都打发走了，那只会让他更快地走向灭亡。我亲了亲哈里顿，跟他告别。从那之后他就和我成了陌生人，虽然这样想起来会很奇怪，但是我肯定他已经把艾伦·迪安完全忘记了，忘了他曾经是她在这个世上最重要的人，而她也曾是他最重要的人！

女管家的故事讲到这里时，她刚好往烟囱上的钟瞥了一眼，让她惊讶的是，时间已经到一点半了。她再无法让自己多待一秒钟。老实说，我自己也希望她能把这个故事的结局推迟一下。此时她已经回去休息了，我又接着思考了一两个小时，虽然我的头和四肢痛得不想动，但我还是得振作精神继续想一想。

Chapter 10
第十章

A charming introduction to a hermit's life! Four weeks' torture, tossing and sickness! Oh, these bleak winds and bitter northern skies, and impassable roads, and dilatory country surgeons!

And, oh, this dearth of the human physiognomy! And, worse than all, the terrible intimation of Kenneth that I need not expect to be out of doors till spring!

Mr. Heathcliff has just honoured me with a call. About seven days ago he sent me a brace of grouse—the last of the season. Scoundrel! He is not altogether guiltless in this illness of mine; and that I had a great mind to tell him. But, alas! how could I offend a man who was charitable enough to sit at my bedside a good hour, and talk on some other subject than pills, and draughts, blisters, and leeches①? This is quite an easy interval. I am too weak to read; yet I feel as if I could enjoy something interesting. Why not have up Mrs. Dean to finish her tale? I can recollect its chief incidents, as far as she had gone. Yes: I remember her hero had run off, and never been heard of for three

对于一个隐士来说，这样的生活真是一个绝好的开端！四个星期的折磨、颠簸、疾病缠身！啊，还有阴冷的寒风，难挨的北方的气候，难以通行的道路，拖拖拉拉的乡村大夫！

还有很少看到陌生人的面孔，更加糟糕的是，肯尼斯宣布了一个可怕的消息，说我在春天之前别想能够出门走走了！

希斯克利夫先生来探望过我一次，我受宠若惊。大概在七天之前他给我送来两只松鸡，是这个季节里最后的两只了。卑鄙的家伙！我这场病，他也全然脱不了干系，我真想告诉他其中的原委。可是，唉！我怎么可以冒犯这么一个仁慈的人，他在我床边足足坐了一个钟点，完全没有提到药丸、药水、脓疱、大夫之类的东西，而是谈了一些别的事情。这真是一段非常安逸的休养期。我身体太虚弱，没法看书，不过我觉得似乎可以享受一些有趣的事情。何不叫迪安太太过来讲完她的故事呢？我还能回忆起她已经讲到的主要情节。没错，我

---

① leeches: 水蛭。过去曾被医生用于为病人放血。

years; and the heroine was married. I'll ring: she'll be delighted to find me capable of talking cheerfully. Mrs. Dean came.

"It wants twenty minutes, sir, to taking the medicine," she commenced.

"Away, away with it!" I replied;"I desire to have—"

"The doctor says you must drop the powders."

"With all my heart! Don't interrupt me. Come and take your seat here. Keep your fingers from that bitter phalanx of vials. Draw your knitting out of your pocket—that will do—now continue the history of Mr. Heathcliff, from where you left off, to the present day. Did he finish his education on the Continent, and come back a gentleman? or did he get a sizar's place at college, or escape to America, and earn honours by drawing blood from his foster country? Or make a fortune more promptly, on the English highways①?"

"He may have done a little in all these vocations, Mr. Lockwood; but I couldn't give my word for any. I stated before that I didn't know how he gained his money; neither am I aware of the means he took to raise his mind from the savage ignorance into which it was sunk: but, with your leave, I'll proceed in my own fashion, if you think it will amuse and not weary you. Are you feeling better this morning?"

"Much."

"That's good news."

I got Miss Catherine and myself to Thrushcross Grange, and, to my agreeable dis-

记得她故事里的男主角跑了，而且三年来一直杳无音讯；而女主角已经结了婚。我拉了响铃。如果她发现我已经能够兴高采烈地聊天，她一定会很高兴的。迪安太太来了。

"先生，还要等二十分钟才吃药呢。"她说道。

"算了，不用去管它！"我回答她，"我想要……"

"医生说你必须要服药的。"

"我很愿意吃这些药，先不要打断我的话。过来，坐在这里。不要碰那些苦得要命的药罐子。把你的针织活从口袋里拿出来吧。行了，现在继续讲希斯克利夫先生的故事吧，从你结束的地方一直讲到今天。他是不是在欧洲大陆完成了自己的学业，变成一位绅士回来了？还是他得到了知名大学减费生的名额？或是逃到了美洲，在他的第二故乡吸取膏血而获得别人的敬重？又或还是直接在英国的公路上打劫发了财？"

"所有这些职业也许他都做过一点，洛克伍德先生，不过我也不清楚他究竟做过什么，之前我已经说过我不知道他怎么得到这些钱！我也不知道他是如何把自己本已堕入野蛮无知的心灵解救出来。不过我先要求得到你的同意，如果你认为这故事能让你得到消遣而没有让你烦扰的话，那我就要用我自己的方式讲下去了。今天早上感觉好点了吗？"

"好多了。"

"是个好消息。"

我带着凯瑟琳小姐一起来到画眉

---

① 暗指拦路打劫。

appointment, she behaved infinitely better than I dared to expect. She seemed almost over fond of Mr. Linton; and even to his sister, she showed plenty of affection. They were both very attentive to her comfort, certainly. It was not the thorn bending to the honeysuckles[①], but the honeysuckles embracing the thorn. There were no mutual concessions: one stood erect, and the others yielded: and who can be ill-natured and bad-tempered when they encounter neither opposition nor indifference? I observed that Mr. Edgar had a deep-rooted fear of ruffling her humour. He concealed it from her; but if ever he heard it answer sharply, or saw any other servant grow cloudy at some imperious order of hers, he would show his trouble by a frown of displeasure that never darkened on his own account. He many a time spoke sternly to me about my pertness; and averred that the stab of a knife could not inflict a worse pang than he suffered at seeing his lady vexed. Not to grieve a kind master, I learned to be less touchy; and, for the space of half a year, the gunpowder lay as harmless as sand, because no fire came near to explode it. Catherine had seasons of gloom and silence, now and then: they were respected with sympathizing silence by her husband, who ascribed them to an alteration in her constitution, produced by her perilous illness; as she was never subject to depression of spirits before. The return of sunshine was welcomed by answering sunshine from him. I believe I may assert that they were really in possession of deep and growing happiness.

It ended. Well, we *must* be for ourselves

---

① honeysuckle: 忍冬,半常绿灌木,茎蔓生,初夏开白花,有香气,叶花可入药,俗名金银花。

in the long run; the mild and generous are only more justly selfish than the domineering; and it ended when circumstances caused each to feel that the one's interest was not the chief consideration in the other's thoughts. On a mellow evening in September, I was coming from the garden with a heavy basket of apples which I had been gathering. It had got dusk, and the moon looked over the high wall of the court, causing undefined shadows to lurk in the corners of the numerous projecting portions of the building. I set my burden on the house steps by the kitchen door, and lingered to rest, and drew in a few more breaths of the soft, sweet air; my eyes were on the moon, and my back to the entrance, when I heard a voice behind me say—

"Nelly, is that you?"

It was a deep voice, and foreign in tone; yet there was something in the manner of pronouncing my name which made it sound familiar. I turned about to discover who spoke, fearfully; for the doors were shut, and I had seen nobody on approaching the steps. Something stirred in the porch; and, moving nearer, I distinguished a tall man dressed in dark clothes, with dark face and hair. He leant against the side, and held his fingers on the latch as if intending to open for himself. "Who can it be?" I thought. "Mr. Earnshaw? Oh, no! The voice has no resemblance to his."

"I have waited here an hour," he resumed, while I continued staring; "and the whole of that time all round has been as still as death. I dared not enter. You do not know me? Look, I'm not a stranger!"

A ray fell on his features; the cheeks were

幸福还是结束了。唉，从头到尾我们必定是为了自己；温柔慷慨的人只不过比作威作福的人可以更有理由自私一点罢了，当种种情况都导致两个人觉得一方所关心的并不是对方挂念的主要内容的时候，幸福就结束了。在一个九月的醉人的傍晚，我提着一大篮子自己摘的苹果从花园里回来。那时天已经稍稍变暗了，月光从庭院的高墙外照进来，映出了一些模糊的影子，潜藏在这房子无数突出部分的角落里。我把篮子放在厨房门口的台阶上，停留了一会儿，让自己休息一下，再吸几口柔和甘美的空气，我背对着门口，望着月亮，这时我听见背后有个声音说：

"内莉，是你吗？"

是个深沉的嗓音，而且夹杂着外地口音，不过叫我名字时的发音又让人觉得很熟悉。我害怕地转过头来看看是谁在说话，因为那时门是关着的，我也没看见有人走上台阶。我看到门廊那里有什么东西在移动，而且越来越近，我看出是个身材高大的男人，穿着黑色衣服，脸和头发都很黑。他斜靠在墙边，手握着门闩，好像想要自己开门。"到底是谁呢？"我心里盘算着，"恩肖先生吗？不对！声音跟他一点都不像。"

"我已经在这儿等了一个小时了，"正当我目不转睛地看着他时，他开口道，"这一个小时里，四周好像死一般的寂静，我又不敢进去。你还没认出我来吗？看，我不是陌生人啊！"

一道光线照在他的脸上，两颊发

sallow, and half covered with black whiskers; the brows lowering, the eyes deep set and singular. I remembered the eyes.

"What!" I cried, uncertain whether to regard him as a worldly visitor, and I raised my hands in amazement. "What! you come back? Is it really you? Is it?"

"Yes, Heathcliff," he replied, glancing from me up to the windows, which reflected a score of glittering moons, but showed no lights from within. "Are they at home? where is she? Nelly, you are not glad! you needn't be so disturbed. Is she here? Speak! I want to have one word with her—your mistress. Go, and say some person from Gimmerton desires to see her."

"How will she take it?" I exclaimed. "What will she do? The surprise bewilders me—it will put her out of her head! And you *are* Heathcliff? But altered! Nay, there's no comprehending it. Have you been for a soldier?"

"Go and carry my message," he interrupted impatiently. "I'm in hell till you do!"

He lifted the latch, and I entered; but when I got to the parlour where Mr. and Mrs. Linton were, I could not persuade myself to proceed. At length, I resolved on making an excuse to ask if they would have the candles lighted, and I opened the door.

They sat together in a window whose lattice lay back against the wall, and displayed, beyond the garden trees and the wild green park, the valley of Gimmerton, with a long line of mist winding nearly to its top (for very soon after you pass the chapel, as you may have noticed, the sough that runs from the

黄，一半脸被黑胡须盖住了，眉头阴沉，眼睛深陷，非常特别。我记起这双眼睛了。

"什么！"我叫道，不敢确定他是人还是鬼，我惊讶地举起双手，"什么！你回来了？真是你吗？是吗？"

"是我，希斯克利夫，"他回答道，从我身上抬眼看了一下窗户，上面反射出闪闪的月亮，不过并没有灯光从里面透出来。"他们在家吗，她在哪儿？内莉，你好像有点不高兴，用不着这么心慌意乱啊！她在这里吗？说啊！我想跟她说句话，你的女主人。快去通报一声，说有个从吉默顿来的人要见她。"

"她会如何接受这个消息呢？"我惊叫道，"她会怎么办呢？这个惊喜真让我不知如何是好，也会让她不知所措的！你真是希斯克利夫！但是变了好多！而且真是让人无法明白，你已经当过兵了吗？"

"快去帮我送口信啊。"他不耐烦地打断了我的问话，"你不去，我就像在地狱里一样！"

他抬起门闩，我进去了，但是当我走到林顿夫妇待的客厅那儿时，我无法说服自己继续往前走。最后我下定决心找借口问他们要不要点上蜡烛，于是我开了门。

他们一起坐在窗前，格子窗打开着靠在墙上，从这儿望出去，可以看到在那园林树木与生机勃勃的绿色花园的远处，吉默顿山谷被一团浓雾环绕着，几乎到了山顶之上（因为在过了这个小礼拜教堂没多久，你就能看到，从沼泽那边吹来的阵阵凉风，吹

marshes joins a beck which follows the bend of the glen). Wuthering Heights rose above this silvery vapour; but our old house was invisible; it rather dips down on the other side. Both the room and its occupants and the scene they gazed on, looked wondrously peaceful. I shrank reluctantly from performing my errand; and was actually going away leaving it unsaid, after having put my question about the candles, when a sense of my folly compelled me to return, and mutter, "A person from Gimmerton wishes to see you, ma'am."

"What does he want?" asked Mrs. Linton.

"I did not question him," I answered.

"Well, close the curtains, Nelly," she said;"and bring up tea. I'll be back again directly."

She quitted the apartment; Mr. Edgar inquired, carelessly, who it was.

"Some one mistress does not expect," I replied. "That Heathcliff—you recollect him, sir—who used to live at Mr. Earnshaw's."

"What, the gipsy—the plough-boy?" he cried."Why did you not say so to Catherine?"

"Hush! you must not call him by those names, master," I said."She'd be sadly grieved to hear you. She was nearly heart-broken when he ran off. I guess his return will make a jubilee to her."

Mr. Linton walked to a window on the other side of the room that overlooked the court. He unfastened it, and leant out. I suppose they were below, for he exclaimed quickly, "Don't stand there, love! Bring the person in, if it be any one particular." Ere long, I heard the click of the latch, and Catherine flew up-stairs, breathless and wild; too excited to show glad-

动着一条沿着峡谷弯曲流动的小溪）。呼啸山庄就从这银色雾气之上拔地而起，但是看不见我们的老房子，它在山谷另一面的下面。这房子和房子里的人，以及他们凝视着的景色，都显得极其平和。我畏畏缩缩极不情愿地做着我的差事。实际上在问过是否需要点蜡烛之后，我差点就默默无语地退出来，这时我那愚蠢的意识又迫使我回去，嘀咕着："太太，一个从吉默顿来的人想见你。"

林顿太太问道："他有什么事？"

我回答说："我没问他。"

"好吧，把窗帘拉上，内莉，"她说，"端杯茶过来，我马上就回来。"

她走出房间。埃德加先生不经意地问起外面是谁。

"是太太意料之外的人，"我回答他，"那个希斯克利夫——你还记得他吧，先生——就是原来住在恩肖先生家的那个人。"

"什么！那个吉普赛人，那个乡巴佬？"他叫了起来，"为什么你不跟凯瑟琳说清楚呢？"

"嘘！你可千万别这么叫他，主人，"我说道，"如果被她听到你这么说希斯克利夫，她会非常伤心的。他离家出走的时候她可是快伤心欲绝呢，我猜他这次回来肯定会让她欢欣鼓舞。"

林顿先生走到房间另一边可以看到院子的窗户前，打开窗户，探身向外张望。我猜他们就在下面，因为他很快就大声叫道："别站在那儿，亲爱的！如果是贵客，就请他进来吧。"没过多久，我就听见门闩的响动声，

ness; indeed, by her face, you would rather have surmised an awful calamity.

"Oh, Edgar, Edgar!" she panted, flinging her arms round his neck. "Oh, Edgar, darling! Heathcliff's come back—he is!" And she tightened her embrace to a squeeze.

"Well, well," cried her husband, crossly, "don't strangle me for that! He never struck me as such a marvellous treasure. There is no need to be frantic!"

"I know you didn't like him," she answered, repressing a little the intensity of her delight. "Yet, for my sake, you must be friends now. Shall I tell him to come up now?"

"Here?" he said, "into the parlour?"

"Where else?" she asked.

He looked vexed, and suggested the kitchen as a more suitable place for him. Mrs. Linton eyed him with a droll expression—half angry, half laughing at his fastidiousness.

"No," she added, after a while; "I cannot sit in the kitchen. Set two tables here, Ellen: one for your master and Miss Isabella, being gentry; the other for Heathcliff and myself, being of the lower orders. Will that please you, dear? Or must I have a fire lighted elsewhere? If so, give directions. I'll run down and secure my guest. I'm afraid the joy is too great to be real!"

She was about to dart off again; but Edgar arrested her.

"*You* bid him step up," he said, addressing me; "and, Catherine, try to be glad, without being absurd! The whole household need not witness the sight of your welcoming a runaway servant as a brother."

I descended, and found Heathcliff waiting

看到凯瑟琳飞奔上楼，气喘吁吁，非常兴奋，兴奋得不知该如何表达自己的喜悦心情。没错，只要看看她脸上的表情，你就能猜到将会发生一件可怕的事情。

"啊，埃德加，埃德加！"她搂着埃德加的脖子，气喘吁吁地叫道，"啊，埃德加，亲爱的！希斯克利夫回来了，他真的回来了！"然后又紧紧地搂住他。

"够了，够了，"她丈夫生气地叫道，"不要为了这事把我给勒死！我从没想到他居然是个这么了不起的宝贝。没必要那么疯疯癫癫的！"

"我知道你不喜欢他。"她回答道，稍微克制了自己强烈的喜悦心情，"不过就算是为了我好，你们现在一定要成为朋友。我可以叫他上来吗？"

"来这里？"他说，"到客厅来吗？"

"那还能去哪里呢？"她问道。

他看起来有点生气，暗示说厨房对他来说更合适些。林顿太太带着一种滑稽可笑的表情看着他，对于他的严格要求感到既生气又好笑。

"不行！"过了一会儿她说道："我不能坐在厨房里。艾伦，在这儿摆两张桌子，一张给你主人和伊莎贝拉小姐用，他们是贵族；另一张就给希斯克利夫和我自己用，我们的档次比他们低。这样你高兴了吧，亲爱的？又或是我去其他地方生个火呢？如果是这样，那就直接跟我说吧，我要下楼去招呼我的客人了。太让我高兴了，真怕这不是真的！"

她正想要再冲出去，就被埃德加拦住了。

"你叫他上来吧。"他对我说道，

under the porch, evidently anticipating an invitation to enter. He followed my guidance without waste of words, and I ushered him into the presence of the master and mistress, whose flushed cheeks betrayed signs of warm talking. But the lady's glowed with another feeling when her friend appeared at the door: she sprang forward, took both his hands, and led him to Linton; and then she seized Linton's reluctant fingers and crushed them into his. Now fully revealed by the fire and candlelight, I was amazed, more than ever, to behold the transformation of Heathcliff. He had grown a tall, athletic, well-formed man; beside whom, my master seemed quite slender and youth-like. His upright carriage suggested the idea of his having been in the army. His countenance was much older in expression and decision of feature than Mr. Linton's; it looked intelligent, and retained no marks of former degradation. A half-civilised ferocity lurked yet in the depressed brows and eyes full of black fire, but it was subdued; and his manner was even dignified: quite divested of roughness, though too stern for grace. My master's surprise equalled or exceeded mine: he remained for a minute at a loss how to address the ploughboy, as he had called him. Heathcliff dropped his slight hand, and stood looking at him coolly till he chose to speak.

"Sit down, sir," he said, at length. "Mrs. Linton, recalling old times, would have me give you a cordial reception; and, of course, I am gratified when anything occurs to please her."

"And I also," answered Heathcliff, "especially if it be anything in which I have a part. I

"还有，凯瑟琳，尽量玩开心点，但不要做得太荒唐！也没必要让全家人看着你把一个逃跑的仆人当兄弟一样欢迎。"

我走下楼去，发现希斯克利夫等在门廊下边，很显然已经预料会请他进来。他没有多说一句话便跟着我进来。我带着他来到主人和女主人面前，他们发红的两颊泄露了刚才争吵的痕迹。但是当他出现在门口时，她的脸上浮现出另一种情感。她跳上前去，拉住他的双手，带他来到林顿面前。然后她又抓住林顿那不情愿伸出的手指，硬塞到希斯克利夫的手里。这时在炉火和烛光的照耀下，我更加惊讶地看着希斯克利夫的变化。他已经成了一个高大、健壮、匀称的男人，在他旁边，我的主人显得那么纤瘦和年幼。他那笔挺的仪态说明他已经在军队里当过兵，他脸上的神情要比林顿先生要老成果断，而且看起来非常聪明伶俐，从前堕落的痕迹在他脸上荡然无存。虽然在他那下凹的眉毛和充满黑色火焰的眼睛里还潜伏着一种半开化的野性，但已经被克制住了。他的举手投足都显得那么高贵，完全不带一点粗野，尽管稍显冷酷，尚欠优美。我的主人和我一样惊讶，甚至还超过了我，他呆呆地站在那儿将近一分钟之久，不知该如何招呼这个他所谓的乡巴佬。希斯克利夫放开他那瘦小的手，镇定自若地站在那儿看着他，等他先开口说话。

"坐吧，先生。"他终于说话了，"回想当年，林顿太太还要我热诚地接待你。当然，任何能让她开心的事情，我也就乐意去做。"

"我也一样。"希斯克利夫回答

shall stay an hour or two willingly."

He took a seat opposite Catherine, who kept her gaze fixed on him as if she feared he would vanish were she to remove it. He did not raise his to her often: a quick glance now and then sufficed; but it flashed back, each time more confidently, the undisguised delight he drank from hers. They were too much absorbed in their mutual joy to suffer embarrassment. Not so Mr. Edgar: he grew pale with pure annoyance: a feeling that reached its climax when his lady rose, and stepping across the rug, seized Heathcliff's hands again, and laughed like one beside herself.

"I shall think it a dream tomorrow!" she cried."I shall not be able to believe that I have seen, and touched, and spoken to you once more. And yet, cruel Heathcliff! you don't deserve this welcome. To be absent and silent for three years, and never to think of me!"

"A little more than you have thought of me," he murmured."I heard of your marriage, Cathy, not long since; and, while waiting in the yard below, I meditated this plan: —just to have one glimpse of your face: a stare of surprise, perhaps, and pretended pleasure; afterwards settle my score with Hindley; and then prevent the law by doing execution on myself. Your welcome has put these ideas out of my mind; but beware of meeting me with another aspect next time! Nay, you'll not drive me off again. You were really sorry for me, were you? Well, there was cause. I've fought through a bitter life since I last heard your voice; and you must forgive me, for I struggled only for you!"

"Catherine, unless we are to have cold

道,"特别是那些我可以参与进来的事,我将很愿意待上一两个小时。"

他在凯瑟琳对面坐了下来,而凯瑟琳则一直盯着他,好像害怕她的视线一离开他,他就会消失不见一样。不过希斯克利夫并不常抬眼看她,只要时不时地快速瞥她一眼就满足了。但是每次偷看完后,都可以从她那里得到毫无掩饰的喜悦,而且变得越来越大胆。他们完全沉浸在这种喜悦当中,并不觉得有什么尴尬。可埃德加先生并不是这样,他心里只觉得苦恼,脸色变得苍白。当他的太太站起身来,走过地毯,再次抓住希斯克利夫的手,大笑到得意忘形的时候,这种感觉到达了顶点。

"明天我应该会觉得这是一场梦啦!"她叫道,"我肯定不会相信自己居然能够再次见到你,摸到你,还能跟你说话。但是,你这个狠心的希斯克利夫!你不应受到这种欢迎。三年来你一直都不出现,杳无音讯,从来都没有想过我!"

"比你想我还要多一点呢。"他轻声地咕哝着,"凯茜,不久以前我才听说你结婚了。而且我在下面院子等你的时候,我打算着只要看一下你的脸就行,也许只是不经意地瞅一眼,还假装很满足,然后就去找辛德雷算账,接着就自杀来逃避法律的制裁。你的欢迎让我把这些念头都抛到了脑后,不过你可要当心下次见我的时候要换个表情喽!不,你不会再赶走我了,你真的为我感到难过,是不是?嗯,说来话长。自从最后一次听你说话的声音之后,我就一直努力着挺过那段痛苦的生活,你一定要原谅

tea, please to come to the table," interrupted Linton, striving to preserve his ordinary tone, and a due measure of politeness."Mr. Heathcliff will have a long walk, wherever he may lodge tonight; and I'm thirsty."

She took her post before the urn; and Miss Isabella came, summoned by the bell; then, having handed their chairs forward, I left the room. The meal hardly endured ten minutes. Catherine's cup was never filled: she could neither eat nor drink. Edgar had made a slop in his saucer, and scarcely swallowed a mouthful. Their guest did not protract his stay that evening above an hour longer. I asked, as he departed, if he went to Gimmerton?

"No, to Wuthering Heights," he answered: "Mr. Earnshaw invited me, when I called this morning."

Mr. Earnshaw invited *him*! and *he* called on Mr. Earnshaw! I pondered this sentence painfully after he was gone. Is he turning out a bit of a hypocrite and coming into the country to work mischief under a cloak? I mused: I had a presentiment, in the bottom of my heart, that he had better have remained away.

About the middle of the night, I was wakened from my first nap by Mrs. Linton eiding into my chamber, taking a seat on my bedside, and pulling me by the hair to rouse me.

"I cannot rest, Ellen," she said, by way of apology."And I want some living creature to keep me company in my happiness! Edgar is sulky, because I'm glad of a thing that does not interest him: he refuses to open his mouth, except to utter pettish, silly speeches; and he affirmed I was cruel and selfish for wishing to talk when he was so sick and sleepy. He always

我，因为我都是为了你而努力的！"

"凯瑟琳，除非我们都要喝凉茶，要不然就请到桌子这边来。"林顿打断了他们，努力保持他平常的语调以及应有的礼貌，"无论希斯克利夫先生今晚住在哪里，都还得走很长一段路呢，而且我也有点渴了。"

她立刻回到茶壶前面的座位上，伊莎贝拉小姐也被铃声叫了过来。接着等我把他们的椅子向前摆好之后，就走出了房间。这顿茶餐持续了不到十分钟时间。凯瑟琳的茶杯一直没有倒上茶，她吃不下，也喝不下。埃德加把茶倒得溢出了茶托，连一口也没喝下。那天傍晚他们的客人逗留了还不到一个小时。在他临走的时候，我问他是不是去吉默顿？

"不，去呼啸山庄，"他回答我，"今天早上我去拜访时，恩肖先生邀请我去的。"

恩肖先生邀请他！他拜访了恩肖先生！在他走之后，我一直苦苦地思索着这句话。他是不是变成了伪君子，乔装打扮之后来郡里害人呢？我陷入了沉思，心底产生了一种预感，他最好还是不要留在这里。

大约夜半时分，我刚打了个盹，就被林顿太太吵醒了，她溜进我的卧室，在我的床边坐下，拉我的头发把我叫醒了。

"我睡不着，艾伦，"她对我说，当作是道歉，"我要找个活人跟我分享我的快乐！埃德加在生闷气，因为我为一件他并不感兴趣的事而高兴。除了说一些闹情绪的无聊蠢话，他不肯开口说其他的。而且他还说我既残忍又自私，在他这么不舒服想睡觉的

contrives to be sick at the least cross! I gave a few sentences of commendation to Heathcliff, and he, either for a head-ache or a pang of envy, began to cry: so I got up and left him."

"What use is it praising Heathcliff to him?" I answered. "As lads they had an aversion to each other, and Heathcliff would hate just as much to hear him praised: it's human nature. Let Mr. Linton alone about him, unless you would like an open quarrel between them."

"But does it not show great weakness?" pursued she. "I'm not envious: I never feel hurt at the brightness of Isabella's yellow hair and the whiteness of her skin, at her dainty elegance, and the fondness all the family exhibit for her. Even you, Nelly, if we have a dispute sometimes, you back Isabella at once; and I yield like a foolish mother: I call her a darling, and flatter her into a good temper. It pleases her brother to see us cordial, and that pleases me. But they are very much alike: they are spoiled children, and fancy the world was made for their accommodation; and though I humour both, I think a smart chastisement might improve them, all the same."

"You're mistaken, Mrs. Linton," said I. "They humour you: I know what there would be to do if they did not. You can well afford to indulge their passing whims as long as their business is to anticipate all your desires. You may, however, fall out, at last, over something of equal consequence to both sides; and then those you term weak are very capable of being as obstinate as you."

"And then we shall fight to the death, shan't we, Nelly?" she returned, laughing. "No! I tell you, I have such faith in Linton's love, that I believe I might kill him, and he wouldn't wish to retaliate."

I advised her to value him the more for his affection.

"I do," she answered, "but he needn't resort to whining for trifles. It is childish; and, instead of melting into tears because I said that Heathcliff was now worthy of any one's regard, and it would honour the first gentleman in the country to be his friend, he ought to have said it for me, and been delighted from sympathy. He must get accustomed to him, and he may as well like him: considering how Heathcliff has reason to object to him, I'm sure he behaved excellently!"

"What do you think of his going to Wuthering Heights?" I inquired. "He is reformed in every respect, apparently: quite a Christian: offering the right hand of fellowship to his enemies all aroumd!"

"He explained it," she replied. "I wondered as much as you. He said he called to gather information concerning me from you, supposing you resided there still, and Joseph told Hindley, who came out and fell to questioning him of what he had been doing, and how he had been living; and finally, desired him to walk in. There were some persons sitting at cards; Heathcliff joined them; my brother lost some money to him, and, finding him plentifully supplied, he requested that he would come again in the evening: to which he consented. Hindley is too reckless to select his acquaintance prudently: he doesn't trouble himself to reflect on the causes he might have for mistrusting one whom he has basely injured. But, Heathcliff affirms his principal reason for

"然后我们就会闹得不可开交，是吗，内莉？"她笑着回我一句，"不会的！我告诉你，我对林顿的爱非常有信心，我相信即便我差点杀了他，他也不会想要报复我。"

我劝她为了他的爱情得更加尊重他。

"我尊重他啊，"她回答说，"可他也用不着为了一些琐事就哭哭啼啼，有点太幼稚了。而且，就因为我说如今希斯克利夫值得别人尊重，郡里第一名的绅士也会以与他成为挚友为荣，他就哭起来，他本不应该哭得那样伤心，而应该由他来替我说这话才对，而且我们会因为有同感而觉得高兴呢。他必须习惯希斯克利夫，而且还要喜欢他，想想希斯克利夫有多少理由反对他，我肯定希斯克利夫做得好极了！"

"你对他去呼啸山庄这件事有什么看法？"我问她，"很明显他已经完全洗心革面了，简直就是个基督徒，可以向他周围的敌人伸出友好的右手！"

"他解释过了，"她回答说，"我也跟你一样感到很惊讶。他说他去那里是想从你这儿得到关于我的消息，以为你还住在那里。约瑟夫通知了辛德雷，辛德雷出来后，就问他一直在干什么，生活过得如何，最后还请他进去。家里有几个人坐在那儿打牌，希斯克利夫就跟他们一起玩。我哥哥输给他一些钱，发现他有很多钱，就请他今天晚上再去，因此他就答应了。辛德雷也太粗心大意了，不会谨慎地选择朋友，他从没费神想一想自己不应信任一个曾经被他伤害过的人。但希斯克利夫说他之所以会跟从前迫害过他的人重新联系，主要还是

resuming a connection with his ancient persecutor is a wish to install himself in quarters at walking distance from the Grange, and an attachment to the house where we lived together; and likewise a hope that I shall have more opportunities of seeing him there than I could have if he settled in Gimmerton. He means to offer liberal payment for permission to lodge at the Heights; and doubtless my brother's covetousness will prompt him to accept the terms: he was always greedy; though what he grasps with one hand he flings away with the other."

"It's a nice place for a young man to fix his dwelling in!" said I. "Have you no fear of the consequences, Mrs. Linton?"

"None for my friend," she replied: "his strong head will keep him from danger; a little for Hindley: but he can't be made morally worse than he is; and I stand between him and bodily harm. The event of this evening has reconciled me to God and humanity! I had risen in angry rebellion against Providence. Oh, I've endured very, very bitter misery, Nelly! If that creature knew how bitter, he'd be ashamed to cloud its removal with idle petulance. It was kindness for him which induced me to bear it alone: had I expressed the agony I frequently felt, he would have been taught to long for its alleviation as ardently as I. However, it's over, and I'll take no revenge on his folly; I can afford to suffer anything hereafter! Should the meanest thing alive slap me on the cheek, I'd not only turn the other, but I'd ask pardon for provoking it; and, as a proof, I'll go make my peace with Edgar instantly. Good-night! I'm an angel!"

In this self-complacent conviction she de-

因为想要找个离庄不远的住处，而且对于我们曾经一起居住过的房子也有一种依恋。还有就是希望我可以有更多的机会去那里见见他，如果他住在吉默顿，那相比起来机会就会少很多。他打算慷慨地支付一笔费用以便能够住在山庄里，而且毫无疑问我哥哥贪婪的本性会接受他的条件，辛德雷总是那么贪心，虽然他一只手抓住了，但另一只手又会扔出去。"

"那是个适合他这样的年轻人居住的好地方！"我说道，"难道你没有担心过会有什么后果吗，林顿太太？"

"对于我的朋友，我当然不担心，"她回答说，"他聪明的头脑会让他远离危险的。对于辛德雷我倒是有点担心。精神方面的迫害总不会比现在更坏吧，至于身体方面的伤害，我会从中阻挠的。今晚的事情使我顺从了上帝与人类！我曾经愤怒地违抗过上帝。唉，内莉！我曾经忍受过非常非常痛苦的事情。如果那个人（指埃德加）知道我曾是多么的痛苦，他就该对他那因为无聊的愤怒就走得不知去向的往事引以为羞哩。只让我独自一人受苦，那是对他的仁慈，如果我表达出自己时常感受到的悲痛，他也会像我这样急切地渴望着能缓和这种悲痛了。不过这些都已经过去，我也不会报复他的愚蠢，从今往后任何事情我都可以忍受得了了！即便是这世上最卑鄙的人打了我一巴掌，我也只会转过另一边脸给他打，还要请他原谅我激怒了他。而且，为了得到验证，我立刻就去跟埃德加讲和。晚

parted; and the success of her fulfilled resolution was obvious on the morrow: Mr. Linton had not only abjured his peevishness (though his spirits seemed still subdued by Catherine's exuberance of vivacity), but he ventured no objection to her taking Isabella with her to Wuthering Heights in the afternoon; and she rewarded him with such a summer of sweetness and affection in return, as made the house a paradise for several days; both master and servants profiting from the perpetual sunshine.

Heathcliff—Mr. Heathcliff I should say in future—used the liberty of visiting at Thrushcross Grange cautiously, at first: he seemed estimating how far its owner would bear his intrusion. Catherine, also, deemed it judicious to moderate her expressions of pleasure in receiving him; and he gradually established his right to be expected. He retained a great deal of the reserve for which his boyhood was remarkable; and that served to repress all startling demonstrations of feeling. My master's uneasiness experienced a lull, and further circumstances diverted it into another channel for a space.

His new source of trouble sprang from the not anticipated misfortune of Isabella Linton evincing a sudden and irresistible attraction towards the tolerated guest. She was at that time a charming young lady of eighteen; infantile in manners, though possessed of keen wit, keen feelings, and a keen temper, too, if irritated. Her brother, who loved her tenderly, was appalled at this fantastic preference. Leaving aside the degradation of an alliance with a nameless man, and the possible fact that his property, in default of heirs male, might pass into such a

安！我是位天使！"

她就这样怀着自我满足的信心走了，很显然第二天她已经成功地完成了自己的决心。林顿先生不但没有抱怨（虽然他的情绪看起来仍被凯瑟琳旺盛的快乐克制着），而且居然没有冒险反对下午的时候她带着伊莎贝拉一起去呼啸山庄。她用尽所有的甜言蜜语来作为回报奖赏他，使得几天来家里就像天堂一样，不论主仆都从这无尽的欢乐中获益不少。

希斯克利夫——以后我得叫他希斯克利夫先生了——刚开始时还小心地使用着拜访画眉田庄的特权，似乎在估计着田庄的主人会容忍他的打扰到何时。凯瑟琳也认为在接待他时稍稍节制一下自己兴奋的表情会比较明智一些，渐渐地希斯克利夫就确立了自己被接待的权利。他还保留了很多在他少年时就很显著的矜持，而这种矜持压抑住了所有感情上令人吃惊的表现。我主人的不安也就平息了，之后的情况又让他的不安暂时转向了另一方面。

他烦恼的新根源是一件不曾预料到的不幸引起的，伊莎贝拉对这位被容忍的客人表示出一种意外而又无法抗拒的爱慕之情。当时她还是个十八岁的充满魅力的小姐，行为举止还很孩子气，尽管拥有敏锐的才智，敏锐的情绪，如果被惹恼了，还有一种敏锐的脾气。她哥哥本非常体贴地爱护着她，对她这个荒谬的选择万分惊讶。暂且不提和一个没名没姓的人结婚有失身份，也不提他若日后没有男嗣继承人，那自己的财产便有可能落

one's power, he had sense to comprehend Heathcliff's disposition: to know that, though his exterior was altered, his mind was unchangeable, and unchanged. And he dreaded that mind: it revolted him: he shrank forebodingly from the idea of committing Isabella to its keeping. He would have recoiled still more had he been aware that her attachment rose unsolicited, and was bestowed where it awakened no reciprocation of sentiment; for the minute he discovered its existence, he laid the blame on Heathcliff's deliberate designing.

We had all remarked, during some time, that Miss Linton fretted and pined over something. She grew cross and wearisome; snapping at and teazing Catherine continually, at the imminent risk of exhausting her limited patience. We excused her to a certain extent, on the plea of ill-health: she was dwindling and fading before our eyes. But one day, when she had been particularly wayward, rejecting her breakfast, complaining that the servants did not do what she told them; that the mistress would allow her to be nothing in the house, and Edgar neglected her; that she had caught a cold with the doors being left open, and we let the parlour fire go out on purpose to vex her, with a hundred yet more frivolous accusations, Mrs. Linton peremptorily insisted that she should get to bed; and, having scolded her heartily, threatened to send for the doctor. Mention of Kenneth caused her to exclaim, instantly, that her health was perfect, and it was only Catherine's harshness which made her unhappy.

"How can you say I am harsh, you naughty fondling?" cried the mistress, amazed at the unreasonable assertion. "You are surely

入这个人的手中，他还是可以理解希斯克利夫的性格：要知道，虽然希斯克利夫的外貌发生了改变，但他的内心是不会改变，也没有改变的。他非常害怕，也非常反感，一想到要把伊莎贝拉交托给希斯克利夫，他就有不祥的预感。如果他知道她的爱情是自己主动产生，而对方毫无感情回报时，他就更要畏缩了。因为他一发现这段恋情的存在，就把责任归咎于希斯克利夫经过深思熟虑的策划。

有一段时间，我们都发现林顿小姐为了什么事情而感到忧伤烦躁。她变得易怒而且消沉，常常叱骂揶揄凯瑟琳，眼看就有耗尽凯瑟琳那有限耐性的危险。我们都在一定程度上原谅了她，借口说她身体欠佳，她就在我们面前萎靡憔悴下去。但是有一天，她变得特别任性，不肯吃早餐，还抱怨仆人没有按照她的吩咐办事，于是女主人不准她在家里做任何事情，埃德加也不理她；她又抱怨房门开着让她感冒了，我们就把客厅的炉火熄了，存心想惹她生气。不过她还有百来条琐碎的抱怨，林顿太太不容分说地要她上床睡觉，还痛骂了她，吓唬她要去请大夫来。一提到肯尼斯，她又大喊大叫起来，说她身体非常健康，只是凯瑟琳的苛刻让她很不开心。

"你怎么可以说我苛刻呢，你这被宠坏的淘气鬼？"女主人喊道，对这不合情理的断言感到莫名其妙，

losing your reason. When have I been harsh, tell me?"

"Yesterday," sobbed Isabella, "and now!"

"Yesterday!" said her sister-in-law. "On what occasion?"

"In our walk along the moor: you told me to ramble where I pleased, while you sauntered on with Mr. Heathcliff!"

"And that's your notion of harshness?" said Catherine, laughing. "It was no hint that your company was superfluous: we didn't care whether you kept with us or not; I merely thought Heathcliff's talk would have nothing entertaining for your ears."

"Oh no," wept the young lady; "you wished me away, because you know I liked to be there!"

"Is she sane?" asked Mrs. Linton, appealing to me. "I'll repeat our conversation, word for word, Isabella; and you point out any charm it could have had for you."

"I don't mind the conversation," she answered. "I wanted to be with—"

"Well!" said Catherine, perceiving her hesitate to complete the sentence.

"With him: and I won't be always sent off!" she continued, kindling up. "You are a dog in the manger[①], Cathy, and desire no one to be loved but yourself!"

"You are an impertinent little monkey!" exclaimed Mrs. Linton, in surprise. "But I'll not believe this idiocy! It is impossible that you can covet the admiration of Heathcliff—that

"你真是不讲理。你说，我什么时候苛刻了？"

"昨天，"伊莎贝拉呜咽着，"还有现在！"

"昨天！"她嫂嫂说，"什么时候？"

"在我们沿着荒野散步的时候，你叫我去自己喜欢的地方溜达，而你却跟希斯克利夫先生一起去散步！"

"这就是你对苛刻的定义吗？"凯瑟琳笑着说道，"这并没暗示你的陪伴是多余的，我们才不介意你是不是跟我们在一起呢。我只不过以为希斯克利夫的话会让你觉得很无趣罢了。"

"绝对不是，"小姐哭着，"你希望我走开是因为你知道我想留在那儿！"

"她脑子还正常吗？"林顿太太转向我问道，"我一个字一个字地把我们的谈话重复一遍，伊莎贝拉，你把那些对你有任何吸引力的话指出来。"

"我不在乎你们的谈话内容，"她回答说，"我只想要跟……"

"什么？"凯瑟琳说，察觉到她犹豫着要不要说完这句话。

"我要跟他在一起，不想总被人打发走！"她激动起来，接着说道，"凯茜，你是马槽里的一条狗，你希望除了你自己谁也不要被别人爱上！"

"你这个放肆的淘气鬼！"林顿太太惊讶地大叫起来，"我不会相信这件蠢事的！你根本不可能博得希斯克利夫的爱慕，你也不可能把他当作情

---

① 马槽里的一只狗，引自《伊索寓言》，一条狗躺在马槽里，自己不吃草，也不让马吃草。指自己不能享用，而又不肯与人的鄙夫，即心术不正者

you can consider him an greeable person! I hope I have misunderstood you, Isabella?"

"No, you have not," said the infatuated girl. "I love him more than ever you loved Edgar; and he might love me, if you would let him!"

"I wouldn't be you for a kingdom, then!" Catherine declared, emphatically; and she seemed to speak sincerely. "Nelly, help me to convince her of her madness. Tell her what Heathcliff is: an unreclaimed creature, without refinement, without cultivation: an arid wilderness of furze and whinstone. I'd as soon put that little canary into the park on a winter's day, as recommend you to bestow your heart on him! It is deplorable ignorance of his character, child, and nothing else, which makes that dream enter your head. Pray, don't imagine that he conceals depths of benevolence and affection beneath a stern exterior! He's not a rough diamond—a pearl-containing oyster of a rustic: he's a fierce, pitiless, wolfish man. I never say to him, 'Let this or that enemy alone, because it would be ungenerous or cruel to harm them'; I say, 'Let them alone, because I should hate them to be wronged'; and he'd crush you like a sparrow's egg, Isabella, if he found you a troublesome charge. I know he couldn't love a Linton; and yet he'd be quite capable of marrying your fortune and expectations: avarice is growing with him a besetting sin. There's my picture: and I'm his friend—so much so, that had he thought seriously to catch you, I should, perhaps, have held my tongue, and let you fall into his trap."

Miss Linton regarded her sister-in-law with indignation.

"For shame! For shame!" she repeated, angrily. "You are worse than twenty foes, you poisonous friend!"

"Ah! You won't believe me, then?" said Catherine. "You think I speak from wicked self-ishness?"

"I'm certain you do," retorted Isabella; "and I shudder at you!"

"Good!" cried the other. "Try for your-self, if that be your spirit I have done, and yield the argument to your saucy insolence."

"And I must suffer for her egotism!" she sobbed, as Mrs. Linton left the room. "All, all is against me: she has blighted my single con-solation. But she uttered falsehoods, didn't she? Mr. Heathcliff is not a fiend: he has an honourable soul, and a true one, or how could he remember her?"

"Banish him from your thoughts, Miss," I said. "He's a bird of bad omen: no mate for you. Mrs. Linton spoke strongly, and yet I can't contradict her. She is better acquainted with his heart than I, or any one besides; and she never would represent him as worse than he is. Honest people don't hide their deeds. How has he been living? how has he got rich? why is he staying at Wuthering Heights, the house of a man whom he abhors? They say Mr. Earnshaw is worse and worse since he came. They sit up all night together continually, and Hindley has been borrowing money on his land, and does nothing but play and drink: I heard only a week ago-it was Joseph who told me—I met him at Gimmerton: 'Nelly,' he said, 'we's hae a Crahnr's 'quest enah, at ahr folks. One on 'em's a'most getten his finger cut off wi' hauding t' other froo' sticking hisseln

"真可耻，真是可耻！"她生气地重复着，"你比那二十个敌人还要坏，你这恶毒的帮凶！"

"啊，那么你还是不肯相信我喽？"凯瑟琳说，"你认为我是因为阴险的自私自利才说出这些话吗？"

"我肯定你就是这样，"伊莎贝拉反驳她，"一想到你我就全身发抖！"

"很好！"另一个叫道，"如果你有勇气，那就自己试试吧。我不说什么了，对于你的傲慢无礼，我也不想争辩了。"

"可我还是要为她的自尊自大受罪！"当林顿太太离开这屋子的时候，她哭诉着，"所有人都反对我。她毁了我的惟一的安慰。但她完全是在撒谎，是不是？希斯克利夫先生不是恶魔，他有一个可敬的灵魂，一个真实的灵魂，不然他怎么还会记得她呢？"

"让他从你脑子里消失吧，小姐，"我说道，"他是一只不祥的小鸟，不是你要的白马王子。虽然林顿太太说得有些强硬，但我不能驳斥她。她比我，或比任何其他人，都更了解他的内心。而且她绝不会把他说得比本人还坏。诚实的人不会隐瞒他们的所作所为。他是怎么生活过来的？他是怎么富有起来的？他为什么要住在呼啸山庄，那山庄的主人可是让他深恶痛绝的人啊？别人说自从他来了之后恩肖先生就变得越来越糟了。他们常常整夜都不睡觉，辛德雷把他的地都抵押换钱了，除了打牌喝酒，什么事都不做。我一星期前才刚刚听说，是我在吉默顿遇到约瑟夫时，他告诉我的。他说：'内莉！我们家的人得请个验尸官来看看了。有

loike a cawlf. That's maister, yah knaw, ut's soa up uh going tuh t' grand 'sizes. He's noan feard uh t' Bench uh judges, norther Paul, nur Peter, nur John, nor Mathew①, nor noan on 'em, nut he! He fair like's he tangs tuh set his brazened face agean 'em! And yon bonny lad Heathcliff, yah mind, he's a rare un! He can girn a laugh, as weel's onybody at a raight divil's jest. Does he niver say nowt of his fine living amang us, when he goas tuh t' Grange? This is t' way on 't—up at sun-dahn; dice, brandy, cloised shutters, und can'le lught till next day, at nooin: then, t' fooil gangs banning un raving tuh his cham'er, makking dacent fowks dig thur fingers i' thur lugs fur varry shaume; un' the knave, wah, he carn cahnt his brass, un' ate, un' sleep, un' off tuh his neighbour's tuh gossip wi' t' wife. I' course, he tells Dame Catherine hah hor father's goold runs intuh his pocket, and her fathur's son gallops dahn t' Broad road, while he flees afore tuh oppen t' pikes? ' Now, Miss Linton, Joseph is an old rascal, but no liar; and, if his account of Heathcliff's conduct be true, you would never think of desiring such a husband, would you?"

"You are leagued with the rest, Ellen!" she replied. "I'll not listen to your slanders. What malevolence you must have to wish to convince me that there is no happiness in the world!"

Whether she would have got over this fancy if left to herself, or persevered in nursing it perpetually, I cannot say: she had little time to reflect. The day after, there was a justice-meeting at the next town; my master was obliged to

---

① 保罗、彼得、约翰、马太，全是耶稣的使徒。

attend; and Mr. Heathcliff, aware of his absence, called rather earlier than usual. Catherine and Isabella were sitting in the library, on hostile terms, but silent. The latter alarmed at her recent indiscretion, and the disclosure she had made of her secret feelings in a transient fit of passion; the former, on mature consideration, really offended with her companion; and, if she laughed again at her pertness, inclined to make it no laughing matter to her. She did laugh as she saw Heathcliff pass the window. I was sweeping the hearth, and I noticed a mischievous smile on her lips. Isabella, absorbed in her meditations, or a book, remained till the door opened; and it was too late to attempt an escape, which she would gladly have done had it been practicable.

"Come in, that's right!" exclaimed the mistress, gaily, pulling a chair to the fire. "Here are two people sadly in need of a third to thaw the ice between them; and you are the very one we should both of us choose. Heathcliff, I'm proud to show you, at last, somebody that dotes on you more than myself. I expect you to feel flattered. Nay, it's not Nelly; don't look at her! My poor little sister-in-law is breaking her heart by mere contemplation of your physical and moral beauty. It lies in your own power to be Edgar's brother! No, no, Isabella, you sha'n't run off," she continued, arresting, with feigned playfulness, the confounded girl, who had risen indignantly. "We were quarrelling like cats about you, Heathcliff, and I was fairly beaten in protestations of devotion and admiration; and, moreover, I was informed that if I would but have the manners to stand aside, my rival, as she will have

人不得不去参加，而希斯克利夫知道他不在家，就比平常来得早了些。凯瑟琳和伊莎贝拉坐在书房里，怀着敌意，谁也不吭声。伊莎贝拉因她近来的莽撞行为，还有她一时性急败露了自己的暗恋感情，有点惊惶不安。而太太已经充分考虑过这件事情，真的在跟她的同伴怄气。如果伊莎贝拉再敢嘲笑她的傲慢，就得让她知道这对她来说没什么可笑的。当她看见希斯克利夫走过窗前的时候，她真的笑了。当时我正在清扫壁炉，注意到她的嘴角上露出一丝淘气的微笑。伊莎贝拉全神贯注地沉思着，或许是在专心看书，直到门开时她依旧那样坐着。这时想要溜走已经太迟了，如果能溜走的话，她真愿意这样做。

"进来啊，来得正好！"女主人高兴地叫道，拖了一把椅子到火炉旁，"这里有两个处于伤心中的人急需一个第三者来融化她们之间的坚冰呢。你正是我俩选择的人。希斯克利夫，我真荣幸，终于给你找到一个比我还要迷恋你的人，我希望你会高兴。不对，不是内莉，不用看着她！我那可怜的小姑子只要想着你身体上与道德上的美，她的芳心就碎了。这完全取决于你想不想做埃德加的妹夫！别，别走，伊莎贝拉，你不要跑啊，"她带着假装开玩笑的口气接着说，抓住那个愤怒起身离开的惊惶失措的姑娘，"希斯克利夫，我们为了你吵得跟两只猫一样。在爱的宣言方面，我可是完全被她打败了。此外，我还被告知，如果我懂得靠边站的规矩，我的情敌（她自己认为是这样）就要把爱情之箭射进你的心灵，永远俘虏你，

herself to be, would shoot a shaft into your soul that would fix you for ever, and send my image into eternal oblivion!"

"Catherine!" said Isabella, calling up her dignity, and disdaining to struggle from the tight grasp that held her."I'd thank you to adhere to the truth and not slander me, even in joke! Mr. Heathcliff, be kind enough to bid this friend of yours release me: she forgets that you and I are not intimate acquaintances; and what amuses her is painful to me beyond expression."

As the guest answered nothing, but took his seat, and looked thoroughly indifferent what sentiments she cherished concerning him, she turned and whispered an earnest appeal for liberty to her tormentor.

"By no means!" cried Mrs. Linton in answer."I won't be named a dog in the manger again. You *shall* stay: now then! Heathcliff, why don't you evince satisfaction at my pleasant news? Isabella swears that the love Edgar has for me is nothing to that she entertains for you. I'm sure she made some speech of the kind; did she not, Ellen? And she has fasted ever since the day before yesterday's walk, from sorrow and rage that I despatched her out of your society under the idea of its being unacceptable."

"I think you belie her," said Heathcliff, twisting his chair to face them."She wishes to be out of my society now, at any rate!"

And he stared hard at the object of discourse, as one might do at a strange repulsive animal: a centipede from the Indies, for instance, which curiosity leads one to examine in spite of the aversion it raises. The poor thing couldn't bear that: she grew white and red in

而且还要你永远遗忘我的身影!"

"凯瑟琳!"伊莎贝拉鼓起尊严说道,不屑于去挣脱那紧紧抓住她的拳头,"就算你这是在说笑话,我也得谢谢你实话实说,没有诽谤我! 希斯克利夫先生,求求你行行好叫你这位朋友放开我吧,她忘了你和我并不是什么亲密朋友。那些让她觉得有趣的事,正是让我无法表达清楚的痛苦啊。"

客人并没回答,而是坐下来,对于伊莎贝拉对他怀有什么样的感情仿佛完全不关心。她转过身来,低声而又急切地请求折磨她的人放开她。

"绝对不放!"林顿太太回答她,"我可不想再被别人叫成马槽里的一条狗,从现在起就留在这里。希斯克利夫,你为什么没有对我这个振奋人心的消息表示满意呢? 伊莎贝拉发誓说埃德加对我的爱比起她对你的爱来真是微不足道呢。我肯定她说过类似的话,是不是,艾伦? 而且自从前天散步之后她就开始绝食了,觉得非常痛苦愤怒,就因为我把她从你身边打发走,她认为不被欢迎。"

"我想你是误会她了,"希斯克利夫说,把椅子转过来面向她们,"无论如何,她现在希望能够离开我身边!"

他死死盯着这个谈话对象,像是盯着一只长相古怪可憎的动物一样,比如说从印度来的蜈蚣,虽然它的样子那么让人讨厌,但人的好奇心总会驱使他观察一番。这个可怜的家伙无法忍受他的眼神,脸色一阵红一阵

rapid succession, and, while tears beaded her lashes, bent the strength of her small fingers to loosen the firm clutch of Catherine; and perceiving that as fast as she raised one finger off her arm another closed down, and she could not remove the whole together, she began to make use of her nails; and their sharpness presently ornamented the detainer's with crescents of red.

"There's a tigress!" exclaimed Mrs. Linton, setting her free, and shaking her hand with pain. "Begone, for God's sake, and hide your vixen face! How foolish to reveal those talons to *him*. Can't you fancy the conclusions he'll draw? Look, Heathcliff! they are instruments that will do execution—you must beware of your eyes."

"I'd wrench them off her fingers, if they ever menaced me," he answered, brutally, when the door had closed after her. "But what did you mean by teasing the creature in that manner, Cathy? You were not speaking the truth, were you?"

"I assure you I was," she returned. "She has been pining for your sake several weeks; and raving about you this morning, and pouring forth a deluge of abuse, because I represented your failings in a plain light, for the purpose of mitigating her adoration. But don't notice it further: I wished to punish her sauciness, that's all. I like her too well, my dear Heathcliff, to let you absolutely seize and devour her up."

"And I like her too ill to attempt it," said he, "except in a very ghoulish fashion. You'd hear of odd things if I lived alone with that mawkish, waxen face: the most ordinary

"真是个母老虎！"林顿太太大叫，放开了她，痛得甩了甩手，"看在上帝的份上，快滚开，把你那母老虎的脸藏好。居然当着他的面露出那些爪子，你可真笨啊！你难道想像不出他会得出什么结论吗？你看，希斯克利夫！这就是她伤人的工具，你一定要当心你自己的眼睛啊。"

"如果这些手指威胁到我，我就把她上面的指甲全部拔下来，"当伊莎贝拉跑出去关上门后，他野蛮地回答道，"可你这样戏弄这个家伙是什么意思呢，凯茜？你说的不是真的吧，对不对？"

"我向你保证我说的是真的，"她回答他说，"她已经苦苦思念你好几个星期了，今天早上又为你胡言乱语一阵呢，而且还发疯似的大骂，就因为我清楚明白地说出你的缺点，想减少她对你的爱慕。不过不要再聊这事儿了，我只想惩罚她的傲慢，仅此而已。亲爱的希斯克利夫，我真的非常喜欢她，因此我不会让你完全占有她，把她吃掉。"

"我并不喜欢她，因此不会想要这样做，"他说，"除非用非常残酷的方法。如果我跟那个让人恶心的苍白的脸在一起，你会听到很多奇怪的

would be painting on its white the colours of the rainbow, and turning the blue eyes black, every day or two: they detestably resemble Linton's."

"Delectably!" observed Catherine. "They are dove's eyes—angel's!"

"She's her brother's heir, is she not?" he asked, after a brief silence.

"I should be sorry to think so[①]," returned his companion. "Half a dozen nephews shall erase her title, please Heaven. Abstract your mind from the subject at present: you are too prone to covet your neighbour's goods; remember *this* neighbour's goods are mine."

"If they were *mine*, they would be none the less that," said Heathcliff; "but though Isabella Linton may be silly, she is scarcely mad; and, in short, we'll dismiss the matter, as you advise."

From their tongues, they did dismiss it; and Catherine, probably, from her thoughts. The other, I felt certain, recalled it often in the course of the evening. I saw him smile to himself—grin rather—and lapse into ominous musing whenever Mrs. Linton had occasion to be absent from the apartment.

I determined to watch his movements. My heart invariably cleaved to the master's, in preference to Catherine's side: with reason I imagined, for he was kind, and trustful, and honourable; and she—she could not be called the *opposite*, yet she seemed to allow herself such wide latitude, that I had little faith in her principles, and still less sympathy for her feel-

---

① 如果伊莎贝拉成为林顿的遗产继承人，那意味着林顿没有儿子，因此凯瑟琳说"I shoule be sorry"。她接着说会有五六个侄子取消伊莎贝拉的继承权，意指自己希望生下五六个男孩。

ings. I wanted something to happen which might have the effect of freeing both Wuthering Heights and the Grange of Mr. Heathcliff, quietly; leaving us as we had been prior to his advent. His visits were a continual nightmare to me; and, I suspected, to my master also. His abode at the Heights was an oppression past explaining. I felt that God had forsaken the stray sheep① there to its own wicked wanderings, and an evil beast prowled between it and the fold, waiting his time to spring and destroy.

画眉田庄都平静地与希斯克利夫脱离关系，让我们像他没出现之前那样生活。对我来说他的拜访就像是一阵袭来的梦魇，我想对我的主人来说也是一样。他住在山庄的行为已经成了一种无法解释的压迫。我觉得是上帝把这个迷途的羔羊遗弃在那儿的，任它在那里胡乱游荡，一只恶毒的野兽正徘徊在那只羊与羊圈之间，伺机跳起来摧毁它。

Chapter 11
第十一章

Sometimes, while meditating on these things in solitude, I've got up in a sudden terror, and put on my bonnet to go and see how all was at the farm. I've persuaded my conscience that it was a duty to warn him how people talked regarding his ways; and then I've recollected his confirmed bad habits, and, hopeless of benefiting him, have flinched from re-entering the dismal house, doubting if I could bear to be taken at my word. One time I passed the old gate, going out of my way, on a journey to Gimmerton. It was about the period that my

有时，我一个人思索着这些的时候，常常会被吓得突然站起来，戴上帽子，走出去，看看庄园是否安然无恙。良心告诉我，我应该去提醒他们是怎么谈论他的行动的，但是一想起他那些无可救药的顽固恶习，一想到我的话根本就不会被接受，我就畏缩不前，不愿再走进那所阴沉的房子。有一回我去吉默顿，特地绕道，好路过那扇古老的大门。那是一个寒冷但阳光很好的下午——刚好是我故事讲到的地方——地面光秃秃的，道

---

① 指伊莎贝拉。

第十一章

narrative has reached: a bright frosty afternoon; the ground bare, and the road hard and dry. I came to a stone where the highway branches off on to the moor at your left hand; a rough sand-pillar, with the letters W. H. ① cut on its north side, on the east, G②, and on the south-west, T. G. ③ It serves as guide-post to the Grange, and Heights, and village. The sun shone yellow on its grey head, reminding me of summer; and I cannot say why, but all at once, a gush of child's sensations flowed into my heart. Hindley and I held it a favourite spot twenty years before. I gazed long at the weather-worn block; and, stooping down, perceived a hole near the bottom still full of snail-shells and pebbles, which we were very fond of storing there with more perishable things; and, as fresh as reality, it appeared that I beheld my early playmate seated on the withered turf: his dark, square head bent forward, and his little hand scooping out the earth with a piece of slate. "Poor Hindley!" I exclaimed, involuntarily. I started: my bodily eye was cheated into a momentary belief that the child lifted its face and stared straight into mine! It vanished in a twinkling; but immediately I felt an irresistible yearning to be at the Heights. Superstition urged me to comply with this impulse: supposing he should be dead! I thought—or should die soon!—supposing it were a sign of death! The nearer I got to the house the more agitated I grew; and on catching sight of it I trembled every limb. The apparition had outstripped me: it stood

路又硬又干。有一块大石头出现在我面前，这儿是大路的分岔口。左边通往原野，有一根粗糙的沙柱，沙柱的北面刻着W.H.，东面是G.，西南面是T.G.。这就算是去田庄、山庄和村子的路标了。金色的阳光照在暗淡的柱顶上，我不知怎么想起了夏天。孩提时的情感猛然间涌上心头，我不知道这是为什么。二十年前，这儿是我和辛德雷流连忘返的天堂。我目不转睛地盯着这块饱经风雨的岩石看了很长时间；又俯下身子，看到石头的底部，那个塞满了鹅卵石和蜗牛壳的小洞还在。当年这些东西以及另外一些不易保存的东西总是被我们欢天喜地地藏在那儿。突然间，我儿时的游伴出现在我面前，历历在目。他坐在那干枯的草皮上，低着黑黑的大脑袋，小手拿着一块瓦片正在掘土。"可怜的辛德雷！"我情不自禁地喊了出来。我吓了一跳——我的玩伴突然抬起头，直直地盯着我！我眼睛一花，那张脸又消失了，可是，一种无法抗拒的渴望立刻占据了我：我想到山庄去。迷信逼着我顺从了这个渴望——"他可能死了！"我心里想，"或者快死了吧！——恐怕这是死亡的兆头！"离那所房子越近，我就越激动，等它出现在我眼前，我已经抖得跟筛糠一样了。那个幽灵却已经先我而到，它躲在栅栏后面向外张望。当我第一眼看到那个卷头发，红脸蛋，棕色眼睛的小男孩靠在门栏上时，我心里的第

---

① Wuthering Heights 之缩写，即呼啸山庄。
② Gimmerton 之缩写，即吉默顿。
③ Thrushcross Grange 之缩写，即画眉田庄。

looking through the gate. That was my first idea on observing an elf-locked, brown-eyed boy setting his ruddy countenance against the bars. Further reflection suggested this must be Hareton, *my* Hareton, not altered greatly since I left him, ten months since.

"God bless thee, darling!" I cried, forgetting instantaneously my foolish fears. "Hareton, it's Nelly! Nelly, thy nurse."

He retreated out of arm's length, and picked up a large flint.

"I am come to see thy father, Hareton," I added, guessing from the action that Nelly, if she lived in his memory at all, was not recognised as one with me.

He raised his missile to hurl it; I commenced a soothing speech, but could not stay his hand: the stone struck my bonnet; and then ensued, from the stammering lips of the little fellow, a string of curses, which, whether he comprehended them or not, were delivered with practised emphasis, and distorted his baby features into a shocking expression of malignity. You may be certain this grieved more than angered me. Fit to cry, I took an orange from my pocket, and offered it to propitiate him. He hesitated, and then snatched it from my hold; as if he fancied I only intended to tempt and disappoint him. I showed another, keeping it out of his reach.

"Who has taught you those fine words, my bairn?" I inquired. "The curate?"

"Damn the curate, and thee! Gie me that," he replied.

"Tell us where you got your lessons, and you shall have it," said I. "Who's your master?"

"Devil daddy," was his answer.

"上帝保佑你，宝贝！"我大声喊道，我那可笑的恐惧立刻飞到了九霄云外。"哈里顿，我是内莉呀！内莉，你的保姆。"

他向后退，好让我没法碰到他，而且还从地上拣起一块大石头。

"哈里顿，我是来看你父亲的。"我解释道，从他的举动中我可以猜到，即使他还没有忘记内莉的话，他也不会认得我就是那个内莉了。

尽管我不住对他软言软语，可那块石头还是从他手里飞出来砸中我的帽子，接着一段结结巴巴的脏话从这小家伙的口里吐出来，真不知道他是否知道自己在说些什么，但他显得又老练又凶恶，脸蛋也扭曲成一种恶狠狠的样子。你应该猜得出，此情此景，我的痛苦更多于生气。我强忍住眼泪，从口袋里掏出一只桔子，想用它来讨他欢心，同他讲和。他迟疑着，然后一把从我手里把桔子夺去，好像担心我是打算逗他，拿他开心。我又掏出一只桔子来给他看，可这回让他的手够不着。

"那些脏话是谁教你的，我的孩子？"我问，"副牧师吗？"

"去他妈的副牧师，还有你！把那个给我。"他说。

"告诉我你在哪儿念书，我就给你，"我说："你的老师是谁？"

"该死的爸爸，"他答道。

"And what do you learn from daddy?" I continued.

He jumped at the fruit; I raised it higher. "What does he teach you?" I asked.

"Naught," said he, "but to keep out of his gait. Daddy cannot bide me, because I swear at him."

"Ah! and the devil teaches you to swear at daddy?" I observed.

"Ay-nay," he drawled.

"Who, then?"

"Heathcliff."

I asked if he liked Mr. Heathcliff.

"Ay!" he answered again.

Desiring to have his reasons for liking him, I could only gather the sentences—"I known't he pays dad back what he gies to me he curses daddy for cursing me. He says I mun do as I will."

"And the curate does not teach you to read and write, then?" I pursued.

"No, I was told the curate should have his—teeth dashed down his—throat, if he stepped over the threshold—Heathcliff had promised that!"

I put the orange in his hand, and bade him tell his father that a woman called Nelly Dean was waiting to speak with him, by the garden gate. He went up the walk, and entered the house; but, instead of Hindley, Heathcliff appeared on the door stones; and I turned directly and ran down the road as hard as ever I could race, making no halt till I gained the guide post, and feeling as scared as if I had raised a goblin. This is not much connected with Miss Isabella's affair; except that it urged me to resolve further on mounting vigilant guard, and

"你爸爸都教了你什么？"我继续问。

他跳起来够那个桔子，我把它举得更高。"他还教了你什么？"我问。

"没了，"他说："就让我离他远点儿。他根本受不了我，因为我老是骂他。"

"哦！那么是魔鬼教你去乱骂爸爸的了？"我说。

"嗯——不，"他吞吞吐吐地说。

"那么，谁？"

"希斯克利夫。"

我问他喜不喜欢希斯克利夫先生。

"嗯，"他回答。

我又问他喜欢的理由，可他只告诉我："我不知道——爸爸怎么对待我，他就怎么对待爸爸——爸爸骂我的话，他就会骂爸爸。他说我想做什么，就可以做什么。"

"那么副牧师他不教你读书写字吗？"我追问下去。

"不教了，听说副牧师只要敢跨进门口一步，就会被打得满地找牙——希斯克利夫那么说的！"

我把桔子给他，让他去告诉父亲，有一个名叫内莉·迪安的女人在园子门口等着，要跟他讲几句话。他顺着小路穿过园子，走进屋里。可出现的是希斯克利夫，而不是辛德雷。我立刻转过身，用尽所有的力气拼命往大路跑去，直到指路碑那儿我才敢站住脚，就像见鬼了一样。这件事和伊莎贝拉小姐的事情并无关系，但是促使我进一步坚定决心，尽我最大力量严加提防，不允许这类邪恶势力影响到画眉田庄，哪怕为此得罪林顿太

doing my utmost to check the spread of such bad influence at the Grange; even though I should wake a domestic storm, by thwarting Mrs. Linton's pleasure.

The next time Heathcliff came, my young lady chanced to be feeding some pigeons in the court. She had never spoken a word to her sister-in-law for three days; but she had likewise dropped her fretful complaining, and we found it a great comfort. Heathcliff had not the habit of bestowing a single unnecessary civility on Miss Linton, I knew. Now, as soon as he beheld her, his first precaution was to take a sweeping survey of the house-front. I was standing by the kitchen window, but I drew out of sight. He then stept across the pavement to her, and said something; she seemed embarrassed, and desirous of getting away; to prevent it, he laid his hand on her arm. She averted her face; he apparently put some question which she had no mind to answer. There was another rapid glance at the house, and supposing himself unseen, the scoundrel had the impudence to embrace her.

"Judas[①]! Traitor!" I ejaculated. "You are a hypocrite, too, are you? A deliberate deceiver."

"Who is, Nelly?" said Catherine's voice at my elbow: I had been overintent on watching the pair outside to mark her entrance.

"Your worthless friend!" I answered warmly: "the sneaking rascal yonder. Ah, he has caught a glimpse of us—he is coming in! I wonder will he have the art to find a plausible excuse for making love to Miss, when he told

---

① Judas: 犹大, 耶稣十二门徒之一, 后来背信弃义将耶稣出卖给敌人。

希斯克利夫再来时, 恰好我家小姐在院子里喂鸽子。虽然整整三天来她没有跟她嫂嫂说过话, 可她好像再也不满腹牢骚了, 这使我们都放心不少。我知道, 希斯克利夫向来没有那个习惯, 对林顿小姐献没必要的殷勤。如今, 他一看见她, 第一反应就是朝房前屋后环顾一遍。我刚好站在厨房窗子后面, 可是我退后了好让他看不见我。他顺着石子路走到她跟前, 跟她说了些什么。她似乎显得很窘, 想走开。他不让她走, 一把抓住她的手臂。她扭过头去, 好像为了躲避他提出的一些她不想回答的问题。希斯克利夫又很快地扫视了一眼房屋, 以为周围没人, 这个流氓竟厚颜无耻地抱住了林顿小姐。

"犹大! 叛徒!"我脱口而出。"你这伪善的家伙, 是吧? 你这老谋深算的骗子!"

"谁呀, 内莉?"旁边传来了凯瑟琳的声音。我注意力过分集中到外面两个人身上, 竟没有注意她的到来。

"你的一文不值的朋友!"我激动地答道: "就是那边那个鬼鬼祟祟摸到别人家里来的流氓。哦, 他看见我们啦——正朝这边来! 既然他告诉过你他恨小姐, 我倒想看看现在他还有什

you he hated her?"

Mrs. Linton saw Isabella tear herself free, and run into the garden; and a minute after, Heathcliff opened the door. I couldn't withhold giving some loose to my imagination; but Catherine angrily insisted on silence, and threatened to order me out of the kitchen, if I dared to be so presumptuous as to put in my insolent tongue.

"To hear you, people might think you were the mistress!" she cried."You want setting down in your right place! Heathcliff, what are you about, raising this stir? I said you must let Isabella alone! —I beg you will, unless you are tired of being received here, and wish Linton to draw the bolts against you!"

"God forbid that he should try!" answered the black villain. I detested him just then."God keep him meek and patient! Every day I grow madder after sending him to heaven!"

"Hush!" said Catherine, shutting the inner door."Don't vex me. Why have you disregarded my request? Did she come across you on purpose?"

"What is it to you?" he growled."I have a right to kiss her, if she chooses; and you have no right to object. I'm not *your* husband: *you* needn't be jealous of me!"

"I'm not jealous of you," replied the mistress;"I'm jealous for you. Clear your face: you shan't scowl at me! If you like Isabella, you shall marry her. But do you like her? Tell the truth, Heathcliff! There, you won't answer. I'm certain you don't!"

"And would Mr. Linton approve of his sister marrying that man?" I inquired.

"Mr. Linton should approve," returned

第十一章

么巧妙的借口来解释他向小姐求爱的举动?"

林顿太太看着伊莎贝拉自己挣开希斯克利夫,消失在花园里。不一会儿,希斯克利夫推门而入。我忍不住要发泄一下怒火,可凯瑟琳却生气地叫我闭嘴,威胁说如果我再胡言乱语,她会命令我离开厨房。

"听你的口气,人家还以为你是这个家的女主人哩!"她嚷道。"你要明白自己的本分!希斯克利夫,你都干了些什么,惹出这样的事?我告诉过你不要再惹伊莎贝拉!——求你啦,除非你不想再待在这里,想让林顿给你吃闭门羹!"

"他敢这么做试试!"这个恶棍回答。这时,我充满了对他的愤恨。"上帝会让他老实而忍耐!我要发狂了,恨不得早点把他送到天堂!"

"别说了!"凯瑟琳说,一边把里面的门关上。"不要再烦我了。为什么你不接受我的请求呢?难道是她故意找你的么?"

"这跟你有什么关系?"他满腹牢骚。"我有权吻她,如果她愿意。你没权利反对。我不是你的丈夫,你用不着嫉妒!"

"我不是嫉妒,"女主人回答,"我是替你担心。脸色开朗些,不要那样瞪我!如果你真心喜欢伊莎贝拉,就娶她为妻。可你真的喜欢她么?要说实话,希斯克利夫!答不上来吧。我就知道你不喜欢她!"

"难道林顿先生会允许他妹妹嫁给这个人吗?"我问。

"林顿先生当然会同意,"太太果

my lady decisively.

"He might spare himself the trouble," said Heathcliff: "I could do as well without his approbation. And as to you, Catherine, I have a mind to speak a few words now, while we are at it. I want you to be aware that I *know* you have treated me infernally—infernally! Do you hear? And if you flatter yourself that I don't perceive it, you are a fool; and if you think I can be consoled by sweet words, you are an idiot; and if you fancy I'll suffer unrevenged, I'll convince you of the contrary, in a very little while! Meantime, thank you for telling me your sister-in-law's secret: I swear I'll make the most of it. And stand you aside!"

"What new phase of his character is this?" exclaimed Mrs. Linton, in amazement. "I've treated you infernally—and you'll take revenge! How will you take it, ungrateful brute? How have I treated you infernally?"

"I seek no revenge on you," replied Heathcliff less vehemently. "That's not the plan. The tyrant grinds down his slaves and they don't turn against him; they crush those beneath them. You are welcome to torture me to death for your amusement, only allow me to amuse myself a little in the same style, and refrain from insult as much as you are able. Having levelled my palace, don't erect a hovel and complacently admire your own charity in giving me that for a home. If I imagined you really wished me to marry Isabella, I'd cut my throat!"

"Oh, the evil is that I am *not* jealous, is it?" cried Catherine. "Well, I won't repeat my offer of a wife: it is as bad as offering Satan a lost soul. Your bliss lies, like his, in inflicting

断地回答。

"他可以省掉这份心了,"希斯克利夫说,"即使他不批准,我也照样会做。至于你,凯瑟琳,既然我们已经到了这一步,我倒有些话说。我要你明白,我知道你恶毒地对待过我——恶毒!你听清了吗?如果你自以为我一直都被蒙在鼓里,你就是个傻子。如果你以为几句好话就可以安慰我,那你就是个白痴。如果你幻想我会一直忍下去而不报复,我会让你相信事实会截然相反!这用不了多少时间。同时,谢谢你告诉我你小姑的心思,我发誓我会好好利用它的。滚一边去吧!"

"他的性格里又翻出了什么新花样啊?"林顿太太惊叫起来。"我对你很恶毒——所以你要报复!你打算怎样报复呢?你这毫不领情的畜生?我对你怎么恶毒啦?"

"我不是报复你,"希斯克利夫不那么激动地答道:"那不是我的计划。暴君压迫奴隶,他们是不会反抗的;他们会转而欺压比他们更下贱的人。你为了开心,可以把我折磨到死,我毫无怨言;可你也要允许我以相同方式给自己找点乐子,同时请你尽量不要侮辱我。你铲平了我的宫殿,给我搭一个草屋,然后心满意足地欣赏你的仁慈。要是我相信你真心希望我娶伊莎贝拉为妻的话,我还不如抹脖子自杀。"

"哦!问题就在于我不嫉妒,是吧?"凯瑟琳喊叫着。"好吧,我不会再提这段亲事啦,那就等于把一个迷失的灵魂献给撒旦。你跟魔鬼一样,把

misery. You prove it. Edgar is restored from the ill-temper he gave way to at your coming; I begin to be secure and tranquil; and you, restless to know us at peace, appear resolved on exciting a quarrel. Quarrel with Edgar, if you please, Heathcliff, and deceive his sister: you'll hit on exactly the most efficient method of revenging yourself on me."

The conversation ceased. Mrs. Linton sat down by the fire, flushed and gloomy. The spirit which served her was growing intractable: she could neither lay nor control it. He stood on the hearth with folded arms, brooding on his evil thoughts; and in this position I left them to seek the master, who was wondering what kept Catherine below so long.

"Ellen," said he, when I entered, "have you seen your mistress?"

"Yes; she's in the kitchen, sir," I answered. "She's sadly put out by Mr. Heathcliff's behaviour: and, indeed, I do think it's time to arrange his visits on another footing. There's harm in being too soft, and now it's come to this—" And I related the scene in the court, and, as near as I dared, the whole subsequent dispute. I fancied it could not be very prejudicial to Mrs. Linton; unless she made it so afterwards, by assuming the defensive for her guest. Edgar Linton had difficulty in hearing me to the close. His first words revealed that he did not dear his wife of blame.

"This is insufferable!" he exclaimed. "It is disgraceful that she should own him for a friend, and force his company on me! Call me two men out of the hall, Ellen. Catherine shall linger no longer to argue with the low ruffian—I have humoured her enough."

自己的幸福建立在别人的痛苦上。你证明了这一点。埃德加现在平静多了，不像你刚来时那样愤怒。我也感到安心多了。而你见不得我们相安无事，存心想挑起事端是吧？如果你高兴的话，去和埃德加吵吧，希斯克利夫，还可以把他妹妹骗走！你正好找到了报复我的最有效的办法。"

谈话停止了，林顿太太坐在火炉边，两颊通红，神情郁闷。缠着她的这种念头越来越难以处理。她放不开，又控制不住。他双手交叉放在胸前，站在炉边，不知道在动着哪些坏念头。就在这时，我离开他们，去找主人，主人正为凯瑟琳在楼下待了老半天感到奇怪呢。

"艾伦，"我刚推门进去，他就问道，"你看见你的女主人了吗？"

"是的，她在厨房里，先生。"我回答。"她在为希斯克利夫先生的举动而闷闷不乐呢。我认为，确实该重新考虑他到我们家的事情了，过分的宽松反而有害，现在事情都到这个地步了——"我接着就把院子里的一幕述说一番，而且鼓足勇气，把这之后的整个争执也一五一十地说了。我觉得这样做对林顿太太并不会很不利，除非她后来还为客人辩护。埃德加·林顿很费劲地听我把话讲完，他第一句话就表明他并不以为他妻子完全没有过错。

"这是不能忍受的！"他嚷起来。"这样的人，她还会把他当朋友，还强迫我去应酬他，真是可耻！给我从下面叫两个人来，艾伦。凯瑟琳不能再留在那儿，跟那下贱的流氓争论——我对她已经够迁就了。"

He descended, and bidding the servants wait in the passage, went, followed by me, to the kitchen. Its occupants had recommenced their angry discussion: Mrs. Linton, at least, was scolding with renewed vigour; Heathcliff had moved to the window, and hung his head, somewhat cowed by her violent rating apparently. He saw the master first, and made a hasty motion that she should be silent; which she obeyed, abruptly, on discovering the reason of his intimation. "How is this?" said Linton, addressing her; "what notion of propriety must you have to remain here, after the language which has been held to you by that blackguard? I suppose, because it is his ordinary talk, you think nothing of it: you are habituated to his baseness, and, perhaps, imagine I can get used to it too!"

"Have you been listening at the door, Edgar?" asked the mistress, in a tone particularly calculated to provoke her husband, implying both carelessness and contempt of his irritation. Heathcliff, who had raised his eyes at the former speech, gave a sneering laugh at the latter; on purpose, it seemed, to draw Mr. Linton's attention to him. He succeeded; but Edgar did not mean to entertain him with any high flights of passion.

"I have been so far forbearing with you, sir," he said, quietly; "not that I was ignorant of your miserable, degraded character, but I felt you were only partly responsible for that; and Catherine wishing to keep up your acquaintance, I acquiesced—foolishly. Your presence is a moral poison that would contaminate the most virtuous: for that cause, and to prevent worse consequences, I shall deny you hereafter

他下了楼，吩咐仆人守在过道里，便向厨房走去，我在后面跟着。厨房里的两个人又重新开始了激烈的争论。至少，林顿太太重新精神抖擞地咒骂起来。希斯克利夫退到窗前，低着头，显然多少有点蔫了。他第一个看见了主人，便赶忙做了个停止的动作，她一发现他暗示的原因，立刻就服从地闭上了嘴。"这是怎么了？"林顿对她说："你倒是忍得住，那个流氓对你这样的话都说得出来，你还待在这里。我想，因为这就是他平时的谈话方式，所以你不以为然。你习惯了他的下流无耻，而且可能还以为我也能容忍！"

"你在门外偷听，埃德加？"女主人问，她故意用了一种语气来激怒她的丈夫，既满不在乎，又鄙视他的愤怒。希斯克利夫在林顿说那番话时还抬了一下眼，听到凯瑟林的话时，就发出一声冷笑，大概是想故意引起林顿先生的注意。他成功了。可埃德加却并不打算对他大发脾气。

"我一直在容忍你的存在，先生。"他平静地说，"并非我对你那卑鄙无耻的品行毫无耳闻，只是我想这并不能完全怪罪于你，而且凯瑟琳希望和你来往，我同意了——愚蠢的做法。你的存在是一种道德上的毒素，会把最纯洁的人都给玷污。所以为了杜绝更糟的事情发生，从现在开始，你不再被允许进入这个房子。现在我

admission into this house, and give notice now that I require your instant departure. Three minutes' delay will render it involuntary and ignominious."

Heathcliff measured the height and breadth of the speaker with an eye full of derision.

"Cathy, this lamb of yours threatens like a bull!" he said. "It is in danger of splitting its skull against my knuckles. By God! Mr. Linton, I'm mortally sorry that you are not worth knocking down!"

My master glanced towards the passage, and signed me to fetch the men: he had no intention of hazarding a personal encounter. I obeyed the hint; but Mrs. Linton, suspecting something, followed; and when I attempted to call them, she pulled me back, slammed the door to, and locked it.

"Fair means!" she said, in answer to her husband's look of angry surprise. "If you have not the courage to attack him, make an apology, or allow yourself to be beaten. It will correct you of feigning more valour than you possess. No, I'll swallow the key before you shall get it! I'm delightfully rewarded for my kindness to each! After constant indulgence of one's weak nature, and the other's bad one, I earn, for thanks, two samples of blind ingratitude, stupid to absurdity! Edgar, I was defending you and yours; and I wish Heathcliff may flog you sick, for daring to think an evil thought of me!"

It did not need the medium of a flogging to produce that effect on the master. He tried to wrest the key from Catherine's grasp, and for safety she flung it into the hottest part of the

就通知你马上离开。如果三分钟之后还不动身，你将会被迫离开，不过那样就难看了。"

希斯克利夫打量着这个说话的人，眼中满是嘲笑。

"凯茜，你这只羊羔吓唬起人来倒挺像只公牛的！"他说："他可别让脑袋碰上我的拳头，不然可会开花的。上帝啊！林顿先生，我非常抱歉，你根本不值得我出手！"

我的主人朝过道方向瞥了一眼，暗示我叫人来——我知道，他可没有单打独斗的打算。我接受暗示，但是林顿太太起了疑心，跟了过来，我刚想叫他们过来时，她把我拖了回来，把门一甩，并且锁住了。

"好公平的办法！"她说，以此来回答她丈夫愤怒惊奇的神情。"如果你没有足够的勇气打他，那你就道歉，或者自己挨打。也好给你个教训，以后不要硬充好汉。别过来抢钥匙，我会先把它吞下去的！我对你们两个这么好，你们却这样回报我，真是我的好报应！我一直纵容你们，一个软蛋，一个坏蛋，最后我得到的报答却是两种莫明其妙的忘恩负义，愚蠢得简直到了荒谬的程度！埃德加，我一直在保护你和你的一切，现在却希望希斯克利夫狠狠抽你一顿，你竟敢用那么坏的心思来揣度我！"

并不需要借助鞭子，主人整个就蔫了下来。他尽力想从凯瑟琳手里把钥匙夺过来。可她一下把钥匙丢到火炉烧得最旺的地方去了，以防出什么

fire; whereupon Mr. Edgar was taken with a nervous trembling, and his countenance grew deadly pale. For his life he could not avert that access of emotion: mingled anguish and humiliation overcame him completely. He leant on the back of a chair, and covered his face.

"Oh! Heavens! In old days this would win you knighthood!" exclaimed Mrs. Linton. "We are vanquished! we are vanquished! Heathcliff would as soon lift a finger at you as the king would march his army against a colony of mice. Cheer up! you sha'n't be hurt! Your type is not a lamb, it's a sucking leveret."

"I wish you joy of the milk-blooded coward, Cathy!" said her friend. "I compliment you on your taste. And that is the slavering, shivering thing you preferred to me! I would not strike him with my fist, but I'd kick him with my foot, and experience considerable satisfaction. Is he weeping, or is he going to faint for fear?"

The fellow approached and gave the chair on which Linton rested a push. He'd better have kept his distance: my master quickly sprang erect, and struck him full on the throat a blow that would have levelled a slighter man. It took his breath for a minute; and, while he choked, Mr. Linton walked out by the back door into the yard, and from thence, to the front entrance.

"There! you've done with coming here," cried Catherine. "Get away, now; he'll return with a brace of pistols, and half a dozen assistants. If he did overhear us, of course, he'd never forgive you. You've played me an ill turn, Heathcliff! But, go—make haste! I'd rather see Edgar at bay than you."

"Do you suppose I'm going with that blow

差错。于是埃德加先生浑身发抖，脸色像死人一样惨白。他一生中从来都不能抵挡这种感情的泛滥，痛苦和耻辱交错混杂，把他完全击垮了。他双手掩面，靠在椅背上。

"哦，天啊！在过去，你会赢得骑士的爵位呢！"林顿太太喊着。"我们被击败啦！我们被击败啦！希斯克利夫用一根手指头对付你，简直就像一个国王用他的整个军队去攻打一窝小耗子一样。别怕，谁也不会揍你的！你根本就是一只还没断奶的小兔子，连一只小绵羊都算不上！"

"但愿你在这个浑身奶味的胆小鬼身上得到快乐，凯茜！"她的朋友说。"我欣赏你的品位。你宁愿要他，这个抖成一团、眼泪鼻涕一大把的家伙，却不要我！我不想侮辱我的拳头，我只会用我的脚去踹他，就会非常满足。他是在哭吗，还是快吓晕了？"

这家伙走上前，推了一把林顿靠着的椅子。他还不如站远点好，因为我的主人立刻跳了起来，扎扎实实地给了他喉咙一拳。这一拳可以把一个瘦弱一点的人打倒。希斯克利夫为此窒息了足足有一分钟。趁着这个时候，林顿先生从后门走到院子里，又走向前面的大门。

"好啦！你以后别想再来这儿。"凯瑟琳叫道："立刻就走——他一会儿会带着一对手枪、半打仆人回来的。如果他真的偷听了我们的谈话，他肯定不会饶过你。你刚才的所作所为可给我带来大麻烦了，希斯克利夫！可是，还是逃吧——快点！我宁愿看见

burning in my gullet?" he thundered. "By hell, no! I'll crush his ribs in like a rotten hazelnut, before I cross the threshold! If I don't floor him now, I shall murder him some time; so, as you value his existence, let me get at him!"

"He is not coming," I interposed, framing a bit of a lie. "There's the coachman, and the two gardeners; you'll surely not wait to be thrust into the road by them! Each has a bludgeon; and master will, very likely, be watching from the parlour windows to see that they fulfil his orders."

The gardeners and coachman were there; but Linton was with them. They had already entered the court. Heathcliff, on second thoughts, resolved to avoid a struggle against three underlings: he seized the poker, smashed the lock from the inner door, and made his escape as they tramped in.

Mrs. Linton, who was very much excited, bade me accompany her up stairs. She did not know my share in contributing to the disturbance, and I was anxious to keep her in ignorance.

"I'm nearly distracted, Nelly!" she exclaimed, throwing herself on the sofa. "A thousand smiths' hammers are beating in my head! Tell Isabella to shun me; this uproar is owing to her; and should she or any one else aggravate my anger at present, I shall get wild. And, Nelly, say to Edgar, if you see him again tonight, that I'm in danger of being seriously ill. I wish it may prove true. He has startled and distressed me shockingly! I want to frighten him. Besides, he might come and begin a string of abuse or complainings; I'm certain I should

埃德加走投无路,也不想看到你那样。"

"难道你以为我喉头挨那一拳是白挨的吗?"他大声咆哮。"见鬼去吧!我不会走的。在我跨出门槛之前,我要把他的肋骨捣烂,就像一颗烂掉的榛子!如果我现在不把他放倒在地,总有一天我会杀了他。所以,如果你还在乎他的小命,就让我找到他吧!"

"他不会来了,"我插嘴说,编了个小谎。"那儿有一个马夫和两个园丁,你该不会等着被他们扔到马路上吧!他们每人都有棍子。而且很可能,主人正在客厅的窗户前看他们执行自己的命令呢。"

园丁和马夫的确在那儿,可林顿也和他们待在一起。他们走进了院子。希斯克利夫念头一动,决定不和这三个仆人打架。在他们大踏步进来的时候,他拿了根拨火棍,敲掉里门的锁,逃了出去。

林顿太太大受了刺激,让我陪她上楼。她并不知道我也掺和进了这场乱子,我自然尽力不让她知道。

"我快疯啦,内莉!"她嚷道,一头倒在了沙发上。"一千把铁匠的大锤子在我头里敲打!告诉伊莎贝拉离我远点儿,这场争吵都是因她而起的;现在,如果她或是任何人再来火上浇油,我就要发疯啦。而且,内莉,告诉埃德加,如果你今晚能看到他的话,我有病死的危险——但愿这是真的。他吓了我一大跳,让我非常难过!我也要吓他一下。而且,他也许会来,还会带来一阵咒骂和抱怨。我一定会反唇相讥,天晓得闹到哪里才

recriminate, and God knows where we should end! Will you do so, my good Nelly? You are aware that I am no way blameable in this matter. What possessed him to turn listener? Heathcliff's talk was outrageous, after you left us; but I could soon have diverted him from Isabella, and the rest meant nothing. Now, all is dashed wrong by the fool's-craving to hear evil of self that haunts some people like a demon! Had Edgar never gathered our conversation, he would never have been the worse for it. Really, when he opened on me in that unreasonable tone of displeasure, after I had scolded Heathcliff till I was hoarse for *him*, I did not care, hardly, what they did to each other; especially as I felt that, however the scene closed, we should all be driven asunder for nobody knows how long! Well, if I cannot keep Heathcliff for my friend—if Edgar will be mean and jealous, I'll try to break their hearts by breaking my own. That will be a prompt way of finishing all, when I am pushed to extremity! But it's a deed to be reserved for a forlorn hope; I'd not take Linton by surprise with it. To this point he has been discreet in dreading to provoke me; you must represent the peril of quitting that policy, and remind him of my passionate temper, verging, when kindled, on frenzy. I wish you could dismiss that apathy out of your countenance, and look rather more anxious about me!"

The stolidity with which I received these instructions was, no doubt, rather exasperating: for they were delivered in perfect sincerity; but I believed a person who could plan the turning of her fits of passion to account, beforehand, might, by exerting her will, manage

是尽头！你也会这么做吗，我的好内莉？你知道这件事上我没有什么可以责怪的地方。谁允许他偷听了？你走了以后，希斯克利夫的话就好歹不分，让人难以忍受了，可我马上就可以让他把对伊莎贝拉的心思丢开，其他事就没什么要紧了。现在，一切都乱了套，都怪这个傻子神经兮兮地拼命想偷听人家说他的坏话，就像魔鬼缠身了一样！如果埃德加不来偷听我们的话，现在什么都不会发生了。真的，我为了他骂希斯克利夫骂得喉咙都哑了，他却用那种不快的无理腔调对我说话，现在我对他们两个如何对待彼此是一点都不关心了。特别是我感到，无论戏怎样收场，我们的关系都会支离破碎，谁也知道何时才会恢复！好吧，如果我不能拥有希斯克利夫这个朋友——如果埃德加自私又嫉妒，我就揉碎自己的心，好伤透他们的心。要是把我逼得走投无路，这倒是结束一切的捷径！但我不会放弃最小的希望，我不想突然吓着林顿。这一点，他一直很谨慎，就怕刺激到我。你一定要让他明白，我放弃这个策略的危险性，提醒他我的暴躁脾气，如果受到刺激的话就会发狂的。我希望你能够消除你脸上的冷漠无情，对我稍微表现一点关心吧！"

我听着这些话时表现得又迟钝又麻木，这无疑很让人生气：因为这些话的确是她发自肺腑的话。但是我相信，如果一个人能够在事先把自己脾气计算好，那么就算真的爆发出来，如果她尽力的话，也可以把自己控制

to control herself tolerably, even while under their influence; and I did not wish to "frighten" her husband, as she said, and multiply his annoyances for the purpose of serving her selfishness. Therefore I said nothing when I met the master coming towards the parlour; but I took the liberty of turning back to listen whether they would resume their quarrel together. He began to speak first.

"Remain where you are, Catherine," he said; without any anger in his voice, but with much sorrowful despondency. "I shall not stay. I am neither come to wrangle nor be reconciled; but I wish just to learn whether, after this evening's events, you intend to continue your intimacy with—"

"Oh, for mercy's sake," interrupted the mistress, stamping her foot, "for mercy's sake, let us hear no more of it now! Your cold blood cannot be worked into a fever: your veins are full of ice-water; but mine are boiling, and the sight of such chillness makes them dance."

"To get rid of me, answer my question," persevered Mr. Linton. "You *must* answer it; and that violence does not alarm me. I have found that you can be as stoical as any one, when you please. Will you give up Heathcliff hereafter, or will you give up me? It is impossible for you to be *my* friend and *his* at the same time; and I absolutely *require* to know which you choose."

"I require to be let alone!" exclaimed Catherine, furiously. "I demand it! Don't you see I can scarcely stand? Edgar, you—you leave me!"

She rung the bell till it broke with a twang; I entered leisurely. It was enough to try the

第十一章

得很好；因此我也不愿意去"吓唬"她的丈夫，就像她说的那样，只是为了增加他的烦恼来满足她的自私自利。因此当主人正向客厅走来时，我碰到了他，却什么也没说，而是转过身来，去看看他们是不是又重新开始吵架。他先开口。

"你待在那儿好了，凯瑟琳，"他说，他的声调很平静，毫无怒气，可是充满了悲伤失望。"我不会待很久。我不是来争吵，也不是来和解。我只想知道，今晚的事发生以后，你是不是还想保持那种亲密的关系，跟那……"

"啊，仁慈一点吧，"女主人打断了他的话，跺着脚，"仁慈一点吧，让我们不要再听到和这事有关的东西了！你的冷血是兴奋不起来的，你的血管尽是冰水，而我的血却在沸腾了。是你这副冷冰冰的模样让它沸腾的。"

"回答我的问题，我就走开。"林顿先生坚持道："装疯卖傻是吓不倒我的，你必须回答。我发现，如果你愿意的话，你可以和任何人一样冷静。从此以后，你是要放弃希斯克利夫，还是放弃我？同时成为我们两个的朋友是不可能的；我绝对要求知道你的选择是什么。"

"我要一个人呆着！"凯瑟琳疯狂地大叫。"我要求这样！你没有看见我站都站不住了吗？埃德加，你——你离开我！"

她拼命拉铃，一直到把它拉断为止；我悠悠地走进来。这样的狂暴，

temper of a saint, such senseless, wicked rages! There she lay dashing her head against the arm of the sofa, and grinding her teeth, so that you might fancy she would crash them to splinters! Mr. Linton stood looking at her in sudden compunction and fear. He told me to fetch some water. She had no breath for speaking. I brought a glass full; and, as she would not drink, I sprinkled it on her face. In few seconds she stretched herself out stiff, and turned up her eyes, while her cheeks, at once blanched and livid, assumed the aspect of death. Linton looked terrified.

"There is nothing in the world the matter," I whispered. I did not want him to yield, though I could not help being afraid in my heart.

"She has blood on her lips!" he said, shuddering.

"Never mind!" I answered, tardy. And I told him how she had resolved, previous to his coming, on exhibiting a fit of frenzy. I incautiously gave the account aloud, and she heard me; for she started up-her hair flying over her shoulders, her eyes flashing, the muscles of her neck and arms standing out preternaturally. I made up my mind for broken bones, at least; but she only glared about her for an instant, and then rushed from the room. The master directed me to follow; I did, to her chamber door: she hindered me from going farther by securing it against me.

As she never offered to descend to breakfast next morning, I went to ask whether she would have some carried up. "No!" she replied, peremptorily. The same question was repeated at dinner and tea; and again on the

这样的毫无理智，可以用来考验圣徒的脾气！她躺在那儿，用头不断撞沙发的扶手，牙齿咬得咯咯响，你还会以为她要把牙齿都咬碎呢！林顿先生看着他，突然间又悔恨又恐惧，让我赶紧去拿点水来，他已经说不出话来了。我端来满满一大杯，她不喝，我就把水洒到她脸上。几秒钟后，她就伸展开僵直的身体，眼睛上翻，脸颊一阵白一阵青，像是快死的样子。林顿看起来吓得要死。

"一点事也没有，"我低声说。我不希望他屈服，虽然我也禁不住害怕。

"她嘴唇上有血！"他边说边颤抖。

"不用担心！"我尖酸地回答。接着告诉他在他来之前她就准备发狂给人看了。我大意了，声音太高，让她听见了。因为她站了起来——头发披散在肩上，目光闪闪，脖子和胳膊上的肌肉都反常地突出来。我准备着至少要断几根骨头了，可她只向周围环视了一下，就冲出屋子去。主人让我跟着，我照做了，一直跟到她的卧房门口。她把房门关紧，把我挡在外面。

第二天早上，她没有下来吃早餐，于是我就去问她要不要我送早餐上楼。"不！"她一口回绝。午饭和下午茶还是一样。第二天也是一样，连回答都一样。林顿先生自己躲在书房

morrow after, and received the same answer. Mr. Linton, on his part, spent his time in the library, and did not inquire concerning his wife's occupations. Isabella and he had had an hour's interview, during which he tried to elicit from her some sentiment of proper horror for Heathcliff's advances: but he could make nothing of her evasive replies, and was obliged to close the examination unsatisfactorily; adding, however, a solemn warning, that if she were so insane as to encourage that worthless suitor, it would dissolve all bonds of relationship between herself and him.

里打发时间，也不过问他太太的事情。伊莎贝拉和他一起待过一个小时。他试图从她的情绪中推测出她是否因为希斯克利夫的求婚而感到一些恐惧；可她闪烁其词，他也推断不出任何东西，只能很不满意地结束了这次问话；不过最后给了她一个严肃的警告，如果她真的疯到竟然鼓励那个下贱的求婚者，那么她和他之间就会断绝一切关系。

Chapter 12
第十二章

While Miss Linton moped about the park and garden, always silent, and almost always in tears; and her brother shut himself up among books that he never opened—wearying, I guessed, with a continual vague expectation that Catherine, repenting her conduct, would come of her own accord to ask pardon, and seek a reconciliation—and *she* fasted pertinaciously, under the idea, probably, that at every meal, Edgar was ready to choke for her absence, and pride alone held him from running to cast himself at her feet; I went about my

林顿小姐终日在园子里没精打采地转悠，一句话也不说，而且总是泪眼汪汪。她哥哥则整天把自己关在书房，盯着那些他从未打开过的书看——我猜，他一直在苦苦地暗自巴望着凯瑟琳痛改前非，自己下来恳求他的原谅，重归于好——而她呢，一直在固执地绝食，大概她以为，埃德加看见饭桌上没有她也会吃不下饭，只是面子上过不去，他才没有跑到楼上，跪倒在她脚下。我照样忙着做我的家务活，确信在这个画眉田庄里只

household duties, convinced that the Grange had but one sensible soul in its walls, and that lodged in my body. I wasted no condolences on miss, nor any expostulations on my mistress; nor did I pay attention to the sighs of my master, who yearned to hear his lady's name, since he might not hear her voice. I determined they should come about as they pleased for me; and though it was a tiresomely slow process, I began to rejoice at length in a faint dawn of its progress: as I thought at first.

Mrs. Linton on the third day, unbarred her door, and having finished the water in her pitcher and decanter, desired a renewed supply, and a basin of gruel, for she believed she was dying. That I set down as a speech meant for Edgar's ears; I believed no such thing, so I kept it to myself, and brought her some tea and dry toast. She eat and drank eagerly; and sank back on her pillow again, clenching her hands and groaning. "Oh, I will die," she exclaimed, "since no one cares anything about me. I wish I had not taken that." Then a good while after I heard her murmur, "No, I'll not die—he'd be glad—he does not love me at all—he would never miss me!"

"Did you want anything, ma'am?" I inquired, still preserving my external composure, in spite of her ghastly countenance and strange exaggerated manner.

"What is that apathetic being doing?" she demanded, pushing the thick entangled locks from her wasted face. "Has he fallen into a lethargy or is he dead?"

"Neither," replied I; "if you mean Mr. Linton. He's tolerably well, I think, though his studies occupy him rather more than they

有一个头脑是清醒的，而这个头脑就是我的。我既没有浪费精力去劝慰小姐，也不空费心思去安慰我的女主人；就是对主人的叹息声，我也不加理会。他听不到他太太的声音，就巴望着有人能提起她的名字。我断定，如果他们愿意，肯定会自己来找我的。虽然这个过程缓慢得让人心烦，但我还是非常高兴地看到曙光终于出现：正如我开始预料的那样。

到了第三天，林顿太太打开了房门，她的水壶和水瓶里的水都已经喝光了，她要我重新满上，还跟我要了一盆粥，她相信自己快死了。我估计这话是说给埃德加听的。我根本不信会有这回事，所以我也就把它闷在肚子里。我给她拿了点热茶和烤面包。她狼吞虎咽地吃掉这些食物，又重新倒在枕头上，攥紧拳头，大声呻吟起来。"唉哟，我还是死了算了，"她大叫着："反正没有任何人会来关心我。我真希望刚才我没有吃那些东西。"又过了大半天，我听见她嘟囔着："不，我才不要死——他一定会因此而高兴的——他根本不爱我——他从来都不会挂念我！"

"有什么吩咐吗，太太？"我问道，尽管她脸色苍白得可怕，举动也古怪夸张，我还像以前一样保持我外表的平静。

"那个没心没肺的家伙在干什么？"她问道，抬起手来把她纠缠在一起的浓密卷发从那憔悴的脸上拨开。"他是得了昏睡病，还是死啦？"

"都不是，"我回答，"如果你指的是林顿先生的话。我看他身体挺好，

ought; he is continually among his books, since he has no other society."

I should not have spoken so, if I had known her true condition, but I could not get rid of the notion that she acted a part of her disorder.

"Among his books!" she cried, confounded. "And I dying! I on the brink of the grave! My Cod! does he know how I'm altered?" continued she, staring at her reflection in a mirror hanging against the opposite wall. "Is that Catherine Linton? He imagines me in a pet—in play, perhaps. Cannot you inform him that it is frightful earnest? Nelly, if it be not too late, as soon as I learn how he feels, I-'ll choose between these two; either to starve at once—that would be no punishment unless he had a heart—or to recover, and leave the country. Are you speaking the truth about him now? Take care. Is he actually so utterly indifferent for my life?"

"Why, ma'am," I answered, "the master has no idea of your being deranged; and of course he does not fear that you will let yourself die of hunger."

"You think not? Cannot you tell him I will?" she returned. "Persuade him! speak of your own mind: say you are certain I will!"

"No, you forget, Mrs. Linton," I suggested, "that you have eaten some food with a relish this evening, and tomorrow you will perceive its good effects."

"If I were only sure it would kill him," she interrupted, "I'd kill myself directly! These three awful nights, I've never closed my lids—and oh, I've been tormented! I've been haunted, Nelly! But I begin to fancy you

第十二章

一点毛病也没有。就是看书用了他过多的时间。他一直在埋头苦读，因为现在没有人跟他做伴。"

要是我了解她的真实状况的话，我是不会这么说的，可我总也摆脱不了这样的想法：她的病多半是装出来的。

"在他那些书本堆里！"她惊叫起来，不知所措。"我快要死了！我都站到坟墓边上了！我的天啊！他知不知道我变成什么模样啦？"她盯着对面墙上镜子中自己的影子，接着说："这就是凯瑟琳·林顿么？他也许认为我在撒娇——闹着玩吧。你就不能告诉他说情况非常严重吗？内莉，只要不是太迟，我一知道他心里想的是什么，就要在这两者之间选择：要么立刻饿死——这算不上是惩罚，除非他还有良心；要么恢复健康，离开乡下。喂，你说的关于他的话是不是真的？听着，他对我的生命真的是这样毫不在乎吗？"

"哎呀，太太，"我回答，"主人根本没想到你会气成这样，当然也就不会担心你把自己饿死。"

"你认为不会吗？你就不能告诉他我就要死了吗？"她回答道。"去劝劝他！就说是你自己的看法：你告诉他我一定会死的！"

"不，林顿太太，你不记得啦，"我提醒着，"今天晚上你已经吃了一些东西，还吃得津津有味呢，明天你就会好起来。"

"只要我确信这样能让他死，"她打断了我的话，"我一定会立刻自杀！这可怕的三天三夜，我就没有合过眼——啊，我受尽了痛苦！我已经被鬼给缠住啦，内莉！不过，我已经开

don't like me. How strange! I thought, though everybody hated and despised each other, they could not avoid loving me. And they have all turned to enemies in a few hours: *they* have, I'm positive; the people *here*. How dreary to meet death, surrounded by their cold faces! Isabella, terrified and repelled, afraid to enter the room, it would be so terrible to watch Catherine go. And Edgar standing solemnly by to see it over; then offering prayers of thanks to God for restoring peace to his house, and going back to his *books*! What in the name of all that feels, has he to do with *books*, when I am dying?"

She could not bear the notion which I had put into her head of Mr. Linton's philosophical resignation. Tossing about, she increased her feverish bewilderment to madness, and tore the pillow with her teeth; then raising herself up all burning, desired that I would open the window. We were in the middle of winter, the wind blew strong from the north-east, and I objected. Both the expressions flitting over her face, and the changes of her moods, began to alarm me terribly; and brought to my recollection her former illness, and the doctor's injunction that she should not be crossed. A minute previously she was violent; now, supported on one arm, and not noticing my refusal to obey her, she seemed to find childish diversion in pulling the feathers from the rents she had just made, and ranging them on the sheet according to their different species: her mind had swayed to other associations.

"That's a turkey's," she murmured to herself;"and this is a wild duck's; and this is a pigeon's. Ah, they put pigeons'feathers in the

始怀疑，我怀疑你并不喜欢我。多奇怪啊！我原以为，虽然人们之间都会互相憎恨和蔑视，可他们不会不爱我。谁知只是过了几个小时，他们都变成仇敌了：他们全都变了，我确信这儿的人都变了。临死的时候，身边被这些冰冷的脸孔围着，那是多么惨的一件事啊！伊莎贝拉又害怕，又嫌恶，肯定不会踏进这个房门一步的；眼睁睁地看着凯瑟琳去世会是多可怕啊。埃德加则会一脸严肃地站在一边看着事情了结，然后向上帝感恩，感谢他的家又恢复了往日的平静，然后回去看他的书！我快要死的时候，他还把自己埋在书堆里，他这到底是存的什么心啊？"

我试图让她了解林顿先生那种哲人般的达观态度，可她怎么可能受得了这种看法？她在床上翻来覆去，本就发着高烧，脑子已经迷乱，现在已经发展成了疯狂。她用牙齿撕咬着枕头，又撑起滚烫的身子，要我把窗户打开。那时正当隆冬季节，呼啸的东北风刮得正急，我坚决抵制她的要求。她脸上飞快闪过的神情和情绪变化使我大为惊恐，这时我想起她上次生的病，医生当时一再嘱咐千万不能惹她生气。就在一分钟以前，她还在暴跳如雷，现在却支起一只胳膊，也不管我有没有听从她的命令，自顾自玩得像一个小孩子给自己解闷似的。她从刚刚咬开的枕头上的裂口中拉出一片片羽毛来，分门别类地把它们一一排列在床单上：她的魂早已经飘到不知什么地方去了。

"那是火鸡的，"她对自己嘀嘀咕咕，"这是野鸭的，这是鸽子的。啊，

pillows—no wonder I couldn't die[①]! Let me take care to throw it on the floor when I lie down. And here is a moor-cock's; and this—I should know it among a thousand—it's a lapwing's. Bonny bird; wheeling over our heads in the middle of the moor. It wanted to get to its nest, for the clouds had touched the swells, and it felt rain coming. This feather was picked up from the heath, the bird was not shot: we saw its nest in the winter, full of little skeletons. Heathcliff set a trap over it, and the old ones dare not come. I made him promise he'd never shoot a lapwing after that, and he didn't. Yes, here are more! Did he shoot my lapwings, Nelly? Are they red, any of them? Let me look."

"Give over with that baby-work!" I interrupted, dragging the pillow away, and turning the holes towards the mattress, for she was removing its contents by handfuls. "Lie down and shut your eyes: you're wandering. There's a mess! The down is flying about like snow."

I went here and there collecting it.

"I see in you, Nelly," she continued, dreamily, "an aged woman: you have grey hair and bent shoulders. This bed is the fairy cave under Penistone Crag, and you are gathering elf-bolts to hurt our heifers; pretending, while I am near, that they are only locks of wool. That's what you'll come to fifty years hence: I know you are not so now. I'm not wandering: you're mistaken, or else I should believe you really *were* that withered hag, and I should think I *was* under Penistone Crag; and I'm con-

他们把鸽子的羽毛放进枕头里啦——怪不得我死不了！这我得小心，一会儿我躺下去的时候，得把它扔到地板上。这是雷鸟的，这个——就是把它放在一千个别的羽毛里，我也能把它认出来——这是田凫的羽毛。多么漂亮的鸟儿啊，在旷野里，在我们头顶上盘旋。它要回家去了，因为云层已经压过来，它知道要下雨啦。这根羽毛是从石楠荒原里捡到的，并没有谁杀死鸟儿。冬天的时候，我们看见过它的窝，里面都是小骨头。希斯克利夫在鸟窝上装了个捕鸟机，老鸟就不敢来了。我叫他答应，以后连一只田凫也不要打。他就再也没打过。是的，这里还有更多！他真的没有打死过我的田凫吗，内莉？这些羽毛是不是红的，有没有红的？让我瞧瞧。"

"别再搞这种小孩子的把戏了！"我打断她的话，把枕头拉到一边去，破洞朝着被褥，因为她正把羽毛大把大把地往外掏。"躺下，把眼睛闭上，你脑袋发昏啦。把东西搞得一团糟！弄得羽毛像雪片似的满屋子乱飞。"

我为了捡羽毛忙得团团转。

"内莉，我看你呀，"她像说梦话似的，继续说道："是个老女人啦：灰灰的头发，背也驼啦。这张床是盘尼斯吞岩底下的精灵山洞，你正在收集小精灵用的石镞来伤害我们的小牝牛；因为我在旁边，所以你就假装这些是羊毛团。五十年后，那就是你会变成的样子：我知道你现在还不是这个样子。我没有头脑发昏，你搞错啦。要

[①] 英国有习俗认为，在垂死的病人身上放鸽子的羽毛，其灵魂就不会离开身体，直到亲人赶来，拿去羽毛，才能安然死去。

scious it's night, and there are two candles on the table making the black press shine like jet."

"The black press? where is that?" I asked. "You are talking in your sleep!"

"It's against the wall, as it always is," she replied. "It *does* appear odd—I see a face in it!"

"There is no press in the room, and never was," said I, resuming my seat, and looping up the curtain that I might watch her.

"Don't you *see* that face?" she enquired, gazing earnestly at the mirror.

And say what I could, I was incapable of making her comprehend it to be her own; so I rose and covered it with a shawl.

"It's behind there still!" she pursued, anxiously. "And it stirred. Who is it? I hope it will not come out when you are gone! Oh! Nelly, the room is haunted! I'm afraid of being alone!"

I took her hand in mine, and bid her be composed; for a succession of shudders convulsed her frame, and she *would* keep straining her gaze towards the glass.

"There's nobody here!" I insisted. "It was *yourself*, Mrs. Linton: you knew it a while since."

"Myself!" she gasped, "and the clock is striking twelve! It's true, then! That's dreadful!"

Her fingers clutched the clothes, and gathered them over her eyes. I attempted to steal to the door with an intention of calling her husband; but I was summoned back by a piercing shriek—the shawl had dropped from the frame.

"Why, what is the matter?" cried I. "Who is coward now? Wake up! That is the glass—the mirror, Mrs. Linton; and you see

不然，我就真的会认为你是那个满脸皱纹的老巫婆啦，而且我还会认为我真的是在盘尼斯吞岩底下了；我知道现在是夜晚，桌子上有两支蜡烛，把那个黑柜子照得像乌玉一样亮。"

"黑柜子？在哪儿？"我问。"你是在说梦话！"

"就靠在墙上，一直在那儿，"她回答。"真奇怪——我看到它里面有张脸！"

"这屋里没有柜子，从来都没有，"我说，重新坐到座位上，我钩起帐子，这样可以仔细地盯着她。

"你看到那张脸吗？"她追问道，十分认真地盯着镜子。

不管怎么解释，我都不能使她明白那就是她自己的脸。所以我只好站起来，用一块围巾把镜子盖上。

"但它还是在那后面！"她追问，非常焦虑。"它在动，那是谁？但愿你离开后它别出来！啊！内莉，这屋子里闹鬼！我害怕一个人待在这！"

我握住她的手，让她镇静下来，一连串的战栗使她浑身发抖，可她还是死死盯着那面镜子。

"这儿没别人！"我一遍又一遍地劝解她。"镜子里是你自己，林顿太太，你刚才不是还知道的吗？"

"我自己！"她气喘吁吁地说，"钟敲十二点啦！那样的话，那是真的了！真是太可怕了！"

她一把抓住她的衣服，拉到一起好遮住自己的眼睛。我正想偷偷溜出去把她丈夫叫来，但是一声刺耳的尖叫又把我拉回来，原来是那围巾从镜子上掉下来了。

"哎呀，这是怎么回事呀？"我快

yourself in it, and there am I, too, by your side."

Trembling and bewildered, she held me fast, but the horror gradually passed from her countenance; its paleness gave place to a glow of shame.

"Oh, dear! I thought I was at home," she sighed. "I thought I was lying in my chamber at Wuthering Heights. Because I'm weak, my brain got confused, and I screamed unconsciously. Don't say anything; but stay with me. I dread sleeping: my dreams appal me."

"A sound sleep would do you good, ma'am," I answered; "and I hope this suffering will prevent your trying starving again."

"Oh, if I were but in my own bed in the old house!" she went on bitterly, wringing her hands. "And that wind sounding in the firs by the lattice. Do let me feel it—it comes straight down the moor—do let me have one breath!"

To pacify her, I had the casement ajar a few seconds. A cold blast rushed through; I closed it, and returned to my post. She lay still now, her face bathed in tears. Exhaustion of body had entirely subdued her spirit: our fiery Catherine was no better than a wailing child.

"How long is it since I shut myself in here?" she asked, suddenly reviving.

"It was Monday evening," I replied, "and this is Thursday night, or rather Friday morning, at present."

"What! of the same week?" she exclaimed. "Only that brief time?"

"Long enough to live on nothing but cold water and ill-temper," observed I.

"Well, it seems a weary number of hours," she muttered doubtfully: "it must be

哭出来了。"现在到底谁是胆小鬼呀？快醒醒！那是镜子——镜子，林顿太太，你在里面看到了自己，还有我，在你边上。"

林顿太太浑身发抖，满脸惊惶，把我抓得死死的，但是，恐怖渐渐从她脸上消退；苍白的脸色转而呈现出一种害羞的红色。

"哦，天啊！我还以为是在自己家里呢，"她叹息道。"我以为我是躺在呼啸山庄自己的卧房里。因为身子有点弱，脑子也有点不清醒，不知不觉就喊了出来。什么都不要说，就这样陪着我。我害怕睡觉，我做的尽是噩梦。"

"睡个好觉会对你大有裨益的，太太，"我答道，"希望这场遭遇让你不要再傻傻地想要饿死自己。"

"啊，如果现在是躺在老家我自己的床上，那该多好啊！"她绞着双手苦涩地说，"还有那在窗外枞树林间呼啸着的狂风。让我感受一下它吧——它是直接从荒原吹来的——让我呼吸一口吧！"

为了让她平静下来，我把窗子打开了几秒钟。一阵冷风灌了进来；我急忙关上窗，又回到我原来的位置。她现在安安静静地躺在那儿，满脸都是泪水。身体的虚弱已经完全摧垮了她的精神：火爆脾气的凯瑟琳现在并不比一个哭哭啼啼的孩子强多少。

"我把自己关在这儿多久了？"她问，精神也突然恢复了。

"那天是星期一晚上，"我答道："现在是星期四晚上，或者不如说是星期五早上。"

"什么！还是这个星期？"她叫了

more. I remember being in the parlour after they had quarrelled, and Edgar being cruelly provoking, and me running into this room desperate. As soon as ever I had barred the door, utter blackness overwhelmed me, and I fell on the floor. I couldn't explain to Edgar how certain I felt of having a fit, or going raging mad, if he persisted in teasing me! I had no command of tongue, or brain, and he did not guess my agony, perhaps: it barely left me sense to try to escape from him and his voice. Before I recovered sufficiently to see and hear, it began to be dawn, and, Nelly, I'll tell you what I thought, and what has kept recurring and recurring till I feared for my reason. I thought as I lay there, with my head against that table leg, and my eyes dimly discerning the grey square of the window, that I was enclosed in the oak-panelled bed at home; and my heart ached with some great grief which, just waking, I could not recollect. I pondered, and worried myself to discover what it could be, and, most strangely, the whole last seven years of my life grew a blank! I did not recall that they had been at all. I was a child; my father was just buried, and my misery arose from the separation that Hindley had ordered between me and Heathcliff. I was laid alone, for the first time; and, rousing from a dismal dose after a night of weeping, I lifted my hand to push the panels aside: it struck the tabletop! I swept it along the carpet, and then memory burst in: my late anguish was swallowed in a paroxysm of despair. I cannot say why I felt so wildly wretched: it must have been temporary derangement, for there is scarcely cause—But, supposing at twelve years old, I had been wrenched from the Heights,

起来。"就这么短短几天?"

"仅仅靠冷水和火爆脾气维生,这也够长的了。"我说。

"唉,我感觉好像过了不知有多久"她怀疑地嘟囔着,"一定不止这么多天。我记得他们翻脸之后,我还呆在客厅里,埃德加狠心地用话伤害我,我就拚命跑到这个房间里。我刚闩上门,黑暗就涌来,把我淹没,我随即就昏倒在地板上。我已经没有能力向埃德加解释了。我真真切切地感到,要是他惹我生气,我一定会旧病复发或者发疯的!我的舌头和脑袋已经不听使唤,他也许根本就没有想我的痛苦有多深,我只想要避开他和他的声音。在我的听力和视力还没有完全恢复的时候,天就亮了。内莉,让我告诉你我当时到底在想什么,还有,什么念头一直萦绕在我脑海里,搞得我担心自己会发疯。我躺在那儿,头顶着桌腿,眼睛还能模模糊糊地分辨出灰蒙蒙的窗玻璃,我以为我是在家里那张橡木大床上。我的心由于极度的忧伤而痛苦得要命。可是我一醒过来,就又想不起来是为了什么而忧伤了。我想着,苦苦地思索,想搞清楚到底是为什么。最奇怪的是,我过去整整七年的生活变成了一张白纸!我根本无法确信是否有过这段生活。我当时还是个孩子,父亲的葬礼刚刚结束,由于辛德雷命令我和希斯克利夫分开,我生活中第一次有了痛苦。我第一次孤零零地被扔在一边。哭了一整夜之后,我又迷迷糊糊地睡了一觉才醒来。醒来之后,我伸手想把围板推开,谁知我的手竟碰到了桌面!我顺着桌毯一拂,记忆突然自己

and every early association, and my all in all, as Heathcliff was at that time, and been converted at a stroke into Mrs. Linton, the lady of Thrushcross Grange, and the wife of a stranger: an exile, and outcast, thenceforth, from what had been my world—You may fancy a glimpse of the abyss where I grovelled! Shake your head as you will, Nelly, *you* have helped to unsettle me! You should have spoken to Edgar, indeed you should, and compelled him to leave me quiet! Oh, I'm burning! I wish I were out of doors! I wish I were a girl again, half savage and hardy, and free... and laughing at injuries, not maddening under them! Why am I so changed? why does my blood rush into a hell of tumult at a few words? I'm sure I should be myself were I once among the heather on those hills. Open the window again wide: fasten it open! Quick, why don't you move?"

"Because I won't give you your death of cold," I answered.

"You won't give me a chance of life, you mean," she said sullenly. "However, I'm not helpless yet; I'll open it myself."

And sliding from the bed before I could hinder her, she crossed the room, walking very uncertainly, threw it back, and bent out, careless of the frosty air that cut about her shoulders as keen as a knife. I entreated, and finally attempted to force her to retire. But I soon found her delirious strength much surpassed mine (she *was* delirious, I became convinced by her subsequent actions and ravings). There was no moon, and everything beneath lay in misty darkness: not a light gleamed from any house, far or near—all had been extinguished long a-

就恢复了：我原来的悲伤突然就被一阵绝望给吞没。我说不出为什么觉得自己这么可怜：肯定是神经有问题了，因为根本就没有任何原因。可是，如果你可以想像在十二岁的时候我就被迫离开呼啸山庄，跟童年的一切断绝联系，包括我当时的一切——希斯克利夫，而突然就变成林顿太太，画眉田庄的女主人，一个陌生人的妻子，从此我就成了原来的小世界里的局外人，一个流浪者，那么你就可以想像我沉沦的深渊是什么样子！你尽管摇头吧，随便你，内莉，你也帮他让我无法安宁！你应该去对埃德加说明，你真的应该去，叫他千万不要惹我！啊，我被惹火了！但愿我现在是在外面！但愿我重新变成女孩子，粗野、勇敢、自由，笑着面对任何伤害，绝不会被它们逼得发疯！为什么我会变成现在这样？为什么几句话就让我激动得血气上涌？我保证如果让我去那边山上的石楠丛里，我就会恢复的。再把窗户开得大一点，完全打开，再把窗钩给钩上！快，你为什么不动呀？"

"因为我不想让你被冻死，"我回答。

"你的意思是你想夺走给我继续活下去的机会，"她愤怒地说："无论如何，我还能动，我自己来。"

我还来不及拦住她，她已经从床上滑下来，跟跟跄跄地从房间这头走到那头，一把推开窗户，身子就探了出去，毫不在意那凛冽的寒风像锋利的刀子一样割着她的肩膀。我恳求着，最后打算强行把她拉回来。可我很快意识到，精神错乱的凯瑟琳力气远远超过我（从她后来地胡言乱语和

go; and those at Wuthering Heights were never visible—still she asserted she caught their shining.

"Look!" she cried eagerly, "that's my room with the candle in it, and the trees swaying before it. . . and the other candle is in Joseph's garret. . . Joseph sits up late, doesn't he? He's waiting till I come home that he may lock the gate. . . Well, he'll wait a while yet. It's a rough journey, and a sad heart to travel it; and we must pass by Gimmerton Kirk[①], to get that journey! We've braved its ghosts often together, and dared each other to stand among the graves and ask them to come. . . But Heathcliff, if I dare you now, will you venture? I-f you do, I'll keep you. I'll not lie there by myself: they may bury me twelve feet deep, and throw the church down over me, but I won't rest till you are with me. I never will!"

She paused, and resumed with a strange smile."He's considering—he'd rather I'd come to him! Find a way, then! not through that Kirkyard. . . You are slow! Be content, you always followed me!"

Perceiving it vain to argue against her insanity, I was planning how I could reach something to wrap about her, without quitting my hold of herself, for I could not trust her alone by the gaping lattice, when, to my consternation, I heard the rattle of the door-handle, and Mr. Linton entered. He had only then come from the library; and, in passing through the lobby, had noticed our talking and been attracted by curiosity, or fear, to examine what it signified, at that late hour.

---

① 教堂旁边有墓地,所以凯瑟琳会害怕经过教堂。

举止,我确信她已经神经错乱了)。外面没有月亮,地上的一切都笼罩在朦朦胧胧的黑暗之中。远近没有一间亮着灯的房子——所有的灯光早就熄灭了:呼啸山庄的灯光从这里是压根也看不到的——可她硬说看见了那儿的灯光。

"看!"她热切地喊道,"那就是我的房间,里面亮着蜡烛,树枝在窗前摇晃,约瑟夫的阁楼里也亮着一支蜡烛呢……约瑟夫夜里是不睡的,不是吗? 他是在等我回家,好把大门给锁上。好吧,他还得再等一会呢。那段路不好走,每次走都心惊胆战。而且我们走那段路肯定要经过吉默顿教堂! 我们以前经常一起在那儿利用鬼魂来比胆量,站在那些坟墓中间叫他们过来。可是,希斯克利夫,如果我现在跟你比,你还敢吗? 要是你敢,我就奉陪到底。我不愿一个人躺在那里:他们会把我埋到十二英尺深的地底下的,还会把一座教堂压在我身上。要是你不跟我在一起,我是不会安息的,永远不会!"

她停住了,接着又继续说,带着一丝古怪的微笑:"他正在思考呢——他要我去找他! 那就另找一条路呀! 我不要穿过那个教堂墓地。你太慢了! 这下满意了吧,你一直跟着我的呀!"

意识到跟她的疯狂争执是件徒劳的事情,我就开始考虑如何才能找些东西给她裹上,同时又不放开她。因为我不敢放任她一个人把身子探出敞开的窗子。这时,我听到门把手转动的声音,大吃一惊,林顿先生进来

"Oh, sir!" I cried, checking the exclamation risen to his lips at the sight which met him, and the bleak atmosphere of the chamber. "My poor Mistress is ill, and she quite masters me: I cannot manage her at all; pray, come and persuade her to go to bed. Forget your anger, for she's hard to guide any way but her own."

"Catherine ill?" he said, hastening to us. "Shut the window, Ellen! Catherine! why…"

He was silent; the haggardness of Mrs. Linton's appearance smote him speechless, and he could only glance from her to me in horrified astonishment.

"She's been fretting here," I continued, "and eating scarcely anything, and never complaining: she would admit none of us till this evening, and so we couldn't inform you of her state, as we were not aware of it ourselves; but it is nothing."

I felt I uttered my explanations awkwardly; the master frowned. "It is nothing, is it, Ellen Dean?" he said sternly. "You shall account more clearly for keeping me ignorant of this!" And he took his wife in his arms, and looked at her with anguish.

At first she gave him no glance of recognition: he was invisible to her abstracted gaze. The delirium was not fixed, however; having weaned her eyes from contemplating the outer darkness, by degrees she centred her attention on him, and discovered who it was that held her.

"Ah! you are come, are you, Edgar Linton?" she said with angry animation… "You are one of those things that are ever found when least wanted, and when you are wanted, never! I suppose we shall have plenty of lamenta-

第十二章

了。原来他刚刚走出书房，经过走廊时，听到我们的说话，受到好奇心或恐惧感的影响，他决定进来看看我们深更半夜的有什么话好说。

"啊，先生！"我喊道，他看到室内的情形和那狂涌进来的凛冽的寒风，正要大声惊叫，却被我给拦住了。"我可怜的女主人病了，她力气比我大得多！我一点儿也没法照顾她。求求你来，快劝劝她，让她赶紧上床。别再生她的气了，她很任性，听不下别人的话。"

"凯瑟琳病了？"他惊道，连忙走上前来。"把窗子关上，艾伦！凯瑟琳！为什么？"

他说不下去了。林顿太太憔悴的神色给了他巨大的打击，他一个字都吐不出来，能做的只是惊恐地看看她，又看看我。

"她一直在这儿生闷气呢，"我接着说，"什么东西都没吃，也从不抱怨：她不允许任何人进来，直到今天晚上，才让我来这里。所以我们也无法向你通报她的状况，因为我们自己也没意识到。不过，这也没什么。"

我觉得我的解释非常笨拙；主人皱紧了眉头。"这没什么，是吗，艾伦·迪安？"他厉声说道。"日后你得给我说清楚，为什么把我蒙在鼓里！"说完，他把妻子搂在怀里，伤心欲绝地望着她。

一开始，她看着他，好像没看到似的：在她那空洞的眼神里，他好像是透明的。不过，她的神经错乱并不是一直持续的。她放弃继续凝视外面的黑暗了，渐渐地把注意力集中到他身上，认出了搂住她的到底是谁。

tions now. . . I see we shall. . . but they can't keep me from my narrow home out yonder: my resting-place, where I'm bound before spring is over! There it is: not among the Lintons, mind, under the chapel-roof, but in the open air, with a headstone; and you may please yourself, whether you go to them or come to me!"

"Catherine, what have you done?" commenced the master. "Am I nothing to you any more? Do you love that wretch Heath—"

"Hush!" cried Mrs. Linton. "Hush, this moment! You mention that name and I end the matter instantly, by a spring from the window! What you touch at present you may have; but my soul will be on that hill-top before you lay hands on me again. I don't want you, Edgar: I'm past wanting you. Return to your books. I'm glad you possess a consolation, for all you had in me is gone."

"Her mind wanders, sir," I interposed. "She has been talking nonsense the whole evening; but, let her have quiet, and proper attendance, and she'll rally. . . Hereafter, we must be cautious how we vex her."

"I desire no further advice from you," answered Mr. Linton. "You knew your mistress's nature, and you encouraged me to harass her. And not to give me one hint of how she has been these three days! It was heartless! Months of sickness could not cause such a change!"

I began to defend myself, thinking it too bad to be blamed for another's wicked waywardness. "I knew Mrs. Linton's nature to be headstrong and domineering," cried I; "but I didn't know that you wished to foster her fierce

"啊！你终于来了，是吗，埃德加·林顿？"她说，愤怒而激动。"你就是那种东西，不需要的时候总在眼前出现，需要的时候却怎么也找不着！我想我们将要有许多悲痛的事啦——我看出我们会有的——不过这些悲伤是不能拦住我去那边的，我那狭小的家——我安息的地方。我挨不过春天了，在那之前我就会去那儿的。就是那儿，注意，不是在教堂里林顿家族的中间，而是在露天旷野里，只有一块墓碑。你愿意去他们那儿，还是到我这儿来，随你的便！"

"凯瑟琳，你都做了什么？"主人说。"难道我在你心里已经没有任何地位了吗？你是不是爱那个混蛋希斯——"

"别说了！"林顿太太大声喊道。"马上给我住口！你胆敢再提那个名字，我就从窗户里跳出去，让这一切立刻结束！眼前你抱着的，还算是你的，可等不到你再把手放在我身上的时候，我的灵魂就已经飞到那边的小山顶啦。我不需要你，埃德加，我需要你的时候已经过去了。回到你的书本里去吧。我很高兴你还可以找到一个安慰你的地方，因为你在我心里已经什么都不剩下了。"

"她心智已经迷失了，先生。"我插嘴说。"她已经说了一个晚上的胡话，让她安静一会，然后好好照顾她，她就会好起来的。从今以后，我们一定要小心，千万不要再惹她生气了。"

"我不需要你的任何劝告。"林顿先生回答。"你明知道你的女主人的脾气，还鼓动我去惹她生气。这三天她是怎么过来的，你也不给我任何暗

temper! I didn't know that, to humour her, I should wink at Mr. Heathcliff. I performed the duty of a faithful servant in telling you, and I have got a faithful servant's wages! Well, it will teach me to be careful next time. Next time you may gather intelligence for yourself!"

"The next time you bring a tale to me, you shall quit my service, Ellen Dean," he replied.

"You'd rather hear nothing about it, I suppose, then, Mr. Linton?" said I. "Heathcliff has your permission to come a-courting to Miss, and to drop in at every opportunity your absence offers, on purpose to poison the mistress against you?"

Confused as Catherine was, her wits were alert at applying our conversation.

"Ah! Nelly has played traitor," she exclaimed, passionately. "Nelly is my hidden enemy. You witch! So you do seek elf-bolts to hurt us! Let me go, and I'll make her rue! I'll make her howl a recantation!"

A maniac's fury kindled under her brows; she struggled desperately to disengage herself from Linton's arms. I felt no inclination to tarry the event; and, resolving to seek medical aid on my own responsibility, I quitted the chamber.

In passing the garden to reach the road, at a place where a bridle hook is driven into the wall, I saw something white moved irregularly, evidently by another agent than the wind. Notwithstanding my hurry, I staid to examine it, lest ever after I should have the conviction impressed on my imagination that it was a creature of the other world. My surprise and perplexity were great to discover, by touch more than vision, Miss Isabella's springer, Fanny, suspended to a handkerchief, and nearly at its

示！你真是没心没肺的东西！就是病上几个月也不能有这么大的变化呀！"

我开始为我自己辩解。别人蛮不讲理、任性，却要我背黑锅，这太过分了。"我知道林顿太太顽固又任性，"我喊叫，"可我不知道是你想要培养她的暴烈性格！我不知道，为了取悦她，我就得假装没看见希斯克利夫先生。我尽了一个忠心仆人的责任去告诉你，我现在已经得到这样的报酬啦，好吧，我得到教训了，下次可要小心点了。下次你想知道什么事，就自己去去打听吧！"

"下次你要是再在我面前搬弄是非，你就准备收拾东西走人吧，艾伦·迪安。"他回答。

"这么说，林顿先生，我想这件事你还是宁愿被蒙在鼓里吧？"我说，"希斯克利夫是得到你的允许来向小姐求爱的，而每次你不在家，他就溜进来，目的就是唆使女主人反对你，是吧？"

凯瑟琳虽然糊涂着，但她的神智还是对我们的谈话很警觉。

"啊！内莉是叛徒，"她激动地大叫起来。"内莉是我暗处的敌人。你这个老巫婆！你真的在寻找小精灵用的石镞来伤害我们呀！放开我，我要叫她后悔！我要让她嚎叫着收回她说的话！"

熊熊的怒火在她眉毛下燃烧起来。她拼命挣扎着，想从林顿先生的胳膊里挣脱出来。我没有兴趣等着事情恶化，决定自己负责去找医生来帮忙，于是就离开了房间。

我一路走过花园，来到大路上，在墙上一个钉了马缰绳钩子的地方，

last gasp. I quickly released the animal, and lifted it into the garden. I had seen it follow its mistress up-stairs, when she went to bed; and wondered much how it could have got out there, and what mischievous person had treated it so. While untying the knot round the hook, it seemed to me that I repeatedly caught the beat of horses' feet galloping at some distance; but there were such a number of things to occupy my reflections that I hardly gave the circumstance a thought: though it was a strange sound, in that place, at two o'clock in the morning.

Mr. Kenneth was fortunately just issuing from his house to see a patient in the village as I came up the street; and my account of Catherine Linton's malady induced him to accompany me back immediately. He was a plain rough man; and he made no scruple to speak his doubts of her surviving this second attack; unless she were more submissive to his directions than she had shown herself before.

"Nelly Dean," said he, "I can't help fancying there's an extra cause for this. What has there been to do at the Grange? We've odd reports up here. A stout, hearty lass like Catherine does not fall ill for a trifle; and that sort of people should not either. It's hard work bringing them through fevers, and such things. How did it begin?"

"The master will inform you," I answered; "but you are acquainted with the Earnshaws' violent dispositions, and Mrs. Linton caps them all. I may say this; it commenced in a quarrel. She was struck during a tempest of passion with a kind of fit. That's her account, at least; for she flew off in the height of it, and

看见一团白的东西在乱动，很显然那不是风吹的结果，而是另一个什么东西在使它动。尽管我忙着赶路，但还是停下来看个究竟，免得日后在我想像中留下一个阴影，以为那是个鬼魂呢。我的惊讶和看不清楚让我碰了它一下，发现那是伊莎贝拉的小狗芬妮，被一条手帕吊着，只剩下最后一口气了。我赶快把它放开，抱到花园里去。伊莎贝拉睡觉的时候，我看到它跟着上楼的。我很诧异，它怎么会到外面来，又是哪个坏蛋这样对待它。在解钩子上的结的时候，我好像多次听见远处有奔跑的马蹄声；可我脑子里这么一大堆乌七八糟的事，也没有功夫稍微关注一下，尽管在凌晨两点钟，在那样的地方，这样的声音是非常奇怪的。

我刚到街上，就非常幸运的碰到了肯尼斯先生刚从家里出来，他是去给村里一个病人看病。我说了凯瑟琳·林顿的情况，他马上就陪我往回走。他是一个有话直说的人，直截了当地说出他很怀疑她是否能抵挡住病魔的第二次打击，除非她对他的话言听计从，不要再像以前那样。

"内莉·迪安，"他说，"我总觉得这场病肯定还有别的原因。最近田庄里出了什么事没有？我们这儿有一些奇怪的传闻。一个像凯瑟琳那样身体健壮、精神饱满的女人是不会为了一点小事就病倒的。那样的人也本不该是这个样子。要使她在这次热病中痊愈是一件很不容易的事。这次是怎么发病的？"

"主人会告诉你，"我回答，"恩肖家的火爆脾气你可是知道的，林顿太

locked herself up. Afterwards, she refused to eat, and now she alternately raves and remains in a half-dream; knowing those about her, but having her mind filled with all sorts of strange ideas and illusions."

"Mr. Linton will be sorry?" observed Kenneth, interrogatively.

"Sorry? he'll break his heart should anything happen!" I replied. "Don't alarm him more than necessary."

"Well, I told him to beware," said my companion;"and he must bide the consequences of neglecting my warning! Hasn't he been thick with Mr. Heathcliff lately?"

"Heathcliff frequently visits at the Grange," answered I, "though more on the strength of the mistress having known him when a boy, than because the master likes his company. At present, he's discharged from the trouble of calling; owing to some presumptuous aspirations after Miss Linton which he manifested. I hardly think he'll be taken in again."

"And does Miss Linton turn a cold shoulder on him?" was the doctor's next question.

"I'm not in her confidence," returned I, reluctant to continue the subject.

"No, she's a sly one," he remarked, shaking his head."She keeps her own counsel! But she's a real little fool. I have it from good authority, that, last night (and a pretty night it was!) she and Heathcliff were walking in the plantation at the back of your house, above two hours; and he pressed her not to go in again, but just mount his horse and away with him! My informant said she could only put him off by pledging her word of honour to be prepared on their first meeting after that: when it was to

太更是出类拔萃。我可以告诉你的是，这是由一场口角引起的。她大发雷霆，随后就像发狂似的昏了过去。至少，这是她自己的说法；因为她在吵得最激烈的时候跑了出去，把她自己锁在房间里。后来，她就一直不肯吃东西，现在她一会乱说胡话，一会儿又进入半昏迷状态。周围的人她都认识，不过心里满是各种各样奇怪的念头和幻觉。"

"林顿先生一定非常难过吧？"肯尼斯带着询问的口吻说。

"难过？要是真的发生了什么事，他的心都会碎的！"我回答说，"如果不是真的有必要，就不要吓唬他了。"

"唉，我早就提醒他要多加小心，"我的同行者说，"他没有把我的警告放在心上，这样的后果是肯定会到来的！最近他和希斯克利夫先生不是还挺友好的吗？"

"希斯克利夫常来田庄，"我回答，"但多半是因为女主人的缘故。他俩从小就熟识，倒并不一定是因为主人欢迎他来做伴。目前他是来不了了，因为他竟然对林顿小姐动起了歪脑筋。我看他以后再也别想踏进大门了。"

"林顿小姐是不是对他不理不睬呢？"医生又问。

"我可不是她信得过的人。"我回答，不愿把这件事继续谈下去。

"不，她可淘气的很，"他一边摇头，一边感慨。"她一直有自己的想法！可她是个真正的小傻瓜。从我得到的可靠消息说，昨天夜里（真是倒霉的一夜呀！）她和希斯克利夫在你们屋后的园子里散步散了两个多小时。他硬要她不要再进屋，干脆骑上

be, he didn't hear; but you urge Mr. Linton to look sharp!"

This news filled me with fresh fears; I outstripped Kenneth, and ran most of the way back. The little dog was yelping in the garden yet. I spared a minute to open the gate for it, but instead of going to the house door, it coursed up and down snuffing the grass, and would have escaped to the road, had I not seized and conveyed it in with me. On ascending to Isabella's room, my suspicions were confirmed: it was empty. Had I been a few hours sooner, Mrs. Linton's illness might have arrested her rash step. But what could be done now? There was a bare possibility of overtaking them if I pursued instantly. *I* could not pursue them, however; and I dare not rouse the family, and fill the place with confusion; still less unfold the business to my master, absorbed as he was in his present calamity, and having no heart to spare for a second grief! I saw nothing for it but to hold my tongue, and suffer matters to take their course; and Kenneth being arrived, I went with a badly composed countenance to announce him. Catherine lay in a troubled sleep: her husband had succeeded in soothing the access of frenzy; he now hung over her pillow, watching every shade, and every change of her painfully expressive features.

The doctor, on examining the case for himself, spoke hopefully to him of its having a favourable termination, if we could only preserve around her perfect and constant tranquillity. To me, he signified the threatening danger was not so much death, as permanent alienation of intellect.

I did not close my eyes that night, nor did

马跟他一块走算了！据向我报告的人说，她认真地保证，说要准备一下，下次再见面时就跟他走，这才把他打发了——至于下次到底是哪天，那个人没有听见，不过你得提醒林顿先生提防着点！"

这个消息使我又有了新的恐惧，我把肯尼斯抛在老后，急忙赶回田庄，大部分路几乎都是用跑的。小狗还在花园里狂叫着。我停下一小会儿，给它开了门，可它怎么也不进屋，只是来回在草地上嗅，要不是我把它给抓住，抱进去，它还要跑到大路上去呢。我跑到楼上，走到伊莎贝拉的房间一看，怀疑终于被证实了：那里一个人影都没有。要是我早来几个小时，林顿太太的病也许会让她不这么鲁莽。可现在还能有什么办法呢？就算我立刻去追，也不一定追得上他们。总而言之，我是不能去追他们的。而我也不敢惊动这家人，搞得人心惶惶；更不敢把这件事告诉我的主人，眼前的事已经够他烦的了，再也受不了再一次的打击！除了一声不吭，听天由命之外，我也实在想不出什么办法；肯尼斯已经来了，我带着一副勉强镇定下来的神色通报。凯瑟琳正在睡觉，但在床上辗转反侧。她的丈夫成功地让她从过分的狂躁中平静下来。现在他正弯身守在她的枕边，仔细地看着她痛苦的脸上每一丝的表情和每一分的变化。

医生给病人检查病情之后，很有希望地跟他说，只要我们给她维持完全平静的环境，病就有希望好转。但他向我暗示，凯瑟琳最大的危险其实倒不是死亡，而是永久性的神经失常。

Mr. Linton; indeed, we never went to bed; and the servants were all up long before the usual hour, moving through the house with stealthy tread, and exchanging whispers as they encountered each other in their vocations. Every one was active, but Miss Isabella; and they began to remark how sound she slept: her brother, too, asked if she had risen, and seemed impatient for her presence, and hurt that she showed so little anxiety for her sister-in-law. I trembled lest he should send me to call her; but I was spared the pain of being the first proclaimant of her flight. One of the maids, a thoughtless girl, who had been on an early errand to Gimmerton, came panting up stairs, open-mouthed, and dashed into the chamber, crying—

"Oh, dear, dear! What mun we have next? Master, master, our young lady—"

"Hold your noise!" cried I hastily, enraged at her clamorous manner.

"Speak lower, Mary—What is the matter?" said Mr. Linton. "What ails your young lady?"

"She's gone, she's gone! Yon' Heathcliff's run off wi' her!" gasped the girl.

"That is not true!" exclaimed Linton, rising in agitation. "It cannot be: how has the idea entered your head? Ellen Dean, go and seek her. It is incredible: it cannot be."

As he spoke he took the servant to the door, and then repeated his demand to know her reasons for such an assertion.

"Why, I met on the road a lad that fetches milk here," she stammered, "and he asked whether we wern't in trouble at the Grange. I thought he meant for missis's sickness, so I answered, yes. Then says he, 'they's somebody gone after 'em, I guess?' I stared. He saw I knew naught about it, and he told how a gentleman and lady had stopped to have a horse's shoe fastened at a blacksmith's shop, two miles out of Gimmerton, not very long after midnight! and how the blacksmith's lass had got up to spy who they were: she knew them both directly. And she noticed the man—Heathcliff it was, she felt certain, nob'dy could mistake him, besides—put a sovereign in her father's hand for payment. The lady had a cloak about her face; but having desired a sup of water, while she drank, it fell back, and she saw her very plain. Heathcliff held both bridles as they rode on, and they set their faces from the village, and went as fast as the rough roads would let them. The lass said nothing to her father, but she told it all over Gimmerton this morning."

I ran and peeped, for form's sake, into Isabella's room; confirming, when I returned, the servant's statement. Mr. Linton had resumed his seat by the bed; on my re-entrance, he raised his eyes, read the meaning of my blank aspect, and dropped them without giving an order, or uttering a word.

"Are we to try any measures for overtaking and bringing her back," I inquired. "How should we do?"

"She went of her own accord," answered the master; "she had a right to go if she pleased. Trouble me no more about her. Hereafter she is only my sister in name: not because I disown her but because she has disowned me."

And that was all he said on the subject: he did not make a single inquiry further, nor men-

答,是啊。接着他就说,'那我猜应该有人去追他们了吧?'我呆住了。他看出我根本不知道那事,便告诉我说,昨儿午夜后没多久,有位先生和一位小姐路过离吉默顿两英里远的一个铁匠铺,停下来在那儿钉马掌!刚好那铁匠家的女儿起来偷偷看他们到底是谁。她一下就认出他们来。她注意到那个男的——是希斯克利夫,她可以肯定,没人会把他认错——他交了一个金镑在她父亲手里。那位小姐的脸被斗篷遮着;不过她很想喝水,喝水的时候,斗篷滑到了后面,这会儿那个铁匠女儿看得清清楚楚。之后,他们骑马继续向前走。希斯克利夫抓着两匹马的缰绳,他们都把脸别了过去,背着村子那一面。而且在那高低不平的路上以最快速度狂奔。那姑娘什么都没有跟她父亲说,可是今天早上,她把这事儿传遍了整个吉默顿。"

为了走个过场,我急忙跑到伊莎贝拉的房间看了看;然后回来证实了女仆的话。林顿先生已经坐回床边他的椅子上了。我再进来时,他抬起眼睛,从我呆呆的表情中看出了一切,便垂下眼睛,什么都没有吩咐,连一个字都没有。

"我们要不要去把她追回来?"我问道。"我们该怎么办呢?"

"是她自愿离开的,"主人回答,"如果她高兴,她有权离开。不要再拿她来烦我了。从今以后她只在名义上是我妹妹;不是我不认她,是她不认我。"

那就是他对这件事所说的所有的话:连一句都没有多问,或者以任何方

tion her in any way, except directing me to send what property she had in the house to her fresh home, wherever it was, when I knew it.

式提到过她,除了吩咐我说,不管在哪儿,不管什么时候,如果我知道了她的新家,就把她在家里的所有东西都给她送过去。

Chapter 13
第十三章

For two months the fugitives remained absent; in those two months, Mrs. Linton encountered and conquered the worst shock of what was denominated a brain fever. No other could have nursed an only child more devotedly than Edgar tended her. Day and night he was watching and patiently enduring all the annoyances that irritable nerves and a shaken reason could inflict; and, though Kenneth remarked that what he saved from the grave would only recompense his care by forming the source of constant future anxiety—in fact, that his health and strength were being sacrificed to preserve a mere ruin of humanity—he knew no limits in gratitude and joy when Catherine's life was declared out of danger; and hour after hour he would sit beside her, tracing the gradual return to bodily health, and flattering his too sanguine hopes with the illusion that her mind would settle back to its right balance also, and she would soon be entirely her former self.

两个月过去了,那对私奔的人一点消息也没有。在这两个月中,林顿太太受到了一种叫做脑膜炎的凶险疾病的侵袭,但总算挺过了最危险的时期。在此期间,埃德加照料林顿太太的尽心程度,就是一个做母亲的看护自己的独生子也比不上。他夜以继日地守着林顿太太,耐心地忍受着这个精神错乱、丧失理智的人带给他的一切烦恼;尽管肯尼斯说,他把这个人从鬼门关那拉回来,只会成为他日后经常陷入焦虑的根源——事实上,他牺牲的健康和精力换来的只是一个废人——当得知凯瑟琳已经没有生命危险的时候,他心中充满的感激和欢乐简直是无限的;他长时间地坐在她的床边,亲眼看着她的健康逐渐恢复,而且满怀希望,一直幻想着她的神志也会恢复正常,不久就能完全恢复成以前一样。

The first time she left her chamber was at the commencement of the following March. Mr. Linton had put on her pillow, in the morning, a handful of golden crocuses; her eye, long stranger to any gleam of pleasure, caught them in waking, and shone delighted as she gathered them eagerly together.

"These are the earliest flowers at the Heights," she exclaimed. "They remind me of soft thaw winds, and warm sunshine, and nearly melted snow. Edgar, is there not a south wind, and is not the snow almost gone?"

"The snow is quite gone down here, darling," replied her husband; "and I only see two white spots on the whole range of moors: the sky is blue, and the larks are singing, and the becks and brooks are all brim full. Catherine, last spring at this time, I was longing to have you under this roof: now, I wish you were a mile or two up those hills: the air blows so sweetly, I feel that it would cure you."

"I shall never be there, but once more," said the invalid; "and then you'll leave me, and I shall remain for ever. Next spring you'll long again to have me under this roof, and you'll look back and think you were happy today."

Linton lavished on her the kindest caresses, and tried to cheer her by the fondest words; but, vaguely regarding the flowers, she let the tears collect on her lashes and stream down her cheeks unheeding. We knew she was really better, and, therefore, decided that long confinement to a single place produced much of this despondency, and it might be partially removed by a change of scene. The master told me to light a fire in the many-weeks deserted parlour, and to set an easy chair in the sunshine by the

她第一次走出卧室是在那年三月初的时候。那天早上，林顿先生在她枕边放了一束金色的番红花。她的眼睛已经很久没有流露出欢乐的神采了，但那天她一醒来，看见这束花，就急急忙忙地把它们拢在一起，眼睛里露出了快乐的光彩。

"这是山庄上开花最早的花，"她叫了起来。"它们让我想起轻暖的和风，温柔的阳光，还有就要融尽的残雪。埃德加，外面是不是吹起了南风，雪融化了吗？"

"这儿的雪差不多全化掉了，亲爱的，"她丈夫回答。"在整个旷野上我只看到两个白点：天空非常蓝，百灵在歌唱，小河小溪里涨满了水。凯瑟琳，去年春天的这时候，我正巴望着把你迎进我家来呢；可现在，我倒希望你到一两英里外的那小山上去：风吹得这么和暖，我相信这能治好你的病。"

"我不会再去了，除非是最后一次，我去了就不会回来了，"病人说，"然后你就会离开我，我则会永远躺在那儿。明年春天，你又会想我，希望我到这个家来，你会想起过去，想起今天你还是幸福的。"

林顿先生给了她最温存的爱抚和最亲昵的话，想让她高兴起来。可她茫然地凝望着那些花，毫不在意地听任泪珠在睫毛上聚集，然后顺着双颊流下来。我们知道她的确好了一些，所以认为只是长期待在一个地方，她才会产生如此沮丧的情绪，要是换一个场所，也许就会好一些。主人吩咐我在那空了好几个星期的客厅里把炉火烧起来，然后在窗口的阳光下放一

window; and then he brought her down, and she sat a long while enjoying the genial heat, and, as we expected, revived by the objects round her: which, though familiar, were free from the dreary associations investing her hated sick-chamber. By evening, she seemed greatly exhausted; yet no arguments could persuade her to return to that apartment, and I had to arrange the parlour sofa for her bed, till another room could be prepared. To obviate the fatigue of mounting and descending the stairs, we fitted up this, where you lie at present: on the same floor with the parlour; and she was soon strong enough to move from one to the other, leaning on Edgar's arm. Ah, I thought myself, she might recover, so waited on as she was. And there was double cause to desire it, for on her existence depended that of another: we cherished the hope that in a little while, Mr. Linton's heart would be gladdened, and his lands secured from a stranger's gripe, by the birth of an heir.

I should mention that Isabella sent to her brother, some six weeks from her departure, a short note, announcing her marriage with Heathcliff. It appeared dry and cold; but at the bottom was dotted in with pencil an obscure apology, and an entreaty for kind remembrance and reconciliation, if her proceeding had offended him: asserting that she could not help it then, and being done, she had now no power to repeal it. Linton did not reply to this, I believe; and, in a fortnight more, I got a long letter which I considered odd, coming from the pen of a bride just out of the honeymoon. I'll read it: for I keep it yet. Any relic of the dead is precious, if they were valued living.

张椅子。他把林顿太太从楼上抱下来。她在那儿呆了很久,享受着舒适的温暖。正如我们预想的那样,四周的变化使她高兴了起来:虽然这些东西都是她再熟悉不过的,但毕竟使她摆脱了在可厌的病床上缠绕她的那些痛苦的联想。到了晚上,她看来好像十分疲惫,但是没法劝动她回卧室去。由于另外一个房间还没布置好,我只得先把客厅沙发铺好,让她睡着。为了不让她上下楼过于劳累,我们收拾了这个房间,就是你现在住着的这间,跟客厅在同一层楼。不久,她又恢复一点,可以扶着埃德加的胳膊从这间走到那间了。啊,我私下忖度,她得到这样的照顾,肯定会复原的。而且还有一个原因,是因为另一个小生命还在她的肚子里;我们都暗暗希望林顿先生不久就会心花怒放,他的土地将因此而后继有人,而不至于落入一个陌生人之手。

有一件事,我在这里应该提一提:伊莎贝拉在出走大约六个星期后,给她哥哥寄了一封短信,宣布她已经跟希斯克利夫结婚了。信写得很冷淡,不过在信的下面用铅笔写了隐约有道歉意思的话,说要是她的行为得罪了他,希望能看在兄妹的情分上原谅她;说她当时不得不这样做,事已至此,无法回头。我认为林顿先生没有给她回信。又过了两个多星期,我收到了她的一封长信,这信来自一个刚度完蜜月的新娘,我觉得里面透着古怪。现在我来把这封信念一遍,因为我还一直保存着它呢。死者的任何遗物都是珍贵的,要是他们生前就

Dear Ellen, it begins.

I came last night to Wuthering Heights, and heard, for the first time, that Catherine has been, and is yet, very ill. I must not write to her, I suppose, and my brother is either too angry or too distressed to answer what I send him. Still, I must write to somebody, and the only choice left me is you.

Inform Edgar that I'd give the world to see his face again-that my heart returned to Thrushcross Grange in twenty-four hours after I left it, and is there at this moment, full of warm feelings for him, and Catherine! *I can't follow it though*—(those words are underlined) they need not expect me, and they may draw what conclusions they please; taking care, however, to lay nothing at the door of my weak will or deficient affection.

The remainder of the letter is for yourself alone. I want to ask you two questions; the first is—How did you contrive to preserve the common sympathies of human nature when you resided here? I cannot recognise any sentiment which those around share with me.

The second question, I have great interest in; it is this—Is Mr. Heathcliff a man? If so, is he mad? And if not, is he a devil? I shan't tell my reasons for making this inquiry; but I beseech you to explain, if you can, what I have married: that is, when you call to see me; and you must call, Ellen, very soon. Don't write but come, and bring me something from Edgar.

Now, you shall hear how I have been received in my new home, as I am led to imagine the Heights will be. It is to amuse myself that I dwell on such subjects as the lack of external comforts: they never occupy my thoughts, ex-

被人看重的话。

亲爱的艾伦，信开头这么写道——

我昨天晚上到了呼啸山庄，这才听说凯瑟琳生了一场大病，到现在还没有好。我想我是无论如何不能给她写信了，而我哥哥不是因为太生气，就是因为太难过，根本就不回我的信。可是，我一定要给什么人写封信，想来想去，就只有你合适了。

告诉埃德加，我非常想再见他一面，就是用整个世界来换也愿意——我离开还不到二十四小时，我的心就回到画眉田庄了。就是现在，我的心也还在那儿，对他，还有对凯瑟琳充满了炽烈的感情！可是我身不由己——(这几个字下面划了下划线)——他们用不着等我，他们爱下什么结论就下什么结论好了；可是，注意，不要怪我意志薄弱或者缺乏情感。

这封信剩下的部分是写给你一个人的。我要问你两个问题：第一——你当初住在这里的时候，是怎样来尽量保持着人与人之间通常的感情交流的？我看不出我和周围的人之间有什么共同的感受可以分享。

第二个问题是我非常关心的，就是——希斯克利夫是不是个人？如果是，那么他是疯了吗？如果不是，他是恶魔吗？问这话的原因我不想告诉你。可是如果你知道，我求你解释一下，我到底嫁给了一个什么东西——我的意思是，等你来看望我的时候，告诉我。而且，艾伦，你一定要尽快赶来。不要写信，直接来，把埃德加的话也捎来。

现在，你听听我这个新家是怎样招待我的吧——我不得不把呼啸山庄

cept at the moment when I miss them. I should laugh and dance for joy, if I found their absence was the total of my miseries, and the rest was an unnatural dream!

The sun set behind the Grange, as we turned on to the moors; by that, I judged it to be six o'clock; and my companion halted half-an-hour, to inspect the park, and the gardens, and, probably, the place itself, as well as he could; so it was dark when we dismounted in the paved yard of the farm-house, and your old fellow servant, Joseph, issued out to receive us by the light of a dip candle. He did it with a courtesy that redounded to his credit. His first act was to elevate his torch to a level with my face, squint malignantly, project his under lip, and turn away. Then he took the two horses, and led them into the stables; reappearing for the purpose of locking the outer gate, as if we lived in an ancient castle.

Heathcliff stayed to speak to him, and I entered the kitchen—a dingy, untidy hole; I dare say you would not know it, it is so changed since it was in your charge. By the fire stood a ruffianly child, strong in limb and dirty in garb, with a look of Catherine in his eye and about his mouth.

"This is Edgar's legal nephew," I reflected—"mine in a manner; I must shake hands, and—yes—I must kiss him. It is right to establish a good understanding at the beginning."

I approached, and, attempting to take his chubby fist, said—

"How do you do, my dear?"

He replied in a jargon I did not comprehend.

"Shall you and I be friends, Hareton?"

was my next essay at conversation.

An oath, and a threat to set Throttler on me if I did not "frame off" rewarded my perseverance.

"Hey, Throttler, lad!" whispered the little wretch, rousing a half-bred bull-dog from its lair in a comer. "Now, wilt tuh be ganging?" he asked authoritatively.

Love for my life urged a compliance; I stepped over the threshold to wait till the others should enter. Mr. Heathcliff was nowhere visible; and Joseph, whom I followed to the stables, and requested to accompany me in, after staring and muttering to himself, screwed up his nose and replied—

"Mim! mim! mim! Did iver Christian body hear owt like it? Minching un' munching! Hah can Aw tell whet ye say?"

"I say, I wish you to come with me into the house!" I cried, thinking him deaf, yet highly disgusted at his rudeness.

"Nor nuh me! Aw getten summut else to do," he answered, and continued his work; moving his lantern jaws meanwhile, and surveying my dress and countenance (the former a great deal too fine, but the latter, I'm sure, as sad as he could desire) with sovereign contempt.

I walked round the yard, and through a wicket, to another door, at which I took the liberty of knocking, in hopes some more civil servant might shew himself. After a short suspense, it was opened by a tall, gaunt man, without neckerchief, and otherwise extremely slovenly; his features were lost in masses of shaggy hair that hung on his shoulders; and *his* eyes, too, were like a ghostly Catherine's,

乎乎的小拳头,说:
"亲爱的,你好吗?"
他嚷了一句我听不懂的话。
"和我交个朋友怎样,哈里顿?"这是我第二次试图跟他说话。
我的坚持换来的回报就是一声咒骂,而且哈里顿威胁说,如果我不"滚开",就要叫勒头儿出来咬我。
"喂,勒头儿,伙计!"这小坏蛋低声唤道,一只杂种的斗牛狗被他从墙角的窝里唤了出来。"现在你走不走?"他盛气凌人地问道。
为了珍惜自己的生命,我只好听他的话。我退到门槛外面,等着别人进来。到处都找不到希斯克利夫的身影。我跟着约瑟夫来到马厩,想请他陪我进去。他先瞪着我,自言自语地咕哝着,接着就皱起鼻子回答:
"咪!咪!咪!哪个基督徒听到过有这样说话的?扭扭捏捏,装模作样!我怎么知道你在说什么?"
"我说,我想请你陪我到屋里去!"我喊着,以为他是个聋子,但他的无礼让我感到十分厌恶。
"我犯不着!而且我还有别的事要做呢,"他回答,继续干他的活。同时还摇晃着他那尖尖的下巴,用一种非常轻蔑的神色来打量我的衣着和容貌(衣服过于华丽了,但是容貌,我相信和他想像的一样惨)。
我绕过院子,穿过一个小门,来到另一个门前,我鼓足勇气敲了敲门,希望能碰到一个客气点的仆人。过了一会儿,一个高大而憔悴的男子把门打开了。他没戴围巾,全身上下的衣服都非常邋遢,他的脸被一直披到肩头的乱发遮住;他的眼睛就像变

with all their beauty annihilated.

"What's your business here?" he demanded, grimly. "Who are you?"

"My name was Isabella Linton," I replied. "You've seen me before, sir. I'm lately married to Mr. Heathcliff, and he has brought me here—I suppose by your permission."

"Is he come back, then?" asked the hermit, glaring like a hungry wolf.

"Yes—we came just now," I said; "but he left me by the kitchen door; and when I would have gone in, your little boy played sentinel over the place, and frightened me off by the help of a bull-dog."

"It's well the hellish villain has kept his word!" growled my future host, searching the darkness beyond me in expectation of discovering Heathcliff; and then he indulged in a soliloquy of execrations, and threats of what he would have done had the "fiend" deceived him.

I repented having tried this second entrance, and was almost inclined to slip away before he finished cursing, but ere I could execute that intention, he ordered me in, and shut and re-fastened the door. There was a great fire, and that was all the light in the huge apartment, whose floor had grown a uniform grey; and the once brilliant pewter dishes, which used to attract my gaze when I was a girl, partook of a similar obscurity, created by tarnish and dust. I inquired whether I might call the maid, and be conducted to a bed-room? Mr. Earnshaw vouchsafed no answer. He walked up and down, with his hands in his pockets, apparently quite forgetting my presence; and his abstraction was evidently so deep, and his whole aspect so misanthropical,

成鬼魂后的凯瑟琳的眼睛，原先所有的美一点都看不到了。

"你来这儿干吗？"他恶狠狠地问道。"你是谁？"

"我叫伊莎贝拉·林顿，"我回答。"先生，你以前见过我。我刚嫁给希斯克利夫先生，是他叫我带到这儿来的——我猜是已经得到了你的允许的。"

"这么说，他回来了？"这个隐士问道，像饿狼一样瞪着我。

"是的——我们刚刚一起到的，"我说，"不过他把我留在了厨房门口。我刚想进去的时候，你的小孩守在那儿，就像一个哨兵。他叫来一只斗牛狗，把我给吓跑了。"

"这该死的流氓，说话倒还挺讲信用的，不错！"我未来的房东大声嚷嚷着，朝着我身后的黑暗张望，希望能发现希斯克利夫。接着他又自言自语地诅咒一番，威胁说，如果那"恶魔"骗了他，他便要如何如何对付他。

我对于第二次进屋的尝试感到很后悔。在他结束诅咒之前，我已经想偷偷开溜了。可在我实施这个打算之前，他就命令我进去，然后把门关上，并且上了锁。屋子里炉火烧得很旺，这间大屋子里所有的光亮也就这点儿了，地板已经全部变成灰色；曾经吸引过还是小女孩的我的那些锃亮的白镴盘子，如今也都蒙上了污垢和灰尘，变得暗淡无光了。我问他是不是可以叫一个女仆送我到卧室去！恩肖先生没有回答我，只是在屋子里来来回回走着，手插在口袋里，很显然已经完全忘记了我的存在。看到他是那样心不在焉，灵魂出窍，还有那样一脸的愤世嫉俗，我不敢再去打扰

that I shrank from disturbing him again.

You'll not be surprised, Ellen, at my feeling particularly cheerless, seated in worse than solitude on that inhospitable hearth, and remembering that four miles distant lay my delightful home, containing the only people I loved on earth; and there might as well be the Atlantic to part us, instead of those four miles: I could not overpass them! I questioned with myself—where must I turn for comfort? and—mind you don't tell Edgar, or Catherine—above every sorrow beside, this rose pre-eminent: despair at finding nobody who could or would be my ally against Heathcliff! I had sought shelter at Wuthering Heights, almost gladly, because I was secured by that arrangement from living alone with him; but he knew the people we were coming amongst, and he did not fear their intermeddling.

I sat and thought a doleful time; the clock struck eight, and nine, and still my companion paced to and fro, his head bent on his breast, and perfectly silent, unless a groan or a bitter ejaculation forced itself out at intervals. I listened to detect a woman's voice in the house, and filled the interim with wild regrets and dismal anticipations, which, at last, spoke audibly in irrepressible sighing and weeping. I was not aware how openly I grieved, till Earnshaw halted opposite, in his measured walk, and gave me a stare of newly-awakened surprise. Taking advantage of his recovered attention, I exclaimed—

"I'm tired with my journey, and I want to go to bed! Where is the maid-servant? Direct me to her, as she won't come to me!"

"We have none," he answered; "you must

他。

艾伦，对我这种特别不快活的感觉你应该不会感到奇怪吧。坐在那光秃秃的壁炉旁，比孤独还要难受。想到四英里之外就是我的令人愉快的家，还住着我在世上最爱的人。而现在这四英里却不再是四英里了，简直就像大西洋一样把我们隔开，我再也越不过它了！我扪心自问——我该向哪儿寻求安慰呢？而且——千万不要告诉埃德加或凯瑟琳——撇开一切悲苦不谈，最重要的是：我该到哪儿找一个能够或是愿意和我一起来反对希斯克利夫的人呢！我感到绝望。我原来几乎是兴高采烈地来到呼啸山庄的，因为这样的话，我从此就可以不必与他单独过日子了。但他知道跟我们在一起的都是些什么样的人，他一点儿也不担心他们会管闲事。

我坐在那儿，脑子里胡思乱想着，挨着时间。时钟敲响了八点、九点，我的那位同伴仍然在来回踱步。他的头垂到胸前，一声不吭，只是偶尔发出一声呻吟或一声辛酸的叹息。我留心听着，想知道屋子里有没有女人的声音，我心里万分悔恨，充满了不妙的预感，终于我控制不住，出声地叹息着，并且哭了起来。我没想过自己是怎么当着别人面痛哭流涕起来的，直到踱着方步的恩肖在我面前停住了脚步，瞪着我，如梦初醒，非常惊讶。趁他恢复了注意力的时候，我就大声喊道：

"我路上走累了，想上床睡觉！女仆在哪里？要是她不肯来见我的话，就带我去找她好了！"

"我家没有女仆，"他回答，"你得

wait on yourself!"

"Where must I sleep, then?" I sobbed; I was beyond regarding selfrespect, weighed down by fatigue and wretchedness.

"Joseph will show you Heathcliff's chamber," said he;"open that door—he's in there."

I was going to obey, but he suddenly arrested me, and added in the strangest tone—

"Be so good as to turn your lock, and draw your bolt-don't omit it!"

"Well!" I said. "But why, Mr. Earnshaw?" I did not relish the notion of deliberately fastening myself in with Heathcliff.

"Look here!" he replied, pulling from his waistcoat a curiously constructed pistol, having a double-edged spring knife attached to the barrel."That's a great tempter to a desperate man, is it not? I cannot resist going up with this every night, and trying his door. If once I find it open, he's done for! I do it invariably, even though the minute before I have been recalling a hundred reasons that should make me refrain: it is some devil that urges me to thwart my own schemes by killing him— you fight against that devil for love as long as you may; when the time comes, not all the angels in heaven shall save him!"

I surveyed the weapon inquisitively; a hideous notion struck me: how powerful I should be possessing such an instrument! I took it from his hand, and touched the blade. He looked astonished at the expression my face assumed during a brief second: it was not horror, it was covetousness. He snatched the pistol back, jealously; shut the knife, and returned it to its concealment.

"I don't care if you tell him," said he."Put

第十三章

自己伺候自己!"

"那么,我该睡在哪儿呢?"我抽泣着,完全顾不得体面了,疲劳和狼狈已经夺走了我的自尊心。

"约瑟夫会领你到希斯克利夫的卧室去,"他说,"打开那扇门,他就在里面。"

我正要遵命行事,可他忽然喊住我,用最古怪的腔调跟我说:

"你最好把门锁上,上好门闩——别忘了!"

"可以!"我说。"但这是为什么呢,恩肖先生?"我并不欣赏特地把自己和希斯克利夫锁在一起这样的念头。

"瞧这儿!"他回答,从他的背心里拔出一把做得很特别的手枪,枪管上装着一把双刃的弹簧刀。"对一个绝望的人,这是件很诱人的东西,不是吗?每天晚上我都不能不带着这个上楼,我要试试他的门。如果有一次让我发现门是开着的,他可就完蛋了;即使一分钟之前我还想出一百条理由告诉我自己要克制,我也还是要这么做:一个魔鬼逼我推翻自己的计划,去杀他。你可以和魔鬼对着干,爱多久就多久;可是时间一到,所有的天使也救不了他!"

我好奇地注视着这武器。心中出然冒出一个可怕的念头:要是我有这么一件武器,我会变得多么强大。我从他手里拿过枪来,抚摸刀刃。我脸上一瞬间所流露出的表情使他大为惊讶:那表情不是恐怖,而是贪婪。他猜疑地急忙把手枪夺回去,合拢刀子,又放到原来藏它的地方。

"你就是去告诉他,我也不在

him on his guard, and watch for him. You know the terms we are on, I see: his danger does not shock you."

"What has Heathcliff done to you?" I asked. "In what has he wronged you, to warrant this appalling hatred? Wouldn't it be wiser to bid him quit the house?"

"No!" thundered Earnshaw; "should he offer to leave me, he's a dead man: persuade him to attempt it, and you are a murderess! Am I to lose *all*, without a chance of retrieval? Is Hareton to be a beggar? Oh, damnation! I *will* have it back: and I'll have *his* gold too: and then his blood; and hell shall have his soul! It will be ten times blacker with that guest than ever it was before!"

You've acquainted me, Ellen, with your old master's habits. He is clearly on the verge of madness: he was so last night at least I shuddered to be near him, and thought on the servant's ill-bred moroseness as comparatively agreeable. He now recommenced his moody walk, and I raised the latch, and escaped into the kitchen. Joseph was bending over the fire, peering into a large pan that swung above it; and a wooden bowl of oatmeal stood on the settle close by. The contents of the pan began to boil, and he turned to plunge his hand into the bowl; I conjectured that this preparation was probably for our supper, and, being hungry, I resolved it should be eatable; so, crying out sharply, "I'll make the porridge!" I removed the vessel out of his reach, and proceeded to take off my hat and riding habit. "Mr. Earnshaw," I continued, "directs me to wait on myself: I will. I'm not going to act the lady among you, for fear I should starve."

乎,"他说。"叫他多提防点儿,注意替他看着。我看得出来,你知道我们的关系:他处于危险之中,可你一点儿也不惊慌。"

"希斯克利夫对你做了什么?"我问道。"他什么地方得罪你了,让你这样对他恨之入骨?叫他离开这所房子不是更明智吗?"

"不行!"恩肖勃然大怒,吼道,"要是他提出要离开我,那他就死定了啦:你要是劝他这么做,你就是一个杀人犯!难道我得输光一切,再也没有翻本的机会吗?难道让哈里顿作一个乞丐?啊,该死的!我一定要把它赢回来。我要他的金子,还有他的血,我要把他的灵魂送到地狱里!有了这位客人,地狱要比以前黑暗十倍!"

艾伦,你曾经给我讲过你的旧主人的习惯。他分明是快要疯了:至少昨天晚上是这样。我一靠近他就浑身发抖,相比之下,仆人的粗暴无礼反倒比较讨人喜欢。现在,他又开始阴郁地来回踱步了,我急忙拔起门闩,逃到厨房里去。约瑟夫正在躬着腰对着火炉,盯着挂在火炉上的一只大锅看,身边的高背椅上摆着一木盆麦片。锅里的东西开始沸腾了,他转过来把手朝木盆里伸去。我想大概是在准备我们的晚饭吧。我已经饿了,觉得有必要把它烧得能够下咽,于是提高嗓门叫道,"让我来吧!"一边说,一边把那个木盆挪开,不让他够到,而且飞快地脱下我的帽子和骑马服。"恩肖先生,"我接着说,"让我自己伺候自己:我就这样办。我可不想在你们中间摆大小姐的谱,我怕自己会活活饿死。"

第十三章

"Gooid Lord!" he muttered, sitting down, and stroking his ribbed stockings from the knee to the ankle. "If they's tuh be fresh or the rings just when aw getten used tuh two maisters, if aw mun hev a *mistress* set o'er my heead, it's loike time tuh be flitting. Aw niver *did* think tuh say t' day ut aw mud lave th' owld place—but aw daht it's nigh at bend!"

This lamentation drew no notice from me: I went briskly to work, sighing to remember a period when it would have been all merry fun; but compelled speedily to drive off the remembrance. It racked me to recall past happiness, and the greater peril there was of conjuring up its apparition, the quicker the thible ran round, and the faster the handfuls of meal fell into the water. Joseph beheld my style of cookery with growing indignation.

"Thear!" he ejaculated. "Hareton, thah willut sup thy porridge tuh neeght; they'll be nowt bud lumps as big as maw nave. Thear, agean! Aw'd fling in bowl un all, if aw wer yah! Thear, pale t' guilp off, un' then yah'll hae done wi't. Bang, bang. It's a marcy t' bothom isn't deaved aht!"

It *was* rather a rough mess, I own, when poured into the basins; four had been provided, and a gallon pitcher of new milk was brought from the dairy, which Hareton seized and commenced drinking and spilling from the expansive lip. I expostulated, and desired that he should have his in a mug; affirming that I could not taste the liquid treated so dirtily. The old cynic chose to be vastly offended at this nicety; assuring me, repeatedly, that "the barn was every bit as gooid" as I, "and every bit as wollsome," and wondering how I could fashion to

"老天爷!"他咕哝着坐下,抚摩着他那罗纹袜子,从膝盖一直摸到脚踝。"又要有新差使啦——我刚习惯了同时有两个东家,现在又来了个女主人骑到我头上来,真是时光如流水啊。我从没想到过会有离开这个老地方的时候——不过,恐怕就近在眼前喽!"

我并没注意到他的悲叹,一个人匆匆地干活,我在叹息中想起,曾经有过一个时期,一切都是那么美好和快乐,可我不得不马上赶跑这些回忆,回忆只能使我心里感到难过。过去的幻影越要出现,我就把粥搅动得越快,大把大把的麦片往水里撒得也越快。约瑟夫看到我这煮粥的方式,心里的火越来越大。

"瞧瞧!"他大叫起来。"哈里顿,今天晚上你可没有麦片粥喝啦,只有像我拳头那么大的疙瘩。瞧,又扔进去了一大把!我要是你的话,就把木盆子什么的扔下去了!瞧呀,你非得把这锅粥都糟蹋光才算完事吧。砰,砰。锅底没敲掉真是谢天谢地啊!"

我得承认,倒在事先准备好的四个盆子里的粥简直是一塌糊涂。有人从牛奶场用罐子装来一加伦的新鲜牛奶,哈里顿一把抢过来就大口大口地喝着。一边喝,一迳漏。我告诉他把牛奶倒在一个杯子里再喝,还声明:这么脏的牛奶我肯定是碰都不会碰的。那个爱挑剔的刻薄老头对我的讲究满腹牢骚,再三跟我说,"这孩子每一丁点儿"都跟我"一样的好","每一丁点儿都一样健康"。他觉得很奇怪,我怎么会这样看不起别人。同

be so conceited. Meanwhile, the infant ruffian continued sucking; and glowered up at me defyingly, as he slavered into the jug.

"I shall have my supper in another room," I said. "Have you no place you call a parlour?"

"*Parlour*!" he echoed, sneeringly, "*parlour*! Nay, we've noa *parlours*. If yah dunnut loike wer company, they's maister's; un' if yah dunnut loike maister, they's us."

"Then I shall go up-stairs," I answered; "shew me a chamber."

I put my basin on a tray, and went myself to fetch some more milk. With great grumblings, the fellow rose, and preceded me in my ascent: we mounted to the garrets; he opening a door, now and then, to look into the apartments we passed.

"Here's a rahm," he said, at last, flinging back a cranky board on hinges. "It's weel enough tuh ate a few porridge in. They's a pack uh corn i' t' corner, thear, meetely clane; if yah're feared uh muckying yer grand silk does, spread yer hankerchir ut t' top on 't."

The "rahm" was a kind of lumber-hole smelling strong of malt and grain; various sacks of which articles were piled around, leaving a wide, bare space in the middle.

"Why, man!" I exclaimed, facing him angrily, "this is not a place to sleep in. I wish to see my bed-room."

"*Bed-rume*!" he repeated, in a tone of mockery. "Yah's see all t' *bedrumes* thear is—yon's mine."

He pointed into the second garret, only differing from the first in being more naked about the walls, and having a large, low, curtainless bed, with an indigo-coloured quilt, at

时,那小恶徒继续喝着他的牛奶,还有意向着罐子里淌口水,一脸挑衅似的朝我怒目而视。

"我要到另外的房间吃晚饭,"我说。"难道你们没有可以叫做客厅的地方吗?"

"客厅!"他学着我的口气轻蔑地说,"客厅!没有,我们没有客厅。要是你不喜欢跟我们一起,就去主人那儿好了。要是你不喜欢主人,就待在我们这儿。"

"那我上楼去。"我回答到,"领我到一间卧室去。"

我把我的盆子放在一个托盘上,自己又去取了点牛奶,那个老家伙唠唠叨叨好一阵子才站起来,领我上楼。我们登上了阁楼,他时不时地打开这扇那扇房门,我们经过的所有房间都被他看遍了。

"这儿有间屋子,"他终于撞开一扇有铰链的摇摇晃晃的木板门。"在这里头喝麦片粥很好啦。墙角里有堆稻草,那儿,还挺干净。你要是怕弄脏你那漂亮的绸衣服,就铺块手绢在上面吧。"

他说的"屋子"是间堆东西的破屋子,一股强烈的麦子和谷子气味直冲鼻子。屋子的四周堆满了各种粮食的袋子,中间留下一大块空地。

"你,怎么这样?"我生气地对他大声嚷嚷,"这是睡觉的地方吗?我要看看我的卧室。"

"卧室!"他嘲弄的口气又出现了,重复了我的话。"所有的卧室你都看过了——那边那间是我的。"

他朝着第二个阁楼指了指,这一间跟先前一间的惟一区别就是墙上东

one end.

"What do I want with yours?" I retorted. "I suppose Mr. Heathcliff does not lodge at the top of the house, does he?"

"Oh, it's Maister *Hathecliff's* yah're wenting?" cried he, as if making a new discovery. "Couldn't ye uh said soa, at onst? un then, aw mud uh telled ye, baht all this wark, ut that's just one yah cannut sea-he allas keeps it locked, un' nob'dy iver mells on 't but hisseln."

"You've a nice house, Joseph," I could not refrain from observing, "and pleasant inmates; and I think the concentrated essence of all the madness in the world took up its abode in my brain the day I linked my fate with theirs! However, that is not to the present purpose—there are other rooms. For Heaven's sake, be quick, and let me settle somewhere!"

He made no reply to this adjuration; only plodding doggedly down the wooden steps, and halting before an apartment which, from that halt and the superior quality of its furniture, I conjectured to be the best one. There was a carpet: a good one, but the pattern was obliterated by dust; a fireplace hung with cut paper, dropping to pieces; a handsome oak-bedstead with ample crimson curtains of rather expensive material and modern make; but they had evidently experienced rough usage; the valances hung in festoons, wrenched from their rings, and the iron rod supporting them was bent in an arc, on one side, causing the drapery to trail upon the floor. The chairs were also damaged, many of them severely; and deep indentations deformed the panels of the walls. I was endeavouring to gather resolution for entering, and taking pos-

西少些，还多了一张没有帐子的矮脚大床。床的一头有一床深蓝色的棉被。

"我要你的卧室干吗？"我回嘴道。"我想希斯克利夫先生总不至于睡在阁楼上，是吗？"

"啊！你是要希斯克利夫少爷的房间呀？"他叫道，好像发现了新大陆似的。"你早说不就行了吗？免得大家麻烦。我可要告诉你，不用费心了，那间屋子你是看不到的——他总是把门锁着，除了他自己，谁也别想进去。"

"你们这家真好，约瑟夫。"我忍不住讽刺道，"多讨人喜欢的一家子。我看自打把自己的命运跟这家人连在一起的那天起，世界上所有疯狂的精髓都集中到我脑子里来了！不过，现在说这些话也于事无补——还有别的房间呢。看在老天的分上，赶快给我安排个地方吧！"

他没有理会我的请求，只是固执地拖着沉重缓慢的步子走下了木制楼梯，在一个房间门口停了下来。从他停步不前以及房间里的上等家具看来，我想这应该是最好的一间了。房间内铺有地毯——质量非常好，可是图案已经被灰尘蒙蔽，再也看不清了。壁炉上贴着的带花纹的墙纸，已经七零八落了。一张漂亮的橡木大床上挂着很大的深红色帷帐。材料非常高档，式样也很时新，但是使用的人显然非常粗心大意：原先挂着一只只花球的帐幔，已经被拉脱了挂钩，挂帐子的铁杆有一边已经弯成弧形，于是帷帐就拖在地板上。椅子也都残缺不全，有好几把坏得相当厉害。墙上的嵌板上有深深的凹痕，非常难看。

我正要拿定主意进去住下来,我的笨蛋向导向我宣布说:"这是主人的房间。"这时,我的晚饭冰冷了,而我一点胃口也没有了,耐性也终于耗尽。我坚持要他马上给我安排一个安身之处和可供休息的地方。

"该死的去哪儿呢?"这个虔诚的老头说道。"上帝保佑我们吧!主饶恕我们吧!你到底要到哪儿去呢!你这讨人厌的废物!除了哈里顿的小房间,这里什么东西你都看过啦。在这所房子里没有别的房间可以让你住啦!"

我简直气坏了,把手里托盘和上面的东西一股脑儿都摔到地上,一屁股坐在楼梯口,双手捂着脸,大哭起来。

"哎呀!哎呀!"约瑟夫大叫。"摔得好,凯茜小姐①!摔得好,凯茜小姐!不过,主人会踩在这些破盆子上摔倒的,到时我们就等着挨骂吧。我们就走着瞧。你这个不学好的疯子呀!为了你的任性,就这样把上帝恩赐的东西摔在地上,你就活该从现在起一直饿到圣诞节!我不信你会一直这么任性下去。你以为希斯克利夫会受得了你这种好腔调?我巴不得他在这会儿看到你使性子呢。但愿他能看到。"

他就这么一直骂骂咧咧地回到楼下他的窝里去,蜡烛也被带走了:留下我一个人呆在黑暗里。干了这样的蠢事之后,我仔细考虑了一番,最后不得不承认,我应该克制我的骄傲,咽下我的愤怒,并且动手把这些东西收拾干净。没过多久,意外地出现了

---

① 凯茜以前在家经常发脾气摔东西,约瑟夫看到伊莎贝拉生气,把她看作另一个"凯茜小姐"。

appeared in the shape of Throttler, whom I now recognised as a son of our old Skulker: it had spent its whelp-hood at the Grange, and was given by my father to Mr. Hindley. I fancy it knew me: it pushed its nose against mine by way of salute, and then hastened to devour the porridge; while I groped from step to step, collecting the shattered earthenware, and drying the spatters of milk from the banister with my pocket-handkerchief. Our labours were scarcely over when I heard Earnshaw's tread in the passage; my assistant tucked in his tail, and pressed to the wall: I stole into the nearest doorway. The dog's endeavour to avoid him was unsuccessful; as I guessed by a scutter down stairs, and a prolonged, piteous yelping. I had better luck: he passed on, entered his chamber, and shut the door. Directly after Joseph came up with Hareton, to put him to bed. I had found shelter in Hareton's room, and the old man, on seeing me, said—

"They's rahm fur boath yah, un yer pride, nah, aw sud think i' th' hahse. It's empty; yah muh hev it all tuh yerseln, un Him as allas maks a third, i' sich ill company!"

Gladly did I take advantage of this intimation; and the minute I flung myself into a chair, by the fire, I nodded, and slept. My slumber was deep and sweet, though over far too soon. Mr. Heathcliff awoke me; he had just come in, and demanded, in his loving manner, what I was doing there? I told him the cause of my staying up so late—that he had the key of our room in his pocket. The adjective *our* gave mortal offence. He swore it was not, nor ever should be mine; and he'd—but I'll not repeat his language, nor describe his habitual conduct; he is ingenious and unresting in seeking to gain my abhorrence! I sometimes wonder at him with an intensity that deadens my fear; yet, I assure you, a tiger or a venomous serpent could not rouse terror in me equal to that which he wakens. He told me of Catherine's illness, and accused my brother of causing it; promising that I should be Edgar's proxy in suffering, till he could get hold of him.

I do hate him—I am wretched—I have been a fool! Beware of uttering one breath of this to any one at the Grange. I shall expect you every day—don't disappoint me!

Isabella

不愿叙述他一贯的行为了：他无休止地用尽心机想激起我的憎恶！有时，我觉得他真是奇怪，奇怪得使我心中的恐惧都减轻了。不过，我跟你说，一只老虎或一条毒蛇给我的恐怖也比不上他所给予的。他告诉我凯瑟琳病了，怪罪是我哥哥逼出来的；他发誓要把我当作埃德加的替身来受罪，直到他干掉他为止。

我恨死他了——我真不幸——我是一个傻瓜！千万不要把这事告诉田庄的任何人。我天天都盼望着你来——不要让我失望！

伊莎贝拉

Chapter 14
第十四章

As soon as I had perused this epistle, I went to the master, and informed him that his sister had arrived at the Heights, and sent me a letter expressing her sorrow for Mrs. Linton's situation, and her ardent desire to see him; with a wish that he would transmit to her, as early as possible, some token of forgiveness by me.

"Forgiveness!" said Linton. "I have nothing to forgive her, Ellen. You may call at Wuthering Heights this afternoon, if you like, and say that I am not angry, but I'm sorry to

我一看完这封信，就立刻去找主人，告诉他说他的妹妹已经到了呼啸山庄，而且还寄给我一封信，表达了她对林顿太太病情的挂念，并热切地渴望见到他。我希望他能尽早让我去山庄转达对她的一点原谅。

"原谅！"林顿说，"我没什么可原谅她的，艾伦。如果你愿意，今天下午就可以去呼啸山庄，说我并不生气，但我非常痛惜失去了她，尤其是

have lost her; especially as I can never think she'll be happy. It is out of the question my going to see her, however: we are eternally divided; and should she really wish to oblige me, let her persuade the villain she has married to leave the country."

"And you won't write her a little note, sir?" I asked imploringly.

"No," he answered. "It is needless. My communication with Heathcliff's family shall be as sparing as his with mine. It shall not exist!"

Mr. Edgar's coldness depressed me exceedingly; and all the way from the Grange I puzzled my brains how to put more heart into what he said, when I repeated it; and how to soften his refusal of even a few lines to console Isabella. I dare say she had been on the watch for me since morning: I saw her looking through the lattice, as I came up the garden causeway, and I nodded to her; but she drew back, as if afraid of being observed. I entered without knocking. There never was such a dreary, dismal scene as the formerly cheerful house presented! I must confess, that if I had been in the young lady's place, I would, at least, have swept the hearth, and wiped the tables with a duster. But she already partook of the pervading spirit of neglect which encompassed her. Her pretty face was wan and listless; her hair uncurled: some locks hanging lankly down, and some carelessly twisted round her head. Probably she had not touched her dress since yester evening. Hindley was not there. Mr. Heathcliff sat at a table, turning over some papers in his pocket-book; but he rose when I appeared, asked me how I did, quite friendly,

我绝不认为她会幸福。无论如何，我是绝不会去见她的，我们已经永远一刀两断。如果她真的想给我做件好事，那就让她说服跟她结婚的那个流氓离开这个地方。"

"你不想给她写个便条吗，先生？"我恳求地问道。

"不，"他回答说，"没这个必要，我跟希斯克利夫家人之间的往来应该像他和我家之间的来往一样，越少越好，根本不应该存在。"

埃德加先生的冷漠让我感到非常沮丧，从田庄出来之后，一路上我都绞尽脑汁地想着，在我重述他这番话的时候该如何加一点感情进去，如何把他甚至拒绝写一两行字来安慰伊莎贝拉说得委婉一些。我料想伊莎贝拉从早上开始就已经盼望着我了：我一走上花园的砌道，就看见她从窗格里向外张望，我对她点了点头；可她把头缩了回去，好像怕被人看到似的。我没敲门就走了进去。这幢曾经充满欢乐的房子从来没有呈现出如此荒凉阴沉的景象！我必须承认，如果我是这位年轻的太太，我至少会扫一扫壁炉，用鸡毛掸子擦一擦桌子。但是她已经沾染了那些包围着她的、遍及整幢房子的懒散气。她那动人的脸蛋显得苍白而无精打采，一头直发，有的直直垂下来，有的则乱七八糟地盘在头上。或许从昨天晚上起她就没有梳洗过。辛德雷不在家。希斯克利夫坐在桌旁，翻阅着他的袖珍记事本，不过我一出现，他就站了起来，非常友好地问候我，还给我张罗了一把椅子。他是那里惟一一个看上去比较像

and offered me a chair. He was the only thing there that seemed decent; and I thought he never looked better. So much had circumstances altered their positions, that he would certainly have struck a stranger as a born and bred gentleman, and his wife as a thorough little slattern! She came forward eagerly to greet me; and held out one hand to take the expected letter. I shook my head. She wouldn't understand the hint, but followed me to a sideboard, where I went to lay my bonnet, and importuned me in a whisper to give her directly what I had brought. Heathcliff guessed the meaning of her manoeuvres, and said—

"If you have got anything for Isabella (as no doubt you have, Nelly), give it to her. You needn't make a secret of it: we have no secrets between us."

"Oh, I have nothing," I replied, thinking it best to speak the truth at once. "My master bid me tell his sister that she must not expect either a letter or a visit from him at present. He sends his love, ma'am, and his wishes for your happiness, and his pardon for the grief you have occasioned but he thinks that after this time, his household and the household here should drop intercommunication, as nothing good could come of keeping it up."

Mrs. Heathcliff's lip quivered slightly, and she returned to her seat in the window. Her husband took his stand on the hearthstone, near me, and began to put questions concerning Catherine. I told him as much as I thought proper of her illness, and he extorted from me, by crossexamination, most of the facts connected with its origin. I blamed her, as she deserved, for bringing it all on herself; and ended

模像样的人，我觉得他从来都没有这样好看过。环境使他们的地位变换得如此之多，陌生人乍一看来，肯定会认为他生来就是个有教养的绅士，而他的妻子则是个彻头彻尾的懒婆子！她急切地走上前来迎接我，还伸出一只手来取她期待着的来信。我摇了摇头。她不明白这个暗示，一直跟着我来到一个餐具柜旁边，我在那儿放下了我的帽子，她轻声地央求我马上把带来的东西交给她。希斯克利夫猜出了她这举动的意思，就说：

"如果你有什么东西要给伊莎贝拉（毫无疑问，你一定带了，内莉），那就给她吧。你没必要搞得那样神神秘秘的，我们之间没有秘密。"

"哦，我什么都没有带，"我回答道，心想最好还是马上说出真相，"我的主人要我告诉他妹妹，她现在不用指望他会来信或是拜访。他让我向你传达他的爱，太太，还有他祝你幸福，也原谅了你所引起的悲伤。但他觉得从现在起，他的家应该和这个家断绝来往，因为保持联系也没什么意义。"

希斯克利夫太太的嘴唇微微地颤抖着，她又回到窗前的座位上。她的丈夫站在壁炉前，靠近我，开始询问有关凯瑟琳的情况。我尽量告诉他一些我认为恰当的关于她病情的事，他却没完没了地逼问我，让我说出跟她病因有关的大部分事实。我责怪了凯瑟琳，她活该受到责怪，这都是她自找苦吃。最后我希望他能学学林顿先

by hoping that he would follow Mr. Linton's example, and avoid future interference with his family, for good or evil.

"Mrs. Linton is now just recovering," I said; "she'll never be like she was, but her life is spared: and if you really have a regard for her, you'll shun crossing her way again: nay, you'll move out of this country entirely; and that you may not regret it, I'll inform you Catherine Linton is as different now from your old friend Catherine Earnshaw, as that young lady is different from me. Her appearance is changed greatly, her character much more so; and the person who is compelled, of necessity, to be her companion, will only sustain his affection hereafter by the remembrance of what she once was, by common humanity, and a sense of duty!"

"That is quite possible," remarked Heathcliff, forcing himself to seem calm: "quite possible that your master should have nothing but common humanity and a sense of duty to fall back upon. But do you imagine that I shall leave Catherine to his *duty* and *humanity*? and can you compare my feelings respecting Catherine to his? Before you leave this house, I must exact a promise from you, that you'll get me an interview with her: consent, or refuse, I *will* see her! What do you say?"

"I say, Mr. Heathcliff," I replied, "you must not: you never shall, through my means. Another encounter between you and the master would kill her altogether."

"With your aid, that may be avoided," he continued; "and should there be danger of such an event—should he be the cause of adding a single trouble more to her existence—why, I

"林顿太太现在正在康复中，"我说，"她永远都没法恢复到生病前的模样，不过命是保住了。如果你真的关心她，那就不要再去纠缠她，不仅如此，你还要彻底搬出这个地方。为了不让你后悔，我要告诉你，如今的凯瑟琳·林顿已经和你的老朋友凯瑟琳·恩肖大不相同了，正如那位年轻太太和我不同一样。她的面貌改变了很多，而她的性格变得更多。那个必须而且不得不作她伴侣的人，今后只能依靠对她往昔的回忆，以及世俗的仁爱与责任心，来维持他的感情了！"

"那倒是挺有可能的，"希斯克利夫说，强迫自己表现出一副平静的样子，"你家主人除了那种世俗的仁爱和责任感之外已经没什么可支撑的了，这是非常有可能的。但是你觉得我会把凯瑟琳丢给他的责任和仁爱吗？你能拿我对凯瑟琳的感情跟他的相比吗？在你离开这所房子之前，我一定要你答应，让我跟她见上一面，你答应也好，拒绝也好，我一定要见到她！你觉得呢？"

"我说，希斯克利夫先生，"我回答道，"千万不能，你永远都别想通过我来想方设法见到她。如果你再和我的主人碰一次面，就会要了她的命。"

"有你的帮助，就可以避免这种事情的发生，"他接着说道，"如果真有这么大的危险，如果是因为他使凯瑟琳的生活增加烦恼，那么，我觉得

think, I shall be justified in going to extremes! I wish you had sincerity enough to tell me whether Catherine would suffer greatly from his loss: the fear that she would restrains me. And there you see the distinction between our feelings: had he been in my place and I in his, though I hated him with a hatred that turned my life to gall, I never would have raised a hand against him You may look incredulous, if you please! I never would have banished him from her society as long as she desired his. The moment her regard ceased, I would have torn his heart out, and drank his blood! But, till then—if you don't believe me, you don't know me—till then, I would have died by inches before I touched a single hair of his head!"

"And yet," I interrupted, "you have no scruples in completely ruining all hopes of her perfect restoration, by thrusting yourself into her remembrance now, when she has nearly forgotten you, and involving her in a new tumult of discord and distress."

"You suppose she has nearly forgotten me?" he said. "Oh, Nelly! you know she has not! You know as well as I do, that for every thought she spends on Linton, she spends a thousand on me! At a most miserable period of my life, I had a notion of the kind: it haunted me on my return to the neighbourhood last summer; but only her own assurance could make me admit the horrible idea again. And then, Linton would be nothing, nor Hindley, nor all the dreams that ever I dreamt. Two words would comprehend my future—*death* and *hell*: existence, after losing her, would be hell. Yet I was a fool to fancy for a moment that

我正有理由走一次极端！我希望你能诚恳地告诉我，如果失去了他，凯瑟琳会不会非常难过：就是因为怕她难过，我才一直强忍着。从这里你就可以看出我们两个感情之间的区别了：如果他处在我的位置，而我处在他的位置，虽然我憎恨他把我的生活变得如此痛苦，但我绝不会反抗他。如果你喜欢，尽可以怀疑我！只要凯瑟琳还需要他的陪伴，我就绝对不会把他从她的身边赶走。一旦她对他的关心停止了，我就会掏出他的心，喝光他的血！可是，在那之前——如果不相信我，那就是你还不了解我——在那之前，我宁愿慢慢死去，也不会碰他一根头发！"

"可是，"我打断他说，"你毫不犹豫地想要彻底地毁掉她完全康复的一切希望，如今在她快要忘了你的时候，却硬要让自己挤到她的记忆里，还把她卷进一场新的争端与苦恼的轩然大波中去。"

"你以为她快要忘了我吗？"他说，"哦，内莉！你知道她没有忘记我！你和我一样都知道她每挂念林顿一次，就会挂念我一千次！在我人生中最痛苦的时期，我曾经有过这样的想法，去年夏天在我回到这附近的时候，这想法还一直萦绕着我，可是只有她亲口对我说明才能让我再次接受这可怕的想法。到了那个时候，林顿才可以算不得什么，辛德雷也算不得什么，我幻想过的所有梦想也都算不得什么。两个词可以概括我的未来——死亡与地狱：失去她之后，人生就是地狱。但是，我曾傻傻地以为

she valued Edgar Linton's attachment more than mine. If he loved with all the powers of his puny being, he couldn't love as much in eighty years as I could in a day. And Catherine has a heart as deep as I have: the sea could be as readily contained in that horse-trough, as her whole affection be monopolised by him. Tush! He is scarcely a degree dearer to her than her dog, or her horse. It is not in him to be loved like me: how can she love in him what he has not?"

"Catherine and Edgar are as fond of each other as any two people can be," cried Isabella, with sudden vivacity."No one has a right to talk in that manner, and I won't hear my brother depreciated in silence!"

"Your brother is wondrous fond of you too, isn't he?" observed Heathcliff scornfully. "He turns you adrift on the world with surprising alacrity."

"He is not aware of what I suffer," she replied."I didn't tell him that."

"You have been telling him something, then: you have written, have you?"

"To say that I was married, I did write—you saw the note."

"And nothing since?"

"No."

"My young lady is looking sadly the worse for her change of condition," I remarked. "Somebody's love comes short in her case, obviously: whose, I may guess; but, perhaps, I shouldn't say."

"I should guess it was her own," said Heathcliff."She degenerates into a mere slut! She is tired of trying to please me, uncommonly early. You'd hardly credit it, but the very

她把埃德加·林顿的爱恋看得比我的还要重。即便林顿用他那软弱的身躯竭尽全力爱她八年,也抵不上我爱她一天。凯瑟琳和我一样有一颗深沉的心:她的所有情感都被林顿独占着,就像海水轻而易举就被装进马槽一样。呸!对于凯瑟琳来说,他不见得比她的狗或是她的马更亲密些。他身上没有像我一样可以被凯瑟琳爱的东西,她又如何去爱上他本来就没有的东西呢?"

"凯瑟琳与埃德加和任何一对夫妇一样相互爱着对方,"伊莎贝拉突然振作起来,大声叫道,"没有人可以用那样的态度讲话,我不能听见有人诋毁我哥哥还继续保持沉默。"

"你哥哥也非常喜欢你,是不是?"希斯克利夫轻蔑地说道,"他令人惊讶地任你在这世上漂泊。"

"他并不知道我所受的痛苦,"她回答说,"我没有告诉他。"

"那么你告诉他别的什么了,你给他写过信,对不对?"

"我是写过,我告诉他我结婚了,你见过那封短信。"

"那之后就没写了吗?"

"没有。"

"自从改变环境之后我家小姐看起来憔悴了很多,"我说,"很显然,有人已经不再爱她了。我可以猜得到是谁,但也许我不该说出来。"

"我倒觉得是她自己不爱自己了,"希斯克利夫说道,"她已经堕落成一个地道的懒婆娘!很早以前她就不想再讨我欢喜了。虽然你几乎不会

morrow of our wedding, she was weeping to go home. However, she'll suit this house so much the better for not being over nice, and I'll take care she does not disgrace me by rambling abroad."

"Well, sir," returned I, "I hope you'll consider that Mrs. Heathcliff is accustomed to be looked after and waited on; and that she has been brought up like an only daughter, whom every one was ready to serve. You must let her have a maid to keep things tidy about her, and you must treat her kindly. Whatever be your notion of Mr. Edgar, you cannot doubt that she has a capacity for strong attachments, or she wouldn't have abandoned the elegancies, and comforts, and friends of her former home, to fix contentedly, in such a wilderness as this, with you."

"She abandoned them under a delusion," he answered; "picturing in me a hero of romance, and expecting unlimited indulgences from my chivalrous devotion. I can hardly regard her in the light of a rational creature, so obstinately has she persisted in forming a fabulous notion of my character, and acting on the false impressions she cherished. But, at last, I think she begins to know me. I don't perceive the silly smiles and grimaces that provoked me at first; and the senseless incapability of discerning that I was in earnest when I gave her my opinion of her infatuation and herself. It was a marvellous effort of perspicacity to discover that I did not love her. I believed, at one time, no lessons could teach her that! And yet it is poorly learnt; for this morning she announced, as a piece of appalling intelligence, that I had actually succeeded in making her hate me! A

相信，但就在我们结婚后的第二天早上，她就哭着想要回娘家。不管怎样，她自己这么不修边幅，正好和这房子相配，我也会多加注意，不让她在外面乱跑，丢我的脸。"

"噢，先生，"我回答他说，"我希望你能考虑到希斯克利夫太太是个习惯于被人照护和侍候的人，她是像个独生女一样被带大的，每个人都随时准备着伺候她。你一定得给她找个女仆来帮她收拾东西，而且你也要好好地对待她。不管你对埃德加先生有什么看法，你都不能怀疑她是否拥有强烈的迷恋之情，不然她也不会放弃以前家中优雅舒适的生活和朋友，安心跟你住在这个荒凉的地方。"

"她是因为错觉才会放弃那些东西的，"他回答道，"她把我想像成一个浪漫的英雄，希望从我的侠义的爱慕中获得无穷无尽的宠爱。我简直无法把她当成一个有理性的人，她固执地坚持要给我的性格构建一种荒谬的看法，硬要凭她怀抱着的错误印象行事。不过，我想她到底还是开始了解我了。刚开始我并没有理会她那些让我恼火的傻笑和鬼脸，也没理会那些愚蠢的无能，当我告诉她我对她那些痴迷和对她本身的看法时，她竟没有意识到我是真诚的。她真的费了好大劲才发现我并不爱她。有一阵子我相信，这是没办法让她明白的！可现在她居然勉勉强强明白了，因为今天早上，她宣布了一件了不起的事，说我已经成功地让她恨我了！我向你保证，这绝对是费了九牛二虎之力的！

positive labour of Hercules, I assure you! If it be achieved, I have cause to return thanks. Can I trust your assertion, Isabella? Are you sure you hate me? If I let you alone for half a day, won't you come sighing and wheedling to me again? I dare say she would rather I had seemed all tenderness before you: it wounds her vanity to have the truth exposed. But I don't care who knows that the passion was wholly on one side; and I never told her a lie about it. She cannot accuse me of showing a bit of deceitful softness. The first thing she saw me do, on coming out of the Grange, was to hang up her little dog; and when she pleaded for it, the first words I uttered were a wish that I had the hanging of every being belonging to her, except one: possibly she took that exception for herself. But no brutality disgusted her: I suppose she has an innate admiration of it, if only her precious person were secure from injury! Now, was it not the depth of absurdity-of genuine idiocy, for that pitiful, slavish, mean-minded brach Il3 to dream that I could love her? Tell your master, Nelly, that I never, in all my life, met with such an abject thing as she is. She even disgraces the name of Linton, and I've sometimes relented, from pure lack of invention, in my experiments on what she could endure, and still creep shamefully cringing back! But tell him, also, to set his fraternal and magisterial heart at ease, that I keep strictly within the limits of the law. I have avoided, up to this period, giving her the slightest right to claim a separation; and, what's more, she'd thank nobody for dividing us. If she desired to go, she might: the nuisance of her presence outweighs the gratification to be derived from

如果真的成功了，那我还有理由来感谢她呢。我能相信你的话吗，伊莎贝拉？你确定真的恨我吗？如果我让你独自一人待上半天，你会不会又叹着气过来跟我甜言蜜语呢？我想她宁愿我当着你的面表现出柔情蜜意的样子，如果暴露了真相，可就要伤她的虚荣心了。可我并不在乎有人知道这份热情完全是片面的：而且我也从来没有在这件事上对她说过一句谎话。她不能指责我表露过一点虚假的温柔。从田庄出来后，她看见我做的第一件事就是把她的小狗吊起来。当她恳求我放了它时，我说的第一句话就是我希望把她家的所有人一个一个地吊死，只有一个人除外，也许她把那个例外当成她自己了吧。但无论多么残忍，都无法让她感到厌恶，我想，只要她自己的宝贝身子安全不受伤害，她内心里还很崇拜这种残忍呢！如今，这可怜、专横、卑贱的母狗，这纯粹的白痴居然还幻想我能爱她，这岂不是荒谬至极！转告你的主人，内莉，说我一生都没遇见过像她这样下贱的东西，她甚至玷辱了林顿家的名声。我试验着她到底能忍多久，可她还是会羞答答地带着一副谄媚样爬回来，因为实在想不出什么新的招数，有时我还真动了恻隐之心！但是，也请你告诉他，请他放宽那颗盛气凌人、充满手足之情的心吧。我严格遵守着法律。迄今为止，我一直避免给她任何一点点的借口来要求离异；不仅如此，任何拆散我们俩的人，她都不会感谢。如果她想走，她可以走；她在我面前的那副讨厌样已经超过了我折磨她时所得到的满足。"

tormenting her!"

"Mr. Heathcliff," said I, "this is the talk of a madman, and your wife, most likely, is convinced you are mad; and, for that reason, she has borne with you hitherto: but now that you say she may go, she'll doubtless avail herself of the permission. You are not so bewitched, ma'am, are you, as to remain with him of your own accord?"

"Take care, Ellen!" answered Isabella, her eyes sparkling irefully; there was no misdoubting by their expression, the full success of her partner's endeavours to make himself detested. "Don't put faith in a single word he speaks. He's a lying fiend! a monster, and not a human being! I've been told I might leave him before; and I've made the attempt, but I dare not repeat it! Only, Ellen, promise you-'ll not mention a syllable of his infamous conversation to my brother or Catherine. Whatever he may pretend, he wishes to provoke Edgar to desperation: he says he has married me on purpose to obtain power over him; and he shan't obtain it—I'll die first! I just hope, I pray, that he may forget his diabolical prudence, and kill me! The single pleasure I can imagine, is to die, or to see him dead!"

"There—that will do for the present!" said Heathcliff. "If you are called upon in a court of law, you'll remember her language, Nelly! And take a good look at that countenance: she's near the point which would suit me. No; you're not fit to be your own guardian, Isabella, now; and I, being your legal protector, must retain you in my custody, however distasteful the obligation may be. Go up stairs; I have something to say to Ellen Dean in private.

"希斯克利夫先生，"我说，"这是一个疯子才会说的话，你的妻子很可能以为你已经疯了。因为这个缘故，她才一直容忍你直到现在。可如今你说她可以走，她毫无疑问会好好利用这个许可的。太太，你总不会被他如此迷惑，还心甘情愿地跟他一起住下去吧？"

"可别这么说，艾伦！"伊莎贝拉答道，她的眼里闪烁着怒火，从这表情可以毫无疑问地看出，她丈夫让她憎恨他的努力已经完全取得了成功。"不要相信他所说的任何话。他是一个撒谎的恶魔！是个怪物，他不是人！之前他也跟我说过我可以离开；我也尝试过，但我现在再也不敢试了！艾伦，我只求你答应我不要对我哥哥或凯瑟琳提起他那些无耻话中的任何一个字。无论他怎么伪装，他只希望能激怒埃德加来跟他拼命。他说过，他娶我只是为了想要跟他夺权，但他是得不到的，因为我会先死！我只希望，我祈求，他会忘记他那恶魔般的谨慎而把我杀掉！我所能想像到的惟一欢乐就是死亡，或是看着他死！"

"好了——说够了吧！"希斯克利夫说道，"内莉，如果你被法庭传讯，可要记住她这番话啊！好好看看她那张脸吧：她很快就要配得上我了。不对，现在你不适合做你自己的保护人了，伊莎贝拉；既然我是你合法的保护人，那一定得把你放在我的监护之下，不管这职责有多么令人厌恶。上楼去，我有些话想要私下跟艾伦·迪安说。不是这边，我叫你上楼！哎

That's not the way: upstairs, I tell you! Why, this is the road up-stairs, child!"

He seized, and thrust her from the room; and returned muttering—

"I have no pity! I have no pity! The more the worms writhe, the more I yearn to crush out their entrails! It is a moral teething; and I grind with greater energy, in proportion to the increase of pain."

"Do you understand what the word pity means?" I said, hastening to resume my bonnet. "Did you ever feel a touch of it in your life?"

"Put that down!" he interrupted, perceiving my intention to depart. "You are not going yet. Come here now, Nelly: I must either persuade or compel you to aid me in fulfilling my determination to see Catherine, and that without delay. I swear that I meditate no harm. I don't desire to cause any disturbance, or to exasperate or insult Mr. Linton; I only wish to hear from herself how she is, and why she has been ill; and to ask if anything that I could do would be of use to her. Last night, I was in the Grange garden six hours, and I'll return there tonight; and every night I'll haunt the place, and every day, till I find an opportunity of entering. If Edgar Linton meets me, I shall not hesitate to knock him down, and give him enough to insure his quiescence while I stay. If his servants oppose me, I shall threaten them off with these pistols. But wouldn't it be better to prevent my coming in contact with them, or their master? And you could do it so easily. I'd warn you when I came, and then you might let me in unobserved as soon as she was alone, and watch till I departed, your conscience quite calm: you

呀,孩子,这才是上楼的路!"

他一把抓住她,把她推出了房门,然后嘀咕着走回来:

"我没有同情心!我没有同情心!虫子越是扭动,我越是想要挤出它们的五脏六腑!这是一种精神上的出牙,越是痛,我越要使劲磨。"

"你知道'同情'这个词是什么意思吗?"我一边说着,一边匆忙地戴上帽子,"你这一生都没有感到过一丝同情吗?"

"放下帽子!"他看出我想要走,就打断了我。"你还不能走。马上过来,内莉,我一定要说服你或是强迫你帮助我,实现我见到凯瑟琳的决心,而且绝不耽搁。我发誓一定不会伤害任何人:我并不想惹出什么乱子,也不想激怒或是侮辱林顿先生;我只希望能听她亲口告诉我她怎么样,为什么会生病:问她我能为她做些什么。昨天晚上我在田庄的花园里待了六个小时,今天晚上我还会去;每天夜里我都会去,直到找到机会进去。如果埃德加·林顿碰到我,我会毫不犹豫地把他打倒在地,在我待在那里的时候保证让他休息个够。如果他的仆人们反抗我,我就会拿手枪威胁他们。可是,如果可以不用碰到他们或是他们的主人,岂不更好?你可以轻而易举就办到的。等我到的时候,我会先通知你,等到她一个人独处的时候,你就让我神不知鬼不觉地进去,然后在外面守着,一直到我离开为止,你的良心也会非常平静:你可以防止事情的恶化。"

would be hindering mischief."

I protested against playing that treacherous part in my employer's house: and besides, I urged the cruelty and selfishness of his destroying Mrs. Linton's tranquillity for his satisfaction. "The commonest occurrence startles her painfully," I said. "She's all nerves, and she couldn't bear the surprise, I'm positive. Don't persist, sir! or else, I shall be obliged to inform my master of your designs; and he'll take measures to secure his house and its inmates from any such unwarrantable intrusions!"

"In that case, I'll take measures to secure you, woman!" exclaimed Heathcliff; "you shall not leave Wuthering Heights till tomorrow morning. It is a foolish story to assert that Catherine could not bear to see me; and as to surprising her, I don't desire it: you must prepare her—ask her if I may come. You say she never mentions my name, and that I am never mentioned to her. To whom should she mention me if I am a forbidden topic in the house? She thinks you are all spies for her husband. Oh, I've no doubt she's in hell among you! I guess by her silence, as much as anything, what she feels. You say she is often restless, and anxious looking: is that a proof of tranquillity? You talk of her mind being unsettled. How the devil could it be otherwise in her frightful isolation? And that insipid, paltry creature attending her from *duty* and *humanity*! From *pity* and *charity*! He might as well plant an oak in a flowerpot, and expect it to thrive, as imagine he can restore her to vigour in the soil of his shallow cares! Let us settle it at once; will you stay here, and am I to fight my way to Catherine over Linton and his footmen? Or will you be

我说自己不会在主人家里做出这些背信弃义的事情，除此之外，我还极力劝他，若为了自己的满足而破坏林顿太太的安宁是残忍而自私的。"最普通的事都会让她非常震惊和痛苦，"我说道，"她的神经已经非常脆弱了，我敢肯定她承受不住这种惊吓。不要坚持了，先生！不然我就不得不把你的计划告诉我家主人。他会采取手段保护他的住所和家人，防止你的无理入侵！"

"如果是这样，我就得采取手段来保护你了，娘们！"希斯克利夫叫了起来，"明天早上之前不准你离开呼啸山庄。说凯瑟琳不能见我一面，这真是胡说八道；至于说我会吓到她，这并不是我想要的；你可以先让她有个准备，问她我可不可以来。你说她从来都没提过我的名字，也从来没人向她提起我。既然我在那个家里是一个禁止谈论的话题，那她又能跟谁提起我呢？她以为你们都是她丈夫的间谍。哦，我一点都不怀疑，她生活在你们中间就像是生活在地狱一样！我从她的沉默以及其他各个方面，都可以猜到她的感觉。你说她经常坐立不安，神色焦躁：难道这就是安宁的证据吗？你说她心绪紊乱，但她处于这种可怕的孤独中，又能有怎样的表现呢？那个乏味而又卑鄙无耻的家伙还说是什么出于责任和仁爱、怜悯和慈悲来照顾她！他想像凯瑟琳能在他那浅薄的照料中恢复精力，就像把一棵橡树种在一个花盆里，期待它枝繁叶茂一样！我们快点决定吧：你是想留在这里，让我干掉林顿和他

my friend, as you have been hitherto, and do what I request? Decide! because there is no reason for my lingering another minute, if you persist in your stubborn ill-nature!"

Well, Mr. Lockwood, I argued and complained, and flatly refused him fifty times; but in the long run he forced me to an agreement. I engaged to carry a letter from him to my mistress; and should she consent, I promised to let him have intelligence of Linton's next absence from home, when he might come, and get in as he was able: I wouldn't be there, and my fellow servants should be equally out of the way. Was it right or wrong? I fear it was wrong, though expedient. I thought I prevented another explosion by my compliance; and I thought, too, it might create a favourable crisis in Catherine's mental illness: and then I remembered Mr. Edgar's stern rebuke of my carrying tales; and I tried to smooth away all disquietude on the subject, by affirming, with frequent iteration, that that betrayal of trust, if it merited so harsh an appellation, should be the last. Notwithstanding, my journey homeward was sadder than my journey thither; and many misgivings I had, ere I could prevail on myself to put the missive into Mrs. Linton's hand.

But here is Kenneth; I'll go down, and tell him how much better you are. My history is *dree*, as we say, and will serve to wile away another morning.

Dree, and dreary! I reflected as the good woman descended to receive the doctor; and not exactly of a kind which I should have chosen to amuse me. But never mind! I'll extract wholesome medicines from Mrs. Dean's bitter herbs; and firstly, let me beware of the

第十四章

的仆人们，杀出一条血路去见凯瑟琳？还是愿意跟从前一样当我的朋友，按照我的请求去做？快决定吧！如果还要坚持你那冥顽不灵的本性，我就没理由再耽搁一分钟！"

好了，洛克伍德先生，我争辩过，抱怨过，明白地拒绝了他五十次，可到最后他还是逼迫我同意。我答应把他的一封信带给我的女主人；如果凯瑟琳同意，等他来的时候，我就答应把下次林顿出门的消息告诉他，让他进来：我不会待在那儿，我的仆役同伴也全都避开。这样做到底是对还是错？恐怕这是不对的，虽然只是权宜之计。我想我的顺从，可以避免另一场混乱的发生；我也认为，对于凯瑟琳的心病来说，这也许会创造一个有利的转机：接着我又想起埃德加先生严厉责骂我搬弄是非的情景；我反复对自己说，这次背信弃义的事，如果真该背上如此严酷的罪名，那也应该是最后一次了。我想由此来消除因为这件事而带来的一切不安。虽然如此，在回家的路上我还是比来时感到更加悲哀了些；在我说服自己把信交到林顿太太的手中之前，我心里疑虑重重。

不过肯尼斯大夫来啦，我得下去告诉他你已经好多了。照我们这样的说法，我这段历史可真够乏味的，而且还可以再消磨一个早晨呢。

乏味，沉闷！在这个好女人下楼招呼医生的时候，我这样想：其实这并不是我原本想要听来解闷的那类故事。但是没关系！我会从迪安太太的苦味药草中吸取有益的药物。首先，我要小心潜藏在凯瑟琳·希斯克利夫

fascination that lurks in Catherine Heathcliff's brilliant eyes. I should be in a curious taking if I surrendered my heart to that young person, and the daughter turned out a second edition of the mother!

那双明亮眼睛里的魔力。如果我对那个年轻人倾心,我一定会陷入不可思议的苦恼中,那个女儿正是她母亲的翻版啊!

Chapter 15
第十五章

Another week over—and I am so many days nearer health, and spring! I have now heard all my neighbour's history, at different sittings, as the housekeeper could spare time from more important occupations. I'll continue it in her own words, only a little condensed. She is, on the whole, a very fair narrator, and I don't think I could improve her style.

In the evening, she said, the evening of my visit to the Heights, I knew, as well as if I saw him, that Mr. Heathcliff was about the place; and I shunned going out, because I still carried his letter in my pocket, and didn't want to be threatened, or teased any more. I had made up my mind not to give it till my master went somewhere, as I could not guess how its receipt would affect Catherine. The consequence was, that it did not reach her before the lapse of three days. The fourth was Sunday, and I brought it into her room after the family

又过了一个星期——春天即将来临,我的身体也快要康复了!我现在已经听完了那位邻居的全部故事,因为这位管家总是可以从相对更为重要的工作中腾出时间来。我会用她自己的话继续把故事讲下去,只是会稍微压缩一点。总的说来,她是个讲故事的能手,我可不认为自己能在她的风格上锦上添花。

她说,那天晚上,就是我去拜访山庄的那个晚上,我知道而且也仿佛看到希斯克利夫先生就在田庄附近。我没有出门,因为他那封信还搁在我的口袋里,而且我也不愿再被吓唬或是戏弄。我下定决心,等到我家主人出门的时候,才把这信交给凯瑟琳,因为我猜不出凯瑟琳收到信后会有怎样的反应。结果,过了三天这封信还没有到她手里。第四天是星期日,等到全家都去教堂之后,我就把信带到

were gone to church. There was a man servant left to keep the house with me, and we generally made a practice of locking the doors during the hours of service; but on that occasion the weather was so warm and pleasant that I set them wide open, and, to fulfil my engagement, as I knew who would be coming, I told my companion that the mistress wished very much for some oranges, and he must run over to the village and get a few, to be paid for on the morrow. He departed, and I went up-stairs.

Mrs. Linton sat in a loose, white dress, with a light shawl over her shoulders, in the recess of the open window, as usual. Her thick, long hair had been partly removed at the beginning of her illness, and now she wore it simply combed in its natural tresses over her temples and neck. Her appearance was altered, as I had told Heathcliff; but when she was calm, there seemed unearthly beauty in the change. The flash of her eyes had been succeeded by a dreamy and melancholy softness; they no longer gave the impression of looking at the objects around her: they appeared always to gaze beyond, and far beyond-you would have said out of this world. Then, the paleness of her face—its haggard aspect having vanished as she recovered flesh—and the peculiar expression arising from her mental state, though painfully suggestive of their causes, added to the touching interest which she awakened; and—invariably to me, I know, and to any person who saw her, I should think—refuted, more tangible proofs of convalescence, and stamped her as one doomed to decay.

A book lay spread on the sill before her, and the scarcely perceptible wind fluttered its

她房里。家里还有一个男仆留下来和我一起看家。通常我们在做礼拜的那几个小时都会把门锁上,可是那天天气非常温暖舒适,我就把门大开着,而且,因为我知道谁会来,所以为了履行我的诺言,我就对我的同伴说女主人很想吃桔子,他必须得跑去村里买几个来,明天再付钱。他走了,我则上了楼。

和平常一样,林顿太太身上穿着一件宽松的白衣服,肩上披着一条薄薄的披巾,坐在一扇敞开着的窗子前面。她那头浓密的长发在她初病时被剪过一点,现在她就简单地梳一梳头发,让它非常自然地披在鬓角和颈子上。正如我对希斯克利夫所说的那样,她的外表已经变了;但是当她平静的时候,仿佛在这变化中存在着一种超凡脱俗的美。她眼睛里的亮光已经被一种梦幻、忧郁的温柔所取代,这光亮给人的印象不再是看着她周围的东西,看上去总是在凝视着遥远的地方,你也可以说是望着世外。她那苍白的脸色(她康复之后,那种憔悴的面貌已经消失了),还有从她内心中表现出来的特殊表情,虽然非常痛苦地暗示着原因,却格外增加了她的动人之处。我知道,无论是我,还是其他人看到她都会想,这些变化足以反驳那些说她是更为明显的康复,却表明她注定是要凋谢的。

她面前的窗台上放着一本摊开的书,一阵阵几乎无法让人感觉到的微

leaves at intervals. I believe Linton had laid it there; for she never endeavoured to divert herself with reading, or occupation of any kind, and he would spend many an hour in trying to entice her attention to some subject which had formerly been her amusement. She was conscious of his aim, and in her better moods endured his efforts placidly, only showing their uselessness by now and then suppressing a wearied sigh, and checking him at last with the saddest of smiles and kisses. At other times, she would turn petulantly away, and hide her face in her hands, or even push him off angrily; and then he took care to let her alone, for he was certain of doing no good.

Gimmerton chapel bells were still ringing; and the full, mellow flow of the beck in the valley came soothingly on the ear. It was a sweet substitute for the yet absent murmur of the summer foliage, which drowned that music about the Grange when the trees were in leaf. At Wuthering Heights it always sounded on quiet days following a great thaw or a season of steady rain. And of Wuthering Heights Catherine was thinking as she listened: that is, if she thought or listened at all; but she had the vague, distant look I mentioned before, which expressed no recognition of material things either by ear or eye.

"There's a letter for you, Mrs. Linton," I said, gently inserting it in one hand that rested on her knee. "You must read it immediately, because it wants an answer. Shall I break the seal?" "Yes," she answered, without altering the direction of her eyes. I opened it—it was very short. "Now," I continued, "read it." She drew away her hand, and let it fall. I replaced it

风掀动着书页。我想应该是林顿放在那儿的：因为凯瑟琳从不会费劲读书或是干其他事情消遣，而林顿则会花上个把小时，试图吸引她注意那些曾经让她消遣过的东西。她明白林顿的用心，在她心情稍微好点的时候，就会温顺地听他摆布，只是时不时强忍着一声厌倦的叹息，表示这些毫无用处，到最后就用最可怜的微笑和亲吻来制止他。在其他时候，她会突然转身，用手掩着脸，甚至愤怒地把他推开；然后他就小心翼翼地让她一个人待着，因为他确信自己已经无能为力了。

吉默顿教堂的钟声还在响着。山谷里的小溪涨满了水，传来一阵阵非常悦耳的潺潺流水声，这美妙的声音代替了现在还没到来的夏日里树叶的飒飒声，等到树上枝繁叶茂的时候，这飒飒声就会湮没田庄附近的那美妙音乐。在呼啸山庄附近，在冰雪融化或是雨季之后的平静日子里，小溪总是潺潺地响着。凯瑟琳一边听着，一边想着呼啸山庄，当然，如果她真的在想或真的在听的话！可她就像我刚才提到过的那样，两眼空洞地望着远方，说明不论是她的耳朵还是她的眼睛，都无法辨识外界的东西了。

"有一封给你的信，林顿太太，"我一边说着，一边轻轻把信塞到她放在膝上的一只手里，"你得马上看一看，因为还等着回信呢。要不要我把信拆开？""好的。"她回答着，并没改变她视线的方向。我拆开信，信非常短。"现在，"我接着说，"你看吧。"她缩回手，由着这封信掉到地

in her lap, and stood waiting till it should please her to glance down; but that movement was so long delayed that at last I resumed—

"Must I read it, ma'am? It is from Mr. Heathcliff."

There was a start and a troubled gleam of recollection, and a struggle to arrange her ideas. She lifted the letter, and seemed to peruse it; and when she came to the signature she sighed: yet still I found she had not gathered its import, for, upon my desiring to hear her reply, she merely pointed to the name, and gazed at me with mournful and questioning eagerness.

"Well, he wishes to see you," said I, guessing her need of an interpreter."He's in the garden by this time, and impatient to know what answer I shall bring."

As I spoke, I observed a large dog lying on the sunny grass beneath, raise its ears as if about to bark, and then smoothing them back, announce, by a wag of the tail, that some one approached whom it did not consider a stranger. Mrs. Linton bent forward, and listened breathlessly. The minute after a step traversed the hall; the open house was too tempting for Heathcliff to resist walking in: most likely he supposed that I was inclined to shirk my promise, and so resolved to trust to his own audacity. With straining eagerness Catherine gazed towards the entrance of her chamber. He did not hit the right room directly; she motioned me to admit him; but he found it out, ere I could reach the door, and in a stride or two was at her side, and had her grasped in his arms.

He neither spoke nor loosed his hold for some five minutes, during which period he bestowed more kisses than ever he gave in his

上。我捡起来重新把它放到她的膝上，站在那里，等她高兴的时候往下看几眼；可那一刻迟迟都没到来，最后我终于开了口：

"要我帮你念吗，太太？这是希斯克利夫先生写来的。"

她一惊，露出一种苦苦回忆的神色，竭力整理着自己的思绪。她拿起信，像是在细细阅读；当她看到签名时，叹了一口气。可我发现她依旧没有领会信的意思，因为在我急着要听她有何答复时，她却仅仅指了指签名，带着悲哀、疑问的急切心情盯着我。

"唉，他想要见见你，"我说，心想她需要找个人给她解释解释，"现在他就在花园里，迫不及待地想要知道我会给他带去什么样的答复呢。"

在我说话的时候，我看见躺在楼下向阳草地上的一条大狗竖起耳朵，好像要吠叫的样子，然后耳朵又耷拉下来，摇着尾巴宣布家里来了一个它并不认为陌生的客人。林顿太太探身向前，凝神屏气地倾听着。片刻之后，有个脚步声穿过大厅；对于希斯克利夫来说这幢敞开着门的房子实在是太诱惑了，他情不自禁地走了进来：很可能他以为我有意逃避诺言，因此就决定相信自己，大胆行事了。凯瑟琳紧张而又急切地盯着她卧室的门口。希斯克利夫并没有马上找到正确的房间，她就示意我去把他带过来，可还没等我走到门口，他就已经找到这里，一两个大步走到她的身旁，把她抱在自己怀里。

过了差不多五分钟时间，他既没说话，也没松开拥抱。我敢说在这段时间

life before, I dare say: but then my mistress had kissed him first, and I plainly saw that he could hardly bear, for downright agony, to look into her face! The same conviction had stricken him as me, from the instant he beheld her, that there was no prospect of ultimate recovery there—she was fated, sure to die.

"Oh, Cathy! Oh, my life! how can I bear it?" was the first sentence he uttered, in a tone that did not seek to disguise his despair. And now he stared at her so earnestly that I thought the very intensity of his gaze would bring tears into his eyes; but they burned with anguish: they did not melt.

"What now?" said Catherine, leaning back, and returning his look with a suddenly clouded brow: her humour was a mere vane for constantly varying caprices. "You and Edgar have broken my heart, Heathcliff! And you both come to bewail the deed to me, as if you were the people to be pitied! I shall not pity you, not I. You have killed me-and thriven on it, I think. How strong you are! How many years do you mean to live after I am gone?"

Heathcliff had knelt on one knee to embrace her; he attempted to rise, but she seized his hair, and kept him down.

"I wish I could hold you," she continued, bitterly, "till we were both dead! I shouldn't care what you suffered. I care nothing for your sufferings. Why shouldn't you suffer? I do! Will you forget me? Will you be happy when I am in the earth? Will you say twenty years hence, 'That's the grave of Catherine Earnshaw. I loved her long ago, and was wretched to lose her; but it is past. I've loved many others since: my children are dearer to me than she

里,他给予的吻比他这一生所给的还要多:不过是我家女主人先吻他的,而且我清清楚楚地看到,因为极大的痛苦,希斯克利夫简直不能直视她的脸!当他看到凯瑟琳时,就同我一样地确信,她是没有最终痊愈的希望了,她已经命中注定,一定是要死的。

"哦,凯茜!哦,我的生命!我怎能忍受得了?"这是他说出的第一句话,那声调毫不掩饰他的绝望。此刻他如此热诚地凝视着她,让我觉得他这样盯着会掉眼泪。但那双眼睛燃烧着极度的痛苦:并没化作泪水。

"现在你想怎么样?"凯瑟琳向后一退,说道,脸色突然阴沉下来,以此回应他的凝视:她的脾气不过是她那变化无常的内心的风向标而已。"你和埃德加都伤痛了我的心,希斯克利夫!你们俩都对我哭诉那件事,好像你们才是那个该被同情的人!我不会可怜你的,绝对不会。你已经把我给毁了,我想,你应该感到心满意足了吧。你身体多强壮啊!我死了以后你还打算活多少年呢?"

希斯克利夫本来一直是单膝下跪抱着她。他想要站起来,可凯瑟琳抓住他的头发,又把他按了下去。

"但愿我可以抓着你不放,"她接着痛楚地说道,"直到我们俩都死去!我不该在乎你受了什么苦,也不会在乎你的痛苦。你为什么就不该受苦?我一直都在受苦啊!你会把我忘掉吗?等我埋进土里的时候,你会快乐吗?二十年后你会不会说,'那是凯瑟琳·恩肖的坟。很久很久以前我爱过她,因为失去了她而万分悲痛;可这

was; and, at death, I shall not rejoice that I am going to her: I shall be sorry that I must leave them!' Will you say so, Heathcliff?"

"Don't torture me till I'm as mad as yourself," cried he, wrenching his head free, and grinding his teeth.

The two, to a cool spectator, made a strange and fearful picture. Well might Catherine deem that heaven would be a land of exile to her, unless with her mortal body she cast away her mortal character also. Her present countenance had a wild vindictiveness in its white cheek, and a bloodless lip and scintillating eye; and she retained in her closed fingers a portion of the locks she had been grasping. As to her companion, while raising himself with one hand, he had taken her arm with the other; and so inadequate was his stock of gentleness to the requirements of her condition, that on his letting go I saw four distinct impressions left blue in the colourless skin.

"Are you possessed with a devil," he pursued, savagely, "to talk in that manner to me when you are dying? Do you reflect that all those words will be branded in my memory, and eating deeper eternally after you have left me? You know you lie to say I have killed you; and, Catherine, you know that I could as soon forget you as my existence! Is it not sufficient for your infernal selfishness, that while you are at peace I shall writhe in the torments of hell?"

"I shall not be at peace," moaned Catherine, recalled to a sense of physical weakness by the violent, unequal throbbing of her heart, which beat visibly and audibly under this excess of agitation. She said nothing further till the

都已经过去。从那之后我又爱过很多人；对我来说，我的孩子比起她来要亲近多了；而且，死了之后，我也不会因为要去她那儿而高兴：我会很难过，因为我要离开孩子们了！'你会这么说吗，希斯克利夫？"

"不要把我折磨得和你一样疯疯癫癫，"他大声嚷道，咬着牙扭过头。

在一个冷静的旁观者看来，这两个人构成了一幅奇异而恐怖的图画。凯瑟琳完全有理由认为天堂对她来说就是个流放地，除非她把自己的精神也随同她的肉体一起抛开。此刻在她脸上，那惨白的双颊，毫无血色的双唇，和那闪烁的双眼都显现出一种狂野的复仇心理；在她握紧的手指里还留着刚才抓住的一绺头发。至于在她旁边的人，一只手撑着自己，另一只手则抓着她的胳膊；他那满腔的温情非常不适合她当时的健康状况。在他松手的时候，我看见在她那没有血色的皮肤上清清楚楚地留下了四条紫色印记。

"你是不是被恶魔附身了，"他恶狠狠地追问着，"在你快要死的时候居然还用这样的口气跟我说话？你有没有想过所有这些话都会烙在我记忆里，而且在你离开我以后，将会一直深深地啃食着我？你知道你在撒谎，说我害死了你；而且，凯瑟琳，你知道只要我还活着就不会忘记你！当你安息的时候，我却要在地狱般的煎熬中翻滚，这些还不够满足你那狠毒而又自私的心吗？"

"我不会安息的，"凯瑟琳呻吟着，感到自己身体的虚弱，因为这次过度的激动，她的心猛烈地、漫无规

paroxysm was over; then she continued, more kindly—

"I'm not wishing you greater torment than I have, Heathcliff. I only wish us never to be parted: and should a word of mine distress you hereafter, think I feel the same distress underground, and for my own sake, forgive me! Come here and kneel down again! You never harmed me in your life. Nay, if you nurse anger, that will be worse to remember than my harsh words! Won't you come here again? Do!"

Heathcliff went to the back of her chair, and leant over, but not so far as to let her see his face, which was livid with emotion. She bent round to look at him; he would not permit it: turning abruptly, he walked to the fireplace, where he stood, silent, with his back towards us. Mrs. Linton's glance followed him suspiciously: every movement woke a new sentiment in her. After a pause, and a prolonged gaze, she resumed; addressing me in accents of indignant disappointment—

"Oh, you see, Nelly, he would not relent a moment to keep me out of the grave. *That* is how I'm loved! Well, never mind. That is not *my* Heathcliff. I shall love mine yet; and take him with me: he's in my soul. And," added she musingly, "the thing that irks me most is this shattered prison, after all. I'm tired, tired of being enclosed here. I'm wearying to escape into that glorious world, and to be always there: not seeing it dimly through tears, and yearning for it through the walls of an aching heart; but really with it, and in it. Nelly, you think you are better and more fortunate than I; in full health and strength: you are sorry for me—very

则地跳动着，甚至可以看到听出心脏的跳动。她没有继续说下去，直到这阵激动过去之后，才稍微温和地接着说道：

"我并不希望你受的折磨比我还大，希斯克利夫。我只希望我们能够永远不分离：如果我的一句话就让你今后难过不已，想一想我在地下也一样会难过的，看在我的分上，原谅我吧！过来，再跪下！你这一生从来没有伤害过我。不，如果你还生气，那今后回想起来就要比我那些粗暴的话更让你难受了！你不想过来了吗？来啊！"

希斯克利夫走到她椅子的背后，俯身向前，不过并没有让她看到他那因激动而发青的脸。她转过身来看他，而他又不许她看，突然转身走到火炉旁边，默默地站在那儿，背对着我们。林顿太太疑惑不解地看着他：每一个动作都在她心里唤起一种新的感情。在一阵沉默和良久的凝视之后，她又讲话了，带着愤慨而又失望的语气对我说：

"啊，你看到了，内莉，他一刻都不肯发发慈悲，让我远离那个坟墓。他就是这样爱我的！算了，没关系。那不是我的希斯克利夫。我还是会爱着我的那个希斯克利夫，把他随身带着：他就在我的灵魂里。而且，"她沉思了一会儿又说道，"说到底，让我最厌烦还是这间破烂的监狱，我不愿再被关在这里了。我多想逃进那个充满欢乐的世界，永远留在那儿：不用再隔着泪水模糊地眺望着它，不用再穿过痛楚心灵的高墙渴望着它，而是真的跟它在一起，待在那里面。内莉，你觉得你比我更好，更幸运，更

soon that will be altered. I shall be sorry for *you*. I shall be incomparably beyond and above you all. I *wonder* he won't be near me!" She went on to herself. "I thought he wished it. Heathcliff, dear! you should not be sullen now. Do come to me, Heathcliff."

In her eagerness she rose and supported herself on the arm of the chair. At that earnest appeal he turned to her, looking absolutely desperate. His eyes wide, and wet at last, flashed fiercely on her; his breast heaved convulsively. An instant they held asunder, and then how they met I hardly saw, but Catherine made a spring, and he caught her, and they were locked in an embrace from which I thought my mistress would never be released alive: in fact, to my eyes, she seemed directly insensible. He flung himself into the nearest seat, and on my approaching hurriedly to ascertain if she had fainted, he gnashed at me, and foamed like a mad dog, and gathered her to him with greedy jealousy. I did not feel as if I were in the company of a creature of my own species: it appeared that he would not understand, though I spoke to him; so I stood off, and held my tongue, in great perplexity.

A movement of Catherine's relieved me a little presently: she put up her hand to clasp his neck, and bring her cheek to his as he held her; while he, in return, covering her with frantic caresses, said wildly—

"You teach me now how cruel you've been—cruel and false. Why did you despise me? Why did you betray your own heart, Cathy? I have not one word of comfort. You deserve this. You have killed yourself. Yes, you may kiss me, and cry; and wring out my kisses and tears; they'll blight you—they'll damn you. You loved me—then what *right* bad you to leave me? What right—answer me—for the poor fancy you felt for Linton? Because misery, and degradation, and death, and nothing that God or satan could inflict would have parted us, *you*, of your own will, did it. I have not broken your heart—*you* have broken it; and in breaking it, you have broken mine. So much the worse for me, that I am strong. Do I want to live? What kind of living will it be when you— oh, God! would *you* like to live with your soul in the grave?"

"Let me alone. Let me alone," sobbed Catherine."If I've done wrong, I'm dying for it. It is enough! You left me too; but I won't upbraid you! I forgive you. Forgive me!"

"It is hard to forgive, and to look at those eyes, and feel those wasted hands," he answered. "Kiss me again; and don't let me see your eyes! I forgive what you have done to me. I love *my* murderer—but *yours*! How can I?"

They were silent—their faces hid against each other, and washed by each other's tears. At least, I suppose the weeping was on both sides; as it seemed Heathcliff *could* weep on a great occasion like this.

I grew very uncomfortable, meanwhile; for the afternoon wore fast away, the man whom I had sent off returned from his errand, and I could distinguish, by the shine of the westering sun up the valley, a concourse thickening outside Gimmerton chapel porch.

"Service is over," I announced."My master will be here in half an hour."

Heathcliff groaned a curse, and strained Catherine closer; she never moved.

话，这是你罪有应得。你害死了你自己。是的，你可以亲吻我，可以哭出来，也可以让我吻你，让我流眼泪；但我的吻和眼泪会摧残你，会诅咒你。你是爱我的，那你又有什么权利离开我呢？有什么权利，回答我，是你对林顿心存的那种可怜幻想吗？苦难、耻辱和死亡，以及上帝或撒旦所能造就的一切东西都无法让我们分开，而你，就因为自己的意愿，居然要让我们分开。我没有让你心碎，是你自己让自己心碎；而你在这同时，也让我心碎。就因为我体格强壮，而让我多受些痛苦吗。我还要活着吗？那会是一种怎样的生活，当你——哦，上帝啊！你愿意让你的灵魂留在坟墓里而继续生活吗？"

"不要管我，不要再管我了，"凯瑟琳呜咽着，"如果我曾经曾做错了什么，就让我为此而死吧。够了！你也抛弃过我，可我并没有责备你！我原谅了你，你也原谅我吧！"

"看看这双眼睛，摸摸这双消瘦的手，让我如何原谅你，"他回答道，"再亲亲我吧，不要让我看到你的眼睛！我原谅你对我做过的事。我爱你这个伤害我的人，可伤害了你的人呢？我又如何能饶恕他呢？"

他们沉默了——两个人的脸彼此紧贴着，相互以泪洗面，至少，我想两个人都在哭吧，在这样一个特别的场合中，就连希斯克利夫好像都会流眼泪。

与此同时，我越来越焦急不安，因为下午很快就过去了，被我支使出去的仆人也已经完成任务回来，借着阳光照在山谷那边西照的夕阳中我可以看出吉默顿教堂门外已经涌出一大

Ere long I perceived a group of the servants passing up the road towards the kitchen wing. Mr. Linton was not far behind; he opened the gate himself and sauntered slowly up, probably enjoying the lovely afternoon that breathed as soft as summer.

"Now he is here," I exclaimed. "For Heaven's sake, hurry down! You'll not meet any one on the front stairs. Do be quick; and stay among the trees till he is fairly in."

"I must go, Cathy," said Heathcliff, seeking to extricate himself from his companion's arms. "But, if I live, I'll see you again before you are asleep. I won't stray five yards from your window."

"You must not go!" she answered, holding him as firmly as her strength allowed. "You shall not, I tell you."

"For one hour," he pleaded, earnestly.

"Not for one minute," she replied.

"I *must*—Linton will be up immediately," persisted the alarmed intruder.

He would have risen, and unfixed her fingers by the act—she clung fast, gasping: there was mad resolution in her face.

"No!" she shrieked. "Oh, don't, don't go. It is the last time! Edgar will not hurt us. Heathdiff, I shall die! I shall die!"

"Damn the fool! There he is," cried Heathdiff, sinking back into his seat. "Hush, my darling! Hush, hush, Catherine! I'll stay. If he shot me so, I'd expire with a blessing on my lips."

And there they were fast again. I heard my master mounting the stairs—the cold sweat ran from my forehead: I was horrified.

"Are you going to listen to her ravings?" I

堆人潮。

"做完礼拜了,"我宣布道,"我家主人半个小时之内就要到家啦。"

希斯克利夫呻吟着骂出一声脏话,把凯瑟琳抱得更紧了,而她则一直没有动弹。

没过多久,我看见一群仆人走过大路,朝着厨房的方向过去了。林顿先生在后面不远处。他自己开了大门,慢慢地蹓跶过来,也许是在享受这个可爱的、风和日丽、宛若夏日的下午。

"他到这儿来了,"我大叫道,"看在上帝的份上,快下去吧!走前面的楼梯,谁也不会遇到你。快点吧,待在树林里,等他进来你再走。"

"我必须得走了,凯茜,"希斯克利夫说,试图从他同伴的胳膊中挣脱出来,"不过,只要我还活着,在你睡觉之前,我还会再来看你的。我不会离开你的窗户五码之外的。"

"你不能走!"她回答着,竭尽全力紧紧地抱着他,"我告诉你,你不要走。"

"只走开一个小时。"他诚恳地乞求着。

"一分钟也不行,"她回答道。

"我非走不可——林顿马上就会上来。"这位受惊的不速之客坚持着。

他想要站起来,用力松开她的手指,可她却紧紧搂着,喘着气:在她脸上显现出一种疯狂的决心。

"不!"她尖叫着,"哦,不,你别走。这是最后一次!埃德加不会伤害我们的。希斯克利夫,我要死了!我要死了!"

"该死!他来了,"希斯克利夫叫着,又倒回在他的座位上,"嘘,亲爱的!嘘,不要闹了,凯瑟琳!我留

said, passionately."She does not know what she says. Will you ruin her, because she has not wit to help herself? Get up! You could be free instantly. That is the most diabolical deed that ever you did. We are all done for—master, mistress, and servant."

I wrung my hands, and cried out; and Mr. Linton hastened his step at the noise. In the midst of my agitation, I was sincerely glad to observe that Catherine's arms had fallen relaxed, and her head hung down.

"She's fainted, or dead," I thought; "so much the better. Far better that she should be dead, than lingering a burden and a misery-maker to all about her."

Edgar sprang to his unbidden guest, blanched with astonishment and rage. What he meant to do, I cannot tell; however, the other stopped all demonstrations, at once, by placing the lifeless-looking form in his arms.

"Look there!" he said. "Unless you be a fiend, help her first—then you shall speak to me!"

He walked into the parlour, and sat down. Mr. Linton summoned me, and with great difficulty, and after resorting to many means, we managed to restore her to sensation; but she was all bewildered; she sighed, and moaned, and knew nobody. Edgar, in his anxiety for her, forgot his hated friend. I did not. I went, at the earliest opportunity, and besought him to depart; affirming that Catherine was better, and he should hear from me in the morning, how she passed the night.

"I shall not refuse to go out of doors," he answered;"but I shall stay in the garden; and, Nelly, mind you keep your word tomorrow. I

下来。如果他就这么开枪崩了我，就让我嘴唇上带着一个祝福咽气吧。"

他们又紧紧地抱在了一起。我听到主人上楼——我的额头上直冒冷汗；我吓坏了。

"你就听由她胡说八道吗？"我激动地说道，"她根本不知道自己说了些什么。因为她神志不清，无法自主，你就要毁了她吗？快起来！你马上就可以挣脱的。这是你生平做过最恶毒的事。我们，包括主人，女主人，仆人可全都完蛋啦！"

我急得直绞手，大叫着；林顿先生一听到这动静，便加快了脚步，在我惊惶失措的时候，我非常高兴地看到凯瑟琳的胳膊松了下来，她的头也垂了下来。

"她是昏迷了，还是死了，"我心想着，"这样最好不过了。与其活着成为周围人的负担，给别人制造不幸，倒不如死掉了事。"

埃德加扑向这位不速之客，脸色因惊愕和愤怒变得惨白。我不知道他打算怎么做，不过，另一个人立刻停止了所有的示威，把那看起来已没有生命的东西送到埃德加的怀里。

"看看这个！"他说道，"除非你是个恶魔，不然就先救救她吧，然后跟我说话！"

他走到客厅里坐下。林顿先生招呼我过去，费了好大的劲，用了很多方法，我们才让她苏醒过来，可她完全神志不清了。她一声声地叹息着，呻吟着，谁也不认识了。埃德加一心替她焦急，忘了她那个可恨的朋友。不过我可没忘，早早地找了个机会走出去劝他离开；告诉他凯瑟琳已经好多了，明天早

shall be under those larch trees. Mind! or I pay another visit, whether Linton be in or not."

He sent a rapid glance through the half-open door of the chamber, and, ascertaining that what I stated was apparently true, delivered the house of his luckless presence.

晨我再告诉他这一夜她过的怎样。

"我并不拒绝走出这扇门,"他回答说,"但是我要待在花园里:内莉,明天你一定要遵守诺言。我会在那些落叶松下等你,记住!不然我还会再闯进来,不管林顿在不在家。"

卧室的门半开着,他匆匆往里瞥了一眼,证实了我所说的都是实话之后,这个倒霉的人才离开这所房子。

Chapter 16
第十六章

About twelve o'clock, that night, was born the Catherine you saw at Wuthering Heights: a puny, seven months' child; and two hours after the mother died, having never recovered sufficient consciousness to miss Heathcliff, or know Edgar. The latter's distraction at his bereavement is a subject too painful to be dwelt on; its after effects showed how deep the sorrow sunk. A great addition, in my eyes, was his being left without an heir. I bemoaned that, as I gazed on the feeble orphan; and I mentally abused old Linton for (what was only natural partiality) the securing his estate to his own daughter, instead of his son's. An unwelcomed infant it was, poor thing! It might have wailed out of life, and nobody cared a morsel, during those first hours of existence. We redeemed the neglect afterwards; but its beginning was as friendless as its end is likely to be.

Next morning—bright and cheerful out of doors—stole softened in through the blinds of the silent room, and suffused the couch and its occupant with a mellow, tender glow. Edgar Linton had his head laid on the pillow, and his eyes shut. His young and fair features were almost as deathlike as those of the form beside

大概在那天夜里十二点左右，你在呼啸山庄里见到的那个凯瑟琳出生了，一个瘦小的才怀了七个月的婴儿。两个小时之后，她的母亲就死了，她还没有完全恢复神志，既不知道希斯克利夫已经离开，也不认识埃德加。埃德加因为妻子去世经受的悲痛无法用言语来形容，从事后的影响可以看出他陷入了多么深切的悲痛之中。在我看来，还有一件雪上加霜的烦恼，就是他没有继承人了。在我盯着这个虚弱的孤儿时，我为此感到哀叹，在心里咒骂着老林顿，因为他规定只把财产传给自己的女儿，而没有考虑到他儿子的女儿（这应该只是天生的偏爱而已吧）。这是个不受欢迎的婴儿，可怜的小家伙！在她来到人世的头几个小时里，她很可能会嚎啕大哭而死去，也不会有人稍微去照顾她一下。虽然后来我们弥补了这个疏忽，但是她人生一开始遭遇的无依无靠，很有可能也是她生命结束时的情景。

第二天早晨——屋外晴空万里、舒适怡人，阳光悄悄地透过窗帘，溜进这寂静的屋子，一道柔美而温和的光线映照在睡椅和躺在上面的人的身上。埃德加·林顿头靠在枕头上，紧闭双眼，

him, and almost as fixed: but *his* was the hush of exhausted anguish, and *hers* of perfect peace. Her brow smooth, her lids closed, her lips wearing the expression of a smile; no angel in heaven could be more beautiful than she appeared. And I partook of the infinite calm in which she lay: my mind was never in a holier frame than while I gazed on that untroubled image of Divine rest. I instinctively echoed the words she had uttered a few hours before: "Incomparably beyond and above us all! Whether still on earth or now in heaven, her spirit is at home with God!"

I don't know if it be a peculiarity in me, but I am seldom otherwise than happy while watching in the chamber of death, should no frenzied or despairing mourner share the duty with me. I see a repose that neither earth nor hell can break, and I feel an assurance of the endless and shadowless hereafter—the Eternity they have entered—where life is boundless in its duration, and love in its sympathy, and joy in its fulness. I noticed on that occasion how much selfishness there is even in a love like Mr. Linton's, when he so regretted Catherine's blessed release! To be sure, one might have doubted, after the wayward and impatient existence she had led, whether she merited a haven of peace at last. One might doubt in seasons of cold reflection; but not then, in the presence of her corpse. It asserted its own tranquillity, which seemed a pledge of equal quiet to its former inhabitant.

Do you believe such people *are* happy in the other world, sir? I'd give a great deal to know.

I declined answering Mrs. Dean's ques-

第十六章

他那年轻俊美的容貌几乎跟他旁边的尸体一样死气沉沉,差不多是静止不动。不过他的脸因悲痛过后而显得平静,而凯瑟琳却是真正的宁静。她眉头舒展,眼眸紧闭,嘴唇上带着一丝微笑的表情,天堂里的天使也不能比她的容貌更美丽了。我沉浸在包围着她的无限恬静中,当我凝视着这神圣的安息者那无人惊扰的面容时,我的内心从没有感到如此圣洁。我不自觉地重复着几小时前她所说的那些话,"无与伦比地超越我们,在我们所有人之上!无论现在她尚在人间,抑或是已入天堂,她的灵魂仍与上帝同在!"

我不知这算不算是我的怪癖,在我守灵的时候,如果没有疯疯癫癫或是呼天抢地的哀悼者跟我一起担守灵的义务,我就很少有伤心难过的时候。我看到了一种无论人间或是地狱都无法打破的安宁,我深信从今往后他们的将来会无穷无尽、没有阴影,他们会进入一个永恒的世界,在那儿,生命可以无限延续,爱情变得和谐一致,生活充满欢乐。如果是这样,我发现,即使像林顿先生这样的爱情,在他痛惜凯瑟琳的美好超脱时,也多少存在着自私的成分!当然有人会怀疑,在她如此刁蛮任性、焦躁急切地度过一生后,最终是否可以得到一个宁静的港湾呢。在我们冷静回想的时候确实可以怀疑一下;但是,在她的遗体面前,绝对不行。遗体保持着自己的宁静,仿佛保证了这个人生前也过着同样宁静的生活。

先生,你相信这样的人在另一个世界里会幸福吗?我真的很想知道。

我拒绝回答迪安太太的问题,这

tion, which struck me as something heterodox. She proceeded:

Retracing the course of Catherine Linton, I fear we have no sight to think she is; but we'll leave her with her Maker.

The master looked asleep, and I ventured soon after sunrise to quit the room and steal out to the pure refreshing air. The servants thought me gone to shake off the drowsiness of my protracted watch; in reality, my chief motive was seeing Mr. Heathcliff. If he had remained among the larches all night, he would have heard nothing of the stir at the Grange; unless, perhaps, he might catch the gallop of the messenger going to Gimmerton. If he had come nearer, he would probably be aware, from the lights flitting to and fro, and the opening and shutting of the outer doors, that all was not right within. I wished, yet feared, to find him. I felt the terrible news must be told, and I longed to get it over; but *how* to do it, I did not know. He was there—at least a few yards further in the park; leant against an old ash tree, his hat off, and his hair soaked with the dew that had gathered on the budded branches, and fell pattering round him. He had been standing a long time in that position, for I saw a pair of ousels passing and repassin g scarcely three feet from him, busy in building their nest, and regarding his proximity no more than that of a piece of timber. They flew off at my approach, and he raised his eyes and spoke:

"She's dead!" he said; "I've not waited for you to learn that. Put your handkerchief away—don't snivel before me. Damn you all! she wants none of *your* tears!"

I was weeping as much for him as her:

让我觉得与信仰有些背道而驰。她接着说道：

追溯凯瑟琳·林顿的一生，恐怕我们大家都没有权利认为她是幸福的，只能把她交由她的造物主处置了。

主人看起来好像睡着了。日出之后，我便壮起胆子溜出房间，偷偷出去呼吸一下清新提神的空气。仆人们以为我是去摆脱那因长时间守夜而产生的睡意，实际上，我的主要目的是想见见希斯克利夫。如果他整夜都待在那一丛落叶松里，他根本听不到田庄里的骚动，但他也许会听到送信人前往吉默顿时那马蹄的声音。如果再靠近些，他或许会因为看到灯光来回闪动，和外面那些门的开开关关而意识到里面有点不对劲。虽然我很害怕，但还是想见到他。我觉得必须得告诉他这个糟糕的消息，同时也渴望这事能快点过去，但我又不知该如何开口。他在那儿，离花园至少有几码远。他靠在一棵老杨树旁，没戴帽子，他的头发被那些聚在发芽的树枝上的露水浸湿了，还滴答滴答地掉在他周围。他就一直保持这个姿势站了很久，因为我看见有一对乌鸫在离他不到三英尺的地方，来来回回地忙着建它们的爱巢，完全把在这附近的他当成了一块木头。我一走过去，它们就飞走了，他抬起眼睛，开口说话了。

"她死了！"他说，"我在这儿等你不是为了听你这个消息。把你的手绢收起来，别在我面前哭哭啼啼的。你们都该死！她才不会稀罕你们的眼泪！"

我哭泣，是为了埃德加，也是为

we do sometimes pity creatures that have none of the feeling either for themselves or others; and when I first looked into his face, I perceived that he had got intelligence of the catastrophe; and a foolish notion struck me that his heart was quelled and he prayed, because his lips moved and his gaze was bent on the ground.

"Yes, she's dead!" I answered, checking my sobs and drying my cheeks. "Gone to heaven, I hope; where we may, every one, join her, if we take due warning and leave our evil ways to follow good!"

"Did *she* take due warning, then?" asked Heathcliff, attempting a sneer. "Did she die like a saint? Come, give me a true history of the event. How did—"

He endeavoured to pronounce the name, but could not manage it; and compressing his mouth he held a silent combat with his inward agony, defying, meanwhile, my sympathy with an unflinching, fero cious stare. "How did she die?" he resumed, at last—fain, notwithstanding his hardihood, to have a support behind him; for, after the struggle, he trembled, in spite of himself, to his very finger-ends.

"Poor wretch!" I thought; "you have a heart and nerves the same as your brother men! Why should you be anxious to conceal them? Your pride cannot blind God! You tempt him to wring them, till he forces a cry of humiliation."

"Quietly as a lamb!" I answered, aloud. "She drew a sigh, and stretched herself, like a child reviving, and sinking again to sleep; and five minutes after I felt one little pulse at her heart, and nothing more!"

了凯瑟琳。有时候我们确实会同情那些对自己或是对别人都冷漠无情的人。当看到他脸上的表情时，我就感到他已经知道了这场灾祸。我忽然想到了一个愚蠢的念头，觉得他的心是平静的，而且他还在祷告，因为他的嘴唇在颤动，目光向下盯着地上。

"是的，她死了！"我压抑着自己的哽咽回答他，擦干脸上的泪水，"我希望她上了天堂。如果我们能够接受应得的警告，能够避恶从善，那我们每个人都可以去那里和她相会。"

"那她也接受了应得的警告吗？"希斯克利夫问道，想要讥讽一番，"她是不是像个圣徒一样死去的？来，告诉我这件事的真相。到底……？"

他努力地想要说出那个名字，但是又说不出口。他闭紧着嘴巴，跟自己内心的痛苦默默地斗争着，同时他又以一种毫不畏惧、凶神恶煞的目光蔑视着我的同情。"她是怎么死的？"最后，他终于又开口了。虽然他很刚毅，但是也很想在他身后找个依靠的地方，因为在斗争过后，他不由自主地颤抖起来，连他的手指尖都在发抖。

"真是个可怜的家伙！"我心里想，"原来你也有和其他人一样的心和神经啊！为什么你那么想要隐藏这些呢？你的自尊蒙蔽不了上帝！你是在诱惑上帝来折磨你的心和神经，直到逼迫你发出羞耻的喊叫为止。"

"像羔羊一样平静地去了！"我大声回答他，"她吸了口气，舒展一下身子，就像个孩子一样苏醒过来，接着又沉睡过去，五分钟后我发觉她的心头微微跳了一下，然后就再也不跳了！"

"And—did she ever mention me?" he asked, hesitating, as if he dreaded the answer to his question would introduce details that he could not bear to hear.

"Her senses never returned: she recognised nobody from the time you left her," I said. "She lies with a sweet smile on her face; and her latest ideas wandered back to pleasant early days. Her life closed in a gentle dream—may she wake as kindly in the other world!"

"May she wake in torment!" he cried, with frightful vehemence, stamping his foot, and groaning in a sudden paroxysm of ungovernable passion. "Why, she's a liar to the end! Where is she? Not *there*—not in heaven—not perished—where? Oh! you said you cared nothing for my sufferings! And I pray one prayer—I repeat it till my tongue stiffens— Catherine Earnshaw, may you not rest as long as I am living! You said I killed you— haunt me, then! The murdered *do* haunt their murderers. I believe—I know that ghosts *have* wandered on earth. Be with me always—take any form—drive me mad! only *do* not leave me in this abyss, where I cannot find you! Oh, God! it is unutterable! I *cannot* live without my life! I *cannot* live without my soul!"

He dashed his head against the knotted think; and, lifting up his eyes, howled, not like a man, but like a savage beast getting goaded to death with knives and spears. I observed several splashes of blood about the bark of the tree, and his hand and forehead were both stained; probably the scene I witnessed was a repetition of others acted during the night. It hardly moved my compassion—it appalled me: still I felt re-

"那——她有没有提起过我？"他犹豫不决地问道，好像害怕这个问题的答案会引出一些他不忍倾听的细节一样。

"她的神志一直都没恢复，从你离开她的那刻起，她就谁都认不出来了！"我说道，"她面带甜蜜的微笑躺在那里，她最后的思想徘徊在愉快的童年时光里。她的生命在一个温和的梦境中结束了，愿她在另一个世界里能温和地醒过来！"

"愿她在痛苦中醒来！"他带着令人恐慌的激奋大叫着，跺着自己的脚，因为一阵突如其来的难以控制的激动发作而呻吟起来。"为什么，她到死还要当一个说谎的人啊！她在哪里？不在那里，她不在天堂，也没有死去，到底在哪里？啊！你说过你完全不在乎我的痛苦！我会为你做个祷告，会一直重复地说，直到我的舌头僵硬：凯瑟琳·恩肖，只要我还活着，愿你永远不要安息！你说是我害死你的，那么就来缠着我吧！我相信被杀的人总是会缠着杀害他们的凶手的。我知道鬼魂会在人间徘徊，那你就永远跟着我，不管你用什么方法，把我逼疯吧！只要你别把我丢在这深渊里，让我无法寻找到你！啊，上帝！叫我该怎么说呢！没有生命，我会活不下去！没有灵魂，我也活不下去啊！"

他用头猛撞着那节瘤密布的树干，又抬起眼睛，嚎啕大哭起来，完全不像个人，而像一头被刀和矛刺得奄奄一息的野兽。我看见树皮上留下好多血迹，他的双手和前额上也都血迹斑斑，也许我亲眼目睹的这一幕他在夜里已经重复上演很多次了。这并没让我产生同情，反而让我感到惊骇，不

luctant to quit him so. But the moment he recollected himself enough to notice me watching, he thundered a command for me to go, and I obeyed. He was beyond my skill to quiet or console!

Mrs. Linton's funeral was appointed to take place on the Friday following her decease; and till then her coffin remained uncovered, and strewn with flowers and scented leaves, in the great drawing-room. Linton spent his days and nights there, a sleepless guardian; and—a circumstance concealed from all but me—Heathcliff spent his nights, at least, outside, equally a stranger to repose. I held no communication with him: still I was conscious of his design to enter, if he could; and on the Tuesday, a little after dark, when my master, from sheer fatigue, had been compelled to retire a couple of hours, I went and opened one of the windows, moved by his perseverance to give him a chance of bestowing on the fading image of his idol one final adieu. He did not omit to avail himself of the opportunity, cautiously and briefly: too cautiously to betray his presence by the slightest noise. Indeed, I shouldn't have discovered that he had been there, except for the disarrangement of the drapery about the corpse's face, and for observing on the floor a curl of light hair, fastened with a silver thread; which, on examination, I ascertained to have been taken from a locket hung round Catherine's neck. Heathdiffhad opened the trinket and cast out its contents, replacing them by a black lock of his own. I twisted the two, and enclosed them together.

Mr. Earnshaw was, of course, invited to attend the remains of his sister to the grave; and

过我还是不愿就这样离开他。但当他一回过神来，发现我在看他，就咆哮着命令我走开，我遵从了。我可没法子让他安静下来，或是给他一些安慰！

林顿太太的葬礼定在她去世的那个星期五举行。在这之前，她的灵柩一直没有上盖，里面点缀着鲜花和香草，安放在大厅。林顿日日夜夜地守在那里，成了不休不眠的守灵人。还有一件除了我以外其他人都不知道的事，希斯克利夫每天都在外面度过这几个夜晚，差不多也是个同样没有休息的客人。我没有跟他互通消息，不过我知道如果有机会的话，他肯定会想办法进来的。星期二的时候，刚天黑不久，我的主人因为疲劳过度，不得不去休息一两个小时，这时我就走过去打开一扇窗户。我被希斯克利夫的坚定不移感动了，于是就给他一个机会，让他跟自己偶像那凋谢的面容做最后的道别。他没有让自己错过这次机会，谨慎而迅速地走进屋来，非常小心地不让那些微弱的声音败露他的出现。说真的，要不是看到尸体脸上的盖布有点凌乱，还有地板上那一绺淡色的头发，我根本不会发现他来过这里。那一绺头发是用一根银线捆扎着的，仔细观察之后，我肯定这是从挂在凯瑟琳脖子上的那只小金盒里拿出来的。希斯克利夫打开这个小盒子，扔掉了里面的头发，用他自己的一绺黑发代替它们放在里面。我把这两绺头发拧成一缕，一起放了进去。

恩肖先生当然受到邀请来参加妹妹的遗体下葬仪式，他没有说过任何

he sent no excuse, but he never came; so that, besides her husband, the mourners were wholly composed of tenants and servants. Isabella was not asked.

The place of Catherine's interment, to the surprise of the villagers, was neither in the chapel, under the carved monument of the Lintons, nor yet by the tombs of her own relations, outside. It was dug on a green slope in a corner of the kirkyard, where the wall is so low that heath and bilberry plants have climbed over it from the moor; and peat mould almost buries it. Her husband lies in the same spot now; and they have each a simple headstone above, and a plain grey block at their feet, to mark the graves.

推辞的话，但是一直都没有出现，因此，除了她丈夫以外，送葬的都是佃户和仆人。伊莎贝拉没有受到邀请。

让村里人感到讶异的是，凯瑟琳的安葬地点既不在礼拜教堂里林顿家族那刻字的石碑下，也不是在外面她自己家人的坟墓旁边，而是在墓园一角的青草坡上，那边的围墙如此低矮，以至于那些石楠和越橘之类的都从旷野那边爬过围墙，泥煤土差不多把整个土坯掩没了。如今她丈夫的坟也在那里，他们的坟上各立着一块简单的墓碑，下面各放着一块普通的灰石块，作为坟墓的标记。

Chapter 17
第十七章

That Friday made the last of our fine days, for a month. In the evening, the weather broke; the wind shifted from south to northeast, and brought rain first, and then sleet and snow. On the morrow one could hardly imagine that there had been three weeks of summer: the primroses and crocuses were hidden under wintry drifts; the larks were silent, the young leaves of the early trees smitten and blackened.

那个星期五是我们这一个月以来最后一个好天气。到了晚上的时候就变天了，南风变成了东北风，先是下起了雨，接着又变成了雨夹雪。第二天早上，人们很难想像已经过了三个星期的夏天：樱草和番红花被埋在积雪下面，百灵鸟静寂无声，幼树的嫩叶也被吹打得变黑了。那个早晨就在沉闷、寒冷和凄凉中慢慢地捱过去

第十七章

And dreary, and chill, and dismal that morrow did creep over! My master kept his room; I took possession of the lonely parlour, converting it into a nursery: and there I was sitting, with the moaning doll of a child laid on my knee; rocking it to and fro, and watching, meanwhile, the still driving flakes build up the uncurtained window, when the door opened, and some person entered, out of breath and laughing! My anger was greater than my astonishment for a minute. I supposed it one of the maids, and I cried—

"Have done! How dare you show your giddiness here? What would Mr. Linton say if he heard you?"

"Excuse me!" answered a familiar voice; "but I know Edgar is in bed, and I cannot stop myself."

With that the speaker came forward to the fire, panting and holding her hand to her side.

"I have run the whole way from Wuthering Heights!" she continued, after a pause; "except where I've flown. I couldn't count the number of falls I've had. Oh, I'm aching all over! Don't be alarmed! There shall be an explanation as soon as I can give it; only just have the goodness to step out and order the carriage to take me on to Gimmerton, and tell a servant to seek up a few clothes in my wardrobe."

The intruder was Mrs. Heathcliff. She certainly seemed in no laughing predicament: her hair streamed on her shoulders, dripping with snow and water; she was dressed in the girlish dress she commonly wore, befitting her age more than her position: a low frock with short sleeves, and nothing on either head or neck. The

了！我的主人一直待在他的屋子里，我就占据了这个孤寂的客厅，把它变成了一间育婴室。我坐在那里，把那个呜咽啜泣的婴儿放膝盖上，摇来晃去，同时望着那依旧纷纷扬扬下着的雪片堆积在那没装窗帘的窗户上。这时门开了，有个人走了进来，一边喘气一边大笑。当时我的怒气胜过了我的惊诧，还以为是某个女仆，就大喊道：

"够了！你怎么敢在这放肆，如果被林顿先生听到，他会怎么说？"

"请原谅我！"一个熟悉的声音回答道，"不过我知道埃德加还在睡觉，我又控制不了自己。"说话的人说着就走到火炉边，手撑着腰喘息着。

"我从呼啸山庄一路跑到这里来！"停顿了一会，她接着说道，"除了那些飞过的路。我都记不清自己跌倒多少次了。啊，我全身都很痛！不要被我吓到了！只要我能解释我自会跟你说清楚的！先请你行行好，准备一辆马车把我送去吉默顿吧，再叫个佣人去我衣橱里找几件衣服来。"

闯进来的正是希斯克利夫太太。看她那副样子实在叫人笑不出来：她的头发披散在肩上，湿漉漉地滴着雪水；身上穿的是她平常做姑娘时穿的衣服，比起她的身份，更适合她的年龄；短袖的露胸上衣，头上和脖子上什么都没戴，上衣是薄丝绸做的，湿

frock was of light silk, and clung to her with wet, and her feet were protected merely by thin slippers; add to this a deep cut under one ear, which only the cold prevented from bleeding profusely, a white face scratched and bruised, and a frame hardly able to support itself, through fatigue; and you may fancy my first fright was not much allayed when I had leisure to examine her.

"My dear young lady," I exclaimed, "I'll stir nowhere, and hear nothing, till you have removed every article of your clothes, and put on dry things; and certainly you shall not go to Gimmerton tonight, so it is needless to order the carriage."

"Certainly, I shall," she said; "walking or riding: yet I've no objection to dress myself decently. And—ah, see how it flows down my neck now! The fire does make it smart."

She insisted on my fulfilling her directions, before she would let me touch her; and not till after the coachman had been instructed to get ready, and a maid set to pack up some necessary attire, did I obtain her consent for binding the wound and helping to change her garments.

"Now, Ellen," she said, when my task was finished, and she was seated in an easy chair on the hearth, with a cup of tea before her, "you sit down opposite me, and put poor Catherine's baby away: I don't like to see it! You mustn't think I care little for Catherine, because I behaved so foolishly on entering: I've cried too, bitterly—yes, more than any one else has reason to cry. We parted unreconciled, you remember, and I shan't forgive myself. But, for all that, I was not going to sympathise with

答答地贴在身上；脚上只穿了一双单薄的拖鞋；除此之外，一只耳朵下面还有一道很深的伤痕，幸亏天气寒冷，才没有失血过多，那张白净的脸满是抓痕，到处都是淤青，还有一副过度疲劳而难以支撑的身躯。你可以想像，等我定下心来仔细打量她的时候，我最初的惊恐并没有减轻多少。

"我亲爱的小姐，"我叫道，"除非你把衣服一件件都脱下，换上干的，要不然我哪儿都不去，什么都不听。当然今晚你不能去吉默顿，因此也不需要准备马车。"

"我当然得去，"她说，"不管是走路，还是坐车，不过我不反对自己穿得体面些。而且，哦，看看这会儿血怎么顺着脖子流下来了！被火一烤觉得更刺痛了。"

她坚持要我先完成她的命令，然后才肯让我碰她，而且直到我吩咐马夫准备好，又叫女仆打包了一些必要的衣物后，她才同意我给她包扎伤口，帮她换衣服。

"现在，艾伦，"此时我的工作已经完成，她坐在壁炉旁的一张安乐椅上，前面放着着一杯茶，对我说道，"你坐到我对面去吧，把那可怜的凯瑟琳的孩子放在一边，我不喜欢见到她！你可不要因为我进来时那副傻乎乎的模样，就以为我一点儿都不关心凯瑟琳，我也哭了，哭得很伤心。是啊，我比任何人都有哭的理由。你还记得吗，我们还没有和好就分开了，我不能原谅我自己。但是，尽管如此，我还是不会同情他——那个残忍

第十七章

him—the brute beast! O, give me the poker! This is the last thing of his I have about me:" she slipped the gold ring from her third finger, and threw it on the floor. "I'll smash it!" she continued, striking it with childish spite, "and then I'll burn it!" and she took and dropped the misused article among the coals. "There! he shall buy another, if he gets me back again. He'd be capable of coming to seek me, to tease Edgar—I dare not stay, lest that notion should possess his wicked head! And besides, Edgar has not been kind, has he? And I won't come suing for his assistance; nor will I bring him into more trouble. Necessity compelled me to seek shelter here; though, if I had not learnt he was out of the way, I'd have halted at the kitchen, washed my face, warmed myself, got you to bring what I wanted, and departed again to anywhere out of the reach of my accursed—of that incarnate goblin! Ah, he was in such a fury! If he had caught me! It's a pity Earnshaw is not his match in strength: I wouldn't have run till I'd seen him all but demolished, had Hindley been able to do it!"

"Well, don't talk so fast, Miss!" I interrupted, "you'll disorder the handkerchief I have tied round your face, and make the cut bleed again. Drink your tea, and take breath, and give over laughing: laughter is sadly out of place under this roof, and in your condition!"

"An undeniable truth," she replied. "Listen to that child! It maintains a constant wail—send it out of my hearing for an hour; I shan't stay any longer."

I rang the bell, and committed it to a servant's care; and then I inquired what had urged her to escape from Wuthering Heights in such

的畜生！哦，快给我拨火棍！这是留在我身边的他的最后一样东西了！"她把那只金戒指从中指上摘下来，丢在地板上。"我要敲碎它！"她带着孩子气的泄愤敲打着，接着说道，"然后我还要把它烧掉！"她捡起那个被敲得不成形的东西，扔进煤堆里。"好了！如果他想要我回去，就得再买一个了。为了挑衅埃德加，他一定会来找我。我不敢留在这儿，免得他心存恶意，况且，埃德加也并不是那么友好，不是吗？而且我并不想来求他帮忙，也不想给他带来更多烦恼。我是迫不得已才来这里躲躲的。尽管如此，但要不是我听说他不在这，我还不得不待在厨房，洗洗脸，暖和暖和身子，叫你帮我拿那些我要的东西，然后再离开，随便去什么地方，只要是那被我诅咒的恶魔化身找不到的地方就行！啊，如果让他捉住我，他就会非常残暴的！真可惜恩肖在力气上比不过他，如果辛德雷能够做到的话，在没看到他被打得稀巴烂之前，我才不会逃跑呢！"

"好啦，小姐，别说得那么快！"我打断她的话说道，"你会把我包扎在脸上的手绢弄松的，伤口又要流血了。先喝口茶，缓口气，别再笑了。在这个屋子里，加上你现在这样的情况，笑是不合时宜的！"

"这倒是不可否认的事实，"她回答说，"你听听那孩子！她一直没完没了地嚎啕大哭。快把她抱开一小时，别让我听见她的哭声，我不会久留的。"

我拉了拉铃，把孩子交给仆人照看，然后盘问她是什么事情逼迫她这么狼狈的情况下逃出呼啸山庄的，

an unlikely plight, and where she means to go, as she refused remaining with us.

"I ought, and I wish to remain," answered she, "to cheer Edgar and take care of the baby, for two things, and because the Grange is my right home. But I tell you he wouldn't let me! Do you think he could bear to see me grow fat and merry; and could bear to think that we were tranquil, and not resolve on poisoning our comfort? Now, I have the satisfaction of being sure that he detests me to the point of its annoying him seriously to have me within ear-shot, or eye-sight: I notice, when I enter his presence, the muscles of his countenance are involuntarily distorted into an expression of hatred; partly arising from his knowledge of the good causes I have to feel that sentiment for him, and partly from original aversion. It is strong enough to make me feel pretty certain that he would not chase me over England, supposing I contrived a clear escape; and therefore I must get quite away. I've recovered from my first desire to be killed by him: I'd rather he'd kill himself! He has extinguished my love effectually, and so I'm at my ease. I can recollect yet how I loved him; and can dimly imagine that I could still be loving him, if—no, no! Even if he had doted on me, the devilish nature would have revealed its existence somehow. Catherine had an awfully per verted taste to esteem him so dearly, knowing him so well. Monster! would that he could be blotted out of creation, and out of my memory!"

"Hush, hush! He's a human being," I said. "Be more charitable: there are worse men than he is yet!"

"He's not a human being," she retorted;

"我应该也愿意留下来，"她回答说，"可以安慰一下埃德加，还可以照顾一下孩子，一举两得，而且毕竟田庄才是我真正的家。不过我告诉你，那畜生肯定不允许我这么做！你觉得他会眼睁睁地看着我发胖而兴高采烈吗；他会想着我们过得风平浪静而决计不来破坏我们舒服的日子吗？现在，让我满意的是，我已经确切地知道他讨厌我，讨厌到了只要他听到或是见到我，就非常恼火的程度，我注意到，当我走到他面前时，他脸上的肌肉就会不由自主地扭曲，变成一副憎恨的表情。这其中的缘由有部分是因为他知道我有充分的理由憎恨他，部分是因为原本就存在的反感。他对我的憎恨如此强烈，以至于让我相信，如果我想方设法溜之大吉，他肯定不会跑遍全英格兰来追我。因此我一定要逃跑，我已经没有自己最初那种甘愿被他杀死的愿望了，现在我宁可他自杀！他已经彻底地熄灭了我的爱情，因此我现在很轻松，尽管还记得我曾多么爱他，也能朦朦胧胧地想像到我仍旧会爱他，如果——不，不，即使他曾经宠爱过我，总有一天他那魔鬼的天性还是会暴露无遗。凯瑟琳那么了解他，却还那么深切地重视他，这感觉还真是奇怪。他是个怪物！但愿他能从人世间消失，从我的记忆里消失！"

"嘘，别说了！他是个人啊，"我说道，"要放慈悲些，这世上还有比他更坏的人呢！"

"他不是人，"她反驳我说，"他没

"and he has no claim on my charity. I gave him my heart, and he took and pinched it to death; and flung it back to me. People feel with their hearts, Ellen: and since he has destroyed mine, I have not power to feel for him: and I would not, though he groaned from this to his dying day, and wept tears of blood for Catherine! No, indeed, indeed, I wouldn't!" And here Isabella began to cry; but, immediately dashing the water from her lashes, she recommenced. "You asked, what has driven me to flight at last? I was compelled to attempt it, because I had succeeded in rousing his rage a pitch above his malignity. Pulling out the nerves with red hot pincers requires more coolness than knocking on the head. He was worked up to forget the fiendish prudence he boasted of, and proceeded to murderous violence. I experienced pleasure in being able to exasperate him: the sense of pleasure woke my instinct of self-preservation, so I fairly broke free; and if ever I come into his hands again he is welcome to a signal revenge.

"Yesterday, you know, Mr. Earnshaw should have been at the funeral. He kept himself sober for the purpose—tolerably sober: not going to bed mad at six o'clock and getting up drunk at twelve. Consequently, he rose, in suicidal low spirits, as fit for the church as for a dance; and instead, he sat down by the fire and swallowed gin or brandy by tumblerfuls.

"Heathcliff—I shudder to name him! has been a stranger in the house from last Sunday till today. Whether the angels have fed him, or his kin beneath, I cannot tell; but he has not eaten a meal with us for nearly a week. He has just come home at dawn, and gone up-stairs to his chamber; locking himself in—as if anybody

有权利要求得到我的仁慈。我把心交给了他,他却拿过去捏碎了,然后再丢还给我。人是用他们的心来感觉的,艾伦,既然他毁了我的心,那么我就无力去同情他了。而且,虽然从今以后他会一直呻吟到他死去的那天,为凯瑟琳哭出血来,但我仍旧不会同情他,不,真的,我真的不会同情他!"说到这儿,伊莎贝拉哭了起来,不过很快她就擦干睫毛上的眼泪,继续说道,"你刚才问我,是什么事最终逼迫我逃跑?我是不得不这么做啊,因为我已经把他的愤怒煽得比他的狠毒还要强烈了。用烧得通红的铁钳拨弄神经比敲打脑袋更需要冷静。他已经被我惹得忘记了他自夸的那种恶魔般的谨慎,要使用暴力的凶杀手做了。能够激怒他让我体验到了一种快感,这种快感唤醒了我自我保护的本能,因此我就跑了出来。如果再落入他的手里,他肯定会狠狠地报复我的。"

"你知道,昨天恩肖先生本应该来送殡的,为此他还特意让自己保持清醒,还算是比较清醒的:没有像往常那样六点钟就疯疯癫癫地上床,十二点才醉醺醺地起来。因此,他起来的时候,情绪低沉得像要自杀一样,不适合去教堂,就像不适合跳舞一样。他没去任何地方,光坐在火炉旁边,一杯杯地灌着杜松子酒或白兰地。

"希斯克利夫——提起这个名字我就发抖!从上星期日开始直到今天他就像是这家里的陌生人一样。是天使养活了他,还是他地狱里的同类养活了他,我说不上来,佀是他已经将近一个星期没跟我们一起吃饭了。到天亮他才回家,上楼到他的卧房里,然后

dreamt of coveting his company! There he has continued, praying like a methodist: only the deity he implored is senseless dust and ashes; and God, when ad dressed, was curiously confounded with his own black father! After concluding these precious orisons—and they lasted generally till he grew hoarse and his voice was strangled in his throat—he would be off again; always straight down to the Grange! I wonder Edgar did not send for a constable, and give him into custody! For me, grieved as I was about Catherine, it was impossible to avoid regarding this season of deliverance from degrading oppression as a holiday.

"I recovered spirits sufficient to hear Joseph's eternal lectures without weeping, and to move up and down the house less with the foot of a frightened thief than formerly. You wouldn't think that I should cry at anything Joseph Could say; but he and Hareton are detestable compan ions. I'd rather sit with Hindley, and hear his awful talk, than with 't' little maister' and his staunch supporter, that odious old man! When Heathcliff is in, I'm often obliged to seek the kitchen and their society, or starve among the damp uninhabited chambers; when he is not, as was the case this week, I establish a table and chair at one corner of the house fire, and never mind how Mr. Earnshaw may occupy himself; and he does not interfere with my arrangements. He is quieter now than he used to be, if no one provokes him: more sullen and depressed, and less furious. Joseph affirms he's sure he's an altered man: that the Lord has touched his heart, and he is saved 'so as by fire.' I'm puzzled to detect signs of the favourable

把自己锁在里面，好像有人梦想着要陪他一样！他就这样一直在里面待着，像个循道宗信徒似的祈祷着，只不过他所祈求的神明是那些毫无知觉的尘埃灰烬而已。至于上帝，每每提及，都是很奇怪地跟他自己的黑鬼父亲混在一起！做完这些真爱的祷告之后（他经常会坚持到自己嗓子嘶哑，喉咙哽住才结束），他就又出门了，总是直奔田庄！我很惊讶埃德加居然没找治安官，把他给羁押起来！至于我，虽然为凯瑟琳感到伤心，但还是情不自禁地把这段从受侮辱的压迫中解脱出来的这段时光当成一个节日呢。

"我已经恢复了精力，可以忍受约瑟夫的絮絮叨叨的说教而不掉眼泪，也可以在这屋子里上下走动，而不用像以前那样惊恐的小偷似的蹑手蹑脚了。你可不要以为无论约瑟夫说什么我都会哭哭啼啼的，可是他和哈里顿都是非常让人讨厌的同伴。我宁愿坐在辛德雷旁边，听他那些骇人听闻的言语，也不愿跟那个'小主人'和他那个得力助手，那讨人厌的糟老头子在一起！希斯克利夫在家的时候，我常常不得不跑去厨房找伴，要不就在那些潮湿而无人居住的卧室里挨饿。当他不在家时，就像这个星期一样，我就在大厅壁炉的一角摆上一张桌子和一把椅子，从来不管恩肖先生在忙什么，他也不干涉我的事。如果没人去激怒他，他要比往常安静多了，更加沉闷沮丧，也很少发脾气。约瑟夫说他肯定恩肖先生已经变了一个人：说是上帝触动了他的心，他就像那'浴火凤凰'一样重生了。我也察觉到了这种好转的迹象，颇感诧

第十七章

change: but it is not my business.

"Yester-evening I sat in my nook reading some old books till late on towards twelve. It seemed so dismal to go up-stairs, with the wild snow blowing outside, and my thoughts continually reverting to the kirkyard and the new-made grave! I dared hardly lift my eyes from the page before me, that melancholy scene so instantly usurped its place. Hindley sat opposite, his head leant on his hand; perhaps meditating on the same subject. He had ceased drinking at a point below irrationality, and had neither stirred nor spoken during two or three hours. There was no sound through the house but the moaning wind which shook the windows every now and then, the faint crackling of the coals, and the click of my snuffers as I removed at intervals the long wick of the candle. Hareton and Joseph were probably fast asleep in bed. It was very, very sad: and while I read I sighed, for it seemed as if all joy had vanished from the world, never to be restored.

"The doleful silence was broken at length by the sound of the kitchen latch: Heathcliff had returned from his watch earlier than usual; owing, I suppose, to the sudden storm. That entrance was fastened, and we heard him coming round to get in by the other. I rose with an irrepressible expression of what I felt on my lips, which induced my companion, who had been staring towards the door, to turn and look at me.

"'I'll keep him out five minutes,' he exclaimed. 'You won't object?'

"'No, you may keep him out the whole night for me,' I answered. 'Do! put the key in the lock, and draw the bolts.'

异,但那又不关我的事。

"昨天晚上,我坐在我的小角落里看一些旧书,一直看到将近十二点钟。外面大雪纷飞,我的思绪不断转向那墓园和新建的墓穴,这时上楼的话好像很凄惨!我几乎不敢从面前的书页上抬起眼睛,只要一抬眼,那幅忧郁的景象就立刻乘虚而入占据了书本的位置。辛德雷坐在对面,头靠在手上,也许他也在思考着同一件事。他已经不再喝酒,到了比失去理性更糟糕的地步,两三个小时里他既没有动弹一下,也没有开口说话。整个屋子没有什么声响,除了呼啸的风时不时地吹动着窗户、煤块微弱的爆裂声,以及我偶尔剪掉长长的烛芯时剪刀发出的咔嚓声。哈里顿和约瑟夫大概早已经躺在床上睡着了。周围真是非常凄凉!我一边看书,一面叹着气,因为看起来所有的欢乐好像要从这世上消失了,永远不再恢复。

"这阵阴沉的寂静终于被厨房的门闩声打破了:希斯克利夫守夜回来了,比平时要早一点。我想应该是由于这场突如其来的暴风雪的缘故吧。厨房那扇门被闩住了,我们听见他绕到另一个门口想要走进来。我站了起来,自己感觉到嘴上带着一种抑制不住的表情,这表情吸引了我那原本盯着门口看的同伴转过头来看着我。

"'我要让他在外面关上五分钟,'他叫道,'你不会反对吧?'

"'不会,你可以替我把他关在外面一整夜,'我回答道,'快去吧!把钥匙插在钥匙孔里,拉上门闩。'

"Earnshaw accomplished this ere his guest reached the front; he then came and brought his chair to the other side of my table, leaning over it, and searching in my eyes, a sympathy with the burning hate that gleamed from his: as he both looked and felt like an assassin, he couldn't exactly find that; but he discovered enough to encourage him to speak.

"'You, and I,' he said, 'have each a great debt to settle with the man out yonder! If we were neither of us cowards, we might combine to discharge it. Are you as soft as your brother? Are you willing to endure to the last, and not once attempt a repayment?'

"'I'm weary of enduring now,' I replied; 'and I'd be glad of a retaliation that wouldn't recoil on myself; but treachery and violence are spears pointed at both ends: they wound those who resort to them, worse than their enemies.'

"'Treachery and violence are a just return for treachery and violence!' cried Hindley. 'Mrs. Heathcliff, I'll ask you to do nothing, but sit still and be dumb. Tell me now, can you? I'm sure you would have as much pleasure as I in witnessing the conclusion of the fiend's existence; he'll be *your* death unless you overreach him; and he'll be *my* ruin. Damn the hellish villain! He knocks at the door as if he were master here already! Promise to hold your tongue, and before that clock strikes—it wants three minutes of one you're a free woman!'

"He took the implements which I described to you in my letter from his breast, and would have turned down the candle. I snatched it away, however, and seized his arm.

"'I'll not hold my tongue!' I said; 'you

"恩肖在他的客人还没来得及走到门口之前就做完了这件事,然后他走过来,把他的椅子搬到我桌子对面,靠在桌子上,他眼里闪烁着一股熊熊燃烧的愤恨,想从我眼里寻求同情。因为看起来和感觉上去他都像个凶手,就无法肯定自己能否从我的眼里寻求到同情,但是他发现的东西足以让他鼓起勇气说话了。

"他说:'你和我跟外面那个人有一大笔帐要算!如果我们俩都不是胆小鬼,我们也许可以联合起来让他清偿。你真的和你哥哥一样软弱吗?你情愿忍受到底,一点都不想报仇吗?'

"'我现在不想再忍下去了,'我回答他,'我比较喜欢用一种不会伤到我自己的方法来报复,可是阴谋和暴力两头都有利矛,它们会刺伤那些使用它们的人,比刺伤他们的敌人更严重。'

"'阴谋和暴力就是对阴谋和暴力的公正报复!'辛德雷大声叫道,'希斯克利夫太太,我什么都不让你做,只要你安静地坐在这里别出声就行。现在告诉我,你做不做得到?我相信当你亲眼目睹这恶魔一命呜呼的时候,会和我一样高兴的。除非你先下手干掉他,不然他就会害死你,他也会毁了我。该死的恶棍!他这敲门的架势仿佛他已经成了这里的主人一样!答应我不要出声,在钟声敲响之前,还差三分钟就到一点了,你就是个自由的女人了!'

"他从自己胸前取出我在信里跟你描述过的武器,正想要吹蜡烛,不过我把蜡烛夺过来,抓住他的胳膊。

"'我不会不吭气!'我说,'你千

mustn't touch him. Let the door remain shut, and be quiet!'

"'No! I've formed my resolution, and by God, I'll execute it!' cried the desperate being. 'I'll do you a kindness in spite of yourself, and Hareton justice! And you needn't trouble your head to screen me; Catherine is gone. Nobody alive would regret me, or be ashamed, though I cut my throat this minute—and it's time to make an end!'

"I might as well have struggled with a bear, or reasoned with a lunatic. The only resource left me was to run to a lattice and warn his intended victim of the fate which awaited him.

"'You'd better seek shelter somewhere else tonight!' I exclaimed in a rather triumphant tone. 'Mr. Earnshaw has a mind to shoot you, if you persist in endeavouring to enter.'

"'You'd better open the door, you—,' he answered, addressing me by some elegant term that I don't care to repeat.

"'I shall not meddle in the matter,' I retorted again. 'Come in and get shot, if you please! I've done my duty.'

"With that I shut the window and returned to my place by the fire; having too small a stock of hypocrisy at my command to pretend any anxiety for the danger that menaced him. Earnshaw swore passionately at me: affirming that I loved the villain yet; and calling me all sorts of names for the base spirit I evinced. And I, in my secret heart, (and conscience never reproached me) thought what a blessing it would be for *him*, should Heathcliff put him out of misery; and what a blessing for *me*, should he send Heathcliff to his right abode! As I sat nursing these reflections, the casement behind me was banged on to the floor by a blow from the latter individual, and his black countenance looked blightingly through. The stanchions stood too close to suffer his shoulders to follow, and I smiled, exulting in my fancied security. His hair and clothes were whitened with snow, and his sharp cannibal teeth, revealed by cold and wrath, gleamed through the dark.

"'Isabella, let me in, or I'll make you repent!' he 'girned,' as Joseph calls it.

"'I cannot commit murder,' I replied. 'Mr. Hindley stands sentinel with a knife and loaded pistol.'

"'Let me in by the kitchen door,' he said.

"'Hindley will be there before me,' I answered: 'and that's a poor love of yours that cannot bear a shower of snow! We were left at peace in our beds as long as the summer moon shone, but the moment a blast of winter returns, you must run for shelter! Heathcliff, if I were you, I'd go stretch myself over her grave and die like a faithful dog. The world is surely not worth living in now, is it? You had distinctly impressed on me the idea that Catherine was the whole joy of your life: I can't imagine how you think of surviving her loss.'

"'He's there, is he?' exclaimed my companion, rushing to the gap. 'If I can get my arm out I can hit him!'"

"I'm afraid, Ellen, you'll set me down as really wicked; but you don't know all, so don't judge. I wouldn't have aided or abetted an attempt on even his life for anything. Wish that he were dead, I must; and therefore I was fearfully disappointed, and unnerved by terror for the consequences of my taunting speech, when he

坐在那里这么想像的时候，希斯克利夫一拳敲落了我背后的一扇窗户，砰地一声掉在地上，他那黑森森的脸阴沉地往里望着。因为窗户的栏杆太密，他的肩膀没办法挤进来。我笑着，自以为非常安全而颇感得意。他的头发和衣服都被雪盖了层白色，他那锋利的野人般的牙齿，因为寒冷和愤怒而呲露出来，在黑暗中闪闪发光。

"'伊莎贝拉，让我进去，不然我会让你后悔的，'他'咆哮'着，就像约瑟夫所说的那样。

"'我不能做杀人的勾当，'我回答道，'辛德雷先生拿着一把刀和上了膛的枪站在门后守着呢。'

"'让我从厨房门进来，'他说。

"'辛德雷会先我一步赶到那里的，'我回答道，'原来你的爱情这么可怜，竟承受不住一场大雪！只要夏日月光闪耀的时候，就让我们安安稳稳地躺在床上睡觉，可是冬天的寒风一刮回来，你就非得找安身之处不可了！希斯克利夫，如果我是你，我就直挺挺地躺在她的坟上，像条忠诚的狗一样死去。如今这世界当然不值得再留恋下去了！对吧？你已经很明显地给我留下了这个印象，凯瑟琳是你生命中全部的欢乐：我无法想像在失去她之后你怎么还想活下去。'

"'他在那里，是不是？'我的同伴大叫，冲到那扇破窗前，'如果我能伸出胳臂，我就可以揍到他！'

"艾伦，我担心你会以为我真的那么恶毒，可你不了解所有的事实，因此请不要妄下定论。即便有人想要谋害他的性命，我也无论如何都不会去帮忙或教唆的。但愿他已经死掉，

flung himself on Earnshaw's weapon and wrenched it from his grasp.

"The charge exploded, and the knife, in springing back, closed into its owner's wrist. Heathcliff pulled it away by main force, slitting up the flesh as it passed on, and thrust it dripping into his pocket. He then took a stone, struck down the division between two windows, and sprung in. His adversary had fallen senseless with excessive pain, and the flow of blood that gushed from an artery or a large vein. The ruffian kicked and trampled on him, and dashed his head repeatedly against the flags, holding me with one hand, meantime, to prevent me summoning Joseph. He exerted preter-human self-denial in abstaining from finishing him completely; but getting out of breath he finally desisted, and dragged the apparently inanimate body onto the settle. There he tore off the sleeve of Earnshaw's coat, and bound up the wound with brutal roughness; spitting and cursing during the opera tion as energetically as he had kicked before. Being at liberty, I lost no time in seeking the old servant; who, having gathered by degrees the purport of my hasty tale, hurried below, gasping, as he descended the steps two at once.

"'Whet is thur tuh do, nah? whet is thur tuh do, nah?'

"'There's this to do,' thundered Heathcliff, 'that your master's mad; and should he last another month, I'll have him to an asylum. And how the devil did you come to fasten me out, you toothless hound? Don't stand muttering and mumbling there. Come, I'm not going to nurse him. Wash that stuff away; and mind the sparks of your candle— it is more than half

我一定不会。因此当他扑向恩肖的武器，把它从恩肖手中夺过去时，我失望至极！而且一想到我那嘲弄的话将要引起的后果，我就吓成一团。

"枪响了，那把刀弹了回去，正好切到这把刀的主人的手腕上。希斯克利夫用劲往回一拉，把皮肉割开一道长口子，然后把那直滴血的刀塞进他口袋里。接着他捡起一块石头，砸落两扇窗户之间的窗框，跳了进来。他的对手由于剧烈的疼痛，以及那从动脉或是大血管里涌出的大量鲜血，倒下不省人事了。那个恶棍对他猛踢猛踩，一再地把他的头往石板地上撞，同时另一只手紧抓着我，不让我去叫约瑟夫。他使出超人般的自制力，才没有完全断送恩肖的性命，可他也累得喘不过气来，终于罢手了，把那显然已经死气沉沉的身体拖到高背椅上，把恩肖外衣上的袖子扯下来，粗暴得如同野兽一样帮他包扎伤口，在包扎的时候，他又是唾弃又是诅咒，就跟刚才踢他时一样精力充沛。此时我已经获得了自由，就立刻去找那个老仆人，他好容易从我那慌里慌张的叙述中一点点地明白了我的意思，便两步并作一步地匆忙赶下楼，气喘吁吁。

"'现在该怎么办？现在该怎么办呀？'

"'按我说的办．'希斯克利夫吼道，'你的主人已经疯了；如果他再活上一个月，我就把他送去疯人院。怎么会那么恶毒，想把我关在外面，你这掉了牙的狼狗？别站在那儿嘀嘀咕咕的，过来，我可不想照顾他。把那摊血擦干净，还有小心你蜡烛的火星，那摊血里可有一半是白兰地呢！'

brandy①!'

"'Und soa, yah been murthering on him?' exclaimed Joseph, lifting his hands and eyes in horror. 'If iver Aw seed a seeght loike this! May the Lord—'

"Heathcliff gave him a push onto his knees in the middle of the blood, and flung a towel to him; but instead of proceeding to dry it up, he joined his hands, and began a prayer which excited my laughter from its odd phraseology. I was in the condition of mind to be shocked at nothing: in fact, I was as reckless as some malefactors show themselves at the foot of the gallows.

"'Oh, I forgot you,' said the tyrant. 'You shall do that. Down with you. And you conspire with him against me, do you, viper? There, that is work fit for you!'

"He shook me till my teeth rattled, and pitched me beside Joseph, who steadily concluded his supplications and then rose, vowing he would set off for the Grange directly. Mr. Linton was a magistrate, and though he had fifty wives dead, he should inquire into this. He was so obstinate in his resolution, that Heathcliff deemed it expedient to compel from my lips a recapitulation of what had taken place; standing over me, heaving with malevolence, as I reluctantly delivered the account in answer to his questions. It required a great deal of labour to satisfy the old man that he was not the aggressor; especially with my hardly wrung replies. However, Mr. Earnshaw soon convinced him that he was alive still; he hastened to administer a dose of spirits, and by their suc-

"'那么是你谋害了他？'约瑟夫大叫道，惊慌地举起双手，瞪大了双眼，'我从来没见过这种情景啊，愿主……'

"希斯克利夫推了他一把，正好把他推倒跪在那摊血中间，又给他扔了一条毛巾，可是他并没有动手擦血迹，而是交叉着双手，开始祈祷起来。他那古怪的措词真是让我哈哈大笑。当时的我已经天不怕地不怕了，事实上，我就像那些犯人在绞架下面表现出来的那样漠不关心了。

"'啊，我把你给忘了，'这个暴君说道，'应该由你来做这件事，快跪下。你和他合谋起来算计我，是不是，奸诈胚子？过去，那才是你该干的事儿！'

"他狠狠地摇晃我，直到我的牙齿咔嗒作响，然后一把将我推到约瑟夫身边。约瑟夫不慌不忙地念完他的祈祷，然后站起来，发誓说他要立刻动身去田庄。林顿先生是地方官，就算他死了五十个妻子，也得管管这件事。他的决心如此坚定，以至于希斯克利夫认为最好还是逼我把刚才发生的事情简单地复述一遍。当我很不情愿地回答着他的问题，说出事情的经过时，他满腔怒火地站在我旁边。费了很大的劲才让那个老头子满意，相信希斯克利夫没有主动攻击人，特别是因为我那些回答都是硬挤出来的。不过，很快恩肖先生就让约瑟夫相信他还活着；约瑟夫赶忙给他拿来一杯酒，借着酒气，他的主人很快就能动

---

① 因为辛德雷酗酒，希斯克利夫在这里讽刺辛德雷，说他的血里一半多都是酒。

cour his master presently regained motion and consciousness. Heathcliff, aware that he was ignorant of the treatment received while insensible, called him deliriously intoxicated; and said he should not notice his atrocious conduct further, but advised him to get to bed. To my joy, he left us, after giving this judicious counsel, and Hindley stretched himself on the hearth-stone. I departed to my own room, marvelling that I had escaped so easily.

"This morning, when I came down, about half an-hour before noon, Mr. Earnshaw was sitting by the fire, deadly sick; his evil genius, almost as gaunt and ghastly, leant against the chimney. Neither appeared inclined to dine, and, having waited till all was cold on the table, I commenced alone. Nothing hindered me from eating heartily, and I experienced a certain sense of satisfaction and superiority, as, at intervals, I cast a look towards my silent companions, and felt the comfort of a quiet conscience within me. After I had done, I ventured on the unusual liberty[①] of drawing near the fire, going round Earnshaw's seat, and kneeling in the comer beside him.

"Heathcliff did not glance my way, and I gazed up, and contemplated his features almost as confidently as if they had been turned to stone. His forehead, that I once thought so manly, and that I now think so diabolical, was shaded with a heavy cloud; his basilisk eyes were nearly quenched by sleeplessness—and weeping, perhaps, for the lashes were wet then; his lips devoid of their ferocious sneer, and

弹,恢复了知觉。希斯克利夫知道他的对手并不知道他在昏迷时所受的待遇,就说他发酒疯,神志不清,还说自己已经不介意他这些凶神恶煞的举动,劝他上床睡觉去。让我高兴的是,在他说完这么一番有见识的劝告后,就离开了我们。辛德雷舒展着身子躺在炉边的石块上,我则离开这里回到自己房间。一想到可以这么容易地逃过一劫,就感到大为惊讶。

"今天上午,大概十一点半的时候,我下楼了。恩肖先生坐在火炉旁边,病得很重。那个恶魔脸色差不多和他一样憔悴惨白,身子靠在烟囱上。两个人看起来都好像不想吃饭,一直等到桌上的饭菜都冷了,我才自己一人开始吃起来,没有什么可以阻止我大快朵颐。我不时瞅瞅那两个沉默的同伴,心里觉得很平静,很舒服,体验着一种满足与优越感。等我吃完后,壮起胆子随意地走近火炉旁,绕过恩肖的椅子,跪在他旁边的角落里烤火。

"希斯克利夫没有往我这边看一眼,我就抬起头来看着他,心安理得地注视着他的面容,仿佛它们已经变成了石头。我曾认为他的前额很有男子汉气概,而现在觉得它变得那么凶狠,笼罩着一层云雾;他那双鬼怪似的眼睛由于缺乏睡眠变得暗淡无光,或是由于哭泣,因为眼睫毛是湿的;他的嘴唇也没有了那凶狠的讥嘲表

---

① 按照礼节,正餐后女士们先到休息室喝茶;男士们继续在饭厅待约摸一个小时饮酒畅谈,最后到休息室和女士们一起喝茶。女士餐后留在厅里便是违反礼数。

sealed in an expression of unspeakable sadness. Had it been another, I would have covered my face, in the presence of such grief. In *his* case, I was gratified; and, ignoble as it seems to insult a fallen enemy, I couldn't miss this chance of sticking in a dart: his weakness was the only time when I could taste the delight of paying wrong for wrong."

"Fie, fie, Miss!" I interrupted. "One might suppose you had never opened a Bible in your life. If God afflict your enemies, surely that ought to suffice you. It is both mean and presumptuous to add your torture to his!"

"In general, I'll allow that it would be, Ellen," she continued; "but what misery laid on Heathcliff could content me, unless I have a hand in it—I'd rather he suffered *less*, if I might cause his sufferings and he might *know* that I was the cause. Oh, I owe him so much. On only one condition can I hope to forgive him. It is, if I may take an eye for an eye, a tooth for a tooth; for every wrench of agony return a wrench: reduce him to my level. As he was the first to injure, make him the first to implore pardon; and then—why then, Ellen, I might show you some generosity. But it is utterly impossible I can ever be revenged, and therefore I cannot forgive him. Hindley wanted some water, and I handed him a glass, and asked him how he was.

"'Not as ill as I wish,' he replied. 'But leaving out my arm, every inch of me is as sore as if I had been fighting with a legion of imps!'

"'Yes, no wonder,' was my next remark. 'Catherine used to boast that she stood between you and bodily harm: she meant that certain

情,被一种难以形容的悲哀封住了。如果他是别人,我在看到这样的悲伤时会遮住自己的脸不忍面对。可换了他,我感到很满足;侮辱一个倒下的敌人看起来确实有点不光彩,可我不会失去这个在伤口上撒盐的机会,唯有趁他虚弱无能的时候,我才能体验到以怨报怨的快感。"

"呸,呸,小姐!"我打断她说,"人家还以为你这一辈子没有看过圣经呢。如果上帝惩罚了你的敌人,那你就该知足了。如果再加上你对他的折磨,那就显得太卑劣狂妄了。"

"一般情况下我也这样承认,艾伦,"她接着说,"但除非是我自己动手所为,不然无论希斯克利夫遭受多大的痛苦,都不会让我满足。如果是我引起他的痛苦,而他也知道是我所为,那我倒宁愿他能少受点苦。啊,我应向他报的仇真是太多了。只有一种情况,可以有希望让我饶恕他。那就是如果我能以眼还眼,以牙还牙,每次他拧我一把,我就还他一把,让他也尝尝我受过的罪。既然他先伤害我,那就让他先求饶,然后,到那时,艾伦,我也许可以向你表现出些宽宏大量来。但我完全不可能报得了仇的,因此我不能饶恕他。这时辛德雷想喝水,我就递给他一杯,问他觉得怎样了?

"'不像我希望的那么严重,'他回答说,'可是除了胳臂,我浑身上下都很酸痛,就像我跟一大群小鬼打了一仗似的。'

"'是的,不用那么奇怪,'我说,'凯瑟琳过去常自诩说她会站在你和肉体伤害之间:她是说有些人会因为

persons would not hurt you for fear of offending her. It's well people don't really rise from their grave, or, last night, she might have witnessed a repulsive scene! Are not you bruised, and cut over your chest and shoulders?'

"'I can't say,' he answered: 'but what do you mean? Did he dare to strike me when I was down?'

"'He trampled on, and kicked you, and dashed you on the ground,' I whispered. 'And his mouth watered to tear you with his teeth; because, he's only half a man—not so much.'

"Mr. Earnshaw looked up, like me, to the countenance of our mutual foe; who, absorbed in his anguish, seemed insensible to anything around him: the longer he stood, the plainer his reflections revealed their blackness through his features.

"'Oh, if God would but give me strength to strangle him in my last agony, I'd go to hell with joy,' groaned the impatient man, writhing to rise, and sinking back in despair, convinced of his inadequacy for the struggle.

"'Nay, it's enough that he has murdered one of you,' I observed aloud. 'At the Grange, every one knows your sister would have been living now, had it not been for Mr. Heathcliff. After all, it is preferable to be hated than loved by him. When I recollect how happy we were—how happy Catherine was before he came I'm fit to curse the day.'

"Most likely, Heathcliff noticed more the truth of what was said, than the spirit of the person who said it His attention was roused, I saw, for his eyes rained down tears among the ashes, and he drew his breath in suffocating sighs. I stared full at him, and laughed scornfully. The clouded windows of hell flashed a moment towards me; the fiend which usually looked out, however, was so dimmed and drowned that I did not fear to hazard another sound of derision.

"'Get up, and begone out of my sight,' said the mourner.

"I guessed he uttered those words, at least, though his voice was hardly intelligible.

"'I beg your pardon,' I replied. 'But I loved Catherine too; and her brother requires attendance which, for her sake, I shall supply. Now that she's dead, I see her in Hindley: Hindley has exactly her eyes, if you had not tried to gouge them out, and made them black and red; and her—'

"'Get up, wretched idiot, before I stamp you to death!' he cried, making a movement that caused me to make one also.

"'But then,' I continued, holding myself ready to flee; 'if poor Catherine had trusted you, and assumed the ridiculous, contemptible, degrading title of Mrs. Heathcliff, she would soon have presented a similar picture! She wouldn't have borne your abominable behaviour quietly: her detestation and disgust must have found voice.'

"The back of the settle and Earnshaw's person interposed between me and him; so instead of endeavouring to reach me, he snatched a dinner knife from the table and flung it at my head. It struck beneath my ear, and stopped the sentence I was uttering; but, pulling it out, I sprang to the door and delivered another which I hope went a little deeper than his missile. The last glimpse I caught of him was a furious rush on his part, checked by the embrace of his host;

的地狱之窗（他的眼睛）朝我闪了一下。不管怎样，那个平时常会出来的魔王此时居然如此暗淡，淹没于泪水之中，因此我毫不畏惧地再次嘲笑了他几声。

"'起来，别再让我看到你，'这个悲哀的人说。

"我猜他至少说出了这几个字，虽然他的声音很难让人听清。

"'请问你在说什么，'我答道，'但是我也爱凯瑟琳，她哥哥现在需要人照顾，为了她我应该来担这个义务。如今，她已经死了，看见辛德雷我就好像看见她：要不是你曾想挖掉他的眼睛，把它们弄得又黑又红，这眼睛就跟凯瑟琳的一模一样，而且她的——'

"'在我踩死你之前，快给我起来，卑鄙的傻瓜！'他大叫着，动了一下，使得我也跟着动了一下。

"'但是当初，'我继续说，并做好了逃跑的准备，'如果可怜的凯瑟琳相信了你，接受了希斯克利夫太太这个荒谬、卑贱、可耻的头衔，她也会很快落到这步田地！她才不会默默地忍受着你那令人讨厌的行为，她一定会发泄自己的厌恶和憎恨。'

"高背椅的椅背和恩肖的身子挡在了我和他之间，因此他没有狠命扑过来，只是从桌上抓起一把餐刀往我头上猛掷过来。刀子刚好打在我的耳朵下面，打断了我正在说的话。可我把刀拔出之后，跳到门口，又说了一句，我希望这句话能比他的刀子刺得更深一些。我最后一眼看到的是他愤怒地猛冲过来，却被他的房东拦腰抱住挡了下来，两个人抱成一团倒在炉

and both fell locked together on the hearth. In my flight through the kitchen I bid Joseph speed to his master; I knocked over Hareton, who was hanging a litter of puppies from a chair-back in the doorway; and, blest as a soul escaped from purgatory, I bounded, leaped, and flew down the steep road; then, quitting its windings, shot direct across the moor, rolling over banks, and wading through marshes: precipitating myself, in fact, towards the beacon light of the Grange. And far rather would I be condemned to a perpetual dwelling in the infernal regions, than, even for one night, abide beneath the roof of Wuthering Heights again."

　　Isabella ceased speaking, and took a drink of tea; then she rose, and bidding me put on her bonnet, and a great shawl I had brought, and turning a deaf ear to my entreaties for her to remain another hour, she stepped onto a chair, kissed Edgar's and Catherine's portraits, bestowed a similar salute on me, and descended to the carriage, accompanied by Fanny, who yelped wild with joy at recovering her mistress. She was driven away, never to revisit this neighbourhood: but a regular correspondence was established between her and my master when things were more settled. I believe her new abode was in the south, near London; there she had a son born, a few months subsequent to her escape. He was christened Linton, and, from the first, she reported him to be an ailing, peevish creature.

　　Mr. Heathcliff, meeting me one day in the village, inquired where she lived. I refused to tell. He remarked that it was not of any moment, only she must beware of coming to her brother: she should not be with him, if he had to

边。在我飞快地跑过厨房时,我叫约瑟夫赶快到他主人那里。我还撞倒了哈里顿,他正在门口把一窝小狗吊在一张椅背上。我跑啊跳啊,就像从炼狱中逃脱出来的灵魂一样,飞一般的顺着陡峭的山路飞奔下来,然后避开弯路,直接穿过旷野,滚下岸坡,蹚过沼泽:其实我是直扑向田庄灯塔的光亮。我宁可被判处永久打入地狱,也无法再容忍在呼啸山庄的屋檐下住一夜了。"

　　伊莎贝拉停下话来,喝了口茶,然后站起身来,叫我帮她戴上帽子,围上我给她拿来的大披巾。我恳求她再多待一个小时,可她死活都听不进去。她站在一把椅子上,亲吻了一下埃德加和凯瑟琳的肖像,也对我抱以同样的礼数,就带着凡尼上了马车。凡尼又找到了自己的女主人,高兴得乱叫一阵。她就这样走了,再也没有回到这附近,但等事情安定下来之后,她和我的主人就建立了正常的书信往来,我想她的新居应该在南方,靠近伦敦。在她逃跑后没几个月,就在那儿生了个儿子,取名叫林顿,从一开始,她就在信里说他是个病快快的倔强的小家伙。

　　有一天希斯克利夫在村子里遇到我,问她在哪里。我拒绝回答他。他说那也没什么关系,只要她当心不要去她哥哥那儿就行。即便她哥哥想收留她,她也不应跟埃德加住在一起。

keep her himself. Though I would give no information, he discovered, through some of the other servants, both her place of residence and the existence of the child. Still he didn't molest her: for which forbearance she might thank his aversion, I suppose. He often asked about the infant, when he saw me; and on hearing its name, smiled grimly, and observed—

"They wish me to hate it too, do they?"

"I don't think they wish you to know any thing about it," I answered.

"But I'll have it," he said, "when I want it. They may reckon on that!"

Fortunately, its mother died before the time arrived, some thirteen years after the decease of Catherine, when Linton was twelve, or a little more.

On the day succeeding Isabella's unexpected visit, I had no opportunity of speaking to my master: he shunned conversation, and was fit for discussing nothing. When I could get him to listen, I saw it pleased him that his sister had left her husband; whom he abhorred with an intensity which the mildness of his nature would scarcely seem to allow. So deep and sensitive was his aversion, that he refrained from going anywhere where he was likely to see or hear of Heathcliff. Grief, and that together, transformed him into a complete hermit: he threw up his office of magistrate, ceased even to attend church, avoided the village on all occasions, and spent a life of entire seclusion within the limits of his park and grounds; only varied by solitary rambles on the moors, and visits to the grave of his wife, mostly at evening, or early morning before other wanderers were abroad. But he was too good to be

虽然我没有告诉他，但他却从别的仆人口中得知了她的住处以及孩子的存在，不过他并没去骚扰她。我猜想，为了希斯克利夫这份宽宏大量，她也许要谢谢他对自己的反感呢。当他见到我的时候，常常会向我打听孩子的事情。一听说这孩子的名字，他就冷酷地笑笑，说道：

"他们希望我连这孩子也一起恨，是不是？"

"我想他们不希望你知道关于这孩子的事情。"我回答他。

"但等我需要他的时候，"他说，"我会得到他的。他们应该会想到这点！"

幸亏孩子的母亲在那时刻到来之前就死了，大概在凯瑟琳死后的第十三年，林顿十二岁，或者稍大一点。

伊莎贝拉忽然造访的第二天，我没机会跟主人说话。他回避谈天，而且他的心情也不适于讨论事情。当我能让他听我说话时，我看出他妹妹离开她丈夫的事让他很高兴，他对她丈夫的憎恶感之强烈，似乎不是他那柔和的天性所能容许的。他的憎恶是如此深刻而敏感，以致任何他可能看到或听到希斯克利夫的地方他都决不涉足。悲痛，加上这种憎恶，使他变成了一个地地道道的隐士，他辞去了地方官的职务，甚至连教堂都不去，避免任何去村里的机会，在他的庄园里过着完全与世隔绝的生活，只是偶尔会改变一下，独自一人到旷野散步，去看妻子的坟前看看，多半是在晚间或大清早没有游人的时候。但他这人太善良了，不会一直这么闷闷不乐。他并不祈求凯瑟琳的灵魂能伴他左

thoroughly unhappy long. *He* didn't pray for Catherine's soul to haunt him: Time brought resignation, and a melancholy sweeter than common joy. He recalled her memory with ardent, tender love, and hopeful aspiring to the better world, where, he doubted not, she was gone.

And he had earthly consolation and affections, also. For a few days, I said, he seemed regardless of the puny successor to the departed: that coldness melted as fast as snow in April, and ere the tiny thing could stammer a word or totter a step, it wielded a despot's sceptre in his heart. It was named Catherine; but he never called it the name in full, as he had never called the first Catherine short: probably because Heathcliff had a habit of doing so. The little one was always Cathy: it formed to him a distinction from the mother, and yet, a connection with her; and his attachment sprang from its relation to her, far more than from its being his own.

I used to draw a comparison between him and Hindley Earnshaw, and perplex myself to explain satisfactorily why their conduct was so opposite in similar circumstances. They had both been fond husbands, and were both attached to their children; and I could not see how they shouldn't both have taken the same road, for good or evil. But, I thought in my mind, Hindley, with apparently the stronger head, has shown himself sadly the worse and the weaker man. When his ship struck, the captain abandoned his post; and the crew, instead of trying to save her, rushed into riot and confusion, leaving no hope for their luckless vessel. Linton, on the contrary, displayed the true courage

右。时间会让人听天由命，带来一种比日常的快乐还甜美的忧郁。他以热烈而温柔的爱来回忆她，期望她能到那个更好的世界去，他毫不怀疑她已经去了那里。

在尘世间他也有能得到慰藉和施以情感的事物。我说过，最初那几天他好像并不关心亡妻留下的后嗣，这种冷淡有如四月雪一样融化得那么快，在这小东西还不会吐出一个字，或是跟跟跄跄地走一步之前，她已经在林顿心中挥起了权杖。孩子名字叫凯瑟琳，但他从来都不叫她的全名，正如他从来不叫头一个凯瑟琳小名一样，也许是因为希斯克利夫习惯于叫她的小名吧。这小家伙常常被叫做凯茜，对她爸爸说来这跟她母亲既有区别又有联系。而他对孩子宠爱的原因，与其说因为她是自己的骨肉，还不如说因为她和凯瑟琳的关系。

我常拿他和辛德雷·恩肖做比较，但都迷迷糊糊地难以满意地解释为什么他们的处境如此相似，行为却截然相反。他们曾经都是深情的丈夫，都疼爱自己的孩子，我不明白无论是好是坏，他们为什么没能走上一条路。但我心里想，辛德雷看起来明显更坚强，但却表现得更糟糕更软弱。当他的船触礁时，船长就擅离职守，全体船员并没有尽力挽救这条船，而是惊慌失措，乱成一团，使得这条不幸的船毫无获救的希望。相反，林顿显示出了一个忠诚守信的灵魂具备的真正勇气，他信赖上帝，上帝也安慰着他。一个是希望，一个则是绝望；他

of a loyal and faithful soul: he trusted God; and God comforted him. One hoped, and the other despaired: they chose their own lots, and were righteously doomed to endure them. But you'll not want to hear my moralizing, Mr. Lockwood; you'll judge as well as I can, all these things: at least, you'll think you will, and that's the same. The end of Earnshaw was what might have been expected; it followed fast on his sister's: there were scarcely six months between them: We, at the Grange, never got a very succinct account of his state preceding it; all that I did learn was on occasion of going to aid in the preparations for the funeral. Mr. Kenneth came to announce the event to my master.

"Well, Nelly," said he, riding into the yard one morning, too early not to alarm me with an instant presentiment of bad news, "It's yours and my turn to go into mourning at present. Who's given us the slip now, do you think?"

"Who?" I asked in a flurry.

"Why, guess!" he returned, dismounting, and slinging his bridle on a hook by the door. "And nip up the corner of your apron: I'm certain you'll need it."

"Not Mr. Heathcliff, surely?" I exclaimed.

"What! would you have tears for him?" said the doctor. "No, Heathcliff's a tough young fellow: he looks blooming today. I've just seen him. He's rapidly regaining flesh since he lost his better half."

"Who is it, then, Mr. Kenneth?" I repeated impatiently.

"Hindley Earnshaw! Your old friend Hindley," he replied, "and my wicked gossip: though he's been too wild for me this long while. There! I said we should draw water. But

们各自选择了自己的命运，自然也就各得其所。不过洛克伍德先生，你一定不想要听我说教吧，你会和我一样对这一切作出判断。至少，你觉得自己会这样，那也是一样的。恩肖的死在人们的预料之中，就紧跟在他妹妹逝世后不久，两者中间相隔不到六个月。住在田庄这边的我们从没收到过关于恩肖临死前的情况，哪怕三言两语都没有。我所知道的一切都是在帮忙准备葬礼时才听说的。肯尼斯先生过来告诉了我家主人这件事。

一天早晨他骑着马走进院子，对我说："你好，内莉，"他来得那么早，着实让我吃了一惊，马上想到可能有坏消息了。"现在该轮到你我去奔丧了。你猜这次又是谁不辞而别？"

"谁？"我慌慌张张地问道。

"哎，你猜啊！"他一边回答我，一边跳下马，然后把马缰绳吊在门边的钩子上，"把你的围裙角撩起来吧，我肯定你会用得着的。"

"该不是希斯克利夫先生吧？"我惊呼。

"什么！你会为他掉眼泪吗？"医生说。"不，希斯克利夫是个健壮的年轻人，今天他气色看来好得很，我刚才还见到他了。自从他失去另一半后，很快就长胖了。"

"那到底是谁呢，肯尼斯先生？"我急不可耐地重复问道。

"辛德雷·恩肖！你的老朋友辛德雷，"他回答说，"也是我那堕落的老朋友啊，虽然很长一段时间里，他都

cheer up! He died true to his character: drunk as a lord①. Poor lad; I'm sorry, too. One can't help missing an old companion: though he had the worst tricks with him that ever man imagined, and has done me many a rascally turn. He's barely twenty-seven, it seems; that's your own age: who would have thought you were born in one year?"

I confess this blow was greater to me than the shock of Mrs. Linton's death: ancient associations lingered round my heart; I sat down in the porch and wept as for a blood relation, desiring Kenneth to get another servant to introduce him to the master. I could not hinder myself from pondering on the question—"Had he had fair play?" Whatever I did, that idea would bother me: it was so tiresomely pertinacious that I resolved on requesting leave to go to Wuthering Heights, and assist in the last duties to the dead. Mr. Linton was extremely reluctant to consent, but I pleaded eloquently for the friendless condition in which he lay; and I said my old master and foster-brother had a claim on my services as strong as his own. Besides, I reminded him that the child Hareton was his wife's nephew, and, in the absence of nearer kin, he ought to act as its guardian; and he ought to and must inquire how the property was left, and look over the concerns of his brother-in-law. He was unfit for attending to such matters then, but he bid me speak to his lawyer; and at length permitted me to go. His lawyer had been Earnshaw's also: I called at the village, and asked him to accompany me. He

---

① as drunk as a lord:烂醉如泥。英国乔治三世统治时期,平民不大喝酒,只有贵族才常常喝醉,所以醉酒被认为是绅士的标志。

shook his head, and advised that Heathcliff should be let alone; affirming, if the truth were known, Hareton would be found little else than a beggar.

"His father died in debt," he said; "the whole property is mortgaged, and the sole chance for the natural heir is to allow him an opportunity of creating some interest in the creditor's heart, that he may be inclined to deal leniently towards him."

When I reached the Heights, I explained that I had come to see everything carried on decently; and Joseph, who appeared in sufficient distress, expressed satisfaction at my presence. Mr. Heathcliff said he did not perceive that I was wanted; but I might stay and order the arrangements for the funeral, if I chose.

"Correctly," he remarked, "that fool's body should be buried at the cross-roads, without ceremony of any kind. I happened to leave him ten minutes yesterday afternoon, and in that interval he fastened the two doors of the house against me, and he has spent the night in drinking himself to death deliberately! We broke in this morning, for we heard him snorting like a horse; and there he was, laid over the settle: flaying and scalping would not have wakened him. I sent for Kenneth, and he came; but not till the beast had changed into carrion; he was both dead and cold, and stark; and so you'll allow, it was useless making more stir about him!"

The old servant confirmed this statement, but muttered—

"Aw'd rayther he'd goan hisseln fur t' doctor! Aw sud uh taen tent uh t' maister better nur him—un he warn't deead when Aw left, nowt uh t' soart!"

头，劝我别去招惹希斯克利夫；还说，一旦真相大白，就会发现哈里顿跟乞丐相差无几了。

"他的父亲背着一身债务死去，"他说，"全部财产都被抵押了，现在对于这位合法继承人来说惟一的机会，就是设法让他在债权人心中引起一点好感，这样债权人还能对他仁慈些。"

当我到达山庄时，我解释说自己是来看看是否一切都已经搞得像模像样了，带着满面愁容出现的约瑟夫对于我的到来感到很满意。希斯克利夫先生说他看不出有什么地方需要我帮忙，不过如果我愿意的话，可以留下来，安排一下丧礼的事情。

"确切来讲，"他说，"那个傻瓜的尸体应该被埋在十字路口，什么仪式都用不着。昨天下午我碰巧离开他十分钟，就在那段时间里，他关上大厅的两扇门，不让我进去，他就整夜地在里面喝酒，故意把自己给喝死了。今天早上我们是破门进来的，因为听到他像匹马似的直喘气。他就在那儿，躺在高背椅上：即使剥掉他的皮，也没办法叫醒他。我派人去请肯尼斯，他来了，可那时这畜生已经变成一具死尸，他死了，冷了，变硬了。因此你得承认，再怎么折腾他也是无济于事。"

老仆人证实了说法，可他嘀咕着：

"我宁愿他自己去请医生！我照顾主人当然要比他好，我走的时候，他还没死呢，一点儿死的迹象都没有！"

第十七章

I insisted on the funeral being respectable. Mr. Heathcliff said I might have my own way there too: only, he desired me to remember that the money for the whole affair came out of his pocket. He maintained a hard, careless deportment, indicative of neither joy nor sorrow: if anything, it expressed a flinty gratification at a piece of difficult work successfully executed. I observed once, indeed, some thing like exultation in his aspect: it was just when the people were bearing the coffin from the house. He had the hypocrisy to represent a mourner: and previous to following with Hareton, he lifted the unfortunate child on to the table and muttered, with peculiar gusto, "Now, my bonny lad, you are *mine*! And we'll see if one tree won't grow as crooked as another, with the same wind to twist it!" The unsuspect ing thing was pleased at this speech: he played with Heathcliff's whiskers, and stroked his cheek; but I divined its meaning, and observed tartly, "That boy must go back with me to Thrushcross Grange, sir. There is nothing in the world less yours than he is!"

"Does Linton say so?" he demanded.

"Of course—he has ordered me to take him," I replied.

"Well," said the scoundrel, "we'll not argue the subject now: but I have a fancy to try my hand at rearing a young one; so intimate to your master that I must supply the place of this with my own, if he attempt to remove it. I don't engage to let Hareton go, undisputed; but I'll be pretty sure to make the other come! Remember to tell him."

This hint was enough to bind our hands. I repeated its substance on my return; and Edgar

我坚持要把丧礼办得体面些。希斯克利夫先生说这些都由我做主，只是他要我记住办丧事的这些钱都是从他口袋里掏的。他始终保持一种冷酷无情、漠不关心的态度，既没有开心，也没有悲哀，如果有什么的话，那就是在顺利完成这件艰难的工作后，他表露出一种满足的冷酷。其实，有一次我看到他脸上有一种近乎狂喜的神情：那就是在人们把灵柩抬出大厅的时候，他竟如此伪善，假装自己是个吊丧者，在跟着哈里顿出去之前，他把这不幸的孩子抱到桌子上，带着罕见的兴致嘀咕着："现在，我的好孩子，你是我的了！我们来看看用同样的风吹扭一棵树，它会不会和另外一棵树一样长得一样弯曲！"那个天真无邪的小家伙听到这些话很开心，把玩着希斯克利夫的胡子，抚摩着他的脸颊，但我想到这话的含义，尖刻地说道："先生，那孩子必须跟我一起回画眉田庄。在这世上，他跟你毫不相干。"

"林顿也是这么说的吗？"他质问道。

"当然，是他叫我来带走他的。"我回答他。

"好啊，"这个恶棍说道，"现在我们不要为这事儿争执了，不过我很想试着自己养养这个孩子，因此请通知你的主人，如果想要带走他，那我就得去找我自己的孩子补这个空位了。我才不会一声不吭地就放哈里顿走，不过我肯定会找回另外一个的！记住一定要告诉他。"

这个暗示已经足以让我们束手无策。回去之后，我把这段话的内容重

Linton, little interested at the commencement, spoke no more of interfering. I'm not aware that he could have done it to any purpose, had he been ever so willing.

The guest was now the master of Wuthering Heights: he held firm possession, and proved to the attorney—who, in his turn, proved it to Mr. Linton—that Earnshaw had mortgaged every yard of land he owned, for cash to supply his mania for gaming; and he, Heathcliff, was the mortgagee. In that manner Hareton, who should now be the first gentleman in the neighbourhood, was reduced to a state of complete dependence on his father's inveterate enemy; and lives in his own house as a servant, deprived of the advantage of wages, and quite unable to right himself, because of his friendlessness, and his ignorance that he has been wronged.

复了一遍，埃德加·林顿一开始就没多大兴趣，也就不再提及干涉的话头"。就算他愿意这么做，我想他也不会干出什么结果来。

如今客人成了呼啸山庄的主人，他牢牢地掌握着所有权，而且他还向律师证明，律师又转过来向林顿先生证明，恩肖已经抵押了他所有的每一寸土地，换成现金，来满足他疯狂的赌博，而他，希斯克利夫，就是承受抵押的人。因此，原本该成为附近一带首屈一指的绅士的哈里顿，却沦落到完完全全需要靠他父亲的死敌来养活自己。他在自己家里就像个仆人一样，还被剥夺了领取工钱的权利。他完全没办法让自己翻身了，因为现在他无亲无故，而且还对自己遭受的冤屈一无所知。

Chapter 18
第十八章

The twelve years, continued Mrs. Dean, following that dismal period, were the happiest of my life: my greatest troubles in their passage rose from our little lady's trifling illnesses, which she had to experience in common with all children, rich and poor. For the rest, after the

在这段伤心日子之后的十二年是我这一生中最快乐的，迪安太太接着说下去。在这些年里我最大的烦恼也不过是我们家小姐闹些微不足道的小毛病，这些都是她和所有其他孩子，不论是贫是富，都会有的毛病。其他

first six months, she grew like a larch, and could walk and talk too, in her own way, before the heath blossomed a second time over Mrs. Linton's dust She was the most winning thing that ever brought sunshine into a desolate house: a real beauty in face, with the Earnshaws' handsome dark eyes, but the Lintons' fair skin, and small features, and yellow curling hair. Her spirit was high, though not rough, and qualified by a heart sensitive and lively to excess in its affections. That capacity for intense attachments reminded me of her mother: still she did not resemble her; for she could be soft and mild as a dove, and she had a gentle voice and pensive expression: her anger was never furious; her love never fierce: it was deep and tender. However, it must be acknowledged, she had faults to foil her gifts. A propensity to be saucy was one; and a perverse will, that indulged children invariably acquire, whether they be good tempered or cross. If a servant chanced to vex her, it was always—"I shall tell papa!" And if he reproved her, even by a look, you would have thought it a heartbreaking business: I don't believe he ever did speak a harsh word to her. He took her education entirely on himself, and made it an amusement. Fortunately, curiosity and a quick intellect urged her into an apt scholar: she learnt rapidly and eagerly, and did honour to his teaching.

Till she reached the age of thirteen, she had not once been beyond the range of the park by herself. Mr. Linton would take her with him a mile or so outside, on rare occasions; but he trusted her to no one else. Gimmerton was an unsubstantial name in her ears; the chapel, the only building she had approached or entered,

的时间里，在出生六个月之后，她就像一棵落叶松一样长大了，而且在林顿太太墓上的石楠第二次开花之前，她就能用自己的方式说话走路了。她是最讨人喜欢的小家伙，把阳光带进了这座凄凉的宅子。她的脸真的很漂亮，有着恩肖家大大的黑眼睛，又有林顿家白皙的皮肤、精致的五官和金黄的鬈发。她总是活力十足，又不粗野，还有一颗敏感而又过度活跃的心。她那种对人极其亲热的态度让我想起了她的母亲，不过她又不像母亲，因为她可以像鸽子一样的温顺柔和，而且她有文雅的声音和深邃的表情，生气起来从不狂暴，爱起人来也从不猛烈，而是非常深沉、温和。不过必须得承认，她也有缺点来衬托这些优点，调皮捣蛋就是一个，还有任性倔强，这些都是被娇惯的孩子们的通病，不管他们脾气温顺还是暴躁。如果有个仆人碰巧惹怒了她，她总会说，"我要告诉爸爸！"如果她父亲责备了她，哪怕是瞪她一眼，你准会认为这是件令人心碎的事呢。我相信他从来都没对凯瑟琳粗声大气过。他完全亲自来教育这孩子，以此作为一种乐趣。幸亏好奇心和聪慧的头脑让她成了一个好学生，她学得又快又热切，也给他的教学增添了光彩。

直到她到了十三岁，她还没有独自一人迈出过庄园一步。林顿先生偶尔会带她去外面走上一英里，但他从不肯把她交给别人。在她听起来吉默顿是个虚无缥缈的名字，除了她自己的家，小礼拜堂是她惟一靠近或走进过的建筑。对她来说呼啸山庄和希斯

except her own home. Wuthering Heights and Mr. Heathcliff did not exist for her: she was a perfect recluse; and, apparently, perfectly contented. Sometimes, indeed, while surveying the country from her nursery window, she would observe—

"Ellen, how long will it be before I can walk to the top of those hills? I wonder what lies on the other side—is it the sea?"

"No, Miss Cathy," I would answer; "it is hills again, just like these."

"And what are those golden rocks like, when you stand under them?" she once asked.

The abrupt descent of Penistone Craggs particularly attracted her notice; especially when the setting sun shone on it and the topmost heights, and the whole extent of landscape besides lay in shadow. I explained that they were bare masses of stone, with hardly enough earth in their clefts to nourish a stunted tree.

"And why are they bright so long after it is evening here?" she pursued.

"Because they are a great deal higher up than we are," replied I; "you could not climb them, they are too high and steep. In winter the frost is always there before it comes to us; and deep into summer I have found snow under that black hollow on the north-east side!"

"Oh, you have been on them!" she cried, gleefully. "Then I can go, too, when I am a woman. Has papa been, Ellen?"

"Papa would tell you, Miss," I answered, hastily, "that they are not worth the trouble of visiting. The moors, where you ramble with him, are much nicer; and Thrushcross park is the finest place in the world."

"But I know the park, and I don't know

克利夫先生根本是不存在的,她是一个地地道道的隐居者,而且,很显然她也满足于这样的生活。但确实,有时从育儿室的窗子向外眺望乡间时,她也会说:

"艾伦,我走到那些山顶要花多少时间呢?我非常好奇山的那边是什么,是海吗?"

"不,凯茜小姐,"我会回答说,"那边还是跟这里一样的山。"

"那如果你站在那些山头的时候,这些金色的石头会是什么样的呢,"有一次她这样问我。

盘尼斯吞悬崖的陡峭山坡特别吸引她的注意,尤其当夕阳照射在岩石和最高峰上,而其余景观都被掩藏在阴影中的时候。我就解释说它们不过是一堆堆石头,石头缝里的那些泥土还不够养活一棵小树呢。

"那为什么这里的傍晚过了很久,那些石头还闪闪发亮呢?"她追问道。

"因为它们那里要比我们这里高很多啊,"我回答她,"你爬不上去的,因为那里很高很陡。冬天的时候,那里总比我们这里先霜霜;盛夏的时候,我还在那东北面的黑洞里看到过雪呢!"

"哇,你已经去过那里啦!"她兴奋地大叫起来,"那等我长大的时候也能去那里啦。艾伦,爸爸有没有去过呢?"

"爸爸会告诉你,小姐,"我慌忙地回答她,"那地方并不值得跑去游玩。你和你爸爸散步的那片旷野比那儿要好得多了,而且画眉山庄是世界上最好的地方。"

"我知道画眉山庄,但我还不知

第十八章

those," she murmured to herself. "And I should delight to look round me from the brow of that tallest point: my little pony Minny shall take me sometime."

One of the maids mentioning the Fairy cave, quite turned her head with a desire to fulfil this project: she teased Mr. Linton about it; and he promised she should have the journey when she got older. But Miss Catherine measured her age by months, and, "Now, am I old enough to go to Penistone Craggs?" was the constant question in her mouth. The road thither wound close by Wuthering Heights. Edgar had not the heart to pass it; so she received as constantly the answer, "Not yet, love: not yet."

I said Mrs. Heathcliff lived above a dozen years after quitting her husband. Her family were of a delicate constitution: she and Edgar both lacked the ruddy health that you will generally meet in these parts. What her last illness was, I am not certain: I conjecture, they died of the same thing, a kind of fever, slow at its commencement, but incurable, and rapidly consuming life towards the dose. She wrote to inform her brother of the probable conclusion of a four months" indisposition under which she had suffered; and entreated him to come to her, if possible; for she had much to settle, and she wished to bid him adieu, and deliver Linton safely into his hands. Her hope was, that Linton might be left with him, as he had been with her: his father, she would fain convince herself, had no desire to assume the burden of his maintenance or education. My master hesitated not a moment in complying with her request: reluctant as he was to leave home at ordinary calls, he flew to answer this; commending Catherine to

道那些地方啊，"她自言自语地说道，"如果能从那最高峰的边上向四周眺望，我一定会很开心的。总有一天我的小马敏妮会带我去的。"

有个女仆提起了仙人洞，这着实让她着了迷，使她想要实现这个计划，她硬缠着林顿先生答应这事，他答应等到她再长大一点就让她去一趟。可凯瑟琳小姐是按月份来计算年龄的，"现在，我是不是已经长大，可以去盘尼斯吞悬崖了？"这是她常常挂在嘴边的问题。到那边的路蜿蜒曲折，而且靠近呼啸山庄，埃德加无心从那里经过，所以小姐得到的回答常常是，"还不行，宝贝，还不行。"

我说过希斯克利夫太太在离开她丈夫以后还活了十二年左右。她们一家都是体弱多病的人：她和埃德加都缺乏你在这一带常见到的健康血色。她最后得的是什么病，我不是非常清楚，我猜他们应该患同样的病死去的吧，就是一种热病，病来得很慢，但无法医治，到最后就很快地耗尽人的生命。她写信告诉哥哥说自己已经病了四个月，结果可能会怎样，并恳求他，如果可能的话去她那里一趟，因为她有很多事情需要处理，并希望能和他告别，把林顿安安全全地托付到他手里。她的心愿就是把林顿交给他，就像过去和她在一起时一样。她自己也一心认为，这孩子的父亲是不会承担抚养和教育他的义务的。我家主人毫不犹豫地答应了她。为了普通的事他是不情愿离开家的，这次他却飞快地答应了。他把凯瑟琳交给我特别照顾，还反复交代我，说他不在家的时候，即便有我陪着，也不能让她

my peculiar vigilance, in his absence, with reiterated orders that she must not wander out of the park, even under my escort: he did not calculate on her going unaccompanied.

He was away three weeks: the first day or two, my charge sat in a corner of the library, too sad for either reading or playing: in that quiet state she caused me little trouble; but it was succeeded by an interval of impatient, fretful weariness; and being too busy, and too old then, to run up and down amusing her, I hit on a method by which she might entertain herself. I used to send her on travels round the grounds-now on foot, and now on a pony: indulging her with a patient audience of all her real and imaginary adventures, when she returned.

The summer shone in full prime; and she took such a taste for this solitary rambling that she often contrived to remain out from breakfast till tea; and then the evenings were spent in recounting her fanciful tales. I did not fear her breaking bounds; because the gates were generally locked, and I thought she would scarcely venture forth alone, if they had stood wide open. Unluckily, my confidence proved misplaced. Catherine came to me, one morning, at eight o'clock, and said she was that day an Arabian merchant, going to cross the Desert with his caravan; and I must give her plenty of provision for herself and beasts: a horse, and three camels, personated by a large hound and a couple of pointers. I got together good store of dainties, and slung them in a basket on one side of the saddle; and she sprang up as gay as a fairy, sheltered by her wide brimmed hat and gauze veil from the July sun, and trotted off with a merry laugh, mocking my cautious coun-

游荡到田庄外面，不过他没有想到，她可以单独一人就出门。

林顿走了三个星期。刚开始的一两天，我负责照顾的小家伙坐在书房的角落里，难过得不想读书，也不想玩，她那样安静的待着并没给我添什么麻烦，但紧接着她就变得不耐烦，急躁起来。当时我太忙，岁数也太大，没办法跑上跑下逗她开心，于是就想出一个办法让她自己玩。我总是打发她出去走走，有时走路，有时骑匹小马。等她回来的时候，我就作个耐心的听众，听她讲述那一切真实和想像的冒险经历。

当时正是盛夏时节，她已经喜欢上了独自一人出去闲逛，在用完早餐到喝茶这段时间里，她经常想方设法在外面逗留，到了傍晚的时候就讲她那些幻想的故事。我并不怕她越过边界，因为大门通常都是紧锁着的，而且即便大门敞开，我也认为她没有胆量独自一人出去冒险。可不幸的是，我的自信被证实错了。某天早晨，八点钟的时候，凯瑟琳过来找我，说这天她是一个阿拉伯商人，要带着她的商队穿过沙漠，我必须得给她足够多的食粮给她自己和牲口吃，这牲口就是一匹马和三只骆驼，那三只骆驼是用一只大猎狗和两只小猎狗来代替的。我做了一大堆可口的食物，扔进一只挂在马鞍边上的篮子里。她高兴得像个仙女似的跳起来，戴上她的宽边帽子、披上面纱用来遮挡七月的太阳，大笑着骑马跑去，对我劝她不要骑太快、早点回家的叮嘱，她只是挖

sel to avoid galloping, and come back early. The naughty thing never made her appearance at tea. One traveller, the hound, being an old dog and fond of its ease, returned; but neither Cathy, nor the pony, nor the two pointers were visible in any direction; and I despatched emissaries down this path, and that path, and at last went wandering in search of her myself. There was a labourer working at a fence round a plantation, on the borders of the grounds. I enquired of him if he had seen our young lady.

"I saw her at morn," he replied; "she would have me to cut her a hazel switch, and then she leapt her galloway over the hedge yonder, where it is lowest, and galloped out of sight."

You may guess how I felt at hearing this news. It struck me directly she must have started for Penistone Craggs. "What will become of her?" I ejaculated, pushing through a gap which the man was repairing, and making straight to the high road. I walked as if for a wager, mile after mile, till a turn brought me in view of the Heights; but no Catherine could I detect, far or near. The Craggs lie about a mile and a half beyond Mr. Heathcliff's place, and that is four from the Grange, so I began to fear night could fall ere I could reach them. "And what if she should have slipped in clambering among them," I reflected, "and been killed, or broken some of her bones?" My suspense was truly painful; and, at first, it gave me delightful relief to observe, in hurrying by the farm-house, Charlie, the fiercest of the pointers, lying under a window, with swelled head and bleeding ear. I opened the wicket and ran to the door, knocking vehemently for admittance. A woman whom I

苦一番。这顽皮的家伙直到喝茶时还没回来。不过有个旅行者，那只大猎狗，因为上了年纪，再加上喜欢安逸，所以先回来了。但不管是凯瑟琳还是小马，抑或那两只小猎狗都没有一点影子，于是我派人顺着这条路，那条路找，到最后我自己也到处去找她。在田庄边上有个工人在一片种植园的四周修篱笆。我问他有没有看见我们家小姐。

"早上的时候我见到过她，"他回答说，"她要我给她截一根榛木条，接着她就抽着她的小马跳过那边最矮的篱笆，跑得无影无踪了。"

你可以猜想当我听到这个消息时是什么样的感觉。我立刻想到她肯定跑去盘尼斯吞悬崖了。"她会发生什么事啊？"我脱口叫起来，冲过那人正在修补的缺口，直接往大路跑去。我就像去赌博一样焦急地走着，走了一英里又一英里，直到转了个弯后，我看到了呼啸山庄，可是远近我都看不见凯瑟琳的影子。悬崖距离希斯克利夫的住处有一英里半左右，离田庄有四英里，因此我开始担心在我到那儿之前，夜幕已经降临了。"如果她在爬上来的时候滑了下来了该怎么办，"我心里想着，"如果摔死，或者摔断了骨头该怎么办？"我的担忧真是让人痛苦，因此当我匆匆忙忙经过农舍，看到那只最凶猛的猎狗查理肿着脑袋，耳朵流着血，卧在窗子底下时，我这才高兴地松了口气。我打开边门，跑到大门前，拼命地敲门想要进去。一个我认识的女人出来应门，

knew, and who formerly lived at Gimmerton, answered: she had been servant there since the death of Mr. Earnshaw.

"Ah," said she, "you are come a seeking your little mistress! don't b e frightened. She's here safe: but I'm glad it isn't the master."

"He is not at home then, is he?" I panted, quite breathless with quick walking and alarm.

"No, no," she replied: "both he and Joseph are off, and I think they won't return this hour or more. Step in and rest you a bit."

I entered, and beheld my stray lamb seated on the hearth, rocking herself in a little chair that had been her mother's when a child. Her hat was hung against the wall and she seemed perfectly at home, laughing and chattering, in the best spirits imaginable, to Hareton— now a great, strong lad of eighteen—who stared at her with considerable curiosity and astonishment: comprehending precious little of the fluent succession of remarks and questions which her tongue never ceased pouring forth.

"Very well, Miss!" I exclaimed, concealing my joy under an angry countenance. "This is your last ride, till papa comes back. I'll not trust you over the threshold again, you naughty, naughty girl!"

"Aha, Ellen!" she cried, gaily, jumping up, and running to my side. "I shall have a pretty story to tell tonight: and so you've found me out. Have you ever been here in your life before?"

"Put that hat on, and home at once," said I. "I'm dreadfully grieved at you, Miss Cathy: you've done extremely wrong! It's no use pouting and crying: that won't repay the trouble I've had, scouring the country after you. To

以前她住在吉默顿，自从恩肖死后就成了这里的女仆。

"啊，"她说，"你是来找你家小姐的吧！不用担心。她在这很安全，不过我很高兴不是主人回来了。"

"他不在家，是不是？"我气喘吁吁地问道，因为走得太快，再加上惊慌，我已经上气不接下气了。

"不在家，不在家。"她回答道，"他和约瑟夫都出去了。我想这一个多小时还不会回来。快进来休息一下吧。"

我走进屋子，看见我那迷途的羔羊坐在火炉旁，坐在她母亲小时候用过的椅子上摇来摇去。她的帽子挂在墙上，而她待在这里显得十分自在，跟哈里顿有说有笑，兴致要多好就有多好。哈里顿现在已经是一个高大健壮的十八岁小伙子了，极其好奇而又惊讶地瞪着凯茜看，无法理解从她嘴里滔滔不绝吐出的言语和问题。

"好啊，小姐！"我对她喊道，装出一副生气的样子来掩盖自己的兴奋，"在你爸爸回来之前，这可是你最后一次骑马了。我不会再相信你了，你这个淘气的姑娘！"

"哎呀，艾伦！"她兴高采烈地叫着，跳起来跑到我身边，"今天晚上我有个非常好听的故事要说给你听呢，你到底还是找到我了。这辈子你有没有来过这里啊？"

"快戴上帽子，马上回家，"我说道，"我真替你感到难过，凯茜小姐，这次你可犯大错误了。撅嘴和哭都没用了，那都弥补不了我吃的苦，为了找你，我跑遍了整个村子。想想林顿

think how Mr. Linton charged me to keep you in; and you stealing off so! it shows you are a cunning little fox, and nobody will put faith in you any more."

"What have I done?" sobbed she, instantly checked. "Papa charged me nothing: he'll not scold me, Ellen—he's never cross, like you!"

"Come, come!" I repeated. "I'll tie the riband. Now, let us have no petulance. Oh, for shame. You thirteen years old, and such a baby!"

This exclamation was caused by her pushing the hat from her head, and retreating to the chimney out of my reach.

"Nay," said the servant, "don't be hard on the bonny lass, Mrs. Dean. We made her stop: she'd fain have ridden forwards, afeard you should be uneasy. But Hareton offered to go with her, and I thought he should: it's a wild road over the hills."

Hareton, during the discussion, stood with his hands in his pockets, too awkward to speak; though he looked as if he did not relish my intrusion.

"How long am I to wait?" I continued, disregarding the woman's interference. "It will be dark in ten minutes. Where is the pony, Miss Cathy? And where is Phoenix? I shall leave you unless you be quick; so please yourself."

"The pony is in the yard," she replied, "and Phoenix is shut in there. He's bitten-and so is Charlie. I was going to tell you all about it; but you are in a bad temper, and don't deserve to hear."

I picked up her hat, and approached to reinstate it; but perceiving that the people of the house took her part, she commenced capering

第十八章

先生是怎么叮嘱我把你关在家里的吧,你居然偷偷溜出来!这说明你是个狡猾的小狐狸,没有人会再信任你的!"

"我做了什么啊?"她呜咽啜泣起来,但马上又忍住,说道,"爸爸什么都没有嘱咐过我,他不会骂我的,艾伦,他从来都不会发脾气的,就像你一样!"

"过来,快过来!"我又说,"我帮你把帽子戴好。现在我们都不要耍性子了。唉,羞死人了,你都已经十三岁了,怎么还像个小孩子似的!"

我这么吼她是因为她把帽子推开,退缩到烟囱那边,不让我靠近她。

"别这样,"那女仆说道,"迪安太太,不要对这个漂亮的小姑娘那么凶啊。是我们叫她停在这儿的。她想继续往前骑,但又怕你不放心。哈里顿说他可以陪着去,我想他应该陪着,山上的路都很荒凉。"

在我们说话的时候,哈里顿一直把手插在口袋里站着,尴尬得说不出话来,不过看样子他好像并不喜欢我突然闯进来。

"我还得等多久?"我接着说,完全不理那女人的干涉。"十分钟后天就要黑了。小马在哪里,凯茜小姐,'凤凰'呢?如果你再不快点,我就要把你丢下了。随你。"

"小马在院子里,"她回答说,"'凤凰'关在那里。它被咬了,查理也是。我正想告诉你发生了什么事,可你那么凶,不配听这个故事。"

我捡起她的帽子,走过去想再给她戴上,可是她察觉到那房子里的人都站在她那边,因此开始在屋子里乱

round the room; and on my giving chase, ran like a mouse over and under and behind the furniture, rendering it ridiculous for me to pursue. Hareton and the woman laughed, and she joined them, and waxed more impertinent still; till I cried, in great irritation—

"Well, Miss Cathy, if you were aware whose house this is, you'd be glad enough to get out."

"It's *your* father's, isn't it?" said she, turning to Hareton.

"Nay," he replied, looking down, and blushing bashfully.

He could not stand a steady gaze from her eyes, though they were just his own.

"Whose, then—your master's?" she asked.

He coloured deeper, with a different feeling, muttered an oath, and turned away.

"Who is his master?" continued the tiresome girl, appealing to me. "He talked about 'our house' and 'our folk' I thought he had been the owner's son. And he never said, Miss: he should have done, shouldn't he, if he's a servant?"

Hareton grew black as a thunder-cloud, at this childish speech. I silently shook my questioner, and at last succeeded in equipping her for departure.

"Now, get my horse," she said, addressing her unknown kinsman as she would one of the stable-boys at the Grange. "And you may come with me. I want to see where the goblin-hunter rises in the marsh, and to hear about the *fairishes,* as you call them: but make haste! What's the matter? Get my horse, I say."

"I'll see thee damned before I be thy ser-

窜。我一过去追她，她就像个老鼠一样在家具的四周乱跑，搞得我这样追她显得很可笑。哈里顿和那女人都大笑起来，她也跟着他们一起笑，变得越来越放肆无礼，直到我极为恼怒地大叫道：

"行，凯茜小姐，如果你知道这是谁的房子，你就巴不得想快点出去了。"

"这是你父亲的房子，不是吗？"她转过身来向哈里顿问道。

"不是，"他回答说，眼睛看着地上，脸涨得通红。

他受不了凯茜紧盯着他的目光，尽管那双眼睛和自己的非常相像。

"那这房子是谁的，是你主人的吗？"她问。

他的脸更红了，不过却是另一种感觉，嘀咕着咒骂了一句，就转过身去。

"他的主人是谁？"这烦人的姑娘又问我说，"他一直说'我们家的房子'和'我们家的人'，我还以为他是这房主的儿子呢。可他从没叫过我一声小姐，他应该这样的，如果他是个仆人，他是不是应该这样叫我？"

听到这段孩子气的话，哈里顿脸就像乌云一样变得铁黑。我默默地摇了摇发问的人，最后终于让她穿戴好准备走了。

"现在，把我的马牵过来，"她对那不认识的亲戚说道，就像对田庄里的马夫说话一样。"你可以跟我一起去。我想去看看那个捉鬼的人在沼泽的哪个地方出现，还要听听你说的'小妖精'。动作可要快点啊，怎么了？我说，把马牵过来啊。"

"在做你的仆人之前，我还是先

vant!" growled the lad.

"You'll see me *what*?" asked Catherine in surprise.

"Damned—thou saucy witch!" he replied.

"There, Miss Cathy! you see you have got into pretty company," I interposed. "Nice words to be used to a young lady! Pray don't begin to dispute with him. Come, let us seek for Minny ourselves, and begone."

"But Ellen," cried she, staring, fixed in astonishment. "How dare he speak so to me? Mustn't he be made to do as I ask him? You wicked creature, I shall tell papa what you said.—Now then!"

Hareton did not appear to feel this threat; so the tears sprung into her eyes with indignation. "You bring the pony," she exclaimed, turning to the woman, "and let my dog free this moment!"

"Softly, Miss," answered the addressed: "you'll lose nothing by being civil. Though Mr. Hareton, there, be not the master's son, he's your cousin; and I was never hired to serve you."

"*He* my cousin!" cried Cathy, with a scornful laugh.

"Yes, indeed," responded her reprover.

"Oh, Ellen! don't let them say such things," she pursued in great trouble. "Papa is gone to fetch my cousin from London: my cousin is a gentleman's son. That my—" she stopped, and wept outright; upset at the bare notion of relationship with such a clown.

"Hush, hush!" I whispered, "people can have many cousins and of all sorts, Miss Cathy, without being any the worse for it; only they needn't keep their company, if they be dis-

看着你下地狱吧!"那个小伙子粗声地吼道。

"你要看我什么?"凯瑟琳莫名其妙地问道。

"下地狱——你这没礼貌的巫婆!"他回答。

"够了,凯瑟琳小姐!你看你已经找到一个很好的伙伴啦,"我插嘴说道,"这些话对一个小姐说会有多好啊!求你不要再跟他争辩了。来,我们自己去找敏妮,快过来。"

"可是,艾伦,"她叫喊着,惊讶地瞪着眼,"他怎么敢那样跟我说话!他不是要按我的吩咐办事吗?你这狠毒的家伙,我要把你说的话都告诉我爸爸,等着吧!"

哈里顿对这威吓并不在意,因此她气得眼泪盈眶。"你去把马牵来,"她又转身对那女仆大叫道,"马上放了我的狗!"

"温柔点,小姐,"那女仆回答说,"你客气点又不会有什么损失。虽然那位哈里顿先生不是主人的儿子,但他也是你表哥啊。而且我又不是雇来伺候你的。"

"他是我的表哥!"凯瑟琳叫着,轻蔑地大笑起来。

"是的,千真万确。"斥责她的人回答说。

"哦,艾伦!别让他们说这些话了,"她心慌意乱地对我说道,"爸爸去伦敦接我的表弟了,我表弟可是绅士的儿子。我的——"她停住了,大声哭起来,一想到和这样的粗人有亲戚关系就大为苦恼。

"嘘,不要再说了!"我低声说,"人可以有很多表亲,各种各样的表亲,凯瑟琳小姐,并没有那么糟糕,

agreeable and bad."

"He's not—he's not my cousin, Ellen!" she went on, gathering fresh grief from reflection, and flinging herself into my arms for refuge from the idea.

I was much vexed at her and the servant for their mutual revelations; having no doubt of Linton's approaching arrival, communicated by the former, being reported to Mr. Heathcliff; and feeling as confident that Catherine's first thought on her father's return would be to seek an explanation of the latter's assertion concerning her rude-bred kindred. Hareton, recovering from his disgust at being taken for a servant, seemed moved by her distress; and, having fetched the pony round to the door, he took, to propitiate her, a fine crooked-legged terrier whelp from the kennel, and putting it into her hand bid her wisht! for he meant naught. Pausing in her lamentations, she surveyed him with a glance of awe and horror, then burst forth anew.

I could scarcely refrain from smiling at this antipathy to the poor fellow; who was a well made, athletic youth, good looking in features, and stout and healthy, but attired in garment befitting his daily occupations of working on the farm, and lounging among the moors after rabbits and game. Still, I thought I could detect in his physiognomy a mind owning better qualities than his father ever possessed. Good things lost amid a wilderness of weeds, to be sure, whose rankness far over-topped their neglected growth; yet, notwithstanding, evidence of a wealthy soil, that might yield luxuriant crops under other and favourable circumstances. Mr. Heathcliff, I believe, had not treated him physi-

如果他们让人讨厌或是很坏的话，不要跟他们在一起就好了。"

"他不是——他不是我的表哥，艾伦！"她接着说，想了想又觉得很难过，扑到我的怀里想逃避这念头。

她和那仆人互相泄露秘密让我觉得很恼火，毫无疑问，凯瑟琳所说的林顿即将回来的消息肯定会被报告到希斯克利夫先生那里，同样我也确信，等凯瑟琳的父亲回来之后，她的第一个念头，就是要她父亲解释一下那女仆所说的关于那个野蛮亲戚的关系。哈里顿已经从他被误认为仆人的憎恶感中恢复了，好像反而被凯瑟琳的忧伤打动。他把小马牵到门前，为了与她和解，他又从窠里拿出一只漂亮的弯腿小猎狗，放在她的手里，叫她不要再哭，因为他并无恶意。凯瑟琳停止了哭泣，用敬畏的眼神打量着他，接着又哭起来。

看到凯瑟琳这么讨厌这孩子，我简直忍不住想要笑出来。哈里顿是个体格匀称而健壮的青年，五官长得也挺漂亮，结实而又健康，可是这身衣服只适合每天在田里干活，在旷野里追追兔子、打打猎之类。不过我仍然能够在他的相貌上看出他拥有比他父亲还要好的品质。当然好东西埋没在一片荒草丛中，无人过问它们的生长，就会被野草遮盖起来。尽管如此，但既然证明这是一块肥沃的土地，在其他有利的情况下，它也会有丰厚的收成。我相信希斯克利夫先生并没有在肉体上虐待过他。多亏这孩子那无所畏惧的天性，没有诱使人家

cally ill; thanks to his fearless nature, which offered no temptation to that course of oppression: it had none of the timid susceptibility that would have given zest to ill-treatment, in Heathcliff's judgment. He appeared to have bent his malevolence on making him a brute: he was never taught to read or write; never rebuked for any bad habit which did not annoy his keeper; never led a single step towards virtue, or guarded by a single precept against vice. And from what I heard, Joseph contributed much to his deterioration, by a narrow minded partiality which prompted him to flatter and pet him, as a boy, because he was the head of the old family. And as he had been in the habit of accusing Catherine Earnshaw and Heathcliff, when children, of putting the master past his patience, and compelling him to seek solace in drink by what he termed their "offalld ways," so at present he laid the whole burden of Hareton's faults on the shoulders of the usurper of his property. If the lad swore, he wouldn't correct him: nor however culpably he behaved. It gave Joseph satisfaction, apparently, to watch him go the worst lengths: he allowed that he was ruined: that his soul was abandoned to perdition; but then, he reflected that Heathcliff must answer for it. Hareton's blood would be required at his hands; and there lay immense consolation in that thought. Joseph had instilled into him a pride of name, and of his lineage; he would, had he dared, have fostered hate between him and the present owner of the Heights: but his dread of that owner amounted to superstition; and he confined his feelings regarding him to muttered innuendoes and private comminations. I don't pretend to be intimately acquainted with the

对他进行压迫。根据希斯克利夫判断，这孩子身上没有那种引起虐待狂怯懦的敏感。看来希斯克利夫想把自己的恶意用来将他培养成一个粗野的人。从来没人教这孩子念书或写字；只要他的坏习惯不惹恼到他主人，就没有人会来斥责他；从来没有人指引他向美德靠近一步，也没有人给他一句斥责恶行的教诲。据我耳闻，他之所以会变坏，约瑟夫可是"功不可没"，出于一种狭隘的偏心，约瑟夫从小就惯着他、宠着他，就因为他是这古老家族的主人。从前，他习惯于责骂孩提时代的凯瑟琳、恩肖和希斯克利夫，怪他们用他所谓的"可怕的行为"吵得老主人失去了耐心，逼得老主人只好借酒浇愁。如今他又把哈里顿过错的责任完全推到篡夺他家产那人的肩上。如果这孩子骂粗话，他也不会去纠正他，不管他做出什么该受责罚的行为，他都听之任之。很显然，看着这孩子坏到极点，就让约瑟夫感到很满足。他承认这孩子已经被毁了，他的灵魂永劫难覆，但接着他又想到这些都得由希斯克利夫负责，哈里顿所要的气质的养成全要靠他了，这么一想他就感到极大的安慰。约瑟夫慢慢地给哈里顿灌输了一种对家族姓氏的骄傲感，如果他敢的话，他就会培养哈里顿和现在山庄主人之间的仇恨。但他对这位主人的害怕程度已近于迷信，因此他只好约束自己对主人的感觉，只是低声讽刺他或是暗中诅咒他。对于那段日子里呼啸山庄中的日常生活方式，我不想假装出很熟悉的样子，这些都只是我道听途说，我亲眼目睹的很少。村里人都说

mode of living customary in those days at Wuthering Heights: I only speak from hearsay; for I saw little. The villagers affirmed Mr. Heathcliff was near, and a cruel hard landlord to his tenants; but the house, inside, had regained its ancient aspect of comfort under female management, and the scenes of riot common in Hindley's time were not now enacted within its walls. The master was too gloomy to seek companionship with any people, good or bad; and he is yet.

This, however, is not making progress with my story. Miss Cathy rejected the peace-offering of the terrier, and demanded her own dogs, Charlie and Phoenix. They came limping, and hanging their heads; and we set out for home, sadly out of sorts, every one of us. I could not wring from my little lady how she had spent the day; except that, as I supposed, the goal of her pilgrimage was Penistone Craggs; and she arrived without adventure to the gate of the farmhouse, when Hareton happened to issue forth, attended by some canine followers, who attacked her train. They had a smart battle, before their owners could separate them: that formed an introduction. Catherine told Hareton who she was, and where she was going; and asked him to show her the way; finally, beguiling him to accompany her. He opened the mysteries of the Fairy cave, and twenty other queer places. But, being in disgrace, I was not favoured with a description of the interesting objects she saw. I could gather, however, that her guide had been a favourite till she hurt his feelings by addressing him as a servant; and Heathcliff's housekeeper hurt hers by calling him her cousin. Then the language he had held

希斯克利夫很"吝啬",对他的佃户们来说,他是个残酷无情的地主。但这房子在女仆的打理下恢复了从前的舒适。辛德雷时代触目可见的骚乱如今在这高墙之内也不再上演了。过去这房子的主人非常阴郁,不与任何人来往,不论他们是好人还是坏人,现在这主人仍然如此。

不过这些都跟故事进展没什么关系。凯茜小姐不要那只作为求和礼物的猎狗,她只要她自己的狗,"查理"和"凤凰"。它们一瘸一拐垂头丧气地进来了,我们就出发回家,一个个都没精打采、垂头丧气。我无法从小姐口中盘问出她是如何消磨这一天的。我猜想,她这番长途跋涉的目的是去盘尼斯吞悬崖,她一路平安地到达农舍的门前,碰巧哈里顿走了出来,几条狗跟随其后,它们就袭击了凯瑟琳的队列,在它们的主人把它们分开之前,肯定来了一场恶战,就这样他们互相认识了。凯瑟琳告诉哈里顿她是谁,要去哪里,还请他为自己指路,最后还诱惑他陪她一起去。他把仙人洞这神秘世界和其他二十个怪异地方全告诉了她。但是,现在我已经失宠,得罪了凯瑟琳,就没法听她把她见到的有趣事情描述一番了。无论如何,我可以猜到她的向导曾很得她的欢心,直到她把他叫做仆人,伤了他的感情。而希斯克利夫的女仆又说他是凯瑟琳的表兄,伤害了她的感情。接着他对凯瑟琳的言语又刺痛了她的心。在田庄里,每个人总是称她

to her rankled in her heart; she who was always "love", and "darling", and "queen", and "angel", with everybody at the Grange, to be insulted so shockingly by a stranger! She did not comprehend it; and hard work I had to obtain a promise that she would not lay the grievance before her father. I explained how he objected to the whole household at the Heights, and how sorry he would be to find she had been there; but I insisted most on the fact, that if she revealed my negligence of his orders, he would perhaps be so angry, that I should have to leave; and Cathy couldn't bear that prospect: she pledged her word, and kept it, for my sake. After all, she was a sweet little girl.

为"亲爱的"、"宝贝"、"皇后"、"天使",如今却被一个陌生人如此骇人地侮辱了!她实在无法理解。我费尽口舌才让她答应不把这伤心事告诉父亲。我跟她解释说他父亲是多么的讨厌山庄那户人家!如果让他知道她去过那里,他会多么难过。但是我最为强调的是,就是如果她揭露了我玩忽职守,没有遵从他的命令,那么她爸爸也许会非常气愤,非让我离开不可。凯茜无法承受那种假设:她发了誓,为我而保守秘密。毕竟,她还是个可爱的小姑娘。

Chapter 19
第十九章

A letter, edged with black, announced the day of my master's return. Isabella was dead; and he wrote to bid me get mourning for his daughter, and arrange a room, and other accommodations, for his youthful nephew. Catherine ran wild with joy at the idea of welcoming her father back; and indulged most sanguine anticipations of the innumerable excellences of her "real" cousin. The evening of their expected arrival came. Since early morning, she had been

一封镶着黑边的信通知了我们主人的归期,伊莎贝拉死了。他写信来吩咐我给他女儿准备孝服,再腾出个房间,打点一下床铺,准备迎接他的小外甥。凯瑟琳一想到要欢迎父亲回来,就兴高采烈起来,还满怀希望地想像着她"真正的"表弟那数不尽的优点。预计他们到家的那个晚上来临了。从一大清早开始,她就忙着吩咐我们做她自己的那些琐碎事情,此刻

busy ordering her own small affairs; and now, attired in her new black frock—poor thing! her aunt's death impressed her with no definite sorrow—she obliged me, by constant worrying, to walk with her down through the grounds to meet them.

"Linton is just six months younger than I am," she chattered, as we strolled leisurely over the swells and hollows of mossy turf, under shadow of the trees. "How delightful it will be to have him for a playfellow! Aunt Isabella sent papa a beautiful lock of his hair; it was lighter than mine—more flaxen, and quite as fine. I have it carefully preserved in a little glass box; and I've often thought what pleasure it would be to see its owner. Oh! I am happy—and papa, dear, dear papa! Come, Ellen, let us run! come run!"

She ran, and returned and ran again, many times before my sober footsteps reached the gate, and then she seated herself on the grassy bank beside the path, and tried to wait patiently, but that was impossible: she couldn't be still a minute.

"How long they are!" she exclaimed. "Ah, I see some dust on the road— they are coming! No! When will they be here? May we not go a little way—half a mile, Ellen: only just half a mile? Do say yes, to that clump of birches at the turn!"

I refused staunchly: and, at length, her suspense was ended: the travelling carriage rolled in sight. Miss Cathy shrieked, and stretched out her arms, as soon as she caught her father's face looking from the window. He descended, nearly as eager as herself; and a considerable interval elapsed ere they had a

"林顿才比我小六个月,"当我们来到树荫下,悠闲地漫步于那坑坑洼洼长满苔藓的草地时,她喋喋不休地说着,"有他做我的玩伴真是让人兴奋啊!伊莎贝拉姑姑曾剪了他一绺漂亮的头发送给爸爸,颜色比我的还要浅,更黄一些,而且还非常细。我已经小心地把它保存在一个小玻璃盒子里。我常常在想,如果能见到这头发的主人会是一件多么愉快的事啊。哦,我真是太高兴了,爸爸,亲爱的,亲爱的爸爸!来呀,艾伦,我们快跑过去!来呀,快跑!"

她跑过去,又转过身跑回来,在我那沉重的脚步走到大门的时候,她已经跑了好几个来回,然后就坐在小路旁边那绿油油的草地上,想要耐心地等待他们,但那又怎么可能呢,她连一分钟都不能安静。

"他们还要多久才会到呀!"她大叫起来,"啊,我看到了,路上扬起一阵尘土,他们来了!不是他们!他们什么时候能到这里啊?我们不能走一点路吗,半英里,艾伦,就走半英里!快点答应啊!就走到转弯处那丛白桦树那里!"

我一口拒绝了她。最后,她的焦虑终于结束了,一辆长途马车缓缓驶来,映入我们的眼帘。凯瑟琳小姐一看到她父亲的脸从车窗向外望,就尖叫起来,伸出她的双臂。埃德加走下马车,几乎和她一样急切,在很长一

thought to spare for any but themselves. While they exchanged caresses, I took a peep in to see after Linton. He was asleep in a corner, wrapped in a warm, fur-lined cloak, as if it had been winter. A pale, delicate, effeminate boy, who might have been taken for my master's younger brother, so strong was the resemblance: but there was a sickly peevishness in his aspect that Edgar Linton never had. The latter saw me looking; and having shaken hands, advised me to close the door, and leave him undisturbed; for the journey had fatigued him. Cathy would fain have taken one glance, but her father told her to come on, and they walked together up the park, while I hastened before to prepare the servants.

"Now, darling," said Mr. Linton, addressing his daughter, as they halted at the bottom of the front steps: "your cousin is not so strong or so merry as you are, and he has lost his mother, remember, a very short time since; therefore, don't expect him to play and run about with you directly. And don't harass him much by talking: let him be quiet this evening, at least, will you?"

"Yes, yes, papa," answered Catherine: "but I do want to see him; and he hasn't once looked out."

The carriage stopped; and the sleeper, being roused, was lifted to the ground by his uncle.

"This is your cousin Cathy, Linton," he said, putting their little hands together. "She's fond of you already; and mind you don't grieve her by crying tonight. Try to be cheerful now; the travelling is at an end, and you have nothing to do but rest and amuse yourself as you please."

"Let me go to bed, then," answered the boy, shrinking from Catherine's salute; and he put his fingers to his eyes to remove incipient tears.

"Come, come, there's a good child," I whispered, leading him in. "You'll make her weep too—see how sorry she is for you!"

I do not know whether it were sorrow for him, but his cousin put on as sad a countenance as himself, and returned to her father. All three entered, and mounted to the library, where tea was laid ready. I proceeded to remove Linton's cap and mantle, and placed him on a chair by the table; but he was no sooner seated than he began to cry afresh. My master inquired what was the matter.

"I can't sit on a chair," sobbed the boy.

"Go to the sofa, then, and Ellen shall bring you some tea," answered his uncle, patiently.

He had been greatly tried during the journey, I felt convinced, by his fretful ailing charge. Linton slowly trailed himself off, and lay down. Cathy carried a foot-stool and her cup to his side. At first she sat silent; but that could not last: she had resolved to make a pet of her little cousin, as she would have him to be; and she commenced stroking his curls, and kissing his cheek, and offering him tea in her saucer, like a baby. This pleased him, for he was not much better: he dried his eyes, and lightened into a faint smile.

"Oh, he'll do very well," said the master to me, after watching them a minute. "Very well, if we can keep him, Ellen. The company of a child of his own age will instil new spirit into him soon, and by wishing for strength he'll

开心，做什么都可以。"

"那就让我上床睡觉吧，"那个男孩子答道，躲开凯瑟琳的热情招呼，用手擦掉刚刚流出的眼泪。

"来，过来吧，真是个好孩子，"我低声说着，把他带了进去，"你都快把她惹哭了，瞧瞧她为了你多么伤心啊！"

我不知道这是不是为他而难过，不过他的表姐也跟他一样哭丧着脸，回到她父亲身边。三个人都进去，上楼去了书房，茶点已经准备好放在那里了。我帮林顿脱掉身上的帽子和斗篷，把他安置在桌旁椅子上，但他刚一坐下就又哭了起来。我的主人问他这是怎么了。

"我不能坐在椅子上。"那孩子抽泣着说道。

"那就坐到沙发上去吧，艾伦会帮你把茶端过去的，"他舅舅耐心地回答他。我确信，在这一路上，为了这心情沮丧、体弱多病的孩子，他已经疲惫不堪了。林顿慢慢地走过去，躺在沙发上。凯茜搬来一条板凳，拿着自己的茶杯，走到他身旁。刚开始她还安静地坐在那，但没多久，她已经下定决心把这个小表弟当成自己的宠儿了，她也希望他能乖乖听话。她开始抚摸他的卷发，亲吻他的脸颊，用她的茶托给他端茶，就像照顾一个婴儿一样。这倒让他很高兴，因为他本来就不比婴孩好多少。他擦干眼睛，露出一丝淡淡的微笑。

"啊，他会过得很好的，"主人注视了他们一会儿之后对我说，"艾伦，只要我们能留住他，他就会过得很好的。有个像他这样年纪的孩子做伴，

gain it."

"Ay, if we can keep him!" I mused to myself; and sore misgivings came over me that there was slight hope of that. And then, I thought, however will that weakling live at Wuthering Heights, between his father and Hareton? What playmates and instructors they'll be. Our doubts were presently decided even earlier than I expected. I had just taken the children up stairs, after tea was finished, and seen Linton asleep—he would not suffer me to leave him till that was the case—I had come down, and was standing by the table in the hall, lighting a bed-room candle for Mr. Edgar, when a maid stepped out of the kitchen and informed me that Mr. Heathcliff's servant Joseph was at the door, and wished to speak with the master.

"I shall ask him what he wants first," I said, in considerable trepidation. "A very unlikely hour to be troubling people, and the instant they have returned from a long journey. I don't think the master can see him."

Joseph had advanced through the kitchen as I uttered these words, and now presented himself in the hall. He was donned in his Sunday garments, with his most sanctimonious and sourest face, and, holding his hat in one hand and his stick in the other, he proceeded to clean his shoes on the mat.

"Good evening, Joseph," I said, coldly. "What business brings you here tonight?"

"It's Maister Linton Aw mun spake tull," he answered, waving me disdainfully aside.

"Mr. Linton is going to bed; unless you have something particular to say, I'm sure he won't hear it now," I continued. "You had better sit down in there, and entrust your message

很快就会给他灌输新的精神，而且只要他想获得力量，他就会得到的。"

"唉，如果我们能留住他！"我自言自语着，一阵痛心的疑虑涌上心头，只怕希望渺茫。后来，我又想到，这个弱不禁风的小家伙该如何生活在呼啸山庄，如何周旋在他父亲和哈里顿中间呢？他们又会是怎样的玩伴和导师呢！很快我们的疑虑就见了分晓，甚至比我预料的还要早一些。吃过茶点之后，我刚把孩子们带上楼，看着林顿睡着（我不忍心离开他，一直等到他睡着），我走下楼，站在大厅的桌子旁边，给埃德加先生点上一支卧室用的蜡烛，这时一个女仆从厨房走来，告诉我希斯克利夫的仆人约瑟夫在门口，想要跟主人说句话。

"我要先问问他想干什么，"我非常惊恐地说道，"这时还来打扰人肯定没好事，况且主人他们刚刚才长途旅行回到家。我想主人不能见他。"

正当我说出这些话的时候，约瑟夫已经走过厨房，到了客厅。他穿着那件做礼拜用的衣服，绷着他那张伪善孤僻的脸，一手拿着帽子，一手拿着手杖，在垫子上擦了擦他的皮鞋。

"晚上好，约瑟夫，"我冷冷地对他说，"今晚是什么风把你吹来了啊？"

"我一定要跟林顿少爷说话。"他回答道，轻蔑地挥一下手，示意我走开。

"林顿先生睡觉了，除非你有什么特别的事要说，不然我肯定他现在不会听的，"我接着说道，"你最好先在这里坐下，把你的口信告诉我。"

to me."

"Which is his rahm?" pursued the fellow, surveying the range of closed doors.

I perceived he was bent on refusing my mediation, so very reluctantly I went up to the library, and announced the unseasonable visitor, advising that he should be dismissed till next day. Mr. Linton had no time to empower me to do so, for he mounted close at my heels, and, pushing into the apartment, planted himself at the far side of the table, with his two fists clapped on the head of his stick, and began in an elevated tone, as if anticipating opposition—

"Hathecliff has send me for his lad, un Aw munn't goa back baht him."

Edgar Linton was silent a minute; an expression of exceeding sorrow overcast his features: he would have pitied the child on his own account; but, recalling Isabella's hopes and fears, and anxious wishes for her son, and her commendations of him to his care, he grieved bitterly at the prospect of yielding him up, and searched in his heart how it might be avoided. No plan offered itself: the very exhibition of any desire to keep him would have rendered the claimant more peremp tory: there was nothing left but to resign him. However, he was not going to rouse him from his sleep.

"Tell Mr. Heathcliff," he answered, calmly, "that his son shall come to Wuthering Heights tomorrow. He is in bed, and too fired to go the distance now. You may also tell him that the mother of Linton desired him to remain under my guardianship; and, at present, his health is very precarious."

"Noa!" said Joseph, giving a thud with his prop on the floor, and assuming an authoritative

"他的卧室是哪一间？"那个家伙追问着，打量着那一排紧闭着的房门。

我察觉到他拒绝了我的调停，因此很不情愿地走到书房，通报了这个不合时宜的拜访者，建议主人先让他离开，明天再说。林顿先生根本没时间授予我这么做的权利，因为约瑟夫紧跟着我的脚步上来了，而且还闯进书房，站定在桌子的另一边，两只拳头放在他手杖的顶端，提高了嗓门开始讲话，仿佛已经预测到会遭遇反对似的。

"希斯克利夫派我来要回他的孩子，没有他我就不能回去。"

埃德加·林顿沉默了一会儿，一种极度悲痛的表情笼罩了他的面容：他自己很同情这孩子，但是，一回想起伊莎贝拉的希望与恐惧，对她儿子的热切希望，以及把孩子托付给他时所说的称赞，再一想到将要把孩子交给别人，真让他痛苦极了，在心中思索着该如何避免这件事情的发生。但最终还是无计可施：如果显露出想要留住他的渴望，反而会让对方更加专横跋扈。除了放弃孩子没有别的办法可行。可是，他又不想把他从睡梦中唤醒。

"告诉希斯克利夫先生，"他平静地回答道，"他的儿子明天就会去呼啸山庄。他现在已经睡着了，况且累得无法再走远路。你也可以告诉他，林顿的母亲希望由我来做他的监护人，而且当下他的健康状况非常不稳定。"

"不行！"约瑟夫一边说，一边用手杖在地板上砰地一顿，摆出一种威

air. "Noa! that manes nowt—Heathcliff maks noa 'cahnt uh t' mother, nur yah norther; bud he'll hev his lad; und Aw mun tak him—soa nah yah knaw!"

"You shall not tonight!" answered Linton, decisively. "Walk down stairs at once, and repeat to your master what I have said. Ellen, show him down. Go—"

And, aiding the indignant elder with a lift by the arm, he rid the room of him, and closed the door.

"Varrah wed!" shouted Joseph, as he slowly drew off. "Tuh morn, he's come hisseln, un' thrust *him* aht, if yah dart!"

风凛凛的神气。"不行！再怎么说也没用。希斯克利夫根本不管那母亲，也不管你，他只要他的孩子。我一定要带他走，这回你应该明白了吧！"

"今晚你不能带他走！"林顿坚决地回答道，"马上给我下楼，把我讲的话说给你主人听。艾伦，带他下去，快——"

他抓住这个愤怒的老头子的膀子一提，把他推到门外，之后便关上了门。

"很好！"约瑟夫大叫道，慢慢地走出去，"明天他亲自过来，看你还敢不敢把他推出去！"

Chapter 20
第二十章

To obviate the danger of this threat being fulfilled, Mr. Linton commissioned me to take the boy home early, on Catherine's pony; and, said he—

"As we shall now have no influence over his destiny, good or bad, you must say nothing of where he is gone to my daughter: she cannot associate with him hereafter, and it is better for her to remain in ignorance of his proximity; lest she should be restless, and anxious to visit the Heights—merely tell her, his father sent for him

为了避免这恐吓得以兑现，林顿先生派我一早就送这孩子回家，让他骑着凯瑟琳的小马过去了。埃德加对我说：

"既然现在我们无法对他的命运产生影响，不论是好还是坏，你千万不要对我女儿说他去了哪里，从今往后她不能和他有任何往来，最好也别让她知道他就在这附近，以免她寝食难安，急着想去呼啸山庄。你就告诉她说他父亲忽然派人来接他，他不得

suddenly, and he has been obliged to leave us."

Linton was very reluctant to be roused from his bed at five o'clock, and astonished to be informed that he must prepare for further travelling; but I softened off the matter by stating that he was going to spend some time with his father, Mr. Heathcliff, who wished to see him so much, he did not like to defer the pleasure till he should recover from his late journey.

"My father!" he cried, in strange perplexity. "Mamma never told me I had a father. Where does he live? I'd rather stay with uncle."

"He lives a little distance from the Grange," I replied; "just beyond those hills: not so far, but you may walk over here when you get hearty. And you should be glad to go home, and to see him. You must try to love him, as you did your mother, and then he will love you."

"But why have I not heard of him before?" asked Linton. "Why didn't mamma and he live together, as other people do?"

"He had business to keep him in the north," I answered, "and your mother's health required her to reside in the south."

"And why didn't mamma speak to me about him?" persevered the child. "She often talked of uncle, and I learnt to love him long ago. How am I to love papa? I don't know him."

"Oh, all children love their parents," I said. "Your mother, perhaps, thought you would want to be with him if she mentioned him often to you. Let us make haste. An early ride on such a beautiful morning is much preferable to an hour's more sleep."

不离开我们走了。"

五点钟的时候，林顿很不情愿地被人从床上唤醒，一听说自己还要准备继续赶路，他大吃一惊。但我还是让他缓下心来，告诉他要和他的父亲希斯克利夫先生住段日子，还说他父亲有多想见他，不愿再拖延这种见面的快乐，不想等他恢复旅行的疲惫才见他。

"我的父亲！"他感到莫名其妙，叫了出来，"妈妈从来没跟我说过我还有个父亲。他住在哪儿？我宁愿跟舅舅住在一起。"

"他住在离山庄不远的地方，"我回答他，"就在那些山头的那边，不是很远，等你精神好些的时候，你可以散步来这里啊。你应该高高兴兴地回家去见他才对。你一定得试着爱他，就像爱你母亲一样，那么他也会爱你的。"

"那为什么我从前都没听说过他呢？"林顿问道，"为什么妈妈没有像别人家那样跟他住在一起？"

"因为他在北方还有事情要做，"我回答道，"而你母亲的健康需要她常住南方。"

"那为什么妈妈没跟我提起过他呢？"这孩子坚持要刨根问底，"她常常会说起舅舅，很早我就学会了要爱他。我要怎么去爱爸爸？我根本不认识他。"

"啊，所有的孩子都爱他们的父母。"我说，"也许你母亲以为如果经常跟你提起他，你就会想要跟他住一起了。我们动作快点吧。在这样一个美丽的早晨，赶早骑马出去走走比多睡一个小时强多了。"

"Is *she* to go with us," he demanded: "the little girl I saw yesterday?"

"Not now," replied I.

"Is uncle?" he continued.

"No, I shall be your companion there," I said.

Linton sank back on his pillow, and fell into a brown study.

"I won't go without uncle," he cried at length; "I can't tell where you mean to take me."

I attempted to persuade him of the naughtiness of showing reluctance to meet his father; still he obstinately resisted any progress towards dressing, and I had to call for my master's assistance in coaxing him out of bed. The poor thing was finally got off with several delusive assurances that his absence should be short; that Mr. Edgar and Cathy would visit him, and other promises, equally ill-founded, which I invented and reiterated at intervals throughout the way. The pure heather-scented air, and the bright sunshine and the gentle canter of Minny, relieved his despondency, after a while. He began to put questions concerning his new home, and its inhabitants, with greater interest and liveliness.

"Is Wuthering Heights as pleasant a place as Thrushcross Grange?" he inquired, turning to take a last glance into the valley, whence a light mist mounted and formed a fleecy cloud on the skirts of the blue.

"It is not so buried in trees," I replied, "and it is not quite so large, but you can see the country beautifully, all round; and the air is healthier for you—fresher and dryer. You will, perhaps, think the building old and dark at first;

"她也要跟我们一起去吗？"他问道，"就是昨天我见到的那个小姑娘。"

"现在还不行。"我回答他。

"舅舅呢？"他又问。

"不去，我陪着你去。"我说。

林顿又躺回自己的枕头上，心里琢磨起来。

"舅舅不去那我也不去。"他终于叫了起来，"我不知道你到底打算把我带去哪儿。"

我企图想说服他，说他如果不愿去他父亲那里，那就不听话了。可他依旧固执地坚持着不穿衣服，我只好去请主人来帮忙哄他起床。最后，这可怜的小家伙终于出发了，留给他很多虚假渺茫的诺言，说什么他很快就能回来，什么埃德加先生和凯茜会去看他，以及其他一些诺言，都是毫无根据，我临时编造出来的，而且一路上我还时不时地重复着这些。过了一会，那夹杂着石楠花香的纯净空气，那灿烂的阳光，以及敏妮轻柔的漫步缓和了他那沮丧的心情。他开始饶有兴趣、精神抖擞地问起他的新家，问起家里都住了些什么人。

"呼啸山庄是不是跟画眉田庄一样好玩呢？"他问我，同时还转过头来向山谷望了最后一眼，山谷中升起了一阵薄雾，在蓝色天空的边际形成了一朵蓬松的白云。

"那里没有像这样隐没在树荫里，"我回答道，"而且也没这儿这么大，但你可以在四周看到美丽的乡村景色，而且那里空气有助于你的健康，更加新鲜干燥。起初你也许会觉

though it is a respectable house: the next best in the neighbourhood. And you will have such nice rambles on the moors. Hareton Earnshaw—that is Miss Cathy's other cousin, and so yours in a manner—will show you all the sweetest spots; and you can bring a book in fine weather, and make a green hollow your study; and, now and then, your uncle may join you in a walk: he does, frequently, walk out on the hills."

"And what is my father like?" he asked. "Is he as young and handsome as uncle?"

"He's as young," I said; "but he has black hair and eyes, and looks sterner; and he is taller and bigger altogether. He'll not seem to you so gentle and kind at first, perhaps, because it is not his way still, mind you be frank and cordial with him; and naturally he'll be fonder of you than any uncle, for you are his own."

"Black hair and eyes!" mused Linton. "I can't fancy him. Then I am not like him, am I?"

"Not much," I answered. Not a morsel, I thought, surveying with regret the white complexion and slim frame of my companion, and his large languid eyes, his mother's eyes, save that, unless a morbid touchiness kindled them a moment, they had not a vestige of her sparkling spirit.

"How strange that he should never come to see mama, and me!" he murmured. "Has he ever seen me? If he have, I must have been a baby—I remember not a single thing about him!"

"Why, Master Linton," I said, "three hundred miles is a great distance; and ten years seem very different in length to a grown-up

得那房子又旧又黑，尽管那是一所非常体面的宅邸，在这一带也是数一数二的。而且你还可以在旷野里优哉游哉地散步。哈里顿·恩肖，就是凯茜小姐的另一个表哥，也是你的表哥，他会带你去玩遍所有最好玩的地方。天气好的时候，你还可以带上一本书，把那绿色的山谷当作是你的书房，而且，你舅舅还可以时不时和你一起散步，他可是常常会在山中散步的呢。"

"那我父亲长什么样？"他问，"是不是跟舅舅一样的年轻帅气呢？"

"他也一样年轻，"我说道，"可他有黑头发和黑眼睛，看上去严厉些，个子也高大威猛些。刚开始你也许会觉得他不怎么温柔亲切，因为这不是他的作风，不过你一定得记住，对他要坦诚热情，那么他自然会比任何一个舅舅还要喜欢你，因为你是他的亲生儿子嘛。"

"黑头发，黑眼睛，"林顿沉思着，"我想像不出他是什么样子。那我长得不像他喽，对不对？"

"不太像，"我回答道，但我心里想着：一点都不像，很遗憾地打量着我同伴白皙的皮肤和纤瘦的身躯，还有他那硕大而无神的眼睛，他母亲的眼睛也是这样，除了某种病态的焦虑会偶尔点亮这双眼睛外，没有一点她那种炯炯有神的痕迹。

"真奇怪，他居然从来没有去看望过我和妈妈！"他嘀咕着，"他有没有见过我？如果他见过，那我一定还是个婴儿——我一点都不记得他！"

"哎呀，林顿少爷，"我说道，"三百英里是很长一段距离，而十年对一个大人和对你来说却是完全不同

person compared with what they do to you. It is probable Mr. Heathcliff proposed going, from summer to summer, but never found a convenient opportunity; and now it is too late. Don't trouble him with questions on the subject, it will disturb him for no good."

The boy was fully occupied with his own cogitations for the remainder of the ride, till we halted before the farm-house garden gate. I watched to catch his impressions in his countenance. He surveyed the carved front and low-browed lattices, the straggling gooseberry bushes and crooked firs, with solemn intentness, and then shook his head, his private feelings entirely disapproved of the exterior of his new abode. But he had sense to postpone complaining: there might be compensation within. Before he dismounted, I went and opened the door. It was half-past six; the family had just finished breakfast; the servant was clearing and wiping down the table. Joseph stood by his master's chair telling some tale concerning a lame horse; and Hareton was preparing for the hay-field.

"Hallo, Nelly!" cried Mr. Heathcliff, when he saw me. "I feared I should have to come down and fetch my property myself. You've brought it, have you? Let us see what we can make of it."

He got up and strode to the door, Hareton and Joseph followed in gaping curiosity. Poor Linton ran a frightened eye over the faces of the three.

"Surely," said Joseph after a grave inspection, "he's swopped wi' ye, maister, an' yon's his lass!"

Heathcliff, having stared his son into an ague of confusion, uttered a scornful laugh.

的。也许每年夏天希斯克利夫都打算去看你们,可一直都没能找到适当的机会,现在又已经太晚了。不要老是问这些问题去打扰他,这会让他不安的,一点好处都没有。"

在剩下来的这段路程里,这孩子就只顾着想他的心事,直到我们停在山庄的花园门前。我留心从他脸上的表情看看他对这里是什么印象。他一本正经地观察着那浮雕正门与矮檐格子窗,以及那蔓生的醋栗丛和弯曲的冷杉,然后就摇了摇头,他内心完全不喜欢这个新居的外表。不过他还很有理智,没急着抱怨:或许里面还可以弥补一下。在他下马之前,我先走过去开门。那时刚好六点半,全家人刚用完早餐,仆人正在收拾碗筷、擦桌子。约瑟夫站在他主人的椅子旁边,正在讲一个关于一匹跛马的故事,哈里顿则正准备去田里干活。

"你好,内莉!"希斯克利夫看见我,就对我说,"我还担心要亲自下山一趟,拿回属于我的东西呢。你已经把他带来了,是不是?让我们看看这孩子到底有多少能耐。"

他站起身来,大步走向门口,哈里顿和约瑟夫紧随其后,好奇地张着大嘴。可怜的林顿吓得惊慌失措,瞥了一眼这三个人的脸。

"一定是这样,"约瑟夫仔细地审视一番后,说道,"他给你掉换啦,主人,这是他家的女娃!"

希斯克利夫盯着自己的儿子,盯得他不知所措、直打冷战,然后他发出一声轻蔑的笑声。

"God! what a beauty! what a lovely, charming thing!" he exclaimed. "Haven't they reared it on snails and sour milk①, Nelly? Oh, damn my soul! but that's worse than I expected—and the devil knows I was not sanguine!"

I bid the trembling and bewildered child get down, and enter. He did not thoroughly comprehend the meaning of his father's speech, or whether it were intended for him; indeed, he was not yet certain that the grim, sneering stranger was his father; but he clung to me with growing trepidation; and on Mr. Heathcliff's taking a seat, and bidding him come here, he hid his face on my shoulder, and wept.

"Tut, tut!" said Heathcliff, stretching out a hand and dragging him roughly between his knees, and then holding up his head by the chin. "None of that nonsense! We're not going to hurt you, Linton—isn't that your name? You are your mother's child, entirely! Where is *my* share in you, puling chicken?"

He took off the boy's cap and pushed back his thick flaxen curls, felt his slender arms and his small fingers; during which examination Linton ceased crying, and lifted his great blue eyes to inspect the inspector.

"Do you know me?" asked Heathcliff, having satisfied himself that the limbs were all equally frail and feeble.

"No," said Linton, with a gaze of vacant fear.

"You've heard of me, I dare say?"

"No," he replied again.

"No? What a shame of your mother, never

"上帝啊，一个多么漂亮的小孩！一个多么可爱娇媚的小家伙！"他惊叫道，"他们不会是用蜗牛和酸奶养活他的吧，内莉？真是该死！比我预料的还要糟糕，鬼才知道我过去从来不是个盲目乐观的人啊！"

我叫那浑身颤抖、不知所措的孩子下马，走进屋来。他还不能完全理解他父亲话里的意思，也不知道这话是不是对他说的：说真的，他还不是非常肯定这个冷嘲热讽着的陌生人就是他父亲。但是他哆嗦得越来越厉害，紧贴着我，而当希斯克利夫坐下来，叫他过去时，他干脆把脸伏在我肩膀上哭了起来。

"啧，啧！"希斯克利夫边说，边伸出一只手粗鲁地把他拉到自己的两膝中间，然后扳着他的下巴抬起他的头，"不要害怕！我们不会伤害你的，林顿，这是不是你的名字？你可真是你母亲的孩子啊，整个身子都是！我的那部分又在哪里呢，爱哭的胆小鬼？"

希斯克利夫摘下这孩子的帽子，向后撸了撸他那浓密的淡黄卷发，摸一摸他那瘦弱的胳膊和细小的手指。在被如此检查的时候，林顿停止了哭泣，抬起他那蓝色的大眼睛审视着这个检查他的人。

"你认识我吗？"希斯克利夫问道，确认了这孩子的四肢都是一样的脆弱。

"不认识。"林顿说道，眼里带着一种茫然的恐惧注视着他。

"那我猜你应该听说过我吧？"

"没有。"他又回答道。

"没有！你母亲可真不知廉耻，

---

① snails and sour milk：蜗牛和酸奶，西方认为蜗牛和酸奶都是美食。

to waken your filial regard for me! You are my son, then, I'll tell you; and your mother was a wicked slut to leave you in ignorance of the sort of father you possessed. Now, don't wince, and colour up! Though it is something to see you have not white blood. Be a good lad; and I'll do for you. Nelly, if you be tired you may sit down; if not, get home again. I guess you'll report what you hear, and see, to the cipher at the Grange; and this thing won't be settled while you linger about it."

"Well," replied I, "I hope you'll be kind to the boy, Mr. Heathcliff, or you'll not keep him long; and he's all you have akin in the wide world, that you will ever know—remember."

"I'll be very kind to him, you needn't fear," he said, laughing. "Only nobody else must be kind to him, I'm jealous of monopolizing his affection. And, to begin my kindness, Joseph! Bring the lad some breakfast. Hareton, you infernal calf, begone to your work. Yes, Nelly," he added when they had departed, "my son is prospective owner of your place, and I should not wish him to die till I was certain of being his successor. Besides, he's mine, and I want the triumph of seeing my descendant fairly lord of their estates, my child hiring their children to till their father's lands for wages. That is the sole consideration which can make me endure the whelp: I despise him for himself, and hate him for the memories he revives! But that consideration is sufficient: he's as safe with me, and shall be tended as carefully as your master tends his own. I have a room upstairs, furnished for him in handsome style; I've engaged a tutor, also, to come three times a week, from twenty miles distance, to teach him what he pleases to learn. I've ordered Hareton to obey him, and in fact I've arranged every thing with a view to preserve the superior and the gentleman in him, above his associates. I do regret, however, that he so little deserves the trouble, if I wished any blessing in the world, it was to find him a worthy object of pride; and I'm bitterly disappointed with the whey-faced whining wretch!"

While he was speaking, Joseph returned, bearing a basin of milk porridge, and placed it before Linton. He stirred round the homely mess with a look of aversion, and affirmed he could not eat it. I saw the old man-servant shared largely in his master's scorn of the child; though he was compelled to retain the sentiment in his heart, because Heathcliff plainly meant his underlings to hold him in honour.

"Cannot ate it?" repeated he, peering in Linton's face, and subduing his voice to a whisper, for fear of being overheard. "But Maister Hareton never ate other else, when he were a little un: und what wer gooid eneugh fur him's gooid eneugh fur yah, Aw's rayther think!"

"I cann't eat it!" answered Linton, snappishly. "Take it away."

Joseph snatched up the food indignantly, and brought it to us.

"Is there owt ails th' victuals?" he asked, thrusting the tray under Heathcliff's nose.

"What should be them?" he said.

"Wah!" answered Joseph, "your dainty child says he cann't ate, either. But I guess it's right! His mother was just so—we wer a'most too mucky tuh sowt' corn fur makking her breead."

在他说话的时候，约瑟夫端着一盆牛奶麦片粥回来了，把它放在林顿面前。林顿带着厌恶的神色搅着这盆难看的粥，说他吃不下去。我发现那个老仆人跟他主人一样，也看不起这孩子，尽管他被迫把这种情绪藏在心里，因为希斯克利夫明白地告诉他的下人们要尊敬他。

"吃不下去吗？"他重复了一遍，凝视着林顿的脸，压低了声音咕噜着，怕被别人听见。"可是哈里顿少爷小的时候就吃这个，从来不吃别的东西，我想他吃得下的东西你也一样能吃下吧！"

"我不吃！"林顿暴躁地回答他，"把它端走。"

约瑟夫气冲冲地把食物拿过来，端到我们跟前。

"这吃的有什么不好？"他问道，把盘子推到希斯克利夫鼻子底下。

"这有什么不好？"他说。

"对啊！"约瑟夫答道，"你这挑剔的孩子说他吃不下去。不过我猜也是这样，他母亲就是这样，我们给她种粮食做面包，她还嫌我们脏呢。"

"Don't mention his mother to me," said the master, angrily. "Get him something that he can eat, that's all. What is his usual food, Nelly?"

I suggested boiled milk or tea; and the housekeeper received instructions to prepare some. Come, I reflected, his father's selfishness may contribute to his comfort. He perceives his delicate constitution, and the necessity of treating him tolerably. I'll console Mr. Edgar by acquainting him with the turn Heathcliff's humour has taken. Having no excuse for lingering longer, I slipped out, while Linton was engaged in timidly rebuffing the advances of a friendly sheep-dog. But he was too much on the alert to be cheated: as I closed the door, I heard a cry, and a frantic repetition of the words—

"Don't leave me! I'll not stay here! I'll not stay here!"

Then the latch was raised and fell: they did not suffer him to come forth. I mounted Minny and urged her to a trot; and so my brief guardianship ended.

"别跟我提起他的母亲，"主人生气地说道，"给他拿点他能吃的东西就行了。内莉，平常他都吃什么？"

我建议给他煮牛奶或茶，管家便奉命去准备。我心想，他父亲的自私自利倒让他过得舒舒服服的。他知道林顿体格娇弱，只能对他宽厚些。我要去告诉埃德加先生，说希斯克利夫的脾气有了转变，让他得到些安慰。既然已经没有理由再逗留下去，我就在林顿忙着胆怯地拒绝一条牧羊犬的友好问候时溜了出去。但是他太警觉，根本骗不了他：我一关上门，就听见一声喊叫，发了疯似的重复着这几句话："不要离开我，我不要待在这儿！我不要待在这儿！"

跟着，门闩抬起来又落下：他们没让他跟出来。我骑上敏妮，催它快跑。就这样，我短暂的监护职责结束了。

Chapter 21
第二十一章

We had sad work with little Cathy that day: she rose in high glee, eager to join her cousin; and such passionate tears and lamentations followed the news of his departure, that Edgar himself was obliged to sooth her, by affirming he should come back soon, he added, however, "if I can get him;" and there were no hope of that. This promise poorly pacified her; but time was more potent; and though still at intervals she inquired of her father when Linton would return, before she did see him again his features had waxed so dim in her memory that she did not recognise him.

When I chanced to encounter the housekeeper of Wuthering Heights, in paying business visits to Gimmerton, I used to ask how the young master got on; for he lived almost as secluded as Catherine herself, and was never to be seen. I could gather from her that he continued in weak health, and was a tiresome inmate. She said Mr. Heathcliff see med to dislike him ever longer and worse, though he took some trouble to conceal it. He had an antipathy to the sound of his voice, and could not do at all with his sitting in the same room with him many minutes together. There seldom passed much talk be-

那天小凯茜把我们折腾得够呛：她兴高采烈地从床上爬起来，一心渴望去陪她的表弟，但听到的却是他已经离开的消息，小凯茜伤心不已，坐在一旁边抹眼泪边叹气，以至于埃德加先生不得不亲自去安慰她，向她表明小表弟不久一定会回来。但他又在后面添上一句，"如果我能把他弄回来；"而那是完全无望的。这个承诺难以使小凯茜平静下来，幸好时间是消除伤痛的有力武器。虽然有时她还会问父亲林顿何时才能回来，但可以肯定的是在她真的再见到他之前，在她的记忆里他的容貌会变得模糊以至见面的时候也认不出来。

每当我到吉默顿去办事，如果能遇到呼啸山庄的管家，总会问到小少爷的近况；因为和凯瑟琳本人一样，他也基本上是与世隔绝从不被人看见的。我从管家那里获悉他的身体还很虚弱，而且还是个很难相处的人。她说虽然希斯克利夫先生在努力掩饰自己的感情，但他似乎越来越讨厌他了。他厌恶他的声音，不能忍受和他共处一室。他们之间也很少交谈。晚上林顿常常在一间他们所谓客厅的小

tween them. Linton learnt his lessons and spent his evenings in a small apartment they called the parlour; or else lay in bed all day; for he was constantly getting coughs, and colds, and aches, and pains of some sort.

"And I never knew such a faint-hearted creature," added the woman; "nor one so careful of himself. He will go on, if I leave the window open a bit late in the evening. Oh! it's killing, a breath of night air! And he must have a fire in the middle of summer; and Joseph's bacca pipe is poison; and he must always have sweets and dainties, and always milk, milk for ever—heeding naught how the rest of us are pinched in winter; and there he'll sit, wrapped in his furred cloak in his chair by the fire, and some toast and water or other slop on the hob to sip at; and if Hareton, for pity, comes to amuse him—Hareton is not bad natured, though he's rough—they're sure to part, one swearing and the other crying. I believe the master would relish Earnshaw's thrashing him to a mummy, if he were not his son; and I'm certain he would be fit to turn him out of doors, if he knew half the nursing he gives himself. But then, he won't go into danger of temptation: he never enters the parlour, and should Linton show those ways in the house where he is, he sends him up stairs directly."

I divined, from this account, that utter lack of sympathy had rendered young Heathcliff selfish and disagreeable, if he were not so originally; and my interest in him, consequently, decayed, though still I was moved with a sense of grief at his lot, and a wish that he had been left with us.

Mr. Edgar encouraged me to gain information, he thought a great deal about him, I fancy, and would have run some risk to see him; and he told me once to ask the housekeeper whether he ever came into the village? She said he had only been twice, on horseback, accompanying his father; and both times he pretended to be quite knocked up for three or four days afterwards. That housekeeper left, if I recollect rightly, two years after he came; and another, whom I did not know, was her successor, she lives there still.

Time wore on at the Grange in its former pleasant way, till Miss Cathy reached sixteen. On the anniversary of her birth we never manifested any signs of rejoicing, because it was also the anniveisary of my late mistress's death. Her father invariably spent that day alone in the library; and walked, at dusk, as far as Gimmerton kirkyard, where he would frequently prolong his stay beyond midnight. Therefore Catherine was thrown on her own resources for amusement.

This twentieth of March was a beautiful spring day, and when her father had retired, my young lady came down dressed for going out, and said she had asked to have a ramble on the edge of the moors with me; and Mr. Linton had given her leave, if we went only a short distance and were back within the hour.

"So make haste, Ellen!" she cried. "I know where I wish to go; where a colony of moor-game are settled: I want to see whether they have made their nests yet."

"That must be a good distance up," I answered; "they don't breed on the edge of the moor."

"No, it's not," she said. "I've gone very

near with papa."

I put on my bonnet and sallied out, thinking nothing more of the matter. She bounded before me, and returned to my side, and was off again like a young greyhound; and, at first, I found plenty of entertain ment in listening to the larks singing far and near, and enjoying the sweet, warm sunshine; and watching her, my pet, and my delight, with her golden ringlets flying loose behind, and her bright cheek, as soft and pure in its bloom as a wild rose, and her eyes radiant with cloudless pleasure. She was a happy creature, and an angel, in those days. It's a pity she could not be content.

"Well," said I, "where are your moor-game, Miss Cathy? We should be at them; the Grange park-fence is a great way off now."

"Oh, a little further—only a little further, Ellen," was her answer, continually. "Climb to that hillock, pass that bank, and by the time you reach the other side I shall have raised the birds."

But there were so many hillocks and banks to climb and pass, that, at length, I began to be weary, and told her we must halt, and retrace our steps. I shouted to her, as she had outstripped me, a long way; she either did not hear or did not regard, for she still sprang on, and I was compelled to follow. Finally, she dived into a hollow and before I came in sight of her again, she was two miles nearer Wuthering Heights than her own home; and I beheld a couple of persons arrest her, one of whom I felt convinced was Mr. Heathcliff himself.

Cathy had been caught in the fact of plundering, or, at least, hunting out the nests of the grouse. The Heights were Heathcliff's land,

我去过,很近的。"

于是我戴上帽子和小姐出发了,不再去想远近的事。小姐高兴极了,在我前面不停地跑着跳着,蹦回到我身旁,接着又马上跑掉,就像一只兴奋不已的小猎狗似的。开始我倒觉得挺有意思,听着或远或近的百灵鸟空灵的歌声,沐浴着甘甜温暖的阳光,再瞧着她,我的宝贝,我的快乐,只见她那一头金黄色的卷发披散在后面,随着她上下波动;因为兴奋而放光的小脸蛋是那样温柔纯洁,就像春天里绽放的野玫瑰,从她的眼睛里放出来的是无忧无虑快乐的光辉。那时的她是快乐的,像个天使。可惜她并不满足。

"好啦,"我说,"你的松鸡在哪呢,凯茜小姐?我们应该可以见到它们了,现在田庄的篱笆已经离我们很远啦。"

"哦,艾伦,再往前走一点点——就一点点,"她不停地说道。"爬上那座小山,再过了那个斜坡,就可以到啦。我们只要一到那边,鸟儿们就会出现了。"

可是等在前面的却是那么多小山和斜坡需要我们去翻越,终于我开始感到疲倦,于是告诉她我们必须就此打住往回走。可她已经把我远远地落在后面,我只能朝她大喊,但她似乎没有听见,或是不愿理我,还是继续往前走,我被迫跟在后面。最后,她闪身钻进一个山谷。当我再见到她时,她离呼啸山庄的距离已经比离她自己家还要近二英里;同时我看见她被两个人抓住了,我敢肯定其中一个就是希斯克利夫先生本人。

凯茜被抓是因为她被怀疑成小

and he was reproving the poacher.

"I've neither taken any nor found any," she said, as I toiled to them, expanding her hands in corroboration of the statement. "I didn't mean to take them; but papa told me there were quantities up here, and I wished to see the eggs."

Heathcliff glanced at me with an ill-meaning smile, expressing his acquaintance with the party, and, consequently, his malevolence towards it, and demanded who "papa" was?

"Mr. Linton of Thrushcross Grange," she replied. "I thought you did not know me, or you wouldn't have spoken in that way."

"You suppose papa is highly esteemed and respected, then?" he said, sarcastically.

"And what are you?" inquired Catherine, gazing curiously on the speaker. "That man I've seen before. Is he your son?"

She pointed to Hareton, the other individual, who had gained nothing but increased bulk and strength by the addition of two years to his age, he seemed as awkward and rough as ever.

"Miss Cathy," I interrupted, "it will be three hours instead of one that we are out, presently. We really must go back."

"No, that man is not my son," answered Heathcliff, pushing me aside. "But I have one, and you have seen him before, too; and, though your nurse is in a hurry, I think both you and she would be the better for a little rest. Will you just turn this nab of heath, and walk into my house? You'll get home earlier for the ease; and you shall receive a kind welcome."

I whispered Catherine that she mustn't, on any account, accede to the proposal: it was entirely out of the question.

偷，或者至少因为她在山庄里搜寻松鸡窝。山庄是属于希斯克利夫的土地，他正在惩罚偷猎者。

"我什么也没拿，并且什么也没找到，"凯茜辩解着，摊开自己的双手来证明自己，此时我已经向他们走去。"爸爸告诉我有很多松鸡在这儿筑巢下蛋，我只想看看那些蛋而已，并不想拿走什么。"

希斯克利夫带着不怀好意的微笑扫了我一眼，暗示他已经认出了对方，同时，也表明他起了歹心，他问道："谁是你爸爸？"

"画眉田庄的林顿先生，"她答道，"我想你肯定不认识我，要不你不会用那样的语气和我说话。"

"看来你认为你爸爸是个很伟大很受人尊敬的人喽？"他的话充满了讽刺。

"那你是谁呢？"凯瑟琳好奇地盯着这个说话的人问。她接着说："那个人我以前见过。他是你的儿子吗？"

她用手指着哈里顿——另一个抓他的人；这两年他没有什么变化，就是身体比以前更粗壮更有力气了，跟从前一样，他看上去既笨拙又粗鲁。

"凯茜小姐，"我打断说，"我们出来三个小时而不是一个小时，真的必须回去了。"

"不，那个人不是我儿子，"希斯克利夫把我推开，继续说，"但我是有个儿子，你以前也见过他；虽然你的保姆这么着急回去，但我觉得你们最好休息一会儿。我家就在山那头，你愿不愿意翻过这长满常青灌木的山头去我家里呢？你歇上一会儿，就有力气早些回家了，而且在那里你会受到

"Why?" she asked, aloud. "I'm tired of running, and the ground is dewy: I can't sit here. Let us go, Ellen. Besides, he says I have seen his son. He's mistaken, I think; but I guess where he lives. At the farm-house I visited in coming from Penistone Craggs. Don't you?"

"I do. Come, Nelly, hold your tongue it will be a treat for her to look in on us. Hareton, get forwards with the lass. You shall walk with me, Nelly."

"No, she's not going to any such place," I cried, struggling to release my arm, which he had seized. But she was almost at the doorstones already, scampering round the brow at full speed. Her appointed companion did not pretend to escort her, he shied off by the roadside, and vanished.

"Mr. Heathcliff, it's very wrong," I continued, "you know you mean no good. And there she'll see Linton, and all will be told, as soon as ever we return; and I shall have the blame."

"I want her to see Linton," he answered; "he's looking better these few days, it's not often he's fit to be seen. And we'll soon persuade her to keep the visit secret, where is the harm of it?"

"The harm of it is that her father would hate me if he found I suffered her to enter your house; and I am convinced you have a bad design in encouraging her to do so," I replied.

"My design is as honest as possible. I'll inform you of its whole scope," he said. "That the two cousins may fall in love, and get married. I'm acting generously to your master, his young chit has no expecta tions, and should she second my wishes, she'll be provided for at

第二十一章

款待的。"

我低声对凯瑟琳说她无论如何不能接受这邀请——这是绝对不可能的。

"为什么?"她大声问我。"我跑累了,而且地上这么多露水,我不能坐在这。艾伦,我们去吧。何况,他说我见过他的儿子。我想他一定是搞错了,但我能猜出他住在哪里。在我从盘尼斯吞岩来时去过的那个农房。对不对?"

"对。来吧,内莉,不要再说什么了——去我们家看看,这对她来说将是件天大的喜事。哈里顿,陪着这姑娘继续往前走吧。内莉,你就跟我一道走。"

"不,她不能到你们那去,"我叫着,想抽出被他紧紧拽住的胳膊。但小姐已经接近门前的石阶了,她飞快地跑着绕过了屋檐。那个被派去陪伴她的伙伴似乎并没完成护送她的任务,他哆哆嗦嗦地向路边溜去,转眼就消失了。

"希斯克利夫先生,你不能这样做,"我接着说,"我知道你没怀好意。她马上就会见到林顿,等我们一回去,老爷就会知道所有的事,我也会受到责备。"

"我就是要她见见林顿,"他回答说,"这几天他看来好些了,他并不是总有这样好的状态去见人的。等会儿我们可以劝她保密。这又有什么害处呢?"

"害处就是,如果她父亲发现我竟然答应她到你家来,他会恨我的;我肯定你蛊惑她这样做是有不可告人的目的。"我回答道。

"我的目的是很光明正大的,我可以一字不漏地告诉你。"他说,"那就是要让这对表姐弟坠入爱河并结婚。对

once as joint successor with Linton."

"If Linton died," I answered, "and his life is quite uncertain, Catherine would be the heir."

"No, she would not," he said. "There is no clause in the will to secure it so, his property would go to me; but, to prevent disputes, I desire their union, and am resolved to bring it about."

"And I'm resolved she shall never approach your house with me again," I returned, as we reached the gate, where Miss Cathy waited our coming.

Heathcliff bid me be quiet; and, preceding us up the path, hastened to open the door. My young lady gave him several looks, as if she could not exactly make up her mind what to think of him; but now he smiled when he met her eyes, and softened his voice in addressing her; and I was foolish enough to imagine the memory of her mother might disarm him from desiring her injury. Linton stood on the hearth. He had been out, walking in the fields, for his cap was on, and he was calling to Joseph to bring him dry shoes. He had grown tall of his age, still wanting some months of sixteen. His features were pretty yet, and his eye and complexion brighter than I remembered them, though with merely temporary lustre borrowed from the salubrious air and genial sun.

"Now, who is that?" asked Mr. Hearhcliff, turning to Cathy. "Can you tell?"

"Your son?" she said, having doubtfully surveyed, first one and then the other.

"Yes, yes," answered he, "but is this the only time you have beheld him? Think! Ah! you have a short memory. Linton, don't you recall your cousin, that you used to tease us so

你的主人我已经仁至义尽了！他年轻的小女儿并没有什么值得期盼的，不过要是她能完成我的心愿，她就跟林顿一起成为继承人，也就有了依靠。"

"如果林顿离开人世了呢，"我说，"他的命要是保不住了，那么凯瑟琳将会成为继承人的。"

"不，不会的，"他回答，"在遗嘱里并没有条文会做出如此保证，他的财产将会成为我的。但为了避免争执，我希望他们能结合，我决心促成这桩婚事。"

"我决心以后决不再带她接近你家。"我回敬道，这时我们已经走到门口，凯茜小姐正在那等着。

希斯克利夫叫我安静，走在我们前面赶紧把门打开。我的小姐瞟了他好几眼，似乎还拿不定主意怎么样看待这个人。但当他们的目光相遇时，他微笑着，并且轻声细语地和她说话；我居然傻到认为他对她母亲的记忆会使他放弃伤害她的打算。林顿站在炉边，他刚到田野散步过，因为他还戴着他的小帽，正在叫约瑟夫给他拿双干净的鞋过来。他还差几个月才满十六周岁，相对于年龄而言，他的个子已经很高了。相貌也英俊了，眼睛和气色比我印象中的有精神些，虽然那只是从清新健康的空气与温暖的阳光中暂时借来的光辉而已。

"他是谁？"希斯克利夫回头问凯茜，"你还记得吗？"

"你的儿子？"她疑惑地在他俩身上轮流打量着。

"是啊，是啊，"他回答，"难道这是你们初次见面吗？想想！天啊！你的记性实在不太好。林顿，你不记得

with wishing to see?"

"What, Linton!" cried Cathy, kindling into joyful surprise at the name. "Is that little Linton? He's taller than I! Are you, Linton?"

The youth stepped forward, and acknowledged himself, she kissed him fervently, and they gazed with wonder at the change time had wrought in the appearance of each. Catherine had reached her full height; her figure was both plump and slender, elastic as steel, and her whole aspect sparkling with health and spirits. Linton's looks and movements were very languid, and his form extremely slight; but there was a grace in his manner that mitigated these defects, and rendered him not unpleasing. After exchanging numerous marks of fondness with him, his cousin went to Mr. Heathcliff, who lingered by the door, dividing his attention between the objects inside and those that lay without: pretending, that is, to observe the latter, and really noting the former alone.

"And you are my uncle, then!" she cried, reaching up to salute him. "I thought I liked you, though you were cross, at first. Why don't you visit at the Grange with Linton? To live all these years such close neighbours, and never see us, is odd: what have you done so for?"

"I visited it once or twice too often before you were born," he answered. "There—damn it! If you have any kisses to spare, give them to Linton: they are thrown away on me."

"Naughty Ellen!" exclaimed Catherine, flying to attack me next with her lavish caresses. "Wicked Ellen! To try to hinder me from entering. But I'll take this walk every morning in future, may I, uncle? and sometimes bring papa. Won't you be glad to see us?"

第二十一章

你的表姐啦，你不是总嚷着要我们带你去见她吗？"

"什么，林顿！"凯茜惊叫，听到这个名字，她异常惊喜，"那就是小林顿吗？他比我还高啦！是你吗，林顿？"

年轻人走上前来，承认他就是小林顿。她狂热地亲吻他，然后他们互相凝视，为时间在彼此容貌上刻下的变化感到惊奇。凯瑟琳已经长得很高；她拥有丰腴迷人的身材，像钢一样的弹性，健康并精神焕发。林顿的神情和举止非常懒散，体形也过于单薄，但他文雅的风度遮盖了他的缺点，使他看上去并不那么讨厌。在他们表达了一通彼此之间的喜爱之情后，他的表姐走到希斯克利夫面前，他正呆在门口，一边注意屋里的人，一边关注外面的情况，换句话说，假装在看外面，实际上只关注前者。

"这么说你就是我姑父啦！"她欢快地叫着，走上前去向他行礼。"我本来就感觉挺喜欢你的，即使你开始对我不大友好。你干嘛不带林顿到我们田庄来呢？这些年我们住得这么近，却从没来看过我们，真是奇怪：这样做为什么呢？"

"你出生前，我去过太多次了，"他答道，"哦——可恶！你要是有多余的吻的话，就送给林顿吧——给我可是浪费了。"

"淘气的艾伦！"凯瑟琳叫着，用她那过于热情的拥抱向我袭来。"坏艾伦！竟想阻止我进来。但从今以后每天早上我都要散步来这儿，可以吗，姑父？有时还会带上爸爸，你难道不高兴见到我们吗？"

"Of course!" replied the uncle, with a hard-ly suppressed grimace, resulting from his deep aversion to both the proposed visitors. "But stay," he continued, turning towards the young lady. "Now I think of it, I'd better tell you. Mr. Linton has a prejudice against me, we quarrelled at one time of our lives, with unchristian ferocity; and, if you mention coming here to him, he'll put a veto on your visits altogether. Therefore, you must not mention it, unless you be careless of seeing your cousin hereafter, You may come, if you will, but you must not mention it."

"Why did you quarrel?" asked Catherine, considerably crest-fallen.

"He thought me too poor to wed his sister," answered Heathcliff, "and was grieved that I got her, his pride was hurt, and he'll never forgive it."

"That's wrong!" said the young lady: "some time, I'll tell him so. But Linton and I have no share in your quarrel. I'll not come here, then; he shall come to the Grange."

"It will be too far for me," murmured her cousin, "to walk four miles would kill me. No, come here, Miss Catherine, now and then, not every morning, but once or twice a week."

The father launched towards his son a glance of bitter contempt.

"I am afraid, Nelly, I shall lose my labour," he muttered to me. "Miss Catherine, as the ninny calls her, will discover his value, and send him to the devil. Now, if it had been Hareton! —Do you know that, twenty times a day, I covet Hareton, with all his degradation? I'd have loved the lad had he been some one else. But I think he's safe from her love. I'll pit him

"当然可以，"姑父回答，出于对两位访客的深深厌恶，他情不自禁地露出狰狞的笑容。"但是等一下，"他转身对小姐说，"既然这样，我最好告诉你。林顿先生对我有很深的成见。我们吵过一次，吵得十分厉害，你要是提到来过这儿，他会禁止你再来的，所以千万不要提这事，除非你并不在意以后能不能见到你的表弟。只要你愿意随时可以来，但你决不能说出去。"

"你们为什么吵架呢？"凯瑟琳听完后唉声叹气地问。

"他嫌我太穷，没有资格娶他的妹妹，"希斯克利夫回答，"但最终我赢得了她的芳心，他很不快，自尊心受到了伤害，他永远不会原谅了。"

"那太不应该啦！"小姐说，"我早晚会告诉他这些。可林顿和我是无辜的。如果这样我就不来这儿了，让林顿来田庄好啦。"

"这对我实在太远了，"她的表弟嘀咕着，"走四英里路会要我的命的。不，还是你来吧，凯瑟琳小姐，随时都行——不过不要每天早晨来，一星期能来一两次就好了。"

他父亲轻蔑地扫了儿子一眼。

"内莉，我恐怕要白费工夫了，"他小声对我说："凯瑟琳小姐——这个小傻子就是这样称呼她的——会发现他一文不值，并将他一脚踢开。要是哈里顿的话就好了——别看他被糟蹋成这样子，我一天倒会羡慕他二十回！他要是换成另一个人我会喜欢的。不过我想他不可能得到她的爱

against that paltry creature, unless it bestir itself briskly. We calculate it will scarcely last till it is eighteen. Oh, confound the vapid thing! He's absorbed in drying his feet, and never looks at her.—Linton!"

"Yes, father," answered the boy.

"Have you nothing to show your cousin, anywhere about; not even a rabbit, or a weasel's nest? Take her into the garden, before you change your shoes; and into the stable to see your horse."

"Wouldn't you rather sit here?" asked Linton, addressing Cathy in a tone which expressed reluctance to move again.

"I don't know," she replied, casting a longing look to the door, and evidently eager to be active.

He kept his seat, and shrank closer to the fire. Heathcliff rose, and went into the kitchen, and from thence to the yard, calling out for Hareton. Hareton responded, and presently the two entered. The young man had been washing himself, as was visible by the glow on his cheeks, and his wetted hair.

"Oh, I'll ask you, uncle," cried Miss Cathy, recollecting the house keeper's assertion. "That is not my cousin, is he?"

"Yes," he replied, "your mother's nephew. Don't you like him?"

Catherine looked queer.

"Is he not a handsome lad?" he continued.

The uncivil little thing stood on tiptoe, and whispered a sentence in Heathcliffs ear. He laughed; Hareton darkened, I perceived he was very sensitive to suspected slights, and had obviously a dim notion of his inferiority. But his master or guardian chased the frown by ex-

情。我要让他来反对那个没用的废物，除非他能赶紧振作起来。可惜满打满算，他也很难活到十八岁。哦，那个该死的窝囊废！他正聚精会神地擦他的脚，却不看她一眼。——林顿！"

"什么事啊，父亲，"那孩子应和着。

"附近没有什么地方可以带你表姐去看看的吗？哪怕兔子或者鼬鼠的窝？你换鞋之前，可以先带她到花园里去，或者到马厩去看看你的马。"

"你不是宁愿坐在这儿吗？"林顿问凯瑟琳，声调里充满了不情愿。

"我不知道，"她回答，用渴望的眼神看着门口，显然她想走走。

他依然坐在那儿，还向火边缩了缩。希斯克利夫站起身来走进厨房，又走进院子去叫哈里顿。哈里顿满口答应着，两人随即又进来了。从他脸上的光泽和潮湿的头发不难看出，那个年轻人刚刚才洗了澡。

"啊，姑夫，我要问问你，"凯瑟琳记起了那个管家的话，"那不是我的表哥，是吗？"

"没错，"他回答，"他是你母亲的侄子。你不喜欢他吗？"

凯瑟琳脸上露出古怪的神情。

"难道他不是个帅小伙吗？"他接着问。

这个没有礼貌的小家伙踮起了脚尖，小声在希斯克利夫耳边说了句话。顿时他大笑，哈里顿的脸也阴沉下来；我想他对可以猜到的轻视是很敏感的，而且显然，他对自己的卑微已经有了模糊的认识。不过他的主人

claiming—

"You'll be the favourite among us, Hareton! She says you are a—what was it? Well, something very flattering. Here! you go with her round the farm. And behave like a gentleman, mind! Don't use any bad words; and don't stare, when the young lady is not looking at you, and be ready to hide your face when she is; and, when you speak, say your words slowly, and keep your hands out of your pockets. Be off, and entertain her as nicely as you can."

He watched the couple walking past the window. Earnshaw had his countenance completely averted from his companion. He seemed studying the familiar landscape with a stranger's and an artist's interest. Catherine took a sly look at him, expressing small admiration. She then turned her attention to seeking out objects of amusement for herself, and tripped merrily on, lilting a tune to supply the lack of conversation.

"I've tied his tongue," observed Heathcliff. "He'll not venture a single syllable, all the time! Nelly, you recollect me at his age—nay, some years younger. Did I ever look so stupid: so 'gaumless', as Joseph calls it?"

"Worse," I replied, "because more sullen with it."

"I've a pleasure in him," he continued reflecting aloud. "He has satisfied my expectations. If he were a born fool I should not enjoy it half so much. But he's no fool; and I can sympathise with all his feelings, having felt them myself. I know what he suffers now, for instance, exactly, it is merely a beginning of what he shall suffer, though. And he'll never be able to emerge from his bathos of coarseness

或者说是保护人的话让他怒气全消：

"你就要成为我们的宝贝啦，哈里顿！她说你是一个——什么来着？恩，反正是说你的好话。这样吧，你陪这位小姐在田庄到处转转。切记，你的举止要像个绅士！不要使用任何坏字眼；在这位小姐没有看你的时候，你千万不要盯着她看，当她看着你的时候，你要准备好闪开你的脸；说话要慢条斯理，不要把手放在口袋里。走吧，尽可能好好款待她。"

他目送着这一对从窗前走过。恩肖转过脸去，不看他的同伴一眼。他仿佛以一个陌生人和艺术家的兴趣在那儿审视着熟悉的风景，凯瑟琳偷偷瞟了他一眼，眼光里没流露出什么爱慕的神情。而后，她就把注意力转移到可以令她高兴的事情上去了，还高兴地轻快地向前走，嘴里哼着曲子，以消除无话可说的尴尬。

"我已经把他的舌头捆住了，"希斯克利夫注视着。"他自始至终都不敢透露任何一个字！内莉，你还记得我像他那么大的时候吧——不，应该是比他要小些。我也是这样笨手笨脚的么，或者像约瑟夫说的那样'莫名其妙'吗？"

"更糟糕，"我回答，"因为你当时比他更阴郁些。"

"他让我心里舒服，"他继续大声说出他的想法。"他满足了我的期望。如果他天生是个呆子，我肯定享受不到现在一半的乐趣。但他不是呆子；他所有的感受，都能引起我的共鸣，因为我自己也曾真切地感受过。比如，我现在能准确地知道他的痛苦；而这只不过是个开始而已。他永远也

and ignorance. I've got him faster than his scoundrel of a father secured me, and lower; for he takes a pride in his brutishness. I've taught him to scorn everything extra-animal as silly and weak. Don't you think Hindley would be proud of his son, if he could see him? Almost as proud as I am of mine. But there's this difference; one is gold put to the use of paving-stones, and the other is tin polished to ape a service of silver. Mine has nothing valuable about it; yet I shall have the merit of making it go as far as such poor stuff can go. His had first rate qualities, and they are lost, rendered worse than unavailing. I have nothing to regret; he would have more than any, but I, are aware of. And the best of it is, Hareton is damnably fond of me! You'll own that I've out-matched Hindley there. If the dead villain could rise from his grave to abuse me for his offspring's wrongs, I should have the fun of seeing the said offspring fight him back again, indignant that he should dare to rail at the one friend he has in the world!"

Heathcliff chuckled a fiendish laugh at the idea. I made no reply, because I saw that he expected none. Meantime, our young companion, who sat too removed from us to hear what was said, began to evince symptoms of uneasiness, probably repenting that he had denied himself the treat of Catherine's society for fear of a little fatigue. His father remarked the restless glances wandering to the window, and the hand irresolutely extended towards his cap.

"Get up, you idle boy!" he exclaimed with assumed heartiness. "Away after them! they are just at the corner, by the stand of hives."

Linton gathered his energies, and left the hearth. The lattice was open, and, as he stepped out, I heard Cathy inquiring of her unsociable attendant, what was that inscription over the door? Hareton stared up, and scratched his head like a true clown.

"It's some damnable writing," he answered. "I cannot read it."

"Can't read it?" cried Catherine; "I can read it, it's English. But I want to know why it is there."

Linton giggled—the first appearance of mirth he had exhibited.

"He does not know his letters," he said to his cousin. "Could you believe in the existence of such a colossal dunce?"

"Is he all as he should be?" asked Miss Cathy seriously; "or is he simple—not right? I've questioned him twice now, and each time he looked so stupid I think he does not understand me. I can hardly understand him, I'm sure!"

Linton repeated his laugh, and glanced at Hareton tauntingly; who certainly did not seem quite clear of comprehension at that moment.

"There's nothing the matter, but laziness, is there, Earnshaw?" he said. "My cousin fancies you are an idiot. There you experience the consequence of scorning 'book learning,' as you would say. Have you noticed, Catherine, his frightful Yorkshire pronunciation?"

"Why, where the devil is the use?" growled Hareton, more ready in answering his daily companion. He was about to enlarge further, but the two youngsters broke into a noisy fit of merriment; my giddy Miss being delighted to discover that she might turn his strange talk to matter of amusement.

林顿抖起精神，离开火炉。窗子开着，当他走出去时，我听见凯茜正在问她那个不善言辞的侍从门上刻的是什么？哈里顿盯着上面，像个傻瓜一样抓了抓头。

"是些乱七八糟的鬼字，"他回答。"我不认识。"

"不认识？"凯瑟琳惊叫，"那是英文，我能念出来。可我想知道它们为什么在那儿。"

林顿笑了，这是他第一次表现出开心的神情。

"他连一个字母都不认识，"他对他的表姐说，"你相信世界上存在这样的大傻瓜吗？"

"一直这样吗？"凯茜小姐严肃地问道，"或是他的头脑比较简单——不是吗？我已经问他两次了，每次他都显得很傻，我还以为他听不懂呢。我确信我也不能理解他！"

林顿又大笑起来，嘲笑地瞟着哈里顿。他那时还不大理解发生了什么。

"没有其他原因，只有懒惰，是吧，恩肖？"他说，"我的表姐认为你是一个白痴呢。你一直嘲笑所谓的'啃书本'，现在你尝到后果了吧。凯瑟琳，你注意到没有，他有吓人的约克郡口音？"

"哼，那能有什么鬼用处？"哈里顿嘀咕着，更熟练地跟他的同伴回嘴。他还想再说些什么，突然两个年轻人一起大笑起来；而我轻浮的小姐也高兴地发现，她可以把哈里顿那些奇怪的话当作笑柄。

"Where is the use of the devil in that sentence?" tittered Linton. "Papa told you not to say any bad words, and you can't open your mouth without one. Do try to behave like a gentleman, now do!"

"If you weren't more a lass than a lady, I'd fell you this minute, I would; pitiful lath of a crater!" retorted the angry boor, retreating, while his face burnt with mingled rage and mortification; for he was conscious of being insulted, and embarrassed how to resent it.

Mr. Heathcliff having overheard the conversation, as well as I, smiled when he saw him go; but immediately afterwards cast a look of singular aversion on the flippant pair, who remained chattering in the door-way: the boy finding animation enough while discussing Hareton's faults and deficiencies, and relating anecdotes of his goings on; and the girl relishing his pert and spiteful sayings, without considering the ill nature they evinced, but I began to dislike, more than to compassion ate, Linton, and to excuse his father, in some measure, for holding him cheap.

We stayed till afternoon, I could not tear Miss Cathy away, before; but happily my master had not quitted his apartment, and remained ignorant of our prolonged absence. As we walked home, I would fain have enlightened my charge on the characters of the people we had quitted; but she got it into her head that I was prejudiced against them.

"Aha!" she cried, "you take papa's side, Ellen. You are partial, I know; or else you wouldn't have cheated me so many years into the notion that Linton lived a long way from here. I'm really extremely angry, only, I'm so

"在那句话加个'鬼'字能有什么用呢?"林顿嗤笑着。"爸爸告诉你不要说任何坏字眼,可你不说坏字眼就没法开口。努力表现得像个绅士吧,现在开始!"

"要不是你不像男的反像女的,我马上会给你打趴下,我会这么做的,你这可怜的瘦板条!"这乡下人勃然大怒,骂骂咧咧地跑开了,愤怒和羞耻让他的脸变得通红,因为他意识到被侮辱了,可又窘迫得不知该如何表达自己的怨恨。

希斯克利夫跟我都听到了这番话,他见哈里顿走开,脸上露出了微笑,但随即又用特别厌恶的目光瞅了一眼这轻薄的一对,他们还在门口继续闲聊。男孩子一提到到哈里顿的毛病和缺点,以及他怪异的举动和可笑的趣闻时,精神就振奋起来;而那小姑娘也爱听他讲那些尖酸刻薄的话,并没意识到这些话所表现的恶意。我对林顿的厌恶大过了同情,也开始有点理解为什么他父亲这样贬低他了。

我们一直待到下午才走,因为我没办法早点将凯瑟琳拉走。万幸的是,主人一直都没离开他的屋子,所以不知道我们很久都没回来。在回家的路上,我想谈谈我们刚离开的那些人的性格,希望以此来开导那个我所照顾的人;但她却觉得我对他们有偏见。

"啊哈,"她叫着,"你是站在我爸爸这边的,艾伦。我知道你存有偏心,要不这么多年你也不会一直骗我说林顿住得很远。我真的很生气,只是我又很高兴,所以就发不出什么脾

pleased, I can't show it! But you must hold your tongue about my uncle, he's my uncle, remember; and I'll scold papa for quarrelling with him."

And so she ran on, till I dropped endeavouring to convince her of her mistake. She did not mention the visit that night, because she did not see Mr. Linton. Next day it all came out, sadly to my chagrin; and still I was not altogether sorry, I thought the burden of directing and warning would be more efficiently borne by him than me, but he was too timid in giving satisfactory reasons for his wish that she would shun connection with the household of the Heights, and Catherine liked good reasons for every restraint that harassed her petted will.

"Papa!" she exclaimed, after the morning salutations, "guess whom I saw yesterday, in my walk on the moors. Ah, papa, you started! You've not done right, have you, now? I saw— But listen, and you shall hear how I found you out, and Ellen, who is in league with you, and yet pretended to pity me so, when I kept hoping, and was always disappointed about Linton's coming back!"

She gave a faithful account of her excursion and its consequences; and my master, though he cast more than one reproachful look at me, said nothing till she had concluded. Then he drew her to him, and asked if she knew why he had concealed Linton's near neighbourhood from her? Could she think it was to deny her a pleasure that she might harmlessly enjoy?

"It was because you disliked Mr. Heathcliff," she answered.

"Then you believe I care more for my own feelings than yours, Cathy?" he said. "No, it was

气来！但以后你不许再说我姑夫的坏话，他始终是我的姑夫，你要记住；我还要责怪爸爸跟他吵过架。"

她就这样说着，直到我放弃让她认识到自己错误的努力。那天晚上她并没提起这次拜访，因为她没有见到林顿先生。但第二天她就统统说出来了，这使我非常沮丧，但我并不十分难过，因为我认为由他来担负这个指导和警戒的担子要有效得多，可是他竟懦弱得给不出令人信服的理由，好让她主动和山庄的那家断绝交往，因为对每件压制凯瑟琳骄纵意愿的事，必须要有充分的理由她才肯听。

向林顿先生请过早安之后，她说："爸爸，猜猜昨天我在旷野散步的时候看见谁了。啊，爸爸，你吃惊啦！你做错了，是吧？我看见——你只需要听着，看我是怎样把你识破的，还有艾伦，她跟你结成联盟，在我盼着林顿回来可又总是大失所望的时候，还假装可怜我。"

她把昨天的出游以及结果都如实跟林顿先生说了，我的主人，虽然不止一次责备地看着我，但一言不发，直到她说完。然后林顿先生把她拉到跟前，问她知不知道为什么他要隐瞒林顿住在附近的事实！难道只为了不让她去享受那些毫无害处的欢乐吗？

"那是因为你讨厌希斯克利夫先生，"她回答。

"那你相信我关心自己的感觉胜过关心你啦，凯茜？"他说，"你错了，

not because I disliked Mr. Heathcliff, but because Mr. Heathcliff dislikes me; and is a most diabolical man, delighting to wrong and ruin those he hates, if they give him the slightest opportunity. I knew that you could not keep up an acquaintance with your cousin, without being brought into contact with him; and I knew he would detest you, on my account; so for your own good, and nothing else, I took precautions that you should not see Linton again. I meant to explain this some time as you grew older, and I'm sorry I delayed it."

"But Mr. Heathcliff was quite cordial, papa," observed Catherine, not at all convinced; "and he didn't object to our seeing each other, he said I might come to his house when I pleased; only I must not tell you, because you had quarrelled with him, and would not forgive him for marrying Aunt Isabella. And you won't. You are the one to be blamed, he is willing to let us be friends, at least; Linton and I; and you are not ."

My master, perceiving that she would not take his word for her uncle in-law's evil disposition, gave a hasty sketch of his conduct to Isabella, and the manner in which Wuthering Heights became his property. He could not bear to discourse long upon the topic; for though he spoke little of it, he still felt the same horror and detestation of his ancient enemy that had occupied his heart ever since Mrs. Linton's death. "She might have been living yet, if it had not been for him!" was his constan bitter reflection; and, in his eyes, Heathcliff seemed a murderer. Miss Cathy—conversant with no bad deeds except her own slight acts of disobedience, injustice, and passion, rising from hot temper and

那不是因为我讨厌希斯克利夫先生，而是因为他憎恶我。他是个极其凶恶的人，喜欢陷害和毁掉他所厌恶的人，只要给他一点点机会。我知道你想跟你表弟交往，就必须跟他接触，我也清楚他会因为我而痛恨你；因此为了你好，而不是别的，我才提防着不让你跟林顿见面。我原想等你长大一点再向你解释这些，我很懊悔把它拖下来了。"

"可我觉得希斯克利夫先生挺诚实的，爸爸。"凯瑟琳说，一点没被她爸爸说服。"而且他并不反对我们见面，他说我什么时候愿意都可以去他家，但就是不能告诉你，因为你曾跟他吵过架，还不能原谅他娶了伊莎贝拉姑姑。你不会的。你才该被责备，他是希望我们能够成为朋友的，至少希望林顿和我是这样，但你不是。"

我的主人看出她接受不了他说她姑夫的坏话，于是便把希斯克利夫对伊莎贝拉的罪行，以及他如何把呼啸山庄变成他的产业的过程说了个大概。他不想将这件事说得太详细；因为即便他只说了一点点，却依然能深切地感受到林顿太太死后一直萦绕在他心头的对宿敌的恐惧和痛恨。"如果不是他，她或许还活着！'是经常存在于他脑海里的痛苦的想法。在他眼中，希斯克利夫像个杀人犯。凯茜小姐却完全没有接触过任何罪恶的行为，只有她自己因脾气暴躁或任性妄为而不听教导，发小姐脾气。而且总是当天就能悔改——因此她对于人灵

thought lessness, and repented of on the day they were committed—was amazed at the blackness of spirit that could brood on and cover revenge for years, and deliberately prosecute its plans without a visitation of remorse. She appeared so deeply impressed and shocked at this new view of human nature—excluded from all her studies and all her ideas fill now-that Mr. Edgar deemed it unnecessary to pursue the subject. He merely added —

"You will know hereafter, darling, why I wish you to avoid his house and family; now, return to your old employments and amusements, and think no more about them!"

Catherine kissed her father, and sat down quietly to her lessons for a couple of hours, according to custom; then she accompanied him into the grounds, and the whole day passed as usual. But in the evening, when she had retired to her room, and I went to help her to undress, I found her crying, on her knees by the bedside.

"Oh, fie, silly child!" I exclaimed. "If you had any real griefs, you'd be ashamed to waste a tear on this little contrariety. You never had one shadow of substantial sorrow, Miss Catherine. Suppose, for a minute, that master and I were dead, and you were by yourself in the world, how would you feel then? Compare the present occasion with such an affliction as that, and be thankful for the friends you have, instead of coveting more."

"I'm not crying for myself, Ellen," she answered, "it's for him. He expected to see me again tomorrow, and there, he'll be so disappointed, and he'll wait for me, and I shan't come!"

"Nonsense!" said I, "do you imagine he

魂可以黑暗到报复之念能够盘算和隐藏这么多年,不择手段不达目的誓不罢休而且毫无悔恨之念感到震惊。这种对人性的新观点使她大为震撼——这种看法一直在她的学习和思考范围之外——因此埃德加先生认为没必要再谈这个话题了。他只是又补充了一句:

"亲爱的,你以后会明白的,为什么我希望你远离他的家。去做该做的事吧,去玩吧,不要再想这些了!"

凯瑟琳亲吻了她的父亲,安静地坐下来跟往常一样温习了两小时功课;然后她陪着林顿先生到园子里溜达,和平常一样平淡地过了一整天。但是到晚上,她回到房间里,当我过去帮她脱衣服时,却发现她正跪在床边哭泣。

"啊,真是令人害羞啊,傻孩子!"我叫着。"如果你经历过真正的痛苦,就会为因这点小事掉眼泪感到羞愧。你连真正痛苦的影子都没见过,凯瑟琳小姐。假如主人和我突然一下子全都死了,世界上就剩下你自己,你的感觉会是什么样的?把现在的情形同这样的痛苦比一比,你就会为有朋友而庆幸,而不是贪得无厌啦。"

"我不是在为自己哭,艾伦,"她回答,"是为了他。他期待明天可以再见到我。这下他会失望啦,他会在那等我,可是我又去不了!"

"真是无稽之谈!"我说,"你以为

has thought as much of you as you have of him? Hasn't he Hareton for a companion? Not one in a hundred would weep at losing a relation they had just seen twice, for two afternoons. Linton will conjecture how it is, and trouble himself no further about you."

"But may I not write a note to tell him why I cannot come?" she asked, rising to her feet. "And just send those books I promised to lend him? His books are not as nice as mine, and he wanted to have them extremely, when I told him how interesting they were. May I not, Ellen?"

"No, indeed! no, indeed!" replied I with decision. "Then he would write to you, and there'd never be an end of it. No, Miss Catherine, the acquaintance must be dropped entirely, so papa expects, and I shall see that it is done."

"But how can one little note—" she recommenced, putting on an imploring countenance.

"Silence!" I interrupted. "We'll not begin with your little notes. Get into bed."

She threw at me a very naughty look, so naughty that I would not kiss her good night at first. I covered her up, and shut her door, in great displeasure; but, repenting half-way, I returned softly, and look! There was Miss, standing at the table with a bit of blank paper before her and a pencil in her hand, which she guiltily slipped out of sight, on my entrance.

"You'll get nobody to take that, Catherine," I said, "if you write it; and at present I shall put out your candle."

I set the extinguisher on the flame, receiving as I did so a slap on my hand, and a petulant "cross thing"! I then quitted her again, and she drew the bolt in one of her worst, most peevish

他会跟你一样在想你吗？他不是已经有哈里顿做伴吗？一百个人里也找不着一个会因为失去一个才见过两次——而且只有两个下午的亲戚而伤心落泪的。林顿会猜到是怎么回事，他才不会为你而自寻烦恼呢。"

"可是我可不可以写一张便条，告诉他我不能去的原因呢？"她站起身来问我说，"并且把答应借给他的书送过去？他的书没有我的好，当我告诉他我的书是多么有趣的时候，他非常想看。这样也不可以吗，艾伦？"

"不行，绝对不行！"我斩钉截铁地回答。"这样的话他也会回信给你，那可就永远没完了。不，凯瑟琳小姐，你们必须完全断绝往来，你爸爸希望这样，我就必须照着他的意思办。"

"就一张小纸条会怎么样呢——"她开口说，一副恳求的神情。

"别再瞎扯啦！"我打断了她的话。"我们不要再谈论你的小纸条啦。乖乖上床去。"

她冲我做出一副非常淘气的鬼脸，淘气得我起初都不想吻她跟她说晚安了，我极不高兴地帮她盖好被子，而后又将门关上。但在半路我又突然后悔了，于是我蹑手蹑脚地回去，看哪！小姐站在桌边，她面前摊着一张白纸，手里拿着一支铅笔，我进去的时候，她正想把它偷偷藏起来。

"就算你写好了信，也不会有人帮你送，凯瑟琳，"我说，"现在我要把你的蜡烛熄掉了。"

当我把熄烛帽盖到火苗上，我的手被打了一下，同时还伴着一声焦躁的"混账东西"！然后我再次离开了，

humours. The letter was finished and forwarded to its destination by a milk-fetcher who came from the village, but that I didn't learn till some time afterwards. Weeks passed on, and Cathy recovered her temper; though she grew wondrous fond of stealing off to corners by herself; and often, if I came near her suddenly while reading, she would start and bend over the book, evidently desirous to hide it; and I detected edges of loose paper sticking out beyond the leaves. She also got a trick of coming down early in the morning, and lingering about the kitchen, as if she were expecting the arrival of something, and she had a small drawer in a cabinet in the library, which she would trifle over for hours, and whose key she took special care to remove when she left it.

One day, as she inspected this drawer, I observed that the play-things and trinkets, which recently formed its contents, were transmuted into bits of folded paper. My curiosity and suspicions were roused; I determined to take a peep at her mysterious treasures; so, at night, as soon as she and my master were safe up stairs, I searched and readily found among my house keys one that would fit the lock. Having opened, I emptied the whole contents into my apron, and took them with me to examine at leisure in my own chamber. Though I could not but suspect, I was still surprised to discover that they were a mass of correspondence—daily, almost, it must have been—from Linton Heathcliff, answers to documents forwarded by her. The earlier dated were embarrassed and short; gradually, however, they expanded into copious love letters, foolish as the age of the writer rendered natural, yet with

她插上了门闩。最终信还是写好了，而且是由一个村里来送牛奶的人送到目的地去的，不过很久以后我才知道。几个星期后，凯茜的脾气好转了，不过她变得非常喜欢一个人偷偷躲在角落里，常常当她看书的时候，如果我忽然靠近她，她就会大吃一惊，把身体伏在书本上，很显然是想盖住那书，我还看得出来，在书页中露出了散张的纸边。她还有个诡计，就是大清早下楼来，在厨房里转悠，好像正在期待着某种东西到来。此外她有小抽屉在图书室的书橱里，她常在那里翻腾上半天，而且走开的时候总小心翼翼地带上那把抽屉的钥匙。

一天，她正在翻抽屉，我发现先前放在里面的玩具和零碎都变成了一张张折叠整齐的纸。这激起了我的好奇和疑惑，我决定偷看她那堆神秘宝藏。晚上，当她和我的主人都已经楼上，我找出了那堆钥匙中最合适的一把。一打开抽屉，我就把里面所有东西都倒在围裙里，再带回我的屋子从容地检查。即使我早有疑心，我仍然惊奇地发现那些原来是一大堆书信——应该差不多每天一封——从林顿·希斯克利夫那里发来的，都是给她写的回信。早期的信短而拘谨，但慢慢地，这些信发展成饱含感情的情书了，内容写得很笨拙，与他们的年龄相称。不过一些细节是从一个更有经验的人那里抄来的。有些混合着热情和平淡的信让我感到莫名其妙，以强烈的感情开头，结尾处矫揉造作、啰里啰唆，好像一个中学生写给他幻

touches, here and there, which I thought were borrowed from a more experienced source. Some of them struck me as singularly odd compounds of ardour and flatness; commencing in strong feeling, and concluding in the affected, wordy way that a schoolboy might use to a fancied, incorporeal sweetheart. Whether they satisfied Cathy, I don't know; but they appeared very worthless trash to me. After turning over as many as I thought proper, I tied them in a handkerchief and set them aside, relocking the vacant drawer.

Following her habit, my young lady descended early, and visited the kitchen. I watched her go to the door, on the arrival of a certain little boy; and, while the dairy maid filled his can, she tucked something into his jacket pocket, and plucked something out. I went round by the garden, and laid wait for the messenger; who fought valorously to defend his trust, and we spilt the milk between us; but I succeeding in abstracting the epistle; and, threatening serious consequences if he did not look sharp home, I remained under the wall and perused Miss Cathy's affectionate composition. It was more simple and more eloquent than her cousin's, very pretty and very silly. I shook my head, and went meditating into the house. The day being wet, she could not divert herself with rambling about the park; so, at the conclusion of her morning studies, she resorted to the solace of the drawer. Her father sat reading at the table; and I, on purpose, had sought a bit of work in some unripped fringes of the window curtain, keeping my eye steadily fixed on her proceedings. Never did any bird flying back to a plundered nest which it had left brimful of

想中的梦中情人一样。这些信能否让凯茜满意,我不得而知,但在我看来,那都是一些没用的废纸。看过我认为足够多的信件后,我用手绢将它们包起来,放在一边,并且重新给这个空抽屉上了锁。

还是以往的习惯,我的小姐很早就下楼,跑到厨房里去了。我发现某个小男孩到来的时候,她马上走到门口,趁着挤奶的女工往罐子里倒牛奶时,她把一个东西塞进了他背心的口袋里,又掏出一个东西。于是我绕到花园里,在那儿等那位送信的,不过他英勇地为保卫受委托的东西而战斗,以致打翻了牛奶。最终我成功地拿到信,并威胁他说如果他不马上回家去后果更加严重。我呆在墙根底下拜读凯茜小姐的爱情大作。她的信要比她表弟的简洁流利,文字也写得漂亮,但也傻里傻气。我摇了摇头,沉思着走进屋子。这一天天气很潮湿,她不能去花园里闲逛散心,所以早读一结束,她就到抽屉那寻找心灵的安慰去了。她父亲坐在桌旁看书,我呢,故意找点事做,去整理窗帘上那几条扯不开的繐子,但是眼睛死盯着她的一举一动。任何一只鸟儿飞回它那离开时还满是叽叽喳喳的小雏鸟,而后却被洗劫一空的巢时所发出的悲鸣与惊惶,都比不上那一声"啊!"和她那快乐的脸色的突变。林顿先生抬

chirping young ones, express more complete despair in its anguished cries and flutterings, than she by her single "Oh"! And the change that transfigured her late happy counte nance. Mr. Linton looked up.

"What is the matter, love? Have you hurt yourself?" he said.

His tone and look assured her he had not been the discoverer of the hoard.

"No, papa —"she gasped."Ellen! Ellen! come upstairs—I'm sick!"

I obeyed her summons, and accompanied her out.

"Oh, Ellen! You have got them," she commenced immediately, dropping on her knees, when we were enclosed alone."O, give them to me, and I'll never never do so again! Don't tell papa. You have not told papa, Ellen, say you have not! I've been exceedingly naughty, but I won't do it any more!"

With a grave severity in my manner, I bid her stand up.

"So," I exclaimed, "Miss Catherine, you are tolerably far on, it seems you may well be ashamed of them! A fine bundle of trash you study in your leisure hours, to be sure why it's good enough to be printed! And what do you suppose the master will think, when I display it before him? I haven't shown it yet, but you needn't imagine I shall keep your ridiculous secrets. For shame! and you must have led the way in writing such absurdities: he would not have thought of beginning, I'm certain."

"I didn't! I didn't!" sobbed Cathy, fit to break her heart."I didn't once think of loving him till —"

"Loving!" cried I, as scornfully as I could

头看了看。

"怎么啦，亲爱的？你哪儿碰伤啦？"他问。

他的语气和神情令她确信发现宝藏那个人不是他。

"没有，爸爸！"她喘息着。"艾伦！艾伦！我们上楼吧——我病了！"

我听从了她的指示，陪着她出去了。

"哦，艾伦！是你把那些拿去啦，"当只有我们在屋里时她立刻问我，还跪下来求我！"啊，还给我吧，我再也不这样做啦！不要告诉爸爸。你还没有告诉爸爸，艾伦？快告诉我你没有，我的确是太淘气啦，但是以后不会啦！"

我十分严肃地叫她起来。

"所以，"我说，"凯瑟琳小姐，你真的是太任性了，你应该为你做的事情感到羞耻！你把你的时间都花在这些垃圾上了，呵，写得真好啊，可以拿去出版啦，我要是拿给主人看，你说他会怎么想？我还没有把这些交给他，但是不必幻想我会为你保守这个荒唐的秘密。羞！想到要写这些的一定是你！我肯定他不会有这样的天赋。"

"我没有！我没有！"凯茜开始啜泣，我的话刺伤了她。"我从来没有想过自己会爱上他，直到——"

"爱！"我惊叫，极尽嘲讽。"爱！

utter the word. "Loving! Did anybody ever hear the like! I might just as well talk of loving the miller who comes once a year to buy our corn. Pretty loving, indeed! And both times together you have seen Linton hardly four hours in your life! Now here is the babyish trash. I'm going with it to the library; and we'll see what your father says to such loving."

She sprang at her precious epistles, but I held them above my head; and then she poured out further frantic entreaties that I would burn them—do anything rather than show them. And being really fully as inclined to laugh as scold—for I esteemed it all girlish vanity—I at length relented in a measure, and asked —

"If I consent to burn them, will you promise faithfully, neither to send nor receive a letter again, nor a book (for I perceive you have sent him books), nor locks of hair, nor rings, nor playthings?"

"We don't send playthings!" cried Catherine, her pride overcoming her shame.

"Nor anything at all, then, my lady!" I said. "Unless you will, here I go."

"I promise, Ellen!" she cried, catching my dress. "Oh, put them in the fire, do, do!"

But when I proceeded to open a place with the poker, the sacrifice was too painful to be borne. She earnestly supplicated that I would spare her one or two.

"One or two, Ellen, to keep for Linton's sake!"

I unknotted the handkerchief, and commenced dropping them in from an angle, and the flame curled up the chimney.

"I will have one, you cruel wretch!" she screamed, darting her hand into the fire, and

有人听到过这样的事么！如果这样的话，我也可以跟那个一年过来买一次谷子的磨坊主大谈其爱啦。好一个爱，真是的！这辈子你见过林顿不到四个小时！喏，这些孩童的胡言乱语。我要带它们到书房里去；我们看看你父亲对这种爱有什么看法。"

她跳起来要抢回她的宝贝信，但是我把它们高举过头顶，然后她作出了大量疯狂的恳求，恳求我烧掉它们——除了公开随便怎么都行。我真是哭笑不得——因为我猜这完全是代表女孩子的虚荣心——最后我退了一步，问道——

"如果我同意把它们烧掉，你能不能真诚地保证不再送出或收进任何一封信，或者一本书（因为我知道你送过书给他），或者一卷头发，一枚戒指，或是其他的玩意儿？"

"我们从来都不送什么玩意儿的，"凯瑟琳嚷道，她的骄傲胜过了她的羞耻心。

"那好，就什么也不送，我的小姐？"我说。"除非你心甘情愿，不然我就走啦。"

"我答应，艾伦，"她叫着，拽住我的衣服。"啊，你把它们丢到火里去吧，丢吧，丢吧！"

但是当我用火钳把一块地方给拨开时，这样的牺牲对她而言的确非常痛苦。她苦苦哀求我能留下一两封信给她。

"就一两封，艾伦，看在林顿的分上，求你给我留下来吧！"

我打开手绢，开始将它们从手绢的一角里倒出来，火焰顿时卷上了烟囱。

"我只要一封就好了，你这无情

drawing forth some half consumed fragments, at the expense of her fingers.

"Very well—and I will have some to exhibit to papa!" I answered, shaking back the rest into the bundle, and turning anew to the door.

She emptied her blackened pieces into the flames, and motioned me to finish the immolation. It was done; I stirred up the ashes, and interred them under a shovel full of coals; and she mutely, and with a sense of intense injury, retired to her private apartment. I descended to tell my master that the young lady's qualm of sickness was almost gone, but I judged it best for her to lie down a while. She wouldn't dine; but she reappeared at tea, pale, and red about the eyes, and marvellously subdued in outward aspect.

Next morning, I answered the letter by a slip of paper, inscribed, "Master Heathcliff is requested to send no more notes to Miss Linton, as she will not receive them." And, thenceforth, the little boy came with vacant pockets.

的坏蛋！"她尖叫着，把手伸进火里，把一些烧了一半的纸片给抓了出来，不过她的手指也因此受了伤。

"很好——我也要留下一点拿去给你爸爸看，"我回答道，把剩下那些信件又重新抖回手绢中去，然后转身朝门口走去。

她把抓出来的那些快要烧焦了的纸片又扔回火里，并且向我打手势，意思是让我继续完成这个祭祀。烧完以后，我把剩下的灰烬搅了搅，再铲来一些煤把这些东西埋起来，她一言不发，怀着委屈悲痛的心情，退回她自己的屋里去了，于是我下楼告诉主人说，小姐的急病已经差不多痊愈了。可我还是认为最好可以再让她躺一会。她不肯吃饭；但在喝茶的时候她却出现了，面色苍白，两眼红红的，但在外表上克制得令人吃惊。

第二天早上我写了一张纸条当作给他的回信，上面写着，"请希斯克利夫少爷不要再给林顿小姐写信了，她是绝对不会接受的。"从那以后，每当那个小男孩来我们这里时，口袋里总是空空如也。

Chapter 22
第二十二章

Summer drew to an end, and early Autumn, it was past Michaelmas①, but the harvest was late that year, and a few of our fields were still uncleared. Mr. Linton and his daughter would frequently walk out among the reapers; at the carrying of the last sheaves, they stayed till dusk, and the evening happening to be chill and damp, my master caught a bad cold, that settling obstinately on his lungs, confined him indoors throughout the whole of the winter, nearly without intermission.

Poor Cathy, frightened from her little romance, had been considerably sadder a nd duller since its abandonment; and her father insisted on her reading less, and taking more exercise. She had his companionship no longer; I esteemed it a duty to supply its lack, as much as possible, with mine, an inefficient substitute, for I could only spare two or three hours, from my numerous diurnal occupations, to follow her footsteps, and then my society was obviously less desirable than his.

On an afternoon in October, or the beginning of November—a fresh watery afternoon,

夏天结束了，已是早秋时节，秋节已经过了，但那年收成晚，我们的庄稼田有些还没清理完毕。林顿先生和他的女儿经常走到收割者中间，在搬运最后几捆作物的时候，他们逗留到黄昏，赶上那晚湿冷，我的主人患了重感冒。感冒顽强地滞留在他的肺部，使他整个冬天都待在家里，几乎没有出门。

可怜的凯茜，因为她那小小的罗曼史而受了惊吓，尔后一直郁郁寡欢。凯茜的父亲坚持要她少读些书，多做些运动。她再也不能找他做伴了，我认为我有义务尽可能去填补这个缺口，但我也只是个于事无补的替代者，因为我只能从我繁忙的日常工作中挤出两三个小时来陪伴她，所以我的陪伴很明显没有他那样合乎凯茜的要求。

十月的一个下午，或者已是十一月初了吧———一个清新欲雨的下午，

---

① Michaelmas：米迦勒节，9月29日。英国四结账日之一，雇佣人、履行租约多在此日。

when the turf and paths were rustling with moist, withered leaves, and the cold, blue sky was half hidden by clouds—dark grey streamers, rapidly mounting from the west, and boding abundant rain—I requested my young lady to forego her ramble because I was certain of showers. She refused; and I unwillingly donned a cloak, and took my umbrella to accompany her on a stroll to the bottom of the park, a formal walk which she generally affected if low-spirited—and that she invariably was when Mr. Edgar had been worse than ordinary; a thing never known from his confession, but guessed both by her and me from his increased silence, and the melancholy of his countenance. She went sadly on, there was no running or bounding now, though the chill wind might well have tempted her to a race. And often, from the side of my eye, I could detect her raising a hand, and brushing something off her cheek. I gazed round for a means of diverting her thoughts. On one side of the road rose a high, rough bank, where hazels and stunted oaks, with their roots half exposed, held uncertain tenure, the soil was too loose for the latter; and strong winds had blown some nearly horizontal. In summer, Miss Catherine delighted to climb along these trunks, and sit in the branches, swinging twenty feet above the ground; and I, pleased with her agility and her light, childish heart, still considered it proper to scold every time I caught her at such an elevation, but so that she knew there was no necessity for descending. From dinner to tea she would lie in her breeze-rocked cradle, doing nothing except singing old songs—my nursery lore-to herself, or watching the birds, joint tenants, feed and entice their young ones to fly, or

潮湿的枯叶落在草皮与小径上发出簌簌的响声，寒冷的蓝天有一半被云遮住了——深灰色的流云从西边迅速升起，预示着暴雨即将来临——我请求我的小姐，希望她取消这次散步，因为我确信暴雨就要来了。她拒绝了，我只好不情愿地披上一件外套，并且带上我的伞，陪着她到园林的深处散步。当她情绪低落的时候，她总爱走这条路——当埃德加先生的病情比平时厉害的时候，她总是这样。虽然埃德加先生自己从不承认他的病势加重，可是，凯茜和我却可以通过他脸上的神色猜出来，因为他的神色比以前更加沉默忧郁了。她默默地向前走着，满脸愁云，本来这刺骨的寒风完全可以引诱她跑上一跑，可她现在却不跑也不跳了。而且我时不时能从眼角里瞅见，她抬起一只手从面颊上把什么擦拭掉。我向四周望去，想找到转移她思绪的办法。路的一旁有一条不平坦的高坡，榛树和短小的橡树半露着根，歪歪斜斜地竖在上面。这种土质对于橡树实在太疏松了，强烈的风把有些树吹得差不多和地面平行了。夏天的时候，凯瑟琳小姐喜欢爬上这些树干，并坐在离地面两丈高的树枝上摇摆；每一次，我看到她爬得那么高时，我就觉得该骂骂她，虽然我很喜欢看她这种活泼的举动，也喜欢她能拥有一颗轻松的童心。可是，听着我这样骂，她也知道没有下来的必要。从午饭后到吃茶的这段时间里，她就躺在她那随微风摇动的摇篮里，无所事事，只哼着一些老歌——我唱的催眠曲——给自己听；或是观察和她栖在同一枝头上的鸟儿喂它们

nestling with closed lids, half thinking, half dreaming, happier than words can express.

"Look, Miss!" I exclaimed, pointing to a nook under the roots of one twisted tree. "Winter is not here yet. There's a little flower, up yonder, the last bud from the multitude of bluebells that clouded those turf steps in July with a lilac mist. Will you clamber up, and pluck it to show to papa?"

Cathy stared a long time at the lonely blossom trembling in its earthy shelter, and replied, at length —

"No, I'll not touch it, but it looks melancholy, does it not, Ellen?"

"Yes," I observed, "about as starved and sackless as you: your cheeks are bloodless; let us take hold of hands and run. You're so low, I dare say I shall keep up with you."

"No," she repeated, and continued sauntering on, pausing, at intervals, to muse over a bit of moss, or a tuft of blanched grass, or a fungus spreading its bright orange among the heaps of brown foliage; and, ever and anon, her hand was lifted to her averted face.

"Catherine, why are you crying, love?" I asked, approaching and putting my arm over her shoulder. "You mustn't cry because papa has a cold; be thankful it is nothing worse."

She now put no further restraint on her tears; her breath was stifled by sobs.

"Oh, it will be something worse," she said. "And what shall I do when papa and you leave me, and I am by myself? I can't forget your words, Ellen; they are always in my ear. How life will be changed, how dreary the world will be, when papa and you are dead."

"None can tell, whether you won't die be-

的小雏鸟,逗引它们飞起来;或是闭上眼睛舒适地靠着,半思索,半做梦,沉浸在无比的快乐中。"

"小姐,你瞧!"我叫道,指着一棵扭曲的树根下一个凹进去的洞穴。"对这里来说冬天还没有到来哩。那边有一朵小花,七月里跟紫丁香一起布满在那些草皮台阶的蓝钟花就剩这一朵啦。你想不想爬上去,把它摘下来给爸爸看?"

凯茜久久地凝视着这朵在土洞中颤抖着的孤寂的花,最后回答道:

"不了,我不要去碰它,它看上去很忧郁,是不是,艾伦?"

"是的,"我答道,"就如同你一样又瘦又干:你的脸都没有血色了,让我们拉着手跑吧。你的情绪这样低落,我敢说,我一定能赶得上你了。"

"不了,"她答道,继续向前闲荡着,间或停下来,望着一点青苔,或一丛变白的草,不然就是望着散布在成堆的棕黄色叶子中间鲜艳、橘黄色的菌陷入沉思;并且,她还时不时把手举到她那张扭转过去的脸上。

"凯瑟琳,你为什么要哭呀,宝贝儿?"我问道,走上前去搂住她的肩膀。"你千万不要为了爸爸受凉的事而哭泣,放心吧,那不是什么重病。"

她不再抑制自己的眼泪,抽泣了起来。

"啊,那会变成重病的,"她说。"当爸爸和你都离开我,只剩下我孤零零一个人的时候,我该怎么办?艾伦,我无法忘记你说过的话。这些话总是萦绕在我耳边。等到爸爸和你都死了,我的生活将变成什么样,世界又将变得多么凄凉啊。"

fore us," I replied. "It's wrong to anticipate evil. We'll hope there are years and years to come before any of us go: master is young, and I am strong, and hardly forty-five. My mother lived till eighty, a canty dame to the last. And suppose Mr. Linton were spared till he saw sixty, that would be more years than you have counted, Miss. And would it not be foolish to mourn a calamity above twenty years beforehand?"

"But Aunt Isabella was younger than papa," she remarked, gazing up with timid hope to seek further consolation.

"Aunt Isabella had not you and me to nurse her," I replied. "She wasn't as happy as master, she hadn't as much to live for. All you need do, is to wait well on your father, and cheer him by letting him see you cheerful; and avoid giving him anxiety on any subject, mind that, Cathy! I'll not disguise but you might kill him, if you were wild and reckless, and cherished a foolish, fanciful affection for the son of a person who would be glad to have him in his grave; and allowed him to discover that you fretted over the separation he has judged it expedient to make."

"I fret about nothing on earth except papa's illness," answered my companion. "I care for nothing in comparison with papa. And I'll never—never —oh, never, while I have my senses, do an act or say a word to vex him. I love him better than myself, Ellen; and I know it by this. I pray every night that I may live after him; because I would rather be miserable than that he should be, that proves I love him better than myself."

"Good words," I replied. "But deeds must

"没有人能预测你会不会先我们而去，"我回答。"预测不祥是错误的。我们要这样希望，就是在我们任何人走之前还有好多好多年能一起度过：主人还年轻，我也还强壮，都还不到四十五岁。我母亲活到八十岁，而且自始至终都是个活泼开朗的女人。假定林顿先生活到六十，小姐，那往后的日子比你现在活过的年纪还多得多呢。现在就为一个二十多年后将发生的不幸提前悲痛不是很愚蠢吗？"

"但伊莎贝拉姑姑比爸爸还年轻哩，"她抬起头凝望着我，胆怯地盼望能得到我的进一步安慰。

"那是因为伊莎贝拉姑姑没有你和我的照顾啊，"我答道。"她没有主人那样幸福，也不像主人那样生活得有意义。你现在要做的就是好好照顾你的父亲，让他因看到你的高兴而高兴，尽量避免因任何事令他担忧，记住，凯茜！如果你轻率胡来，竟然对一个希望他早日进坟墓的人的儿子怀有愚蠢而又空想的感情的话；如果你让他发现你在为他断定的应尽早作出的分离而烦恼的话，那我明白地对你说，你会把他活活气死的。"

"除了爸爸的病，在世界上没什么能令我感到烦恼了，"我的同伴答道。"和爸爸相比，其他任何事我都不关心。而且我永远不——永远不——啊，在我还有知觉时，我永远不会做一件事或说一个字使他烦恼。我爱他胜过爱自己，艾伦。每天晚上我都向上帝祈祷让他死在我前头，因为我宁可自己忍受不幸，也不愿他遭受这一切。从这件事中就可以证明我爱他胜过爱自己。"

prove it also; and after he is well, remember you don't forget resolutions formed in the hour of fear."

As we talked, we neared a door that opened on the road; and my young lady, lightening into sunshine again, climbed up, and seated herself on the top of the wall, reaching over to gather some hips that bloomed scarlet on the summit branches of the wild rose trees, shadowing the highway side, the lower fruit had disappeared, but only birds could touch the upper, except from Cathy's present station. In stretching to pull them, her hat fell off; and as the door was locked, she proposed scrambling down to recover it. I bid her be cautious lest she got a fall, and she nimbly disappeared. But the return was no such easy matter: the stones were smooth and neatly cemented, and the rosebushes and blackberry stragglers could yield no assistance in re-ascending. I, like a fool, didn't recollect that, till I heard her laughing and exclaiming —

"Ellen, you'll have to fetch the key, or else I must run round to the porter's lodge. I can't scale the ramparts on this side!"

"Stay where you are," I answered, "I have my bundle of keys in my pocket, perhaps I may manage to open it; if not, I'll go."

Catherine amused herself with dancing to and fro before the door, while I tried all the large keys in succession. I had applied the last, and found that none would do; so, repeating my desire that she would remain there, I was about to hurry home as fast as I could, when an approaching sound arrested me. It was the trot of a horse; Cathy's dance stopped; and in a minute the horse stopped also.

"说得好，"我回答，"可是你也必须用行动来证明它。等他病好之后，你要记住你在担惊受怕时所下的决心。"

说着说着，我们走到了一扇通往大路的门口。我年轻的小姐因为又走到阳光中而轻松起来，她爬上墙，坐在墙头上，伸手去摘一些遮蔽了道边的野蔷薇树顶上的鲜红果实。结在树下面的果子早已不见了，除了从凯茜现在的位置，只有鸟儿才能接触到上面的果子。她伸出手去扯这些果子的时候，帽子掉了。因为门被锁住了，所以她打算爬下去把帽子捡回来。我叫她当心，以免跌下去，但她却灵敏地消失得无影无踪。然而她想返回可就不是件容易的事了。石头很光滑，而且还平整地涂上了水泥，那些蔷薇丛和黑莓的蔓枝对她的返回也没有任何帮助。我活像个傻子，一直等到听她笑着大叫后才明白过来：

"艾伦！你得去拿钥匙啦，不然我必须绕道跑到守门人住的地方去。我没办法从这边爬上围墙啊！"

"你就呆在那儿，"我回答，"我口袋里有我那串钥匙，也许我有办法把门打开；不行的话，我就去拿钥匙。"

我挨个把所有的大钥匙试了一遍，凯瑟琳就在门前跳来跳去地自己玩。我试到最后一个时，发现没有一个能把门打开的；因此，我就又嘱咐她呆在原地。就在我想尽快赶回家时，一个越来越近的声音使我停了下来。那是飞奔的马蹄声；凯茜停止了蹦跳，很快那马也停了下来。

"Who is that?" I whispered.

"Ellen, I wish you could open the door," whispered back my companion, anxiously.

"Ho, Miss Linton!" cried a deep voice, (the rider's.) "I'm glad to meet you. Don't be in haste to enter, for I have an explanation to ask and obtain."

"I shan't speak to you, Mr. Heathcliff," answered Catherine. "Papa says you are a wicked man, and you hate both him and me; and Ellen says the same."

"That is nothing to the purpose," said Heathcliff. (He it was.) "I don't hate my son, I suppose; and it is concerning him that I demand your attention. Yes! you have cause to blush. Two or three months since, were you not in the habit of writing to Linton? making love in play, eh? You deserved, both of you, flogging for that! You especially, the elder, and less sensitive, as it turns out. I've got your letters, and if you give me any pertness I'll send them to your father. I presume you grew weary of the amusement and dropped it, didn't you? Well, you dropped Linton with it, into a Slough of Despond.He was in earnest: in love, really. As true as I live, he's dying for you; breaking his heart at your fickleness: not figuratively, but actually. Though Hareton has made him a standing jest for six weeks, and I have used more serious measures, and attempted to frighten him out of his idiocy, he gets worse daily; and he'll be under the sod before summer, unless you restore him!"

"How can you lie so glaringly to the poor child!" I called from the inside."Pray ride on! How can you deliberately get up such paltry falsehoods? Miss Cathy, I'll knock the lock off

"那人是谁?"我低声说。

"艾伦,希望你能马上把门打开,"我的同伴焦急地低声回话。

"喂,林顿小姐!"一个深沉的声音(骑马人的声音)叫道,"很高兴遇见你。别急着进去,因为我有些事要求你能解释一下。"

"我不想同你讲话,希斯克利夫先生,"凯瑟琳回答:"爸爸说你是个邪恶的人,不仅憎恨他,也恨我;艾伦也是这么说的。"

"那跟件事毫不相干,"希斯克利夫(正是他)说道,"我想我并不憎恨我的儿子,正是因为他我才要求你的注意。是的,你完全有理由脸红。两三个月前,你不是还习惯给林顿写信吗?玩弄感情,呃?你们两个都该挨鞭子!尤其是你,年纪比他大,却比他更无情。我手中可有你的信,如果你对我有任何不敬的举动,我就把它们寄给你父亲。我猜你只是把这份感情当成儿戏,厌烦了就把它丢到一边,是不是?好呀,你把林顿和这样的消遣一起丢入'绝望的深渊'之中啦。他可是认真的在爱了,真的。就如同我现在还活着一样的真实,他为了你都快死了。就是因为你的三心二意,他的心都碎啦。我不是夸张,事实就是如此。尽管哈里顿为这事已经讥笑了他六个星期了,我也使用了更严厉的措施,企图把他的痴情吓走,但他的情况还是越来越糟。除非你去挽救他,否则不用等到夏天他就入土啦!"

"你怎么能对这可怜的孩子如此明目张胆地撒谎呢?"我从里面叫喊着。"请你快骑上马走吧!你怎么能够蓄意编造出如此卑鄙的谎话啊?凯茜

with a stone. you won't believe that vile nonsense. You can feel in yourself, it is impossible that a person should die for the love of a stranger."

"I was not aware there were eaves-droppers," muttered the detected villain. "Worthy Mrs. Dean, I like you, but I don't like your double dealing," he added, aloud. "How could you lie so glaringly, as to affirm I hated the 'poor child?' and invent bugbear stories to terrify her from my door-stones? Catherine Linton (the very name warms me), my bonny lass, I shall be from home all this week; go and see if I have not spoken truth. Do, there's a darling! Just imagine your father in my place, and Linton in yours; then think how you would value your careless lover if he refused to stir a step to comfort you, when your father, himself, entreated him; and don't, from pure stupidity, fall into the same error. I swear, on my salvation, he's going to his grave, and none but you can save him!"

The lock gave way, and I issued out.

"I swear Linton is dying," repeated Heathcliff, looking hard at me. "And grief and disappointment are hastening his death. Nelly, if you won't let her go, you can walk over yourself. But I shall not return till this time next week; and I think your master himself would scarcely object to her visiting her cousin!"

"Come in," said I, taking Cathy by the arm and half forcing her to enter; for she lingered, viewing with troubled eyes the features of the speaker, too stern to express his inward deceit.

He pushed his horse close, and, bending down, observed —

"Miss Catherine, I'll own to you that I have little patience with Linton; and Hareton and Joseph have less. I'll own that he's with a harsh set. He pines for kindness, as well as love; and a kind word from you would be his best medicine. Don't mind Mrs. Dean's cruel cautions; but be generous, and contrive to see him. He dreams of you day and night, and cannot be persuaded that you don't hate him, since you neither write nor call."

I closed the door, and rolled a stone to assist the loosened lock in holding it; and spreading my umbrella, I drew my charge underneath, for the rain began to drive through the moaning branches of the trees, and warned us to avoid delay. Our hurry prevented any comment on the encounter with Heathcliff, as we stretched towards home; but I divined instinctively that Catherine's heart was clouded now in double darkness. Her features were so sad, they did not seem hers. She evidently regarded what she had heard as every syllable true.

The master had retired to rest before we came in. Cathy stole to his room to inquire how he was; he had fallen asleep. She returned, and asked me to sit with her in the library. We took our tea together; and afterwards she lay down on the rug, and told me not to talk for she was weary. I got a book, and pretended to read. As soon as she supposed me absorbed in my occupation, she recommenced her silent weeping, it appeared, at present, her favourite diversion. I suffered her to enjoy it a while; then I expostulated: deriding and ridiculing all Mr. Heathcliff's assertions about his son, as if I were certain she would coincide. Alas! I hadn't the skill to counteract the effect his account had

弯下腰说——

"凯瑟琳小姐，我向你承认，我对林顿没什么耐心，哈里顿和约瑟夫的耐心更少。我承认他和一些粗暴的人在一起。他渴望和善和爱情。你一句和气的话会是他最好的药。别去管迪安太太那些残忍的警告，慷慨一些，设法去看看他。他无时无刻不在想着你，而且没法相信你不恨他，因为你既不写信，也不去看他。"

我把门关上，推过一块石头把门顶住，因为锁已被撬开。我撑开伞，将我保护的人拉在伞下。雨开始从悲叹的树枝间降下，警告我们避免耽搁。我们匆匆往家赶，顾不上对希斯克利夫的事发表议论。可我下意识地感到，凯瑟琳的心被双重黑暗遮住了。她的脸是如此的悲伤，都不像她的脸了。她显然认为她所听到的字字句句都千真万确。

主人在我们回来前就已经去休息了。凯茜悄悄地到他的房中去看他怎么样了；他已经睡着了。她回来，叫我陪她在书房坐着。我们一块吃茶；后来她躺在地毯上，叫我不要说话，因为她累了。我拿了一本书，假装在看。等她以为我在专心看书时，她就无声地抽泣起来。当时，那好像是她最喜爱的解闷法。我让她这样享受了一阵，然后劝她：嘲讽希斯克利夫所说的关于他儿子的一切，好像我肯定她会赞同。唉！我却没本事消除他那番话所产生的效果：那正是他的打算。

produced: it was just what he intended.

"You may be right, Ellen," she answered; "but I shall never feel at ease till I know. And I must tell Linton it is not my fault that I don't write; and convince him that I shall not change."

What use were anger and protestations against her silly credulity? We parted that night—hostile; but next day beheld me on the road to Wuthering Heights, by the side of my wilful young mistress's pony. I couldn't bear to witness her sorrow: to see her pale, dejected counte nance, and heavy eyes; and I yielded, in the faint hope that Linton himself might prove, by his reception of us, how little of the tale was founded on fact.

"或许你是对的，艾伦，"她回答，"可是，在我知道真相之前，我是永远不会安心的。我必须告诉林顿，我不写信并不是我的错，还要让他知道我是永远不会变心的。"

对于她那样痴心的轻信，愤怒和抗议又有什么用呢，那天晚上我们不欢而散；可第二天我又走在倔强年轻的女主人的小马旁边，陪伴她走在去往呼啸山庄的路上。我不忍心看她难受：看她那苍白的脸，失望的表情和忧郁的眼神。最后，我屈服了，怀着渺茫的希望，只盼着能够通过林顿对我们的接待来证明希斯克利夫的故事完全是他自己杜撰的。

Chapter 23
第二十三章

The rainy night had ushered in a misty morning—half frost, half drizzle and temporary brooks crossed our path, gurgling from the uplands. My feet were thoroughly wetted; I was cross and low: exactly the humour suited for making the most of these disagreeable things. We entered the farm-house by the kitchen way, to ascertain whether Mr. Heathcliff were really absent; because I put slight faith in his own af-

夜雨过后，一个雾气蒙蒙的早晨到来了——有霜、还有绵绵细雨，临时形成的小溪从高处潺潺流下，横穿小径。我的脚湿透了。我很恼火，情绪低落：正好适合做这类令人感到不愉快的事的心境。穿过厨房，我们来到农舍，以确认希斯克利夫是否真的不在家：因为我不大相信他自己承诺的话。

firmation.

Joseph seemed sitting in a sort of elysium alone, beside a roaring fire; a quart of ale on the table near him, bristling with large pieces of toasted oat cake; and his black, short pipe in his mouth. Catherine ran to the hearth to warm herself. I asked if the master was in? My question remained so long unanswered, that I thought the old man had grown deaf, and repeated it louder.

"Na—ay!" he snarled, or rather screamed through his nose. "Na—ay! You must go back where you come from."

"Joseph!" cried a peevish voice, simultaneously with me, from the inner room. "How often am I to call you? There are only a few red ashes now. Joseph! Come this moment."

Vigorous puffs, and a resolute stare into the grate, declared he had no ear for this appeal. The housekeeper and Hareton were invisible; one gone on an errand, and the other at his work, probably. We knew Linton's tones and entered.

"Oh, I hope you'll die in a garret! Starved to death," said the boy, mistaking our approach for that of his negligent attendant.

He stopped, on observing his error; his cousin flew to him.

"Is that you, Miss Linton?" he said, raising his head from the arm of the great chair, in which he reclined. "No—don't kiss me. It takes my breath—dear me! Papa said you would call," continued he, after recovering a little from Catherine's embrace; while she stood by looking very contrite. "Will you shut the door, if you please? You left it open; and those—those detestable creatures won't bring coals to the fire. It's so cold!"

约瑟夫仿佛独自置身于一种极乐世界中，旁边是熊熊燃烧的火炉；在他近旁的桌子上，放着一杯啤酒，杯中还竖着大块的烤麦饼；嘴里是他那又黑又短的烟斗。凯瑟琳跑到炉边取暖。我就问约瑟夫主人是否在家？我的问题许久没有得到回应，我还以为这位老人的耳朵已经不大好了，就大声重复了一遍。

"没——有！"他咆哮道，而这声音仿佛是从他的鼻子中发出来的。"没——有！你们从哪儿来，就滚回哪儿去吧。"

"约瑟夫！"屋中同时传出了一个跟我相同的抱怨声，"我得叫你多少遍？只剩少许红色的灰烬了。约瑟夫！你给我马上过来。"

他用力吸着烟，坚定地盯着炉栅，表明他根本听不见这个请求。管家和哈里顿都没了踪影，一个有事出去了，另一个在忙自己的事。我们听出是林顿的声音，就进去了。

"啊，我希望你死在阁楼上，活活饿死！"这孩子说道，错把我们的脚步声当成他那怠慢的仆人的了。

他一看是自己错了，马上闭了嘴。凯瑟琳向他奔了过去。

"林顿小姐，是你吗？"他说着，把头从他躺的大椅子的扶手上抬了起来，"别——别亲我。弄得我喘不过气来了——天呀！爸爸说你会来的，"他继续说，从凯瑟琳的拥抱中稍稍缓过来一些；而她站在旁边看起来很后悔。"请你把门关上，行吗？你们没把它关上；那些——那些可恶的家伙不肯给我添煤。冻死我了！"

I stirred up the cinders, and fetched a scuttle full myself. The invalid complained of being covered with ashes; but he had a tiresome cough, and looked feverish and ill, so I did not rebuke his temper.

"Well, Linton," murmured Catherine, when his corrugated brow relaxed. "Are you glad to see me? Can I do you any good?"

"Why didn't you come before?" he said. "You should have come, instead of writing. It tired me dreadfully, writing those long letters. I'd far rather have talked to you. Now, I can neither bear to talk, nor anything else. I wonder where Zillah is! Will you," looking at me, "step into the kitchen and see?"

I had received no thanks for my other service; and being unwilling to run to and fro at his behest, I replied —

"Nobody is out there but Joseph."

"I want to drink," he exclaimed, fretfully, turning away. "Zillah is constantly gadding off to Gimmerton since papa went. It's miserable! And I'm obliged to come down here—they resolved never to hear me up stairs."

"Is your father attentive to you, Master Heathcliff?" I asked, perceiving Catherine to be checked in her friendly advances.

"Attentive? He makes them a little more attentive, at least," he cried. "The wretches! Do you know, Miss Linton, that brute Hareton laughs at me! I hate him! indeed, I hate them all: they are odious beings."

Cathy began searching for some water; she lighted on a pitcher in the dresser, filled a tumbler, and brought it. He bid her add a spoonful of wine from a bottle on the table; and having swallowed a small portion, appeared more tran-

我把火炉中的余烬搅了一下，然后自己取了一斗煤。病人抱怨煤灰落了他一身；因为他在不停地咳嗽，样子像是在发烧生病，所以我也没斥责他。

"那，林顿，"他眉头舒展后，凯瑟琳喃喃地说，"你喜欢看到我吗？我能为你做些什么呢？"

"你之前怎么不来呢？"他问。"你本该来的，而不是写信。写这些长信烦死我了。我宁愿和你说话。现在我受不了谈话，也受不了别的。不知道希拉现在去哪了！你能否，"他望着我，"到厨房里去看一下？"

我刚才为他忙来忙去，却连一声谢谢都没听到，所以我不愿听从他的命令跑来跑去，于是我回答说：

"除了约瑟夫外，那儿没人。"

"我想喝水，"他不耐烦地叫嚷着，转过身去。"真是倒霉透了！爸爸走了以后，希拉就常常去吉默顿闲荡。真倒霉！不得不我只得下楼到这来——他们是决心听不到我在楼上叫喊的。"

"希斯克利夫少爷，你父亲把你照顾得周到吗？"我问道，看出凯瑟琳的友好表示遭到了挫折。

"照顾？他吩咐他们把我照顾得好些，至少，"他叫喊道。"那群混蛋！你知道吗？林顿小姐，那个粗鲁的哈里顿还嘲笑我！我恨他！的确，我憎恶他们所有的人：尽是些讨厌的家伙。"

凯瑟琳开始找水。在食橱里，她找到一瓶水，倒了满满一大杯，端了过来。他吩咐她从桌子上的一个瓶子里倒出一匙酒加入水中。他喝了一点后，显得平静多了，还说她很善良。

quil, and said she was very kind.

"And are you glad to see me?" asked she, reiterating her former question, and pleased to detect the faint dawn of a smile.

"Yes, I am. It's something new to hear a voice like yours!" he replied. "But I have been vexed, because you wouldn't come. And papa swore it was owing to me: he called me a pitiful, shuffling, worthless thing; and said you despised me; and if he had been in my place, he would be more the master of the Grange than your father, by this time. But you don't despise me, do you Miss —"

"I wish you would say Catherine, or Cathy," interrupted my young lady. "Despise you? No! Next to papa, and Ellen, I love you better than anybody living. I don't love Mr. Heathcliff, though; and I dare not come when he returns. Will he stay away many days?"

"Not many," answered Linton; "but he goes onto the moors frequently, since the shooting season commenced; and you might spend an hour or two with me, in his absence. Do! say you will! I think I should not be peevish with you: you'd not provoke me, and you'd be always ready to help me, wouldn't you?"

"Yes," said Catherine, stroking his long soft hair; "if I could only get papa's consent, I'd spend half my time with you. Pretty Linton! I wish you were my brother."

"And then you would like me as well as your father?" he observed, more cheerfully. "But papa says you would love me better than him and all the world, if you were my wife; so I'd rather you were that."

"No! I should never love anybody better than papa," she returned gravely. "And people

"你喜欢看到我吗?"她重复着前面的问题,惊喜地发现他脸上显现出的一丝笑容。

"是的,我喜欢,能听到你的声音是一件很新鲜的事!"他回答。"可是我曾经很苦恼,因为你不肯来。爸爸赌咒说,那是因为我:他骂我是个可怜的、怪声怪气的废物;说你瞧不起我;还说如果他在我的位置,那么他就会比你的父亲更像一个山庄的主人。但是,你不会瞧不起我,是吗,小姐?"

"我希望你能叫我凯瑟琳,或者凯茜,"我的小姐打断他的话。"瞧不起你?不!除了爸爸和艾伦,我对你的爱超过我对任何一个活着的人的爱。但是,我不爱希斯克利夫先生;他回来我就不敢来了。他要离开家很多天吗?"

"没几天,"林顿回答,"但是,打猎的季节开始后,他常常到旷野去。他不在的时候,你可以和我呆上一两个小时。答应我!说你会!我想我不会朝你发脾气;你不会惹我生气,总是愿意帮助我,不是吗?"

"是的,"凯瑟琳抚摸着他那柔软的长发,说道,"只要得到爸爸的允许,我将用一半的时间陪伴你。漂亮的林顿!我希望你是我的弟弟。"

"那么你就会像爱你父亲一样爱我?"他这样说着,更加愉悦了。"但是爸爸说,如果你是我的妻子的话,那么你爱我就会胜过你爱他、爱全世界。所以我宁愿你是我的妻子。"

"不!我对其他人的爱决不会胜过对爸爸的爱,"她严肃地回复道。

hate their wives, sometimes; but not their sisters and brothers, and if you were the latter, you would live with us, and papa would be as fond of you as he is of me."

Linton denied that people ever hated their wives; but Cathy affirmed they did, and, in her wisdom, instanced his own father's aversion to her aunt. I endeavoured to stop her thoughtless tongue. I couldn't succeed till everything she knew was out. Master Heathcliff, much irritated, asserted her relation was false.

"Papa told me; and papa does not tell falsehoods!" she answered pertly.

"My papa scorns yours!" cried Linton."He calls him a sneaking fool!"

"Yours is a wicked man," retorted Catherine; "and you are very naughty to dare to repeat what he says. He must be wicked, to have made Aunt Isabella leave him as she did!"

"She didn't leave him," said the boy:"you shan't contradict me!"

"She did!" cried my young lady.

"Well, I'll tell you something!" said Linton."Your mother hated your father, now then."

"Oh!" exclaimed Catherine, too enraged to continue.

"And she loved mine!" added he.

"You little liar! I hate you now," she panted, and her face grew red with passion.

"She did! she did!" sang Linton, sinking into the recess of his chair, and leaning back his head to enjoy the agitation of the other disputant, who stood behind.

"Hush, Master Heathcliff!" I said; "that's your father's tale too, I suppose."

"It isn't: you hold your tongue!" he an-

第二十三章

"某些时候，人们憎恨自己的妻子，但是不憎恨自己的兄弟姐妹，假如你是后者，你就可以和我们住在一起，这样爸爸喜欢你就会像喜欢我一样。"

林顿否认人们会恨他们的妻子，可凯茜肯定他们会这样，并且一时聪明，举出他自己的父亲对她姑姑的反感为例。我试图制止她那欠考虑的多嘴，但却无法办到。于是她把她所知道的一切全说了出来。希斯克利夫少爷大为恼怒，坚决说她所说的全是假的。

"爸爸告诉我的，我爸爸不说假话。"她唐突地回答。

"我爸爸瞧不起你爸爸，"林顿大叫。"他称他是鬼鬼祟祟的傻瓜。"

"你爸爸是一个恶毒的人，"凯瑟琳反唇相讥，"你真可恶，竟敢重复他说的话。他一定很恶毒，才使伊莎贝拉姑姑离开了他。"

"她没有离开他，"男孩说，"你不要反驳我。"

"她是，"我的小姐也嚷道。

"那好，我也告诉你点事吧！"林顿说道，"你的母亲也恨你的父亲，怎么样吧。"

"哦！"凯瑟琳大叫起来，愤怒得说不下去了。

"而且她还爱我的父亲。"他又说。

"你这个小骗子！我现在恨死你啦！"她喘着气，脸因为激动而变得通红。

"她就是这样的！就是这样的！"林顿大叫着，陷进椅子里头，向后仰着头，欣赏着站在他后面的另一个争论者激动的神情。

"闭嘴，希斯克利夫少爷！"我说，"那也是你父亲编造出来的一个故

swered. "She did, she did, Catherine! she did, she did!"

Cathy, beside herself, gave the chair a violent push, and caused him to fall against one arm. He was immediately seized by a suffocating; cough that soon ended his triumph. It lasted so long that it frightened even me. As to his cousin, she wept with all her might; aghast at the mischief she had done: though she said nothing. I held him till the fit exhausted itself. Then he thrust me away, and leant his head down silently. Catherine quelled her lamentations also, took a seat opposite, and looked solemnly into the fire.

"How do you feel now, Master Heathcliff?" I inquired after waiting ten minutes.

"I wish she felt as I do," he replied: "spiteful, cruel thing! Hareton never touches me: he never struck me in his life. And I was better today and there —" his voice died in a whimper.

"I didn't strike you!" muttered Cathy, chewing her lip to prevent another burst of emotion.

He sighed and moaned like one under great suffering, and kept it up for a quarter of an hour; on purpose to distress his cousin, apparently, for whenever he caught a stifled sob from her he put renewed pain and pathos into the inflexions of his voice.

"I'm sorry I hurt you, Linton," she said at length, racked beyond endurance. "But I couldn't have been hurt by that little push, and I had no idea that you could, either: you're not much, are you, Linton? Don't let me go home thinking I've done you harm. Answer! speak to me."

"I can't speak to you," he murmured;

事,我认为。"

"不是的,你闭嘴!"他答道。"她就是这样的,就是这样的,凯瑟琳!她就是这样的,就是这样!"

凯茜再也控制不了自己,猛地推了一把那椅子,就把他推倒在一只扶手上。他立刻像要窒息似的咳嗽起来,很快地结束了他的胜利。他咳了好久,时间长得连我都被吓住了。至于他那位表姐,拼命地大哭起来,被她惹的祸吓坏了:虽然她什么话也没说。我扶着他,直到咳完。他一把将我推开,默默垂下了头。凯瑟琳也停止了悲泣,坐在椅子对面,神色严肃地望着火焰。

十分钟过后,我问他:"你现在觉得怎样了,希斯克利夫少爷?"。

"我希望她也尝尝我的感受,"他回答,"可恶的、残忍的东西!哈里顿从没碰过我,他一生就从未打过我。今天我才好了一点,就——"他的声音在呜咽中戛然而止。

"我没打你!"凯茜嘟囔着,咬住自己的嘴唇,为避免情绪再一次爆发。

他叹息着,呻吟着,像是忍受着极大苦痛,而且持续了一刻钟,显然是故意让他表姐难受。因为她每次发出哽咽的啜泣,他就在他那抑扬顿挫的声调中重新添点痛苦与哀伤。

"我对伤害到你表示抱歉,林顿,"她终于开口了,给折磨得实在受不了。"如果是我的话,被那样轻轻一推,一定没事,我也想不到你会受伤。林顿,你伤得不严重吧,是吗?别让我回到家去还想着我伤害了你。回答我!请和我说话吧。"

"我不能跟你说话了,"他嘟囔着,

"you've hurt me so, that I shall lie awake all night, choking with this cough! If you had it you'd know what it was, but you'll be comfortably asleep, while I'm in agony—and nobody near me! I wonder how you would like to pass those fearful nights!" And he began to wail aloud, for very pity of himself.

"Since you are in the habit of passing dreadful nights," I said, "it won't be Miss who spoils your ease, you'd be the same had she never come. However, she shall not disturb you again; and perhaps you'll get quieter when we leave you."

"Must I go?" asked Catherine dolefully, bending over him. "Do you want me to go, Linton?"

"You can't alter what you've done," he replied pettishly, shrinking form her, "unless you alter it for the worse,by teasing me into a fever."

"Well,then I must go?"she repeated.

"Let me alone,at least,"said he; "I can't bear your talking!"

She lingered,and resisted my persuasions to departure,a tiresome while; but as h e neither looked up nor spoke, she finally made a movement to the door and I fol lowed. We were recalled by a scream. Linton had slid from his seat on to the hea rthstone, and lay writhing in the mere perverseness of an indulged plague of a c hild, determined to be as grievous and harassing as it can. I thoroughly gauged his disposition from his behaviour, and saw at once it would be folly to attempt humouring him. Not so my companion: she ran back in terror, knelt down,and crie d,and soothed, and entreated, till he grew quiet from lack of breath by no means

"你弄伤了我，我会整夜睡不着觉，咳得喘不过气来。如果你得了这种病，你就知道这滋味了。但是，当我痛苦的时候，你却会在舒舒服服地睡觉，没有一个人在我左右。我倒想，如果是你，会怎样度过那些可怕的夜晚？"他因为怜悯自己而大哭起来。

"既然你有度过可怕夜晚的习惯，"我说，"那就不是小姐打扰了你的安宁啦。就算她从没来过，你也是一样。不管怎样，她以后不会再打搅你啦。或许我们离开，你就能安静些了。"

"我必须走吗？"凯瑟琳神情忧愁，俯下身对着他问道。"你想让我走吗？林顿？"

"你改变不了你所做的，"他急躁地回答，躲开她，"除非你把事情弄得更糟，把我气得发烧。"

"好吧，那我必须得走啦？"她重复。

"让我独自呆着，至少，"他说，"我受不了你说话。"

她踌躇起来，我劝她走，她就是不听。可他既不抬头，也不说话，她最后只得向门口走去，我也跟了上去。然而，我们却被一声尖叫唤了回来。林顿从他的椅子上滑落到炉前的石板上，躺在那里身体扭来扭去，就像一个任性的，烦人的小孩在撒赖，决意做出痛苦和受折磨的样子。他的举动使我看透他的性格，立刻看出要迁就他那真是傻了。我的伙伴可不这样想，她惶恐地跑回去，跪下来，哭着，又是安慰，又是哀求，直到他没劲安静下来——绝不是因为看到她难过而感到懊悔。

from compunction at distressing her.

"I shall lift him on the settle," I said, "and he may roll about as he please we can't stop to watch him. I hope you are satisfied, Miss Cathy, that you are not the person to benefit him, and that his condition of health is not occasioned by attachment to you. Now then, there he is! Come away: as soon as he knows there is nobody by to care for his nonsense, he'll be glad to lie still!"

She placed a cushion under his head, and offered him some water; he rejected the latter, and tossed uneasily on the former, as if it were a stone or a block of wood. She tried to put it more comfortably.

"I can't do with that," he said; "It's not high enough!"

Catherine brought another to lay above it.

"That's too high!" murmured the provoking thing.

"How must I arrange it, then?" she asked despairingly.

He twined himself up to her, as she half knelt by the settle, and converted her shoulder into a support.

"No, that won't do," I said. "You'll be content with the cushion, Master Heath cliff. Miss has wasted too much time on you already, we cannot remain five minutes lon ger."

"Yes, yes, we can!" replied Cathy. "He's good and patient now. He's beginnin g to think I shall have far greater misery than he will tonight, if I believe he is t he worse for my visit; and then, I dare not come again. Tell the truth about it, Linton; for I mustn't come, if I have hurt you."

"You must come, to crue me," he an-

"让我把他抱到高背的长靠椅上,"我说,"这样随便他怎么滚都可以。我们不能停下来看着他。我希望你能满意了,凯茜小姐,你不是一个能帮他的人。他的健康状况也不是因为对你的依恋而搞成这样的。好了,让他在那儿吧!走吧,当他看到没人理睬他的胡闹时,他就会很高兴安静地躺着了。"

她在他的头下放置了靠垫,并且想给他喝水。他拒绝了后者,又在靠垫上翻来覆去,表现得十分不舒服,好像那是块石头或者木头。她试着将它放得更舒服些。

"我可不要这个,"他说,"这不够高。"

凯瑟琳又拿来一个靠垫加在上面。

"太高啦,"这个惹人厌的东西嘟囔着。

"那么我该怎么弄呢?"她绝望地问道。

他靠在她身上,因为她半跪在长椅旁,他把她的肩膀当作支撑了。

"不,这不行,"我说,"你枕着靠垫就该知足了,希斯克利夫少爷。小姐已经在你身上浪费了太多时间,我们连五分钟也不能多呆了。"

"不,不,我们能!"凯茜回答。"他现在好多了,耐心多了。他开始认识到,如果我相信是因为我的来访使他病情加重的话,我今晚肯定比他还要痛苦。这样我也就不敢再来了。说实话吧,林顿;要是我弄痛了你,我就不能来啦。"

"你必须来,来医治我,"他回

swered. "You ought to come because you have hurt me, you know you have, extremely! I was not as ill when you entered as I am at present—was I?"

"But you've made yourself ill by crying, and being in a passion."

"I didn't do it all," said his cousin, "However, we'll be friends now. And you want me:you would wish to see me sometimes, really?"

"I told you I did," he replied impatiently. "Sit on the settle and let me lean on your knee. That's as mama used to do, whole afternoon together. Sit quite still, and don't talk, but you may sing a song if you can sing; or you may say a nice long interesting ballad—one of those you promised to teach me; or a story. I'd rather have a ballad, though begin."

Catherine repeated the longest she could remember. The employment pleased both mightily. Linton would have another, and after that another, notwithstanding my strenuous objections; and so they went on until the clock struck twelve, and we heard Hareton in the court, returning for his dinner:

"And tomorrow, Catherine, will you be here tomorrow?" asked young Heathcliff, holding her frock as she rose reluctantly.

"No!" I answered, "nor next day neither." She, however, gave a different response, evidently, for his forehead cleared as she stooped and whispered in his ear.

"You won't go tomorrow, recollect, Miss!" I commenced, when we were out of the house. "You are not dreaming of it, are you?"

She smiled.

"Oh, I'll take good care," I continued: "I'

ll have that lock mended, and you can escape by no way else."

"I can get over the wall," she said, laughing. "The Grange is not a prison, Ellen, and you are not my jailer. And besides, I'm almost seventeen, I'm a woman. And I'm certain Linton would recover quickly if he had me to look after him. I'm older than he is, you know, and wiser, less childish, am I not? And he'll soon do as I direct him, with some slight coaxing. He's a pretty little darling when he's good. I'd make such a pet of him, if he were mine. We should never quarrel, should we, after we were used to each other? Don't you like him, Ellen?"

"Like him?" I exclaimed. "The worst-tempered bit of a sickly slip that ever struggled into its teens! Happily, as Mr. Heathcliff conjectured, he'll not win twenty! I doubt whether he'll see spring, indeed. And small loss to his family whenever he drops off. And lucky it is for us that his father took him: the kinder he was treated, the more tedious and selfish he'd be! I'm glad you have no chance of having him for a husband, Miss Catherine!"

My companion waxed serious at hearing this speech. To speak of his death so regardlessly wounded her feelings.

"He's younger than I," she answered, after a protracted pause of meditation, "and he ought to live the longest, he will—he must live as long as I do. He's as strong now as when he first came into the North; I'm positive of that! It's only a cold that ails him, the same as papa has. You say papa will get better, and why shouldn't he?"

"Well, well," I cried, "after all, we needn't trouble ourselves; for listen, Miss,—and mind,

说,"我会叫人把那把锁修好,这样你没有办法溜走啦。"

"我能爬墙,"她笑着说,"田庄不是监牢,艾伦,而且你也不是我的看守。再说,我就快十七岁啦,我是一个女人了。我敢肯定有我去照顾林顿,他会很快康复的。我年纪比他大,你知道,我也更聪明,不像他那么孩子气,不是吗?我只要稍微说点甜言蜜语,他就会听从我的吩咐。等他好了以后,他将是个漂亮可爱的小孩。如果他是我的,我将把他当成宝贝,等到我们习惯对方后,我们就永远不会吵架了。难道你不喜欢他吗,艾伦?"

"喜欢他!"我大叫起来。"一个勉强才挣扎到十几岁,脾气暴躁的小病孩。幸好,如希斯克利夫预料的那样,他活不到二十岁。真的,我怀疑他是否能看到春天。无论何时他死了,对他的家庭而言,都算不上是个大损失。总算我们运气好,他父亲将他带走了:别人对他越和气,他就越麻烦,越自私。我很高兴你没有机会让他成为你的丈夫,凯瑟琳小姐。"

听着这段话,我的同伴变得神情严肃。我这么漫不经心地谈到他的死,伤害了她的感情。

"他比我年轻,"沉思半晌之后,她答道,"他应该能活到最长,他会一定会活得跟我一样久。现在他同刚来北方的时候一样强壮,这点我敢肯定。他只是受了凉而已,就像爸爸一样,你说过爸爸会康复的,那他为什么不呢?"

"好啦,好啦,"我叫道,"反正我们没有必要给自己添麻烦。听我说,

I'll keep my word—if you attempt going to Wuthering Heights again, with or without me, I shall inform Mr. Linton, and, unless he allow it, the intimacy with your cousin must not be revived."

"It has been revived!" muttered Cathy sulkily.

"Must not be continued, then!" I said.

"We'll see!" was her reply, and she set off at a gallop, leaving me to toil in the rear.

We both reached home before our dinner-time; my master supposed we had been wandering through the park, and therefore he demanded no explanation of our absence. As soon as I entered, I hastened to change my soaked shoes and stockings; but sitting such a while at the Heights had done the mischief. On the succeeding morning I was laid up, and during three weeks I remained incapacitated for attending to my duties, a calamity never experienced prior to that period, and never, I am thankful to say, since.

My little mistress behaved like an angel in coming to wait on me, and cheer my solitude, the confinement brought me exceedingly low. It is wearisome, to a stirring active body, but few have slighter reasons for complaint than I had. The moment Catherine left Mr. Linton's room, she appeared at my bed-side. Her day was divided between us; no amusement usurped a minute: she neglected her meals, her studies, and her play; and she was the fondest nurse that ever watched. She must have had a warm heart, when she loved her father so, to give so much to me!

I said her days were divided between us; but the master retired early, and I generally

小姐——记住，我说话算数——如果你试图再去呼啸山庄的话，不管有没有我陪同，我都会告诉林顿先生。除非他许可，否则你和你表弟的亲密关系绝不可能再复原。"

"已经复原了。"凯茜倔强地嘟囔着。

"那绝不可能再继续，"我说。

"我们走着瞧。"她答道，骑着马疾驰而去，丢下我在后面拼命追赶。

我们两人在午饭前就回到了家。我的主人还以为我们一直在花园里溜达，因此没要我们解释不在家的原因。我一踏进门，就立即把我湿透的鞋袜换掉。可是就在山庄坐了一会儿，就给我带来了不幸。第二天早上我就起不来了，有三个星期我不得不卧床休养，没法干活。这场灾难是以前从未有过的，而且感谢上帝，自这以后就再没发生过。

在我孤单的时候，我的小主人像天使般来侍候我，令我很愉快，这种禁闭使我的情绪很低落。对于一个忙碌勤快的人，这样无聊透了。可是同别人相比，我又毫无理由去抱怨。凯瑟琳一离开林顿先生的房间，就会出现在我的床边。她一天的时间都花在我们两人身上了，没有一分钟是用于玩乐的。她甚至忘掉了吃饭、读书和游戏，真是一个讨人喜欢的看护。在她对父亲的爱是如此强烈时，还能对我这么关心，她得有一颗多么热情的心啊。

我说过她一天的时间全花在我们两人身上了，但主人睡得很早，而我

needed nothing after six o'clock, thus the evening was her own. Poor thing! I never considered what she did with herself after tea. And though frequently, when she looked in to bid me goodnight, I remarked a fresh colour in her cheeks and a pinkness over her slender fingers; instead of fancying the hue borrowed from a cold ride across the moors, I laid it to the charge of a hot fire in the library.

通常六点钟后就没什么需要了,这样晚上就是她的了。可怜的孩子!我从未想过吃茶后她会去做什么。虽然她进来看我跟我道晚安时,我常看见她脸上鲜艳的色彩和纤细手指上的微红;然而我把它们归为在书房烤火的缘故,没想到这是因为冒着严寒骑马经过旷野造成的。

Chapter 24
第二十四章

At the close of three weeks, I was able to quit my chamber, and move about the house. And on the first occasion of my sitting up in the evening, I asked Catherine to read to me, because my eyes were weak. We were in the library, the master having gone to bed, she consented, rather unwillingly, I fancied; and imagining my sort of books did not suit her, I bid her please herself in the choice of what she perused. She selected one of her own favourites, and got forward steadily about an hour; then came frequent questions.

"Ellen, are not you tired? Hadn't you better lie down now? You'll be sick, keeping up so long, Ellen."

"No, no, dear, I'm not tired," I returned.

在床上躺了近三个星期后,我就能起身走出房间在屋里溜达了。我能坐起的第一个晚上,等主人睡着后,我和凯瑟琳到了书房,因为我的眼睛仍很疲劳,所以请凯瑟琳念书给我听。她答应了,但我想她是不大愿意的。我还以为我看的这类书不合她的喜好,就叫她随便挑一本她看过的读给我听。她挑了本她喜欢的,但花了差不多一个小时才念完,接着就不停地问我:"艾伦,你不累吗?你现在躺下休息不是更好吗?你现在还在生病啦,这么晚还不睡,艾伦。"

我也不停答复她道:"不,不,亲爱的,我还不累。"

当她明白无法劝动我时,就尝试

continually.

Perceiving me immovable, she essayed another method of showing her disrelish for her occupation. It changed to yawning, and stretching, and—

"Ellen, I'm tired."

"Give over then and talk," I answered.

That was worse: she fretted and sighed, and looked at her watch till eight, and finally went to her room, completely overdone with sleep; judging by her peevish, heavy look, and the constant rubbing she inflicted on her eyes. The following night she seemed more impatient still; and on the third from recovering my company, she complained of a headache, and left me. I thought her conduct odd; and having remained alone a long while, I resolved on going, and inquiring whether she were better, and asking her to come and lie on the sofa, instead of up stairs in the dark. No Catherine could I discover upstairs, and none below. The servants affirmed they had not seen her. I listened at Mr. Edgar's door; all was silence. I returned to her apartment, extinguished my candle, and seated myself in the window.

The moon shone bright; a sprinkling of snow covered the ground, and I reflected that she might, possibly, have taken it into her head to walk about the garden, for refreshment. I did detect a figure creeping along the inner fence of the park; but it was not my young mistress, on its emerging into the light, I recognised one of the grooms. He stood a considerable period, viewing the carriage-road through the grounds; then started off at a brisk pace, as if he had detected something, and reappeared presently, leading Miss's pony; and there she was, just

了另一种方法，即故意向我显示她对正在干的事提不起精神，不时打打哈欠，伸伸懒腰，又对我说：

"艾伦，我累了。"

"那么别念啦，我们谈话吧，"我答道。

听到这话，她的表现更糟：又是焦躁又是叹气，时不时低头看表，一直到八点钟，她才抱怨着回到房间，一脸的快快不乐，还不停地揉着眼睛，装作非常瞌睡的样子。第二天晚上她更不耐烦。第三天，为了不再陪我，她抱怨说头痛，离开了我。我觉得她的行为很奇怪。在独自待了许久后，我决定去看看她是不是好些了，想叫她躺在楼下沙发上，免得呆在黑漆漆的楼上。但在楼上我却找不到她的踪影，楼下也没有。仆人们都说肯定没看见她。我在埃德加先生门前听了听动静，里面静悄悄的。我走进她的房间，吹灭蜡烛，坐在窗前。

月亮很亮，皎洁的月光为大地披上一件雪的外衣。我想她可能为了清醒一下头脑，到花园散步了。而且我的确看到一个人影顺着花园的篱笆蹑手蹑脚地向前走，但当那人影走到亮处时，我认出那是马夫，而不是我的小主人。他在那儿站了很久，然后穿过园林，敏捷地顺着那条马路迈步走去，好像发现了什么似的，但马上又出现了，手中还牵着小姐的马。我看到小姐刚下了马，走在马旁边。马夫鬼鬼祟祟地牵着马穿过草地向马厩走

dismounted, and walking by its side. The man took his charge stealthily across the grass towards the stable. Cathy entered by the casement window of the drawing-room, and glided noiselessly up to where I awaited her. She put the door gently to, slipped off her snowy shoe, untied her hat, and was proceeding, unconscious of my espionage, to lay aside her mantle, when I suddenly rose and revealed myself. The surprise petrified her an instant, she uttered an inarticulate exclamation, and stood fixed.

"My dear Miss Catherine," I began, too vividly impressed by her recent kindness to break into a scold, "where have you been riding out at this hour? And why should you try to deceive me, by telling a tale? Where have you been? Speak!"

"To the bottom of the park," she stammered. "I didn't tell a tale."

"And nowhere else?" I demanded.

"No," was the muttered reply.

"Oh, Catherine!" I cried, sorrowfully. "You know you have been doing wrong, or you wouldn't be driven to uttering an untruth to me. That does grieve me. I'd rather be three months ill, than hear you frame a deliberate lie."

She sprang forward and bursting into tears, threw her arms round my neck.

"Well Ellen, I'm so afraid of you being angry," she said. "Promise not to be angry, and you shall know the very truth. I hate to hide it."

We sat down in the window-seat; I assured her I would not scold, whatever her secret might be, and I guessed it, of course; so she commenced—

"I've been to Wuthering Heights, Ellen, and I've never missed going a day since you

去。而凯茜却从客厅的窗户那儿爬进来，一声不响地溜到我坐着等她的地方。她轻轻地关上门，脱下沾雪的鞋子和头上的帽子，却没有发觉我正瞅着她，就在她正要脱下斗篷的时候，我忽然站起来，走到她面前。我的出现使她颇为意外，她愣了一下，发出一声模糊的叫声，便站在那里不动了。

"我亲爱的凯瑟琳小姐，"我说道，她这阵子表现出的温柔给我的印象太深，我不忍破口骂她，只说："这么晚了，你还骑马啊，到哪儿去啦？为什么要撒谎骗我呢？说吧！到哪儿去啦？"

"我只是到花园那头去了，"她结结巴巴地答道，"我没有撒谎。"

"没去别的地方吗？"我继续追问道。

"没有，"她喃喃地回答道。

"啊，凯瑟琳！"我难过地大叫起来。"难道你不知道你错了吗？你这样故意跟我说谎使我难过。我宁可再病三个月，也不愿听你故意捏造一套瞎话来骗我。"

她向我扑了上来，搂住我的脖子，忽然放声大哭。

"啊，艾伦，我是害怕你会生气，所以才撒谎的，"她回答道。"答应我不生气，我才把实情告诉你，当然我也不愿一直瞒着你呢。"

我们坐在窗台上，我向她保证无论她的秘密是什么，我都不会骂她，当然，就算她不说，我也猜到了。于是她开始叙述："我是去呼啸山庄了，艾伦，从你病倒后，我每天都去。只

fell ill; except thrice before, and twice after you left your room. I gave Michael books and pictures to prepare Minny every evening, and to put her back in the stable. You mustn't scold him either, mind. I was at the Heights by half-past six, and generally stayed till half past eight, and then galloped home. It was not to amuse myself that I went, I was often wretched all the time. Now and then, I was happy: once in a week perhaps. At first, I expected there would be sad work persuading you to let me keep my word to Linton, for I had engaged to call again next day, when we quitted him; but, as you stayed up stairs on the morrow, I escaped that trouble; and while Michael was refastening the lock of the park door in the afternoon, I got possession of the key, and told him how my cousin wished me to visit him, because he was sick, and couldn't come to the Grange; and how papa would object to my going; and then I negotiated with him about the pony. He is fond of reading, and he thinks of leaving soon to get married; so he offered, if I would lend him books out of the library, to do what I wished, but I preferred giving him my own, and that satisfied him better.

"On my second visit, Linton seemed in lively spirits; and Zillah (that is their housekeeper) made us a clean room and a good fire, and told us that, as Joseph was out at a prayer-meeting and Hareton Eamshaw was off with his dogs-robbing our woods of pheasants, as I heard afterwards—we might do what we liked. She brought me some warm wine and gingerbread, and appeared exceedingly good-natured; and Linton sat in the arm-chair, and I in the little rocking chair on the hearthstone, and we laughed and talked so merrily, and found so much to say. We planned where we would go, and what we would do in summer. I needn't repeat that, because you would call it silly.

"One time, however, we were near quarrelling. He said the pleasantest manner of spending a hot July day was lying from morning till evening on a bank of heath in the middle of the moors, with the bees humming dreamily about among the bloom, and the larks singing high up over head, and the blue sky and bright sun shining steadily and cloudlessly. That was his most perfect idea of heaven's happiness. Mine was rocking in a rustling green tree, with a west wind blowing, and bright white clouds flitting rapidly above; and not only larks, but throstles, and blackbirds, and linnets, and cuckoos pouring out music on every side, and the moors seen at a distance, broken into cool dusky dells; but close by great swells of long grass undulating in waves to the breeze; and woods and sounding water, and the whole world awake and wild with joy. He wanted all to lie in an ecstacy of peace; I wanted all to sparkle, and dance in a glorious jubilee. I said his heaven would be only half alive; and he said mine would be drunk. I said I should fall asleep in his; and he said he could not breathe in mine, and began to grow very snappish. At last, we agreed to try both, as soon as the right weather came; and then we kissed each other and were friends.

"After sitting still an hour, I looked at the great room with its smooth uncarpeted floor, and thought how nice it would be to play in, if we removed the table; and I asked Linton to call Zillah in to help us, and we'd have a game at

话。我们计划了夏天要到哪儿去，要做什么。这里我不想再重复了，因为你一定会说这样是愚蠢的。

"可有一次，我们差点吵了起来。他说，想让酷热的七月过得令人愉快的最佳办法就是从早到晚躺在旷野中的草地上，蜜蜂在花丛中梦幻似的嗡嗡叫，百灵鸟在头顶高高地唱着动听的歌儿，还有蔚蓝的天空和灿烂的太阳，空中一望无云，太阳毫无遮挡地照着大地。他说这就是他脑海中想像的最完美的天堂之乐。而我想的却是能坐在一棵被西风吹得簌簌作响的绿树上摇荡，看着洁白的云朵从头顶飞快地飘过，听着百灵鸟，以及画眉雀、山鸟、红雀和杜鹃到处婉转地啼鸣，遥望旷野上裂成许多凉爽微暗的峡谷。近处能看到浓密的长长的青草随风波浪似的起伏，还有茂密的森林和潺潺的流水，而整个世界都苏醒过来，陷入疯狂的欢乐之中。他想让一切都沉浸在恬静的心醉神迷中；而我要一切都沐浴在灿烂的欢欣兴奋中。我说他的天堂毫无生气，他说我的天堂是发酒疯。我说我处在他的天堂里一定会睡着，他说他身在我的天堂里就会喘不过气，于是他开始变得很暴躁。最后我们同意只要有适宜的天气就去尝试一下。然后彼此亲吻了对方，重新成了好朋友。

"在安静地坐了足有一个小时后，我望着那间地板上光溜溜的未铺地毯的大屋子，我想要是把桌子挪开，到里面去玩那该多有趣啊。所以我把希拉唤进来帮我们，这样就可以玩捉迷

blind-man's buff, she should try to catch us; you used to, you know, Ellen. He wouldn't, there was no pleasure in it, he said; but he consented to play at ball with me. We found two in a cupboard, among a heap of old toys: tops, and hoops, battledores, and shuttlecocks. One was marked C., and the other H.; I wished to have the C., because that stood for Catherine, and the H. might be for Heathcliff, his name; but the bran came out of H., and Linton didn't like it. I beat him constantly and he got cross again, and coughed, and returned to his chair. That night, though, he easily recovered his good humour, he was charmed with two or three pretty songs—*your* songs, Ellen; and when I was obliged to go, he begged and entreated me to come the following evening; and I promised. Minny and I went flying home as light as air; and I dreamt of Wuthering Heights and my sweet, darling cousin, till morning.

"On the morrow, I was sad; partly because you were poorly, and partly that I wished my father knew, and approved of my excursions, but it was beautiful moonlight after tea; and, as I rode on, the gloom cleared. I shall have another happy evening, I thought to myself; and what delights me more, my pretty Linton will. I trotted up their garden, and was turning round to the back, when that fellow Earnshaw met me, took my bridle, and bid me go in by the front entrance. He patted Minny's neck, and said she was a bonny beast, and appeared as if he wanted me to speak to him. I only told him to leave my horse alone, or else it would kick him. He answered in his vulgar accent, 'It wouldn't do mitch hurt if it did'; and surveyed its legs with a smile. I was half inclined to make it try; however, he moved off to open the door, and, as he raised the latch, he looked up to the inscription above, and said, with a stupid mixture of awkwardness and elation —

"'Miss Catherine! I can read yon, nah.'

"'Wonderful,' I exclaimed. 'Pray let us hear you—you *are* grown clever!'

"He spelt, and drawled over by syllables, the name — 'Hareton Earnshaw.'

"'And the figures?' I cried, encouragingly, perceiving that he came to a dead halt.

"'I cannot tell them yet,' he answered.

"'Oh, you dunce?' I said, laughing heartily at his failure.

"The fool stared, with a grin hovering about his lips, and a scowl gathering over his eyes, as if uncertain whether he might not join in my mirth, whether it were not pleasant familiarity, or what it really was, contempt. I settled his doubts, by suddenly retrieving my gravity and desiring him to walk away, for I came to see Linton not him. He reddened—I saw that by the moonlight—dropped his hand from the latch, and skulked off, a picture of mortified vanity. He imagined himself to be as accomplished as Linton, I suppose, because he could spell his own name; and was marvellously discomfited that I didn't think the same."

"Stop, Miss Catherine, dear!" I interrupted."I shall not scold, but I don't like your conduct there. If you had remembered that Hareton was your cousin as much as Master Heathcliff, you would have felt how improper it was to behave in that way. At least, it was praiseworthy ambition for him to desire to be as accomplished as Linton; and probably he did not learn merely to show off. You had made him ashamed

笑。我倒是想让他尝尝被踢的滋味。但他却转身去开了门，拔起门闩，抬头望着刻在门上的字，脸上呈现出又窘迫又得意的傻样，说：

"'凯瑟琳小姐，请让我念给你听吧。'

"'好啊，'我叫道。'让我听听你能念些什么吧——你倒是变聪明了！'

"他念着'哈里顿·恩肖'这个名字，而且还把它拖长声音逐字地读出来。

"看到他停顿下来，我鼓励地大声喊着：'那上面不是还有数字吗？'

"'那些数字我还不会念，'他说。

"看到他不会念我就开心地笑起来，说道：'啊，你真是个傻瓜！'

"那个傻子瞪着双眼发愣，嘴角挂着痴笑，蹙起双眉，看样子好像不知道该不该同我一块笑，也不知我的笑是代表亲热还是鄙视。事实上，我当然是在鄙视他。突然我恢复了尊严，叫他走开，并告诉他我是来看望林顿而非他的。我借着皎洁的月光看到他的脸红了。只见他有一种虚荣心被羞辱的样子，手从门上垂下来，躲躲闪闪地跑开了。我猜测，他还以为只要能念自己的名字，就能像林顿表弟一样聪明呢。我却鄙视了这种法，这使他感到十分狼狈。"

"别说啦，亲爱的凯瑟琳小姐！"我打断她，说道。"我不骂你，但我不喜欢你这种作风。如果你记得表哥哈里顿和希斯克利夫少爷是一样的，那你就该意识到这种做法是多么不恰当。至少他渴望和林顿一样有学问，这是值得称赞的抱负。而他学习也许并不只是为了炫耀。我毫不怀疑你曾因他的无知而羞辱他。而他为了讨你欢

of his ignorance before, I have no doubt; and he wished to remedy it and please you. To sneer at his imperfect attempt was very bad breeding. Had you been brought up in his circumstances, would you be less rude? He was as quick and as intelligent a child as ever you were; and I'm hurt that he should be despised now, because that base Heathcliff has treated him so unjustly."

"Well, Ellen, you won't cry about it, will you?" she exclaimed, surprised at my earnestness. "But wait, and you shall hear if he conned his A B C to please me; and if it were worth while being civil to the brute. I entered; Linton was lying on the settle, and half got up to welcome me.

"'I'm ill tonight, Catherine, love,' he said; 'and you must have all the talk, and let me listen. Come, and sit by me. I was sure you wouldn't break your word, and I'll make you promise again, before you go.'

"I knew now that I mustn't tease him, as he was ill; and I spoke softly and put no questions, and avoided irritating him in any way. I had brought some of my nicest books for him; he asked me to read a little of one, and I was about to comply, when Earnshaw burst the door open, having gathered venom with reflection. He advanced direct to us, seized Linton by the arm, and swung him off the seat.

"'Get to thy own room!' he said in a voice almost inarticulate with passion; and his face looked swelled and furious. 'Take her there if she comes to see thee, thou shalln't keep me out of this. Begone, wi' ye both!'

"He swore at us, and left Linton no time to answer, nearly throwing him into the kitchen; and he clenched his fist as I followed, seemingly longing to knock me down. I was afraid for a moment, and I let one volume fall; he kicked it after me, and shut us out. I heard a malignant, crackly laugh by the fire, and turning, beheld that odious Joseph standing rubbing his bony hands, and quivering.

"'Aw wer sure he'd sarve ye eht! He's a grand lad! He's getten t' raight sperrit in him! *He* knaws—Aye, he knaws, as weel as Aw do, who sud be t' maister yonder—Ech, ech, ech! He mad ye skift properly! Ech, ech, ech!'

"'Where must we go?' I said to my cousin, disregarding the old wretch's mockery.

"Linton was white and trembling. He was not pretty then, Ellen: Oh no! He looked frightful! For his thin face and large eyes were wrought into an expression of frantic, powerless fury. He grasped the handle of the door, and shook it, it was fastened inside.

"'If you don't let me in I'll kill you!—If you don't let me in I'll kill you!' he rather shrieked than said. 'Devil! Devil!—I'll kill you—I'll kill you!'

"Joseph uttered his croaking laugh again.

"'Thear that's t' father!' he cried. 'That's father! We've allas summut uh orther side in us. Niver heed Hareton, lad—dunnut be 'feard—he cannot get at thee!'

"I took hold of Linton's hands, and tried to pull him away; but he shrieked so shockingly that I dared not proceed. At last, his cries were choked by a dreadful fit of coughing; blood gushed from his mouth, and he fell on the ground. I ran into the yard, sick with terror; and called for Zillah, as loud as I could. She soon heard me: she was milking the cows in a shed

房,与其说撑,不如说是扔。我也跟着走出房门,去了厨房,他握紧拳头,好像想打倒我似的。当时我害怕得连手中的书都掉在地上。他把书踢给我,关上门,把我们关到屋外。我听到火炉那边传来一声恶毒的怪笑,于是转过身,瞅见那个可恶的约瑟夫正站着那儿,颤抖地搓着他瘦骨嶙峋的手。

"'我就知道他会去把你们赶出来!他是一个好小伙!他可有劲啦!他同我一样,知道谁才该是这间房子的主人——呃、呃、呃!他干得好!呃、呃、呃!'

"我不理会那老家伙的嘲笑,问表弟:'现在我们该到哪儿去?'

"林顿脸色苍白,浑身哆嗦。那时他的表情可不好看,艾伦。啊,不,他看上去很可怕,因为有一种疯狂无力的愤怒表情从他的瘦脸和大眼睛中透出来。他握住门柄,拼命地摇,但门从里面闩上了,怎么摇也打不开。

"'如果你不让我进去,我就会杀了你——如果你不让我进去,我就会杀了你!'他大叫道,简直是在尖叫,而不是在说话。'你这个恶魔!恶魔!——我要杀了你——我要杀了你!'

"这时,又传来约瑟夫那嘶哑的笑声。

"'喏,就像他的父亲!'他叫道。'就像他的父亲!我们俩都有份。不要理他,哈里顿,孩子,不要害怕,他碰不到你!'

"我抓住林顿的手,想拉开他。可是他叫得那么吓人,我不敢去拉他。他的叫声淹没在一阵可怕的咳嗽中。接着他口吐鲜血倒在地上。我被吓坏了,跑到院子里尽全力呼唤希

behind the barn, and hurrying from her work, she inquired what there was to do? I hadn't breath to explain; dragging her in, I looked about for Linton. Earnshaw had come out to examine the mischief he had caused, and he was then conveying the poor thing upstairs. Zillah and I ascended after him; but he stopped me at the top of the steps, and said I shouldn't go in, I must go home. I exclaimed that he had killed Linton, and I *would* enter. Joseph locked the door, and declared I should do 'no sich stuff,' and asked me whether I were 'born to be as mad as him.' I stood crying, till the housekeeper appeared. She affirmed that he would be better in a bit, but he couldn't do with that shrieking and din; and she took me, and nearly carried me into the house.

"Ellen, I was ready to tear my hair off my head! I sobbed and wept so that my eyes were almost blind; and the ruffian you have such sympathy with stood opposite: presuming every now and then to bid me 'wisht,' and denying that it was his fault; and finally, frightened by my assertions that I would tell papa, and that he should be put in prison and hanged, he commenced blubbering himself, and hurried out to hide his cowardly agitation. Still, I was not rid of him: when at length they compelled me to depart, and I had got some hundred yards off the premises, he suddenly issued from the shadow of the roadside, and checked Minny and took hold of me.

"'Miss Catherine, I'm ill grieved,' he began, 'but it's rather too bad—'

"I gave him a cut with my whip, thinking perhaps he would murder me. He let go, thundering one of his horrid curses, and I galloped

拉。她很快听到了,当时她正在谷包后面的棚子里挤牛奶,赶忙丢下活儿跑来,问我急着叫她干吗?我顾不上解释,就拉着她来到林顿表弟身边。这时恩肖已经出来看到他闯的祸,在我和希拉进来的时候,他正抱着可怜的表弟上楼。希拉和我跟着他上了楼。可他停在楼梯上,不让我跟进去,叫我马上回家。我喊着说,就是他林顿表弟才受到伤害,我非要进去不可。约瑟夫把门锁上,叫我'不要做这种蠢事',又问我是不是'生来就跟他一样疯疯癫癫的'。我站在门口哭,不久,管家来到我面前,对我说他肯定很快就会好的,但像我这样大吵大闹对他不会有好处。于是她拉着我——与其说拉,还不如说拖——进了屋子。

"艾伦,我当时几乎想把我的头发全扯下来!我哭得死去活来,差点眼睛都瞎了,你所同情的那个混蛋就站在对面,竟敢时不时要我'不要吵',而且拒绝承认这是他的错。最后我宣称要把这事告诉爸爸,而这必定导致他被关进牢狱,被判吊死,他才害怕得哭起来,连忙跑出去想以此掩盖他怯弱的感情。但我仍没能摆脱他的纠缠。最后他们强迫我离开,我才不得已走出了屋子。就在我骑上马走了还不过几百码的时候,他忽然从路旁的阴影处穿了出来,拦住敏妮,抓住我。

"'凯瑟琳小姐,我感到非常难过,'他对我说,'这一切实在是糟透了——'

"我还以为他想要谋害我,所以给了他一鞭子。他放开我,让我走,但狠狠地咒骂了我一句,我当时吓的

home more than half out of my senses.

"I didn't bid you good night, that evening, and I didn't go to Wuthering Heights, the next. I wished to, exceedingly; but I was strangely excited, and dreaded to hear that Linton was dead, sometimes; and sometimes shuddered at the thought of encountering Hareton. On the third day I took courage: at least, I couldn't bear longer suspense, and stole off once more. I went at five o'clock, and walked; fancying I might manage to creep into the house, and up to Linton's room, unobserved. However, the dogs gave notice of my approach. Zillah received me, and saying 'the lad was mending nicely,' showed me into a small, tidy, carpeted apartment, where, to my inexpressible joy, I beheld Linton laid on a little sofa, reading one of my books. But he would neither speak to me nor look at me, through a whole hour, Ellen, he has such an unhappy temper. And what quite confounded me, when he did open his mouth it was to utter the falsehood that I had occasioned the uproar, and Hareton was not to blame! Unable to reply, except passionately, I got up and walked from the room. He sent after me a faint 'Catherine!' He did not reckon on being answered so: but I wouldn't turn back; and the morrow was the second day on which I stayed at home, nearly determined to visit him no more. But it was so miserable going to bed, and getting up, and never hearing anything about him, that my resolution melted into air before it was properly formed. It *had* appeared wrong to take the journey once; now it seemed wrong to refrain. Michael came to ask if he must saddle Minny; I said 'Yes,' and considered myself doing a duty as she bore me over the hills. I was

魂都没了，骑着马飞奔回家。

"也是这个原因，那天晚上我没去向你道晚安，第二天我也没去呼啸山庄。我很想去，可我内心一直难以平静，一是怕听说林顿表弟死了，二是想到可能遇见哈里顿就害怕得发抖。第三天我终于鼓起勇气，至少，我再也无法忍受这种心神不定的折磨了，我又偷偷溜出去。我是五点钟时徒步过去的，心想我该用办法爬进房子，直接上楼到林顿的屋里，不被人发现。可是我的行踪被看门的狗发现了。于是希拉出来把我领进屋，并告诉我'这孩子现在好多了'，说着把我带到一间铺着地毯的干净小房间。我一进屋就看见林顿躺在一张小沙发上读我带给他的书，这使我感到无比快乐。可接下来的一个小时里，他不和我说一句话，甚至连看都不看我。艾伦，他这脾气多怪啊。但最使我狼狈的是，他一开口就胡说八道，说是我引起了那场纷扰，不怪哈里顿！听到这，我一下就火了，站起身，一声不吭地走出屋子。他没料想我会做出这样的举动，于是在我身后轻轻呼唤了一声'凯瑟琳！'可我头也不回地走了。第二天，也就是从我回到家的第二天，我几乎决定不再去看他。可是就整天这样睡觉再醒来，永远无法得知一点有关他的消息，这是多么难受啊，因此我的决定在还未正式形成之前就被否决了。以前到那儿去好像是错误的，可现在不去反倒让我觉得不对。迈克尔来询问，是否要为我把敏妮准备好，我说'要。'当敏妮把我驮过山头时，我心想这么做是在尽我的责任。这回我是经过前面的窗子

forced to pass the front windows to get to the court, it was no use trying to conceal my presence.

"'Young master is in the house,' said Zillah, as she saw me making for the parlour. I went in; Earnshaw was there also, but he quitted the room directly. Linton sat in the great arm chair half asleep; waking up to the fire, I began in a serious tone, partly meaning it to be true —

"'As you don't like me, Linton, and as you think I come on purpose to hurt you, and pretend that I do so every time, this is our last meeting, let us say good bye; and tell Mr. Heathcliff that you have no wish to see me, and that he mustn't invent any more falsehoods on the subject.'

"'Sit down and take your hat off, Catherine,' he answered. 'You are so much happier than I am, you ought to be better. Papa talks enough of my defects, and shows enough scorn of me, to make it natural I should doubt myself. I doubt whether I am not altogether as worthless as he calls me, frequently; and then I feel so cross and bitter, I hate everybody! I *am* worthless, and bad in temper, and bad in spirit, almost always; and if you choose, you *may* say goodbye: you'll get rid of an annoyance. Only, Catherine, do me this justice: believe that if I might be as sweet, and as kind, and as good as you are, I would be; as willingly, and more so, than as happy and as healthy. And believe that your kindness has made me love you deeper than if I deserved your love, and though I couldn't, and cannot help showing my nature to you, I regret it and repent it; and shall regret and repent it till I die!'

"希拉看到我正朝客厅方向走,就说:'小少爷现在待在房间里。'我走进去,恩肖也在那儿,但他一看到我就马上起身离开房间。林顿表弟正半醒半睡地躺在一张大扶手的椅子上。我走到火炉前,用一种严肃的声调,半认真地说:

"'林顿,既然你不喜欢我,认为我来只是为了故意伤害你,而且以为我每次都如此,那么这将是我们最后一面。让我们永别吧。告诉希斯克利夫先生叫他不用再编造任何有关这事的瞎话了,因为你压根就不愿见我。'

"'摘下帽子,坐到我面前,凯瑟琳,'他回答道。'你比我幸福多了,我想你应该比我好。爸爸老是数落我的缺点,对我非常轻视,这自然使我开始怀疑自己。我怀疑自己是不是完全像他经常数落我的那样没有出息。我很不高兴,也很苦恼,因此恨上每个人!我没出息,脾气坏,精神差,而且差不多总这样;如果你希望同我永别,那就说吧,这样你可以摆脱一个累赘。可是,凯瑟琳,请对我公道点:相信我,比起让我像你一样幸福健康,我更希望让我像你一样讨人喜欢,和气善良。你要相信:你的善良使我深深爱上了你,比起你的爱——如果我有资格承受——更深,虽然曾经我不得不,而且情不自禁地向你表露我的本性,但我并没有恶意,如果那样伤害了你,我很抱歉,也很悔恨,甚至后悔死了!'

"I felt he spoke the truth; and I felt I must forgive him, and though he should quarrel the next moment, I must forgive him again. We were reconciled; but we cried, both of us, the whole time I stayed, not entirely for sorrow; yet I was sorry Linton had that distorted nature. He'll never let his friends be at ease, and he'll never be at ease himself! I have always gone to his little parlour, since that night; because his father returned the day after.

"About three times, I think, we have been merry and hopeful, as we were the first evening; the rest of my visits were dreary and troubled. Now with his selfishness and spite, and now with his sufferings, but I've learnt to endure the former with nearly as little resentment as the latter. Mr. Heathcliff purposely avoids me; I have hardly seen him at all. Last Sunday, indeed, coming earlier than usual, I heard him abusing poor Linton, cruelly, for his conduct of the night before. I can't tell how he knew of it, unless he listened. Linton had certainly behaved provokingly, however, it was the business of nobody but me, and I interrupted Mr. Heathcliff's lecture by entering and telling him so. He burst into a laugh, and went away, saying he was glad I took that view of the matter. Since then, I've told Linton he must whisper his bitter things. Now, Ellen, you have heard all; and I can't be prevented from going to Wuthering Heights, except by inflicting misery on two people; whereas, if you'll only not tell papa, my going need disturb the tranquillity of none. You'll not tell, will you? It will be very heartless if you do."

"I'll make up my mind on that point by tomorrow, Miss Catherine," I replied. "It re-

"我觉得他所说的是实话,我还认为我必须原谅他,而且,即使过一会他还会吵,我也一定还会原谅他。就这样,我们和好了。但我们俩却哭起来,以至于我在那儿的所有时间都在哭泣中度过。虽然不只悲哀才流泪,但我的确是因为林顿表弟有那么乖僻的天性才难过。他永远不会让他的朋友们安逸,也永远不会让自己安逸。从那天夜晚起,由于他的父亲第二天回来了,我只能到小客厅去陪他。

"我想大概有三次我们过得很快乐,充满希望,就像第一天晚上那样。但其他的几次拜访,都过得既凄惨又烦恼。一方面因为他的自私和怨恨,另一个方面因为他的病痛;但我已学会用最少的反感去容忍他的自私和怨恨,也同样忍受他的病痛。希斯克利夫好像故意避开我,因为我几乎从没见过他。记得是上个礼拜天,没错,就是那天,我去得比平常早了些,我听见他正为林顿表弟头天晚上的行为严厉责骂可怜的他。我不知他是怎么知道的,除非是偷听。林顿头天的举止当然惹人生气;可那全是为了我,所以我闯进去打断希斯克利夫先生的话,而且如实告诉他。他大笑起来,一边走一边说他很欣赏我对这事采取的做法。自从那时起,我就告诉林顿表弟,他还是小声向我诉说他的烦恼为好。现在,艾伦,你已经知道了一切。如果我不能去呼啸山庄,那么就有两个人会痛苦。可只要你不告诉爸爸,我去了,就不会妨碍到任何人的平静。你不会告诉爸爸吧,你会吗?如果你告诉他的话,那你就太残酷无情了。"

quires some study; and so I'll leave you to your rest, and go think it over."

I thought it over aloud, in my master's presence; walking straight from her room to his, and relating the whole story with the exception of her conversations with her cousin, and any mention of Hareton. Mr. Linton was alarmed and distressed more than he would acknowledge to me. In the morning, Catherine learnt my betrayal of her confidence, and she learnt also that her secret visits were to end. In vain she wept and writhed against the interdict, and implored her father to have pity on Linton. All she got to comfort her was a promise that he would write, and give him leave to come to the Grange when he pleased; but explaining that he must no longer expect to see Catherine at Wuthering Heights. Perhaps, had he been aware of his nephew's disposition and state of health, he would have seen fit to withhold even that slight consolation.

"这个问题我明天才答复你,凯瑟琳小姐,"我答道。"给我点时间考虑。你快去休息,让我好好想一下。"

我所谓的考虑,就是去把这事告诉我的主人。从她屋里出来后,我直接走到他的屋内,把除了她跟表弟的对话,以及任何提及哈里顿的内容外,所有事情都告诉他。林顿老爷感到非常惊惶难过,而我想他内心的惊惶难过比他外表表现的要多得多。早晨,凯瑟琳就知道我辜负了她的信赖,也知道她不得不结束那秘密的拜访。她又哭又闹,反抗这道禁令,并乞求她的父亲可怜可怜小林顿。主人答应会写信通知林顿,并答应只要他高兴就可以来田庄。这是凯瑟琳从她父亲那得到的惟一安慰。但主人说他会在信上说清楚,叫他不要抱有希望在呼啸山庄看到凯瑟琳。如果他知道他外甥的脾气和健康状况的话,那么说不定连这点微小的慰藉都不会给她。

Chapter 25
第二十五章

"These things happened last winter, sir," said Mrs. Dean; "hardly more than a year ago. Last winter, I did not think, at another twelve months' end, I should be amusing a stranger to

"这些事全发生在去年冬天,先生,"迪安太太说,"也就是一年以前。去年冬天,我还想不到,在十二个月后,为了解闷,我会将这些向家里的

the family with relating them! Yet, who knows how long you'll be a stranger? You're too young to rest always contented, living by yourself; and I some way fancy, no one could see Catherine Linton, and not love her. You smile; but why do you look so lively and interested, when I talk about her? And why have you asked me to hang her picture over your fireplace? And why—"

"Stop, my good friend!" I cried. "It may be very possible that I should love her; but would she love me? I doubt it too much to venture my tranquillity by running into temptation and then my home is not here. I'm of the busy world, and to its arms I must return. Go on. Was Catherine obedient to her father's commands?"

"She was," continued the housekeeper. "Her affection for him was still the chief sentiment in her heart; and he spoke without anger. He spoke in the deep tenderness of one about to leave his treasure amid perils and foes, where his remembered words would be the only aid that he could bequeath to guide her. He said to me, a few days afterwards.

"'I wish my nephew would write, Ellen, or call. Tell me, sincerely, what do you think of him? Is he changed for the better, or is there a prospect of improvement, as he grows a man?'

"'He's very delicate, sir,' I replied; 'and scarcely likely to reach manhood. But this I can say, he does not resemble his father; and if Miss Catherine had the misfortune to marry him, he would not be beyond her control unless she were extremely and foolishly indulgent. However, master, you'll have plenty of time to get acquainted with him, and see whether he would

一位生客倾诉！可天晓得你还能呆多久？你太年轻了，不会心满意足地希望孤零零地待下去。我总想，不管谁见了凯瑟琳·林顿，都会爱上她的。你笑啦。为什么每次我谈到她，你总显得如此快活而且很感兴趣呢？你为什么让我把她的画像挂在你的壁炉上面？为什么——"

"别说啦，我的好朋友！"我叫道。"说到我会爱上她，这倒是很可能的。可她会爱上我吗？我对这点持怀疑态度，而且十分怀疑，我才不愿因此动心，拿我的平静来冒险，话说回来，我的家也不在这。我来自于一个熙熙攘攘的世界，最后也必然回到它的怀抱中。我们说下去吧，那么凯瑟琳遵从她父亲的命令吗？"

"她服从了，"管家继续说。"她心中对父亲的爱胜过一切，并主宰着她的感情。而主人是不温不火地规劝她的。他以一种看到他所珍爱的人将陷入危境和敌人手中所怀有的那种深沉的柔情来跟她交谈。而我认为记住他的赠言是帮她引导自己的惟一方法。那之后几天，他对我说："对我外甥的来信或拜访，我是可以接受的，艾伦，老实告诉我，你觉得他这个人怎样，他是否变好一些了，或者说当他成人以后，是否有变好的希望？"

"他很娇气，先生，"我回答说，"而且不像有长大成人的可能。可有一点我确定，他不像他的父亲；如果凯瑟琳小姐不幸嫁给他，他将对凯瑟琳小姐百依百顺，除非她极端愚蠢地纵容他。而且，主人，你还有很多时间去熟识他，看他是否配得上你的女儿，因为他还有四年多才成年呢？"

suit her, it wants four years and more to his being of age.'"

Edgar sighed; and, walking to the window, looked out towards Gimmerton Kirk. It was a misty afternoon but the February sun shone dimly, and we could just distinguish the two fir trees in the yard, and the sparely scattered gravestones.

"I've prayed often," he half soliloquised, "for the approach of what is coming; and now I begin to shrink, and fear it. I thought the memory of the hour I came down that glen a bridegroom would be less sweet than the anticipation that I was soon, in a few months, or, possibly, weeks, to be carried up, and laid in its lonely hollow! Ellen, I've been very happy with my little Cathy. Through winter nights and summer days she was a living hope at my side. But I've been as happy musing by myself among those stones, under that old church: lying, through the long June evenings, on the green mound of her mother's grave, and wishing, yearning for the time when I might lie beneath it What can I do for Cathy? How must I quit her? I'd not care one moment for Linton being Heathcliff's son; nor for his taking her from me, if he could console her for my loss. I'd not care that Heathcliff gained his ends, and triumphed in robbing me of my last blessing! But should Linton be unworthy—only a feeble tool to his father—I cannot abandon her to him! And, hard though it be to crush her buoyant spirit, I must persevere in making her sad while I live, and leaving her solitary when I die. Darling! I'd rather resign her to God, and lay her in the earth before me."

"Resign her to God, as it is, sir," I answered,"and if we should lose you—which may

埃德加叹了口气。独自走到窗前，向窗外的吉默顿教堂望去。那天雾气蒙蒙，下午的时候，二月的太阳淡淡地照着大地．墓园里的两棵枞树和那些零零落落的墓碑清晰可见。

"我经常祈祷，"他像是自言自语地说道，"祈祷该来的快些来，但现在我开始畏缩，而且对将要发生的感到害怕。我曾想，与其回忆从前我走下山谷作新郎的情景，还不如预想再过几个月，或者也许只要几星期，我就会被人抬进一个荒凉的土坑，或许这样想会更甜蜜！艾伦，我和我的小凯茜曾在一起生活得非常快乐，我们度过了许多难忘的冬夜和夏日，她是我心中一个实在的希望。当然在那些墓碑中间，或是在那古老的教堂下面，我也能获得同样的快乐，我还时常想：在那些六月的漫长夜晚，我躺在她母亲绿茵的青冢上，希望着——渴求着某个时候我也能躺在下面。我能为凯茜做些什么呢？我要怎样做才能尽到对她的义务呢？其实我一点也不在乎林顿是希斯克利夫的儿子，也不在乎他将会把她从我身边带走，只要他能安慰因失去了我而难过的她。我也不在乎看到希斯克利夫因夺去我最后的幸福，达到目的而洋洋得意！但如果林顿没出息——只是他父亲的一个软弱的工具——我就不能把她交给他，虽然这样会扑灭她的热情，很残忍，但我决不让步，就让她在我活着的时候难过，在我死后孤独好了。亲爱的，我宁愿在我死前就把她埋葬，让她投入上帝的怀抱。"

"让她像现在这样投入上帝的怀抱好了，先生。"我答道，"如果我们

He forbid—under His providence, I'll stand her friend and counsellor to the last. Miss Catherine is a good girl. I don't fear that she will go wilfully wrong; and people who do their duty are always finally rewarded."

Spring advanced; yet my master gathered no real strength, though he resumed his walks in the grounds with his daughter. To her inexperienced notions, this itself was a sign of convalescence; and then his cheek was often flushed, and his eyes were bright, she felt sure of his recovering.

On her seventeenth birthday, he did not visit the churchyard. It was raining, and I observed —

"You'll surely not go out tonight, sir?"

He answered —

"No, I'll defer it, this year, a little longer."

He wrote again to Linton, expressing his great desire to see him; and, had the invalid been presentable, I've no doubt his father would have permitted him to come. As it was, being instructed, he returned an answer, intimating that Mr. Heathcliff objected to his calling at the Grange; but his uncle's kind remembrance delighted him, and he hoped to meet him, sometimes, in his rambles, and personally to petition that his cousin and he might not remain long so utterly divided.

That part of his letter was simple, and probably his own. Heathcliff knew he could plead eloquently enough for Catherine's company, then —

"I do not ask," he said, "that she may visit here; but, am I never to see her, because my father forbids me to go to her home, and you forbid her to come to mine? Do, now and then,

失去你是天意——但愿上帝会禁止这事——我愿做她终生的朋友和顾问。我并不担心凯瑟琳小姐会有意去做错事，因为她是个好姑娘。而我想凡是尽责的人最后都会得到好报的。"

不知不觉快到春天了；虽然我的主人又恢复同他女儿一起到田间散步的习惯，但他并没有康复起来。凯瑟琳小姐以她那不成熟的眼光判断，还以为能出外散步就是痊愈的象征；而且她还看到父亲的面颊常常发红，眼睛发亮；因此相信他完全康复了。

在她十七岁生日那天，天空中下着雨，主人没去墓园，我对他说：

"今天晚上你肯定不外出了吧，先生？"

他回答说：

"不出去了，今年我要晚一点再去墓园。"

他再次给林顿写信，表示自己渴望能见到他。如果那个病人还能外出见人的话，我敢保证他父亲一定会答应让他来的。但就当时的情况而言，他是来不了的，只是回了一封信，信中暗示他的父亲希斯克利夫先生不许他来田庄。但他也为他舅舅的亲切关怀感到高兴，而且希望能在他外出散步时遇见他，以便当面向舅舅请求不要让他和表姐像这样长期断绝往来。

在他的信中，这部分写得很短，也许因为这才是他心中最想说的话。但希斯克利夫还是知道，他为了能同凯瑟琳在一起是愿意向他诚恳央求的。

他在信中写道："我并不要求她天天到这来，但这并不代表我将永远不见她，不要只因为我父亲不许我去您家，所以您也不愿让她来我家。请您

ride with her towards the Heights; and let us exchange a few words, in your presence! We have done nothing to deserve this separation; and you are not angry with me, you have no reason to dislike me, you allow, yourself. Dear uncle! send me a kind note tomorrow, and leave to join you anywhere you please, except at Thrushcross Grange. I believe an interview would convince you that my father's character is not mine: he affirms I am more your nephew than his son; and though I have faults which render me unworthy of Catherine, she has excused them, and, for her sake, you should also. You inquire after my health – it is better; but while I remain cut off from all hope, and doomed to solitude, or the society of those who never did and never will like me, how can I be cheerful and well?"

  Edgar, though he felt for the boy, could not consent to grant his request; because he could not accompany Catherine. He said, in summer, perhaps, they might meet: meantime, he wished him to continue writing at intervals, and engaged to give him what advice and comfort he was able by letter; being well aware of his hard position in his family. Linton complied; and had he been unre strained, would probably have spoiled all by filling his epistles with complaints and lamentations: but his father kept a sharp watch over him; and, of course, insisted on every line that my master sent being shown; so, instead of penning his peculiar personal sufferings and distresses, the themes constantly uppermost in his thoughts, he harped on the cruel obligation of being held asunder from his friend and love; and gently intimated that Mr.. Linton must allow an interview soon, or he should fear

能偶尔骑马带她到山岗这边来，让我们当着您的面说几句话！我们并没有做过任何该受这种隔离惩罚的事；我想您也并未生我的气，您自己也承认找不出不喜欢我的理由。亲爱的舅舅！希望明天您能给我回一封和气的信，也希望能在您指定的任何地点见见你们，当然除了画眉田庄。我相信在我们见过一次面后，您就会相信我的性格并不像我的父亲。而父亲也常说我更像是您的外甥而不是他的儿子。虽然有些缺点让我配不上凯瑟琳，但她已接受了我，为了她的缘故，您也该接受我。您问起我的健康，现在我觉得好多了。但让我总是活在一个割断了一切希望，注定一生孤寂的环境下，或者同那些永远不会恨我，但也永远不会喜欢我的人生活在一起，我又如何能乐观健康的成长呢？"

  埃德加虽同情那孩子的境遇，但他不能同凯瑟琳一起去，所以并没答应他的请求。他说，也许到了夏天，他们就可以相见。同时，他希望他一有空就来信，而且答应会在回信中尽力劝告和安慰他，因为他很了解他在家中的尴尬地位。林顿接受了舅舅的意见。如果他毫无拘束的话，也许会让信中满是抱怨和悲叹，结果就会把一切搞得一团糟。虽然我主人回的每封信中每一行字他都亲自过目，但由于受到父亲严格的监视，他只得尽量避免在信中流露出个人特有的痛苦和悲伤，虽说这是他脑海中最先想到的题目，他却只能表达他与他的朋友和爱人分离之苦。他还向林顿先生暗示让他们早些见面的必要性，否则他就怀疑林顿先生是不是故意用空话来搪

he was purposely deceiving him with empty promises.

　　Cathy was a powerful ally at home; and, between them, they at length persuaded my master to acquiesce in their having a ride or a walk together, about once a week, under my guardianship, and on the moors nearest the Grange: for June found him still declining; and though he had set aside, yearly, a portion of his income for my young lady's fortune, he had a natural desire that she might retain or at least return in a short time to—the house of her ancestors; and he considered her only prospect of doing that was by a union with his heir; he had no idea that the latter was failing almost as fast as himself; nor had any one, I believe: no doctor visited the Heights, and no one saw Master Heathcliff to make report of his condition, among us. I, for my part, began to fancy my forebodings were false, and that he must be actually rallying, when he mentioned riding and walking on the moors, and seemed so earnest in pursuing his object. I could not picture a father treating a dying child as tyrannically and wickedly as I afterwards learnt Heathcliff had treated him, to compel this apparent eagerness: his efforts redoubling the more imminently his avaricious and unfeeling plans were threatened with defeat by death.

塞他。

　　在家里，凯茜小姐是林顿少爷的有力同盟，他俩内外呼应最终收到了效果，主人同意在有我保护时，让他们每星期在靠近田庄的旷野上一起骑马或散步一次。但到了六月，主人发现自己的身体越来越衰弱。虽然每年他都拨出收入的一部分作为小姐的财产，但他还是希望她能留住祖先的房屋，至少短期内能回去住，而他的惟一指望就是让她和他的继承人结合，但任何人都没想到，甚至连他也没有，这个所谓的继承人会和他一样迅速地衰弱。我相信：从未有医生去过山庄，也没人能把希斯克利夫少爷的情况带回来告诉我们。就我本人也开始怀疑起我的预测，当我听到他提起能在旷野骑马和散步，而且如此真挚的想要实现它时，我还以为他是真的康复了。我无法想像作为一位父亲，对待快死的儿子会像希斯克利夫那样暴虐和恶毒，我后来才知道，一想到自己贪婪无情的计划会因为受到死亡的威胁而失败，他就会变本加厉的行动。

Chapter 26
第二十六章

Summer was already past its prime, when Edgar rel uctantly yielded his assent to their entreaties, and Catherine and I set out on our first ride to join her cousin. It was a close, sultry day: devoid of sunshine, but with a sky too dappled and hazy to threaten rain; and our place of meeting had been fixed at the guide-stone, by the cross-roads. On arriving there, however, a little herd-boy, despatched as a messenger, told us that—

"Maister Linton wer just ut this side th' Heights: and he'd be mitch obleeged to us to gang on a bit further."

"Then Master Linton has forgot the first injunction of his uncle," I observed: "he bid us keep on the Grange land, and here we are, off at once."

"Well, we'll turn our horses' heads round, when we reach him," answered my companion, "our excursion shall lie towards home."

But when we reached him, and that was scarcely a quarter of a mile from his own door, we found he had no horse; and we were forced to dismount, and leave ours to graze. He lay on the heath, awaiting our approach, and did not rise till we came within a few yards. Then he

炎热的夏天差不多过去，埃德加才勉强答应了他们的请求，凯瑟琳和我第一次骑着马启程去看她的表弟。那天的天气格外闷热，虽然没有阳光，但天上却一直阴沉沉的，我们相约在十字路口的指路碑那儿见面。然而，当我们抵达那里时，一个奉命来捎口信的小牧童告诉我们说：

"林顿少爷就在山庄这边，如果你们可以再往前走一点的话，他将会很感激你们。"

"这么说来，林顿少爷已经忘记他舅舅发布的第一道禁令了。"我说，"他只让我们老老实实地呆在田庄里，但现在我们马上就要过界了。"

"那么我们等一会儿到达他那儿就掉转马头吧，"我的同伴答道，"我们到时再回头往家里走。"

可是当我们抵达他那里时，发现离他家门口已经不到四分之一英里了，而且发现他并没有骑马，我们只能下马，让马去吃草。他在草地上平躺着等我们过来，而且一直等我们走到离他只有几码远时他才站起来，看

walked so feebly, and looked so pale, that I immediately exclaimed —

"Why, Master Heathcliff, you are not fit for enjoying a ramble, this morning. How ill you do look?"

Catherine surveyed him with grief and astonishment; and changed the ejaculation of joy on her lips, to one of alarm; and the congratulation on their long postponed meeting to an anxious inquiry, whether he were worse than usual?

"No—better—better!" he panted, trembling, and retaining her hand as if he needed its support, while his large blue eyes wandered timidly over her; the hollowness round them transforming to haggard wildness the languid expression they once possessed.

"But you have been worse," persisted his cousin; "worse than when I saw you last— you are thinner, and —"

"I'm tired," he interrupted, hurriedly. "It is too hot for walking, let us rest here. And, in the morning, I often feel sick—papa says I grow so fast."

Badly satisfied, Cathy sat down, and he reclined beside her.

"This is something like your paradise," said she, making an effort at cheerfulness. "You recollect the two days we agreed to spend in the place and way each thought pleasantest? This is nearly yours, only there are clouds; but then they are so soft and mellow, it is nicer than sunshine. Next week, if you can, we'll ride down to the Grange Park, and try mine."

Linton did not appear to remember what she talked of; and he had evidently great difficulty in sustaining any kind of conversation. His lack of interest in the subjects she started, and his equal incapacity to contribute to her entertainment, were so obvious, that she could not conceal her disappointment. An indefinite alteration had come over his whole person and manner. The pettishness that might be caressed into fondness, had yielded to a listless apathy; there was less of the peevish temper of a child which frets and teases on purpose to be soothed, and more of the self-absorbed moroseness of a confirmed invalid, repelling consolation, and ready to regard the good-humoured mirth of others, as an insult. Catherine perceived, as well as I did, that he held it rather a punishment, than a gratification, to endure our company; and she made no scruple of proposing, presently, to depart. That proposal, unexpectedly, roused Linton from his lethargy, and threw him into a strange state of agitation. He glanced fearfully towards the Heights, begging she would remain another half-hour, at least.

"But, I think," said Cathy, "you'd be more comfortable at home than sitting here; and I cannot amuse you today, I see, by my tales, and songs, and chatter: you have grown wiser than I, in these six months; you have little taste for my diversions now; or else, if I could amuse you, I'd willingly stay."

"Stay to rest yourself," he replied. "And, Catherine, don't think, or say that I'm *very* unwell: it is the heavy weather and heat that make me dull and I walked about, before you came, agreat deal, for me. Tell uncle, I'm in tolerable health, will you?"

"I'll tell him that *you* say so, Linton. I couldn't affirm that you are," observed my young lady, wondering at his pertinacious assertion of what was evidently an untruth.

毫不感兴趣，也同样没有能力使她快乐，这些都显而易见，她也不掩饰她的失望。他整个人以及精神态度已经发生了一种难以说出的变化。原先的那种暴烈性格，本还可以用爱抚软化成娇气，但现在却变成淡漠无情，小孩子为了要寻求安慰而打搅别人的那种任性少了一些，但却增加了一个的确有病的人对自己坏脾气的执拗，抗拒别人的安慰，并打算把别人真诚的快乐看作是一种侮辱。和我一样，凯瑟琳也看出来了，他认为我们在这里陪他是对他的一种惩罚，而不是喜悦，于是她毫不犹豫地提议就此分手。出乎意料那个提议却把林顿从昏昏沉沉的状态中唤醒，堕入另一种莫名其妙的兴奋。他胆怯地朝山庄瞟了一眼，求她再逗留至少半个小时。

"但是依我看，"凯茜说，"你待在家要比坐在这里舒服多了，现在我再也不能用我讲的故事、唱的歌儿以及陪你聊天来给你解闷了。在这六个月里，你变得比我还要聪明了，现在你对我的消遣已经不感兴趣了；不过，如果我还可以给你解闷的话，我是愿意继续留下来的。"

"留下来，歇歇吧，"他回答说，"凯瑟琳，不要想、也不要说我很不开心，是这酷热的天气使我无精打采的，何况在你来之前我已经到处走了，对我来说，是走得太多了。请你转告舅舅说我还健康，好吗？"

"我会跟他说是你要我这么说的，林顿。因为我不能确定你的身体是否健康，"我的小姐说，不理解他为什么那样倔强地一味强调那些显然与事

"And be here again next Thursday," continued he, shunning her puzzled gaze. "And give him my thanks for permitting you to come—my best thanks, Catherine. And—and, if you *did* meet my father, and he asked you about me, don't lead him to suppose that I've been extremely silent and stupid: don't look sad and downcast, as you *are* doing— he'll be angry."

"I care nothing for his anger," exclaimed Cathy, imagining she would be its object.

"But I do," said her cousin, shuddering. "*Don't* provoke him against me, Catherine, for he is very hard."

"Is he severe to you, Master Heathcliff?" I inquired. "Has he grown weary of indulgence, and passed from passive, to active hatred?"

Linton looked at me, but did not answer; and, after keeping her seat by his side another ten minutes, during which his head fell drowsily on his breast, and he uttered nothing except suppressed moans of exhaustion or pain, Cathy began to seek solace in looking for bilberries, and sharing the produce of her researches with me: she did not offer them to him, for she saw further notice would only weary and annoy.

"Is it half an hour now, Ellen!" she whispered in my ear, at last. "I can't tell why we should stay. He's asleep, and papa will be wanting us back."

"Well, we must not leave him asleep," I answered; "wait till he wakes, and be patient. You were mighty eager to set off, but your longing to see poor Linton has soon evaporated!"

"Why did *he* wish to see me?" returned Catherine. "In his crossest humours, formerly, I liked him better than I do in his present curious

实不符的话。

"而且下星期四再到这里来,"他接着说,避开她略带困惑的目光。"替我谢谢他答应让你过来——向他致谢——非常感谢,凯瑟琳。还有——还有,假如你真的遇到了我父亲,他向你问起我的话,千万别让他觉得我是极其寡言木讷的,别表现出一付垂头丧气的样子,就像你现在这样——他会生气的。"

"我才不在乎他是不是在生气哩,"凯茜一想到他会生她的气,就嚷道。

"但是我在乎,"她的表弟战栗着说,"千万不要惹他来责怪我,凯瑟琳,因为他对我非常严厉。"

"他对你很凶吗,希斯克利夫少爷?"我问道,"他是不是已经逐渐厌倦了一味的放任和纵容,开始由消极的恨转变成为积极的恨了?"

林顿看了我一眼,一句话也没说,她又在他身旁坐了十分钟,在这十分钟里,他把头低在胸前,昏昏欲睡,什么也不说,只是发出因为疲劳或痛苦而产生的压抑的呻吟,凯瑟琳开始到处寻找覆盆子来解闷,她把找到的覆盆子分了一点给我,不过并没有分给他,因为她看出如果再来理睬他反而会使他不耐烦。

"现在有半个小时了吧,艾伦!"最后,她在我耳边小声说道,"我不知道为什么我们非待在这里不可。他睡着了,爸爸也该正盼着我们回去。"

"不过,我们绝不能丢下他一个人在这睡觉,"我回答说,"等他醒过来再说吧,要忍耐。你本来是非常热心地出来见他的,可你对可怜的林顿的思念这么快就消散啦!"

mood. It's just as if it were a task he was compelled to perform—this interview— for fear his father should scold him. But I'm hardly going to come to give Mr. Heathcliff pleasure; whatever reason he may have for ordering Linton to undergo this penance. And, though I'm glad he's better in health, I'm sorry he's so much less pleasant, and so much less affectionate to me."

"You think *he is* better in health, then?" I said.

"Yes," she answered; "because he always made such a great deal of his sufferings, you know. He is not tolerably well, as he told me to tell papa; but he's better, very likely."

"There you differ with me, Miss Cathy," I remarked; "I should conjecture him to be far worse."

Linton here started from his slumber in bewildered terror, and asked if any one had called his name.

"No," said Catherine; "unless in dreams. I cannot conceive how you manage to dose, out of doors, in the morning."

"I thought I heard my father," he gasped, glancing up to the frowning nab above us. "You are sure nobody spoke?"

"Quite sure," replied his cousin. "Only Ellen and I were disputing concerning your health. Are you truly stronger, Linton, than when we separated in winter? If you be, I'm certain one thing is not stronger— your regard for me—speak, are you?"

The tears gushed from Linton's eyes as he answered, "Yes, yes, I am!" And, still under the spell of the imaginary voice, his gaze wandered up and down to detect its owner. Cathy rose.

"但他为什么想要见我呢？"凯瑟琳回答，"相对于他现在的古怪心情而言，我反倒比较喜欢他从前那种别扭脾气。现在正像他被人强迫过来完成一个任务似的——我是说这次见面——惟恐他父亲会责怪他。可是我来可不是想要给希斯克利夫先生解闷的，我才不管他有什么理由命令林顿来受这种罪。虽然我很欣慰他的健康状况有所改善，但他却变得如此不开心，而且对我也很冷淡，这使我很难过。"

"那么依你之见，他的健康状况有所好转吗？"我说。

"是的，"她回答，"你应该知道他可是很会夸大他所受的痛苦的。虽然他现在不像他叫我告诉爸爸的那样已经好多了，但他确实真的好些了。"

"在这一点上我和你看法不一样，"我说，"我觉得他比以前更糟了。"

此时林顿从睡梦中惊醒过来，问我们刚才是否有人喊过他的名字。

"没有，"凯瑟琳说，"除非刚才你是在做梦。我真难以想像你为什么一大早都要在外面打瞌睡。"

"我觉得好像听到我父亲的声音了，"他喘息着，朝我们头上森严的山顶望了一眼。"你们确定刚才没人说话吗？"

"绝对没有，"他表姐回答，"刚才只有艾伦和我在讨论你的健康状况。林顿，你真的要比我们在冬天分手时更强壮些吗？如果是的话，我确信有一点却没有任何增强——你对我的重视程度——你说呢，到底是不是？"

"是的，是的，我是比那时更强壮一些！"他回答的时候，眼泪夺眶而出。他仍然被那存在于他想像之中

"For today we must part," she said. "And I won't conceal that I have been sadly disappointed with our meeting, though I'll mention it to nobody but you: not that I stand in awe of Mr. Heathcliff!"

"Hush," murmured Linton; "for God's sake, hush! He's coming." And he clung to Catherine's arm, striving to detain her; but at that announcement she hastily disengaged herself, and whistled to Minny, who obeyed like a dog.

"I'll be here next Thursday," she cried, springing to the saddle. "Good-bye. Quick, Ellen!"

And so we left him, scarcely conscious of our departure, so absorbed was he in anticipating his father's approach.

Before we reached home, Catherine's displeasure softened into a perplexed sensation of pity and regret, largely blended with vague, uneasy doubts about Linton's actual circumstances, physical and social: in which I partook, though I counselled her not to say much; for a second journey would make us better judges. My master requested an account of our on-goings. His nephew's offering of thanks was duly delivered, Miss Cathy gently touching on the rest: I also, threw little light on his inquiries, for I hardly knew what to hide, and what to reveal.

的声音控制，眼睛东张西望地寻找那个发出声音的人。凯茜站起来。"现在该是我们分手的时候了，"她说，"我不瞒你，对于我们的这次见面，我感到万分失望，不过除了跟你，我不会跟其他任何人说的，但那不是因为我害怕希斯克利夫先生才这么做。"

"嘘，"林顿喃喃地说，"看在上帝的面子上，什么话都别说！他已经来啦。"他抓住凯瑟琳的手臂，想把她留住，但一听这个宣告，她赶忙挣脱，朝着敏妮的方向呼啸一声，它像条狗一样闻声跑来。

"下星期四我到这儿来，"她喊道，翻身跳上马鞍，"再见。赶快，艾伦！"

于是我们就这样离开了他，但他却还没有注意到我们已经走开，因为他正在全心全意地等待着他父亲的到来。

我们还没到家之前，凯瑟琳内心的不快已经转化成为一种怜惜与同情交织的困惑的感情，其中大部分还掺杂着对林顿身体与处境的实际情况所感到的隐约的、不安的担心，我也有同感，虽然我告诫她不要说得太过分，因为第二次的出游或许有利于我们做出更正确的判断。我的主人要我们向他汇报出去的情形，除了转达他外甥的致谢外，凯茜小姐把其他所有事情都轻描淡写地随口带过了，对于主人的追问，我也没有多说什么，因为我真的不清楚应该隐瞒什么和说出什么。

Chapter 27
第二十七章

Seven days glided away, every one marking its course by the henceforth rapid alteration of Edgar Linton's state. The havoc that months had previously wrought was now emulated by the inroads of hours. Catherine, we would fain have deluded yet; but her own quick spirit refused to delude her: it divined in secret, and brooded on the dreadful probability, gradually ripening into certainty. She had not the heart to mention her ride, when Thursday came round; I mentioned it for her, and obtained permission to order her out of doors: for the library, where her father stopped a short time daily—the brief period he could bear to sit up—and his chamber, had become her whole world. She grudged each moment that did not find her bending over his pillow, or seated by his side. Her countenance grew wan with watching and sorrow, and my master gladly dismissed her to what he flattered himself would be a happy change of scene and society; drawing comfort from the hope that she would not now be left entirely alone after his death.

He had a fixed idea, I guessed by several observations he let fall, that as his nephew resembled him in person, he would resemble him

七天很快过去，埃德加·林顿的病情一天天急剧恶化。前几个月他的身体已经垮了，如今更是一小时一小时地恶化着。我们原本想瞒着凯瑟琳，但以她的机灵，骗过她很难。她暗自揣量着最可怕的事发生的可能，但那可能已逐渐发展为必然了。星期四又来临时，她已没有心情提起骑马的事，于是我建议并得到了许可陪她到户外去。因为图书室（她父亲每天只能待一会儿，而且只能坐很短的时间）和他的卧室，已成为她的全部世界。她愿意每分每秒都伏在他枕旁，或是坐在他身边。她的脸色由于守护和悲哀而变得苍白，主人希望她出去走走，以为这样能使她乐于改变一下环境和同伴，在他死后她也不至于孤零零的，他想用这来安慰自己。

他有一个坚定的想法，那是我从他好几次谈话中猜到的，就是既然他的外甥长得像他，内心也一定像他，

in mind; for Linton's letters bore few or no indications of his defective character. And I, through pardonable weakness, refrained from cor- recting the error; asking myself what good there would be in disturbing his last moments with information that he had neither power nor opportunity to turn to account.

We deferred our excursion till the afternoon; a golden afternoon of August: every breath from the hills so full of life, that it seemed whoever respired it, though dying, might revive. Catherine's face was just like the landscape—shadows and sunshine flitting over it in rapid succession; but the shadows rested longer, and the sunshine was more transient; and her poor little heart reproached itself for even that passing forgetfulness of its cares.

We discerned Linton watching at the same spot he had selected before. My young mistress alighted, and told me that as she was resolved to stay a very little while, I had better hold the pony and remain on horseback; but I dissented: I wouldn't risk losing sight of the charge committed to me a minute; so we climbed the slope of heath together. Master Heathcliff received us with greater animation on the occasion: not the animation of high spirits though, nor yet of joy; it looked more like fear.

"It is late!" he said, speaking short and with difficulty. "Is not your father very ill? I thought you wouldn't come."

"Why won't you be candid?" cried Catherine, swallowing her greeting. "Why cannot you say at once, you don't want me? It is strange Linton, that for the second time, you have brought me here on purpose, apparently, to distress us both, and for no reason besides!"

因为林顿的信中很少或根本没有显示过他的缺点。而我，因为可以原谅他的软弱，克制着不去纠正这错误，我自问：在他生命的最后时刻，对这消息他既无力也无机会扭转，反倒使他心烦意躁，让他知道又有什么好处呢。

我们把出游推迟到下午，是八月里一个难得美妙的下午：山上吹来的风里洋溢着生命的气息，仿佛无论谁吸了它，即便是奄奄一息的人，也会立刻复活。凯瑟琳的脸恰似那道风景——阴影与阳光交替着飞掠而过，但阴影停留的时间更长，阳光则比较短暂，她那颗小小的可怜的心甚至因为偶然忘了忧愁还责备自己呢。

我们看到林顿还在他上次选择的地方等着。我的小女主人跳下马，告诉我，她决定只待一会工夫，我最好骑在马上牵着她的小马，但我不同意，我不能冒险有一分钟看不见我的被监护者，所以我们一起爬上草地的斜坡。这次希斯克利夫少爷迎接我们时显得兴奋多了，不过不是兴高采烈的兴奋，也不是快乐的兴奋，倒更像是害怕。

"来晚了！"他说，说得短促吃力，"你父亲不是病得很重吗？我以为你不来了呢。"

"为什么你不坦白直说呢？"凯瑟琳叫着，把她的问候硬生生吞下去没说，"难道你不能直截了当说你不需要我吗？真特别啊，林顿，你硬要我第二次来这儿，却不过是让我们俩都受罪，此外毫无理由！"

Linton shivered, and glanced at her, half supplicating, half ashamed; but his cousin's patience was not sufficient to endure this enigmatical behaviour.

"My father *is* very ill," she said;"and why am I called from his bedside — why didn't you send to absolve me from my promise, when you wished I wouldn't keep it? Come! I desire an explanation: playing and trifling are completely banished out of my mind; and I can't dance attendance on your affections, now!"

"My affections!" he murmured; "what are they? For Heaven's sake Catherine, don't look so angry! Despise me as much as you please; I am a worthless, cowardly wretch: I can't be scorned enough! but I'm too mean for your anger—hate my father, and spare me, for contempt."

"Nonsense!" cried Catherine, in a passion. "Foolish, silly boy! And there! he trembles, as if I were really going to touch him! You needn't bespeak contempt, Linton: anybody will have it spontaneously, at your service. Get off! I shall return home: it is folly dragging you from the hearth-stone, and pretending—what do we pretend? Let go my frock! If I pitied you for crying and looking so very frightened, you should spurn such pity. Ellen, tell him how disgraceful this conduct is. Rise, and don't degrade yourself into an abject reptile—*don't*."

With streaming face and an expression of agony, Linton had thrown his nerveless frame along the ground: he seemed convulsed with exquisite terror.

"Oh!" he sobbed, "I cannot bear it! Catherine, Catherine, I'm a traitor too, and I

林顿颤抖着，半是乞求、半是羞愧地瞅了她一眼，但他的表姐却没有耐心忍受这种暧昧的态度。

"的确，我父亲病得很重，"她说，"那为什么要叫我离开他的床边呢？你既然希望我不守诺言，为什么不派人送信叫我不要来啦？来！给我一个解释，我完全没有游戏瞎聊的心情，现在我再也不想给你的装腔作势凑趣了！"

"我装腔作势！"他喃喃着，"那是什么呢？凯瑟琳，看在上帝面上请不要这么生气！随你怎么看不起我好了，我是个没出息的软弱的可怜虫，嘲笑我是不够的，但我根本就不配让你生气。恨我父亲吧，蔑视我吧，就是饶了我了。"

"无聊！"凯瑟琳激动地大叫，"糊涂的傻瓜，看啊，他在颤抖，好像我真要碰他似的！你用不着请求蔑视，林顿：任何人随时都会自然而然地鄙视你。滚开！我要回家了。简直可笑之极，把你从壁炉边拖出来，装作——我们还装什么呢？放开我的衣服！假如我因为你的哭泣和你这惊恐万分的神态而怜悯你，你也该拒绝这种怜悯。艾伦，告诉他这种行为多不体面。起来，可别把你自己看成一个下贱的小爬虫——可别！"

林顿泪如雨下，带着一种痛苦的表情，他的身子软弱无力地扑倒在地上，仿佛因为一种强烈的恐惧而不住痉挛。

"啊，"他啜泣着，"我受不了啦！凯瑟琳，凯瑟琳，我是个背信弃义的

dare not tell you! But leave me and I shall be killed! *Dear* Catherine, my life is in your hands: and you have said you loved me— and if you did, it wouldn't harm you. You'll not go, then? kind, sweet, good Catherine! And perhaps you *will* consent—and he'll let me die with you!"

My young lady, on witnessing his intense anguish, stooped to raise him. The old feeling of indulgent tenderness overcame her vexation, and she grew thoroughly moved and alarmed.

"Consent to what?" she asked. "To stay? Tell me the meaning of this strange talk, and I will. You contradict your own words, and distract me! Be calm and frank, and confess at once all that weighs on your heart. You wouldn't injure me, Linton, would you? You wouldn't let any enemy hurt me, if you could prevent it? I'll believe you are a coward, for yourself, but not a cowardly betrayer of your best friend."

"But my father threatened me," gasped the boy, clasping his attenuated fingers, "and I dread him—I dread him! I *dare* not tell!"

"Oh well!" said Catherine, with scornful compassion, "keep your secret, *I'm* no coward—save yourself: I'm not afraid!"

Her magnanimity provoked his tears: he wept wildly, kissing her supporting hands, and yet could not summon courage to speak out. I was cogitating what the mystery might be, and determined Catherine should never suffer to benefit him or any one else, by my good will; when hearing a rustle among the ling, I looked up, and saw Mr. Heathcliff almost close upon us, descending the Heights. He didn't cast a glance towards my companions, though they

人，我不敢告诉你！可如果你离我而去，我就别想活啦！亲爱的凯瑟琳，我的命在你手里。你说过爱我的，你要是真爱，那不会对你不利的。你不要走，好吗？亲爱的好凯瑟琳！或许你会答应——他要我死也要跟你在一起啊！"

我的小姐看他痛苦的样子，就弯腰去扶他。往日宽容的温情彻底压倒她的气恼，她被完全感动而且吓住了。

"答应什么？"她问道，"答应留下吗？告诉我你这奇怪的话的意思，我就留下来。你的话前后矛盾，要把我搞糊涂了！静下心来坦诚些，说说你心里所有的负担。我想你不会伤害我的，林顿，是吗？如果你能制止，你不会让任何敌人伤害我吧？我能确信你只是自己软弱胆小，但总不致会是一个懦弱地背叛你最好朋友的人吧。"

"但我的父亲威胁我，"那孩子喘着气，紧握着他的瘦长手指，"我怕他——我怕他！我不敢说呀！"

"啊！好吧！"凯瑟琳带着讥讽的怜悯说道，"守着你的秘密吧，我可不是懦夫。拯救你自己吧，我可不怕！"

她的宽宏大量激起他的眼泪，他发疯似的大哭，亲吻着她搀扶他的手，但仍不能鼓起勇气说出来。我正思考这是什么秘密，我已决心不让凯瑟琳为了让他或任何其他人受益而委屈自己，这是我的美好愿望。这时我听到石楠林中传来一阵簌簌的响声，抬头一看，只见希斯克利夫正走下山庄，已经离我们很近了。他看都不看我所陪着的这两个人，即使他们离得

were sufficiently near for Linton's sobs to be audible; but hailing me in the almost hearty tone he assumed to none besides, and the sincerity of which, I couldn't avoid doubting, he said—

"It is something to see you so near to my house, Nelly! How are you at the Grange? Let us hear! The rumour goes," he added in a lower tone, "that Edgar Linton is on his deathbed: perhaps they exaggerate his illness?"

"No; my master is dying," I replied: "it is true enough. A sad thing it will be for us all, but a blessing for him!"

"How long will he last, do you think?" he asked.

"I don't know," I said.

"Because," he continued, looking at the two young people, who were fixed under his eye—Linton appeared as if he could not venture to stir, or raise his head, and Catherine could not move, on his account—, "Because that lad yonder, seems determined to beat me; and I'd thank his uncle to be quick, and go before him—Hallo! Has the whelp been playing that game long? I *did* give him some lessons about snivelling. Is he pretty lively with Miss Linton generally?"

"Lively? No—he has shown the greatest distress," I answered. "To see him, I should say, that instead of rambling with his sweetheart on the hills, he ought to be in bed, under the hands of a doctor."

"He shall be, in a day or two," muttered Heathcliff. "But first— get up, Linton! Get up!" he shouted. "Don't grovel on the ground, there—up this moment!"

Linton had sunk prostrate again in another

paroxysm of helpless fear, caused by his father's glance towards him, I suppose: there was nothing else to produce such humiliation. He made several efforts to obey, but his little strength was annihilated for the time, and he fell back again with a moan. Mr. Heathcliff advanced, and lifted him to lean against a ridge of turf.

"Now," said he, with curbed ferocity, "I'm getting angry; and if you don't command that paltry spirit of yours—*Damn* you! Get up, directly!"

"I will, father!" he panted. "Only, let me alone, or I shall faint! I've done as you wished, I'm sure. Catherine will tell you that I—that I —have been cheerful. Ah! keep by me Catherine; give me your hand."

"Take mine," said his father; "stand on your feet. There now—she'll lend you her arm: that's right, look at *her*. You would imagine I was the devil himself, Miss Linton, to excite such horror. Be so kind as to walk home with him, will you? He shudders, if I touch him."

"Linton, dear!" whispered Catherine, "I can't go to Wuthering Heights... papa has forbidden me... He'll not harm you: why are you so afraid?"

"I can never re-enter that house," he answered. "I'm *not* to re-enter i t without you!"

"Stop..." cried his father. "We'll respect Catherine's filial scruples. Nelly, take him in, and I'll follow your advice concerning the doctor, without delay."

"You'll do well," replied I, "but I must remain with my mistress. To mind your son is not my business."

"You are very stiff," said Heathcliff, "I

又伏到地上,我想这是因为他父亲看了他一眼的缘故,没有其他可能产生这种屈辱。他好几次努力想服从,但他仅有的可怜的体力已经消失了,他呻吟了一声又倒下去。希斯克利夫走上前,把他拎起来,靠在一个隆起的草堆上。

"现在,"他带着压抑着的凶狠说,"如果你不能振作你那点精神的话,我要生气了——你这该死的!马上起来!"

"我就起,父亲,"他喘息着,"只是,不要逼我,不然我就要晕倒啦。我保证我已按照你的吩咐做了。凯瑟琳会告诉你的,我——我——本来很高兴的。啊,来我这边待着,凯瑟琳,把你的手给我。"

"抓住我的手,"他父亲说,"站起来。好了——她会把她的胳膊伸给你的,这就对啦,看着她吧。林顿小姐,你该想到,我就是造成这种恐怖的恶魔吧,请你做做好事,陪他一起回家,可以吗? 我一碰他,他就浑身发抖。"

"林顿,亲爱的!"凯瑟琳低声说,"我不能去呼啸山庄……爸爸禁止我去……他不会伤害你的,你为什么这样害怕?"

"我永远不能回到那个房子啦,"他答道,"如果没有你一块回去,我再也不能进去啦!"

"住嘴!"他的父亲喊道,"凯瑟琳出于孝心有所顾忌,我们应当尊重。内莉,带他进去吧,我要听你的建议去请医生,绝不拖延了。"

"你可以自己带他回去,"我回答说,"我必须跟我的小姐在一起,照顾

know that: but you'll force me to pinch the baby, and make it scream, before it moves your charity. Come then, my hero. Are you willing to return, escorted by me?"

He approached once more, and made as if he would seize the fragile being; but shrinking back, Linton clung to his cousin, and implored her to accompany him, with a frantic importunity that admitted no denial. However I disapproved, I couldn't hinder her: indeed how could she have refused him herself? What was filling him with dread we had no means of discerning; but there he was, powerless under its gripe, and any addition seemed capable of shocking him into idiocy. We reached the threshold; Catherine walked in; and I stood waiting till she had conducted the invalid to a chair, expecting her out immediately; when Mr. Heathcliff, pushing me forward, exclaimed —

"My house is not stricken with the plague, Nelly; and I have a mind to be hospitable today: sit down, and allow me to shut the door."

He shut and locked it also. I started.

"You shall have tea, before you go home," he added."I am by myself. Hareton is gone with some cattle to the Lees — and Zillah and Joseph are off on a journey of pleasure. And, though I'm used to being alone, I'd rather have some interesting company, if I can get it. Miss Linton, take your seat by *him*. I give you what I have: the present is hardly worth accepting; but, I have nothing else to offer. It is Linton, I mean. How she does stare! It's odd what a savage feeling I have to anything that seems afraid of me! Had I been born where laws are less strict, and tastes less dainty, I should treat myself to a slow vivisection of those two, as an evening's

你的儿子可不是我的事。"

"你真是顽固,"希斯克利夫说,"我知道的。但你这是在逼我掐痛这婴儿,让他高声尖叫,打动你的慈悲心肠。那么,来吧,我的英雄。现在由我护送,你可愿意回去?"

他再次走近林顿,做出想要抓住那个脆弱东西的模样,但林顿向后退着,粘住他的表姐不放,显出一副疯狂而死乞白赖的神情,简直不容人拒绝。无论我怎样反对,我也不能阻止她,说实话,她又怎忍心拒绝他呢?我们不知道是什么让他充满恐惧,但他就在那儿,无力地在它掌控之中,好像再加上任何一点点吓,就会把他吓成白痴。我们抵达门口后,凯瑟琳走进去,我站在那儿等着她把病人扶到椅子上,希望她马上出来,这时,希斯克利夫先生把我往前一推,叫道:

"我的房子并没有瘟疫,内莉,今天我还想款待一下客人哩,坐下,我去关门。"

他关上门,又锁上。我大吃一惊。

"你们回家之前可以喝点茶,"他又说,"只有我一个人。哈里顿到里斯河边放牛去了,希拉和约瑟夫出去玩了,虽然我习惯一个人呆着,要是可以,我还是希望有几个有趣的伙伴。林顿小姐,坐到他旁边吧。我把我的一切都送给你,虽然这份礼物简直不值得接受,但我没有别的可以献出来啦。我意思是指林顿。你瞪眼干吗!真奇怪,对任何看起来像是怕我的东西,我心里就会涌起一种非常野蛮的感觉!假如我生长在法律不严格、风尚野蛮的地方,我一定会慢慢地对这两位进行活体解剖,作为晚上的娱

amusement."

He drew in his breath, struck the table, and swore to himself, "By hell! I hate them."

"I'm not afraid of you!" exclaimed Catherine, who could not hear the latter part of his speech. She stepped close up; her black eyes flashing with passion and resolution. "Give me that key: I will have it!" she said. "I wouldn't eat or drink here, if I were starving."

Heathcliff had the key in his hand that remained on the table. He looked up, seized with a sort of surprise at her boldness; or, possibly, reminded by her voice and glance, of the person from whom she inherited it. She snatched at the instrument, and half succeeded in getting it out of his loosened fingers: but her action recalled him to the present; he recovered it speedily.

"Now, Catherine Linton," he said, "stand off, or I shall knock you down; and that will make Mrs. Dean mad."

Regardless of this warning, she captured his closed hand and its contents again. "We will go!" she repeated, exerting her utmost efforts to cause the iron muscles to relax; and finding that her nails made no impression, she applied her teeth pretty sharply. Heathcliff glanced at me a glance that kept me from interfering a moment. Catherine was too intent on his fingers to notice his face. He opened them suddenly, and resigned the object of dispute; but, ere she had well secured it, he seized her with the liberated hand, and, pulling her on his knee, administered with the other a shower of terrific slaps on both sides of the head, each sufficient to have fulfilled his threat, had she been able to fall.

At this diabolical violence, I rushed on

乐。"

他倒吸口气，捶着桌子，诅咒着："我愿对着地狱发誓！我恨他们。"

"我不怕你！"凯瑟琳大叫道，她受不了他所说的后半段话。她走到他跟前，黑色的眼眸里闪烁着怒火和决心。"把钥匙给我，我要！"她说："就算饿死，我也不会在这里吃喝。"

希斯克利夫把放在桌上的钥匙拿在手里。他抬头看她，她的勇敢反而使他惊讶，或许，他可能从她的声音和眼神中想起把这些遗传给她的那个人。她抓住钥匙，差点就从他那松开的手指间拽出它，但她的动作让他回到现实，很快，他就恢复过来。

"现在，凯瑟琳·林顿，"他说道，"站开，不然我就把你打倒，不过那样迪安太太会发疯的。"

不顾这警告，她又一次抓住他那紧握的拳头和拳头里的东西。"我们一定要走！"她重复说，使出她全身力量想使这钢铁般的肌肉松开，当发现指甲没有效果时，她便开始使劲用牙齿咬。希斯克利夫瞟了我一眼，这让我分了神，不能马上干预。凯瑟琳只注意他的手指，忽略了他的脸。忽然他松开手指，把这引起争执的东西给扔出去，不过，在她还没拿到那之前，他用那松开的手抓住她，把她拉到面前跪下，另一只手朝她的头脸一通暴风骤雨似的乱打，要是她能倒下，只需一下就能达到他威胁的目的了。

看到这凶恶的狂暴，我愤怒地冲

him furiously. "You villain!" I began to cry, "you villain!" A touch on the chest silenced me: I am stout, and soon put out of breath; and, what with that and the rage, I staggered dizzily back, and felt ready to suffocate, or to burst a blood-vessel.

The scene was over in two minutes; Catherine, released, put her two hands to her temples, and looked just as if she were not sure whether her ears were off or on. She trembled like a reed, poor thing, and leant against the table perfectly bewildered.

"I know how to chastise children, you see," said the scoundrel, grimly, as he stooped to repossess himself of the key, which had dropped to the floor. "Go to Linton now, as I told you; and cry at your ease! I shall be your father, tomorrow— all the father you'll have in a few days—and you shall have plenty of that— you can bear plenty—you're no weakling — you shall have a daily taste, if I catch such a devil of a temper in your eyes again!"

Cathy ran to me instead of Linton, and knelt down, and put her burning cheek on my lap, weeping aloud. Her cousin had shrunk into a corner of the settle, as quiet as a mouse, congratulating himself, I dare say, that the correction had lighted on another than him. Mr. Heathcliff, perceiving us all confounded, rose, and expeditiously made the tea himself. The cups and saucers were laid ready. He poured it out, and handed me a cup.

"Wash away your spleen," he said. "And help your own naughty pet and mine. It is not poisoned, though I prepared it. I'm going out to seek your horses."

Our first thought, on his departure, was to

到他面前,"你这混蛋!"我开始大叫,"你这混蛋!"他当胸一拳就让我住嘴了:我很胖,一下就喘不过气来;加上那一击和内心的愤怒,我昏昏沉沉地踉跄倒退,觉得就快闷死了,或者血管爆裂。

不到两分钟,这场闹剧就结束了,凯瑟琳被放开,她两只手放在太阳穴上,好像还不能准确知道自己的耳朵是否还在上面。她像一根芦苇似的颤抖着,那个可怜的东西则完全六神无主地靠在桌边。

"你看,我知道怎么惩罚孩子们,"这个无赖恶狠狠地说,弯腰捡起掉在地板上的钥匙,"现在,按照我吩咐你的,到林顿那儿去痛快地哭个够吧!我就是你父亲了,明天——在这一两天之内你将只有我这一个父亲了——你还有很多罪要受呢。你倒是能受得住,不是个草包,如果再让我看见你眼里有这种该死的神情,就给我每天尝一次这滋味!"

凯茜并没到林顿那儿去,却跑到我面前,跪下来,把她发烫的脸挨着我的膝,放声大哭。她的表弟则缩在躺椅的一角,静得像只耗子,我敢肯定他在暗自庆幸这场惩罚降临在别人而非他自己头上。希斯克利夫看我们都吓坏了,就站起来,很麻利地自己去沏茶。茶杯和碟子都摆好了。他倒了茶,递给我一杯。

"快把你的臭脾气冲掉,"他说,"帮个忙,给你那淘气宝贝和我的孩子倒杯茶。虽然这是我预备的,可没有下毒。我要出去找你们的马。"

他一走,我们第一个念头就是找

force an exit somewhere. We tried the kitchen door, but that was fastened outside: we looked at the windows—they were too narrow for even Cathy's little figure.

"Master Linton," I cried, seeing we were regularly imprisoned;"you know what your diabolical father is after, and you shall tell us, or I'll box your ears, as he has done your cousin's."

"Yes, Linton; you must tell," said Catherine."It is for your sake I came; and it will be wickedly ungrateful if you refuse."

"Give me some tea, I'm thirsty, and then I'll tell you," he answered. "Mrs. Dean, go away. I don't like you standing over me. Now, Catherine, you are letting your tears fall into my cup! I won't drink that. Give me another."

Catherine pushed another to him, and wiped her face. I felt disgusted at the little wretch's composure, since he was no longer in terror for himself. The anguish he had exhibited on the moor subsided as soon as ever he entered Wuthering Heights; so I guessed he had been menaced with an awful visitation of wrath if he failed in decoying us there; and, that accomplished, he had no further immediate fears.

"Papa wants us to be married," he continued, after sipping some of the liquid. "And he knows your papa wouldn't let us marry now; and he's afraid of my dying, if we wait; so we are to be married in the morning, and you are to stay here all night; and, if you do as he wishes, you shall return home next day, and take me with you."

"Take you with her, pitiful changeling?" I exclaimed. "*You* marry? Why, the man is mad! or he thinks us fools, everyone. And do you imagine that beautiful young lady, that

"林顿少爷,"我叫道,眼看我们已经正式被囚禁了,"你知道你那凶狠的父亲想干什么,快告诉我们,不然我就打你耳光,像他打你表姐那样。"

"没错,林顿,你必须告诉我们,"凯瑟琳说,"因为你,我才来,如果你不说,那也太忘恩负义。"

"给我点茶,我渴啦,然后我就告诉你,"他答道,"迪安太太,走开,我讨厌你站在我面前。瞧,凯瑟琳,你把眼泪滴到我茶杯里了,我不喝那杯,再给我倒一杯。"

凯瑟琳把另一杯茶递给他,擦擦他的脸。这小可怜虫若无其事的态度让我感到极其厌恶,他已不再为他自己感到恐惧了。当他一走进呼啸山庄,他在旷野上所表现出的痛苦就全都消失,所以我猜他一定受了一场暴怒的惩罚的威胁,如果他不能成功地把我们引诱到这里,就饶不过一顿毒打,不过眼下事已成功,他也就没有什么恐惧了。

"爸爸要我俩结婚,"他喝了口茶,接着说,"他知道你爸爸绝对不允许我们现在结婚,但如果我们等着,他又担心我死掉,因此我们明早就结婚,你必须在这儿住一夜,如果一切如他所愿,第二天你就可以回家,还可以带我一起。"

"带你跟她一起去,你这可怜的白痴!"我叫起来,"和你结婚?那个人肯定疯了!要不就是他以为我们是傻子,大家都是。你以为这个美丽

healthy, hearty girl, will tie herself to a little perishing monkey like you? Are you cherishing the notion that *anybody*, let alone Miss Catherine Linton, would have you for a husband? You want whipping for bringing us in here at all, with your dastardly, puling tricks; and—don't look so silly now! I've a very good mind to shake you severely, for your contemptible treachery, and your imbecile conceit."

I did give him a slight shaking; but it brought on the cough, and he took to his ordinary resource of moaning and weeping, and Catherine rebuked me.

"Stay all night? No!" she said, looking slowly round. "Ellen, I'll burn that door down, but I'll get out."

And she would have commenced the execution of her threat directly, but Linton was up in alarm, for his dear self, again. He clasped her in his two feeble arms, sobbing—

"Won't you have me, and save me—not let me come to the Grange? Oh! darling Catherine! you mustn't go, and leave me, after all. You *must* obey my father, you *must*!"

"I must obey my own," she replied, "and relieve him from this cruel suspense. The whole night! What would he think? he'll be distressed already. I'll either break or burn a way out of the house. Be quiet! You're in no danger—but, if you hinder me—Linton, I love papa better than you!"

The mortal terror he felt of Mr. Heathcliff's anger, restored to the boy his coward's eloquence. Catherine was near distraught: still, she persisted that she must go home, and tried entreaty, in her turn, persuading him to subdue his selfish agony.

的小姐，这个健康活泼的姑娘会把自己拴在一个像你这样快死的小猴子身边吗？不说她，你居然妄想自己可以当某人的丈夫吗？你用那怯懦的哭哭啼啼的把戏把我们骗到这儿来，你简直该被鞭子抽；而且——现在，别再现出这样一副呆相啦！我倒想狠狠地摇醒你，就因你无耻的背叛和愚蠢的妄想。"

我真的轻轻摇了他一下，但一下就引发了他的咳嗽，那老一套呻吟和哭泣的闹剧又重新上演，凯瑟琳不由得责备我。

"住一夜？不！'她说，缓缓地环顾四周。"艾伦，我要把那门烧掉，不管怎样，我一定要出去。"

她马上就说到做到的时候，林顿又为了珍惜自己的性命吓得惊慌失措。他伸出两个瘦胳臂将她抱住，啜泣着说：

"你不愿要我，不想救我——不希望带我去田庄吗？啊！亲爱的凯瑟琳！你千万别走，别扔下我。你一定要遵从我父亲，一定要啊！"

"我必须遵从我自己的父亲，"她回答，"免得他为我担惊受怕。一整夜！你说他会想什么呢？他已经够难受了。我一定要找一条路逃出去，或是绕出去。别作声！你没有任何危险——可如果你要妨碍我——林顿，你知道，我对爸爸的爱胜过你！"

对希斯克利夫先生的愤怒所引发的恐惧让他恢复了那懦夫的辩才。凯瑟琳几乎神经错乱了，但她依然坚持说一定要回家，而这次轮到她，来恳求他努力克制由于自私而带来的痛苦。

While they were thus occupied, our jailer re-entered.

"Your beasts have trotted off;" he said, "and—Now, Linton! snivelling again? What has she been doing to you? Come, come—have done, and get to bed. In a month or two, my lad, you'll be able to pay her back her present tyrannies, with a vigorous hand. You're pining for pure love, are you not? nothing else in the world: and she shall have you! There, to bed! Zillah won't be here tonight; you must undress yourself. Hush! hold your noise! Once in your own room, I'll not come near you, you needn't fear. By chance, you've managed tolerably. I'll look to the rest."

He spoke these words, holding the door open for his son to pass; and the latter achieved his exit exactly as a spaniel might, which suspected the person who attended on it of designing a spiteful squeeze. The lock was re-secured. Heathcliff approached the fire, where my mistress and I stood silent. Catherine looked up, and instinctively raised her hand to her cheek: his neighbourhood revived a painful sensation. Anybody else would have been incapable of regarding the childish act with sternness, but he scowled on her, and muttered —

"Oh, you are now afraid of me? Your courage is well disguised: you seem damnably afraid!"

"I *am* afraid now," she replied; "because if I stay, papa will be miserable; and how can I endure making him miserable—when he — when he—Mr. Heathcliff, *let* me go home! I promise to marry Linton: papa would like me to, and I love him—and why should you wish to force me to do what I'll willingly do of my-

就在他俩纠缠不清的时候，我们的狱卒又回来了。

"你们的马都跑掉了，"他说，"而且——嘿，林顿！又哭哭啼啼啦？她对你做了什么？来，来——算了，上床睡觉吧。一两个月内，我的孩子，你就能用一只强壮的手来报复她现在的虐待了。你是为纯洁的爱情而不是这世上其他东西而憔悴的，不是吗？她会要你的！那么，快到床上去吧！今晚希拉不在这里，你必须要自己脱衣服。嘘！别作声啦！只要你一进屋子，我就不会靠近你，你也不要害怕啦。刚巧，这回你总算完成任务。其他的事就交给我来办好了。"

说完这番话，他就把门打开，让他的儿子走过去；后者出去时的神态活像一只摇尾乞怜的小狗，生怕那开门的人想要不怀好意地夹他一下似的。门又被锁上。希斯克利夫走到火炉旁，我的女主人和我都静静地站在那里。凯瑟琳抬头看看，本能地将手举起来放到脸上，好像有他在附近，那疼痛的感觉又会复苏。任何一个人都不会用严厉来对待这孩子气的行为，但他却对她皱眉而且咕噜着：

"啊！你不怕我？倒是装得挺勇敢的，不过你好像非常害怕呢！"

"现在我是怕了，"她回答说，"因为，如果我待在这里，爸爸肯定会难过的，我又怎么忍心让他替我难过呢——当他——当他——希斯克利夫先生，请让我回家吧！我答应嫁给林顿，爸爸会允许我嫁给他的，而且我爱他——为什么希望强迫我做我本

self?"

"Let him dare to force you!" I cried. "There's law in the land, thank God, there is! though we *be* in an out-of-the-way place. I'd inform, if he were my own son, and it's felony without benefit of clergy!"

"Silence!" said the ruffian. "To the devil with your clamour! I don't want *you* to speak. Miss Linton, I shall enjoy myself remarkably in thinking your father will be miserable: I shall not sleep for satisfaction. You could have hit on no surer way of fixing your residence under my roof, for the next twenty-four hours, than informing me that such an event would follow. As to your promise to marry Linton, I'll take care you shall keep it; for you shall not quit this place till it is fulfilled."

"Send Ellen then, to let papa know I'm safe!" exclaimed Catherine, weeping bitterly. "Or marry me now. Poor papa! Ellen, he'll think we're lost. What shall we do?"

"Not he! He'll think you are tired of waiting on him, and run off, for a little amusement," answered Heathcliff. "You cannot deny that you entered my house of your own accord, in contempt of his injunctions to the contrary. And it is quite natural that you should desire amusement at your age; and that you should weary of nursing a sick man, and that man *only* your father. Catherine, his happiest days were over when your days began. He cursed you, I dare say, for coming into the world (I did, at least). And it would just do if he cursed you as *he* went out of it. I'd join him. I don't love you! How should I? Weep away. As far as I can see, it will be your chief diversion hereafter; unless Linton make amends for other

第二十七章

来就愿意做的事呢？"

"看他还敢如何强迫你！"我叫道，"国有国法，感谢上帝，有法律！虽然我们住在一个偏僻的地方。不过就算他是我自己的儿子，我也会去控告他，即使是教会，也绝不能宽赦这样的重罪！"

"闭嘴！"那恶人说道，"你瞎嚷嚷什么！不许你在这里乱说话。林顿小姐，只要我一想到你父亲会难过，我就非常开心，我将会高兴得彻夜难眠。你告诉我会出这样的事，那正是让你在我家呆二十四个小时的最好理由。至于你答应嫁给林顿，我肯定会叫你信守诺言；因为如果你不照办，就休想从这儿离开。"

"要不叫艾伦回去，让爸爸知道我平安吧！"凯瑟琳叫着，苦苦哀求。"又或者是现在就娶我。可怜的爸爸！艾伦，他准会认为我们失踪了。我们该怎么办呢？"

"他才不会！他会认为你侍奉他烦了，跑出来散心，"希斯克利夫回答道。毫无疑问是你违背了他的命令，走到我房子里来的。像你这样年纪，渴望一些娱乐也无可厚非；当然，要你照顾一个病人，即使是你父亲，你也会厌烦的。凯瑟琳，在你生命开始的同时，他生命中最快乐的日子也就结束了。我敢肯定，他诅咒你来到这个世界（至少，我诅咒）。如果他在离开世界时也诅咒你，那正好。我愿意和他一起诅咒。我不喜欢你！我怎么可能呢？你哭去吧。据我所知，今后哭将成为你的主要消遣，除非林顿可以弥补其他损失，你那有远虑的家长仿佛幻想他可以弥补。他

losses: and your provident parent appears to fancy he may. His letters of advice and consolation entertained me vastly. In his last, he recommended my jewel to be careful of his; and kind to her when he got her. Careful and kind – that's paternal. But Linton requires his whole stock of care and kindness for himself. Linton can play the little tyrant well. He'll undertake to torture any number of cats if their teeth be drawn, and their claws pared. You'll be able to tell his uncle fine tales of his *kindness*, when you get home again, I assure you."

"You're right there!" I said; "explain your son's character. Show his resemblance to yourself; and then, I hope, Miss Cathy will think twice before she takes the cockatrice!"

"I don't much mind speaking of his amiable qualities now," he answered; "because she must either accept him or remain a prisoner, and you along with her, till your master dies. I can detain you both, quite concealed, here. If you doubt, encourage her to retract her word, and you'll have an opportunity of judging!"

"I'll not retract my word," said Catherine. "I'll marry him, within this hour, if I may go to Thrushcross Grange afterwards. Mr. Heathcliff, you're a cruel man, but you're not a fiend; and you won't, from *mere* malice, destroy, irrevocably, all my happiness. If papa thought I had left him, on purpose, and if he died before I returned, could I bear to live? I've given over crying: but I'm going to kneel here, at your knee; and I'll not get up, and I'll not take my eyes from your face, fill you look back at me! No, don't turn away! *do* look! You'll see nothing to provoke you. I don't hate you. I'm not angry that you struck me. Have you never

的劝诫和安慰的信让我大为开心。在他最后一封信上，还劝我的宝贝要关心他的宝贝，并且当他得到她时，要对她很温柔。关心同温柔——那是父亲的慈爱。但林顿却只会把他所有的关心和温柔用在自己身上。林顿是很善于扮演小暴君的。随便多少猫，只要拔掉它们的牙齿，削掉爪子，他都会把它们折磨致死。我向你保证，等你再回家时，就能编造出一些关于他的温柔的各种美妙的故事告诉他舅舅了。"

"你说得对！"我说，"你很好地解释了你儿子的性格。因为他表现出和你的相像，那么我想，凯茜小姐在同意接受这毒蛇之前一定会三思的！"

"现在我才不在乎说他那些可爱的品质哩，"他答道，"因为要么她接受他，要么就做一个囚犯，而且还有你陪着，直至你的主人死去。我可以留下你们，而且相当严密，就在这里。如果你怀疑，鼓励她逃走，你倒是叫她试试看！"

"我才不收回我的话，"凯瑟琳说。"如果我结完婚后可以回画眉田庄，那我会在这个小时内就和他结婚，希斯克利夫先生，你真是个残忍的人，可你不是恶魔，你不会只是出于恶意，就不留余地地毁掉我所有的幸福吧。如果爸爸误解我是故意离他而去，如果没等我回去他就离开人世，那要我怎样活下去呢？我不哭了，但我要跪在这儿，就跪在你面前，我不会起来，并且我的眼睛会一直看着你的脸，直到你回头来看我！不，别转过去！看吧！你不会看见惹你生气的。我不恨你。你打我我也不

loved *anybody*, in all your life, uncle? *never?* Ah! you must look once—I'm so wretched— you can't help being sorry and pitying me."

"Keep your eft's fingers off; and move, or I'll kick you!" cried Heathcliff, brutally repulsing her. "I'd rather be hugged by a snake. How the devil can you dream of fawning on me? I *detest* you!"

He shrugged his shoulders: shook himself, indeed, as if his flesh crept with aversion; and thrust back his chair; while I got up, and opened my mouth, to commence a downright torrent of abuse; but I was rendered dumb in the middle of the first sentence, by a threat that I should be shown into a room by myself, the very next syllable I uttered. It was growing dark— we heard a sound of voices at the garden gate. Our host hurried out instantly: *he* had his wits about him; *we* had not. There was a talk of two or three minutes, and he returned alone.

"I thought it had been your cousin Hareton," I observed to Catherine. "I wish he would arrive! Who knows but he might take our part?"

"It was three servants sent to seek you from the Grange," said Heathcliff, overhearing me. "You should have opened a lattice and called out: but I could swear that chit is glad you didn't. She's glad to be obliged to stay, I'm certain."

At learning the chance we had missed, we both gave vent to our grief without control; and he allowed us to wail on till nine o'clock. Then he bade us go up stairs, through the kitchen, to Zillah's chamber; and I whispered my companion to obey: perhaps we might contrive to get through the window there, or into a garret, and

生气。姑父，你一生就没遇到过你爱的人吗？从来没有吗？啊！你一定要看我一眼。我是多么可怜啊，你不能不难过，不能不怜悯我呀。"

"把你那蜥蜴般的手指给我拿开，快滚，不然我就踢你了！"希斯克利夫大叫，残暴地将她推开。"我宁愿被一条毒蛇缠住。你怎么会想到来谄媚我？我恨透了你！"

他耸耸肩，并真的哆嗦了一下，好像憎恶得不寒而栗，还把他的椅子使劲向后推；这时我站起来想要破口大骂，但我还没说完第一句就被他的一声呵斥给堵了回去，他警告我要是再说一个字就把我单独关到一间屋里去。眼看天就黑了——我们听到花园门口有人声。我们的主人立即赶出去，他还保存着理智，而我们已经丧失了。经过两三分钟谈话，他又单独回来了。

"我想是你的表哥哈里顿，"我对凯瑟琳说。"但愿是他！他也许会和我们站在一起，可谁知道呢？"

"是田庄的三个仆人来找你们，"听见我的话，希斯克利夫说，"你本该把窗户打开向外叫的，不过我确定，那个小丫头心里很高兴你没有喊，她很乐意被留下。"

我们知道失去了良机，就再也控制不住情绪，号啕大哭来发泄悲哀，他任由我们哭到九点。然后命我们上楼，穿过厨房，到希拉的卧房去。我低声叫凯瑟琳服从，也许我们可以设法从那边的窗户出去，或是到一间阁楼里，从天窗出去。但窗户和楼下的

out by its skylight. The window, however, was narrow, like those below, and the garret trap was safe from our attempts; for we were fastened in as before. We neither of us lay down: Catherine took her station by the lattice, and watched anxiously for morning; a deep sigh being the only answer I could obtain to my frequent entreaties that she would try to rest. I seated myself in a chair, and rocked, to and fro, passing harsh judgment on my many derelictions of duty; from which, it struck me then, all the misfortunes of all my employers sprang. It was not the case, in reality, I am aware; but it was, in my imagination, that dismal night; and I thought Heathcliff himself less guilty than I.

At seven o'clock he came, and inquired if Miss Linton had risen. She ran to the door immediately, and answered, "Yes." "Here, then," he said, opening it, and pulling her out. I rose to follow, but he turned the lock again. I demanded my release.

"Be patient," he replied; "I'll send up your breakfast in a while."

I thumped on the panels, and rattled the latch angrily; and Catherine asked why I was still shut up? He answered, I must try to endure it another hour, and they went away. I endured it two or three hours; at length, I heard a footstep, not Heathcliff's.

"I've brought you something to eat," said a voice; "oppen t' door!"

Complying eagerly, I beheld Hareton, laden with food enough to last me all day.

"Talk it," he added, thrusting the tray into my hand.

"Stay one minute," I began.

"Nay!" cried he, and retired, regardless of

any prayers I could pour forth to detain him.

And there I remained enclosed, the whole day, and the whole of the next night; and another, and another. Five nights and four days I remained, altogether, seeing nobody but Hareton, once every morn ing; and he was a model of a jailer: surly, and dumb, and deaf to every attempt at moving his sense of justice or compassion.

求他，希望他能留下，但他置之不理。

我一直被关在这里，白天过去了是晚上，接着又是白天和晚上。我一共待了四天五夜，除了每天早上看见一次哈里顿，再也见不到其他人，而他是个典型的狱卒：紧绷着脸，一声不吭，对能激起他的正义感或同情心而作出的各种哀求完全无动于衷。

Chapter 28
第二十八章

On the fifth morning, or rather afternoon, a different st ep approached—lighter and shorter; and, this time, the person entered the room. It was Zillah; donned in her scarlet shawl, with a black silk bonnet on her head, and a willow basket swung to her arm.

"Eh, dear! Mrs. Dean," she exclaimed. "Well! there is a talk about you at Gimmerton. I never thought but you were sunk in the Blackhorse marsh, and Missy with you, till master told me you'd been found, and he'd lodged you here! What, and you must have got on an island, sure? And how long were you in the hole? Did master save you, Mrs. Dean? But you're not so thin—you've not been so poorly, have you?"

第五天上午，或者该说是下午，听见了不一样的脚步声——较为轻而急促，这次，这个人进了屋，是希拉，她披着一条的深红色的围巾，头上戴一顶黑色的丝帽，胳膊上挎着个柳条篮子。

"呃，天哪！迪安太太！"她嚷道。"唉呀！在吉默顿已经有人谈论起你们啦。我做梦都想不到你会陷在黑马沼里，还有小姐跟你一起，后来主人对我说已经找到你们了，他让你们住在这儿了！怎么！你们一定是爬上一个岛了吧？你们在山洞呆了多久？是主人救了你们吗，迪安太太？不过你看起来没怎么瘦——好像没怎么遭罪，是吗？"

"Your master is a true scoundrel!" I replied. "But he shall answer for it. He needn't have raised that tale: it shall all be laid bare!"

"What do you mean?" asked Zillah. "It's not his tale: they tell that in the village—about your being lost in the marsh; and I calls to Earnshaw, when I come in — 'Eh, they's queer things, Mr. Hareton, happened since I went off. It's a sad pity of that likely young lass, and cant Nelly Dean.' He stared. I thought he had not heard aught, so I told him the rumour. The master listened, and he just smiled to himself, and said, 'If they have been in the marsh, they are out now, Zillah. Nelly Dean is lodged, at this minute, in your room. You can tell her to flit, when you go up; here is the key. The bog-water got into her head, and she would have run home, quite flighty, but I fixed her, till she came round to her senses. You can bid her go to the Grange, at once, if she be able, and carry a message from me, that her young lady will follow in time to attend the Squire's funeral.'"

"Mr. Edgar is not dead?" I gasped. "Oh! Zillah, Zillah!"

"No, no; sit you down, my good mistress," she replied; "your right sickly yet. He's not dead; Doctor Kenneth thinks he may last another day. I met him on the road and asked."

Instead of sitting down, I snatched my outdoor things, and hastened below, for the way was free. On entering the house, I looked about for some one to give information of Catherine. The place was filled with sunshine, and the door stood wide open; but nobody seemed at hand. As I hesitated whether to go off at once, or return and seek my mistress, a slight cough drew my attention to the hearth. Linton lay on the

"你主人是个名副其实的无赖！"我答道。"可他要负责任的，用不着编些瞎话来骗别人，真相总会大白的！"

"你这是什么意思？"希拉问，"那绝不是他编的，村里人都这么说——说你们在沼泽地里失踪了，刚才我进来时，对恩肖先生说：'呃，哈里顿先生，我走之后发生了些怪事，只可惜了那个如花似玉的小姑娘，还有能干的内莉·迪安就完了。'他立刻拿眼瞪我。我以为他还没有听到，就把它一五一十告诉他。主人听后，自己微笑着说：'就算她们先前曾掉到沼泽地里，现在已经安然无恙了，希拉。这会儿内莉·迪安就在你的房里，你上楼叫她快走吧，钥匙在这里。她脑子进水了，整天发神经要往家里跑，可我留住了她。等她神志清醒以后，如果她能走的话，你叫她马上回田庄吧，替我带个信，说她的小姐随后就到，保证能赶得及参加她父亲的葬礼。"

"埃德加先生还没死吧？"我喘息着，"啊！希拉，希拉！"

"没有，还没；你好好地坐着吧，我的好太太，"她回答说，"你还在生病呢。他还没死；回来的路上我遇见了肯尼斯医生，他认为埃德加先生还可以再多活一天。"

我没有坐下，一把抓起帽子，连忙下楼，因为路是自由开放的了。一进大厅，我环顾四周，想找个人打听一下关于凯瑟琳的消息。这地方充满了和煦的阳光，门敞开着，可眼前却看不到一个人。我不由得踌躇起来，是马上走呢，还是回去寻找我的女主人，忽然一声轻微的咳嗽吸引了我的注意。我看见林顿独自躺在炉边的躺

settle, sole tenant, sucking a stick of sugar-candy, and pursuing my movements with apathetic eyes. "Where is Miss Catherine?" I demanded, sternly, supposing I could frighten him into giving intelligence, by catching him thus, alone. He sucked on like an innocent.

"Is she gone?" I said.

"No," he replied; "she's up stairs: she's not to go; we won't let her."

"You won't let her, little idiot!" I exclaimed. "Direct me to her room immediately, or I'll make you sing out sharply."

"Papa would make you sing out, if you attempted to get there," he answered. "He says I'm not to be soft with Catherine: she's my wife, and it's shameful that she should wish to leave me! He says, she hates me, and wants me to die, that she may have my money; but she shan't have it: and she shan't go home! She never shall! —she may cry, and be sick as much as she pleases!"

He resumed his former occupation, closing his lids, as if he meant to drop asleep.

"Master Heathcliff," I resumed, "have you forgotten all Catherine's kindness to you, last winter, when you affirmed you loved her, and when she brought you books, and sung you songs, and came many a time through wind and snow to see you? She wept to miss one evening, because you would be disappointed; and you felt then, that she was a hundred times too good to you: and now you believe the lies your father tells, though you know he detests you both! And you join him against her. That's fine gratitude, is it not?"

The corner of Linton's mouth fell, and he took the sugar-candy from his lips.

"Did she come to Wuthering Heights, because she hated you?" I continued. "Think for yourself! As to your money, she does not even know that you will have any. And you say she's sick; and yet, you leave her alone, up there in a strange house! You, who have felt what it is to be so neglected! You could pity your own sufferings, and she pitied them, too, but you won't pity hers! I shed tears Master Heathcliff, you see—an elderly woman, and a servant merely—and you, after pretending such affection, and having reason to worship her, almost, store up every tear you have for yourself, and lie there quite at ease. Ah! you're a heartless, selfish boy!"

"I can't stay with her," he answered crossly. "I'll not stay, by myself. She cries so I can't bear it. And she won't give over, though I say I'll call my father. I did call him once; and he threatened to strangle her, if she was not quiet; but she began again, the instant he left the room; moaning and grieving all night long, though I screamed for vexation that I couldn't sleep."

"Is Mr. Heathcliff out?" I inquired, perceiving that the wretched creature had no power to sympathise with his cousin's mental tortures.

"He's in the court," he replied, "talking to Doctor Kenneth who says uncle is dying, truly, at last. I'm glad, for I shall be master of the Grange after him—and Catherine always spoke of it as *her* house. It isn't hers! It's mine: papa says everything she has is mine. All her nice books are mine; she offered to give me them, and her pretty birds, and her pony Minny, if I would get the key of our room, and let her out; but I told her she had nothing to give, they were

"你觉得她是因为恨你才到呼啸山庄吗?"我接着说,"你想想!至于你的钱,她甚至不知道你会不会有钱。而你说她病了,还把她一人丢在一个陌生人家的楼上!你也曾受过这种被人忽视的滋味!你能怜悯你自己的痛苦,她也怜悯你的痛苦,可是你为什么不能怜悯她的痛苦!我都掉泪了,希斯克利夫少爷,你瞧——我,一个上了年纪的女人,而且不过是个仆人——而你,在假装出那么多柔情,而且几乎有了爱她的理由之后,却把每滴眼泪留下来自己用,还能悠闲地躺在这里。啊!你真是个没良心的、自私的孩子!"

"我没法跟她待在一起,"他焦躁地回答。"我本不想一个人呆着。可她的哭闹让我受不了。即使我说要叫我父亲啦,她还是没完没了。有一次我真的叫来父亲,他威胁说,要是她还不安静,就要勒死她,可一旦他离开那屋,她又哭个不停,虽然我因为睡不着烦得大叫,她还是整夜哭哭啼啼。"

"希斯克利夫先生出去了吗?"我知道这个卑贱的东西一点都不同情他表姐在心灵上所受的创伤,便问道。

"他在院子里,"他回答,"跟肯尼斯医生谈话呢,医生说舅舅快要死了——终于逃不过了。我很开心,因为我会继承他而做田庄的新主人。凯瑟琳总把它看作她的房子。其实那不是她的!是我的。爸爸说她所有的每样东西都是我的。她所有的好书是我的;她说如果我肯拿给她房子的钥匙,放她出去,就把那些书都给我,还有她那可爱的小鸟,还有小马敏

all, all mine. And then she cried, and took a little picture from her neck, and said I should have that two pictures in a gold case—on one side her mother, and on the other, uncle, when they were young. That was yesterday—I said *they* were mine, too; and tried to get them from her. The spiteful thing wouldn't let me: she pushed me off, and hurt me. I shrieked out—that frightens her—she heard papa coming, and she broke the hinges, and divided the case and gave me her mother's portrait; the other she attempted to hide: but papa asked what was the matter and I explained it. He took the one I had away; and ordered her to resign hers to me; she refused, and he—he struck her down, and wrenched it off the chain, and crushed it with his foot."

"And were you pleased to see her struck?" I asked: having my designs in encouraging his talk.

"I winked," he answered. "I wink to see my father strike a dog, or a horse, he does it so hard. Yet I was glad at first—she deserved punishing for pushing me: but when papa was gone, she made me come to the window and showed me her cheek cut on the inside, against her teeth, and her mouth filling with blood; and then she gathered up the bits of the picture, and went and sat down with her face to the wall, and she has never spoken to me since: and I sometimes think she can't speak for pain. I don't like to think so! but she's a naughty thing for crying continually; and she looks so pale and wild, I'm afraid of her!"

"And you can get the key if you choose?" I said.

"Yes, when I am up-stairs," he answered;

"but I can't walk up-stairs now."

"In what apartment is it?" I asked.

"Oh," he cried, "I shan't tell *you* where it is! It is our secret. Nobody, neither Hareton, nor Zillah are to know. There! you've fired me—go away, go away!" And he turned his face onto his arm, and shut his eyes, again.

I considered it best to depart without seeing Mr. Heathcliff; and bring a rescue for my young lady, from the Grange. On reaching it, the astonishment of my fellow servants to see me, and their joy also, was intense; and when they heard that their little mistress was safe, two or three were about to hurry up, and shout the news at Mr. Edgar's door: but I bespoke the announcement of it, myself. How changed I found him, even in those few days! He lay an image of sadness, and resignation, waiting his death. Very young he looked: though his actual age was thirty-nine; one would have called him ten years younger, at least. He thought of Catherine for he murmured her name. I touched his hand, and spoke.

"Catherine is coming, dear master!" I whispered; "she is alive, and well; and will be here I hope tonight."

I trembled at the first effects of this intelligence: he half rose up, looked eagerly round the apartment, and then sunk back in a swoon. As soon as he recovered, I related our compulsory visit, and detention at the Heights. I said Heathcliff forced me to go in: which was not quite true. I uttered as little as possible against Linton; nor did I describe all his father's brutal conduct— my intentions being to add no bitterness, if I could help it, to his already overflowing cup.

说,"可我现在走不到楼上去。"

"那她在哪间屋子?"我问道。

"啊,"他叫道,"我才不会告诉你在哪儿呢!那是我们的秘密。没人知道,哈里顿和希拉也不知道。啊呀!你把我弄累了——快走开,走开!"他转过脸去,靠在胳膊上,又闭上了眼睛。

我觉得最好不见希斯克利夫先生就走,再从田庄带人来救我的小姐。一到家,我的伙伴们看到我,都异常惊喜,他们一听到小女主人仍然平安,就有两三个人想去埃德加先生房门口大声宣告这好消息,但我情愿自己通报。才几天的时间,我发现他变得多么厉害啊!他带着悲伤的、听天由命的神情静静躺在那里等死。他看来还很年轻,虽然他实际年龄是三十九岁,但一般人都会至少把他当作年轻十岁看。他还在思念凯瑟琳,因为他正喃喃地唤着她的名字。我摸着他的手说:

"凯瑟琳马上就回来了,亲爱的主人!"我低声说,"她活着,她没事,她就来了,我希望,就在今天晚上。"

这个消息引起的当场反应让我感到震惊:他把上半身撑起来,用热切的目光环顾这间屋子,接着就晕过去。等他醒来后,我就把我们被骗进山庄,以及被扣留的事详细给他汇报。我说希斯克利夫强迫我进去,那并不是完全真实的。我尽可能少说林顿的坏话,也没把他父亲禽兽不如的行为全都说出来——我的目的是,只要我可以,就不愿在他那已经溢满的苦杯中再增加苦味了。

第二十八章

He divined that one of his enemy's purposes was to secure the personal property, as well as the estate, to his son, or rather himself; yet why he did not wait till his decease, was a puzzle to my master, because ignorant how nearly he and his nephew would quit the world together. However, he felt that his will had better be altered: instead of leaving Catherine's fortune at her own disposal, he determined to put it in the hands of trustees, for her use during life; and for her children, if she had any, after her. By that means, it could not fall to Mr. Heathcliff should Linton die.

Having received his orders, I despatched a man to fetch the attorney, and four more, provided with serviceable weapons, to demand my young lady of her jailer. Both parties were delayed very late. The single servant returned first. He said Mr. Green, the lawyer, was out when he arrived at his house, and he had to wait two hours for his re-entrance; and then Mr. Green told him he had a little business in the village that must be done; but he would be at Thrushcross Grange before morning. The four men came back unaccompanied, also. They brought word that Catherine was ill: too ill to quit her room; and Heathcliff would not suffer them to see her. I scolded the stupid fellows well, for listening to that tale, which I would not carry to my master; resolving to take a whole bevy up to the Heights, at daylight, and storm it, literally, unless the prisoner were quietly surrendered to us. Her father *shall* see her, I vowed, and vowed again, if that devil be killed on his own door-stones in trying to prevent it!

Happily, I was spared the journey, and the trouble. I had gone down stairs at three o'clock

他推测他敌人的目的之一就是夺得他的私人财产以及田地，好给他的儿子，或者也可以说是给他自己；但使我主人大惑不解的是他为什么不等自己死后再动手，因为他不知道他的外甥差不多将要和他一道离开人世。无论如何，他觉得最好修改一下遗嘱：不必让凯瑟琳自己支配他的财产，他决定把这财产交到委托人手里，供她生前使用，如果她有孩子，在她死后就留给孩子用。通过这样的方法，就算林顿死了，财产也不会落到希斯克利夫先生手里。

我按照他的嘱咐，派人去请律师，又找了四个人，装备好可用的武器，去把我的小姐从她的狱卒手里救回来。两拨人都耽搁到很晚才回来。独自出去的仆人先回来。他说当他到律师格林先生家里的时候，他不在家，他不得不等了两个小时，律师才回来；但是格林先生告诉他说要到村里办点小事，不过他保证在早晨之前一定赶到画眉田庄。那四个人也没带着小姐回来。他们带回口信说凯瑟琳病了——病得没法离开她的屋子，希斯克利夫不让他们去见她。我结结实实地痛骂了这伙笨蛋，因为他们竟相信了那套瞎话，我决定先不把这话传给主人，天亮时再带一群人到山庄去，痛快地大干一场，除非他们把被囚禁的人平平安安地交到我们手里，因为她父亲一定要见到她，我发誓，又发誓，如果那魔鬼想阻止这个，即便是让他死在自家门口的石阶上也行！

幸好，我免去了这趟出行和麻烦。三点钟我下楼去拿一罐水，正提

to fetch a jug of water; and was passing through the hall with it in my hand, when a sharp knock at the front door made me jump. "Oh! it is Green," I said, recollecting myself —"only Green," and I went on, intending to send somebody else to open it; but the knock was repeated: not loud, and still importunately. I put the jug on the banister, and hastened to admit him myself. The harvest moon shone clear outside. It was not the attorney. My own sweet little mistress sprung on my neck, sobbing —

"Ellen! Ellen! Is papa alive?"

"Yes!" I cried: "yes, my angel, he is. God be thanked, you are safe with us again!"

She wanted to run, breathless as she was, upstairs to Mr. Linton's room; but I compelled her to sit down on a chair, and made her drink, and washed her pale face, chafing it into a faint colour with my apron. Then I said I must go first, and tell of her arrival; imploring her to say, she should be happy with young Heathcliff. She stared, but soon comprehending why I counselled her to utter the falsehood, she assured me she would not complain.

I couldn't abide to be present at their meeting. I stood outside the chamber-door a quarter of an hour, and hardly ventured near the bed, then. All was composed, however: Catherine's despair was as silent as her father's joy. She supported him calmly, in appearance; and he fixed on her features his raised eyes, that seemed dilating with ecstacy.

He died blissfully; Mr. Lockwood: he died so. Kissing her cheek, he murmured, "I am going to her; and you darling child shall come to us;" and never stirred or spoke again; but continued that rapt, radiant gaze, till his

着它走过大厅时,突然前门传来的一阵猛敲吓了我一跳。"啊!那是格林,"我说,努力保持镇定——"就是格林,"我继续向前走,打算叫别人来开门,可门又响起来,声音不大,但很急促。于是我把水罐放在栏杆上,连忙自己开门让他进来。头顶的满月把外面照得很亮,那不是律师。我可爱的小女主人跳进来,搂住我的脖子哭喊着:

"艾伦,艾伦!爸爸他还活着是吗?"

"是的!"我叫道,"是的,我的小天使,他还活着,感谢上帝,你又平平安安地跟我们在一起啦!"

此时她已气喘吁吁,却想跑上楼到林顿先生的屋里去;但我迫使她坐在椅子上,叫她喝点水,再洗洗她那苍白的脸,并用我的围裙把她的脸擦得微微泛红。然后说我必须先去通报一声她来了,又央求她对林顿先生说,她和小希斯克利夫在一起会幸福的。她愣住了,不过马上就明白我为什么劝她说假话,因此向我保证她不会诉苦的。

我不忍待在那儿看他们见面。我在卧室门外站了将近一刻钟,一直不敢靠近床边。但一切都显得很安宁:凯瑟琳的痛苦同她父亲的快乐一样不露声色,只见她小心翼翼地搀扶着他,他抬起他那双仿佛因为狂喜而张大的眼睛凝视着她的脸。

他临终的时候心里充满幸福,他,洛克伍德先生,就这样去世了:他亲了亲她的脸,低声说:"我要去她那里了,你,我的宝贝孩子,将来你也要到我们那儿去的!"说完就再也

pulse imperceptibly stopped, and his soul departed. None could have noticed the exact minute of his death, it was so entirely without a struggle.

Whether Catherine had spent her tears, or whether the grief were too weighty to let them flow, she sat there dry-eyed till the sun rose: she sat till noon, and would still have remained, brooding over that deathbed, but I insisted on her coming away, and taking some repose. It was well I succeeded in removing her, for at dinner-time appeared the lawyer, having called at Wuthering Heights to get his instructions how to behave. He had sold himself to Mr. Heathcliff, and that was the cause of his delay in obeying my master's summons. Fortunately, no thought of worldly affairs crossed the latter's mind, to disturb him, after his daughter's arrival.

Mr. Green took upon himself to order everything and everybody about the place. He gave all the servants but me, notice to quit. He would have carried his delegated authority to the point of insisting that Edgar Linton should not be buried beside his wife, but in the chapel, with his family. There was the will however, to hinder that, and my loud protestations against any infringement of its directions. The funeral was hurried over; Catherine, Mrs. Linton Heathcliff now, was suffered to stay at the Grange till her father's corpse had quitted it.

She told me that her anguish had at last spurred Linton to incur the risk of liberating her. She heard the men I sent, disputing at the door, and she gathered the sense of Heathcliff's answer. It drove her desperate. Linton, who had been conveyed up to the little parlour soon after

没动，也没说话，但他狂喜的明亮的凝视却一直保持着，直至不知不觉中，他的脉搏停止跳动，他的灵魂离开身体。没有人知道他去世的确切时间，因为他完全连一点挣扎都没有就死去了。

也许凯瑟琳已经哭干了眼泪，也许悲哀太沉重以至哭不出来，她就这样眼中无泪地呆坐在那里直到日出。她一直坐到中午，还要待在那儿对着灵床发呆，但我坚持让她走开，好好休息。幸好我把她劝开，因为午饭时候律师来了，他已经去过呼啸山庄，获得了如何处理的指示。他已经被希斯克利夫先生收买，这也是他在得到我主人召唤后迟迟不来的原因。幸亏在他女儿到来以后，他就根本没为那尘世间的种种事操心了。

格林先生自行担负责安排所有事情以及安排这里的每个人。他把除了我的所有仆人都辞退了。他还要行使他的委托权，坚持说埃德加·林顿不能葬在他妻子旁边，而是要跟他的家族一起葬在教堂。无论如何，遗嘱里并没那样写，于是我高声抗议，反对一切有悖遗嘱的行动。丧事就这样草草了事；凯瑟琳，也就是如今的林顿·希斯克利夫太太，被允许住在田庄，直到她父亲起灵为止。

她告诉我，她的悲惨遭遇终于刺激了林顿，于是他冒险放走了她。她听到我派去的人在门口争吵，明白了希斯克利夫答话里的意思，那更使她不顾一切地设法逃出来。林顿在我走后就被搬到楼上小客厅里去，他趁父

Ileft, was terrified into fetching the key before his father re-ascended. He had the cunning to unlock, and re-lock the door, without shutting it; and when he should have gone to bed, he begged to sleep with Hareton, and his petition was granted, for once. Catherine stole out before break of day. She dare not try the doors, lest the dogs should raise an alarm; she visited the empty chambers, and examined their windows; and, luckily, lighting on her mother's, she got easily out of its lattice, and onto the ground, by means of the fir tree, close by. Her accomplice suffered for his share in the escape, notwithstanding his timid contrivances.

亲还没上楼，偷偷拿到了钥匙。他很聪明地打开门锁，又重新上了锁，但故意没把它关严；到了他该上床睡觉的时间，他要求跟哈里顿睡，这回他的请求总算顺利地被批准了。就这样凯瑟琳得以在天亮前偷偷溜出去。她不敢直接开门，担心会引起那些狗的骚动；她到那些空着的房间，检查那里的窗户；幸运的是，她走到了她母亲的房间，很容易地从那里的窗台上跳了出来，然后从附近的枞树上滑到地上。她的同谋者，尽管想出了这个怯懦的计策，仍然因为这事吃到了苦头。

Chapter 29
第二十九章

The evening after the funeral, my young lady and I were seated in the library; now musing mournfully—one of us despairingly—on our loss, now venturing conjectures as to the gloomy future.

We had just agreed the best destiny which could await Catherine, would be a permission to continue resident at the Grange; at least during Linton's life: he being allowed to join her there, and I to remain a housekeeper. That seemed rather too favourable an arrangement to

丧事办完的那天晚上，小姐和我坐在书房里；一会儿悲哀地（准确点说应该是我们中的一个几近绝望地）思考着我们的所失，一会儿又揣测着黯淡的未来。

我们刚刚达成共识，对凯瑟琳来说，最好的安排就是准许她继续住在田庄，至少在林顿活着的时候，也允许他来这里陪她，而我还是管家。这简直就是不敢奢望的太令人满意的安排，可我还是希望着，而且一想到可

be hoped for; and yet I did hope, and began to cheer up under the prospect of retaining my home, and my employment, and, above all, my beloved young mistress, when a servant— one of the discarded ones, not yet departed—rushed hastily in, and said, "that devil Heathcliff" was coming through the court: should he fasten the door in his face?

If we had been mad enough to order that proceeding, we had not time. He made no ceremony of knocking, or announcing his name: he was master, and availed himself of the master's privilege to walk straight in, without saying a word. The sound of our informant's voice directed him to the library; he entered, and motioning him out, shut the door.

It was the same room into which he had been ushered, as a guest, eighteen years before: the same moon shone through the window; and the same autumn landscape lay outside. We had not yet lighted a candle, but all the apartment was visible, even to the portraits on the wall— the splendid head of Mrs. Linton, and the graceful one of her husband. Heathcliff advanced to the hearth. Time had little altered his person either. There was the same man: his dark face rather sallower, and more composed, his frame a stone[①] or two heavier, perhaps, and no other difference. Catherine had risen, with an impulse to dash out, when she saw him.

"Stop!" he said, arresting her by the arm. "No more runnings away! Where would you go? I'm come to fetch you home; and I hope you'll be a dutiful daughter, and not encourage my son to further disobedience. I was embar-

以保全我的家，我的工作，还有，最重要的，我可爱年轻的女主人，我就开始高兴。可好景不长，此时一个仆人——已经被遣散但还未离去的一个——急匆匆地进来说，"那个魔鬼希斯克利夫"正穿过院子走来，问要不要当着他的面把门闩上？

即使我们真气得吩咐他把门闩上，也来不及了。他完全没有礼貌地进来，没有敲门，或是通报他的姓名。他已经是主人，有作为主人的特权，径直走进来，没说一个字。那个向我们汇报的仆人的声音将他引到书房。他进来后，做个手势，命令仆人出去，关上了门。

这间屋子就是他十八年前做客庄园时被引进来的那间：一样的月光从窗外悄悄爬进来，窗外依然是一样的秋景。虽然我们没点蜡烛，整间屋子在月光下显得如此明亮，甚至墙上的肖像也能看得清楚。那是林顿太太漂亮的肖像和她丈夫文雅的肖像。希斯克利夫走到炉边。时间并没改变他多少，他还是跟以前一样，除了那发黑的脸稍稍发黄，也宁静些，他的身躯，也许就重了一两斤，并没发生其他大的变化。凯瑟琳一见他进来就立刻站起来想冲出去。

"站住！"他大吼着说，抓住她的胳臂。"不要再逃跑啦！你要到哪儿去啊？我是来带你回家的，我希望你能作个孝顺的儿媳妇，不要再鼓动我儿子任性不听话了。当我发现这件事他也有份的时候，我真不知该如何罚他才好，他就像是个蜘蛛网，伸手一抓

---

① stone：石，重量名，常用来表示体重，一石等于十四磅，在实用上因物而异。

rassed how to punish him, when I discovered his part in the business: he's such a cobweb, a pinch would annihilate him; but you'll see by his look that he has received his due! I brought him down one evening, the day before yesterday, and just set him in a chair, and never touched him afterwards. I sent Hareton out, and we had the room to ourselves. In two hours, I called Joseph to carry him up again; and, since then, my presence is as potent on his nerves as a ghost; and I fancy he sees me often, though I am not near. Hareton says he wakes and shrieks in the night by the hour together; and calls you to protect him from me; and, whether you like your precious mate or not, you must come: he's your concern now; I yield all my interest in him to you."

"Why not let Catherine continue here?" I pleaded, "and send Master Linton to her. As you hate them both, you'd not miss them: they *can* only be a daily plague to your unnatural heart."

"I'm seeking a tenant for the Grange," he answered; "and I want my children about me, to be sure—besides, that lass owes me her services for her bread; I'm not going to nurture her in luxury and idleness after Linton is gone. Make haste and get ready now. And don't oblige me to compel you."

"I shall," said Catherine. "Linton is all I have to love in the world, and, though you have done what you could to make him hateful to me, and me to him, you *cannot* make us hate each other! and I defy you to hurt him when I am by, and I defy you to frighten me."

"You are a boastful champion," replied Heathcliff; "but I don't like you well enough to hurt him: you shall get the full benefit of the

"就会让他粉身碎骨,等你看见他那副样子就知道,他已经得到他应得的报应了!有天晚上,就是前天,我把他带下楼来,让他坐在椅子上,这以后再也没碰过他。我让哈里顿出去,屋里就剩我们俩。两个小时后,我叫约瑟夫再把他送回楼上,自此以后,我一出现在他面前,他就仿佛见到鬼一般,就算我不在他身旁,我猜想他也常常看得见我,也许对他来说我就像鬼一样牢牢缠住了他的神经。哈里顿说他在夜里常常睁着眼睛不睡觉,一连几个钟头,还大叫着,叫你保护他,免得遭到我的迫害;不管你喜不喜欢你那亲爱的伴侣,你一定得去——现在他已经属于你了;我把对他的一切兴趣全让给你。"

"为什么不让凯瑟琳呆在这儿?"我恳求道,"也把林顿少爷接过来。既然你这么恨他们,他们不在的话,你也不会想念啊,况且他们的存在只能增添你每天的烦恼罢了。"

"我要为田庄找个房客,"他答道,"而且我的孩子们当然应该呆在我身边。此外,那个丫头既然有面包吃,就得付出劳动。我可不打算在林顿去世后她依然养尊处优、无所事事。现在,赶紧准备去,不要逼我用强硬的手段。"

"我当然要去,"凯瑟琳说。"这世界上我能爱的只剩下林顿了。虽然你费尽心思让我们彼此厌恶,但你不能使我们互相敌视!当有我在旁边的时候,我既不怕你会伤害他,也不怕你来吓唬我!"

"你只是个夸夸其谈的勇士,"希斯克利夫回答,"可我还不至于因为讨厌你而伤害他,但你必须要经受折

torment, as long as it lasts. It is not I who will make him hateful to you—it is his own sweet spirit. He's as bitter as gall at your desertion, and its consequences; don't expect thanks for this noble devotion. I heard him draw a pleasant picture to Zillah of what he would do, if he were as strong as I: the inclination is there, and his very weakness will sharpen his wits to find a substitute for strength."

"I know he has a bad nature," said Catherine: "he's your son. But I'm glad I've a better, to forgive it; and I know he loves me, and for that reason I love him. Mr. Heathcliff, *you* have *nobody* to love you; and, however miserable you make us, we shall still have the revenge of thinking that your cruelty arises from your greater misery! You are miserable, are you not? Lonely, like the devil, and envious like him? *Nobody* loves you—*nobody* will cry for you when you die! I wouldn't be you!"

Catherine spoke with a kind of dreary triumph: she seemed to have made up her mind to enter into the spirit of her future family, and draw pleasure from the griefs of her enemies.

"You shall be sorry to be yourself presently," said her father-in-law, "if you stand there another minute. Begone, witch, and get your things."

She scornfully withdrew. In her absence, I began to beg for Zillah's place at the Heights, offering to resign mine to her; but he would suffer it on no account. He bid me be silent; and then, for the first time, allowed himself a glance round the room, and a look at the pictures. Having studied Mrs. Linton, he said—

"I shall have that home. Not because I need it, but—" He turned abruptly to the fire, and continued, with what, for lack of a better word, I must call a smile —"I'll tell you what I did yesterday! I got the sexton, who was digging Linton's grave, to remove the earth off her coffin-lid, and I opened it. I thought, once, I would have stayed there, when I saw her face again—it is hers yet—he had hard work to stir me; but he said it would change, if the air blew on it, and so I struck one side of the coffin loose, and covered it up: not Linton's side, damn him! I wish he'd been soldered in lead—and I bribed the sexton to pull it away, when I'm laid there, and slide mine out too. I'll have it made so, and then, by the time Linton gets to us, he'll not know which is which!"

"You were very wicked, Mr. Heathcliff!" I exclaimed; "were you not ashamed to disturb the dead?"

"I disturbed nobody, Nelly," he replied; "and I gave some ease to myself. I shall be a great deal more comfortable now; and you'll have a better chance of keeping me underground, when I get there. Disturbed her? No! she has disturbed me, night and day, through eighteen years— incessantly—remorselessly—till yesternight; and yesternight I was tranquil. I dreamt I was sleeping the last sleep by that sleeper, with my heart stopped and my cheek frozen against hers."

"And if she had been dissolved into earth, or worse, what would you have dreamt of then?" I said.

"Of dissolving with her, and being more happy still!" he answered. "Do you suppose I dread any change of that sort? I expected such a transformation on raising the lid, but I'm better pleased that it should not commence till I share

他突然转身面向壁炉，带着一种，我也找不出更好的字眼来说，只能说该算是一种微笑吧，接着说："我要告诉你我昨天都干了什么！我找到了给林顿掘坟的教堂司事，叫他拨开她棺盖上的土，然后打开了棺木。我当时一度想将来死后我也要埋在那里，我还看见了她的脸——还是先前的模样——他费了很大的劲才把我赶开，因为他说如果吹了风就会起变化，因此我就把棺木的一边敲松，又盖了土，不是靠林顿那边，滚他娘的！我宁愿把他用铅焊住——我贿赂了在那掘坟的人，等将来我死后埋在那儿时，就把它抽掉，把我的尸首也扒出来。我要造成这样的效果：等林顿到我们这儿来的时候，他就再也分不清哪个是哪个了！"

"你怎么如此恶毒，希斯克利夫先生！"我叫起来，"你就不为打扰死者感到羞耻吗？"

"我并没打扰到任何人，内莉，"他回答说，"我只想给自己一点安宁而已。现在我觉得舒服多了，等有一天我要到那儿去的时候我也能安详地躺在地下了。我扰及了她吗？不！这十八年以来，是她日日夜夜都在扰着我——不断地——毫不留情地——一直持续到昨夜；昨夜我终于平静了，我梦见我靠着那长眠者睡我生命中的最后一觉，我的心脏停止了跳动，我冰冷的脸紧紧偎依着她的脸。"

"如果她已经化为泥土，或是更糟，那你还会梦到什么呢？"我说。

"梦到和她一起化掉，而且还会更开心些！"他回答说，"你以为我害

it. Besides, unless I had received a distinct impression of her passionless features, that strange feeling would hardly have been removed. It began oddly. You know, I was wild after she died; and eternally, from dawn to dawn, praying her to return to me—her spirit—I have a strong faith in ghosts: I have a conviction that they can, and do exist, among us! The day she was buried, there came a fall of snow. In the evening I went to the churchyard. It blew bleak as winter—all round was solitary: I didn't fear that her fool of a husband would wander up the den so late; and no one else had business to bring them there. Being alone, and conscious two yards of loose earth was the sole barrier between us, I said to myself—'I'll have her in my arms again! If she be cold, I'll think it is this north wind that chills *me* ; and if she be motionless, it is sleep.' I got a spade from the toolhouse, and began to delve with all my might—it scraped the coffin; I fell to work with my hands; the wood commenced cracking about the screws, I was on the point of attaining my object, when it seemed that I heard a sigh from some one above, close at the edge of the grave, and bending down. 'If I can only get this off,' I muttered, 'I wish they may shovel in the earth over us both! ' and I wrenched more desperately still. There was another sigh, close at my ear. I appeared to feel the warm breath of it displacing the sleet-laden wind. I knew no hying thing in flesh and blood was by; but as certainly as you perceive the approach to some substantial body in the dark, though it cannot be discerned, so certainly I felt that Cathy was there: not under me, but on the earth. A sudden sense of relief flowed, from my heart, through every

怕看到那样的变化吗？当我掀起棺盖时，我本来期待着会有这变化，但我很高兴它还没有开始，那就表示要等到我和它一同变化。而且，除非我脑子里真真切切地印下了对她那冷若冰霜的面貌的印象，否则很难消除那种奇异的感觉。开始觉得很古怪，你也知道在她死后我发了狂，每天我都在不断地祈求她的灵魂能够回到我这儿来！我相信这世上有鬼魂，也相信它们可以，而且确实存在于我们中间！她下葬的那天，下了雪。晚上我去了墓园。冬日的寒风凛冽地刮着——周围一片凄凉。我倒不担心她的那个混蛋丈夫这么晚了还会游荡到这幽谷之中，也没有其他人会没事跑到那边去。我孤身一人，而且我知道我们之间惟一的障碍就是这两码厚的松土，于是我对我自己说——'我要再把她抱在我的怀里！如果她身上是冰冷的，我就认为是寒风吹得我冷，如果她一动不动，那么我就认为她是在睡觉。'于是我从工具房里拿到一把铲子，开始竭尽全力去挖——挖到棺木后，我就用手来掀，钉子周围的木头咯吱咯吱响着，就在我马上可以得到我想要的东西时，我仿佛听到上面有人叹气，就在坟边，而且俯身向下。'如果我能掀开这个，'我嘀咕着，'我宁愿他们把我们俩都用土给埋起来！'我就更拼命地想把盖子掀开。这时又有一声叹息在我耳边响起。我好像觉得那叹息的暖气取代了那夹着雨雪的刺骨的风。我知道身边并不存在活的东西，但是，就像人们感到在黑暗中有什么活人走近来，可又并不能辨认出是什么一样，我也能真切地

limb. I relinquished my labour of agony, and turned consoled at once: unspeakably consoled. Her presence was with me: it remained while I re-filled the grave, and led me home. You may laugh, if you will; but I was sure I should see her there. I was sure she was with me, and I could not help talking to her. Having reached the Heights, I rushed eagerly to the door. It was fastened; and, I remember, that accursed Eamshaw and my wife opposed my entrance. I remember stopping to kick the breath out of him, and then hurrying up stairs, to my room, and hers. I looked round impatiently—I felt her by me—I could *almost* see her, and yet I *could not*! I ought to have sweat blood then, from the anguish of my yearning—from the fervour of my supplications to have but one glimpse! I had not one. She showed herself, as she often was in life, a devil to me! And, since then, sometimes more and sometimes less, I've been the sport of that intolerable torture! Infernal—keeping my nerves at such a stretch, that, if they had not resembled catgut, they would, long ago, have relaxed to the feebleness of Linton's. When I sat in the house with Hareton, it seemed that on going out, I should meet her; when I walked on the moors I should meet her coming in. When I went from home, I hastened to return: she *must* be somewhere at the Heights, I was certain! And when I slept in her chamber—I was beaten out of that—I couldn't lie there; for the moment I closed my eyes, she was either outside the window, or sliding back the panels, or entering the room, or even resting her darling head on the same pillow as she did when a child. And I must open my lids to see. And so I opened and closed them a hundred

感到凯茜在那儿，不是在我脚下，而是在地上。突然从我心里涌出一种轻松愉快的感觉，缓缓地流过四肢。于是我放弃了那悲痛的工作，马上获得了慰藉，一种难以言喻的慰藉。她和我同在，在我又填平墓穴时，她逗留着，并且带我回家。如果你想笑，尽管笑好了，可我可以肯定我在那儿看见她了，我也确信她跟我在一起，我也可以跟她说话。到了山庄，我急匆匆地冲到门前。门锁了，我记得那个被诅咒的恩肖和我的妻子不让我进去。我记得我停下来，踢得他喘不过气来，然后就立刻上楼，跑到我的屋子和她的屋子里。我焦躁地环顾四周——我感到她就在我身边——我几乎看得见她，可是我却什么也看不见！我当时急得要冒出血来，苦苦的祈求——出于狂热的祈求只要能够看她一眼！但我一眼也看不到。正如她生前一样魔鬼一般的折磨我！而且，从此以后，我总会或多或少被那难以忍受的折磨所捉弄！地狱呀！我的神经总是紧张兮兮的，假如我的神经不像羊肠线那样坚韧的话，早就松弛到林顿那样衰弱的地步了。每当我同哈里顿坐在屋里的时候，仿佛一走出去就会遇见她，当我漫步在旷野的时候，仿佛我只要回去就会遇见她。当我从家里出来时，我会赶着回去，因为我肯定她一定还在山庄的某个地方。而当我在她的屋子里睡觉时——我又不得不出来，我根本躺不住，只要闭上眼，她要么在窗外徘徊，要么溜进窗格，要么就走进屋里来，要么甚至将她可爱的头靠在我的枕上，像她小时候那样。而我必须睁开眼睛看

第二十九章

times a night—to be always disappointed! It racked me! I've often groaned aloud, till that old rascal Joseph no doubt believed that my conscience was playing the fiend inside of me. Now, since I've seen her, I'm pacified—a little. It was a strange way of killing, not by inches, but by fractions of hairbreadths, to beguile me with the spectre of a hope, through eighteen years!"

Mr. Heathcliff paused and wiped his forehead; his hair clung to it, wet with perspiration; his eyes were fixed on the red embers of the fire; the brows not contracted, but raised next the temples; diminishing the grim aspect of his countenance, but imparting a peculiar look of trouble, and a painful appearance of mental tension towards one absorbing subject. He only half addressed me, and I maintained silence—I didn't like to hear him talk! After a short period, he resumed his meditation on the picture, took it down and leant it against the sofa to contemplate it at better advantage; and while so occupied Catherine entered, announcing that she was ready, when her pony should be saddled.

"Send that over tomorrow," said Heathcliff to me, then turning to her he added, "You may do without your pony: it is a fine evening, and you'll need no ponies at Wuthering Heights; for what journeys you take, your own feet will serve you—Come along."

"Good-bye, Ellen!" whispered my dear little mistress. As she kissed me, her lips felt like ice. "Come and see me Ellen, don't forget."

"Take care you do no such thing, Mrs. Dean!" said her new father. "When I wish to speak to you I'll come here. I want none of

着,因此我在一个晚上往往睁眼闭眼一百次——但永远是失望!它折磨我!我常常大声呻吟,以至于约瑟夫那个老流氓认为是我的良心在身体里面起作用。不过现在,既然我看见了她,我平静了——稍稍平静了一点。那真是一种奇怪的杀人方法:不是一寸寸的,而是像头发丝那样的一丝丝地割,这十八年来就用像幽灵一样的希望来引诱和折磨我!"

希斯克利夫停下来,用手擦擦额头,他的头发粘在上面,完全被汗浸湿了。他的眼睛盯着壁炉里红红的余烬,眉毛并未皱起,只是扬得高高地接近鬓骨,减少了他脸上阴郁的神色,但多了种特别的烦恼神情,还有对待一件全神贯注的事情时那种提心吊胆的痛苦表情。他用一半脸对着我说话,我也一直沉默。我很讨厌听到他的声音!过了一会儿,他又重新对着肖像冥想,他把它取下来,靠放在沙发上,以便更好地凝视;就在他全神贯注欣赏的时候,凯瑟琳进来了,宣布她准备好了,就等给她的小马装鞍了。

"明天送过来吧,"希斯克利夫对我说,然后又转身对小姐说:"你的小马可以不用,今晚天气不错,而且你在呼啸山庄也不用着马儿,不论你想要怎样的旅行,你的脚都能帮你实现的。走吧。"

"再见了,艾伦!"我亲爱的小女主人低声说。当她亲吻我时,我感到她的嘴唇像冰一样。"记得来看我,艾伦,千万别忘了。"

"做这种事情一定要当心,迪安太太!"她的新父亲说,"我有话要对你说时,一定会到这儿来找你。我可

your prying at my house!"

He signed her to precede him; and casting back a look that cut my heart, she obeyed. I watched them from the window, walk down the garden. Heathcliff fixed Catherine's arm under his: though she dis puted the act, at first, evidently; and with rapid strides, he hurried her into the alley, whose trees concealed them.

不希望你偷偷跑到我家去!"

他打了个手势叫她走到前面,她回头看了一眼,我心如刀割,她服从了他的命令。我在窗前望着他们沿着花园走过去,希斯克利夫用自己的胳膊把凯瑟琳的胳膊夹住,虽然她开始显然很反感这样;他昂首阔步地将她带到小路上,最后那边的树木把他们遮住不见了。

Chapter 30
第三十章

I have paid a visit to the Heights, but I have not seen her since she left: Joseph held the door ha his hand, when I called to ask after her, and wouldn't let me pass. He said Mrs. Linton was "thrang," and the master was not in. Zillah has told me something of the way they go on, otherwise I should hardly know who was dead and who living. She thinks Catherine haughty, and does not like her, I can guess by her talk. My young lady asked some aid of her when she first came; but Mr. Heathcliff told her to follow her own business, and let his daughter-in-law look after herself; and Zillah willingly acquiesced, being a narrow-minded selfish woman. Catherine evinced a child's annoyance at this neglect; repaid it with contempt, and thus en-

我曾去过山庄一次,但是自从凯瑟琳走了之后我就再也没有见到过她;当我去看望她的时候,约瑟夫用手把着门,不让我进去。他说林顿太太"完蛋了",主人不在家。希拉告诉了我他们相处过日子的一些情况,要不然我根本不知道到底是谁死了,谁还活着。我可以从她的话里猜出来,她觉得凯瑟琳很傲慢,也不喜欢她。我家小姐刚去山庄时曾要她帮点忙,可是希斯克利夫叫她只做自己的事,让他儿媳妇自己照料自己。希拉本是个心胸狭窄、自私自利的女人,因此很乐意就答应了。凯瑟琳对于这种怠慢表示出孩子气的恼怒,用轻蔑的态度来回应此事,就这样,这个向

listed my informant among her enemies, as securely as if she had done her some great wrong. I had a long talk with Zillah, about six weeks ago, a little before you came, one day, when we foregathered on the moor; and this is what she told me.

"The first thing Mrs. Linton did," she said, "on her arrival at the Heights, was to run upstairs without even wishing good-evening to me and Joseph; she shut herself into Linton's room, and remained till morning. Then, while the master and Earnshaw were at breakfast, she entered the house, and asked all in a quiver if the doctor might be sent for? her cousin was very ill.

"'We know that!' answered Heathcliff; 'but his life is not worth a farthing, and I won't spend a farthing on him.'

"'But I cannot tell how to do,' she said; 'and if nobody will help me, he'll die!'

"'Walk out of the room,' cried the master, 'and let me never hear a word more about him! None here care what becomes of him; if you do, act the nurse; if you do not, lock him up and leave him.'

"Then she began to bother me, and I said I'd had enough plague with the tiresome thing; we each had our tasks, and hers was to wait on Linton, Mr. Heathcliff bid me leave that labour to her.

"How they managed together, I can't tell. I fancy he fretted a great deal, and moaned hisseln, night and day; and she had precious little rest, one could guess by her white face, and heavy eyes—she sometimes came into the kitchen all wildered like, and looked as if she would fain beg assistance; but I was not going to disobey the master: I never dare disobey him, Mrs. Dean, and though I thought it wrong that Kenneth should not be sent for, it was no concern of mine, either to advise or complain; and I always refused to meddle. Once or twice, after we had gone to bed, I've happened to open my door again, and seen her sitting crying, on the stairs' top; and then I've shut myself in, quick, for fear of being moved to interfere. I did pity her then, I'm sure: still I didn't want to lose my place, you know!

"At last, one night she came boldly into my chamber, and frightened me out of my wits, by saying —

"'Tell Mr. Heathcliff that his son is dying—I'm sure he is, this time. Get up, instantly, and tell him!'

"Having uttered this speech, she vanished again. I lay a quarter of an hour listening and trembling. Nothing stirred—the house was quiet.

"'She's mistaken,' I said to myself. 'He's got over it. I needn't disturb them.' And I began to dose. But my sleep was marred a second time, by a sharp ringing of the bell—the only bell we have, put up on purpose for Linton; and the master called to me to see what was the matter, and inform them that he wouldn't have that noise repeated.

"I delivered Catherine's message. He cursed to himself, and in a few minutes came out with a lighted candle, and proceeded to their room. I followed. Mrs. Heathcliff was seated by the bedside, with her hands folded on her knees. Her father-in-law went up, held the light to Linton's face, looked at him, and touched him; afterwards he turned to her.

"'Now—Catherine,' he said, 'how do you

背主人的意思——我从来不敢违背他,迪安太太。虽然我也觉得不请肯尼斯大夫来是不对的,但不管是给点意见还是抱怨,这都跟我没关系,我向来不愿多管闲事。有一两次,在我们都上床睡觉之后,我碰巧打开房门,就看见她坐在楼梯顶上哭,接着我就连忙关上门,生怕自己动摇了就会去干预。当时我真的可怜她,但你知道,我还是不想丢了自己的饭碗啊!

"最后,一天夜里她鼓足勇气走进我的卧室,把我吓得魂飞魄散,她说,'告诉希斯克利夫先生他儿子快要死了——我肯定他这次要死了。快起来,去告诉他!'

"说完这些话后,她又不见了。我接着躺了一刻钟,颤抖着仔细听外面的动静。外头悄无声息,整幢房子一片寂静。

"'她弄错了,'我自言自语着,'他一定已经挺过来了,我用不着去打扰他们。'然后我打起瞌睡来。可是我的睡眠再一次被刺耳的铃声打断了——这是我们仅有的一个铃,专门给林顿安装的。主人叫我去看看发生了什么事,还让我通知他们,他不想再听到那个噪音。

"我把凯瑟琳的口信告诉了他。他自言自语地咒骂了一声,几分钟后拿着一根点着的蜡烛出来,向他们的房间走去,我则跟在他后面。希斯克利夫太太坐在床边,双手抱着膝盖。她公公走上前去,用烛光照了照林顿的脸,看了看他,又摸了摸他,然后转身面对着她。

"'凯瑟琳,'他说,'现在你觉得

feel?'

"She was dumb.

"'How do you feel, Catherine?' he repeated.

"'He's safe, and I'm free,' she answered: 'I should feel well—but,' she continued with a bitterness she couldn't conceal, 'you have left me so long to struggle against death, alone, that I feel and see only death! I feel like death!'

"And she looked like it, too! I gave her a little wine. Hareton and Joseph, who had been wakened by the ringing, and the sound of feet, and heard our talk from outside, now entered. Joseph was fain, I believe, of the lad's removal; Hareton seemed a thought bothered: though he was more taken up with staring at Catherine than thinking of Linton. But the master bid him get off to bed again: we didn't want his help. He afterwards made Joseph remove the body to his chamber, and told me to return to mine, and Mrs. Heathcliff remained by herself.

"In the morning, he sent me to tell her she must come down to breakfast: she had undressed, and appeared going to sleep; and said she was ill; at which I hardly wondered. I informed Mr. Heathcliff, and he replied —

"'Well, let her be till after the funeral; and go up now and then to get her what is needful; and as soon as she seems better, tell me.'"

Cathy stayed upstairs a fortnight, according to Zillah, who visited her twice a-day, and would have been rather more friendly, but her attempts at increasing kindness were proudly and promptly repelled.

Heathcliff went up at once, to show her

Linton's will. He had bequeathed the whole of his, and what had been her moveable property to his father. The poor creature was threatened, or coaxed, into that act during her week's absence, when his uncle died. The lands, being a minor, he could not meddle with. However, Mr. Heathcliff has claimed and kept them in his wife's right, and his also: I suppose legally, at any rate Catherine, destitute of cash and friends, cannot disturb his possession.

"Nobody," said Zillah, "ever approached her door, except that once, but I... and nobody asked anything about her. The first occasion of her coming down into the house, was on a Sunday afternoon. She had cried out, when I carried up her dinner, that she couldn't bear any longer being in the cold; and I told her the master was going to Thrushcross Grange; and Earnshaw and I needn't hinder her from descending; so, as soon as she heard Heathcliff's horse trot off, she made her appearance, donned in black, and her yellow curls combed back behind her ears, as plain as a quaker: she couldn't comb them out."

"Joseph and I generally go to chapel on Sundays." (The Kirk, you know, has no minister now, explained Mrs. Dean; and they call the Methodists' or Baptists' place, I can't say which it is, at Gimmerton, a chapel.) "Joseph had gone," she continued, "but I thought proper to bide at home. Young folks are always the better for an elder's over-looking; and Hareton, with all his bashfulness, isn't a model of nice behaviour. I let him know that his cousin would very likely sit with us, and she had been always used to see the Sabbath respected; so he had as good leave his guns, and bits of in-door work

看林顿的遗嘱。林顿把自己所有的财产，以及曾经属于凯瑟琳的动产全部遗赠给了他父亲；这可怜的东西在他舅舅去世，凯瑟琳不在家的那个星期里被威逼利诱写下了那份遗嘱。至于田产，由于他还未成年，无法过问。但是希斯克利夫先生利用林顿和他妻子的权利把它占为己有。我想这应该是合法的；不管怎样，凯瑟琳无钱无势，根本没办法干预他的产权。

"除了那次我进去之外，"希拉说，"就没有人靠近过她的房门，也没有人问起她的情况。她第一次走下楼来到大厅是在一个星期日的下午。当我给她送饭的时候，她大声叫喊着说她再也受不了待在这个冰冷的地方；我告诉她说主人要去画眉田庄，恩肖和我都不会妨碍她下楼；因此当她听到希斯克利夫的马奔驰离去时，她就出现了，穿着黑衣服，那黄色的卷发梳在耳后，朴素得像个教友派信徒：她没办法把头发梳顺。

"星期天的时候，约瑟夫和我通常都会去礼拜堂。"（你知道，现在那个教堂已经没有牧师了，迪安太太解释着；他们把吉默顿美以美会或是浸礼会的场所，我说不清是哪一个，叫作礼拜堂。）"约瑟夫已经走了，"希拉接着说道，"但是我想我还是留在家里比较好。年轻人有个年纪大的看着总会好一些，况且哈里顿虽然非常羞怯，却不是个品行端正的榜样。我告诉他，他表妹可能会和我们坐在一起，她总是习惯于遵守安息日，因此当她待在那儿的时候，他最好别玩弄

alone, while she stayed. He coloured up at the news, and cast his eyes over his hands and clothes. The train oil and gunpowder were shoved out of sight in a minute. I saw he meant to give her his company; and I guessed, by his way, he wanted to be presentable; so, laughing, as I durst not laugh when the master is by, I offered to help him, if he would, and joked at his confusion. He grew sullen, and began to swear.

"Now, Mrs. Dean," she went on, seeing me not pleased by her manner, "you happen think your young lady too fine for Mr. Hareton; and happen you're right: but, I own, I should love well to bring her pride a peg lower. And what will all her learning and her daintiness do for her, now? She's as poor as you or I: poorer, I'll be bound: you're saving, and I'm doing my little all, that road."

Hareton allowed Zillah to give him her aid; and she flattered him into a good humour; so, when Catherine came, half forgetting her former insults, he tried to make himself agreeable, by the housekeeper's account.

"Missis walked in," she said, "as chill as an icicle, and as high as a princess. I got up and offered her my seat in the arm-chair. No, she turned up her nose at my civility. Earnshaw rose too, and, bid her come to the settle, and sit close by the fire: he was sure she was starved.

"'I've been starved a month and more,' she answered, resting on the word, as scornful as she could.

"And she got a chair for herself, and placed it at a distance from both of us. Having sat till she was warm, she began to look round, and discovered a number of books in the dress-

他的枪,也别管屋里那些琐碎事情。他一听到这消息就脸红了起来,还看一看自己的手和衣服。一转眼功夫鲸油和火药就全被收了起来。我看得出他有意要跟她做伴;而且从他的举动来看,他也想要让自己体面一些;所以,我笑了起来,如果主人在身旁我可不敢笑,告诉他如果他愿意,我可以帮他的忙,还取笑了他那慌张的模样。不过他的脸色马上变得阴沉,开始咒骂起来。

"现在,迪安太太,"希拉看出我对她的行为有点不满,继续说道,"也许你觉得你家小姐太高贵,哈里顿先生配不上她;也许你想得没错,可我承认我很希望能压一压她那股傲气。如今她所有的学问和修养对她来说又有什么用呢?她和你我一样的贫穷,我敢说比我们更穷,你在存钱,我也在这方面尽力呢。"

哈里顿同意希拉帮他的忙,希拉把他奉承得态度变温和了,因此当凯瑟琳过来的时候,据那女管家说,哈里顿把她从前对自己的侮辱也忘了一半,尽量让自己表现得彬彬有礼。

"太太走进来了,"她说,"像个冰柱一样寒气逼人,又像个公主一样高不可攀。我站起身把自己坐的那把扶手椅让给她。可是她却翘起鼻子对待我的礼数。恩肖也站了起来,请她坐在高背椅上,坐到火炉旁边,还说她一定是饿了。

"'我已经饿了一个多月了,'她回答道,极其轻蔑地重读那个'饿'字。

"她自己拿了把椅子,放在离我们俩很远的地方。等到身子坐暖和之后,她开始四处张望,看见柜子上有

er; she was instantly upon her feet again, stretching to reach them: but they were too high up. Her cousin, after watching her endeavours a while, at last summoned courage to help her; she held her frock, and he filled it with the first that came to hand.

"That was a great advance for the lad. She didn't thank him: still, he felt gratified that she had accepted his assistance, and ventured to stand behind as she examined them, and even to stoop and point out what struck his fancy in certain old pictures which they contained; nor was he daunted by the saucy style in which she jerked the page from his finger: he contented himself with going a bit farther back, and looking at her instead of the book. She continued reading, or seeking for something to read. His attention became, by degrees, quite centred in the study of her thick, silky curls: her face he couldn't see, and she couldn't see him. And, perhaps, not quite awake to what he did, but attracted like a child to a candle, at last he proceeded from staring to touching; he put out his hand and stroked one curl, as gently as if it were a bird. Be might have stuck a knife into her neck, she started round in such a taking.

"'Get away, this moment! How dare you touch me? Why are you stopping there?' she cried, in a tone of disgust.'I can't endure you! I'll go upstairs again, if you come near me.'

"Mr. Hareton recoiled, looking as foolish as he could do: he sat down in the settle, very quiet, and she continued turning over her volumes, another half-hour; finally, Earnshaw crossed over, and whispered to me.

"'Will you ask her to read to us, Zillah? I'm stalled of doing naught; and I do like—I could

很多书,她立刻又站了起来,想要拿书,可是它们放的位置太高了。她的表哥看着她试了一会,最后鼓起勇气过去帮她。她兜起衣服,刚刚拿下几本就装满了一兜。

"这对那个小伙子来说已经是个很大的进步了。凯瑟琳没有谢他,可是因为她接受了他的帮助,他还是觉得受宠若惊,而且在她看这些书的时候,他还大胆地站在她后面,甚至还弯腰指出书中那些激发他想像的一些古老插图,他也没有因为凯瑟琳猛翻书页,不让他的手指碰到书的那种无礼态度而感到沮丧。他心满意足地退后了一些,望着她,不再看书了。她继续看书,或者说是找些什么可看的。他的注意力渐渐集中在研究她那浓密发亮的卷发上,他看不见她的脸,她也看不见他。也许,他自己也不清楚自己做了些什么,只是像个孩子似的被一根蜡烛吸引着,最后眼看转变成了手摸。他伸出自己的手抚摸着一绺卷发,温柔得像抚摸一只小鸟一样。而凯瑟琳则猛然转过身来,就像她的脖子被他捅进一把刀子一样。

'马上滚开!你怎么敢碰我?你愣在这里干什么?'她非常厌恶地对他大叫道,'我受不了你了!如果你再靠近我,我就回楼上。'

"哈里顿先生退了回去,那样子要有多蠢就有多蠢。他很安静地坐在高背椅上,而她则接着翻弄了半个小时的书。最后,恩肖走过来,对我耳语道:

"'你能请她读给我们听吗,希拉?我都闷得发慌了,我真的喜欢,

like to hear her! Dunnot say I wanted it, but ask of yourseln.'

"'Mr. Hareton wishes you would read to us, ma'am,' I said, immediately. 'He'd take it very kind—he'd be much obliged.'

"She frowned; and, looking up, answered—

"'Mr. Hareton, and the whole set of you, will be good enough to understand that I reject any pretence at kindness you have the hypocrisy to offer! I despise you, and will have nothing to say to any of you! When I would have given my life for one kind word, even to see one of your faces, you all kept off. But I won't complain to you! I'm driven down here by the cold, not either to amuse you, or enjoy your society.'

"'What could I ha' done?' began Earnshaw. 'How was I to blame?'

"'Oh! you are an exception,' answered Mrs. Heathcliff. 'I never missed such a concern as you.'

"'But, I offered more than once, and asked,' he said, kindling up at her pertness, 'I asked Mr. Heathcliff to let me wake for you—'

"'Be silent! I'll go out of doors, or anywhere, rather than have your disagreeable voice in my ear!' said my lady.

"Hareton muttered, she might go to hell, for him! and unslinging his gun, restrained himself from his Sunday occupations no longer. He talked now, freely enough; and she presently saw fit to retreat to her solitude: but the frost had set in, and, in spite of her pride, she was forced to condescend to our company, more and more. However, I took care there should be no further scorning at my good nature: ever since, I've been as stiff as herself; and she has no

我会喜欢听她读书的！不要说是我要求的，就说你自己请她念的吧。'

"'哈里顿先生希望您把书读给我们听听，太太，'我马上说道，'他会领情，也会非常感谢您。'

"她皱起眉头，抬起头来，回答说：'哈里顿先生，还有你们这帮人，请放明白点：我拒绝你们那些对我表示友好的虚情假意！我看不起你们，也没有任何话要对你们中任何一个人说！在我宁愿舍弃性命想要听到一个温和的字眼，甚至是看看你们的脸时，你们都躲开了。可是我并不怪你们！我是被寒冷赶到楼下来的，不是来逗你们开心或是跟你们做伴的。'

"'我做错什么了吗？'恩肖开口说道，'为什么要责怪我？'

"'啊！你是个例外，'希斯克利夫太太回答说，'我从来都没想要得到你这样的关心。'

"'但是我不止一次提出过，也请求过，'他被她的傲慢无礼激怒了，说道，'我求过希斯克利夫先生让我替你守夜……'

"'住嘴！我宁愿走出房门，或者去其他任何地方，也不想听到你那让人讨厌的声音在我耳边响起！'我的太太说道。

"哈里顿嘀咕着说，在他看来，她会下地狱的！他从墙上取下枪，不再约束自己不做那些他在礼拜天会做的事情，现在他说起话来非常直率。当时她就看出还是回去独守空房比较合适些，但是已经下起寒霜，尽管她很骄傲，但也不得不降尊纡贵，渐渐地跟我们在一起。无论如何，我也小

lover or liker among us: and she does not deserve one; for, let them say the least word to her, and she'll curl back without respect of any one! She'll snap at the master himself, and as good as dares him to thrash her, and the more hurt she gets, the more venomous she grows."

At first, on hearing this account from Zillah, I determined to leave my situation, take a cottage, and get Catherine to come and live with me: but Mr. Heathcliff would as soon permit that, as he would set up Hareton in an independent house; and I can see no remedy, at present, unless she could marry again: and that scheme it does not come within my province to arrange.

Thus ended Mrs. Dean's story. Notwithstanding the doctor's prophecy, I am rapidly recovering strength; and, though it be only the second week in January, I propose getting out on horseback in a day or two, and riding over to Wuthering Heights, to inform my landlord that I shall spend the next six months in London; and, if he likes, he may look out for another tenant to take the place, after October—I would not pass another winter here for much.

心翼翼地不再让她蔑视我对她的好心好意。从那之后，我和她一样板着脸，在我们中间没人爱她或是喜欢她，她也不配，因为，谁对她说一个字，她就蜷缩起来，完全不尊敬其他人。她还会冲撞主人，毫不畏惧主人的毒打；她越是挨打，就变得越狠毒。"

刚开始听到希拉这番话，我就决定辞去自己的职务，找一间茅舍，叫凯瑟琳过来跟我一起生活，但是要让希斯克利夫先生答应，就像要他让哈里顿自立门户一样不可能。目前我还找不到什么补救的方法，除非她能再嫁，而我又无力去筹划这件事。

就这样迪安太太的故事结束了。尽管有大夫的预言在先，不过我还是迅速地恢复了体力；而且虽然现在还只是元月的第二个星期，可是我打算一两天内骑马去呼啸山庄，告诉我的房东我要去伦敦住上半年，如果他愿意的话，可以在十月之后另找房客住进去。无论如何我不会再在这里过一个冬天了。

Chapter 31
第三十一章

Yesterday was bright, calm, and frosty. I went to the Hei ghts as I proposed: my housekeeper entreated me to bear a little note from her to her young lady, and I did not refuse, for the worthy woman was not conscious of anything odd in her request. The front door stood open, but the jealous gate was fastened, as at my last visit; I knocked, and invoked Earnshaw from among the garden beds; he unchained it, and I entered. The fellow is as handsome a rustic as need be seen. I took particular notice of him this time; but then he does his best, apparently, to make the least of his advantages.

I asked if Mr. Heathcliff were at home? He answered, no; but he would be in at dinner-time. It was eleven o'clock, and I announced my intention of going in, and waiting for him, at which he immediately flung down his tools and accompanied me, in the office of watchdog, not as a substitute for the host.

We entered together; Catherine was there, making herself useful in preparing some vegetables for the approaching meal; she looked more sulky, and less spirited than when I had seen her first. She hardly raised her eyes to notice me, and continued her employment with

昨天天气晴朗，结了霜。我按照原先的计划去了呼啸山庄：我的女管家恳求我替她捎个便条给她家小姐，我没有拒绝，因为这个可敬的女仆并不觉得她的请求有什么奇怪。山庄的前门开着，不过那专为防止外人闯入的栅门被拴住了，和我上次来时一样。我敲了敲门，把恩肖从花圃中唤了过来。他解开了锁链，我走了进去。作为一个乡下人来说这家伙还是够帅气的。这次我特别留意了他，不过很显然他一点也不会利用自己的优点。

我问他希斯克利夫先生有没有在家？他回答说，不在，不过吃饭的时候他会在家。那时已经十一点钟了，我就说我想进屋去等他，他听了之后立刻丢下他的工具，陪我进去，并不是代表主人，而是尽一条看门狗的职责而已。

我们一同走进屋子，凯瑟琳在里面，正在为待会儿的午饭准备一些蔬菜，让自己显得有些用处。她比我第一次见到时显得更加沉闷、无精打采。她几乎没有抬起眼睛看我，和从前一样的完全不顾基本的礼数，始终

the same disregard to common forms of politeness, as before; never returning my bow and good-morning by the slightest acknowledgment.

"She does not seem so amiable," I thought, "as Mrs. Dean would persuade me to believe. She's a beauty, it is true; but not an angel."

Earnshaw surlily bid her remove her things to the kitchen. "Remove them yourself," she said, pushing them from her as soon as she had done; and retiring to a stool by the window, where she began to carve figures of birds and beasts out of the turnip parings in her lap. I approached her, pretending to desire a view of the garden; and, as I fancied, adroitly dropped Mrs. Dean's note onto her knee, unnoticed by Hareton—but she asked aloud, "What is that?" and chucked it off.

"A letter from your old acquaintance, the housekeeper at the Grange," I answered, annoyed at her exposing my kind deed, and fearful lest it should be imagined a missive of my own. She would gladly have gathered it up at this information, but Hareton beat her; he seized, and put it in his waistcoat, saying Mr. Heathcliff should look at it first. Thereat, Catherine silently turned her face from us, and, very stealthily, drew out her pocket-handkerchief and applied it to her eyes; and her cousin, after struggling a while to keep down his softer feelings, pulled out the letter and flung it on the floor beside her, as ungraciously as he could. Catherine caught and perused it eagerly; then she put a few questions to me concerning the inmates, rational and irrational, of her former home; and gazing towards the hills, murmured

没有回应我的鞠躬和早安问候。

"她看来并不怎么讨人喜欢。"我心想,"不像迪安太太让我相信的那样。没错,她是个美人,但不是个天使。"

恩肖粗鲁地叫她把那些东西搬到厨房去。"你自己搬。"她一边说,一边把刚收拾完的蔬菜往旁边一推,然后坐在窗前的一张凳子上休息,把萝卜皮放在腿上开始刻些鸟兽图案。我走上前去,假装想要欣赏一下花园的景色,而且,自以为很敏捷地把迪安太太的便条丢在她的膝盖上,没有让哈里顿注意到,但是她却大声问道:"那是什么?"然后一手把它丢开了。

"你的老朋友,田庄的管家给你写的信。"我答道,对于她揭穿我的善行感到颇为恼火,生怕她以为这是我自己给她的信。听到这话她本可以高兴地把信捡起来,不过却被哈里顿抢了先。他一把抓起信,塞进自己的背心里,说先得让希斯克利夫先生看看。因此凯瑟琳默默地把脸转了过去,偷偷地掏出她的手绢擦着眼睛。她的表哥心有些软下来,在内心挣扎了一番之后,又把信抽了出来,十分没礼貌地丢在她旁边的地板上。凯瑟琳捡起信,急切地看着,接着她又问了我一些关于她以前家里那些人的情况,有些问题问得很清楚明白,有些则稀里糊涂;她凝望着那些小山,喃喃自语着:

in soliloquy—

"I should like to be riding Minny down there! I should like to be climbing up there— Oh! I'm fired—I'm *stalled*, Hareton!" And she leant her pretty head back against the sill, with half a yawn and half a sigh, and lapsed into an aspect of abstracted sadness: neither caring nor knowing whether we remarked her.

"Mrs. Heathcliff," I said, after sitting some time mute, "are you not aware that I am an acquaintance of yours? so intimate, that I think it strange you won't come and speak to me. My housekeeper never wearies of talking about and praising you; and she'll be greatly disappointed if I return with no news of, or from you, except that you received her letter and said nothing!"

She appeared to wonder at this speech and asked —

"Does Ellen like you?"

"Yes, very well," I replied unhesitatingly.

"You must tell her," she continued, "that I would answer her letter, but I have no materials for writing: not even a book from which I might tear a leaf."

"No books!" I exclaimed. "How do you contrive to live here without them? if I may take the liberty to inquire. Though provided with a large library, I'm frequently very dull at the Grange; take my books away, and I should be desperate!"

"I was always reading, when I had them," said Catherine: "and Mr. Heathcliff never reads; so he took it into his head to destroy my books. I have not had a glimpse of one, for weeks. Only once, I searched through Joseph's store of theology, to his great irritation; and once, Hare-

"我真想骑着敏妮去那里！真想爬上那些山头！哎！我厌倦了，我被囚禁起来了，哈顿！"她把她那漂亮的头靠在窗台上，半打哈欠半叹息着，陷入了神情恍惚的悲哀之中，既不在乎，也不知道我们是否在注意她。

"希斯克利夫太太，"我安静地坐了一会之后说道，"你还不知道我是你的一个熟人吧？我觉得我们如此亲密，觉得你不肯过来跟我说话真是非常奇怪。我的管家一直都不知疲倦地说起你，赞美你，如果回去之后我没有带回一点关于你或是你给她的消息，只说你收到了她的信，而且没说什么，她肯定会大失所望的！"

她好像对这番话感到很惊讶，就问：

"艾伦喜欢你吗？"

"是的，很喜欢。"我毫不犹豫地回答她。

"你一定得告诉她，"她接着说，"我很想给她回信，但是我没有写字用的东西：甚至没有一本可以撕下一张纸的书。"

"没有书！"我惊叫道，"容我冒昧地问一句，没有书你在这里怎么还过得下去呢？虽然我有一个很大的书房，但我在田庄还是会常常感到闷得慌，如果把我的书拿走了，那我可就要急疯啦！"

"当我有书的时候，我就会一直看书，"凯瑟琳说，"不过希斯克利夫从不看书，因此他就想着要把我的书毁掉。我已经好几个星期没能看到一本书了。只有一次，我翻了翻约瑟夫藏的神学书，就惹得他火冒三丈；还

ton, I came upon a secret stock in your room... some Latin and Greek, and some tales and poetry: all old friends—I brought the last here—and you gathered them, as a magpie gathers silver spoons①, for the mere love of stealing! They are of no use to you; or else you concealed them in the bad spirit, that as you cannot enjoy them, nobody else shall. Perhaps *your* envy counselled Mr. Heathcliff to rob me of my treasures? But I've most of them written on my brain and printed in my heart, and you cannot deprive me of those!"

Earnshaw blushed crimson when his cousin made this revelation of his private literary accumulations, and stammered an indignant denial of her accusations.

"Mr. Hareton is desirous of increasing his amount of knowledge," I said, coming to his rescue. "He is not *envious* but *emulous* of your attainments—He'll be a clever scholar in a few years!"

"And he wants *me* to sink into a dunce, meantime," answered Catherine. "Yes, I hear him trying to spell and read to himself, and pretty blunders he makes! I wish you would repeat Chevy Chase as you did yesterday: it was extremely funny! I heard you... and I heard you turning over the dictionary, to seek out the hard words, and then cursing, because you couldn't read their explanations!"

The young man evidently thought it too bad that he should be laughed at for his ignorance, and then laughed at for trying to remove it. I had a similar notion, and, remembering Mrs. Dean's anecdote of his first attempt at en-

有一次，哈里顿，我在你屋里无意中看到一堆私下里藏起来的书，有些是拉丁文和希腊文的，还有些故事书和诗歌：全都是我的老朋友。诗歌是我带来的，你把它们都收起来，像喜鹊收集银汤勺一样，纯粹是爱偷东西而已，它们对你来说一点用都没有；不然就是你故意把它们藏起来，既然你不会读书，也叫别人不能看。也许是你出于嫉妒建议希斯克利夫先生，让他把我的珍藏抢去的吧？可是大部分书已经写在我的脑子里，刻在我的心里了，这些是你没办法夺走的！"

当恩肖听到他的表妹揭穿了他私下收集文学书时，他的脸变得通红，结结巴巴地，恼怒地否认对他的那些指控。

"哈里顿先生是想要增长他的知识。"我替他解围道，"他不是嫉妒你，而是想超过你的学识。几年之后他就会成为一个聪明的学者了。"

"同时他还想要让我变成一个傻瓜。"凯瑟琳回答说，"没错，我听到他试着想要拼音朗读，而且还错误百出！真希望你能再念一遍'追逐'，就像你昨天念的那样：那真是太可笑了！我听到了，还听到你翻字典查生字，然后又咒骂起来，因为你看不懂那些词的解释！"

这个年轻人显然觉得这很难堪，先是因为愚昧无知而被人嘲笑，然后想要去除愚昧，却又被人嘲笑。我也颇有同感，记起迪安太太所说的那些关于他当初曾想要冲破从小养成的蒙

---

① 欧洲民间传说，认为喜鹊喜欢把闪光发亮的东西衔入窝中，因而喜鹊成了小偷小摸的象征。

lightening the darkness in which he had been reared, I observed —

"But, Mrs. Heathcliff, we have each had a commencement, and each stumbled and tottered on the threshold, and had our teachers scorned, instead of aiding us, we should stumble and totter yet."

"Oh!" she replied, "I don't wish to limit his acquirements... still, he has no right to appropriate what is mine, and make it ridiculous to me with his vile mistakes and mispronunciations! Those books, both prose and verse, were consecrated to me by other associations, and I hate to have them debased and profaned in his mouth! Besides, of all, he has selected my favourite pieces that I love the most to repeat, as if out of deliberate malice!"

Hareton's chest heaved in silence a minute: he laboured under a severe sense of mortification and wrath, which it was no easy task to suppress. I rose and, from a gentlemanly idea of relieving his embarrassment, took up my station in the doorway, surveying the external prospect as I stood. He followed my example, and left the room; but presently re-appeared, bearing half a dozen volumes in his hands, which he threw into Catherine's lap, exclaiming—

"Take them! I never want to hear, or read, or think of them again!"

"I won't have them, now," she answered. "I shall connect them with you, and hate them."

She opened one that had obviously been often turned over, and read a portion in the drawling tone of a beginner; then laughed, and threw it from her. "And listen," she continued provokingly, commencing a verse of an old bal-昧的故事，我就说：

"不过，希斯克利夫太太，我们每个人都有开始，每个人都在起点上跌跌撞撞，如果我们的老师只会嘲弄我们而不来帮助我们，那我们到现在还是跌跌撞撞的呢。"

"哦。"她答道，"我并没有想要限制他上进，但是他也没有权利来把我的东西占为己有，而且他那些讨厌的错误和不正确的发音让我觉得很可笑！这些书，不管散文还是诗集，都有一些其他的联想，因此对我来说是非常神圣的，我讨厌这些书在他的口中被贬低、被亵渎！更何况他居然选了那些我最爱反复阅读的篇章，好像是在存心捣乱一样！"

哈里顿的胸膛默默地上下起伏着：他是在极度屈辱与愤怒的感觉下挣扎着，想要把他们压抑下去是件不容易的事情。我站了起来，出于想要缓解他的困窘的高尚念头，走到了门口，站在那里，浏览着门外的风景。他学着我的样子，也离开了房间，但是很快又回来了，手中捧着六七本书，把它们扔到凯瑟琳的腿上，叫道：

"拿去吧！我永远都不要听，不要读，也不要再想到它们了！"

"我现在不要了，"她回答道，"看见这些书我就会联想到你，我恨它们。"

她翻开一本显然是经常翻阅的书，用一种初学者的语调拖长声音读了一段，然后大笑起来，把书丢在一旁。"听着。"她带着挑衅的语气继续说，用同样的腔调读了一节古歌谣。

lad in the same fashion.

But his self-love would endure no further torment: I heard, and not altogether disapprovingly, a manual check given to her saucy tongue— The little wretch had done her utmost to hurt her cousin's sensitive though uncultivated feelings, and a physical argument was the only mode he had of balancing the account and repaying its effects on the inflicter. He afterwards gathered the books and hurled them on the fire. I read in his countenance what anguish it was to offer that sacrifice to spleen—I fancied that as they consumed, he recalled the pleasure they had already imparted, and the triumph and ever-increasing pleasure he had anticipated from them; and I fancied, I guessed the incitement to his secret studies, also. He had been content with daily labour and rough animal enjoyments, till Catherine crossed his path. Shame at her scorn, and hope of her approval, were his first prompters to higher pursuits; and instead of guarding him from one, and winning him the other, his endeavours to raise himself had produced just the contrary result.

"Yes; that's all the good that such a brute as you can get from them!" cried Catherine, sucking her damaged lip, and watching the conflagration with indignant eyes.

"You'd *better* hold your tongue, now!" he answered fiercely.

And his agitation precluding further speech, he advanced hastily to the entrance, where I made way for him to pass. But, ere he had crossed the door-stones, Mr. Heathcliff, coming up the causeway, encountered him, and laying hold of his shoulder, asked —

"What's to do now, my lad?"

但是他的自爱让他无法再忍受这些折磨。我听见了一种用手来制止她那傲慢舌头的声音（我也并非完全不赞成这种方式）。这个小坏蛋处心积虑地伤害她表哥的感情，虽然这感情未经开化，但是却很敏感，体罚是他向折磨他的人算帐报复的惟一方法。之后哈里顿捡起那些书一股脑儿全扔进火里。我从他脸上看出他心里是多么的痛苦，才让他在愤怒中献上这个祭品。我想像着，在这些书燃烧的时候，他回味着它们带给他的欢乐，以及那些从书中看到的胜利和日益增长的快乐。我想我也猜到了是什么在鼓励着他在私底下学习。从前他满足于日常劳作和野兽般的享乐，直到凯瑟琳出现，他生活的道路才得到了改变。对她的嘲笑感到羞耻，又期待博得她的赞许，这就是他追求上进的最初动机，而他尽力提升自己的努力，既没能让他避开羞辱，也没能让他得到赞许，却产生了恰恰相反的结果。

"是啊，这就是像你这样的畜生能从那些书里得到的所有好处！"凯瑟琳喊道，吮着她那受伤的嘴唇，愤怒地看着那堆熊熊的火焰。

"你最好马上住嘴！"他凶狠地回答道。

他激动得不能开口说话，急匆匆地向大门口走去，我让开路让他走了过去。但是在他跨过门前的石阶时，希斯克利夫先生走上铺道，正好碰到了他，便抓着他的肩膀问道：

"这个时候还要去干什么，我的孩子？"

"没有，没干什么，"他着挣脱了身

第三十一章

"Naught, naught!" he said, and broke away, to enjoy his grief and anger in solitude.

Heathcliff gazed after him, and sighed.

"It will be odd, if I thwart myself!" he muttered, unconscious that I was behind him. "But, when I look for his father in his face, I find *her* every day more! How the devil is he so like? I can hardly bear to see him."

He bent his eyes to the ground, and walked moodily in. There was a restless, anxious expression in his countenance I had never remarked there before; and he looked sparer in person. His daughter-in-law, on perceiving him through the window, immediately escaped to the kitchen, so that I remained alone.

"I'm glad to see you out of doors again, Mr. Lockwood," he said in reply to my greeting, "from selfish motives partly: I don't think I could readily supply your loss in this desolation. I've wondered, more than once, what brought you here."

"An idle whim, I fear, sir," was my answer; "or else an idle whim is going to spirit me away. I shall set out for London, next week; and I must give you warning, that I feel no disposition to retain Thrushcross Grange beyond the twelve-months I agreed to rent it. I believe I shall not live there any more."

"Oh, indeed! you're tired of being banished from the world, are you?" he said. "But, if you be coming to plead off paying for a place you won't occupy, your journey is useless: I never relent in exacting my due, from any one."

"I'm coming to plead off nothing about it!" I exclaimed, considerably irritated. "Should you wish it, I'll settle with you now," and I drew my note-book from my pocket.

"子，独自一人去承受他的悲伤与愤怒。

希斯克利夫凝视着他的背影，叹了口气。

"如果我妨碍了自己，那才奇怪呢，"他嘀咕着，并不知道我在他背后，"可是当我在他的脸上寻找他父亲的影子时，却一天天地看到了她！见鬼了！哈里顿怎么会那么像她？我简直不能看到他。"

他的目光落在地上，闷闷不乐地走进屋去，脸上带着一种不安而又焦虑的表情，那是我从未在他脸上看到过的；而且他本人看起来消瘦了一些。他的儿媳妇从窗里看到他走进屋，就立刻跑去了厨房，因此就只剩下我一个人。

"很高兴看见你又可以出门了，洛克伍德先生，"他回答我的招呼说道，"一部分是出于自私的动机，我觉得自己没办法轻易地弥补你在这荒山野岭的损失。我不止一次地感到非常纳闷，是什么风把你吹到这儿来的。"

"恐怕是种无聊的怪念头吧，先生，"我回答他说，"又或者是一种无聊的怪念头诱使我离开这里。下个星期我要去伦敦了，我必须来先知会你一声，在我约定租用画眉山庄十二个月之后，我无意再保留它，我想自己不会再在那儿住下去了。"

"哦，真的吗！你已经厌倦了被流放在尘世之外的生活了，是吧？"他说，"但是如果你来这里是想要请求停付租金的话，那你这一趟算是白跑了：我在催讨那些我应得的费用时是从来都不会心软的，对谁都一样。"

"我来这儿不是要请求少付租金，"我非常愤怒地说道，"如果你愿意的话，我现在就跟你把账算清。"

"No, no," he replied coolly; "You'll leave sufficient behind to cover your debts if you fail to return: I'm not in such a hurry—sit down and take your dinner with us; a guest that is safe from repeating his visit can generally be made welcome; Catherine! bring the things in: where are you?"

Catherine re-appeared, bearing a tray of knives and forks.

"You may get your dinner with Joseph," muttered Heathcliff aside, "and remain in the kitchen till he is gone."

She obeyed his directions, very punctually: perhaps she had no temptation to transgress. Living among clowns and misanthropists, she probably cannot appreciate a better class of people, when she meets them.

With Mr. Heathcliff, grim and saturnine, on one hand, and Hareton, absolutely dumb, on the other, I made a somewhat cheerless meal, and bid adieu early. I would have departed by the back way, to get a last glimpse of Catherine, and annoy old Joseph; but Hareton received orders to lead up my horse, and my host himself escorted me to the door, so I could not fulfil my wish.

"How dreary life gets over in that house!" I reflected, while riding down the road. "What a realization of something more romantic than a fairy tale it would have been for Mrs. Linton Heathcliff, had she and I struck up an attachment, as her good nurse desired, and migrated together into the stirring atmosphere of the town!"

说着我便从口袋里取出记事簿。

"不，不，"他冷淡地回答道，"如果你不回来了，那你就得留下一笔足够的钱来清偿你欠下的债。我不是很着急，先坐下来，跟我们一块吃个午饭吧。一个将来肯定不会再拜访的客人通常都是受人欢迎的。凯瑟琳！把饭菜端出来，你在哪里？"

凯琴琳又出现了，手里端着一盘刀叉。

"你可以跟约瑟夫一块吃饭，"希斯克利夫在旁边轻声嘀咕着，"在厨房里待着，等她走了再出来。"

她非常顺从地执行他的指示，也许她根本没有受到违抗命令的诱惑。生活在粗人和厌世者之中，即使遇到上流社会的那些人，她大概也不会赏识了。

我的一旁坐着冷酷而阴沉的希斯克利夫先生，另一旁则是一声不吭的哈里顿，这顿饭吃得多少有点不愉快，于是我就早早地告辞离去。我本想着从后门走，可以看凯瑟琳最后一眼，还可以气气那个约瑟夫老头，可是哈里顿奉命把我的马牵了过来，而这位主人亲自陪着我走到门口，因此我未能如愿。

"这一家人的生活可真是沉闷啊！"当我骑着马走在大路上的时候心里想着，"如果林顿·希斯克利夫太太和我一见钟情、谈起恋爱，就像她的好仆人期望的那样，而且一起搬去热热闹闹的城里，那么她就能实现比童话故事还要浪漫的事情了！"

Chapter 32

第三十二章

1802.—This September, I was invited to devastate the moors of a friend, in the North; and, on my journey to his abode, I unexpectedly came within fifteen miles of Gimmerton. The hostler at a roadside public-house was holding a pail of water to refresh my horses, when a cart of very green oats, newly reaped, passed by, and he remarked —

"Yon's frough Gimmerton, nah! They're allas three wick" after other folk wi' ther harvest."

"Gimmerton?" I repeated—my residence in that locality had already grown dim and dreamy. "Ah! I know! How far is it from this?"

"Happen fourteen mile' o'er th' hills, and a rough road," he answered.

A sudden impulse seized me to visit Thrushcross Grange. It was scarcely noon, and I conceived that I might as well pass the night under my own roof, as in an inn. Besides, I could spare a day easily, to arrange matters with my landlord, and thus save myself the trouble of invading the neighbourhood again. Having rested a while, I directed my servant to inquire the

一八〇二年。——这年九月,北方一个朋友邀请我去原野打猎,在我去他的居住地的旅途中,无意来到了一处地方,离吉默顿不到十五英里。路旁一家客栈的仆役正提着一桶水来饮我的马,正在这时,有一辆大车,装着新收割的碧绿的燕麦,从前面经过,他就说:

"你们是从吉默顿来的吧,哪!他们总是落后,人家都收割了三个礼拜了,他们才开始动手。"

"吉默顿?"我重复了一句——我在那儿住过一段时间,但在记忆中已经变得模糊,像梦一般了。"啊!我知道了。那个地方离这儿有多远?"

"翻过山,大概有十四英里吧,路不好走。"他回答道。

一种突如其来的冲动促使我想去画眉田庄,那时还不到中午,我想与其在客栈里过夜,倒不妨在自己宅子的屋顶下过夜呢。更何况,我可以非常方便地腾出一天的时间跟我的房东安排事务,这样一来,就免得以后再到附近这一带来一趟了。休息片刻以后,我打发我的仆人去询问到村子的

way to the village; and, with great fatigue to our beasts, we managed the distance in some three hours.

I left him there, and proceeded down the valley alone. The grey church looked greyer, and the lonely churchyard lonelier. I distinguished a moor sheep cropping the short turf on the graves. It was sweet, warm weather—too warm for travelling; but the heat did not hinder me from enjoying the delightful scenery above and below: had I seen it nearer August, I'm sure it would have tempted me to waste a month among its solitudes. In winter nothing more dreary, in summer nothing more divine, than those glens shut in by hills, and those bluff, bold swells of heath.

I reached the Grange before sunset, and knocked for admittance; but the family had retreated into the back premises, I judged by one thin, blue wreath curling from the kitchen chimney, and they did not hear. I rode into the court. Under the porch, a girl of nine or ten sat knitting, and an old woman reclined on the horse-steps, smoking a meditative pipe.

"Is Mrs. Dean within?" I demanded of the dame.

"Mistress Dean? Nay!" she answered, "shoo doesn't bide here; shoo's up at th' Heights."

"Are you the housekeeper, then?" I continued.

"Eea, Aw keep th' hause," she replied.

"Well, I'm Mr. Lockwood, the master. Are there any rooms to lodge me in, I wonder? I wish to stay here all night."

"T' maister!" she cried in astonishment. "Whet, whoiver knew yah wur coming? Yah

路，于是三个小时之后我们到了那边，真把我们的牲口累得够呛。

我把仆人留在那儿，独自沿着山谷向前走去。那灰色的教堂显得更灰暗了，荒凉的墓地也更见荒凉。我望见有一只沼泽地羊正在吃着坟上的矮草。那正是可爱的、温暖的天气——虽然对于旅行来说太暖和了些；但并不妨碍我尽情欣赏这高高低低的美景；要是我在快到八月时看见这样的美景，我相信它会诱惑我在那寂静的环境中消磨一个月。冬季里再没有什么比它们更为荒凉了，夏季里再没有什么比它们更美妙神奇了——那些被群山环绕的溪谷，以及荒地上那些陡峭醒目连续起伏的波浪。

在太阳落山前，我赶到了田庄，敲了门等着被准许进去；可是从厨房烟囱里冒出的一圈圈细细的蓝色的烟圈，我猜想家里人都已经到后屋去了，所以他们没听见。我骑马进了院子。走廊下面坐着一个九、十岁的女孩子，正在编结东西，一个老妇人靠在门阶上，悠闲地抽着烟斗。

"迪安太太在家吗？"我问那老妇人。

"迪安太太？她不在！"她回答道，"她不在这儿住了；她住到山庄去啦。"

"那么，你是女管家吧？"我接着问。

"是啊，是我掌管着这个家，"她回答。

"那好，我是洛克伍德先生，这儿的主人。不知道有没有房间好让我住进去？我想住一晚上。"

"主人！"她惊叫道。"怎么，怎么也没有料到您会来呀？您应该捎个信

sud ha' send word! They's nowt norther dry— nor mensful abaht t' place: nowt there is n't!"

She threw down her pipe and bustled in, the girl followed, and I entered too; soon perceiving that her report was true, and, moreover, that I had almost upset her wits by my unwelcome apparition. I bid her be composed— I would go out for a walk; and, meantime, she must try to prepare a corner of a sitting-room for me to sup in, and a bed-room to sleep in. No sweeping and dusting, only good fires and dry sheets were necessary. She seemed willing to do her best; though she thrust the hearth-brush into the grates in mistake for the poker, and malappropriate d several other articles of her craft: but I retired, confiding in her energy for a resting-place against my return. Wuthering Heights was the goal of my proposed excursion. An after-thought brought me back, when I had quitted the court.

"All well at the Heights?" I enquired of the woman.

"Eea, f't owt Ee knaw!" she answered, skurrying away with a pan of hot cinders.

I would have asked why Mrs. Dean had deserted the Grange, but it was impossible to delay her at such a crisis, so I turned away and made my exit, rambling leisurely along, with the glow of a sinking sun behind, and the mild glory of a rising moon in front—one fading, and the other brightening, as I quitted the park, and climbed the stony byroad branching off to Mr. Heathcliff's dwelling. Before I arrived in sight of it, all that remained of day was a beamless, amber light along the west: but I could see every pebble on the path, and every blade of grass, by that splendid moon. I had neither to climb

儿来的。这儿还没有收拾过，没有一块地方是干干净净的，真是不像样！"

她丢下烟斗，慌慌张张地进去，女孩子跟在她后面，我也走了进去，立刻就发现她的汇报是真实情况，而我这不受欢迎的突然出现几乎把她搞昏了。我叫她镇静些，我会出去散散步；不过，同时她得在起居室给我清理出一个角落让我吃饭，再收拾好一个卧室让我睡觉。扫地掸灰都不必了，只要生起一炉旺火，铺一床干被单就可以了。她仿佛很愿意卖力，虽说她把炉帚当火钳给插进壁炉里去了，还用错了其他几种工具——反正我离开了，相信在我回来之前，她会尽力为我准备好一个歇息的地方。呼啸山庄是我这次出游的目的地。我刚走出院子，一个念头又使我转了回来。

"山庄那边的人都还好吧？"我问那老妇人。

"都好，只要是我知道的！"她回答道，端着一盆热炭渣急匆匆离开了。

我原打算问她迪安太太为什么抛下田庄，但在这样一个关键时刻跟她打岔是不可能的，所以我就转身出去，一路上悠闲地散步，身后是落日的余晖，前面是正在升起的月亮温和的清辉——一个渐渐暗下去，另一个渐渐亮起来——这时我走出庄园，攀上一条石子路，它的支路通往希斯克利夫的住所。在我还没能望得见那儿以前，西天只剩下一抹若有若无的琥珀色光彩；但借着皎洁的月光，依然可以看清小路上每一颗石子每一根草叶。我不必从栅门上爬过去，也不用

the gate, nor to knock— it yielded to my hand. That is an improvement! I thought. And I noticed another, by the aid of my nostrils; a fragrance of stocks and wall flowers, wafted on the air, from amongst the homely fruit trees.

Both doors and lattices were open; and yet, as is usually the case in a coal district, a fine, red fire illuminated the chimney: the comfort which the eye derives from it, renders the extra heat endurable. But the house of Wuthering Heights is so large, that the inmates have plenty of space for withdrawing out of its influence; and, accordingly, what inmates there were had stationed themselves not far from one of the windows. I could both see them and hear them talk before I entered, and looked and listened in consequence; being moved thereto by a mingled sense of curiosity, and envy that grew as I lingered.

"Con-*trary*!" said a voice, as sweet as a silver bell —"That for the th ird time, you dunce! I'm not going to tell you, again—Recollect, or I pull your hair!"

"Contrary, then," answered another, in deep but softened tones. "And now, kiss me, for minding so well."

"No, read it over first correctly, without a single mistake."

The male speaker began to read: he was a young man, respectably dressed, and seated at a table, having a book before him. His handsome features glowed with pleasure, and his eyes kept impatiently wandering from the page to a small white hand over his shoulder, which recalled him by a smart slap on the cheek, whenever its owner detected such signs of inattention. Its owner stood behind; her light shining ringlets

敲门，门顺手一推就开了。这是一种改进，我想。我的鼻孔又帮助我发现了另一项改进，从那些亲切的果树的空气中飘荡着一种紫罗兰和桂竹兰的芳香。

门窗都敞开着；不过正像产煤地区的通常情况那样，一炉烧得旺旺的火照亮了壁炉：由这一眼望去所得的舒适之感也让那过多的热量成为可以忍受的了。但是呼啸山庄的正屋是那么大，以至于屋里的人有的是空地方来躲开那热力；因此，屋子里的人都一个个呆在离窗口不远的地方。我还没进门之前，就可以望见他们，听见他们讲话，于是我便看着听着；一股好奇心与妒嫉心的混合感觉驱使我这么做，而当我在那儿徘徊的时候，这种混合的感觉还在逐渐滋长。

"相——反！"一个如银铃般甜蜜的声音说道——"这是第三遍了，你这个笨蛋！我可不会再告诉你了——记住，要不我可就要扯你的头发了！"

"好了，相反，"另一个答道，是深沉而又柔和的声调。"现在，亲我一下吧，因为我记得这么好。"

"不，先把它正确地念过一遍，一个错也不能有。"

那说话的男子开始念：他是一个年轻人，穿着体面，坐在一张桌子旁，面前放着一本书。他那英俊的面貌因为欢喜而容光焕发，他的眼睛总是不安分地从书页上溜到一只放在他肩头的白白的小手上，而每当这种不专心的样子被那人发现的时候，这只小手就会在他脸上很快地掴一下。小手的主人站在背后，当她俯身辅导他

blending, at intervals, with his brown locks, as she bent to superintend his studies; and her face—it was lucky he could not see her face, or he would never have been so steady—I could, and I bit my lip, in spite, at having thrown away the chance I might have had, of doing something besides staring at its smiting beauty.

The task was done, not free from further blunders; but the pupil claimed a reward, and received at least five kisses: which, however, he generously returned. Then, they came to the door, and from their conversation, I judged they were about to issue out and have a walk on the moors. I supposed I should be condemned in Hareton Earnshaw's heart, if not by his mouth, to the lowest pit in the infernal regions, if I showed my unfortunate person in his neighbourhood then; and feeling very mean and malignant, I skulked round to seek refuge in the kitchen.

There was unobstructed admittance on that side also; and, at the door, sat my old friend, Nelly Dean, sewing and singing a song, which was often interrupted from within, by harsh words of scorn and intolerance, uttered in far from musical accents.

"Aw'd rayther, by th' haulf, hev'em swearing i' my lugs frough morn tuh neeght, nur hearken yah, hahsiver!" said the tenant of the kitchen, in answer to an unheard speech of Nelly's. "It's a blazing shaime, ut Aw cannut oppen t' Blessed Book, bud yah set up them glories tuh sattan, un' all t' flaysome wickednesses ut iver wer born intuh t' warld! Oh! yah're a raight nowt; un' shoo's another; un' that poor lad'ull be lost, atween ye. Poor lad!" he added, with a groan; "he's witched, Aw'm

学习时，她那轻柔发亮的卷发有时就和他棕色的头发混在一起了；而她的脸——多亏他看不见她的脸，要不他决不会这样定下神来——我却看得见，我怨恨地咬着自己的嘴唇，因为我已经失掉了大好机会，现在就只能傻盯着那令人倾倒的美人了。

任务完成了，可没有少犯大错，但那学生却要求奖励，得了至少五个吻，而他又慷慨地回敬了一番。然后他们来到门口，从他们的谈话中我想他们大概要出去，到荒野上散步。我猜想，如果这时我这个不幸的人出现在他附近的话，哈里顿·恩肖即使嘴里不说，心里也要诅咒我下到地狱的最底层去。因为感到自己非常卑鄙恶劣，我偷偷摸摸地绕道，想到厨房去找个安身之所。

那边同样是畅通无阻，门口坐着我的老朋友内莉·迪安，一边做针线，一边唱歌。她的歌声常被从里面传来的刺耳的嘲笑与不耐烦的话所打断，那声音一点也合不上音乐的节奏。

"我宁可从早到晚，耳朵里只听一个人咒骂，也不要听你这哼哼唧唧！"厨房里的那个人嚷道，可能是回答内莉说的一句连我也没听清的话。"真是太丢脸了，弄得我都不能打开《圣经》，可你把荣耀归于魔鬼撒旦，归于这尘世间产生的一切罪恶！唉！你实在是个一文不值的废物，而她是另一个，可怜那个小伙子落在你们俩手里。可怜的小伙子啊！"他又呻吟着添了一句，"我敢断定，他是受到了蛊惑！哦，

sartin on't! O, Lord, judge 'em, fur they's norther law nur justice amang wer rullers!"

"No! or we should be sitting in flaming fagots, I suppose," retorted the singer. "But wisht, old man, and read your Bible, like a christian, and never mind me. This is 'Fairy Annie's Wedding'—a bonny tune— it goes to a dance."

Mrs. Dean was about to recommence, when I advanced; and recog- nising me directly, she jumped to her feet, crying—

"Why, bless you, Mr. Lockwood! How could you think of returning in this way? All's shut up at Thrushcross Grange. You should have given us notice!"

"I've arranged to be accommodated there, for as long as I shall stay," I answered. "I depart again tomorrow. And how are you transplanted here, Mrs. Dean? tell me that."

"Zillah left, and Mr. Heathcliff wished me to come, soon after you went to London, and stay till you returned. But, step in, pray! Have you walked from Gimmerton this evening?"

"From the Grange," I replied; "and, while they make me lodging room there, I want to finish my business with your master; because I don't think of having another opportunity in a hurry."

"What business, sir?" said Nelly, con- ducting me into the house. "He's gone out at present, and won't return soon."

"About the rent," I answered.

"Oh! then it is with Mrs. Heathcliff you must settle," she observed; "or rather with me. She has not learnt to manage her affairs yet, and I act for her: there's nobody else."

I looked surprised.

上帝啊，审判她们吧，因为我们这些统治者既没有王法，又没有正义！"

"不！我想，否则只怕我们就会给绑在干柴堆上，受着火刑呢，"那歌唱家反驳道，"得了吧，老头，像个信徒一样去念你的《圣经》吧，永远不要来管我。这是'安妮仙子的婚礼'———支动听的曲子——是配着跳舞来用的。"

迪安太太刚要接着开口继续唱，我走上前去；她立刻就认出了我，她跳了起来，嚷道——

"哦，祝福你，洛克伍德先生！你怎么会想到就这样回来了？画眉田庄的一切东西全都收拾起来了。你应该先给我们一个通知！"

"我在那边安排好住宿，为了暂时住下去，"我回答道。"明天我又要离开了。你怎么会搬到这边来了，迪安太太？告诉我吧。"

"在你去伦敦后不久，希拉就离开了，希斯克利夫先生希望我过来，一直住到你回来。但是，请进来啊！你是今天晚上从吉默顿走来的吗？"

"从田庄来，"我答道，"我要乘她们在那边给我收拾房间时，跟你的主人把我的事务处理完，因为我认为以后不会再有一个忙中偷闲的机会了。"

"什么事务啊，先生？"内莉说着，把我引进了正屋。"他现在出去了。并且一时还回不来呢。"

"关于租约的事儿。"我回答道。

"啊！那么你肯定得跟希斯克利夫太太结算了，"她说道，"或者不如跟我谈吧。她还没学会怎么料理她的事务呢，我替她来代理：再没别人啦。"

我露出一幅惊讶的样子。

"Ah! you have not heard of Heathcliff's death, I see!" she continued.

"Heathcliff dead?" I exclaimed, astonished. "How long ago?"

"Three months since: but, sit down, and let me take your hat, and I'll tell you all about it. Stop, you have had nothing to eat, have you?"

"I want nothing. I have ordered supper at home. You sit down too. I never dreamt of his dying! Let me hear how it came to pass. You say you don't expect them back for some time—the young people?"

"No—I have to scold them every evening, for their late rambles: but they don't care for me. At least, have a drink of our old ale; it will do you good: you seem weary."

She hastened to fetch it, before I could refuse, and I heard Joseph asking whether "it warn't a crying scandal that she should have fellies at her time of life? And then, to get them jocks out uh' t' Maister's cellar! He fair shaamed to 'bide still and see it."

She did not stay to retaliate, but re-entered, in a minute, bearing a reaming silver pint, whose contents I lauded with becoming earnest—ness. And afterwards she furnished me with the sequel of Heathcliff's history. He had a "queer" end, as she expressed it.

I was summoned to Wuthering Heights, within a fortnight of your leaving us, she said; and I obeyed joyfully, for Catherine's sake. My first interview with her grieved and shocked me! she had altered so much since our separation. Mr. Heathcliff did not explain his reasons for taking a new mind about my coming here; he only told me he wanted me, and he was tired of seeing Catherine: I must make the little

"哦！我明白了！你还没有听说希斯克利夫去世了。"她接着说道。

"希斯克利夫死了？"我惊呼道，大吃一惊。"多久了？"

"三个月了，不过，请坐下吧，把帽子给我，让我一五一十地都告诉你。等一下，你还没吃过什么东西吧，对不对？"

"我一点儿也不想吃，我已关照家里准备晚饭了。你也坐下吧。我做梦也没想到他已经死了！让我听听是怎么回事。你说你想他们一时不会回来——是说那两个年轻人吗？"

"是的——我每天晚上不得不责备他们半夜三更还在外面闲逛。可他们不理我。至少，你得喝口我们的陈年老酒吧；这会对你有好处的；你看来有些累了。"

她赶紧去拿酒，还没等我来得及拒绝。我听见约瑟夫在问：'像她这样年纪的女佣还有人追求，这不是件惹人耳目的耻辱吗？这还没完，还要从主人的地窖里拿酒！他坐在那儿看着，真替她害臊。"

她并没停下来回嘴，而是立马又进来，端来一个大银壶，我连声称赞那里面的酒。这以后她就把关于希斯克利夫后来的往事讲给我听。按照她所说的，他有一个"奇怪"的结局。

你离开我们还不到两个礼拜，我就被叫到呼啸山庄来，因为凯瑟琳，我高兴地听从了。第一次跟她见面让我又伤心又震惊！自从我们分开以后，她变得这么厉害。希斯克利夫先生并没说明他为什么又改变主意让我到这儿来。他只告诉我说他需要我，他已经厌倦了再看到凯瑟琳；我必须把小客厅当我的起居室，而且把她

parlour my sitting room, and keep her with me. It was enough if he were obliged to see her once or twice a day. She seemed pleased at this arrangement; and, by degrees, I smuggled over a great number of books, and other articles, that had formed her amusement at the Grange; and flattered myself we should get on in tolerable comfort. The delusion did not last long. Catherine, contented at first, in a brief space grew irritable and restless. For one thing, she was forbidden to move out of the garden, and it fretted her sadly to be confined to its narrow bounds, as Spring drew on; for another, in following the house, I was forced to quit her frequently, and she complained of loneliness: she preferred quarrelling with Joseph in the kitchen, to sitting at peace in her solitude. I did not mind their skirmishes: but Hareton was often obliged to seek the kitchen also, when the master wanted to have the house to himself; and though, in the beginning, she either left it at his approach, or quietly joined in my occupations, and shunned remarking or addressing him—and though he was always as sullen and silent as possible-after a while, she changed her behaviour, and became incapable of letting him alone: talking at him; commenting on his stupidity and idleness; expressing her wonder how he could endure the life he lived—how he could sit a whole evening staring into the fire, and dozing.

"He's just like a dog, is he not, Ellen?" she once observed, "or a cart horse? He does his work, eats his food, and sleeps, eternally! What a blank, dreary mind he must have! Do you ever dream, Hareton? And, if you do, what is it about? But you can't speak to me!"

Then she looked at him; but he would nei-

带在身边。如果他每天不得不看到她一两次，那也足够了。凯瑟琳对这一安排十分高兴。我一点一点偷偷运来一大批书，还有她在田庄作为消遣的其他东西；我自鸣得意，以为我们可以比较舒服地生活下去。可惜这一幻想并没持续很久。凯瑟琳开始倒是满足了，不久就变得焦躁不安。一件事是她是被禁止走出花园，春天来了，却把她关禁在狭小的范围之内，这使她十分恼火；另一件就是我为了要料理家务，也被迫要经常离开她，而她就抱怨孤单，她宁愿在厨房里跟约瑟夫吵架，也不愿单独一人安静地坐在那。我并不介意他们的小冲突：可每当主人想要一个人独用正屋时，哈里顿也不得不到厨房去！虽然起初要么是他一靠近她就离开，要么是默默帮我做家务，既不提起他也不跟他说话——而他也总是尽可能沉默寡言——没多久，她就改变了她的做法，也变得再不能让他那样清净了；她议论他，批评他的愚蠢和懒散：对他如何能够忍受他所过的生活表示她的迷惑不解——他怎么能一整晚的坐在那，死盯着炉火，打着瞌睡。

"他就像条狗，不是吗？艾伦？"有一次她这么说，"要不就是一匹套车的马吧！他干他的活，吃他的饭，睡他的觉，永远是这样！他的头脑该是多么空洞和灰暗啊！哈里顿，你从来没有做过梦吗？要是做过，都梦见些什么呢？但是你没法跟我说话！"

接着她便望着他，可他既不开

ther open his mouth nor look again.

"He's perhaps, dreaming now," she continued. "He twitched his shoulder as Juno twitches hers. Ask him, Ellen."

"Mr. Hareton will ask the master to send you up stairs, if you don't behave!" I said. He had not only twitched his shoulder but clenched his fist, as if tempted to use it.

"I know why Hareton never speaks, when I am in the kitchen," she exclaimed, on another occasion. "He is afraid I shall laugh at him. Ellen, what do you think? He began to teach himself to read once; and, because I laughed, he burned his books, and dropped it: was he not a fool?"

"Were not you naughty?" I said; "answer me that."

"Perhaps I was," she went on; "but I did not expect him to be so silly. Hareton, if I gave you a book, would you take it now? I'll try!"

She placed one she had been perusing on his hand; he flung it off, and muttered, if she did not give over, he would break her neck.

"Well, I shall put it here," she said, "in the table drawer; and I'm going to bed."

Then she whispered me to watch whether he touched it, and departed. But he would not come near it; and so I informed her in the morning, to her great disappointment. I saw she was sorry for his persevering sulkiness and indolence: her conscience reproved her for frightening him off improving himself: she had done it effectually.

But her ingenuity was at work to remedy the injury: while I ironed, or pursued other stationary employments I could not well do in the parlour, she would bring some pleasant volume and read it aloud to me. When Hareton was there, she generally paused in an interesting part, and left the book lying about: that she did repeatedly; but he was as obstinate as a mule, and, instead of snatching at her bait, in wet weather he took to smoking with Joseph, and they sat like automatons, one on each side of the fire, the elder happily too deaf to understand her wicked nonsense, as he would have called it, the younger doing his best to seem to disregard it. On fine evenings the latter followed his shooting expeditions, and Catherine yawned and sighed, and teased me to talk to her, and ran off into the court or garden, the moment I began; and, as a last resource, cried and said, she was tired of living: her life was useless.

Mr. Heathcliff, who grew more and more disinclined to society, had almost banished Earnshaw out of his apartment. Owing to an accident, at the commencement of March, he became for some days a fixture in the kitchen. His gun burst while out on the hills by himself; a splinter cut his arm, and he lost a good deal of blood before he could reach home. The consequence was, that, perforce, he was condemned to the fire-side and tranquillity, till he made it up again. It suited Catherine to have him there: at any rate, it made her hate her room upstairs more than ever: and she would compel me to find out business below, that she might accompany me.

On Easter Monday, Joseph went to Gimmerton fair with some cattle; and, in the afternoon, I was busy getting up linen in the kitchen. Earnshaw sat, morose as usual, at the chimney corner, and my little mistress was beguiling an idle hour with drawing pictures on the window panes, varying her amusement by smothered bursts of songs, and whispered ejaculations, and quick glances of annoyance and impatience in the direction of her cousin, who steadfastly smoked, and looked into the grate. At a notice that I could do with her no longer, intercepting my light, she removed to the hearthstone. I bestowed little attention on her proceedings, but, presently, I heard her begin —

"I've found out, Hareton, that I want—that I'm glad—that I should like you to be my cousin, now, if you had not grown so cross to me, and so rough."

Hareton returned no answer.

"Hareton, Hareton, Hareton! do you hear?" she continued.

"Get off wi' ye!" he growled, with uncompromising gruffness.

"Let me take that pipe," she said, cautiously advancing her hand, and abstracting it from his mouth.

Before he could attempt to recover it, it was broken, and behind the fire. He swore at her and seized another.

"Stop," she cried, "you must listen to me, first; and I can't speak while those clouds are floating in my face."

"Will you go to the devil!" he exclaimed, ferociously, "and let me be!"

"No," she persisted, "I won't: I can't tell what to do to make you talk to me; and you are determined not to understand. When I call you stupid, I don't mean anything: I don't mean that I despise you. Come, you shall take notice of me, Hareton: you are my cousin, and you shall own me."

"I shall have naught to do wi' you, and

句歌，轻轻喊一两声，或者向她的表哥投去恼怒和不耐烦的目光，她的表哥则一个劲地抽烟，呆望着炉栅。当我跟她说不要再挡我的光时，她就挪到壁炉边上去。我也没大理会她在做什么，但没过多久，我就听到她开始讲话了——

"我发觉，哈里顿，要是你对我不再那么暴躁，不再那么粗鲁的话，我要——我很高兴——我现在喜欢你做我表哥了。"

哈里顿没答理她。

"哈里顿，哈里顿，哈里顿！你听见没有呀？"她接着说。

"去你的吧！"他用一种顽固的粗暴态度咆哮道。

"让我拿开那烟斗吧，"她说道，小心翼翼地把她的手伸过去，把烟斗从他的嘴里抽了出来。

在他试图把它夺回来之前，那烟斗已经被折断，扔在了火里。他咒骂着她，又抓起了另外一只。

"停一下，"她喊道，"你得先听我说句话；那些烟冲着我脸上飘的时候，我没法说话啊。"

"你给我见鬼去吧！"他凶狠地嚷道，"少来理我！"

"不，"她坚持着，"我偏不：我真不知道怎么样才能让你跟我讲话，而你又下决心不肯理解我的意思。当我说你笨的时候，我并没有什么用意：并没有瞧不起你的意思。来吧，你应该注意到我呀，哈里顿，你是我的表哥，你应该承认我呀。"

"我跟你和你那副臭架子，还有

your mucky pride, and your damned, mocking tricks!" he answered. "I'll go to hell, body and soul, before I look sideways after you again! Side out of t' gait, now; this minute!"

Catherine frowned, and retreated to the window-seat, chewing her lip, and endeavouring, by humming an eccentric tune, to conceal a growing tendency to sob.

"You should be friends with your cousin, Mr. Hareton," I interrupted, "since she repents of her sauciness! It would do you a great deal of good: it would make you another man, to have her for a companion."

"A companion?" he cried; "when she hates me, and does not think me fit to wipe her shoon! Nay, if it made me a king, I'd not be scorned for seeking her good will any more."

"It is not I who hate you, it is you who hate me!" wept Cathy, no longer disguising her trouble. "You hate me as much as Mr. Heathcliff does, and more."

"You're a damned liar," began Earnshaw: "why have I made him angry, by taking your part then, a hundred times? and that, when you sneered at, and despised me, and—Go on plaguing me, and I'll step in yonder, and say you worried me out of the kitchen!"

"I didn't know you took my part," she answered, drying her eyes; "and I was miserable and bitter at everybody; but, now I thank you, and beg you to forgive me, what can I do besides?"

She returned to the hearth, and frankly extended her hand. He blackened, and scowled like a thunder-cloud, and kept his fists resolutely clenched, and his gaze fixed on the ground. Catherine, by instinct, must have divined it was

你那套该死的虚伪的花招没什么好说的!"哈里顿回答。"我宁可从身体到灵魂都下地狱,也不愿再斜着眼看你一眼。滚出门去,现在,马上滚开!"

凯瑟琳皱紧了眉头,退回到窗前的座位上,紧咬着她的嘴唇,试图哼起一支曲调怪怪的曲子,想来掩盖她越来越忍不住想哭的趋势。

"你应该跟你表妹和好,哈里顿先生,"我插嘴说,"既然她已经为以前的无礼忏悔了。那会对你有很大的好处的:你让她和你做个伴,会令你变成另一个人的。"

"做伴?"他叫起来,"在她恨我,觉得我还不配给她擦皮鞋的时候?不,就算是让我当国王,我也再不愿意为了讨她的好而受到取笑了。"

"不是我恨你,是你恨我呀!"凯茜哭着说,不再掩饰她的苦恼了。"你就跟希斯克利夫先生一样恨我,甚至恨得还更厉害些呢。"

"你这个该死的撒谎的家伙,"恩肖开口说,"那么,我为什么要惹他生气呢?有一百次了。都是因为我向着你的缘故。还有,你嘲笑我,瞧不起我,还有——继续折磨我吧,我要到那边去,就说是你把我从厨房里赶出来的!"

"我并不知道你向着我呀,"她回答道,一边擦干她的眼睛,"那一阵子我痛苦难受,对每个人都一肚子气;但现在,我谢谢你,我请求你原谅我:除此以外我还能做什么呢?"

她又回到壁炉边,坦率地把手伸过去。而他,一张脸阴沉沉的,愁眉苦脸的就像雷电交加的乌云,两只拳头握得紧紧的,两只眼睛死死地盯着地面。凯瑟琳凭着她的本能,看出了

obdurate perversity, and not dislike, that prompted this dogged conduct; for, after remaining an instant undecided, she stooped, and impressed on his cheek a gentle kiss. The little rogue thought I had not seen her, and, drawing back, she took her former station by the window, quite demurely. I shook my head reprovingly; and then she blushed, and whispered —

"Well! what should I have done, Ellen? He wouldn't shake hands, and he wouldn't look: I must show him some way that I like him—that I want to be friends."

Whether the kiss convinced Hareton, I cannot tell: he was very careful, for some minutes, that his face should not be seen; and when he did raise it, he was sadly puzzled where to turn his eyes.

Catherine employed herself in wrapping a handsome book neatly in white paper; and having tied it with a bit of riband, and addressed it to "Mr. Hareton Earnshaw," she desired me to be her ambassadress, and convey the present to its destined recipient.

"And tell him, if he'll take it, I'll come and teach him to read it right," she said;"and, if he refuse it, I'll go upstairs, and never tease him again."

I carried it, and repeated the message, anxiously watched by my employer. Hareton would not open his fingers, so I laid it on his knee. He did not strike it off, either. I returned to my work: Catherine leaned her head and arms on the table, till she heard the slight rustle of the covering being removed; then she stole away, and quietly seated herself beside her cousin. He trembled, and his face glowed: all his rudeness and all his surly harshness had de-

那其实是顽固的倔强，并不是因为讨厌她才促成这种顽固的举止。因此，在犹豫了好一阵之后，她俯下身来，在他的脸上轻轻地吻了一下。这个淘气鬼还以为我没看见她，抽回身子，坐在窗前原来的位子上，真是假正经。我不以为然地摇了摇头，于是她脸红了，低声说——

"那么！我应该怎么办呢，艾伦？他不肯握手，他也不肯看我；我必须用某种方式向他表示我喜欢他——我愿意和他交朋友呀。"

我分辨不出是不是那一吻打动了哈里顿：有那么几分钟的时间，他很小心地不让他的脸被人看见，等到把脸抬起来的时候，他非常的慌乱，不知道该把自己的眼睛往哪边看才好。

凯瑟琳一心一意地把一本漂亮的书用一张白纸整整齐齐地包起来，又在上面扎了一条缎带，上面写着送给"哈里顿·恩肖先生"，她让我作她的特使，把这份礼物交给它的指定的接受者。

"告诉他，如果他接受了的话，我就来教他怎样把它读得正确，"她说，"要是他拒绝了，我就上楼去，并且再也不会找他麻烦了。"

我把书送了去，并传达了口信，我的主人焦急地监视着我。哈里顿偏偏不肯松开手指，于是我把书搁在他的膝盖上。他没有把它扔在一边。我又回去干我的活儿。凯瑟琳把胳膊和头都偎依在桌上，直等到她听到拆开包书纸的沙沙声；于是她轻手轻脚地走过去，悄悄地在她表哥的身旁坐下来。他直哆嗦，脸涨得通红，他所有的粗鲁无礼和所有的粗暴无情全都离

serted him: he could not summon courage, at first, to utter a syllable, in reply to her questioning look, and her murmured petition.

"Say you forgive me, Hareton, do! You can make me so happy, by speaking that little word."

He muttered something inaudible.

"And you'll be my friend?" added Catherine, interrogatively.

"Nay! you'll be ashamed of me every day of your life," he answered. "And the more, the more you know me, and I cannot bide it."

"So, you won't be my friend?" she said, smiling as sweet as honey, and creeping close up.

I overheard no further distinguishable talk, but on looking round again, I perceived two such radiant countenances bent over the page of the accepted book, that I did not doubt the treaty had been ratified, on both sides, and the enemies were, thenceforth, sworn allies.

The work they studied was full of costly pictures; and those, and their position, had charm enough to keep them unmoved, till Joseph came home. He, poor man, was perfectly aghast at the spectacle of Catherine seated on the same bench with Hareton Earnshaw, leaning her hand on his shoulder; and confounded at his favourite's endurance of her proximity. It affected him too deeply to allow an observation on the subject that night. His emotion was only revealed by the immense sighs he drew, as he solemnly spread his large bible on the table, and overlaid it with dirty bank-notes from his pocket book, the produce of the day's transactions. At length, he summoned Hareton from his seat.

开了他。起初，他都鼓不起勇气吐出一个字，来回答她那询问的目光和那柔声细气的恳求。

"说你原谅我了吧，哈里顿，说呀！只要说出那么几个字来，你就会使我非常快乐的。"

他咕哝了一句，没人能听得清他在说什么。

"那么你是愿意和我做朋友了吗？"凯瑟琳接着又问了一句。

"不，你这辈子每一天都会因为我而感到羞耻的，"他回答，"你越了解我，就越觉得可耻；我可受不了。"

"那么，你是不肯和我做朋友吗？"她说，微笑得像蜜一样甜，又逐渐向他凑近些。

再往下又谈了些什么，我就听不清了，不过，我再回头望的时候，只看到两张如此容光焕发的脸正凑在那本已经被接受了的书上呢，毫无疑问，双方的合约已经签订好，两个敌人从此以后就是盟友了。

他们阅读的那本书里全是些珍贵的图片，那些图片和他们所在位置的魔力足以使他们坐着不动，一直到约瑟夫回家。这个可怜的人看到凯瑟琳和哈里顿同坐在一张凳子上，她的手还搭在他的肩上，简直完全给吓傻了。他实在是很困惑，他最喜欢的那个人怎能容忍她去接近他，这对他来说打击太沉重了，使他整个夜晚对这事都说不出一句话来。他的情感只能通过长长地叹气来发泄，当时，他正一本正经在桌上把他的《圣经》打开，又从他袖珍书里掏出当天交易所得的那堆脏钞票，都摊在《圣经》上。最后他把哈里顿从他的座位上叫过去。

"Tak' these in tuh t' maister, lad," he said, "un' bide theare; Aw's gang up tuh my awn rahm. This hoile's norther mensful, nor seemly fur us— we mun side aht, and seearch another!"

"Come, Catherine," I said, "we must 'side out' too: I've done my ironing, are you ready to go?"

"It is not eight o'clock!" she answered, rising unwillingly. "Hareton, I'll leave this book upon the chimney-piece, and I'll bring some more tomorrow."

"Ony books ut yah leave, Aw suall tak' in-tuh th' hahse," said Joseph, 'un' it 'ull be mitch if yah find'em agean; soa, yah muh plase yourseln!"

Cathy threatened that his library should pay for hers; and, smiling as she passed Hareton, went singing upstairs: lighter of heart, I venture to say, than ever she had been under that roof before; except, perhaps, during her earliest visits to Linton.

The intimacy thus commenced, grew rapidly: though it encountered temporary interruptions. Earnshaw was not to be civilised with a wish; and my young lady was no philosopher, and no paragon of patience; but both their minds tending to the same point—one loving and desiring to esteem, and the other loving and desiring to be esteemed— they contrived in the end to reach it.

You see, Mr. Lockwood, it was easy enough to win Mrs. Heathcliff's heart. But now, I'm glad you did not try. The crown of all my wishes will be the union of those two. I shall envy no one on their wedding day: there won't be a happier woman than myself in England!

"把这些东西给主人送去，孩子，"他说道，"就待在那儿。我要上楼到我自己屋子里去。这屋子看起来不大合适我们；我们还是溜出去另外找个地方吧。"

"来吧，凯瑟琳，"我说，"我们也得'溜出去'了。我把衣服熨完了，你准备好走了吗？"

"八点钟都还不到呢！"她回答道，很不乐意地站起来。"哈里顿，这本书我放在壁炉架上，明天我再拿些书来。"

"不管你留下些什么书，我都要把它们拿到正屋去，"约瑟夫说，"你要是还能再找出来，那就真是奇迹了。所以，随你的便！"

凯茜威胁他说要拿他的那些藏书来赔她的书；她从哈里顿身边走过时笑了笑，唱着歌上楼去了。我敢说，自从她来到这个家之后，心情从来没有这样轻松过；也许除了她最初来探望林顿的那几次以外。

那亲密的关系就这样迅速地发展着；虽然也偶尔遇到过暂时的挫折。并不是光凭一个愿望恩肖能变得有修养起来的，我家小姐不是个哲学家，也不是一个有耐心的典范。但他们的心都向着同一个目标——一个是爱着，一心想着尊重对方，另一个是爱着，一心想着获得对方的尊重——他们都努力要最后达到这个目标。

你瞧，洛克伍德先生，要赢得希斯克利夫太太的心是很容易的吧。不过现在，我很高兴你没有尝试。在我所有愿望中最高的那个就是这两个人的结合。在他们结婚的那天，我将不会去羡慕任何人了：在全英国也不会有哪个比我更快乐的女人了！

Chapter 33
第三十三章

On the morrow of that Monday, Earnshaw being still unable to follow his ordinary employments, and therefore remaining about the house, I speedily found it would be impracticable to retain my charge beside me, as heretofore. She got downstairs before me, and out into the garden, where she had seen her cousin performing some easy work; and when I went to bid them come to breakfast, I saw she had persuaded him to clear a large space of ground from currant and gooseberry bushes, and they were busy planning together an importation of plants from the Grange.

I was terrified at the devastation which had been accomplished in a brief half hour; the black currant trees were the apple of Joseph's eye, and she had just fixed her choice of a flower bed in the midst of them!

"There! That will be all shewn to the master," I exclaimed, "the minute it is discovered. And what excuse have you to offer for taking such liberties with the garden? We shall have a fine explosion on the head of it: see if we don't! Mr. Hareton, I wonder you should have no more wit, than to go and make that mess at her bidding!"

那个星期一的早上，恩肖仍旧无法去做他日常所干的活儿，因此就留在了屋子里，我很快发现，我还要像从前那样，把由我照顾着的小姐留在身边，是不切实际的了。她比我先下楼，并且跑出去到了花园里，她看见她的表哥在那儿干一些轻便活。当我去喊他们来吃早点的时候，我看到她已经说服他在醋栗和红醋栗的树丛里清理出一大片的空地来。两人正一起忙着计划着怎样从田庄移一些植物过来。

我吓坏了，在这短短的半小时之内，竟完成这样的大破坏。那些黑醋栗树是约瑟夫眼中的宝贝，而她偏偏要选中在这些树中间建她的花圃。

"好呀！他一定会去领主人来看，"我叫道，"这事一旦被他发现的话。你们这样自作主张处理花园，有什么理由能交代呢？为了这事儿，我们可要有一番热闹了：走着瞧吧，要没有才怪呢！哈里顿先生，我不懂你怎么这样昏头昏脑的，竟听了她的话，把事情搞得一团糟！"

"I'd forgotten they were Joseph's," answered Earnshaw, rather puzzled; "but I'll tell him I did it."

We always ate our meals with Mr. Heathcliff. I held the mistress's post in making tea and carving; so I was indispensable at table. Catherine usually sat by me; but today, she stole nearer to Hareton, and I presently saw she would have no more discretion in her friendship, than she had in her hostility.

"Now, mind you don't talk with and notice your cousin too much," were my whispered instructions as we entered the room. "It will certainly annoy Mr. Heathcliff, and he'll be mad at you both."

"I'm not going to," she answered.

The minute after, she had sidled to him, and was sticking priMr.oses in his plate of porridge.

He dared not speak to her, there: he dared hardly look; and yet she went on teasing, till he was twice on the point of being provoked to laugh; and I frowned, and then, she glanced towards the master, whose mind was occupied on other subjects than his company, as his countenance evinced, and she grew serious for an instant, scrutinizing him with deep gravity. Afterwards she turned, and re-commenced her nonsense; at last, Hareton uttered a smothered laugh. Mr. Heathcliff started; his eye rapidly surveyed our faces. Catherine met it with her accustomed look of nervousness, and yet defiance, which he abhorred.

"It is well you are out of my reach," he exclaimed. "What fiend possesses you to stare back at me, continually, with those infernal eyes? Down with them! and don't remind me

"我忘了它们是约瑟夫的树了,"恩肖回答,很有点手足无措,"但是我会告诉他这事儿是我干的。"

我们吃饭的时候总是和希斯克利夫先生一起的。我代替女主人,倒茶切肉,所以在饭桌上是缺不了我的。凯瑟琳平时总坐在我旁边,可今天她却悄悄地挨近了哈里顿一些。我立刻看出比起她以前在敌对关系上,她在友谊上更加不知慎重,不懂克制。

"现在,你要留神,别跟你表哥多说话,也不要太注意他,"我们进屋的时候,我低声嘱咐她。"那一定会惹恼了希斯克利夫先生的,他会对你们俩发脾气的。"

"我才不会呢,"她回答道。

可是才过了一分钟,她就侧着身子靠近他,而且还把几根樱草插在他的粥盆里。

他不敢在饭桌上跟她讲话;他几乎都不敢看她;可她还是逗他,有两次他差点给逗得笑出来。我皱了皱眉,凯瑟琳扫了主人一眼,主人脑子里正在想别的事,没留意到和他在一块的人,这从他的神色可以看出来;有一瞬间,她变得严肃起来,一脸正经地望着他。紧接着,她转过脸来,又开始胡闹起来;哈里顿终于偷偷地发出了一声笑。希斯克利夫先生吃了一惊;他的眼睛很快地审视我们的脸。凯瑟琳仍然是用平时那种既紧张却又蔑视的表情回望他,而他最憎厌的恰恰是这个。

"好在我够不到你,"他嚷道。"你中了哪门子魔了,不停地用那对恶魔般的眼睛瞪着我?低下你的眼睛!别提醒我还有你这个人的存在。

of your existence again. I thought I had cured you of laughing!"

"It was me," muttered Hareton.

"What do you say?" demanded the master.

Hareton looked at his plate, and did not repeat the confession. Mr. Heathcliff looked at him a bit, and then silently resumed his breakfast, and his interrupted musing. We had nearly finished, and the two young people prudently shifted wider asunder, so I anticipated no further disturbance during that sitting; when Joseph appeared at the door, revealing by his quivering lip and furious eyes, that the outrage committed on his precious shrubs was detected. He must have seen Cathy and her cousin about the spot before he examined it, for while his jaws worked like those of a cow chewing its cud, and rendered his speech difficult to understand, he began —

"Aw mun hev my wage, and Aw mun goa! Aw *hed* aimed tuh dee, wheare Aw'd sarved fur sixty year; un' Aw thowt Aw'd lug my books up intuh t' garret,'un all my bits uh stuff, un' they sud hev t' kitchen tuh theirseln; fur t' sake uh quietness. It wur hard tuh gie up my awn hearthstun, bud Aw thowt Aw *could* do that! Bud, nah, shoo's taan my garden frough me, un' by th' heart! Maister, Aw cannot stand it! Yah muh bend tuh th' yoak, an ye will —*Aw*' noan used to 't and an ow'd man doesn't sooin get used tuh new barthens—Aw'd rayther arn my bite, an' my sup, wi' a hammer in th' road!"

"Now, now, idiot!" interrupted Heathcliff, "cut it short! What's your grievance? I'll interfere in no quarrels between you and Nelly—She may thrust you into the coal-hole for any-

我还以为我都已经治好了你的笑呢!"

"那是我,"哈里顿咕哝地说。

"你说什么?"主人问道。

哈里顿看着他的盘子,没有再重复他的供词。希斯克利夫先生看了他一眼,依旧默默地吃他的早饭,重新陷入他那被打断的沉思之中。我们都快吃完了,这两个年轻人也小心翼翼地彼此挪开了一些,我料想这会儿不会再有什么风波了。可就在这时,约瑟夫出现在门口,他那发抖的嘴唇和极端愤怒的眼睛表明,他那宝贝的树丛遭到破坏的事儿已经被他发现了。他准是先看见凯茜和她表哥去过那儿,才过去检查的,因为这时他的下巴磨得起劲,就像母牛在反刍似的,而且说出来什么话都很难听懂,他开口说:

"给我工钱,我一定非走不可!本来,我打算就死在这个我已经干了六十年的地方;我心想,我已经把自己的书和所有的零零碎碎的东西统统搬到阁楼上去了,把厨房让给他们,也就为了图个清静。撂下我自己炉边的位子本来很难,可是我想我也能做到!可谁知她连我的花园也给拿去了,还有我在炉边的位子!老爷,我可忍不下去了!你可以随便受屈——我可受不惯;一个老头儿是没法一下子习惯这些个新花样的。我宁愿扛着个锄头到大路上去挣口饭吃!"

"得了,得了,白痴!"希斯克利夫打断他说,"直截了当点!你有什么不痛快的?我可不管你跟内莉吵架的事儿,她就是把你丢进煤洞里去,也不关我的事儿。"

thing I care."

"It's noan Nelly!" answered Joseph. "Aw sudn't shift fur Nelly— Nasty, ill nowt as shoo is, Thank God! *shoo* cannot stale t' sowl uh nob'dy! Shoo wer niver soa handsome, bud whet a body mud look at her 'baht winking. It's yon flaysome, graceless quean, ut's witched ahr lad, wi' her bold een, un' her forrard ways—till—Nay! It fair brusts my heart! He's forgetten all E done for him, un made on him, un' goan un' riven up a whole row ut t' grandest currant trees, i' t' garden!" and here he lamented outright, unmanned by a sense of his bitter injuries, and Earnshaw's ingratitude and dangerous condition.

"Is the fool drunk?" asked Mr. Heathcliff. "Hareton, is it you he's finding fault with?"

"I've pulled up two or three bushes," replied the young man; "but I'm going to set' em again."

"And why have you pulled them up?" said the master.

Catherine wisely put in her tongue.

"We wanted to plant some flowers there," she cried. "I'm the only person to blame, for I wished him to do it."

"And who the devil gave *you* leave to touch a stick about the place?" demanded her father-in-law, much surprised. "And who ordered *you* to obey her?" he added, turning to Hareton.

The latter was speechless; his cousin replied—

"You shouldn't grudge a few yards of earth, for me to ornament, when you have taken all my land!"

"Your land, insolent slut? you never had

"不关内莉的事!"约瑟夫答道,"我可不会因为内莉就走掉——尽管她现在也挺糟糕。感谢上帝!她还不能把任何人的魂给勾走!她从来都没怎么漂亮过,男人不会因为看到她就眨眼睛。是你那边那个可怕的、无礼的臭丫头,用那双放肆的眼睛和那一贯不害臊的样子迷住了咱们的孩子——到后来——不说了!简直伤透了我的心!他把我为他做过的事,还有我对他的照顾全都给忘记了。如今他竟然把花园里一整排最好的黑醋栗树都给拔掉了!"说到这里,他当场失声痛哭;他感到痛苦的伤害,恩肖的忘恩负义及其危险的处境让他一点男子汉的气概都没有了。

"这蠢货是喝醉了吧?"希斯克利夫先生问道。"哈里顿,他是不是在找你的茬?"

"我是拔掉两三株灌木,"那小伙子回答道,"不过我是要把它们重新种起来的。"

"你干吗要把它们都拔掉?"主人说。

凯瑟琳机灵地插了嘴。

"我们想在那儿种些花。"她嚷道。"这事儿怪我一个人,因为是我让他做的。"

"哪个恶魔准许你碰那地方哪怕是一根树枝的?"她的公公十分吃惊地问道。"又是谁让你去听从她的呢?"他又转过身去问哈里顿。

后者说不上话;他的表妹回答道——

"你不应该吝惜给我几码地,美化一下的,你已经把我所有的土地都占去了!"

"你的土地,你这无礼的懒婆娘!

any!" said Heathcliff.

"And my money," she continued, returning his angry glare, and meantime, biting a piece of crust, the remnant of her breakfast.

"Silence!" he exclaimed. "Get done, and begone!"

"And Hareton's land, and his money," pursued the reckless thing. "Hareton and I are friends now; and I shall tell him all about you!"

The master seemed confounded a moment: he grew pale, and rose up, eyeing her all the while, with an expression of mortal hate.

"If you strike me, Hareton will strike you!" she said; "so you may as well sit down."

"If Hareton does not turn you out of the room, I'll strike him to Hell," thundered Heathcliff. "Damnable witch! dare you pretend to rouse him against me? Off with her! Do you hear? Fling her into the kitchen! I'll kill her, Ellen Dean, if you let her come into my sight again!"

Hareton tried under his breath to persuade her to go.

"Drag her away!" he cried savagely. "Are you staying to talk?" And he approached to execute his own command.

"He'll not obey you, wicked man, any more!" said Catherine; "and he'll soon detest you, as much as I do!"

"Wisht! wisht!" muttered the young man reproachfully. "I will not hear you speak so to him—Have done."

"But you won't let him strike me?" she cried.

"Come then!" he whispered earnestly.

It was too late: Heathcliff had caught hold of her.

你从来就没有过什么土地！"希斯克利夫说。

"还有我的钱，"她继续说，恶狠狠地回瞪他，一边还咬着她早餐吃剩的一片面包皮。

"闭嘴！"他叫道，"吃完了就滚出去！"

"还有哈里顿的土地和他的钱。"那个鲁莽的小家伙紧跟着说。"哈里顿和我现在是朋友了，我会把你的一切都告诉他！"

主人似乎愣了一下。脸色刷地白了，站起身来，两眼死盯着她，带着一种极度仇恨的表情。

"要是你打我，哈里顿就会打你，"她说，"所以你最好还是坐下来吧。"

"要是哈里顿不把你从这间屋子撵出去的话，我就把他打到地狱去，"希斯克利夫怒气冲天。"该死的妖精！你竟敢妄想挑拨他来跟我作对？让她滚！听到没有？把她扔进厨房里去！我会宰了她的，艾伦·迪安，要是你再让她出现在我的视线范围内的话！"

哈里顿低声下气地试着劝她离开。

"快把她拖走！"他粗暴地大叫。"你还想赖在这儿谈下去吗？"他走过来执行他自己的命令了。

"他不会听你的话的，狠毒的人，再也不会啦！"凯瑟琳说，"而且，不久，他就会跟我一样地痛恨你！"

"嘘！嘘！"那年轻人责备地咕哝着，"我不愿意听到你这样跟他讲话——算了吧。"

"可你也总不会让他打我吧？"她嚷道。

"算了，别说啦！"他迫切地低声说道。

"Now *you* go!" he said to Earnshaw. "Accursed witch! this time she has provoked me, when I could not bear it; and I'll make her repent it for ever!"

He had his hand in her hair; Hareton attempted to release the locks, entreating him not to hurt her that once, His black eyes flashed; he seemed ready to tear Catherine in pieces, and I was just worked up to risk coming to the rescue, when of a sudden, his fingers relaxed, he shifted his grasp from her head, to her arm, and gazed intently in her face—Then, he drew his hand over his eyes, stood a moment to collect himself apparently, and turning anew to Catherine, said with assumed calmness, "You must learn to avoid putting me in a passion, or I shall really murder you, some time! Go with Mrs. Dean, and keep with her, and confine your insolence to her ears. As to Hareton Earnshaw, if I see him listen to you, I'll send him seeking his bread where he can get it! Your love will make him an outcast, and a beggar. Nelly, take her, and leave me, all of you! Leave me!"

I led my young lady out: she was too glad of her escape, to resist; the other followed, and Mr. Heathcliff had the room to himself, till dinner. I had counselled Catherine to get hers upstairs; but, as soon as he perceived her vacant seat, he sent me to call her. He spoke to none of us, ate very little, and went out directly afterwards, intimating that he should not return before evening.

The two new friends established themselves in the house, during his absence, where I heard Hareton sternly check his cousin, on her offering a revelation of her father-in-law's conduct to his father. He said he wouldn't suffer a

那已经太迟了：希斯克利夫已经抓住了她。

"现在，你给我走开！"他对恩肖说。"该死的妖精！这次她把我惹得无法忍受了，我要让她为此后悔一辈子！"

他一把抓住她的头发。哈里顿试图想把她的卷发解救出来，恳求他这次别伤害她。希斯克利夫那双黑眼睛射出了凶光。他似乎想要把凯瑟琳撕成碎片；我正要鼓起勇气去冒险搭救，没想到他的手指忽然间松开了；他把紧紧抓住的手从她头上移到胳膊上，一动不动地凝视着她的脸——接着，他用双手捂住了他的眼睛，站了一会，分明是要想要冷静下来，又重新转向凯瑟琳，故作镇静地说，"你必须学会别惹我发火，否则总有一天我当真会把你杀死的！跟迪安太太走吧，和她待在一起，把你那些傲慢无礼的话都说给她听吧。至于哈里顿·恩肖，如果我看出来他听你的，我就会赶走他，由他自己到外面挣面包吃！你的爱情会将他变为一个流浪汉或是一个乞丐。内莉，快带她走，离开我，你们所有的人！都离开我！"

我把我家小姐带了出去；她很高兴自己居然能够逃掉，也不想再抵抗了；另一个也跟了出来，希斯克利夫先生一个人呆在屋子里，一直到吃午饭的时候。我劝凯瑟琳在楼上吃饭，没想到希斯克利夫一看见她的座位空在那儿，就让我去叫她。他没跟我们任何一个说话，吃得很少，之后就径直出去，说是到晚上以前不会回来。

他不在的时候，这两个新朋友占据了正屋；我听到哈里顿坚决制止他的表妹向他揭露她公公是怎样对待

word to be uttered to him, in his disparagement: if he were the devil, it didn't signify; he would stand by him; and he'd rather she would abuse himself, as she used to, than begin on Mr. Heathcliff. Catherine was waxing cross at this; but he found means to make her hold her tongue, by asking, how she would like *him* to speak ill of her father? and then she comprehended that Earnshaw took the master's reputation home to himself; and was attached by ties stronger than reason could break—chains, forged by habit, which it would be cruel to attempt to loosen. She showed a good heart, thenceforth, in avoiding both com plaints and expressions of antipathy concerning Heathcliff; and con fessed to me her sorrow that she had endeavoured to raise a bad spirit between him and Hareton: indeed, I don't believe she has ever breathed a syllable, in the latter's hearing, against her oppressor, since.

When this slight disagreement was over, they were thick again, and as busy as possible, in their several occupations, of pupil, and teacher. I came in to sit with them, after I had done my work; and I felt so soothed and comforted to watch them, that I did not notice how time got on. You know, they both appeared in a measure my children: I had long been proud of one; and now, I was sure, the other would be a source of equal satisfaction. His honest, warm, and intelligent nature shook off rapidly the clouds of ignorance and degradation in which it had been bred; and Catherine's sincere commendations acted as a spur to his industry. His brightening mind brightened his features, and added spirit and nobility to their aspect: I could hardly fancy it the same individual I had beheld on the day I

他父亲的。他说不愿意任何人在她面前讲希斯克利夫一句坏话；就算他是魔鬼，那也无所谓，他还是跟他站在一边；他宁愿她像过去那样辱骂自己一顿，也不愿意她去触犯希斯克利夫先生。凯瑟琳听了这话有些生气；不过他却有办法让她无话可说，他问凯瑟琳如果他也说她父亲的坏话，她会不会高兴呢？这样她才体会到恩肖是把主人的声誉看得如同他自己的一样；他们之间的关系就如同习惯铸成的锁链一样，不是理智所能够打断的，企图去拆开它将非常残忍。从那以后，她显示出她的好心肠来，不再用怨恨或者仇恨的口气提到希斯克利夫了；她还对我承认她心里很难过，因为自己曾经试图去挑起他和哈里顿之间的不和。确实，我相信她从此以后当着哈里顿的面，再也没有吐出过一言半语来反对她的压迫者。

这场小小的摩擦过去之后，他们俩又是好朋友了，而且一个当学生，一个当老师，在他们的职位上忙得不可开交。等我干完了自己的事，进去和他们一起坐着；看着他们，觉得宽心和欣慰，连时间是怎么过去的都没有注意到。你知道，说起来，他们两个都好像是我的孩子：其中的一个我一直都引以为豪；而现在，我敢确定，另一个也会令我同样满意。他那诚恳的、热情的、聪明的天性很快地就摆脱那自小沾染的愚昧与粗野的困境；而凯瑟琳真心真意的称赞对于他的勤奋又成为一种鼓舞。他开了窍的头脑也使他的容貌跟着光彩焕发，增添了一种活力和高贵的身份，我简直难以想像这个人和我家小姐到山岩探

discovered my little lady at Wuthering Heights, after her expedition to the Crags. While I admired, and they laboured, dusk drew on, and with it returned the master. He came upon us quite unexpectedly, entering by the front way, and had a full view of the whole three, ere we could raise our heads to glance at him. Well, I reflected, there was never a pleasanter, or more harmless sight; and it will be a burning shame to scold them. The red fire-light glowed on their two bonny heads, and revealed their faces, animated with the eager interest of children; for, though he was twenty-three, and she eighteen, each had so much of novelty to feel and learn, that neither experienced nor evinced the sentiments of sober disenchanted maturity.

They lifted their eyes together, to encounter Mr. Heathcliff: perhaps you have never remarked that their eyes are precisely similar, and they are those of Catherine Earnshaw. The present Catherine has no other likeness to her, except a breadth of forehead, and a certain arch of the nostril that makes her appear rather haughty, whether she will or not. With Hareton the resemblance is carried farther: it is singular, at all times—then it was particularly striking: because his senses were alert, and his mental faculties wakened to unwonted activity. I suppose this resemblance disarmed Mr. Heathcliff: he walked to the hearth in evident agitation; but it quickly subsided, as he looked at the young man: or, I should say, altered its character; for it was there yet. He took the book from his hand, and glanced at the open page, then returned it without any observation; merely signing Catherine away: her compan ion lingered very little behind her, and I was about to depart also,

第三十三章

险,我追着她找到呼啸山庄的那天所见到的野小子是同一个人。在我欣赏着他们,他们正在用功的时候,天色渐渐渐暗下来,接着主人也回来了。他非常出乎意料地来到我们面前,是从前门进来的,我们还没来得及抬头看他,他已经把我们三个人全看在眼里了。嗯,在我看来,没有比当时的场景更为愉快或是更为无邪的了;如果这时要斥责他们,那将是一个奇耻大辱。熊熊的炉火映照在他们两人漂亮的头上,显出他们那充满孩子气的热切兴趣而生气蓬勃的脸;因为,尽管他二十三岁,她十八岁,但各自都还有那么多新鲜事物要去感受、去学习,两个人都没有经历过或是表现出那种冷静、清醒、成熟的感情。

他们一起抬起眼来,目光碰上了希斯克利夫:或许你从来没有注意到,他们的眼睛非常的相似,都是凯瑟琳·恩肖的眼睛。眼前这个凯瑟琳别的地方都不太像她,除了宽阔的额头和有点拱起的翘鼻子,这使她看上去相当傲慢,不管她本意是不是要那样。至于哈里顿,那份相似的模样就更进一步:这一向都是很明显的,这会儿更引人注目了,因为他的意识正锐敏,他的智力也正觉醒到异常活跃的地步。我估计正是这种相似让希斯克利夫消除了敌意:他走到壁炉边,心里显然非常激动;可在他望着那个年轻人时,那种激动很快就平静了;或者,我可以说,是变了性质,因为那份激动还是存在的。他从哈里顿手中拿过那本书,看了看打开的那页,然后一句话也没说就还给他,只做了个手势让凯瑟琳离开。她的伙伴在她离开后也没

but he bid me sit still.

"It is a poor conclusion, is it not," he observed, having brooded a while on the scene he had just witnessed. "An absurd termination to my violent exertions? I get levers and mattocks to demolish the two houses, and train myself to be capable of working like Hercules①, and when everything is ready, and in my power, I find the will to lift a slate off either roof has vanished! My old enemies have not beaten me; now would be the precise time to revenge myself on their representatives: I could do it; and none could hinder me. But where is the use? I don't care for striking: I can't take the trouble to raise my hand! That sounds as if I had been labouring the whole time, only to exhibit a fine trait of magnanimity. It is far from being the case—I have lost the faculty of enjoying their destruction, and I am too idle to destroy for nothing."

"Nelly, there is a strange change approaching: I'm in its shadow at present. I take so little interest in my daily life, that I hardly remember to eat and drink. Those two, who have left the room are the only objects which retain adistinct material appearance to me; and, that appearance causes me pain, amounting to agony. About *her* I won't speak; and I don't desire to think; but I earnestly wish she were invisible: her presence invokes only maddening sensations. *He* moves me differently: and yet if I could do it without seeming insane, I'd never see him again! You'll perhaps think me rather inclined to become so," he added, making an

"这是个很糟糕的结局，不是吗？"他目睹了刚才的情景，沉思了片刻之后说："我穷凶极恶做了那么多，却得到这样荒唐的结局？我拿着撬杆和锄头要把这两个家都毁掉，我让自己磨炼得能像赫拉克勒斯一样工作，等到一切都布置好，并且是在我掌握之中的时候，我却发现自己连掀起随便哪所房子的一片瓦的意志都已经消失！我往日的敌人并不曾把我打败；现如今正是我向他们的代表者报仇的时机；我可以做得到；没有哪个能阻拦得了我。可是这又有什么用呢？我不想再打人了；我连抬个手都嫌麻烦！这听起来仿佛是我劳碌了一辈子只是为了要显示我的宽宏大量一般。完全不是这回事儿：我已经失去了欣赏他们毁灭的能力了，我懒得去做无谓地破坏了。

"内莉，有个奇异的变化到来了；现在我正笼罩在它的阴影里。我对我的日常生活如此不感兴趣，以至于连吃喝的事都几乎不记起来。刚才走出这间屋子的那两个人，只有他们，还能在我心头保留一个清晰实质的印象；那形象让我感到苦恼，甚至痛苦。关于她，我不想说什么；也不愿去想，但我真心地希望她不要让我看见；她的出现只会引起让人发疯的感觉。而他激起的我的感情就不一样了；但如果我能做得到，又不像是看上去精神错乱的样子，我宁可永远都

---

① Hercules：赫拉克勒斯，宙斯与阿尔克墨涅之子，力大无比的英雄，因完成赫拉要求的十二项任务而获得永生。

effort to smile, "if I try to describe the thousand forms of past associations, and ideas he awakens, or embodies—But you'll not talk of what I tell you; and my mind is so eternally secluded in itself, it is tempting, at last, to turn it out to another."

"Five minutes ago, Hareton seemed a personification of my youth, not a human being: I felt to him in such a variety of ways, that it would have been impossible to have accosted him rationally.

"In the first place, his startling likeness to Catherine connected him fearfully with her. That however which you may suppose the most potent to arrest my imagination, is actually the least: for what is not connected with her to me? and what does not recall her? I cannot look down to this floor, but her features are shaped on the flags! In every cloud, in every tree filling the air at night, and caught by glimpses in every object, by day I am surrounded with her image! The most ordinary faces of men, and women—my own features mock me with a resemblance. The entire world is a dreadful collection of memoranda that she did exist, and that I have lost her!

"Well, Hareton's aspect was the ghost of my immortal love, of my wild endeavours to hold my right, my degradation, my pride, my happiness, and my anguish—

"But it is frenzy to repeat these thoughts to you: only it will let you know, why, with a reluctance to be always alone, his society is no benefit, rather an aggravation of the constant torment I suffer: and it partly contributes to render me regardless how he and his cousin go on together. I can give them no attention, any

不再看到他！你也许真会以为我要发疯了，"他补充道，勉强笑了一下，"要是我试着描绘他所唤醒的，或是他所体现的千百种过去的联想和念头的话——不过我所跟说的，你不要说出去：我的内心永远都是这样关闭着的，到最后它终于忍不住向另一个人倾诉出来。

"五分钟之前，哈里顿似乎就是我青春的化身，而不是一个人，他让我涌起了许多各种各样的感受，以至于我简直不可能理性地跟他讲话。

"首先，他和凯瑟琳惊人的相似，非常可怕把他和她联系在了一起。或许你认为这一点最足以吸引我的想像力，其实却是最微不足道的；因为对我而言，有什么不是和她有联系的呢？有什么不令我回忆起她来呢？我一低头看这间屋子里的地板，就看见她的面容出现在石板中间！在每一朵云里，在每一棵树上——夜晚的时候充满在空中，白天则在任何一件东西上都看得见——她的形象总是围绕着我！最普通的男人和女人的脸——连我自己这张脸——都像她，都在嘲弄我。整个世界成了一个可怕的纪念品收藏馆，到处提醒着我她存在过，而我已经失去了她！

"唉，哈里顿的容貌是我那不朽爱情的幻影；是我想要保持我权力的那些疯狂的努力，我的堕落，我的骄傲，我的幸福，以及我痛苦的幻影——

"翻来覆去地把这些想法说给你听也是发疯：不过这会让你明白为什么，我不情愿永远这样孤独，有他陪伴却又没有好处，反而加重了我所忍受的不断的折磨———部分是这原

more."

"But what do you mean by a *change*, Mr. Heathcliff?" I said, alarmed at his manner, though he was neither in danger of losing his senses, nor dying; according to my judgment he was quite strong and healthy; and, as to his reason, from childhood he had a delight in dwelling on dark things, and entertaining odd fancies. He might have had a monomania on the subject of his departed idol; but on every other point his wits were as sound as mine.

"I shall not know that, till it comes," he said; "I'm only half conscious of it now."

"You have no feeling of illness, have you?" I asked.

"No, Nelly, I have not," he answered.

"Then, you are not afraid of death?" I pursued.

"Afraid? No!" he replied. "I have neither a fear, nor a presentiment, nor a hope of death. Why should I? With my hard constitution and temperate mode of living, and unperilous occupations, I ought to, and probably *shall* remain above ground, till there is scarcely a black hair on my head—And yet I cannot continue in this condition! I have to remind myself to breathe—almost to remind my heart to beat! And it is like bending back a stiff spring: it is by compulsion that I do the slightest act not prompted by one thought, and by compulsion, that I notice anything alive or dead, which is not associated with one universal idea. I have a single wish, and my whole being and faculties are yearning to attain it. They have yearned towards it so long, and so unwaveringly, that I'm convinced it *will* be reached—and *soon*—because it has devoured my existence: I am swal-

因，使我不再去管他和他的表妹如何相处。我没再去注意他们了。"

"可你说的'变化'是什么呢，希斯克利夫先生？"我说，他的举止让我害怕；虽说他并不像是有精神错乱，或是死去的危险。据我判断，他相当结实健康。至于他的理智，他从童年起就喜欢把注意力集中在一些不可思议的事上，他还有有趣的古怪的想像力。或许他对他那死去的偶像有点偏执；不过在别的方面，他的头脑跟我的一样健全。

"在变化到来以前，我也不会知道，"他说道，"现在我只是模模糊糊地意识到罢了。"

"你不是觉得生病了吧，是这样吗？"我问道。

"没有，内莉，我没有生病，"他回答。

"那么你是怕死吗？"我接着问道。

"怕死？不！"他答道。"我对死既没有恐惧，没有预感，也没有期望。我干吗要这样呢？我有强健的体质，有节制的生活方式，工作也不危险，我应该，也可能是这样，活着一直等到我头上再也找不出一根黑发来为止——可我没法让这种情况再继续了！我得提醒自己去呼吸——几乎都要提醒我的心脏去跳动！这就像是要把一根硬弹簧扳弯过来似的；如果没有我的那个思想在提醒，都要十分勉强才能做出，哪怕是最微不足道的动作。无论是什么活的或是死的东西，如果和那一个无所不在的意念联系不起来，我也是强迫自己才能注意到。我只有一个心愿，我整个的身心和能力都渴望如愿以偿，我渴望了那么久，那么

lowed in the anticipation of its fulfilment. My confessions have not relieved me; but they may account for some otherwise unaccountable phases of humour which I show. O, God! It is a long fight, I wish it were over!"

He began to pace the room, muttering terrible things to himself, till I was inclined to believe, as he said Joseph did, that conscience had turned his heart to an earthly hell. I wondered greatly how it would end. Though he seldom before had revealed this state of mind, even by looks, it was his habitual mood, I had no doubt: he asserted it himself; but not a soul, from his general bearing, would have conjectured the fact. You did not, when you saw him, Mr. Lockwood: and at the period of which I speak, he was just the same as then, only fonder of continued solitude, and perhaps still more laconic in company.

的坚定不移，以至于我深信一定能够达到——而且很快就可以——因为，这个心愿已经吞没了我的存在：我已经被吞没在那朝思暮想的预感中了。我的坦白并没能让我轻松；但这些话或许可以说明我为什么会无故地表现出那样的情绪。啊，上帝啊！这是一场漫长的搏斗，我希望它快快结束！"

他开始在屋里踱来踱去，嘴里咕噜着一些可怕的话，这让我不觉相信起来（他说约瑟夫也这样认为），良心把他的那颗心变成人间地狱。我真不知道这将会怎样结束。虽然他从前很少透露过这种心理状态，甚至连神色上也不露出来，但我毫不怀疑这正是他平时的心境。他自己也这么说；但是从他平时的举止上看，没有人能想得到这事实。当你初次见到他的时候，你也没想到，洛克伍德先生：就在我谈到的那一段时期，他也还是和以往一样，只是更喜欢自己一个人呆着罢了，还有，或许在人前更不爱讲话了而已。

Chapter 34
第三十四章

For some days after that evening, Mr. Heathcliff shunned m eeting us at meals; yet he would not consent, formally, to exclude Hareton

那晚之后的好几天里，希斯克利夫先生都避免在吃饭时遇见我们，可他又不愿正式承认自己想把哈里

and Cathy. He had an aversion to yielding so completely to his feelings, choosing rather to absent himself; and eating once in twenty-four hours seemed sufficient sustenance for him.

One night, after the family were in bed, I heard him go downstairs, and out at the front door. I did not hear him re-enter, and in the morning I found he was still away. We were in April then: the weather was sweet and warm, the grass as green as showers and sun could make it, and the two dwarf apple trees, near the southern wall, in full bloom. After breakfast, Catherine insisted on my bringing a chair, and sitting with my work under the fir trees at the end of the house; and she beguiled Hareton, who had perfectly recovered from his accident, to dig and arrange her little garden, which was shifted to that corner by the influence of Joseph's complaints. I was comfortably revelling in the spring fragrance around, and the beautiful soft blue overhead, when my young lady, who had run down near the gate to procure some priMr.ose roots for a border, returned only half laden, and informed us that Mr. Heathcliff was coming in. "And he spoke to me," she added, with a perplexed countenance.

"What did he say?" asked Hareton.

"He told me to begone as fast as I could," she answered. "But he looked so different from his usual look that I stopped a moment to stare at him."

"How?" he enquired.

"Why, almost bright and cheerful—No, almost nothing—*very much* excited, and wild and glad!" she replied.

"Night-walking amuses him, then," I remarked, affecting a careless manner: in reality,

顿和凯茜排除在外。他讨厌自己完全受制于感情，宁可自己不来；而且在二十四小时内只吃一顿饭，对他来说似乎足够了。

有一天晚上，一家人全睡了，我听见他走下楼来，走出前门。我没听见他再进来，到了早晨，我发现他仍然不在。那时正值四月，天气温和舒适，雨水和阳光把青草滋润得要多绿有多绿，那两株靠着南墙的矮苹果树开满了花。早饭后，凯瑟琳非要让我带着一把椅子，连同我的活计一起，坐在这房子末端的枞树底下。她又鼓动那早已从上次事故恢复过来的哈里顿为她挖掘并布置她的小花园——因为约瑟夫的告状，这小花园已经挪到一个角落去了。我正舒畅地在陶醉在周围春天的香气和头顶那美丽柔和的蓝天中，这时我家小姐，跑到栅门外去采集些带根须的樱草，准备种在花床的边圈，可她只采了一半就赶回来，告诉我们说希斯克利夫先生进来了。"他还跟我说话呢，"她添了一句，带着迷惑不解的神情。

"他说什么？"哈里顿问。

"他对我说尽快走开，"她答道。"可他看来跟平常的样子太不一样，以至于我还停下来看了他一会儿。"

"怎么不一样？"他问道。

"呃，几乎是兴高采烈的。不，几乎没有什么可——相当兴奋，狂热，而且快乐！"她回答说。

"那么是夜里的散步让他高兴吧，"我装作毫不在意地说。其实我

as surprised as she was; and, anxious to ascertain the truth of her statement, for to see the master looking glad would not be an everyday spectacle, I framed an excuse to go in. Heathcliff stood at the open door; he was pale, and he trembled: yet, certainly, he had a strange joyful glitter in his eyes that altered the aspect of his whole face.

"Will you have some breakfast?" I said. "You must be hungry, rambling about all night!" I wanted to discover where he had been, but I did not like to ask directly.

"No, I'm not hungry," he answered, averting his head, and speaking rather contemptuously, as if he guessed I was trying to divine the occasion of his good humour.

I felt perplexed: I didn't know whether it were not a proper opportunity to offer a bit of admonition.

"I don't think it right to wander out of doors," I observed, "instead of being in bed: it is not wise, at any rate, this moist season. I dare say you'll catch a bad cold, or a fever: you have something the matter with you now!"

"Nothing but what I can bear," he replied; "and with the greatest pleasure, provided you'll leave me alone: get in, and don't annoy me."

I obeyed; and, in passing, I noticed he breathed as fast as a cat.

"Yes!" I reflected to myself, "we shall have a fit of illness. I cannot conceive what he has been doing!"

That noon, he sat down to dinner with us, and received a heaped-up plate from my hands, as if he intended to make amends for previous fasting.

"I've neither cold nor lever, Nelly," he re-

与她一样吃惊，并很想去证实她所说的事实，因为并不是天天都能看到主人高兴的神色，我编了个借口走进屋去。希斯克利夫站在门口；他脸色苍白，身子发抖，但是眼睛里确实闪着一股奇异的欢乐的光彩，使他整个面容变了样。

"你要吃点早饭吗？"我说。"在外面游荡了一夜，一定饿了！"我的确很想知道他去了哪里，但我不愿直接问。

"不，我不饿，"他答道，掉过头去，有些傲慢地说，仿佛他已猜到我是在捉摸他的好心情的原因。

我感到惶惑。我不知现在是不是一个合适的奉献忠告的时机。

"我认为在该睡觉的时候到外面闲荡，是不对的。"我说，"不管怎样，在这个潮湿的季节里，可不怎么聪明。我敢说，你肯定会受凉，甚至发烧：你现在就有点毛病了！"

"没什么，我受得了，"他答道，"倘若你让我一个人呆着，我还非常高兴：进去吧，别来打扰我。"

我听从了；走过他身边时，我留意到他呼吸急促，像只猫一样。

"是的，"我心想："眼看就要有场大病了。我想不出他都做了什么。"

当天中午他坐下来同我们一道吃饭，并从我手中接过一个堆得满满的盘子，好像他打算补偿一下先前的绝食似的。

"我既没受凉，也没发烧，内

marked, in allusion to my morning's speech; "and I'm ready to do justice to the food you give me."

He took his knife and fork, and was going to commence eating, when the inclination appeared to become suddenly extinct He laid them on the table, looked eagerly towards the window, then rose and went out. We saw him walking to and fro in the garden while we concluded our meal, and Earnshaw said he'd go and ask why he would not dine: he thought we had grieved him some way.

"Well, is he coming?" cried Catherine, when her cousin returned.

"Nay," he answered; "but he's not angry: he seemedrareand pleased indeed; only, I made him impatient by speaking to him twice; and then he bid me be off to you: he wondered how I could want the company of anybody else."

I set his plate to keep warm on the fender: and after an hour or two he re-entered, when the room was clear, in no degree calmer: the same unnatural—it was unnatural—appearance of joy under his black brows; the same bloodless hue, and his teeth visible, now and then, in a kind of smile; his frame shivering, not as one shivers with chill or weakness, but as a tight-stretched cord vibrate—a strong thrilling, rather than trembling.

I will ask what is the matter, I thought, or who should? And I exclaimed —

"Have you heard any good news, Mr. Heathcliff? You look uncom-monly animated."

"Where should good news come from, to me?" he said. "I'm animated with hunger; and, seemingly, I must not eat."

"Your dinner is here," I returned; "why

莉。"他说，针对我早上说的那些话，"你给我这些吃的，我不吃太可惜了。"

他拿起刀叉，刚要开始吃，忽然没了胃口。他放下刀叉，热切地望着窗外，接着站起身来出去了。我们吃完饭之后，还看见他在花园里踱来踱去，恩肖说他要去问问他为什么不吃饭：他觉得我们一定又在什么地方让他伤心了。

"怎么样，他来吗？"看到表哥回转来，凯瑟琳嚷道。

"没有，"他答道，"但他没有生气。说实话，他仿佛难得有这样的高兴；倒是我跟他说了两遍话让他不耐烦，他叫我走开到你这儿来。他奇怪我怎么还要找旁人做伴。"

我把他的盘子放在火炉围栏上热着，一两个小时以后，屋里没有人时，他又走进来，却没有平静多少——在那道浓黑的眉毛下露出的同样是不自然——的确是不自然——仍然面无血色，他的牙齿不时地露出来，像在微笑；他的身子在哆嗦，但不像是一个人冷得发抖，也不是虚弱得发抖，而是像一根绷紧了的弦线在颤动——一种强烈的震颤，而不是颤抖。

我想，我一定要问问这是怎么回事；不然又该谁来问呢？于是我喊道：

"你听到什么好消息了吗，希斯克利夫先生？你看上去充满活力。"

"哪儿会有什么好消息送来给我呢？"他说。"我是饿得兴奋，但又好像吃不下饭。"

"你的午饭就在这儿，"我答道，

won't you get it?"

"I don't want it now," he muttered, hastily:"I'll wait till supper. And, Nelly, once for all, let me beg you to warn Hareton and the other away from me. I wish to be troubled by nobody: I wish to have this place to myself."

"Is there some new reason for this banishment?" I inquired. "Tell me why you are so queer, Mr. Heathcliff? Where were you last night? I'm not putting the question through idle curiosity, but —"

"You are putting the question through very idle curiosity," he interrupted, with a laugh. "Yet, I'll answer it. Last night, I was on the threshold of hell. Today, I am within sight of my heaven. I have my eyes on it hardly three feet to sever me! And now you'd better go—You'll neither see nor hear anything to frighten you, if you refrain from prying."

Having swept the hearth and wiped the table, I departed more perplexed than ever.

He did not quit the house again that afternoon, and no one intruded on his solitude, till, at eight o'clock, I deemed it proper, though unsummoned, to carry a candle and his supper to him.

He was leaning against the ledge of an open lattice, but not looking out: his face was turned to the interior gloom. The fire had smouldered to ashes; the room was filled with the damp, mild air of the cloudy evening; and so still, that not only the murmur of the beck down Gimmerton was distinguishable, but its ripples and its gurgling over the pebbles, or through the large stones which it could not cover. I uttered an ejaculation of discontent at seeing the dismal grate, and commenced shutting

"你为什么不拿去吃呢？"

"现在不想吃，"他赶忙咕哝地说。"我要等到吃晚饭的时候，内莉，跟你说最后一遍，我恳求你去警告哈里顿还有别人都避开我。我希望谁也别来打扰我。我想要自己待在这地方。"

"你这样放逐自己，有什么新的理由吗？"我问道。"告诉我你为什么如此古怪，希斯克利夫先生？昨天晚上你跑到哪儿去啦？我问这句话并不是出于无聊的好奇，但是——"

"你问这话正是出于非常无聊的好奇心，"他打断我，大笑了一声。"不过，我还是要回答你。昨天晚上我是在地狱的门槛上。今天我看得见我的天堂了。我亲眼看见了，离我三尺都不到！现在你最好走开——如果你能克制自己、不窥探的话，你就不会看到或听到什么让你恐惧的事。"

扫完壁炉、擦过桌子之后，我走开了，心里比以前更加困惑。

那天下午，他没再离开正屋，也没人打扰他的孤独，直到八点钟，虽然没有得到召唤，我还是觉得该给他送一支蜡烛和晚饭了。

他正靠着敞开着的格子窗边，但并没向外张望；他的脸朝向屋内的黑暗。炉火已经烧成灰烬；屋里充满了阴天晚上的潮湿、温和的空气。如此安静，不止听得清吉默顿那边淙淙的流水，就连它那涟漪的潺潺声，以及它冲刷过卵石、穿过那些它不能淹没的大石头时的汩汩声也听得见。我一看到那阴暗的壁炉，就发出一声不满的叫喊，同时开始关窗子，一扇接一扇地关，直到我来到他靠着的那扇窗

the casements, one after another, till I came to his.

"Must I close this?" I asked, in order to rouse him; for he would not stir.

The light flashed on his features as I spoke. Oh, Mr. Lockwood, I cannot express what a terrible start I got, by the momentary view! Those deep black eyes! That smile, and ghastly paleness! It appeared to me, not Mr. Heathcliff, but a goblin; and, in my terror, I let the candle bend towards the wall, and it left me in darkness.

"Yes, close it," he replied, in his familiar voice. "There, that is pure awkwardness! Why did you hold the candle horizontally? Be quick, and bring another."

I hurried out in a foolish state of dread, and said to Joseph —

"The master wishes you to take him a light and re-kindle the fire." For I dare not go in myself again just then.

Joseph rattled some fire into the shovel, and went: but he brought it back immediately, with the supper-tray in his other hand, explaining that Mr. Heathcliff was going to bed, and he wanted nothing to eat till morning. We heard him mount the stairs directly; he did not proceed to his ordinary chamber, but turned into that with the panelled bed: its window, as I mentioned before, is wide enough for anybody to get through; and it struck me that he plotted another midnight excursion, which he had rather we had no suspicion of.

"Is he a ghoul, or a vampire?" I mused. I had read of such hideous, incarnate demons. And then I set myself to reflect how I had tended him in infancy; and watched him grow to

户前面。

"要不要关上这扇？"我问，为了把他唤醒，因为他一动不动。

我说话时，烛光闪到他的脸上。哦，洛克伍德先生，那可把我吓了一大跳，我真没法形容！那双深陷的黑眼睛！那种微笑和鬼一样的苍白，在我看来，那不是希斯克利夫先生，而是一个妖怪；我吓坏了，蜡烛竟歪倒了，碰到墙上，我一下被笼罩在黑暗中。

"好吧，关上吧，"他用他平时的声音答道，"瞧，那真是十足的愚蠢！你怎么把蜡烛横着拿呢？快点再去拿一支来。"

我匆忙地跑出去，处于一种吓傻了的状态，跟约瑟夫说道——

"主人让你给他送支蜡烛去，再把炉火生着。"因为那会儿我自己已经不敢再进去了。

约瑟夫哗啦哗啦地在煤斗里装了些燃料，进去了，不过接着又回来，另一只手里托着那只晚餐的盘子，他说希斯克利夫先生要上床睡觉了，今晚什么也不想吃。我们听到他直接上楼去了；可他并没有到他平时睡的那间卧室，而是绕到有板条床的那间；那间卧室的窗户，我之前提到过，宽得足够让任何人爬进爬出；这使我突然想到，他是打算再来一次夜游，可又不想让我们听到动静。

"他是个食尸鬼，还是个吸血鬼呢？"我陷入了沉思。我读到过有关这种狰狞可怕、魔鬼化身的书；接着我又回想在他幼年时我是怎样照料

youth; and followed him almost through his whole course; and what absurd nonsense it was to yield to that sense of horror. "But where did he come from, the little dark thing, harboured by a good man to his bane?" muttered superstition, as I dozed into unconsciousness. And I began, half dreaming, to weary myself with imaging some fit parentage for him; and repeating my waking meditations, I tracked his existence over again, with grim variations; at last, picturing his death and funeral: of which, all I can remember is, being exceedingly vexed at having the task of dictating an inscription for his monument, and consulting the sexton about it; and, as he had no surname, and we could not tell his age, we were obliged to content ourselves with the single word, "Heathcliff." That came true: we were. If you enter the kirkyard, you'll read on his headstone, only that, and the date of his death.

Dawn restored me to common sense. I rose, and went into the garden, as soon as I could see, to ascertain if there were any footmarks under his window. There were none. "He has stayed at home," I thought, "and he'll be all right today."

I prepared breakfast for the household, as was my usual custom, but told Hareton and Catherine to get theirs ere the master came down, for he lay late. They preferred taking it out of doors, under the trees, and I set a little table to accommodate them.

On my re-entrance, I found Mr. Heathcliff below. He and Joseph were conversing about some farming business; he gave clear, minute directions concerning the matter discussed, but he spoke rapidly, and turned his head continually aside, and had the same excited expression, even more exaggerated. When Joseph quitted the room, he took his seat in the place he generally chose, and I put a basin of coffee before him. He drew it nearer, and then rested his arms on the table, and looked at the opposite wall, as I supposed, surveying one particular portion, up and down, with glittering, restless eyes, and with such eager interest that he stopped breathing, during half a minute together.

"Come now," I exclaimed, pushing some bread against his hand. "Eat and drink that, while it is hot: it has been waiting near an hour."

He didn't notice me, and yet he smiled. I'd rather have seen him gnash his teeth than smile so.

"Mr. Heathclif! master!" I cried. "Don't for God's sake, stare as if you saw an unearthly vision."

"Don't, for God's sake, shout so loud," he replied."Turn round, and tell me, are we by ourselves?"

"Of course," was my answer; "of course we are!"

Still, I involuntarily obeyed him, as if I were not quite sure. With a sweep of his hand he cleared a vacant space in front among the breakfast things, and leant forward to gaze more at his ease.

Now, I perceived he was not looking at the wall; for when I regarded him alone, it seemed exactly that he gazed at something within two yards distance. And whatever it was, it communicated, apparently, both pleasure and pain, in exquisite extremes: at least, the anguished, yet raptured expression of his counteance suggest-

带着同样兴奋的神情，甚至更比以前更夸张。当约瑟夫离开这间屋子时，他就坐在他平时坐着的地方，我把一杯咖啡端到他面前。他把杯子挪近些，把胳臂放在桌子上，望着对面的墙上。我猜想，他一定是上上下下地打量一块特别的部分，用他那闪烁不安的眼睛，并且带着一种如此热切的兴趣，以至于有半分钟他几乎停止了呼吸。

"好啦，"我嚷道，把面包塞到他手边，"趁热吃点、喝点吧。等了快一个小时了。"

他没有理会，不过他笑了笑。我宁愿看见他咬牙切齿，也不愿看到他这样的笑。

"希斯克利夫先生！主人！"我喊道，"看在上帝分上，别那样瞪眼，就像是你看见了鬼一样。"

"看在上帝的面上，别这样大喊大叫。"他回答。"看看四周，告诉我，这儿是不是只有我俩在？"

"当然了，"这是我的回答，"当然只有我们俩！"

不过，我仍是不由自主地听从了他，好像我也不太确定似的。他用手一推，把吃早饭用的碗杯推到一旁，腾出一块空地方，好更方便地往前俯着身子凝望。

现在，我意识到他不是在望着墙壁；因为当我仔细打量他时，他像是在凝视着两码之内的某个东西。不管那是什么，显然它传递着极端的快乐和痛苦——至少他脸上那种既是悲痛又是喜悦的表情让人产生这样的想法。那想像中的东西也不是固定的；

ed that idea. The fancied object was not fixed, either; his eyes pursued it with unwearied vigilance, and, even in speaking to me, were never weaned away. I vainly reminded him of his protracted abstinence from food: if he stirred to touch anything in compliance with my entreaties, if he stretched his hand out to get a piece of bread, his fingers clenched before they reached it, and remained on the table, forgetful of their aim.

I sat, a model of patience, trying to attract his absorbed attention from its engrossing speculation; till he grew irritable, and got up, asking why I would not allow him to have his own time in taking his meals? and saying that, on the next occasion, I needn't wait: I might set the things down and go. Having uttered these words he left the house, slowly sauntered down the garden path, and disappeared through the gate.

The hours crept anxiously by: another evening came. I did not retire to rest till late, and when I did, I could not sleep. He returned after midnight, and, instead of going to bed, shut himself into the room beneath. I listened, and tossed about; and, finally, dressed, and descended. It was too irksome to lie up there, harassing my brain with a hundred idle misgivings.

I distinguished Mr. Heathcliff's step, restlessly measuring the floor; and he frequently broke the silence by a deep inspiration, resembling a groan. He muttered detached words also; the only one I could catch was the name of Catherine, coupled with some wild term of endear- ment or suffering; and spoken as one would speak to a person present: low and earnest, and wrung from the depth of his soul. I had not courage to walk straight into the apartment; but I desired to divert him from his reverie, and therefore fell foul of the kitchen fire, stirred it, and began to scrape the cinders. It drew him forth sooner than I expected. He opened the door immediately, and said —

"Nelly, come here — is it morning? Come in with your light."

"It is striking four," I answered. "You want a candle to take upstairs: you might have lit one at this fire."

"No, I don't wish to go upstairs," he said. "Come in, and kindle me a fire, and do anything there is to do about the room."

"I must blow the coals red first, before I can carry any," I replied, getting a chair and the bellows.

He roamed to and fro, meantime, in a state approaching distraction; his heavy sighs succeeding each other so thick as to leave no space for common breathing between.

"When day breaks I'll send for Green," he said; "I wish to make some legal inquiries of him while I can bestow a thought on those matters, and while I can act catlmly. I have not written my will yet; and how to leave my property I cannot determine! I wish I could annihilate it from the face of the earth."

"I would not talk so, Mr. Heathcliff," I interposed. "Let your will be, a while: you'll be spared to repent of your many injustices, yet! I never expected that your nerves would be disordered: they are, at present, marvellously so, however; and almost entirely through your own fault. The way you've passed these three last days might knock up a Titan①. Do take some

"内莉,过来这边——已经是早晨了吗?把你的蜡烛带进来。"

"才敲四点钟呢,"我答道。"你需要支蜡烛上楼去,你可以就着这火点上一支。"

"不,我不想上楼去,"他说道。"进来吧,给我生个炉火,就在这屋里做点什么。"

"我必须把这堆煤先煽红了,才能去送煤。"我答道,搬来了一把椅子和一个风箱。

同时,他只顾来回地走着,那样子像是要精神错乱了;他重重地叹气接连不断,一声接着一声,叹得如此沉重,仿佛连正常呼吸的空间都没有了。

"天亮的时候,我要请格林来,"他说道,"我想向他请教一些有关法律上的事,趁我还能考虑这些问题,能冷静地办事的时候。我还没有立下遗嘱;还没法决定怎样处理我的财产。但愿我能把它们从地面上毁掉。"

"我可不愿说这些,希斯克利夫先生,"我插嘴道,"先别管你的遗嘱吧;你做下许许多多不公正的事,还要空下时间来忏悔哩!我从来没想到你会神经错乱;可这会儿,它的确错乱得令人惊奇;而且这几乎全都是你一个人的错。像你这三天所过的生活方式,就是泰坦也会垮掉的。你吃点

---

① Titan:泰坦,太阳神,巨人。

food, and some repose. You need only look at yourself in a glass to see how you require both. Your cheeks are hollow, and your eyes bloodshot, like a person starving with hunger, and going blind with loss of sleep."

"It is not my fault that I cannot eat or rest," he replied. "I assure you it is through no settled designs. I'll do both, as soon as I possibly can. But you might as well bid a man struggling in the water, rest within arm's length of the shore! I must reach it first, and then I'll rest. Well, never mind Mr. Green: as to repenting of my injustices, I've done no injustice, and I repent of nothing—I'm too happy, and yet I'm not happy enough. My soul's bliss kills my body, but does not satisfy itself."

"Happy, master?" I cried. "Strange happiness! If you would hear me without being angry, I might offer some advice that would make you happier."

"What is that?" he asked. "Give it."

"You are aware, Mr. Heathcliff," I said, "that from the time you were thirteen years old, you have lived a selfish, unchristian life; and probably hardly had a Bible in your hands during all that period. You must have forgotten the contents of the book, and you may not have space to search it now. Could it be hurtful to send for some one—some minister of any denomination, it does not matter which, to explain it, and show you how very far you have erred from its precepts, and how unfit you will be for its heaven, unless a change takes place before you die?"

"I'm rather obliged than angry, Nelly," he said, "for you remind me of the manner that I desire to be buried in—It is to be carried to the churchyard, in the evening. You and Hareton may, if you please, accompany me: and mind, particularly, to notice that the sexton obeys my directions concerning the two coffins! No minister need come; nor need anything be said over me—I tell you, I have nearly attained my heaven; and that of others is altogether unvalued and uncoveted by me!"

"And supposing you persevered in your obstinate fast, and died by that means, and they refused to bury you in the precincts of the Kirk?" I said, shocked at his godless indifference. "How would you like it?"

"They won't do that," he replied: "if they did, you must have me removed secretly; and if you neglect it, you shall prove, practically, that the dead are not annihilated!"

As soon as he heard the other members of the family stirring he retired to his den, and I breathed freer. But in the afternoon, while Joseph and Hareton were at their work, he came into the kitchen again, and with a wild look, bid me come, and sit in the house: he wanted somebody with him. I declined; telling him plainly that his strange talk and manner frightened me, and I had neither the nerve nor the will to be his companion, alone.

"I believe you think me a fiend!" he said, with his dismal laugh: "something too horrible to live under a decent roof!" Then turning to Catherine, who was there, and who drew behind me at his approach, he added, half sneeringly — "Will *you* come, chuck? I'll not hurt you. No! to you, I've made myself worse than the devil. Well, there is *one* who won't shrink from my company! By God! she's relentless. Oh, damn it! It's unutterably too much for flesh

晚上被抬到教堂的墓园。你和哈里顿，如果你们愿意，可以陪我一起去：要特别记住，留意教堂司事要遵从我关于那两口棺木怎样安放的指示！用不着牧师来；也不需要给我念叨些什么——我告诉你，我就要到达我的天堂了，别人的天堂对我来说一点价值都没有，我也不稀罕！"

"可如果你继续绝食下去，并且那样死掉了，他们拒绝把你埋葬在教堂的范围之内呢？"我说，对他不信神的冷淡态度十分震惊。"那你希望怎么样呢？"

"他们不会那样做的，"他回答说，"如果他们真这样做了，你们一定得打发人悄悄把我搬进去；要是你们没有完成，你们就会发现，实际上死者并没有彻底消亡！"

他一听到家里其他成员在走动，就躲到自己的房间去了，我也终于松了口气。可到了下午，当约瑟夫和哈里顿在干活时，他又再次带着狂野的神情来到厨房，让我到正屋坐着：他要有个人陪他。我婉拒了，清楚地告诉他，他那奇怪的谈话和举止把我吓坏了，我没有那份勇气，也没有那个意愿来独个儿和他做伴。

"我相信你觉得我是个魔鬼吧，"他带着阴沉的笑说道，"是个太可怕的东西，不适合住在一个体面的家里。"接着他转向凯瑟琳半带着讥笑地说着。凯瑟琳正好在那儿，一看到他进来，她就躲在我身后了——"你愿意过来吗，小乖乖？我不会伤害你的。绝对不会！你是不是觉得我已经变得比魔鬼还坏了。好吧，有那么一个人不怕跟我做伴！上帝啊！她太狠心

and blood to bear— even mine."

He solicited the society of no one more. At dusk, he went into his chamber. Through the whole night, and far into the morning, we heard him groaning, and murmuring to himself. Hareton was anxious to enter; but I bid him fetch Mr. Kenneth, and he should go in and see him.

When he came, and I requested admittance and tried to open the door, I found it locked; and Heathcliff bid us be damned. He was better, and would be left alone; so the doctor went away.

The following evening was very wet: indeed it poured down, till day dawn; and, as I took my morning walk round the house, I observed the master's window swinging open, and the rain driving straight in. He cannot be in bed, I thought: those showers would drench him through! He must either be up or out. But I'll make no more ado, I'll go boldly and look!

Having succeeded in obtaining entrance with another key, I ran to unclose the panels, for the chamber was vacant; quickly pushing them aside, I peeped in. NIr Heathcliff was there— laid on his back. His eyes met mine so keen and fierce, I started; and then he seemed to smile.

I could not think him dead: but his face and throat were washed with rain; the bed-clothes dripped, and he was perfectly still. The lattice, flapping to and fro, had grazed one hand that rested on the sill; no blood trickled from the broken skin, and when I put my fingers to it, I could doubt no more: he was dead and stark!

I hasped the window; I combed his black long hair from his forehead; I tried to close his eyes: to extinguish, if possible, that frightful,

第三十四章

了。啊，他妈的！这是任何有血有肉的人都受不了的——甚至连我自己都受不了啦！"

他再也不恳求有人陪他。傍晚时候，他到卧室去了。一整夜，直到早上我们还听见他的呻吟和低声抱怨。哈里顿急着想进去；但我让他去请肯尼斯先生，然后再进去看他。

后来肯尼斯先生来了，我请求进去，并试着想打开门，发现门上了锁；希斯克利夫叫我们滚开。他好些了，想要一个人呆着；于是医生就走了。

接下来的晚上下起大雨。倾盆大雨一直下到天亮。早晨我照例绕着屋子散步，看见主人的窗子开着摆来摆去，雨都直接打进去了。他不可能在床上，我想：这场大雨会把他淋透的！他要么是起来了，要么是出去了。不过我也不必再困惑了，我要勇敢地过去看看。

我成功地用另一把钥匙开了门，进去以后，看到卧室是空的，我就跑去打开壁板；我很快把壁板推开了，向里面窥视。希斯克利夫先生在那儿——仰躺着。他的眼睛遇上了我的，既锐利又凶猛，我吃了一惊；接着他仿佛又笑了一下。

我不能想像他已经死去：可他的脸、喉咙都被雨水浸湿了；床单也在滴水，而他却纹丝不动。那格子窗撞来撞去，把放在窗台上的一只手擦破了；没有血从破损的皮肤处滴出来，当我的手指摸上去时，我无法再怀疑了；他死了，并且僵硬了！

我扣上窗户，梳理好他前额上长长的黑色头发；我试着合上他的眼

life-like gaze of exultation, before any one else beheld it. They would not shut: they seemed to sneer at my attempts; and his parted lips and sharp white teeth sneered too! Taken with another fit of cowardice, I cried out for Joseph. Joseph shuffled up and made a noise, but resolutely refused to meddle with him.

"Th' divil's harried off his soul," he cried, "and he muh hey his carcass intuh t' bargin, for ow't Aw care! Ech! What a wicked un he looks girnning at death!" and the old sinner grinned in mockery.

I thought he intended to cut a caper round the bed; but suddenly composing himself, he fell on his knees, and raised his hands, and returned thanks that the lawful master and the ancient stock were restored to their rights.

I felt stunned by the awful event; and my memory unavoidably recurred to former times with a sort of oppressive sadness. But poor Hareton, the most wronged, was the only one that really suffered much. He sat by the corpse all night, weeping in bitter earnest He pressed its hand, and kissed the sarcastic, savage face that every one else shrank from contemplating; and bemoaned him with that strong grief which springs naturally from a generous heart, though it be tough as tempered steel.

Kenneth was perplexed to pronounce of what disorder the master died. I concealed the fact of his having swallowed nothing for four days, fearing it might lead to trouble, and then, I am persuaded he did not abstain on purpose: it was the consequence of his strange illness, not the cause.

We buried him, to the scandal of the whole neighbourhood, as he had wished. Earnshaw,

睛：如果可能的话，想要熄灭那可怕的、像活人一样狂喜的凝视，再不让别的什么人看见。眼睛合不拢，像是在嘲笑我的尝试；他那张开的嘴唇、锋利的白牙齿也在嘲笑着我！我又害怕起来，就大声喊约瑟夫。约瑟夫拖着步子上来了，叫嚷了一声，但却一口拒绝去管他。

"魔鬼夺走他的灵魂了，"他喊道，"那他就该把他的尸体一起拿去，我才不在乎呢！呸！他看上去多么邪恶啊，临死还笑得龇牙咧嘴的！"这个老罪徒也嘲讽地龇牙咧嘴笑了一下。

我还以为他计划要围绕着床手舞足蹈一阵呢；可是忽然间，他马上镇定下来，双膝下跪，并举起了他的双手，感谢上帝让合法的主人和古老的血统又恢复了他们的权利。

这件可怕的事情让我目瞪口呆：我不禁怀着一种压抑的悲哀回想起过去的岁月。可是可怜的哈里顿，虽然是受委屈最多的，却又是惟一真正感到难过的人。他整夜守在尸体旁边，痛苦而真挚地哭泣着。他握住死者的手，吻了吻那张谁都不愿注视的嘲笑的、恶狠狠的脸。他沉痛地哀悼着死者，那种强烈的情绪出于一颗宽宏大量的心，尽管这颗心像回火的铁一样坚韧。

肯尼斯先生为了宣布主人死于什么病一事感到很为难。我隐瞒了他四天没吃东西的事实，因为担心会招来麻烦，不过话说回来，我也相信他不是有意绝食：绝食是他的古怪的病的结果，而不是原因。

我们按照他的希望安葬了他，惹得远近的邻居都议论纷纷。恩肖和

and I, the sexton and six men to carry the coffin, comprehended the whole attendance. The six men departed when they had let it down into the grave: we stayed to see it covered. Hareton, with a streaming face, dug green sods, and laid them over the brown mould himself: at present it is as smooth and verdant as its companion mounds—and I hope its tenant sleeps as soundly. But the country folks, if you asked them, would swear on their bible that he *walks*. There are those who speak to having met him near the church, and on the moor, and even within this house. Idle tales, you'll say, and so say I. Yet that old man by the kitchen fire affirms he has seen two on'em looking out of his chamber window, on every rainy night since his death:— and an odd thing happened to me about a month ago. I was going to the Grange one evening— a dark evening threatening thunder— and, just at the turn of the Heights, I encountered a little boy with a sheep and two lambs before him; he was crying terribly, and I supposed the lambs were skittish, and would not be guided.

"What is the matter, my little man?" I asked.

"They's Heathcliff, and a woman, yonder, under t' Nab," he blubbered, "un' Aw darnut pass 'em."

"I saw nothing; but neither the sheep nor he would go on; so I bid him take the road lower down. He probably raised the phantoms from thinking, as he traversed the moors alone, on the nonsense he had heard his parents and companions repeat—yet still, I don't like being out in the dark, now; and I don't like being left by myself in this grim house: I cannot help it; I shall be glad when they leave it, and shift to the

我、教堂司事，还有另外六个抬棺木的人，这就是所有的出席人数。那六个人在把棺木放进墓穴后就离开了；我们留下来看着它被掩盖好。哈里顿泪流满面，亲手掘起青草皮铺在那棕褐色的坟地上；现在这个坟已经跟周围其他坟地一样地平整青翠了——我希望睡在这里的人也能睡得同样酣畅。不过要是你去问问乡里的人们，他们就会手按在《圣经》上发誓说他走出来了：有些人说在教堂附近遇见过他，在原野里，甚至在这所宅子里。你会说这是无稽之谈，我也是这么说的。可在厨房烤火的那个老头儿一口咬定，自从主人过世后，一到下雨的夜里，从他卧室的窗户向外看，就看见他们两个。大约在一个月之前，我也碰到了一件怪事。有一天晚上我正向田庄走去——那是个漆黑的夜晚，隐隐传来了轰隆的雷声——就在山庄的拐角处，我碰见一个小男孩，他前面有一只绵羊和两只小羊羔；他哭得那么厉害，我还以为是羊羔容易受惊，不听他指挥。

"出什么事儿了，我的小人儿？"我问道。

"希斯克利夫和一个女人在那边，在山脚下，"他边哭边说着，"我不敢从那儿走。"

"我什么也没看到，可那孩子和羊都不愿往前走；因此我就叫他从底下那条路绕过去，可能是在他一个人穿过原野时，想起他从父母、伙伴们那儿听来的无稽之谈而产生了幻觉吧。虽然这么说，但现在我也不想在天黑时出去了，我也不想被一个人留下来，呆在这阴森的屋子里。我无计

Grange!"

"They are going to the Grange then?" I said.

"Yes," answered Mrs. Dean, "as soon as they are married; and that will be on New Year's day."

"And who will live here then?"

"Why, Joseph will take care of the house, and, perhaps, a lad to keep him company. They will live in the kitchen, and the rest will be shut up."

"For the use of such ghosts as choose to inhabit it," I observed.

"No, Mr. Lockwood," said Nelly, shaking her head. "I believe the dead are at peace, but it is not right to speak of them with levity."

At that moment the garden gate swung to; the ramblers were returning.

"*They* are afraid of nothing," I grumbled, watching their approach through the window. "Together, they would brave satan and all his legions."

As they stepped onto the door-stones, and halted to take a last look at the moon—or, more correctly, at each other, by her light—I felt irresistibly impelled to escape them again; and, pressing a remembrance into the hand of Mrs. Dean, and disregarding her expostulations at my rudeness, I vanished through the kitchen as they opened the house door: and so should have confirmed Joseph in his opinion of his fellow servant's gay indiscretions, had he not fortunately recognised me for a respectable character by the sweet ring of a sovereign at his feet.

My walk home was lengthened by a diversion in the direction of the kirk. When beneath its walls, I perceived decay had made progress,

可施。等他们离开这里，搬到田庄去的时候，我才高兴呢！"

"这样说来，他们是要搬到田庄去了？"我说。

"是啊，"迪安太太回答道，"他们一结了婚就过去，就是新年那天。"

"那么谁住这里呢？"

"呃，约瑟夫会照料这宅子的，或许，还有个小伙子和他做伴。他们会住在厨房里，其余的房间都关起来。"

"这样的话，鬼魂想要住进来可就方便了。"我说。

"不，洛克伍德先生，"内莉摇着她的头说。"我相信死者们是安宁的，这样随随便便地提到死者，是不对的呀。"

就在那一刻，花园的门推开了；漫步的人回来了。

"他们可什么也不怕，"我咕哝着说，从窗口看着他们走过来。"两个人在一起，他们就可以勇敢地面对撒旦和他所有的军队。"

他们俩踏上台阶，又停下来对着月亮看了最后一眼——或者，说得更确切些，借着月光，他们彼此对看了一眼——我感到一种不可抗拒的推动力迫使我再次躲开他们。我把一点"纪念品"硬塞进迪安太太手中，顾不得她对我的粗鲁的抗议，就在他们打开房门时，我从厨房里溜掉了；约瑟夫本来就认为他的同事在干那见不得人的轻薄勾当，现在更确定了；幸亏这时他听到很好听的一声脆响——一枚金币落在他的脚下，他这才认可我是品行端正的。

回家的道路因为我改道到教堂去而加长了。当我走到教堂的墙脚下时，

even in seven months: many a window showed black gaps deprived of glass; and slates jutted off, here and there, beyond the right line of the roof, to be gradually worked off in coming autumn storms.

I sought, and soon discovered, the three headstones on the slope next the moor: the middle one grey, and half buried in heath; Edgar Linton's only harmonised by the turf, and moss creeping up its foot; Heathcliff's still bare.

I lingered round them, under that benign sky: watched the moths fluttering among the heath and hare-bells; listened to the soft wind breathing through the grass; and wondered how any one could ever imagine unquiet slumbers for the sleepers in that quiet earth.

THE END

我发现，只不过隔了七个月的时间，它就已经显得愈发破败了。好几扇窗子没有玻璃，露出黑黑的豁口来；屋顶右侧各处都有石板瓦凸出来，等秋季的暴风雨一来，就会逐渐地掉光的。

我在靠近原野的斜坡上寻找那三块墓碑，不久就找到了：中间那块是灰色的，一半被埋在石楠里；埃德加·林顿的墓碑脚下才刚刚被草皮和苔藓覆盖；希斯克利夫的还是光秃秃的。

在那温和的天空下，我在这三块墓碑前徘徊：看着飞蛾在石楠丛和钓钟柳中翩然飞舞，听着轻柔的风在草间吹过，心里想着，可有人能想到，在那静谧的大地下，长眠的人居然会不得安睡。

（完）

An Emily Bronte Chronology

1818	July 30	Emily Jane Bronte born at Thornton
1820	April	The Bronte family moves to Haworth.
1821	September	Mrs. Bronte dies.
1824	November	Emily Bronte enrolls at the Cowan Bridge School.
1825	May 6	Maria Bronte dies.
	June 1	Charlotte and Emily leave Cowan Bridge.
	June 15	Elizabeth Bronte dies.
1826	June	Mr. Bronte brings home twelve wooden soldiers for Branwell--the start of the Brontes' oral literature and imaginative games.
1831		Emily and Anne begin the Gondal saga.
1834	Nov. 24	the earliest dated Emily Bronte manuscript --mentions the Gondals discovering Caaldine.
1835	July--Oct.	A pupil in Miss Wooler's school at Roe Head is sent home after alarming Charlotte with her physical decline.
1836	July 12	The earliest dated poem.
1837	September	Goes to teach at Law Hill School, near Halifax; remains there for about six months--the exact dates of the Law Hill period are disputed.
1838-1842		Over half of Bronte's surviving poems written
1842	Feb.--Nov.	At school in Brussels with Charlotte to study music and foreign languages; writes the essays in French; returns to Haworth after the death of Aunt Branwell
1843		Alone at Haworth with her father; a time of creativity and freedom
1844		Begins to arrange her poems into two notebooks, dividing the Gondalan from the non-Gondalan material

1845		The Brontes give up hopes for a school of their own; Branwell, working on a novel, tells his sisters of the profitable possibilities of novel writing; Emily's birthday note shows her hearty and content, reunited with Anne and as enthusiastic as ever about the Gondalans.
	Oct.	Charlotte discovers Emily's poems and convinces her sister to collaborate on a volume of poems.
	Dec.	*Wuthering Heights* begun.
1846	May	Poems by Currer Ellis and Acton Bell published, with the Brontes paying for costs
	July	*Wuthering Heights* finished and begins to make the round of publishers, along with *Agnes Grey* by Anne Bronte and *The Profrssor* by Charlotte.
	Sep. 14	Last dated complete poem
1847	July	T. C. Newby accepts *Wuthering Heights* and *Agnes Grey* but delays publishing until the success of Jane Eyre arouses interest in the "Bells".
	Dec.	*Wuthering Heights* and *Agnes Grey* published
1848		Confusion in the literary world over the identity and number of the Bells; Anne publishes *The Tenant of Wildfıll Hall*; Emily withdraws more resolutely into herself.
	Sep. 24	Branwell dies.
	Oct. 1	Emily leaves home for the last time to attend Branwell's funeral service--catches a severe cold which develops into inflammation of the lungs
	Dec. 19	Emily Bronte dies.
1850		*Wuthering Heights* reissued, with a selection of poems, and a biographical notice by Charlotte.